RETHINKING THE OTHER
IN ANTIQUITY

⊙ ⊙ ⊙ ⊙ ⊙ ⊙ ⊙ ⊙ ⊙ ⊙ ⊙ ⊙ ⊙ ⊙ ⊙

MARTIN CLASSICAL LECTURES

⦿ ⦿

The Martin Classical Lectures are delivered annually at Oberlin College through a foundation established by his many friends in honor of Charles Beebe Martin, for forty-five years a teacher of classical literature and classical art at Oberlin.

John Peradotto, *Man in the Middle Voice: Name and Narration in the* Odyssey

Martha C. Nussbaum, *The Therapy of Desire: Theory and Practice in Hellenistic Ethics*

Josiah Ober, *Political Dissent in Democratic Athens: Intellectual Critics of Popular Rule*

Anne Carson, *Economy of the Unlost: (Reading Simonides of Keos with Paul Celan)*

Helene P. Foley, *Female Acts in Greek Tragedy*

Mark W. Edwards, *Sound, Sense, and Rhythm: Listening to Greek and Latin Poetry*

Michael C. J. Putnam, *Poetic Interplay: Catullus and Horace*

Julia Haig Gaisser, *The Fortunes of Apuleius and the* Golden Ass: *A Study in Transmission and Reception*

Kenneth J. Reckford, *Recognizing Persius*

Leslie Kurke, *Aesopic Conversations: Popular Tradition, Cultural Dialogue, and the Invention of Greek Prose*

Erich Gruen, *Rethinking the Other in Antiquity*

Simon Goldhill, *Victorian Culture and Classical Antiquity: Art, Opera, Fiction, and the Proclamation of Modernity*

RETHINKING THE OTHER IN ANTIQUITY

ERICH S. GRUEN

PRINCETON UNIVERSITY PRESS

PRINCETON AND OXFORD

Copyright © 2011 by the Trustees of Oberlin College

Requests for permission to reproduce material from this work should be sent to Permissions, Princeton University Press

Published by Princeton University Press, 41 William Street, Princeton, New Jersey 08540

In the United Kingdom: Princeton University Press, 6 Oxford Street, Woodstock, Oxfordshire OX20 1TW

press.princeton.edu

All Rights Reserved

Third printing, and first paperback printing, 2012
Paperback ISBN 978-0-691-15635-4

The Library of Congress has cataloged the cloth edition of this book as follows

Gruen, Erich S.
  Rethinking the other in antiquity / Erich S. Gruen.
    p. cm. — (Martin classical lectures)
  Includes bibliographical references and index.
  ISBN 978-0-691-14852-6 (hardcover : acid-free paper)
  1. Greeks—Attitudes—History—To 1500. 2. Romans—Attitudes—History—To 1500. 3. Aliens—Greece—Public opinion—History—To 1500. 4. Aliens—Rome—Public opinion—History. 5. Greece—Civilization—To 146 B.C.—Foreign influences. 6. Rome—Civilization—Foreign influences. 7. Culture conflict—History. 8. Civilization, Classical. I. Title.
CB251.G78 2011
930.1—dc22   2010014739

British Library Cataloging-in-Publication Data is available

This book has been composed in Janson Text

Printed on acid-free paper. ∞

Printed in the United States of America

10 9 8 7 6 5 4 3

*To the memory of Joan B. Gruen,
who remains ever a vital part of my life*

CONTENTS

⊚ ⊚ ⊚ ⊚ ⊚ ⊚ ⊚ ⊚ ⊚ ⊚ ⊚ ⊚ ⊚ ⊚ ⊚ ⊚

List of Illustrations   xi
Acknowledgments   xiii
Introduction   1

PART I. IMPRESSIONS OF THE "OTHER"

CHAPTER ONE
Persia in the Greek Perception: Aeschylus and Herodotus   09

   Aeschylus' *Persae*   09
   Herodotus   21
   Some Visual Representations   40

CHAPTER TWO
Persia in the Greek Perception: Xenophon and Alexander   53

   Xenophon's *Cyropaedia*   53
   Alexander and the Persians   65

CHAPTER THREE
Egypt in the Classical Imagination   76

   Herodotus   76
   Diodorus   90
   Assorted Assessments   99
   Plutarch   111

CHAPTER FOUR
Punica Fides   115

   The Hellenic Backdrop   116
   In the Shadow of the Punic Wars   122
   The Manipulation of the Image   132
   The Enhancement of the Image   137

CHAPTER FIVE
Caesar on the Gauls   141

   Prior Portraits   141
   The Caesarian Rendering   147

CHAPTER SIX
Tacitus on the Germans 159
- Germans and Romans 159
- Interpretatio Romana? 169

CHAPTER SEVEN
Tacitus and the Defamation of the Jews 179
- The Question 180
- Tacitean Irony 187

CHAPTER EIGHT
People of Color 197
- Textual Images 197
- Visual Images 211

PART II. CONNECTIONS WITH THE "OTHER"

CHAPTER NINE
Foundation Legends 223
- Foundation Tales as Cultural Thievery 224
- Pelops 227
- Danaus 229
- Cadmus 233
- Athenians and Pelasgians 236
- Rome, Troy, and Arcadia 243
- Israel's Fictive Founders 250

CHAPTER TEN
Fictitious Kinships: Greeks and Others 253
- Perseus as Multiculturalist 253
- Athens and Egypt 265
- The Legend of Nectanebos 267
- Numidians and the Near East 272

CHAPTER ELEVEN
Fictitious Kinships: Jews and Others 277
- The Separatist Impression 277
- The Bible's Other Side 287
- Ishmaelites and Arabs 299
- Jews and Greeks as Kinsmen 302

CHAPTER TWELVE
Cultural Interlockings and Overlappings 308
   Jews and Greeks as Philosophers 308
   Jewish Presentations of Gentiles 325
   Phoenicians and Greeks 341
   Roman Adaptation and Appropriation 343

Conclusion 352
Bibliography 359
Index of Citations 385
Subject Index 403

ILLUSTRATIONS

⊙ ⊙ ⊙ ⊙ ⊙ ⊙ ⊙ ⊙ ⊙ ⊙ ⊙ ⊙ ⊙ ⊙ ⊙ ⊙

FIGURE 1. Oinochoe showing Greek warrior and Persian archer, mid–fifth century BCE. Museum of Fine Arts, Boston. — 41

FIGURE 2. "Eurymedon" oinochoe, showing one nude figure and one in "barbarian" attire, first half of fifth century BCE. Hamburg, Museum für Kunst und Gewerbe. — 43

FIGURE 3. Amazon rhyton, showing victorious Persian and fallen Greek, first half of fifth century BCE. Museum of Fine Arts, Boston. — 46

FIGURE 4. Darius volute krater, with scenes of divinities and Persian court, second half of fourth century BCE. Museo Archeologico Nazionale, Naples. — 47

FIGURE 5. Bronze herm with negroid head, Roman period. Ashmolean Museum. — 214

FIGURE 6. Kantharos in form of conjoined heads, white and Negro, late sixth century BCE. Museum of Fine Arts, Boston. — 217

FIGURE 7. Terra-cotta vase with Janiform heads, fourth century BCE. Metropolitan Museum of Art, New York. — 218

FIGURE 8. Kantharos with Janiform heads, early fifth century BCE. Archaeological Museum, Thessaloniki. — 219

ACKNOWLEDGMENTS

⊚ ⊚ ⊚ ⊚ ⊚ ⊚ ⊚ ⊚ ⊚ ⊚ ⊚ ⊚ ⊚ ⊚ ⊚ ⊚ ⊚

Acknowledgments, however heartfelt, are never adequate. Numerous people have shared their thoughts with me on one or more aspects of this study over the past several years. Many more attended lectures or conferences at which I presented ideas connected with the theme, offering their reactions, questions, suggestions, criticisms, dissent, and even (occasionally) assent. Obviously the registering of their names is impossible. But they have earned deep gratitude.

Some, however, deserve to be singled out. First and foremost, the Classics Department at Oberlin College paid me the signal honor of inviting me to deliver the Martin Classical Lectures for 2006, out of which this (much larger, though not necessarily better) work eventually emerged. I note in particular Tom Van Nortwick, who issued the invitation, and Kirk Ormand, who chaired the department. The warmth of their hospitality and the pleasure of their company trumped even the challenging weather of Ohio in February. Comments from Oberlin students and faculty alike enriched my experience and enhanced the book.

Several scholars have very kindly read one or another of the chapters in penultimate form, much to my profit. Their pointed observations, both encouraging and sobering, substantially improved the manuscript — even though they might withhold agreement on many matters. I am happy to record my gratitude to Stan Burstein, Ada Cohen, Mark Griffith, Chris Kraus, Christopher Krebs, Meg Miller, Sarah Morris, Ellen O'Gorman, Margaret Root, Dylan Sailor, Tom Scanlon, Ron Stroud, and Christopher Tuplin. They are, of course, not implicated in the outcome.

I have obtained at least equal advantage from the graduate students at Berkeley who participated in my seminar, The Alien in Antiquity, where I floated a number of these ideas, some of which drew their fire but emerged much the better for the shelling. My thanks go to David DeVore, Vera Hannush, Tom Hendrickson, Chris Johnson, Nandini Pandey, David Rosenberg-Wohl, Amy Russell, Greg Smay, Cai Thorman, and John Tully. And I take special pleasure in acknowledging the help of two incisive and industrious research assistants, Nandini Pandey and Amy Russell.

Two generous invitations to spend time outside my normal environs placed me in stimulating and productive settings that markedly advanced the work. I had the great privilege of serving as "Villa Professor" at the Getty Villa in Malibu during the academic year 2007/8, where I enjoyed the conversations and company of fellow visiting scholars Kevin Butcher,

Ada Cohen, Cecilia D'Ercole, Josephine Quinn, Karen Stern, and Molly Swetnam-Burland, and benefited immeasurably from the learning and congeniality of Ken Lapatin. In the spring of 2009, the hospitality of Merton College, Oxford, and the availability of Oxford's incomparable libraries, effected through the kind offices of Jonathan Prag, allowed me to bring the manuscript to a respectable conclusion.

Certain portions of the book have appeared or will appear elsewhere in modified form. I appreciate the willingness of the publishers, Getty Research Institute, Mohr Siebeck, The Open University, and Eerdmans, to grant permission for republication.

My greatest debt, in countless matters both large and small, is owed to my partner, bride, and loving critic Ann Hasse.

January 2010

RETHINKING THE OTHER IN ANTIQUITY

INTRODUCTION

⊚ ⊚ ⊚ ⊚ ⊚ ⊚ ⊚ ⊚ ⊚ ⊚ ⊚ ⊚ ⊚ ⊚ ⊚ ⊚ ⊚

ALTERITY AND "OTHERNESS" have too often plagued our world. The denigration, even demonization, of the "Other" in order to declare superiority or to construct a contrasting national identity is all too familiar. Trading in stereotypes, manufacturing traits, and branding those who are different as inferior, objectionable, or menacing have had an inordinate grip on imagining the divergent over the centuries. One need not rehearse the devastating consequences that ethnic, racial, or national typecasting of any kind has delivered in human history. And various forms of negative conceptualizations retain force today, creating barriers to communication and understanding, engendering or intensifying hostilities that poison international (and even internal) relations on the contemporary scene.

Analysis of such self-fashioning through disparagement of alien societies has been a staple of academic discourse for more than three decades. A collective self-image, so it is commonly asserted, demands a contrast with other peoples and cultures. Or rather a contrast with the perceptions and representations of other peoples. They can serve as images and creations, indeed as stereotypes and caricatures. Denigration of the "Other" seems essential to shape the inner portrait, the marginalization that defines the center, the reverse mirror that distorts the reflection of the opposite and enhances that of the holder. "Othering" has even taken on verbal form, a discouraging mode of linguistic pollution.

Edward Said's *Orientalism* stands as the classic work, a passionate and powerful voice on the subject.[1] Said focused essentially on the divide between East and West, the Eurocentric design of the "Orient." His linkage of colonialism and imperialism to the portraits of subordinate peoples conceived by hegemonial powers spawned a whole scholarly industry that advanced, deepened, and occasionally criticized his vision. Said's penetrating and highly influential text remains central to discussion of the subject. The sweeping study has transformed "Orientalism" into standard phraseology, a defining characteristic of the discourse. It recently prompted a mirror image, appropriately titled *Occidentalism*, which pointed the lens in exactly the opposite direction: a treatment of the depiction and distortion of westerners by nonwesterners.[2] The alleged confrontation of the societies gained greater public notoriety by Samuel Huntington's *Clash of Civilizations and the Remaking of World Order*,

---
[1] E. Said (1978).
[2] Buruma and Margalit (2004).

which envisioned a fearsome contest of opposites.[3] Most recently, the idea took even more extreme form, reaching a reductio ad absurdum in Anthony Pagden's *Worlds at War: The 2,500-Year Struggle between East and West*. On that perception, continuing hostilities date back to the Greco-Persian wars of the fifth century BCE.[4] The ancients are thus to blame.

The line of reasoning has had a potent impact on scholarship regarding antiquity. Negative images, misrepresentations, and stereotypes permitted ancients to invent the "Other," thereby justifying marginalization, subordination, and exclusion. Creation of the opposite served as a means to establish identity, distinctiveness, and superiority. The Hellenic vision of the easterner cast as "barbarian," inaugurated or intensified by the Persian wars, holds center stage in this interpretation, powerfully argued by scholars of distinction and influence. Francois Hartog's landmark *Mirror of Herodotus* called attention to the modes of representing the "Other" in historical writing.[5] Edith Hall gained wide impact by exploring this thesis in her *Inventing the Barbarian* through the lens of Greek tragedy.[6] The portrait is enshrined in Paul Cartledge's pointed survey of the Hellenic experience.[7] The incisive study of Jonathan Hall further advanced, in nuanced fashion, the idea of the Persian wars as molding Hellenic identity in contrast with the "barbarian."[8] That notion prevails.

The Jews, of course, fared no better. Division of the world between Jew and gentile has its roots in the Bible. The fierce rejection of idolatry entailed the hostile labeling of most neighboring peoples. Jewish writers excoriated Egyptians for zoolatry and shunned admixture with Canaanites, Ammonites, Moabites, and Philistines. That feature has been emphasized and underscored by a number of publications in the past decade and a half.[9] Romans scattered their biases widely with negative pronouncements on easterners and westerners alike. They dismissed Greeks as lightweights and belittled Jews for superstition (not to mention what they thought of Celts, Germans, Sardinians, and Syrians). Data gathered in the works of Balsdon and Dauge provide ample testimony on Roman expressions along these lines, although both works are rather short on analysis.[10] Abusive comments

---

[3] Huntington (1996).
[4] Pagden (2008).
[5] Hartog (1988).
[6] E. Hall (1989).
[7] Cartledge (1993).
[8] J. M. Hall (2002).
[9] See, among others, Cohn (1994); Machinist (1994); Benbessa and Attias (2004); Wills (2008).
[10] Balsdon's cascade of examples (1979) receives little interpretation. Dauge's gargantuan volume (1981), with its idiosyncratic organization, makes it difficult to find one's way around. But his firm stance on the polarity of Romans and non-Romans (or "barbarians") is clear; see, especially, 57, 393–402, 532–579.

can be found without difficulty. Some Greeks, for instance, decried Romans as boors and regarded Jews as having contributed nothing useful to civilization. Egyptians mocked Greeks as recent arrivals in the world's history, and they transformed the Exodus story into a flight of Jewish lepers and pollutants. The list of ethnic aspersions is long. No need to dwell on the matter. Scholarship regularly identifies the construction of the "Other" as a keystone of collective identity. Recent collections of essays attest to continuing scrutiny of the subject.[11] And the most sweeping contribution to this topic, the immensely learned and indispensable volume of Benjamin Isaac, *The Invention of Racism in Classical Antiquity*, assembles a plethora of Greek and Roman adverse attitudes toward an array of foreigners across the Mediterranean, reaching the conclusion that they amounted to either ethnic prejudice or proto-racism.[12]

The present work offers an alternative approach. It argues that Greeks, Romans, and Jews (who provide us with almost all the relevant extant texts) had far more mixed, nuanced, and complex opinions about other peoples. A spark for its inception came from the brilliant study of Arnaldo Momigliano, *Alien Wisdom*. That slim volume of lectures interweaves diverse aspects of Greek intellectual encounters with various folk like Jews, Romans, Celts, and Iranians. The chapters are jammed with insights and unexpected connections, affording a stimulus to thinking on every page. Its compactness and density, however, did not allow for expanded treatment of texts or authors.[13]

It is easy enough to gather individual derogatory remarks (often out of context), piecemeal comments, and particular observations that suggest bias or antipathy. The ancients were certainly not above prejudicial reflections on persons unlike themselves. It is a very different matter, however, to tar them with a blanket characterization of xenophobia and ethnocentrism, let alone racism. The thrust of this study is to argue that ancient societies, while certainly acknowledging differences among peoples (indeed occasionally

---

[11] See, for example, the fine volume of essays in Hölscher (2000). The contrast of Greeks and barbarians has most frequently stimulated scrutiny. A valuable assemblage of articles on the subject may be found in Harrison (2002). Silberstein and Cohn (1994) provide a comparable collection on Jews and "Others." The pieces on this topic gathered in Neusner and Frerichs (1985) are a more mixed bag, but the characteristically acute and far-ranging contribution of J. Smith (1985) is well worth reading. See also the monograph by Benbessa and Attias (2004). For Egyptians and non-Egyptians, see now Vittmann (2003) with telling illustrations. One should note also the visual images of western "barbarians," often harsh and brutal, by Roman or provincial artists, as treated, e.g., in the works of Ferris (2000) and Scott and Webster (2003).

[12] Isaac (2004). An older but still useful study by Haarhoff (1948) collects a broad range of Greek and Roman opinions about aliens with the noble aim of promoting racial harmony in the postwar world.

[13] Momigliano (1975).

emphasizing them) could also visualize themselves as part of a broader cultural heritage, could discover or invent links with other societies, and could couch their own historical memories in terms of a borrowed or appropriated past. When ancients reconstructed their roots or fashioned their history, they often did so by associating themselves with the legends and traditions of others. That practice affords a perhaps surprising but certainly revealing insight into the mentalities of Mediterranean folk in antiquity. It discloses not how they *distinguished* themselves from others but how they transformed or reimagined them for their own purposes. The "Other" takes on quite a different shape. This is not rejection, denigration, or distancing—but rather appropriation. It represents a more circuitous and a more creative mode of fashioning a collective self-consciousness.

The book does not pretend to cover this subject in all its manifestations and ramifications. Of necessity it must be highly selective. It engages, for the most part, with major and extended texts rather than fragments or isolated ruminations. And it investigates a variety of means whereby thinkers and writers conceived connections among peoples instead of creating barriers between them. Much of the material delivers ancient perceptions and impressions, often conveyed through inventions, legends, fictions, and fabrications. It is not part of the purpose here to inquire how closely they correspond to "historical reality," but rather to employ them as a window on ancient mentalities.

The work falls into two parts. The first, "Impressions of the Other," treats attitudes toward and assessments of foreigners by a range of authors and texts. It tackles the prevailing scholarly consensus on the Greek image of Persia, the cornerstone of whose argument traces antipathy and "Otherness" to the aftermath of the Persian wars. Examination of Aeschylus' poignant *Persae*, Herodotus' intricate portrait of Persian practices and personalities, Xenophon's fictive homage to Cyrus in the *Cyropaedia*, and Alexander's remarkable receptivity to collaboration with Iranians presents an important corrective. A similar revisionism applies to Roman attitudes toward their most fearsome and formidable foe, the Carthaginians. The pernicious concept of *Punica fides*, often seen as the defining feature, in fact masks a more differentiated, varied, and even sympathetic appraisal. A summary of sentiments on blacks and "Ethiopians" further illustrates the broad-mindedness of classical authors and artists toward people who have lacked comparable consideration in more modern times. Other chapters apply close scrutiny to pivotal texts that supply some of the most significant surviving evidence on representations of the alien: Herodotus, Diodorus, and Plutarch on the Egyptians, Caesar on the Gauls, Tacitus on Germans and Jews. They endeavor to show that the descriptions and conceptualizations, far from exhibiting simplistic stereotypes, display subtle characterizations that resist reductive placement into negative (or, for that matter, positive) categories.

The second part, "Connections with the Other," explores fictive genealogies, invented kinship relations, foundation legends, and stories of multiple migrations that underscore interconnections and overlappings rather than disassociation and estrangement. The objective here is not to discern cultural "influences," the impact of one people on another, whether in art, artifacts, literature, or mythology.[14] Part II concerns itself rather with the manner in which Mediterranean societies encountered, even embraced, the traditions of others and introduced them into their own self-consciousness. The chapters examine these themes across a wide range. They include analysis of biblical tales like those of Judah and Tamar and of Ruth, postbiblical legends of Jews and Spartans as common descendants of Abraham, and the traditions of Ishmaelites and Arabs, all of which express intimate ties between Jews and "Others." Additional chapters investigate fictive kinships that emerge in the legends of Perseus tying together a number of societies, the connections of Athens and Egyptian Saïs, the story of Nectanebos conceived both as Macedonian and Egyptian, the tales of Roman derivation from mythical Troy, and the fantasized associations of Rome and Arcadia. They proceed to a scrutiny of foundation legends, with a stress on foreign founders like Pelops, Danaus, Cadmus, and the Pelasgians, Greek claims on the origins of Armenians, Medes, and Scythians, Egyptian assertions of responsibility for the inception of Macedonians, Jews, and Thebans, and the variety of stories on Jewish beginnings recorded by Tacitus. The intertwining of divergent peoples surfaces again and again. A final chapter on cultural appropriation encompasses the reciprocal influences imagined between Jewish and Greek philosophers, the refashioning of Hellenic traditions for Jewish purposes by authors like Artapanus, Aristobulus, the *Letter of Aristeas*, and the Sibylline oracles, and the Romans' association of themselves with Greek figures, cults, and history.

Plainly the book, while traversing multiple and disparate territories, is illustrative, not exhaustive. But it aims to demonstrate that the conception of collective identity in terms of (rather than in contrast to) another culture forms a significant ingredient in the ancient outlook. This did not issue in some bland amalgam, a Mediterranean melting pot—let alone any starry-eyed universalism. Of course, prejudices existed, a wariness of those whose habits and beliefs seemed peculiar, even a resort to misrepresentation and stereotype. The multiple mirrors reflect mixed mutual perceptions. But this investigation brings into prominence the powerful ancient penchant (largely unnoticed in modern works) of buying into other cultures to augment one's own. That feature complicated the sense of collective identity—but also substantially enriched it.

---

[14] On this, see, e.g., the important works of M. West (1997) and M. Miller (1997). Cf. now the remarks of Mitchell (2007), 114–124.

PART I

⊙ ⊙ ⊙ ⊙ ⊙ ⊙ ⊙ ⊙ ⊙ ⊙ ⊙ ⊙ ⊙ ⊙ ⊙ ⊙

Impressions of the "Other"

Chapter 1

PERSIA IN THE GREEK PERCEPTION: AESCHYLUS AND HERODOTUS

THE PERSIAN WAR represented a mighty watershed in Hellenic history. Its effects resonated through Greek literature in subsequent centuries. Current scholarly consensus in fact goes further. It designates the conflict with Persia as the pivotal turning point in the conception of Greek identity. The clash prompted Greeks to reconsider the values that gave them distinctiveness and to shape those values by contrast with a constructed "barbarian" who would set them in high relief.[1] The "Orientalizing" of the Persian, therefore, stemmed from that international contest for survival or supremacy. It drove Greeks to distinguish their special characteristics from the despised "Other" who lived contentedly under despotism, scorned freedom, and preferred servility to rationality and self-determination. Such is the overwhelming *communis opinio*.[2] Should we buy it? A fresh look at some key texts might be salutary.

Aeschylus' *Persae*

Aeschylus produced his *Persae* in 472 BCE, a scant seven years since the Greeks had turned back a massive Persian invasion. Hellenic armies and navies had won decisive victories over a numerically superior foe, a highwater mark in their history, a salvation of the land from the fearsome easterner whose conquest would have brought Greece under the heel of the barbarian. So the clash was destined to be celebrated through the ages. And the conflict had by no means ended when the *Persae* hit the stage. Athenians

---

[1] E.g., Hartog (1988), 323–324; E. Hall (1989), 56–69; Nippel (1990), 36; Hornblower (1991), 11; Cartledge (1993), 13, 38–39; Georges (1994), 245; J. M. Hall (1997), 44–46; *idem* (2002), 175; Wiesehöfer (2005), 84–92. Tuplin (1999), 54–57, suggests that the dichotomy may have been formulated by eastern Greeks in the archaic age and picked up by mainland Greeks after 480. A modified view of the polarization appears now in Mitchell (2007), 78–79. 128–132, 136–138, 158–159. The brief but wise observations of Momigliano (1975), 129–132, should be required reading.

[2] See the valuable summary of opinions along these lines collected by Isaac (2004), 257–261.

(and perhaps Greeks generally) could not breathe easily until the next decade, when they smashed the Persian fleet at the Eurymedon and a peace of some sort took hold thereafter. The image of Persia, however, still loomed as the preeminent adversary of Hellas. And Greek statesmen charged with or suspected of leanings toward Persia were branded as "Medizers," emblematic of treachery to the nation. Yet Aeschylus presented a drama set entirely at Susa, the seat of Achaemenid rule, without a single Greek character onstage. And the effects of the great naval victory at Salamis are viewed altogether from the (presumed) perspective of the Persians. What does this signify for Greek attitudes toward the great eastern power?

Aeschylus was not the first to compose a work along these lines. Phrynichus had produced his *Phoenissae* probably in 476 and had carried off the prize. Only the first line of the play survives, but Aeschylus, so we are told, modeled his *Persae* on it and shared its perspective, that is, its presentation of events as seen from the Persian angle. Athens, in the immediate aftermath of the great war, evidently did not discourage the presentation of that vantage point.[3] Just how to interpret the phenomenon remains controversial. Critics fall broadly into two camps. Some find the *Persae* to be the quintessential expression of Hellenic superiority, a celebratory drama that extols the victory of freedom and democracy over barbaric despotism, of western values over eastern degeneracy. Persians appear as effeminate and emotional, softened by luxury and inured to servility, a foil for the egalitarian, hardy, and disciplined Greeks.[4] Others, by contrast, offer a precisely inverted analysis: Aeschylus expresses sympathy for the Persian plight, recognizes the common humanity of both peoples, and provides a universalist perspective that transcends national sentiment or ethnic antagonism.[5]

One need not, however, embrace either end of the dichotomy.[6] There is little or nothing in the drama to promote jingoism. Ethnic distinctions

[3] Hyp. to Aeschylus' *Persae*. Cf. the remarks of Georges (1994), 81–85; Garvie (2009), ix–xi.
[4] E.g., Kranz (1933), 77–78; Lattimore (1943), 82–93; Clifton (1963), 111–117; Goldhill (1988), 189–193; E. Hall (1989), 76–100; *eadem* (1993), 116–130; (1996), 11–13; Georges (1994), 86, 102–109; Hutzfeldt (1999), 62–69, 79–81 (with modifications); Gehrke (2000), 85–86; Harrison (2000b), 51–115, passim; J. M. Hall (2002), 176–177; Kantzios (2004), 3–19. Additional bibliography in Harrison (2000b), 135, n. 1. Rosenmeyer (1982), 318–320, has Aeschylus pit easterners against westerners and kingship against democracy, but in complex and qualified ways.
[5] E.g., Perrotta (1931), 54–55; Broadhead (1960), xvi–xx, xxviii–xxxii; Lesky (1966), 245–246; Vogt (1972), 132; Thalmann (1980), 281–282; Schmal (1995), 75–76; Garvie (2009), xx–xxii. Further bibliography in Hutzfeldt (1999), 92–93; Harrison (2000b), 135, n. 1. Griffith (1998), 44–48, 76, finds Aeschylus' depiction of Persian rulers and practices relatively sympathetic inasmuch as they were compatible with the behavior and aspirations of the Athenian elite; followed by Mendels (2004), 55–58. That is a provocative and original idea, even if not altogether compelling. See the doubts of Harrison (2000b), 105–108.
[6] Gagarin (1976), 29–56, endeavors to embrace both. He finds the play suffused with patriotic propaganda while at the same time presenting a genuine tragedy, i.e., the fall of Persia

play no explicit part and political distinctions only an indirect one. Persians may enjoy wealth and splendor, but Aeschylus nowhere suggests Greek austerity or self-denial as national traits.[7] The idea of luxury and extravagance as signaling Persian decadence, the intimations of Persian effeminacy as against Hellenic manliness, the "Orientalizing," in short, of the barbarian is hard to discern in the *Persae*. Many of the features associated with an opulent lifestyle, in fact, found favor with Greek poets and writers of the archaic era, particularly as they reflected the aspirations of the aristocracy.[8] The receptivity in the Greek world to Persian dress, Persian products, Persian art, and the Persian aesthetic generally as status symbols and modes of cultural expression among the elite was widespread. And the adaptation of such symbols gradually devolved into the lower strata of society as well.[9] Greeks were familiar figures in the Persian empire as envoys, traders, soldiers, artisans, and skilled professionals.[10] The remarkable overlap and interconnections that linked the cultures would discourage any drive to demonize the high life of the "Oriental." Aeschylus, despite claims to the contrary, does not engage in such stigmatization.[11] The play avoids trumpeting any inherent superiority of Hellenes over barbarians.

---

from prosperity to adversity. McCall (1986), 43–49, offers a somewhat comparable analysis but adds the highly speculative suggestion that Aeschylus gave a human dimension to the Persians by playing the role of Xerxes himself. See also Meier (1988), 76–93, who perceives both an advocacy of freedom/west over monarchy/east and a profound sympathy for Persians as part of a broader humanity. Similarly, Pelling (1997a), 13–19; Mitchell (2007), 113–114, 185–187. Cf. also Michelini (1982), 75, 105, 115. Rosenbloom (2006), 139–148, finds a complex combination of Persian pathos and a warning for Athenians, with Darius as pivotal figure emblematizing both. For Hutzfeldt (1999), 79–81, Aeschylus, by putting Persians onstage, both underscored their profound differences from Greeks and allowed the audience to experience a distancing akin to viewing mythic themes in tragedy. He sees the play essentially as falling into two parts, the first stressing the contrast between the cultures, the second focusing on internal Persian tensions between the generations; ibid., 92–96.

[7] In the view of Thalmann (1980), 260–282, Aeschylus dwells on Persian luxury thus to set up the fall from prosperity and power by the end of the play, as symbolized by Xerxes' appearance in torn clothes.

[8] Kurke (1992), 92–101, makes the point convincingly.

[9] See the important book of Miller (1997), passim; esp. 188–217, 243–258.

[10] For some examples, see Lewis (1977), 12–15. Miller (1997), 89–133, provides a valuable collection of evidence and discussion.

[11] It is true that Aeschylus does employ forms of the term ἁβροσύνη, signifying "softness." See Hutzfeldt (1999), 45–47. But not with negative connotations branding Persians as different from and inferior to Greeks. Cf. Garvie (2009), 62–63. He uses the form at *Pers.* 41 to refer to Lydians, not Persians, and couples it, in fact, with a reference to Lydian forces in Xerxes' army as presenting a "fearsome sight" (φοβερὰν ὄψιν); *Pers.* 48. Two other passages apply ἁβροσύνη to Persian women, *Pers.* 134–137, 541–545, which has no implications of effeminacy for Persian males. One final allusion at the end of the play, in the mouth of Xerxes, to those who "step lightly" (*Pers.* 1074) does not have a pejorative meaning; cf. 1070.

On the other hand, compassion for Persians hardly suits a dramatist who fought proudly in the war, whose brother was killed in action, and who, according to Aristophanes, portrayed his work as a lesson to Athenians always to seek conquest of their enemies.[12] The *Persae* eschews universalist preaching—let alone pacifism. A different path to understanding seems called for.

The very fact of the drama itself, produced when wounds had not yet healed and future fighting was in store, remains the most striking point. Persians alone constitute the cast; they suffer the losses, they lament their fate, they encompass both the admirable and the flawed. The tragedy is theirs. And tragic figures, for all their limitations, are not despicable.

The outlook of Aeschylus resists reductionism. Persian rulers are despots, to be sure. The playwright does not disguise their absolutism. All nations of the empire follow the fearsome processions of the monarch.[13] Even kings are subordinate to the Great King.[14] Xerxes, the Achaemenid monarch who ordered the host to Greece, will remain sovereign of the realm, so his mother exclaims, regardless of the outcome of the war: he is not accountable to the polity.[15] He has the power of life and death over his subjects, and, if his forces should allow the enemy to escape, their heads will roll.[16] No wonder that many scholars find the drama as demonstrating the advantages of Greek democracy over oriental despotism.[17] Autocratic governance, to be sure, may have been unappealing to many Hellenes. But Aeschylus is not making a constitutional argument or posing a contrast between political institutions. When he speaks of the Persian drive to set a yoke upon their enemies, he refers to the plan of conquest, not the imposition of a system.[18] And when Greek soldiers were reported to have shouted a battle cry of liberating their native land, wives, children, shrines of ancestral gods, and tombs of forefathers, they were expressing their determination to resist foreign occupation, not their adherence to a political theory.[19]

Monarchic rule is simply the established state of affairs in Persia. Darius, the father of Xerxes and a praiseworthy character in the *Persae*, states the fact without embarrassment: Zeus himself conferred monarchy (as well as empire) on the Persians. Darius acknowledges that there were some good

---

[12] Aristoph. *Frogs* 1026–1027. That Aeschylus fought at Salamis is recorded by Ion of Chios (*FGH* 392 F7).

[13] Aesch. *Pers.* 56–58.

[14] Aesch. *Pers.* 24.

[15] Aesch. *Pers.* 211–214.

[16] Aesch. *Pers.* 369–371.

[17] Goldhill (1988), 189–193; more recently, Harrison (2000b), 76–91, 108–115, and Kantzios (2004), 3–19, the latter an immoderate position.

[18] Aesch. *Pers.* 49–50, 234. On the image of the yoke in the *Persae*, see Michelini (1982), 80–88.

[19] Aesch. *Pers.* 401–405.

and some bad kings, but the institution is not in question.[20] Nothing in the play implies that the playwright questioned it. Persian elders fear that failure in the western expedition would have dire consequences for the eastern holdings of the empire: tribute would no longer be paid, subjects would abandon obeisance to the king, tongues would be untied, and people could speak with freedom once the yoke was lifted.[21] The passage imagines an overthrow of Persian authority, not the installation of a democracy. And the reference to those who would throw off the yoke, in any case, applies to Asians—who would hardly exemplify democratic institutions.[22]

Only once does the play come close to expressing a contrast between competing political systems. This surfaces in the Queen Mother's inquiry of the chorus about the location, resources, and practices of the Athenians. She wonders quite naturally about who exercises sole command over their army (on analogy with the Persian king). The elders' quick retort asserts that Athenians are called neither slaves nor subjects of any one man.[23] This helps to explain, in their eyes, why Athenians have gained success against Persian arms. Do we have here, as is so often claimed, a classic affirmation of the superiority of democracy over tyranny? It would be prudent to avoid jumping to that conclusion. The chorus gives a number of reasons for regarding Athens as a formidable opponent: the size of its army, the silver mines, and the fact that its soldiers employ shields and spears instead of bows and arrows.[24] Reference to Athenian pride in shunning the appellation of slaves and subjects is merely one item in that litany. It hardly encapsulates the message of the drama.

A rarely noticed passage may be more to the point. The chorus of elders, in looking back with pride and nostalgia on the reign of Darius, reckons it a time when Persians enjoyed a well-ordered civil society and when "established practices, a tower of strength, governed all matters."[25]

---

[20] Aesch. Pers. 760–786. Georges (1994), 82–83, 109–112, implies that a darker Darius lurks behind Aeschylus' portrayal, one who embodies the absolutist conqueror remembered all too vividly by the generation of Marathon; similarly, Kantzios (2004), 13–14. But that element, if it exists at all, is decidedly soft-pedaled in the play. Cf. Hutzfeldt (1999), 74–75.

[21] Aesch. Pers. 584–594.

[22] There is no warrant for the assumption of Gagarin (1976), 32–33, that the reference here is to Ionian Greeks. Aeschylus speaks broadly of those who dwell in Asia under Persian rule. The potential calamity from the Persian vantage point would be much diminished if he intended only the Greeks of western Asia Minor. Cf. also Thalmann (1980), 272–273.

[23] Aesch. Pers. 241–242: οὔτινος δοῦλοι κέκληνται φωτὸς οὐδ' ὑπήκοοι.

[24] Aesch. Pers. 235–244.

[25] Aesch. Pers. 852–859. The term πολισσονόμου refers more likely to internal civic order than to governance of cities abroad; cf. Broadhead (1960), 213–214; E. Hall (1996), 166; contra: S. Said (1981), 34, n. 159. Some corruption has certainly entered into the line that is here read as νομίσματα πύργινα πάντ' ἐπεύθυνον. See the discussion of Broadhead (1960), 215–216, 280–281; Garvie (2009), 328–329; cf. S. Said (1981), 33, n. 153; E. Hall (1996), 167.

The praise accentuates a contrast with the current reign of Xerxes, when misfortune has struck and the state is reeling. But monarchy itself could not be held to blame. With a ruler like Darius, kingship and an effective polity founded on stable traditions went hand in hand. The play indeed contrasts the failings of Xerxes most starkly with those of almost all his predecessors.[26] The system was sound enough; the individual practitioner fell short. Aeschylus did not compose this play to advance a particular political philosophy.[27]

The *Persae* on several occasions makes reference to the divine aura of the king. Aeschylus further underscores that aspect of the monarchy by calling attention to the Persian practice of prostration before the king. To a Greek mind such a custom was offensive and intolerable, indeed crossed the line between mortal and immortal, risking vengeance from the gods. Did the playwright then bring this feature to the fore in order to stir revulsion in an Athenian audience and to underscore the differences between Greek rationality and eastern servility? Not necessarily so. Aeschylus indulges in the poetic usage of "godlike," "equivalent to a god," or "divine," which carries a different connotation from actual belief in the divinity of the ruler.[28] The chorus seeks to rouse Darius from the dead and calls him "Susa-born god."[29] But the phrase implies only that (in the play's perspective) Persians deified rulers after death. One passage alone may allude to a living god, and even that is indecisive. Persian elders hail the queen as wife of one god (Darius) and mother of another (Xerxes). The reference, however, could well be to the one divinized after death and the other whose elevation was still to come.[30] In any case, the harvest is meager indeed. And the most explicit statement refutes the proposition of divine rulership. Darius' ghost bemoans the disasters inflicted on Persia in the reign of his son and blasts

---

[26] S. Said (1981), 36–38; cf. Griffith (1998), 54; Schmal (1995), 79–80. Contra: Georges (1994), 109–112, for whom Aeschylus reckoned the Persian regime itself, despite the virtues of Darius' rule, as a slave society and hence the fundamental ingredient in the woes suffered under Xerxes.

[27] We leave aside here the idea that Aeschylus indulged in political partisanship. Podlecki (1966), 8–26, argued that the play, by placing heavy emphasis on Salamis, represents defense of Themistocles' politics and policies. See also Hahn (1981), 73–86. That is hard to credit when the only allusion to Themistocles (without naming him) has him as the trickster who deceitfully lured the Persians into battle; Aesch. *Pers.* 355–361; cf. Herod. 8.74–76. Rosenbloom (2006), 34–35, is properly skeptical. See also Garvie (2009), xvi–xix. As for the emphasis on Salamis, to the exclusion of Artemisium and Thermopylae (Plataea does receive more than mere mention), that has more to do with dramatic unity than with politics. Cf. Pelling (1997a), 9–10. Aristotle would have approved. For a very different political interpretation, see Mendels (2004), 48–59.

[28] Aesch. *Pers.* 80, 634, 651, 654, 711. At 75, even Xerxes' flock of followers is designated as "divine."

[29] Aesch. *Pers.* 643.

[30] Aesch. *Pers.* 157. See E. Hall (1996), 121; Garvie (2009), 99–100.

Xerxes for thinking that, though a mortal, he could surpass all the gods.[31] As for prostration, Persians performed it before their rulers, a mark of respect rather than worship. Aeschylus may well have known that.[32] He avoids use of the offensive term *proskynein*, preferring instead *prospitnein*, which could signify obeisance to humans as well as to gods.[33] The drama hardly serves as a vehicle to denounce Persian proclivity toward (and Greek resistance to) ruler worship. Aeschylus at most reflects his own audience's perception of Persian beliefs about divine kingship.[34]

Persians in the play repeatedly characterize their defeat in Greece as an utter calamity.[35] This was no mere loss of a battle or a frustrated hope for conquest. The results appear as nothing less than catastrophe. The army of the Achaemenids, if one believes the characters, was destroyed root and branch, the flower of Persian youth gone.[36] That is bad enough. But the hyperbole goes further. The capital at Susa is portrayed as denuded of men.[37] And, worse still, the Persian empire has been crushed, and the whole of Asia emptied.[38] That is extravagant exaggeration, as patent to readers as it must have been to Aeschylus and his audience. The defeat had made hardly a dent in the imperial holdings of the Achaemenids, further fighting lay in the future, and Persia had certainly not been stripped of its manpower.[39]

---

[31] Aesch. *Pers.* 749: θνητὸς ὢν θεῶν τε πάντων ᾤετ.

[32] On Aeschylus' knowledge of Persian practices, see Bacon (1961), 34–45, although she believes that Persians did regard their kings as gods or something like it. See the balanced discussion of Hutzfeldt (1999), 58–61, with additional bibliography.

[33] Aesch. *Pers.* 150–154, 589–590. So, rightly, Griffith (1998), 48–49. His statement that no form of *proskynein* appears in the play is not quite accurate. Aeschylus does apply it to Persians supplicating heaven and earth as gods; *Pers.* 497–499. The assertion by Rosenbloom (2006), 50, that *proskynesis* defined Persia as a slave society in the context of the play is plainly problematic.

[34] A balanced analysis in E. Hall (1989), 89–93. Cf. Georges (1994), 113–114; Griffith (1998), 59–60; Harrison (2000b), 87–89; Garvie (2009), 97. For Rosenmeyer (1982), 262, 275, Aeschylus' application of the terms for divinity contains ambiguity and confusion.

[35] See the comments of Avery (1964), 173–179.

[36] Aesch. *Pers.* 251–255, 260, 284, 516, 532–534, 670, 716, 729–733, 918–927, 1014–1024.

[37] Aesch. *Pers.* 118–119, 730, 760–761.

[38] Aesch. *Pers.* 434, 548–549, 714, 718. On this theme, see Harrison (2000b), 71–75. For E. Hall (1993), 117–118, and (1996), 116–117, the passages represent Asia as manless and female; cf. E. Hall (1996), 117–139, 532–547. But Aeschylus places primary stress on the loss of vast numbers, not on a gender distinction. See, e.g., the references to parents deprived of their children; *Pers.* 61–64, 579–583.

[39] Avery (1964), 179–184, reconciles the incongruity by imagining that Xerxes was regarbed in splendor near the end of the drama, after returning with rent robes, thus symbolizing the rehabilitation of Persian power. But nothing in the text implies this; the concluding lines remain mournful; and the statement at 1060 fully refutes the proposition. Cf. the different interpretations of Alexanderson (1967), 6–9, Thalmann (1980), 277–278, and Rosenbloom (2006), 115–118. Gagarin (1976), 40–42, accepts Avery's notion of a Persian recovery by the end of the play but imagines that Xerxes' new clothing would be bestowed after its conclusion.

How to interpret the overstatements? Are we to infer Athenian swaggering, a chauvinistic bellicosity, reveling in the deserved distress of the defeated? The dolorous mourning of the Persians, to be sure, pervades the play.[40] For some, the poet here calls attention to barbarian weakness of character, emasculating their males by having them lament like hysterical females. But that may miss the point. Greek men also mourned in Attic tragedy.[41] Aeschylus went beyond patriotic caricature. Triumphalism hardly captures the tone of the tragedy. The poet refrains from proclaiming the success of Hellenic values over Persian practices.

Not that one should leap to the opposite pole. It would be absurd to imagine that Aeschylus, who had fought in the Athenian ranks, wept for Persia—or expected his audience to do so. This is no antiwar drama. Nor does it resolve itself into a humanitarian reflection on the universal sufferings wrought by conflict among the nations. The play transcends an antithesis of Greek and barbarian, but stops short of dissolving distinctions.

If the playwright wished to spotlight the superiority of Hellas, he missed his opportunity. Aeschylus is quite unequivocal about who brought about the trouncing of the invader. Divine intervention dictated the outcome. Greeks may have wielded the weapons and manned the ships, but the gods determined the Persian disaster. Of course, ascription of responsibility to the gods, as is well known, does not itself diminish human accountability—especially in Athenian tragedy. Persians were no innocent victims. Xerxes' overreaching and impiety roused divine retaliation; aggression and arrogance backfired; vast numbers proved unavailing and produced only myriads of casualties.[42] But the role of the Greeks is decidedly subordinated to the wrath of the gods and the inexorability of fate. There is no more persistent theme in the play than that.

The chorus of elders signals it almost from the very outset. After detailing with pride the flower of Asia's soldiery that had set forth for Greece, they enunciate the darker forebodings. What mortal, they assert, can hope to evade the duplicitous deceit of the god? Fatal delusion itself (*Ate*) is a deity in this choral song. She entices and ensnares men, rendering escape impossible.

Similarly, Rosenmeyer (1982), 327–328. On clothing and costume in the *Persae*, see Hutzfeldt (1999), 35–37.

[40] E.g., Aesch. *Pers.* 61–64, 133–136, 465–470, 512–513, 541–543, 1038–1045, 1054–1074. See Rosenbloom (2006), 122–138.

[41] Griffith (1998), 50, cogently makes this point, summoning the example of Orestes in the *Choephori*—as against E. Hall (1989), 83–84; *eadem* (1993), 122–123. See also Rosenbloom (2006), 125–126.

[42] Gagarin (1976), 46–50, sees the emphasis on divine intervention but unduly minimizes Xerxes' *hybris* and impiety, thus leaving the gods' actions oddly unmotivated. Xerxes' misconduct, folly, irrationality, and overreaching, in fact, gain repeated mention. Cf. S. Said (1981), 18–20.

Persians find themselves in the grips of a heaven-sent fate that had driven them not only to imperialist expansion by land but now fueled overseas ambitions that risked calamity.[43] The elders here herald a fundamental leitmotif of the tragedy: control and manipulation by divine powers.

The Queen Mother strikes the major chord: necessity demands that mortals endure the sufferings sent by the gods.[44] The herald who announced the disastrous debacle at Salamis made certain that the queen would be under no misapprehension. Her nation's forces were not outnumbered; they were simply undone by some divinity who destroyed the forces—for the gods protect the city of Pallas.[45] The root of all this evil, according to the messenger's report, was a vengeful or wicked spirit appearing from nowhere.[46] Xerxes, naive as he was, blundered into battle, deceived by the trickery of a Greek, unaware of what the gods had designed for his future.[47] The herald proceeded to ascribe the massacre of Persians in the prime of life to the most ignoble fate.[48] It was god who bestowed the victory at Salamis on the Greeks.[49] The Queen Mother cries out in pain at the perpetrator of this disaster: the hateful divinity who deceived the minds of her Persians.[50] The grieving messenger insists that his report contains only the truth, adding even at the conclusion that he has omitted numerous other evils that god had flung upon his people at Salamis.[51] Persian elders echo the message of the herald. Their cry goes directly to Zeus as the agent of destruction who eliminated the whole army of Persia and rained misery upon the empire.[52]

The motif persists. When the ghost of Darius emerges from his abode beneath the earth and learns of the catastrophe, he draws the same conclusion. Xerxes' yoking of the Hellespont prompted his comeuppance; indeed it must have been some mighty god who clouded his mind in the first place to motivate such an act.[53] Darius recalls divine prophecies issued by Zeus

---

[43] Aesch. *Pers.* 93–114.
[44] Aesch. *Pers.* 293–294: ἀνάγκη πημονὰς βροτοῖς φέρειν/ θεῶν διδόντων.
[45] Aesch. *Pers.* 344–347. See Garvie (2009), 177–178. This is the only allusion in the play to Athena. E. Hall (1993), 129–130, and (1996), 135, is surprised not to find more reference to the Athenians' particular contribution to victory. In view of the play's general tenor, that should not cause surprise. Hall's suggestions that the author "suppressed" Athena either to create a more panhellenic aura or to further the "masculinisation" of the Athenians are quite unnecessary.
[46] Aesch. *Pers.* 353–354.
[47] Aesch. *Pers.* 361–362, 372–373.
[48] Aesch. *Pers.* 441–444.
[49] Aesch. *Pers.* 454–455: . . . ὡς γὰρ θεὸς / ναῶν ἔδωκε κῦδος Ἕλλησιν μάχης.
[50] Aesch. *Pers.* 472–473.
[51] Aesch. *Pers.* 513–514.
[52] Aesch. *Pers.* 532–536.
[53] Aesch. *Pers.* 723–725. On this passage, see Garvie (2009), 287–288. On the role of Darius in the play, see Alexanderson (1967), 1–11; S. Said (1981), 31–36; Tourraix (1984), 126–131; Garvie (2009), xxvii–xxxii.

18 IMPRESSIONS OF THE "OTHER"

in his own lifetime, oracular pronouncements that forecast this grave misfortune, now brought to fulfillment by the gods.[54] The ghostly apparition left no doubt that superhuman forces controlled the events. Xerxes had offended the gods not only by overweening ambition but by outright sacrilege in the desecration of their shrines, the theft of their images, and the destruction of their temples in Greece. Retribution will come at Plataea, as Darius foresees. Zeus' chastisement will deliver a lesson that the king needs to take to heart.[55] The contrast between father and son resonates with the elders, who bemoan the turns of fortune ordained by the gods.[56]

Xerxes himself explains the circumstances in much the same terms. The dismal outcome of the expedition was the work of a hateful and altogether unanticipated fate, inflicted by a deity in savage fashion on the Persian nation.[57] The chorus censures Xerxes for his heedless actions that sent so many of Persia's finest youths to pack the realm of Hades. But they know that it was a *daimon* who mowed down that fine generation of soldiers.[58]

The role of the Greeks in turning back the Persian invasion is muted and subdued.[59] Aeschylus does have the messenger take note of their discipline, orderliness, confidence, and cleverness at Salamis. Their preparation was impeccable, the plan was shrewd, and the execution flawless. Persians were unprepared and misled, then routed and scattered in flight. Those who were trapped were butchered to a man.[60] Even this account, however, does not purport to contrast Hellenic valor with barbarian cowardice—or to suggest any innate difference in quality or character between the races.[61] The messenger praises the nobility, bearing, and fortitude of the Persian

---

[54] Aesch. *Pers.* 739–741.

[55] Aesch. *Pers.* 807–832.

[56] Aesch. *Pers.* 904–905: νῦν δ' οὐκ ἀμφιλόγως θεότρεπτα τάδ' αὖ φέρομεν πολέμοιο. For Griffith (1998), 53–63, the father/son relationship between Darius and Xerxes is a central element in the drama. Similarly, Rosenbloom (2006), 89–103. Perhaps an overinterpretation.

[57] Aesch. *Pers.* 909–912, 941–943.

[58] Aesch. *Pers.* 918–925, 1005–1007. It is not, of course, inconsistent with divine dictation that "Ionians" are occasionally referred to as the fighters who defeated Persians in battle; Aesch. *Pers.* 563, 950–951, 1011–1012, 1025–1027.

[59] Cf. Griffith (1998), 63: "these victors remain ... curiously colourless."

[60] Aesch. *Pers.* 353–432, 447–464.

[61] E. Hall (1996), 12–13, finds a stark contrast between ordinary Athenian citizens manning the ships and the hierarchicalism of the Persians, thus a celebration of the Athenian democratic system. Similarly, Goldhill (1988), 192–193. But the text does not draw explicit attention to this aspect—and indeed avoids any reference to Athenians themselves in the account of Salamis. The fighters are simply Hellenes. Harrison's characterization of the play as "Athenocentric," (2000b), 63, seems well off the mark. Greek and Persian modes of fighting are symbolized by the spear and the bow respectively; Aesch. *Pers.* 147–148, 817–818. Cf. Hutzfeldt (1999), 54–55; Rosenbloom (2006), 48–49. But this is not put in terms of symbolic cultural differences.

leaders who lost their lives.[62] On the Hellenic side, double-dealing inaugurated the fateful battle. A deceptive Greek (Themistocles is not named) led the Persian fleet into a trap by persuading them that their enemies would flee rather than fight.[63] Cunning intelligence, to be sure, could be a virtue, as Odysseus exemplifies. But trickery as trigger to the pivotal contest at Salamis is hardly the most uplifting of presentations. And, as we have seen, the part played by the gods prevails throughout, even at Salamis.[64] When Darius looks ahead to the Persian disaster at Plataea and warns against any further expeditions to Greece, his reasoning gives no credit to Hellenic superiority. The soil of Greece itself rates a principal role in the outcome. Its very poverty will starve an invading army.[65] Beyond that, the delusions and impieties of Xerxes brought divine vengeance upon his head and those of his troops—a grim warning to Xerxes and counsel for the practice of restraint and humility.[66] Hellenic arms are little more than pawns in the scheme of the gods to drive home the lesson to mortals. Greek values as distinct from those of the barbarians barely surface in the text. The goal of the *Persae* is not disparagement of the Persians.

Indeed a largely neglected element of the play merits emphasis here. Aeschylus alludes briefly and with no elaboration to Xerxes as equal to the gods, for his descent came from a race of gold.[67] The allusion must be to the legend that the Greek hero Perseus was born to an Argive princess impregnated by Zeus in the guise of a golden shower. Perseus later rescued and took as bride Andromeda, daughter of the Persian ruler, and their issue, Perses, became progenitor of the Persians.[68] Both Greeks and Persians, it seems, subscribed to that tale in some form or other. Its fundamental import, whatever else one makes of it, declares a genealogical connection between the two peoples. Aeschylus does not make an issue of it. He did not need to. His audience could be presumed to take the kinship association for granted.[69]

A more striking and expanded citation of this legendary tie comes in the queen's vivid dream prior to news of the cataclysm at Salamis.[70] She had visualized two women surpassingly beautiful in appearance and grand in stature. Each was bedecked in lovely garb, the one in Persian robes, the other in

---

[62] Aesch. *Pers.* 302–331, 441–444. Cf. Broadhead (1960), xviii; Garvie (2009), 161–162.

[63] Aesch. *Pers.* 355–368.

[64] Aesch. *Pers.* 345–347, 353–354, 361–362, 454–455, 472–473.

[65] Aesch. *Pers.* 790–794; cf. 480–491.

[66] Aesch. *Pers.* 800–831.

[67] Aesch. *Pers.* 80: χρυσογόνου γενεᾶς ἰσόθεος φώς.

[68] See Herod. 7.61, 7.150–152; Euripides, *apud* Apollod. 2.1–4. Cf. Georges (1994), 66–67. For a fuller discussion of the Perseus legend, see below, pp. 253–265.

[69] There may be another reference to this genealogy at Aesch. *Pers.* 145 (possibly a mention of Xerxes' descent from Danae, mother of Perseus), but the reading is quite uncertain.

[70] Aesch. *Pers.* 181–199. See, esp., 185–186: κασιγνήτα γένους / ταὐτοῦ.

Doric.[71] They were sisters of the same race. The lot accorded them separate dwellings, one sister in Greece, the other in the land of the barbarians. A conflict of some sort followed. Xerxes endeavored to harness the two by yoking them both to his chariot. One took her place with pride, submitting herself to the reins; the second chafed at them, tore the harness, broke the yoke, and upended the chariot. Xerxes fell from his seat, saw his father before him, and ripped up his robes. The imagery is arresting and powerful. The queen's nightmare plainly convicts Xerxes of seeking to bridle both Europe and Asia, then finding fierce resistance from the Greek west and ending in humiliation, especially bitter as it contrasted with the successes of his father.[72] Still more significant, however, is the unequivocal assertion that the two peoples possessed a single genealogical root. Portrayal as sisters resonates with the legend that the demigod Perseus, of Greek lineage, fathered the ancestor of the Persians.[73] And even if the audience did not catch that connection, they could not miss the dramatic vision that coupled the two nations as sisters. Strife arose later, evidently allusion to the Ionian revolt or to the Marathon campaign. But the serious rift came with Xerxes' effort to harness east and west to his realm under compulsion, obviously a reference to the yoking of the Hellespont. The split can be laid to the ambitions of the Achaemenids. But there is no hint of an ethnic chasm between Greek and Persian. On the contrary. They belong to the same lineage.

The *Persae* has too often been taken as emblematizing the Hellenic perception of an essentialist divide between Greek and barbarian, a perception owed directly to the experience of the Persian wars. Yet the play itself resists that interpretation. The two peoples shared a genealogy; their discord arose from Achaemenid imperialism and the arrogance of a king. The dismal outcome of the expedition had little to do with monarchic institutions or ruler worship, much less with any intrinsic flaws of Persian character or admirable Hellenic values. Coming as it did when the military contest was fresh in mind and its resumption imminent, this play presents quite a remarkable perspective on the Persians. Not that Aeschylus evinced "sympathy" for their plight, let alone took the line that war is hell and that its effects victimize humanity in general. The drama freely castigated the bluster and overreaching of Xerxes, presented a chorus of Persian elders who fluctuated

---

[71] On the difference in attire, see Bacon (1961), 27–28.

[72] The notion that the two women represented western and Asiatic Greeks respectively rather than Europe and Asia is highly implausible. The Greeks of Ionia, under Persian suzerainty, would hardly be characterized as engaging in stasis with European Greeks. So, rightly, Broadhead (1960), 78; E. Hall (1996), 124; Garvie (2009), 116.

[73] The passages are noticed by Griffith (1998), 47, who does not emphasize the kinship aspect. The discussion by Rosenblom (2006), 54–56, also omits it. Mitchell (2007), 186–187, sees it in terms of Aeschylus' universalism. Hutzfeldt (1999), 64–66, argues implausibly for historical allusions to the royal household.

between useless criticism and hapless servility (not to mention excessive lamentation), and judged the actions of Persian forces at Salamis as rather less than sterling.[74] But in the end, the play has neither ethnic distinctions nor a common humanity in view. Events were triggered by heedless impieties, manipulated by gods, and determined by fate. The *Persae* counts as a genuine tragedy, rather than a piece of political propaganda, ethnic antipathy, or moral philosophy. Persians constitute the enemy; their actions engendered divine retaliation; and their failure gratified the audience. But Aeschylus decidedly does not relegate them to the category of the "Other."

Herodotus

Why should we think that the Persian War proved decisive in a Hellenic shift of attitude toward the "Other"? The chronicler of that contest, Herodotus, generally stands as chief witness. His canvas, painted a half century or so after the conflict, portrays, so it is often maintained, a collision between freedom and autocracy, between reason and arbitrariness, between western values and oriental barbarism.[75] Yet the "father of history," insofar as he may be representative of Hellenic thinking in the mid- and later fifth century, possessed a palette with much richer pigmentation.

The classic statement of the antithesis comes in Herodotus' narrative of events that followed the Persian crossing of the Hellespont. The historian constructs a dialogue between Xerxes, ruler of Persia and leader of the invasion, and Demaratus, the exiled Spartan king, now an adviser in Xerxes' entourage. The Persian monarch, having reviewed his enormous forces, unprecedented in numbers, challenged Demaratus to give him reason to believe that Greeks would dare to resist this awesome juggernaut. The Spartan prefaced his remarks by asking Xerxes whether he wanted to hear the truth or something pleasant. Xerxes insisted on the former, which Demaratus proceeded to give him, even with the expectation that it would fall upon deaf ears. The former Spartan king did not profess to speak for all Greeks, but could predict what Spartans would do in the face of such an invasion. They would resist regardless of numbers and heavy adverse odds, for they would not accept any terms that brought slavery to Greece, and they would take up arms even if all other Greeks acceded to Persian demands.[76] Xerxes

---

[74] Georges (1994), 86–109, makes some telling points about the deficiencies of the elders but overplays them as emblematizing the defects of the nation. A similar view in Harrison (2000b), 81–82, with additional bibliography at 151, n. 41. Hutzfeldt (1999), 69–72, offers a more judicious assessment. On the portrayal of Xerxes, see Hutzfeldt (1999), 75–79, with bibliography.

[75] E.g., Walser (1984), 1–8; Hartog (1988), 40, 333–339; E. Levy (1992), 242–244; Cartledge (1993), 60–62, 143–145.

[76] Herod. 7.101–102.

broke out in laughter, quite incredulous at so mad an idea. Perhaps hopelessly outnumbered men would put up a fight, he said, if, like his own troops, they were ruled by a single man and acted out of fear or were impelled by the lash—but certainly not of their own free will. Demaratus held fast. Spartans are indeed free, he replied, but not altogether free. For Law is their master, and one whom they fear far more than Persians fear their ruler. They obey its commands unequivocally, and the basic command is always the same: it enjoins them never to flee, no matter how great the foe, but to stand in their ranks and fight, until they prevail or they perish.[77] Xerxes reacted once again with laughter. Demaratus could not be taken seriously and was gently dismissed.[78]

The celebrated scene has long served as centerpiece for those who see Herodotus' pitting of Greek against Persian, of liberty against servitude, of free choice against tyrannical compulsion as a linchpin for Hellenic identity in contrast to eastern barbarism.[79] In fact, it cannot carry such a burden. Demaratus claims to speak only for Sparta, not for the rest of Greece— indeed Spartans are contrasted with other Greeks on this score.[80] More importantly, the speech that Herodotus sets in his mouth praises a system of discipline, not a constitutional order. Xerxes, to be sure, draws a distinction between men who fight on the orders of an absolute ruler and those who do so (or rather would decline to do so) of their own volition. Demaratus, however, asserts that Spartans, though free, are far from entirely free. Law is their despot, a striking phrase. The system may have been deliberately chosen, but it is no less authoritarian than that of Xerxes. Herodotus places emphasis not on political liberty, let alone on democracy (Sparta was hardly democratic), but on undeviating obedience to Spartan *nomos*, their *despotes*, which they hold in much greater awe than Persians do their king.[81] The famous exchange does nothing to suggest that the Greeks fought to preserve a free system against the imposition of Persian tyranny.

The same holds for another well-known statement in Herodotus' text. The historian ventured the opinion, even knowing that it might be unpopular among most people, that Greece could not have been saved without the actions of Athenians, who alone possessed the naval power to resist

[77] Herod. 7.103–104.
[78] Herod. 7.105.
[79] E.g., Redfield (1985), 115–116; Hartog (1988), 334; Lateiner (1989), 160; Cartledge (1993), 61–62.
[80] Herod. 7.102.2: ἀντιώσονταί τοι ἐς μάχην καὶ ἢν οἱ ἄλλοι Ἕλληνες πάντες τὰ σὰ φρονέωσι.
[81] Herod. 7.104.4: ἔπεστι γάρ σφι δεσπότης νόμος τὸν ὑποδειμαίνουσι πολλῷ ἔτι μᾶλλον ἢ οἱ σοὶ σέ. The point, missed by most interpreters, is persuasively noted by Isaac (2004), 264–266. Cf. Schmal (1995), 98–102. See also the discussion by R. Thomas (2000), 109–112, who stresses the *nomos/physis* distinction in the exchange. Herodotus' allusion (7.102.2) to δουλοσύνη refers to potential Persian subjugation of Greece, not to the substitution of one political system for another.

Persia at sea. Had they chosen to submit, the results would have been fatal for Hellas. The Athenians, he proclaimed, held the balance in their hands, and it was they who decided that Greece should live free.[82] The assertion, however, plainly refers to the maintenance of Hellenic freedom from Persian rule and says nothing about the superiority of the Hellenic form of governance.[83]

One passage does indeed give pause. Spartan envoys, on their way to Susa, stopped along the way to be hosted by Hydarnes, the Persian commander of men who served on the coastlines of Asia. Hydarnes wondered why the Spartans refused the friendship of Xerxes, especially when they could witness in his own case how the king rewards good men. The delegates replied quite pointedly that the Persian satrap could not offer a balanced judgment on the matter, for though he knows what it is like to be a slave he has had no taste of freedom.[84] Does this constitute a condemnation of the Persian system and a celebration of the Greek?[85] That may accord the statement more weight than it can shoulder. Reference to a Persian official, high up in the hierarchical chain, as a "slave" does not have a literal connotation. The terminology is slung about more than once to refer to officials serving under a monarch—used even by the Halicarnassian ruler Artemisia to designate Mardonius.[86] The Lacedaemonian envoys do draw a contrast between the absolutist realm of Xerxes, where all inhabitants technically serve the king, and a society whose members are free to make their own choices (the envoys themselves volunteered for this mission, on which they expected to lose their lives). It would go too far, however, to infer that the contrast here goes to the heart of Herodotus' message in his *Histories*. And it is noteworthy that Xerxes treats the Spartan representatives in a far more generous and humane fashion than his own envoys experienced in Sparta.[87] The episode hardly serves as a compelling advertisement for the superiority of Hellenic values over Persian.

Herodotus does supply one full-scale debate on the relative merits of different constitutional systems, and in a Persian context. The so-called "constitutional debate" stands among the best-known and most discussed segments of the work. It provides no explicit comparison between Greek and Persian institutions. But something even more interesting emerges. The overthrow of usurpers to the Achaemenid throne set the stage. The

---

[82] Herod. 7.139.5: ἑλόμενοι δὲ τὴν Ἑλλάδα περιεῖναι ἐλευθέρην.

[83] Cf. also Herod. 7.157.2: Greek envoys, seeking the support of Gelon, tyrant of Syracuse, to help those fighting for Greek freedom. See Isaac (2004), 270.

[84] Herod. 7.135.3: τὸ μὲν γὰρ δοῦλος εἶναι ἐξεπίστεαι, ἐλευθερίης δὲ οὔκω ἐπειρήθης.

[85] So Cartledge (1993), 143–145.

[86] Herod. 8.102; see also 7.39, 7.96, 8.68, 8.116; so, rightly, Isaac (2004), 266–267, who does not, however, discuss 7.135.

[87] Herod. 7.136; see below, p. 29.

successful conspirators then held a discussion as to the proper form of government with which to administer the realm. Herodotus transmits three speeches, advocating respectively democracy, oligarchy, and monarchy. Whether these speeches—or anything like them—were ever delivered has long been disputed.[88] There is no question that the arguments echo Greek political thinking, and the debate has an unmistakably Hellenic flavor. But a decision on the genuineness of the speeches is unnecessary. What matters is that Herodotus insisted that they were trustworthy, even though aware that some Greeks would find that incredible.[89] He either believed in them or, at the least, wished to assert to his audience his confidence in their authenticity. That itself is noteworthy.

The opening speaker, Otanes, made a case for setting government in the hands of the Persians generally. He delivered strong arguments against monarchy, whose very arbitrariness can corrupt the best of men. Absolute power breeds hubris and jealousy. The monarch is simply a *tyrannos*, hostile to the best men and cultivator of the worst, distrustful of those who show proper respect and even angrier at those who flatter him—in short, one who shatters traditional customs and law. Instead, Otanes urged the institution of *isonomia*, equality under the law, where magistrates are selected by lot, accountable for their actions, and all decisions are made by common consent. Monarchy should be abolished and the power of the people expanded.[90] Megabyzus then took up the cudgels for oligarchy. He sharply criticized the idea of transferring power to the people: there is nothing more stupid or arrogant than the useless mob. It would be intolerable to escape the hubris of the tyrant and fall into that of the undisciplined rabble. Let those hostile to the Persians be governed by the people; Persians should put power into the hands of the best men—who will make the best decisions.[91] The argument for monarchy, suitably enough, is put into the mouth of Darius. Oligarchy rouses private jealousies and partisan violence that issues in monarchy; and popular rule leads to malpractice and corruption until one man emerges, wins the admiration of the people, and is accorded monarchic power. Thus, monarchy plainly takes the prize. And Darius interestingly associates the institution with liberation. He summons up the memory of Cyrus, author of Persia's emancipation from the Medes, a feat accomplished by one-man rule, which in Persia constituted "ancestral

---

[88] E.g., Dihle (1962), 207–220; Bringmann (1976), 266–279; Lassere (1976), 65–84; Bleicken (1979), 148–172; Lateiner (1984), 257–284; *idem* (1989), 163–186; Ostwald (2000), 17–20; Pelling (2002), 123–158. Cf. the remarks of Fornara (1983), 164–165, on these speeches and Herodotus' audience.

[89] Herod. 3.80.1; cf. 6.43. R. Thomas (2000), 115–116, believes that Herodotus is being mischievous here.

[90] Herod. 3.80.

[91] Herod. 3.81.

tradition."[92] Darius, of course, won the day, and was shortly thereafter elevated to the throne.

The debate may or may not be fictitious. The terms in which it was couched certainly resonate with Hellenic political philosophy. Even if (perhaps especially if) it is a construct, however, it speaks to Herodotus' conception of Persian theorizing about government. Autocracy, on this view, was not an integral element in Persian national character. Even the one possible, though indirect, comparison made with Greek practice, the allusion to Persia's enemies as governed by the people, was put in the mouth of Megabyzus, the advocate of oligarchy (and there were plenty of oligarchies in Greece).[93] The scenario, whatever its historicity or lack thereof, presupposes that Persians could reach this momentous decision by rational debate and majority vote (of the conspirators). Democracy (or *isonomia*) and oligarchy were viable alternatives to monarchy, even though reckoned in the end as less preferable. Whatever this tells us about the Persians, it demonstrates that Herodotus presented them as calmly deliberating about their constitutional structure and weighing the advantages of possible options.[94] There was no essentialist impulse to freedom in Greece and slavery in Persia.[95]

To be sure, Herodotus draws attention to some notable differences between Greeks and Persians. The historian-ethnographer was ever alive to peculiarities that differentiated peoples and highlighted their special distinctiveness. But the advantage, if such there was, did not always go to the Hellene. Herodotus' text, in fact, contains more nuance and cleverness on this score than is often recognized.

A memorable episode can serve as example. After the battle of Artemisium, Xerxes asked some Arcadian deserters just what it was the Greeks were engaged in. The Arcadians explained that they were holding the Olympic Games and watching athletic and equestrian contests. The king then inquired what prizes awaited the victors and was told that they would win a crown of olive leaves. On hearing that reply, a prominent Persian turned to the general Mardonius and exclaimed: "against what sort of men

[92] Herod. 3.82.
[93] Herod. 3.81.3.
[94] See also Herodotus' narrative of the rise of Deioces to become ruler of Media. He obtained the position as a consequence of the Medes' deliberations and decision to install a monarchy; Herod. 1.96–97.
[95] Cf. the similar conclusion by Isaac (2004), 268–269, and, more expansively, Pelling (2002), 123–158. Darius' general Mardonius, in fact, removed governments of one-man rule in Ionia and installed democracies instead; Herod. 6.43. For Romm (1998), 176–190, the debate (and Herodotus' views) focused primarily on pragmatic considerations—which would further diminish any ideological component. R. Thomas (2000), 113–117, rightly observes that Herodotus believes in the changeability of ethnic character and that this corresponds to changeability in political *nomoi* as well. Cf. also Ward (2008), 90–100.

26   IMPRESSIONS OF THE "OTHER"

are you leading us into battle—men who compete in contests not for money but for honor!"[96] On the face of it, that looks like a slap at Persians, who could understand exertion for material gain but not for mere accolades, a distinctive Greek virtue. But Herodotus was not making so simplistic a point. For one thing, the remark of the Persian earned him a rebuke from Xerxes, who evidently did appreciate the drive for esteem that motivated Greek competitors. More interesting, however, is a tale told by Herodotus about Cyrus the Great, founder of the Persian empire to which Xerxes eventually fell heir. When a distinguished Spartan envoy arrived in Sardis warning Cyrus to keep his hands off Ionia lest he have to answer to the Lacedaemonians, the king made some inquiries as to just who these Lacedaemonians were. Upon gaining the relevant information, he mocked the Spartan representative, and asserted that he had never yet had any fear of men who designated a place in the middle of their city where they would swear oaths and then cheat one another. Herodotus elaborates on the import of Cyrus' remark: he really addressed those words to all the Greeks because they use markets for buying and selling, whereas Persians are unaccustomed to transactions in markets and indeed have no marketplace anywhere in their land.[97] If Persians are skewered for avidity in the one anecdote, Greeks suffer a similar barb in the other. Whether either conversation ever took place is beyond verification. But Herodotus plainly plays with national characteristics here to his own taste. This is no simple matter of inconsistency or absentmindedness. The historian angles his mirror not only toward his own society but toward the Persians in turn. The contrast between the cultures can work both ways.

Another noteworthy episode illustrates the nuances of Herodotean representations. After the decisive battle of Plataea, Xerxes evacuated his forces from Greece. The victorious Spartan king Pausanias entered the abandoned tent of the Persian commander Mardonius. He found it festooned with handsome decorations and expensive furnishings. Pausanias then ordered Mardonius' cooks and bakers to prepare the sort of meal that they normally produced for their former master, while at the same time instructing his own servants to put together the customary Spartan repast. The great discrepancy between Persian lavishness and Spartan austerity quickly became evident. Pausanias seized the opportunity to summon his officers for a viewing and to make his anticipated joke: "Gentlemen, I brought you here to show you the irrationality of the Persians who, enjoying this opulent lifestyle, came here to rob us of our dreary existence."[98] Once again,

---

[96] Herod. 8.26.2–3: οἳ οὐ περὶ χρημάτων τὸν ἀγῶνα ποιεῦνται ἀλλὰ περὶ ἀρετῆς. On this passage, see the acute comments of Konstan (1987), 61–72.
[97] Herod. 1.153.1–2.
[98] Herod. 9.82.2–3.

Herodotus has ostensibly scored a point on the Persians, denoting the discrepancy between eastern luxury and Hellenic hardiness.

But only ostensibly. As is well known, Herodotus makes much of the luxury/softness motif in his *Histories*.[99] Persia by no means plays a consistent part in the presentation. Cyrus himself emblematizes the ambiguity and inversions with which Herodotus toys with the theme. He has Cyrus stir up the Persians to revolt against Median rule by producing a demonstration (also punctuated by an extravagant banquet) that promised them a prosperous and affluent life rather than one of toil and sacrifice.[100] This is the same Cyrus who heaped scorn on the Spartans for their greedy hucksterism. And the inversions persist. When Croesus, the fabulously wealthy ruler of Lydia, prepared for war against Cyrus and Persia, he ignored the sober advice of a counselor. The adviser warned that Croesus would be waging war on a people who dress in leather, drink water rather than wine, never have enough food for their wants, and enjoy no luxury at all. Croesus had everything to lose and nothing to gain. The Persians, Herodotus adds, enjoyed no material comforts—prior to the war with Lydia.[101] A reversal of roles came later. Cyrus, plagued by rebellious activity in Sardis, considered enslaving the city's population. But he was dissuaded by Croesus, now a trusted adviser of the king. Croesus pointed out that Cyrus could best prevent rebelliousness among the Lydians by encouraging them to wear fine undergarments and boots, play the lute and the harp, and teach their children to be retail merchants. That will turn them swiftly from men to women and eliminate them as a threat.[102] The advice may have been sardonic or tongue in cheek—or indeed never offered. But it suited Herodotus' cunning schema. Cyrus took the advice, thus reaffirming Persia as the tough, rigorous, and severe nation as against the effeminate, soft, and commercial-minded Lydians.[103]

But the schema then comes full circle. Cyrus, in what proved to be his final campaign, took on the fierce Massagetae, ruled by their formidable queen Tomyris. Roles are here reversed once more. The Massagetae are represented (again in a speech of Croesus) as having no experience of Persian advantages or indeed of any of the great material pleasures of life. A sumptuous banquet appears in this story as well, this time to lure the Massagetae into a trap. But the devices cannot prevent Cyrus' failure. The hardier society prevails, and Cyrus perishes.[104] Yet it is no accident, of course,

---

[99] On this theme in Herodotus, see Redfield (1985), 109–114; Gould (1989), 59–60; Georges (1994), 181–186.
[100] Herod. 1.126.
[101] Herod. 1.71.
[102] Herod. 1.155.
[103] Herod. 1.156.
[104] Herod. 1.204–214; see, esp., 1.207.6: Μασσαγέται εἰσὶ ἀγαθῶν τε Περσικῶν ἄπειροι καὶ καλῶν μεγάλων ἀπαθέες.

that Herodotus brings Cyrus back at the very end of his work. He flashes back to a supposed conversation between the king and a counselor who urged him to further imperial conquest and to move from his small and rugged country to a better land. Cyrus, however, spurned the advice, warning that, if he did so, Persians would no longer be rulers but ruled. Soft countries produce soft men, Cyrus declared.[105] The convoluted conversions had indeed come full circle—more than once.

There is no straight antithesis here that sets Greek and Persian qualities at odds with one another. Xerxes' tent in Greece might have brought the infiltration of luxury to its peak, at least as displayed for ridicule by Pausanias. But, as Herodotus' readers knew, without being told in his *Histories*, Pausanias came to a bad end, precisely for succumbing to Persian blandishments and the lure of eastern opulence. He may have played the role of quintessential patriot at Plataea, but the aftermath of the war found him dispatched to the east, where he ran into accusations of dictatorial behavior, arbitrary actions against individuals, and treasonable negotiations with Persia. A Spartan tribunal acquitted him of the charges, but suspicions persisted. Pausanias returned to the east without official sanction, engaged in further dealings with the king of Persia, adopted Persian clothing, employed Persian bodyguards—and indulged in grandiose Persian banquets. The various intrigues, whether real, exaggerated, or fabricated, fell afoul of Spartan opinion, resulting in another arrest, imprisonment, and death.[106] All this occurred after the period covered in Herodotus' work, and receives no mention there.[107] It did not need to be mentioned. Pausanias' fall was notorious. Few readers would miss the irony of Herodotus' portrait of Pausanias as prime champion of Hellenic austerity, counterposed to the man whom everyone knew as prime Medizer and emblematic of indulgence in "Oriental" behavior.[108] Herodotus' manipulation of the luxury motif is shrewd, sophisticated, and complex, a series of inversions that entangled Persian and Greek figures alike. The "self" and the "Other" overlap in intricate ways that defy reduction into ethnic categories.

The double reflection applies also to another episode involving Pausanias. After the victory at Plataea, an Aeginetan approached Pausanias and urged upon him an act of brutal vengeance. He reminded the commander that Xerxes and Mardonius had beheaded Leonidas, leader of the valiant but futile resistance at Thermopylae, and had stuck his head on a pike. It would only be fitting to avenge Leonidas' fate by ordering the fallen Mardonius' body to be impaled on a stake. Pausanias rejected the suggestion

---

[105] Herod. 9.122.
[106] Thuc. 1.94–95, 1.128–135; see, esp., 1.130.1.
[107] An indirect allusion, however, occurs in Herod. 5.32.
[108] Cf. Fornara (1971), 62–66.

unequivocally: such an act would be more appropriate for barbarians to perform than for Greeks—and we would despise it even then.[109] Once more Herodotus seems to deliver the lesson that Greek principles are decidedly different from—and preferable to—Persian practice.

But an earlier event turns that lesson precisely on its head. Xerxes had sent envoys to almost all Greek states, asking for earth and water, tokens of submission. Many yielded; others refused and preferred to resist. At Sparta, the king's representatives experienced an especially rude reception. The envoys were hurled into a well, told to seek their earth and water there, and left to perish. Such a violation of diplomatic immunity angered the gods, who scorned Spartan sacrifices and sent only ominous omens. The state called for volunteers to offer themselves to Persia and yield themselves to vengeance, thus to make amends for their nation's offense and appease the gods. Two brave volunteers accepted the mission and presented themselves at Xerxes' court, prepared to sacrifice their lives in the state's interest. Xerxes, however, responded in magnanimous fashion, as Herodotus describes it, asserting that he would not behave toward them as the Lacedaemonians had toward his envoys. He would keep faith with a practice honored by all nations, the immunity of diplomats—and he would not relieve Sparta of its guilt.[110] The latter motive adds a note of pragmatism to the decision. But, whatever the motivation, Xerxes here takes the part of the high-minded leader, the adherent to principle who refuses to imitate the savage behavior of his adversary, exactly the stance of Pausanias when roles were reversed. Herodotus skillfully undermines any notion of essentialist character traits that divided Hellene and Persian.

As is well known, Herodotus has some admiring comments for Persian practices. In his ethnographic excursus on that people, he presents an array of unusual and distinctive traits, most of them quite different from Hellenic customs, and some of them plainly commendable.[111] Persians teach their sons three things only: to ride a horse, to use the bow, and to speak the truth.[112] They regard lying as the most shameful of acts, the owing of debts the next worse, for the debtor is inevitably led into lies.[113] Persian custom also forbids even the king from executing anyone for a single offense; a similar prohibition holds for masters in penalizing slaves. They prefer to weigh the good deeds against the misdeeds before translating their anger into punishment—a practice that Herodotus explicitly approves.[114]

[109] Herod. 9.78–79. See 9.79.1: τὰ πρέπει μᾶλλον βαρβάροισι ποιέειν ἤ περ Ἕλλησι.
[110] Herod. 7.133–136.
[111] Herod. 1.131–140.
[112] Herod. 1.136.2.
[113] Herod. 1.138.1.
[114] Herod. 1.137.1.

For such verdicts, Plutarch more than five centuries later branded Herodotus a *philobarbaros*.[115] That is a naive and superficial judgment. Herodotus held no brief for Persia. Nor was his a bare list of customs treated in detached matter as a mere collection of curious data. Herodotus approved of Persia's principled aversion to lying. But he had no illusions about the frequent violations of that precept, which he himself records.[116] Indeed he places into the mouth of Darius a striking speech that justifies resort to the lie when necessary or advantageous and even raises the practice to a general principle: men lie or speak the truth in accord with their own interest; if there is no profit either way, the liar is as likely to speak the truth as the truth teller is to lie.[117] With regard to the ban on executing men for a single offense, that was honored more in the breach than in the observance. Xerxes more than once vented his anger without balancing the victim's services with his offenses. One need mention only Xerxes' horrific response to his magnanimously generous Lydian host when he asked the king to spare one of his five sons from military service. Xerxes forthwith ordered the guiltless son to be slain and cut in half, with each half displayed on the road through which the Persian army marched.[118] Another instance is equally dramatic. In his retreat from Greece after the battle of Salamis, Xerxes nearly became shipwrecked in a storm; he was saved only when his ship captain suggested lightening the load by asking for volunteers to jump overboard—which several of them did, thus allowing the ship to arrive safely. Xerxes then awarded a golden crown to the ship captain for his sage advice, only to have him beheaded for sending a number of Persians to their death.[119] No measuring of good deeds and bad deeds here. Herodotus does not himself buy this story, indeed takes pains to refute it. But the very fact of its circulation (and Herodotus' record of it) subverts the notion that Persians were assumed to adhere to their own principles.

How to interpret this complex mosaic? Herodotus, as is clear, did not embark on a mission to hail Persian virtues. Did he aim then to expose hypocrisy, contrasting lofty principles with shabby behavior—thereby giving advantage to Greek steadfastness? Not likely. The historian knew well that Greek practices too could fall short of avowed ideals, like those of all people. He did not conceal sharp practices by Greek leaders, or compromised

---

[115] Plut. *De Malig. Her.* 857a. On this work, see Bowen (1992), 2–13; Marincola (1994), 191–203.

[116] See Gould (1989), 26–27; Ward (2008), 100–106.

[117] Herod. 3.72.4.

[118] Herod. 7.38–39. One should observe, however, that punishment for those who sought special treatment through exemption from military service may have been standard policy in Persia. This tale of Xerxes' anger is matched by a closely comparable one involving Darius; Herod. 4.84.

[119] Herod. 8.118.

principles. Here again Herodotus employs ambiguities and inconsistencies that allow each society to reflect in subtle ways on one another. The Spartans, for instance, so Herodotus tells us, have a custom whereby a new king, upon his accession, remits all debts owed by citizens either to the crown or to the state. This generous custom, he adds, corresponds precisely to that of Persia, where a newly enthroned monarch forgives the accumulated tribute for all citizens of the empire.[120] That suggests shared values. But another shared practice was not so estimable. Herodotus observes, without comment, that Persians are more open to foreign customs than any other people. He cites some examples like Median clothing and Egyptian armor. The one practice that Herodotus claims they learned from the Greeks, however, is pederasty.[121] That is no innocent remark. The double reflection operates here. The questionable Persian practice mirrors the Greek—and vice versa. Herodotus passes no overt judgment, and does not need to. Readers can draw their own conclusions. Both connections and disconnects exist between the cultures, an ambiguous relationship that defies polarization.

The idea that Herodotus depicted Persians as nothing but craven minions of a despotic ruler, by contrast with Hellenic freedom fighters, makes nonsense of the narrative. The Persians had high regard for courage in adversity. Brave leaders and soldiers received great respect, a national trait that Herodotus duly praises. One might note the case of the courageous satrap of Eion, Boges, who was besieged by a Greek invading force a few years after the war, refused surrender, and fought tenaciously to the end in a hopeless cause. Herodotus observes that Xerxes considered him a man of great virtue and that his name resonates in Persia down to Herodotus' own day—and justly so.[122] Persians showed equal admiration for valor among their enemies. The brave Aeginetan sailor who fought fiercely and fearlessly despite massive wounds was greatly honored by the Persians, who treated his wounds, nursed him back to health, and accorded him every respect.[123] Xerxes' vindictive order to have the head of Leonidas cut off and affixed to a pike, after the Spartan leader had fallen at Thermopylae, was a glaring exception to Persian practice. Herodotus pauses to reflect on the matter: Xerxes' fury at Leonidas must have been ferocious indeed, for Persians generally show greater honor to brave warriors than does any other nation.[124] At the climactic battle of Plataea, as Herodotus reports, Persians

[120] Herod. 6.58–59.
[121] Herod. 1.135.
[122] Herod. 7.107.1–2: οὕτω μὲν οὗτος δικαίως αἰνέεται ἔτι καὶ ἐς τόδε ὑπὸ Περσέων.
[123] Herod. 7.181, 8.92.1.
[124] Herod. 7.238: ἐπεὶ τιμᾶν μάλιστα νομίζουσι τῶν ἐγὼ οἶδα ἀνθρώπων Πέρσαι ἄνδρας ἀγαθοὺς τὰ πολέμια. Persians also made it a practice to honor the sons of foreign kings, even restoring them to the thrones of fathers who had rebelled against them; Herod. 3.15.2.

suffered defeat because they lacked armor, were unskilled, and were unequal to their enemies in military know-how, but they were in no way inferior in courage and strength.[125]

Herodotus also valued Persian regard for religious precepts and practices, both their own and those of others. He notes customs quite different from those of the Greeks, such as a strict aniconism and a worship of sun, moon, and other natural powers in addition to a supreme deity whom they consider as equivalent to the whole circle of the heavens, rather than a multitude of gods to be honored by temples, statues, and altars. Herodotus eschews judgment on these modes of worship, but plainly respects them.[126] Although the Persians may have declined to erect images or structures to the divine, they could give proper appreciation to those of others. The Ionians, in their burning of Sardis, had destroyed the temple of the local Lydian deity Cybebe. The Persians later, according to Herodotus, used that event as pretext for burning Greek shrines.[127] Pretext it may have been, but the championing of retaliation for the Lydian religious loss must have had some resonance among Persians. Datis, the Mede whom Darius had appointed as a commander, took on the task of recruiting soldiers in the Aegean or subjugating those islands that resisted. When his forces took the island of Naxos and engaged in destruction that included the burning of shrines, word spread to Delos and caused its inhabitants to abandon their sacred isle. But Datis swiftly sent a herald to reassure the Delians that he would never harm the soil or the people of a land that gave birth to the two gods (Apollo and Artemis). And he punctuated his point by offering a great sacrifice at the altar.[128] This was evidently more than just propagandistic posturing. After the Persian defeat at Marathon, Datis stopped at Mykonos on the way back to Asia. There he discovered a gilded statue of Apollo hidden away in a Phoenician ship, plainly purloined from a Greek shrine. Datis personally took the image in his own ship to Delos and placed it in a temple where it could be secure until returned to its original owners in Boeotian Delium.[129] The commander clearly put his homage to Hellenic reverence on display here. In this matter, as in others, Persians did not consistently live up to such principles (they did, after all, burn shrines in Naxos). But Herodotus' astute portrait of the nation steers away from any dualistic scheme that puts Greek patriotism ahead of discriminating judgment.[130]

---

[125] Herod. 9.62.3: λήματι μέν νυν καὶ ῥώμῃ οὐκ ἥσσονες ἦσαν οἱ Πέρσαι, ἄνοπλοι δὲ ἐόντες καὶ πρὸς ἀνεπιστήμονες ἦσαν καὶ οὐκ ὅμοιοι τοῖσι ἐναντίοισι σοφίην. Cf. 9.71.1.
[126] Herod. 1.131. See Burkert (1990), 14–22.
[127] Herod. 5.102.1.
[128] Herod. 6.96–97.
[129] Herod. 6.118.1–2.
[130] See the judicious remarks of Flower (2006), 284–287.

Persian rulers did, of course, behave in arbitrary, despotic, and occasionally brutal fashion. Herodotus makes no secret of it.[131] But autocracy did not depend on ethnicity. Herodotus has as much to say about Greek tyranny as he does about eastern despotism.[132] As for "barbaric" cruelty, one could hardly find a better example than the order by the *Athenian* commander Xanthippus at the end of the war to crucify the satrap Artayctes and to execute his son before his eyes.[133]

Nor does Herodotus reduce the kings of Persia to cardboard figures posted up to dramatize the advantages of Hellenism over barbarism. The shifting portrait of Cyrus, already alluded to, gives the sense of a complex personality.[134] Herodotus certainly sets some of his qualities in a positive light. The Persians, so he reports, reckoned Cyrus as a father because of his kindness and his efforts to bring them every benefit.[135] Perhaps the most memorable scene occurs when Cyrus ordered the burning alive of Croesus, king of Lydia, after the battle of Sardis and the capture of its ruler. As flames began to rise, Cyrus had a change of heart. He comprehended the fickleness of fate, the instability of human affairs, as he pondered the fact that he was consigning a fellow human being to the flames, and one who had enjoyed a good fortune no less than his own. Cyrus then ordered the extinguishing of the fire.[136] He had behaved in similar fashion, though without elaboration in the Herodotean text, when he led Persians in revolt against the Medes and toppled the regime of Astyages, the Median monarch. Cyrus had treated him with scorn during the revolt but showed magnanimity after his capture. Astyages suffered no harm, and Cyrus kept him, like Croesus, as a member of his court until his death.[137] Herodotus, it appears, had some admiration also for Cyrus' wit and perceptiveness.[138] When Astyages, learning of the revolt, sent a messenger to summon Cyrus to him, Cyrus promptly had the messenger return with the reply that he would arrive rather sooner than Astyages wished.[139] After having rescued Croesus from the pyre, installed him as an adviser, and received excellent counsel from him, Cyrus offered to grant him any wish. Croesus, who believed that the Delphic oracle had treacherously misled him into making war on Persia, asked leave to rebuke Apollo by placing chains at the entrance of the

---

[131] Lateiner (1989), 153–155.
[132] See the recent discussion of Dewald (2003), 25–58. She may exaggerate, however, the supposed Herodotean distinction between the personal tyrannies of Greek rulers and the systemic autocracy of the east.
[133] Herod. 9.120. See Flower and Marincola (2002), 302–303, 308–310, with bibliography.
[134] Cf. Evans (1991), 51–56; Georges (1994), 180–186.
[135] Herod. 3.89.3.
[136] Herod. 1.86.6.
[137] Herod. 1.130.
[138] Cf. Waters (1971), 51.
[139] Herod. 1.127.1–2.

temple at Delphi, symbolizing his own captive status, and to ask the god whether he did not feel ashamed for having deceived him. Cyrus granted the wish—but only after having a hearty laugh over it.[140] On this score at least, the ruler was evidently wiser than his wise counselor. Cyrus displayed his wit again when the Ionians and Aeolians sent envoys requesting the same terms as subjects of his realm as they had enjoyed under Croesus' suzerainty. Cyrus responded with an old fable: the fish who would not come ashore when the flute player cajoled them with music were subsequently hauled in by nets and jumped about accordingly; their captor then duly mocked them, stating that it was too late to dance now. Cyrus employed the tale to rub it in to the Asian Greeks: they had not joined him in revolt against Croesus when he asked, and it was too late for them to make any requests now.[141] We have noticed already Cyrus' equally caustic comment to Spartan representatives who protested his attack on the Ionians. He could not take seriously men who spent their time in the marketplace cheating fellow citizens.[142]

Herodotus, as we have seen, significantly recalls Cyrus to his text at its very conclusion. There he delivers words of wisdom that underscore a central theme for the historian. He parries the advice of Persians who urge a move, now that they are victorious, to a more prosperous land. The king retorted that no land produces both excellent fruit and fine warriors. If Persians choose the good life, they have to prepare to be the ruled rather than the rulers. His interlocutors acknowledged the force of that advice and dropped their case, bested by Cyrus' sagacity.[143] Herodotus closes his work on that note. Cyrus, in the end, becomes the virtual embodiment of sound counsel.

Herodotus, to be sure, has no interest in whitewashing Achaemenid kings. His depiction of Cambyses is almost unrelievedly dark.[144] And Darius hardly emerges as an admirable figure, ruthless, unprincipled, and ferociously ambitious in his imperial expansionism. It is fitting that he expressed the cynical line that all persons lie or speak the truth only in accord with their own interest, and that he obtained his throne through calculated chicanery.[145] Yet Herodotus can redeploy the character in surprising ways. The case that Darius makes for monarchy in the "constitutional debate" voices the idea that no government can be better than that of the "best man"; by following his own counsel he will guide the people faultlessly and

[140] Herod. 1.90.
[141] Herod. 1.141.1–3.
[142] Herod. 1.153.1–3.
[143] Herod. 9.122.
[144] E.g., Herod. 3.14, 3.25, 3.30–38; cf. Waters (1971), 53–56.
[145] Herod. 3.72, 3.84–87. On Herodotus' portrait of Darius generally, see Waters (1971), 57–65; Evans (1991), 56–60.

mature his plans in silence against men of ill will.[146] It would be too simple to interpret the argument for an ideal monarch in the mouth of one who fell well short of that standard as Herodotean irony or as condemnation of hypocrisy. (The king, who overtly praised the value of mendacity, was no hypocrite).[147] Herodotus finds it perfectly reasonable that a Persian could employ concepts familiar to Greek political philosophy in advocating a system of benign one-man rule. Even more striking is Herodotus' celebrated homage to cultural relativism: every nation regards its customs as preferable to those of all others and shrinks in horror at alien practices that violate its own sensibilities, a universal shortsightedness. What is especially notable here is that Herodotus has this lesson delivered to the Greeks, who should have known better, by none other than Darius.[148] Like Cyrus, he could convey maxims of profound significance in broad-minded fashion. The very conception of a Persian with keener insight into cultural sensitivities than the Greeks at his court further subverts any Hellene/barbarian dichotomy.

The figure of Xerxes, of course, looms large in the narrative. He is generally taken as emblematic of the hubristic ruler, the arrogant and foolish aggrandizer, overconfident in the numbers and power of his forces, alternately boastful and fearful, often cruel, lacking balance and good sense, overweening in victory and cowardly in defeat, epitomizing eastern despotism as against Hellenic freedom.[149] We have had occasion already to question the starkness of that antithesis. To be sure, Xerxes' flaws manifest themselves with vividness through the Herodotean text. But that makes all the more arresting those occasions when the historian sets him in a very different light.

A stunning scene occurred at the Hellespont. Xerxes sat on an elevated site to review his extraordinarily vast forces filling the whole of the straits and covering the beaches and plains all around. His first impulse was to rejoice, but shortly thereafter he burst into tears. That remarkable behavior puzzled his uncle and adviser Artabanus, who inquired as to its meaning. Xerxes then made the doleful response that he had realized, after observing these thousands of men, that none would be alive after a century, a pointed reminder of the brief time we have on earth.[150] Herodotus forbears

---

[146] Herod. 3.82.2: ἀνδρὸς γὰρ ἑνὸς τοῦ ἀρίστου οὐδὲν ἄμεινον ἂν φανείη. γνώμῃ γὰρ τοιαύτῃ χρεώμενος ἐπιτροπεύοι ἂν ἀμωμήτως τοῦ πλήθεος, σιγῷτό τε ἂν βουλεύματα ἐπὶ δυσμενέας ἄνδρας οὕτω μάλιστα. Hartog's view (1988), 324–327, that Darius conceives monarchy as equivalent to tyranny, is somewhat reductive.

[147] That Darius could act in magnanimous fashion is illustrated by his sparing of Milesian and Eretrian captives and resettling them in productive lands; Herod. 6.20, 6.119.

[148] Herod. 3.38.

[149] Cf. Hartog (1988), 330–334, who finds no redeeming features. More balanced views in Evans (1991), 60–67, and Romm (1998), 166–170.

[150] Herod. 7.45–46.2. Cf. the comments of Gould (1989), 133–134. Konstan (1987), 64, minimizes the episode.

36 IMPRESSIONS OF THE "OTHER"

to comment, and Xerxes swiftly moves on to more positive matters. But the melancholy reflections put into the king's mouth signal Herodotus' wish to present something considerably more than a caricature.[151] That aim gains reinforcement when the historian does inject an opinion of his own on this score, an even more arresting passage. After Herodotus calculates the astonishing (and utterly fantastic) numbers that made up Xerxes' army, navy, support personnel, and camp followers, he adds a surprising statement. Amidst this vast sea of humanity, he opines, there was not a single man more worthy, in grace and stature, to hold the power than Xerxes.[152] The king here possesses a noble bearing that transcends any "Orientalist" designs. Herodotus provides a compelling image that brings the reader up short, subverts simplistic estimates of Xerxes' character, and demands a deeper probe. The exemplar of "Oriental kingship" turns out to be, at least in Herodotus' hands, a far more complex and intriguing personality.

Xerxes' more attractive side emerges in a variety of contexts. The king acts in impetuous ways but can also feel remorse. After he angrily and insolently rejected Artabanus' sound advice not to undertake the expedition against Greece, Xerxes later expressed his regrets. Before an assembly of Persian leaders he asked forgiveness for his hasty judgment and his rude behavior, reversed himself, and acknowledged the wisdom of Artabanus' judgment.[153] Xerxes' most notorious act of *hybris* came when his bridge across the Hellespont was destroyed by a storm and the king vented his fury by ordering the Hellespont itself to receive three hundred lashes and a pair of fetters to be thrown into its waters.[154] Here was the pinnacle of preposterous arrogance. But it is easy to forget an episode that took place not long thereafter. When the bridge had been repaired and the army prepared to cross, Xerxes poured a libation into the sea from a golden goblet, prayed to the sun for no further mishap, and cast the cup and other objects into the Hellespont. Herodotus suggests two possible explanations for the act: either Xerxes made an offering to the sun or he repented his lashing of the Hellespont and sent the gifts as recompense.[155] Whatever Xerxes' reason may have been in fact, Herodotus leaves his readers with the impression that the king could acknowledge his own failings. This is not the stereotypical tyrant. Other indications confirm the complexity of character. As we

---

[151] The motif of joy giving way to tears is one that appears on several occasions in Herodotus' text; see Flory (1978), 145–153. That does not, however, diminish the poignancy of Xerxes' reaction or the significance attached to it by Herodotus.

[152] Herod. 7.187.2: ἀνδρῶν δ' ἐουσέων τοσουτέων μυριάδων κάλλεός τε εἵνεκα καὶ μεγάθεος οὐδεὶς αὐτῶν ἀξιονικότερος ἦν αὐτοῦ Ξέρξεω ἔχειν τοῦτο τὸ κράτος.

[153] Herod. 7.13. Of course, he subsequently reversed himself again, but only with Artabanus' agreement; 7.15–18.

[154] Herod. 7.35.1.

[155] Herod. 7.54.2.

have seen, Xerxes greeted Demaratus' prediction that Spartans would resist his invasion and fight against overwhelming odds with disbelief. But he showed no anger, gave a laugh, and sent Demaratus off in genial fashion.[156] And, as noted earlier, Xerxes behaved in exemplary fashion when Spartan envoys arrived to atone with their lives for their state's violation of diplomatic sanctity. The king would not retaliate by imitating their sacrilege, a gesture that Herodotus describes as one of noble high-mindedness.[157]

Nor was nobility of mind limited to rulers. Herodotus describes a touching scene on the eve of the climactic battle of Plataea in which Persians and Thebans shared a banquet. At its conclusion one of the Persians spoke in Greek, asked his fellow banqueters to gaze on the vast host of Persian soldiers encamped prior to battle, and observed that within a very short time only a small portion of them would still be alive. And he proceeded to burst into tears. Herodotus claimed to have the story from a Boeotian eyewitness.[158] That makes all the more telling the fact that these sentiments, expressing a deep humanity, are set in the mouth of a Persian.

Herodotus, of course, does not propose to exonerate Persia, let alone to defend its monarchs. But he maneuvers those figures in diverse ways to define political principles, exhibit wit, deliver moral lessons, offer prudent counsel, decry foolishness, feel remorse, acknowledge failings, and reflect on the human condition. How much of this derives from sources and how much constitutes embellishment or manufacture evades determination. But the historian is no passive recorder. Herodotus' kings play multiple roles, take surprising actions, shift between the objectionable and the admirable, and often upset expectations. Their pronouncements and behavior could as easily be ascribed to Greek as to Persian figures. They hardly serve as exemplars of an alien society representing principles irreconcilable with the spirit of Hellas.

Indeed Herodotus even reports a genealogical connection between the peoples. Legend traced that association back to the Argive hero Perseus, son of Danaë who had been impregnated by Zeus in the form of a golden shower. Perseus' most celebrated adventure, the rescue of Andromeda from a sea monster, culminated in a marriage that produced several children including Perses, from whom the Persians took their name.[159] Various forms of that tale circulated. But Herodotus plainly adopted the version that linked Persians and Greeks to the Argive ancestor. Not all Persians bought it in that form. Some made Perseus an Assyrian who only later became Greek.[160] But Xerxes himself embraced the Hellenic tradition, so we are

[156] Herod. 7.105.
[157] Herod. 7.136.2: ὑπὸ μεγαλοφροσύνης.
[158] Herod. 9.16.
[159] Herod. 7.61; cf. Apollod. 2.4.1–5.
[160] Herod. 6.54.

told. He found it especially valuable in negotiating with Argos to procure that city's neutrality in the war. The king could conveniently point to their common ancestry through the bloodline of Perseus. Herodotus does not guarantee the reliability of the report that Xerxes sent a messenger to Argos to appeal to their kinship. But he casts no doubt on the tradition of kinship itself.[161] The idea that Persians and Greeks shared a link in distant antiquity proved perfectly acceptable to some on both sides. And the historian transmitted it without hesitation or embarrassment.

The enmeshing of Persia in Hellenic legend is itself noteworthy. Herodotus notoriously opens his history by citing Persian authorities on the origins of the great war, origins that they set into the distant mists of mythology. They traced its genesis back to the supposed capture by Phoenicians of the Argive princess Io, whom they spirited off to Egypt. This inaugurated a series of body snatches between east and west, including the seizure of Medea, and mutual recriminations culminating in the rape of Helen, which triggered the Trojan War. From the Persian vantage point, abductions of women were no more than irritating and illegitimate (the women must have made themselves available anyway). To mobilize for war on that account was senseless escalation. The Trojan conflict, on their view, engendered the hostility between east and west, and lay at the root of the climactic war between Greece and Persia.[162] Whether Herodotus actually had Persian sources for this tradition has long stirred debate.[163] That need not be decided here. A more pertinent point merits emphasis. Herodotus expected his readers to find perfectly plausible the idea that Persian storytellers embraced legends integral to Hellenic tradition. The point receives reinforcement from Xerxes' burning desire to visit the citadel at Troy and his showy sacrifice of one thousand oxen to Athena of Ilium.[164] This plainly presupposes a shared legendary heritage, even if it put the two people on opposite sides. Xerxes indeed justified his confidence in victory by noting that Pelops from Phrygia, no more than a servant of Xerxes' royal ancestors, had subdued the land and people who still bear his name in Greece.[165]

---

[161] Herod. 7.150–152. Cf. 7.220.4. See the valuable discussion of Georges (1994), 66–71.
[162] Herod. 1.1–5.
[163] Fehling (1971), 39–45, expresses strong skepticism. See the response of Pritchett (1993), 55–63. Cf. E. Levy (1992), 227–229, who ascribes the story to Asian Greeks in the service of Persia—a plausible vehicle for Persian familiarity with Greek myth.
[164] Herod. 7.43.1–2. One might note also the seizure by a Persian official of the shrine of Protesilaus in Elaeus on the grounds that that Achaean hero had unjustly invaded the territory of the king; Herod. 9.116; cf. 7.33. Protesilaus, according to Homer, had been the first of the Greeks to enter Trojan soil; *Il*. 2.701–702. The connection is here once again made between Persia and Troy, an implication that the Trojan legend was familiar to and now deployed by the Persians. See Boedeker (1988); Haubold (2007), 54–56. See also Ctesias *FGH* 688 F16 = Diod. 2.22, who asserts that events of the Trojan War found place in Persian royal records.
[165] Herod. 7.11.4; cf. 8.9g.

Here again, without fanfare or elaboration, Herodotus takes for granted that Persians are steeped in the same traditions familiar to the Greeks.

The chronicler of the great war between Greece and Persia finds numerous reasons for bitter enmity between the nations. But a cultural divide does not take precedence among them.[166] Herodotus presents a motley canvas, no black-and-white images.[167] Heroes and villains appear on both sides. Persians embraced some admirable ideals but did not always adhere to them—like Greeks. Principles (and the breach of principles) allowed Herodotus to have the two societies reflect each on the other. Persian monarchs possessed complex personalities, no mere stereotypes to point out moral or political lessons. Value systems overlapped rather than clashed. Customs and practices could be distinguished, but not necessarily to the advantage of one or the other. And the two peoples shared a legendary and genealogical heritage. Herodotus did not compose a manifesto to advocate the superiority of a constitutional system, to celebrate Hellenic values, or to suggest essentialist characteristics that entailed an irremediable separation between the peoples.[168] Cultural identities are ambiguous and fluid phenomena, as the father of history knew.

---

[166] Cf. the remarks of Schmal (1995), 106–107.

[167] A somewhat similar conclusion, through a different route with different examples, is reached by Pelling (1997), 1–12.

[168] Essentialist distinctions between Greeks and Persians have often been found in the peculiar Hippocratic treatise *Airs, Waters, Places*, probably contemporaneous or nearly contemporaneous with Herodotus. See the edition of Jouanna (1996). The author does believe in a form of environmental determinism, and he draws a pointed contrast between "Asia" and "Europe." The latter appears to come out ahead. The Hippocratic writer oddly claims that because easterners enjoy a mild and pleasant climate the region would not promote courage, hardiness, or energy. The relatively unchangeableness of the climate makes them less warlike, milder, and weaker; *Airs*, 12, 16. Both physical and mental toughness require dramatic changes in the environment; hence, Europeans are braver than Asians; *Airs*, 19.23–24. The author also adds institutions as a contributory cause, since most Asians live under despots and have little incentive to develop warlike traits and military prowess; *Airs*, 16, 23. As testimony to Hellenic belief in an essentialist divide between Greeks and Persians, however, this treatise hardly fits the bill. The author never once mentions Persians. And the sole reference to Greeks speaks of the inhabitants of Asia (presumably Asia Minor) and asserts that both Greeks and non-Greeks in that region are the most warlike of all, so long as they are autonomous and not under despotic rule; *Airs*, 16. This appears to give the nod to institutions rather than physical environment as determinative. But they are determinative for Greeks and non-Greeks alike. Hence they do not serve as an ethnic differentiation. Indeed the author is confused not only about the relative significance of climate and institutions; he acknowledges that there are numerous differences among Europeans, depending on environmental conditions, as there are among Asians, thus undermining his own contrast between the peoples; *Airs*, 16, 23, 24. The treatise is riddled with inconsistencies and with statements inadequately thought through. Even the polarization of east and west is shaky in formulation, and nothing asserts a polarization of Greeks and Persians. *Airs, Waters, Places* cannot be used as witness to Hellenic embrace of such a dichotomy. See the reasoned comments of R. Thomas (2000), 86–98; cf. Tuplin (1999), 62–69; Isaac (2004), 60–69.

Some Visual Representations

Visual representations, to be sure, drew clear distinctions. Battle scenes that pitted Greeks against non-Greeks leave little room for doubt as to who is who. Images of Greek hoplites, generally unclothed, clean shaven, with spear, shield, and helmet, engaged in contests with "Orientals," clad in trousers or leggings with long-sleeved upper garments, striped or spotted, soft headgear, full bearded, armed with quiver and bow, appear on numerous Attic vase paintings. And the easterner, in most cases probably a "Persian," regularly appears as loser in the contests (fig. 1). Numerous variations on this theme exist. Clothing, weaponry, and physiognomy do not follow rigid and consistent formulas. But the general pattern is plain. Although, for example, one cannot always distinguish a Persian from a Scythian or even a Thracian on these paintings, there is no reason to doubt that fifth-century representations of such scenes allude to Hellenic martial superiority as demonstrated in the Persian wars of the early part of that century.[169]

Nothing surprising in that. The Greeks took justifiable pride in their successful defense of the homeland against the dreaded invasion of vast armies bent on their subjugation. Celebration of their victory and repeated depiction of Persians succumbing to the valor of the Hellenes are readily intelligible. The south frieze of the Temple of Athena Nike, dating to the late fifth century BCE, provides a celebrated example. Battle scenes depicted there show Greeks, presumably Athenians, essentially nude in fighting trim and on foot, victorious over fully clothed Persian horsemen and archers, in flight or already fallen. The heroic stances may have echoed a comparable scene from the Marathon painting in the Painted Stoa of the mid–fifth century.[170] Whether the south frieze actually did represent the battle of Marathon or that of Plataea or perhaps the broader conflict need

---

[169] See the valuable discussion of Raeck (1981), 101–163, who observes the variations but maintains that Persians came to stand in for exotic easterners generally in the course of the fifth century; a similar view in Shapiro (2009), 72–83, for whom the scenes are largely fanciful and imaginary. On the battle scenes, see also Bovon (1963), 579–591; Hölscher (1973), 38–49; Muth (2005), 185–209. In important recent works, Miller (1995), 39–44, and (2006), 113–116, argues that portrayal of Persian warriors went through two phases: the first depicted them as worthy and brave opponents; the second, after about 460, represented them in more cowardly and effeminate mode. Just why there should have been a shift in midcentury remains quite unclear—if indeed there was one. Miller offers very few examples. And she does acknowledge that none of them involved demonization of the Persian.

[170] See the full discussion, still the most thorough treatment, by E. Harrison (1972), 353–378, with plates 73–78. On the Marathon painting, see especially Paus. 1.15.3, and the complete listing of literary testimonia in E. Harrison (1972), 370–378. For other important studies of the Nike Temple frieze, see Hölscher (1973), 91–98; Stewart (1985), 53–73. Harrison's more recent study (1997), 109–125, deals largely with other issues than the Greek/Persian confrontation. An extensive bibliography on the temple and its sculpture can be found in Stewart (1985), 70–71.

Figure 1. Oinochoe showing Greek warrior and Persian archer, mid–fifth century BCE. Museum of Fine Arts, Boston (inv. no. 13.196).

not be decided here.[171] But it is well to remember that even this proud commemoration of Hellenic success against the foreign invader did not exhaust the themes of the friezes elsewhere on the Temple of Nike. In the west and north friezes Greeks appear in mortal combat against other Greeks. Whether these scenes reflect specific historical battles and which battles they might represent remain altogether unsettled.[172] But an important fact needs emphasis. The contests with the Persians no more disparage the defeated than do those that pit Greeks against Greeks.[173] Celebration of victory had greater impact by eschewing stigmatization of the vanquished.

Where then do we get a demeaning portrait of the weak, effeminate, cowardly, and despicable Persian, the "Other," whose characteristics starkly contrast with Hellenic values and virtues?

The notorious "Eurymedon vase" has served as a prime exhibit for this interpretation (fig. 2). The red-figure oinochoe, probably of the mid–fifth century, portrays on one side a nude, evidently Greek, male striding forth, with phallus in right hand and left hand outstretched, and on the other side a figure in oriental garb, a quiver slung over his shoulder, in frontal pose, bent over, and hands raised. The inscription, extending between the figures, appears to read "I am Eurymedon, I am bent over."[174] The allusion is generally taken as referring to the battle of the Eurymedon River, a major Athenian naval and land victory over Persian forces in the mid-460s. And it has called forth the interpretation of the imagery as a crude sexual metaphor, the virile Athenian lording it over the womanish Persian, who presents himself as the passive recipient of the victor's thrust.[175]

Several caveats, however, need to be entered here. First, the phrase "I am Eurymedon," on the face of it, should signify a personal name, not a metaphorical allusion. And indeed the name appears with some frequency for Greek gods, heroes, and others.[176] Neither of the figures on the vase

---

[171] See the differing views of Harrison (1997), 353–356; Hölscher (1973), 93, 259, n. 470; Ridgway (1981), 89–93; Stewart (1985), 61.

[172] For some suggestions, see Hölscher (1973), 94–95.

[173] So, rightly, Hölscher (1973), 98. Stewart (1985), 61–62, exaggerates the contrast between the hardiness of the Greek warriors and the "sluggish eastern corpulence" of the Persians.

[174] The initial publication of the piece is Schauenburg (1975), 97–121, and Tafel 25. On the meaning of the inscription, the latter part of which is disputed, see Schauenberg (1975), 103–104. A new reading now in Miller (forthcoming) offers a small variation: "I stand at the ready in a bent-over position."

[175] So the celebrated expression of Dover (1978), 105: "We've buggered the Persians!" A more restrained formulation by Schauenburg (1975), 120: "eine spezielle Form des Triumphs." That view is endorsed more recently by, e.g., Arafat (1997), 101–104; Cartledge (1998), 56–57; Hölscher (2000a), 302; Lissarague (2002), 118–119 (with a slightly different rendering); and Mitchell (2007), 135; Shapiro (2009), 66–72. Miller (forthcoming) concurs but offers a more complex interpretation that has the painter mock both figures on the vase.

[176] This is acknowledged by Schauenburg (1975), 104, with references, although he prefers to see it as a place-name here. Pinney (1984), 181, and Davidson (1998), 171, consider the

AESCHYLUS AND HERODOTUS ON PERSIA 43

Figure 2. "Eurymedon" oinochoe, showing one nude figure and one in "barbarian" attire, first half of fifth century BCE. Hamburg, Museum für Kunst und Gewerbe (inv. vo. 1981.173). Photograph courtesy of the Getty Museum, Los Angeles.

approximates the standard personifications of rivers.[177] Second, the striding figure is no warrior, carries no martial attributes, and gives no hint of a military victory.[178] Third, even the Greek/Persian dichotomy is far from neat and clear. The first figure's "Greekness" appears compromised by his goatee and sideburns.[179] And the second figure could be a Scythian rather

---

name of an individual. Braund (2006), 109–113, postulates a particular individual, Eurymedon of the family of Speusippos who first organized the Scythian archers in Athens, an ingenious but altogether speculative suggestion. Schauenburg's discussion (1975), 104–106, of Greek names ascribed to non-Greeks, presumed that the eastern figure on the vase identifies himself as "Eurymedon." Others regard the words as more likely uttered by the "Greek" than by the easterner on the vase; see Pinney (1984), 180–181; A. Smith (1999), 135. Miller's recent reexamination of the vase (forthcoming) makes the important observation that the words begin at the mouth of the "Greek" figure and confirms Schauenburg's view of the inscription as closely binding the two individuals.

[177] A. Smith (1999), 129–135, makes a good case for the widespread use of personifications in early classical visual representations. But that need not hold in this instance. She concedes that the image does not correspond to personifications of rivers and resorts to seeing it as a personification of the battle.

[178] A. Smith (1999), 136, describes him as a hunter but nonetheless interprets the figure as representing Greek virility by contrast to oriental effeminacy.

[179] Wannagat (2001), 54–63, usefully discusses the variety of figures and types depicted with facial hair on Attic vases, usually foreigners, peasants, pedagogues, and dwarfs, almost never

than a Persian. The fluidity between the two in depictions on Attic vases regularly baffles interpreters.[180] Fourth, the easterner's frontal facing and upraised hands need not indicate political or military surrender. His pose looks more like mockery than submission. And, even if the bent-over posture signifies the prelude to a sexual encounter, with the easterner in the passive role, that hardly demonstrates forcible subordination or the defeat of east by west.[181] And fifth, perhaps most important, this form of representation is essentially unique, with no close or even remote parallels. The notion that the images signal a triumphant proclamation of Hellenic superiority over the degenerate barbarian reads far too much into the imagery, which possesses a decidedly comic flavor, lacking any heavy implications for a clash of Hellenism and barbarism.[182] As evidence for the supposed Greek denigration and disparagement of Persian character, the Eurymedon vase simply fails to qualify.

Attic vase painting of the fifth century in general does not cast the Persian as a despised and inferior being. Far from it. In the two or three decades following immediately upon the Persian wars, portrayals of Greek

---

the ideal and admirable Athenian. He notes also, 63–69, that the cloak, fastened by a knot rather than a clasp, would normally indicate a shepherd, a farmer, or (in a military context) a light-armed soldier, not a respected warrior. Pinney (1984), 181, even regards his mantle as a Thracian one. But, although Wannagat neatly deconstructs the "Greek" character of the striding figure, he fully accepts the standard notion of the easterner as representing the cowardly and effeminate passivity of the oriental barbarian; (2001), 69. Miller (forthcoming) offers the novel and intriguing suggestion that the "Greek" represents a lower-class Athenian, possibly symbolizing the rise of the Athenian navy, a development unwelcome to and thus satirized by the cultural elite. The proposal is ingenious, but the absence of parallels leaves it in the realm of stimulating speculation.

[180] The extended discussion of Schauenburg (1975), 106–118, strains to draw distinctions but only underscores the difficulty of doing so. See also Raeck (1981), 102–104. For the depiction of Scythians on Attic vase painting, see, recently, Osborne (2004), 41–54; Barringer (2004), 13–25; Ivanchik (2005), 100–113. Miller (forthcoming) finds that Scythian imagery gives way to Persian by the early fifth century.

[181] Pinney (1984), 181–183, makes a cogent argument against the political and military interpretation, focusing on the sexual character of the scene. So also Davidson (1998), 170–171, 180–182, who nonetheless views it as a metaphor for the decadence, weakness, and cowardice of the Asiatic. A. Smith (1999), 128–141, claims to steer a middle course between the views of Schauenburg and Pinney, embracing both the sexual and the political implications, but in fact largely adopting the Schauenburg/Dover line, while usefully calling attention to the background of Greek personification. With regard to the sexual implications, one might note that the striding figure is hardly in a menacing posture; even the phallus is at best semierect. It is not easy to reckon this as emblematic of Hellenic superiority over the hapless Persian.

[182] For a similar view, arrived at independently, see A. Cohen (forthcoming). Miller (forthcoming) recognizes the comic character of the scene but postulates that the vase ridicules both the vanquished Persians and the victorious lower-class Greek. That places a heavy burden on the symbolism. It requires us to imagine that the artist simultaneously commemorated an Athenian victory and satirized the victor. On the comic features, see also Shapiro (2009), 70–72.

hoplites defeating Persian warriors became quite popular—unsurprisingly so. But Persians do not appear as craven and feeble. And even these portrayals give way, on the whole, after the middle of the fifth century, to a variety of representations that carry few if any negative connotations. So, for instance, scenes of Persian warriors leaving their families to go off to war parallel depictions of Greeks in closely comparable situations. Elsewhere Persians can be found as hunters in idyllic settings. On the battlefield, even when wearing obviously eastern garb, they also appear in breastplate, with lances, shields, and swords, not limited to bow and arrows. Still more noteworthy, Greek artists refrain from what one might have expected, that is, representing Persians as base slaves of autocratic monarchs or masters. On the contrary, they are worthy opponents, frequently fighting toe to toe with Greeks, giving little quarter. The occasional vase indeed even has Persians as victors in skirmishes (fig. 3).[183] Artists do not appear to have employed the medium to demean the "Other."[184]

The point can be illustrated by perhaps the best known of pictorial representations that depict Greeks and Persians—at the level of both gods and mortals. The elaborate tripartite scene on the "Darius painter" vase now in the Naples archaeological museum carries real importance for our purpose (fig. 4). The volute krater comes from southern Italy, discovered in Canosa in Puglia. A scholarly consensus dates it to the latter part of the fourth century BCE. But the scene itself evidently alludes to the great contest between Greece and Persia in the early fifth century.[185] Its implications warrant scrutiny.

[183] Hölscher (1973), 40–45; Raeck (1981), 109–133; Schauenburg (1977), 91–100; Hölscher (2000a), 312–314; Shapiro (2009), 65. For the depiction of a Persian victor, see Raeck (1981), plate 56. For the Persian "Abschied" scenes, see Raeck (1981), 138–147, with plates 59–61. For the hunt, Raeck (1981), 149–150. Hölscher's recent contribution (2000a), 288–289, 300–316, sees Greeks as defining themselves not in political fashion against external foes but in a cultural sense against barbarism. His further claim, however, that the portrayal of overpowered Persians amounts to an ascription of moral defeatism and an exhibit of democratic superiority over oriental softness goes beyond what the images can establish. Miller (2006), 116–119, rightly recognizes that portraits depicting Persians in "departure" scenes, hunts, symposia, and tomb visits rendered Persians more familiar and Greek-like. That these images were designed to alleviate Greek anxiety about a Persian threat, as Miller proposes, however, is considerably more problematic.

[184] Miller's provocative study (2006), 114–115, maintains that Attic vase paintings in the later fifth century did suggest effeminacy, ineffectiveness, and fear on the part of the Persians. But it is difficult to see, for example, why rendering Persians beardless "effeminizes" them, while beardless Greeks are "heroic." And a sword often accompanies the Persian bow, which surely compromises the notion of cowardice. Miller valuably observes that Greeks appear without defensive armor. But they do carry shields and wield spears—and Persians have no body armor at all. Miller (2006), 120–123, has a better case to make in some comic renditions of Persian throne scenes, as well as equestrian and hunting activities, than in battle scenes.

[185] See the extensive bibliography cited by Anti (1952), 25–26. More recent works appear in the footnotes of Tourraix (1997), 295–324. Anti (1952), 33–34, sets the scene as a debate prior

46   IMPRESSIONS OF THE "OTHER"

Figure 3. Amazon rhyton, showing victorious Persian and fallen Greek, first half of fifth century BCE. Museum of Fine Arts, Boston (inv. no. 21.2286).

Three bands decorate the vase. The upper register portrays a group of gods and personifications, the middle a collection of Persian royalty and elite, the lower a scene of suppliants appealing to what seems to be a financial

---

to the Marathon campaign. For Oliver (1960), 118–120, the vase denotes the Greek championship of liberty at Marathon. Ghiron-Bistagne (1992–1993), 151–153, sees it as celebrating the victory of Greek democracy over oriental tyranny. Taplin (2007), 235–237, treats, with due caution, its possible connection to drama. Shapiro (2009) 84–86, sees it as emblematic of a "clash of civilizations."

Figure 4. Darius volute krater, with scenes of divinities and Persian court, second half of fourth century BCE. Museo Archeologico Nazionale, Naples (inv. no. 81947). Photograph by courtesy of Archivio dell'Arte, Luciano Pedicini.

official. A most intriguing—and much debated—combination. The artist helpfully supplies a few inscriptions to identify key figures: Hellas, Apate, and Asia in the top band; Darius and a pedestal labeled "Persai" on which another figure stands in the middle band. Certain divinities are readily recognizable in the upper register: Zeus, Athena, Nike, Artemis, and Apollo. Other identifications require guesswork—which is best avoided.

To begin at the top. Zeus sits in the center, flanked by Nike on the left, Hellas on the right. That this signifies a Greek victory or the promise thereof can hardly be doubted. Hellas is well buttressed by divine authority. Not only do Zeus and Nike point to her, but Athena on her other side, in her warrior outfit, places a hand on her shoulder. The outcome or expected outcome of the contest is unambiguous. Additional Greek divinities, Apollo and Artemis, line up on the far left—though they seem curiously uninterested in what is going on elsewhere in the scene. On the far right, sits "Asia" on a high pedestal that also carries a female herm. Next to her stands a female figure glancing in her direction, clad in exotic garb, carrying two torches, and named as "Apate" by the inscription. Asia is heavily outnumbered by Greek gods on the side of Hellas.[186] And she has the added disadvantage of Apate, "deception," hovering next to her. It is hardly surprising, and entirely reasonable, that scholars find here a signal or a foreshadowing of the glorious victory of Hellas over Asia in the Persian wars of the early fifth century. If so, however, the posture of Asia merits notice. She is not bent, bowed, weeping, or supplicating. The figure sits, regal and unruffled, on what may be a throne or an altar, bearing a crown and holding a royal scepter. If anything, she looks more serene and secure than Hellas, who seems to need all the divine help she can get. Asia may indeed be on the brink of a calamitous war, led unsuspectingly into disaster by Apate. But the painter in no way demeans this calm and impressive figure. She represents a worthy counterpart to Hellas. Indeed her garb has no trace of "Oriental" features. Were it not for the labels (and surrounding deities), we would have grave difficulty in figuring out who was who. There is no triumphalism here.

The middle scene presents Persian dignitaries in stately and imposing fashion. Darius (so named) sits on a throne in the center, in royal garb and holding a scepter, with an armed guard behind him. Another figure, standing on a round block labeled "Persai," addresses him, perhaps bringing news, perhaps offering advice. The remaining individuals lack designation. Two other august personages sit in regal fashion, one at least with a scepter comparable to those of Darius and Asia. Are they members of the royal family? Or perhaps three different manifestations of Darius?[187] Speculation would not be profitable. A seated figure on the far left appears to be counseling one of the royal personages, and an elderly figure on the extreme right to be supplicating or conversing with the other. One last individual, with no trace of eastern trappings, sits as a curious observer.[188] What to make of this complex scene? Is the figure on the round block advising his king for or against a war with Hellas?[189] Or is he a messenger come to give alarming news about the Ionian revolt or indeed to announce defeat at the hand of Greeks? These and other suggestions emerge from the scholarship and have some force.[190] But a different point needs emphasis. Nothing in the scene shows lamentation, weakness, or anxiety—nor unjustified pride

---

[186] It is difficult to understand how Anti (1952), 28, sees this as a menacing posture and a threatened attack by Asia directed at the demure Hellas.

[187] So Tourraix (1997), 314; cf. Ghiron–Bistagne (1992–1993), 146–148.

[188] He has been identified as the former Athenian tyrant Hippias, now collaborating with the Persians; Anti (1952), 32, or as the devious Milesian Histiaeus, temporarily a refugee at Darius' court; Schmidt (1982), 507.

[189] Anti (1952), 32.

[190] For Schmidt (1982), 507–508, the Ionian revolt is at issue here.

and arrogance before the fall. If we lacked knowledge of a war in which Greece thwarted Persia, we could certainly not infer it from this rendition.

The lower segment of the vase moves into the lower echelon of the social scale. A central character, evidently of some authority, sits with a tablet in his hand doing calculations at a table. Surrounding him are lesser personages, some bringing gifts or offerings, others reaching out with gestures of supplication.[191] All are clad in eastern outfits except the official at the table. He could be a Greek. There were many in the service of the Persian king.[192] To take him, however, as emblematic of Hellenic rule over Persia, with allusion to Alexander the Great's conquests and his new regime, would be altogether incongruous with the rest of the vase.[193] The fundamental impression delivered by this work is one of respect for the proud bearing of Persian sovereignty. If it presumed awareness of a Hellenic victory in the offing, Persia would plainly be a fitting and respected foe.

The vase is the product of a south Italian painter in the later fourth century BCE. What relevance would a portrayal of Darius' empire or an imminent clash of Greece and Persia have for that time and place?[194] The scene might, to be sure, represent a dramatic production, as do so many vase paintings.[195] But this still leaves the question of why such a play about historical events remote in time and place (rather than the more common mythological theme) would have appeal to a south Italian audience. One can, of course, postulate the expedition of Alexander into the Iranian realm as a stimulus for pertinent analogy. That momentous event would certainly resonate with the clash of Hellas and Persia.[196] We do not, alas, know whether the krater came before, during, or after that expedition. But, whatever the timing, the overall import of the representation, as we have seen, is very far from the jingoism of an Isocrates or the celebration of Greek (let alone Macedonian)

---

[191] That they are imploring the representative of the king to urge war against Greece, as Anti (1952), 31, suggests, is most unlikely, for the scene plainly depicts financial transactions.

[192] For Anti (1952), 30, he is a Persian, identified by "ethnic type."

[193] Such is the thesis of Tourraix (1997), 297–298, 316–320. A better interpretation of the "tribute scene" by Villanueva-Puig (1989), 289–295.

[194] Schmidt (1982), 508–517, implausibly links Isocrates' panhellenic propaganda against the "barbarian" with the western Greeks' struggles against the non-Greeks of southern Italy.

[195] The most common suggestions are Aeschylus' *Persae* or Phrynichus' *Phoenissae* or *Persae*—see Anti (1952), 39–45, with references; cf. Hölscher (1973), 177; Villanueva-Puig (1989), 281–284; Ghiron-Bistagne (1992–1993), 148–153. But this scene suits nothing in the *Persae*, and the lost plays of Phrynichus prompt only idle speculation. Schmidt (1982), 507–510, reckons a pictorial representation as a more likely model for the Darius vase but opts ultimately for a literary source, namely Herodotus. That the Apulian painter would be conversant with the details of Herodotus' account of the Ionian revolt, however, is implausible; cf. Villanueva-Puig (1989), 285.

[196] Cf. Hölscher (1973), 178–180; Villaneuva-Puig (1989), 285–289; Tourraix (1997), 297–298, 324.

50 IMPRESSIONS OF THE "OTHER"

superiority. The krater possesses a wider significance. It recalls an episode of major consequence for Hellenic history and self-reflection. But it discloses a real esteem for Persia as a worthy competitor, an august regime, and an imperial power. That form of conceptualizing still held meaning for the Greeks of Magna Graecia a century and a half after the great Persian wars.

The reverse of the coin eludes us. Persia's perspective remains largely out of reach. Extant testimony gives little access to how Iranians perceived Greeks. Nor is that our subject here. But a brief footnote to the discussion along these lines provides some grounds for reflection.

An intriguing Greek statue of a headless seated woman found in Persepolis calls for notice. The figure type bears close resemblance to extant copies that represent Penelope, and it is a fair surmise that the Persepolis woman is that long-suffering, patient, and determined wife of Odysseus celebrated in Homer's *Odyssey*.[197] Its date is disputed, with most scholars opting for the mid–fifth century BCE or the end of the fifth century.[198] It was in all likelihood buried in the rubble when Alexander the Great sacked Persepolis in 330 BCE. What was such a work doing in the possession of the Persian regime? One can, of course, postulate that the statue was carried off as a spoil of war, perhaps from eastern Greeks within reach of Persian plunder. Or else it was purchased by the court. Or indeed it came as a gift from Greek allies of the Achaemenid ruler.[199] Whatever the route, the presence of Penelope in the capital of Persia implies a familiarity with or an interest in the epic tale and with the legends of Hellas.[200] Xerxes, as we have seen, exhibited knowledge of the *Iliad* and employed it to good effect in performing conspicuous sacrifices at Troy.[201] If Xerxes could appropriate

---

[197] On the Penelope type, see the extensive bibliography in Olmstead (1950), 10. That the statue depicts Penelope carries a clear consensus among scholars. See, e.g., Olmstead (1950), 10–18; Ohly (1957), 433–460; Ridgway (1970), 101–105; Gauer (1990), 40–41. The effort of Langlotz (1961), 88–94, to identify her as a mourning Aphrodite has not had takers. Nor that of Kenner (1966), 527–592, that she represented a mourning Hellas bewailing the triumph of Persia marked by the peace of Antalkidas in 386 BCE—hardly a Persian victory over Greece. More recently, Stähler (1990), 10–11, proposed that the figure constitutes a personification of *eleutheria*—not the most likely concept to be embraced by the Persian king.

[198] Langlotz (1961), 77–78; Stähler (1990), 8; Gauer (1990), 41, with references to earlier scholarship.

[199] Palagia (2008), 223–237, proposes that it was a diplomatic gift from the Thasians. The suggestion of Gauer (1990), 47–53, 64, that Greeks sent the statue to Persepolis to summon the Persian king as a new Odysseus to rescue them from the tyranny of the Athenian empire is, at the very least, far-fetched.

[200] It is quite illegitimate to assume that Persian taste would not have extended to an understanding of Hellenic artistic products and that the piece was desired simply for its material worth, as do Langlotz (1961), 81–82; Stähler (1990), 9; cf. also Kenner (1966), 574–575.

[201] Herod. 7.43. See above, pp. 37–39. Xerxes may have heard the legend from Greeks in Asia Minor or in his retinue, if he did not already know it; Georges (1994), 58–63. In either case, he seized the opportunity to embrace the association.

the *Iliad*, a successor could as easily embrace the *Odyssey*. It would be hazardous to build an elaborate superstructure upon this exceptional piece. But the fact that a representation of Penelope proved to be desirable booty or an appropriate gift suggests that the ruler of Persia placed a positive value on the culture and traditions of Hellas.[202]

Reinforcement for that conclusion comes from another Greek artistic product that was definitely spirited away to Persia. The celebrated statue group of the Athenian "Tyrannicides" by Antenor was dedicated, so we are told, in 509 BCE.[203] It commemorated the slaying of Hipparchos, brother of the tyrant Hippias, by Harmodius and Aristogeiton, a deed that at least in popular imagination led eventually to the overthrow of Athenian tyranny itself and the establishment of democracy. After the sack of Athens in 480, Xerxes hauled the statues off to Persia. They were plunder, but no mere plunder. They still stood in Susa, Arrian reports, a century and a half later when Alexander took the city and sent them back to Athens.[204] Whether this was, in fact, Alexander's doing remains in dispute. Other sources claim that either Seleucus or Antiochus effected the return of the statues, which would give them a still longer stay in Susa.[205] A decision on that matter is unimportant. The Achaemenids, in any case, held the statues, and presumably had them on display for at least one hundred and fifty years. Why? For the Athenians the images carried high symbolic significance. They represented, in retrospect, the moment when Athenians first took steps to abolish tyranny (even though this was not accomplished for several years thereafter—and then only through Spartan intervention), and thus to pave the way for democracy. Xerxes' removal of the statues spurred the Athenians to replace them with new replicas within a very short time.[206] And images of Harmodius and Aristogeiton were reproduced again and again in vase painting and other media for many years thereafter, emblematic of Athenian pride in freedom and democracy.[207] But that can hardly be the reason for Xerxes and his successors setting up and retaining these statues in Susa. The Achaemenids had no interest in trumpeting democracy. The exiled Athenian tyrant Hippias had taken refuge at the Persian court

---

[202] One might note also that Xerxes did not plunder indiscriminately. Pausanias observes that he took the cult image of Artemis from Brauron and a bronze statue of Apollo from the Milesians at Branchidae; 8.46.3.

[203] Pliny *NH* 34.16–17.

[204] Arrian *Anab.* 3.16.7–8; cf. 7.19.2. The restoration by Alexander is attested also by Pliny *NH* 34.69–70.

[205] Val. Max. 2.10.ext. 1; Paus. 1.8.5. Brunnsaker (1971), 44–45, prefers Alexander; Bosworth (1980), 317, prefers Seleucus and Antiochus (in their joint reign).

[206] They were set up already in 477/476, according to the evidence of the *Marmor Parium*; *FGH* 239 A54; cf. Diod. 11.41.1.

[207] The classic study is that of Brunnsaker (1971), with full documentation. See also Hölscher (1973), 85–88; Fehr (1984), 5–54; Taylor (1991), 36–76; Ober (2003), 215–250.

and may have exercised some influence with the king. But it would be paradoxical indeed if Hippias prompted the theft and installation of images that recalled the assassination of his brother and the abolition of his own tyranny. Xerxes could only have erected the statues despite, not because of, the wishes of Hippias. Athenians may have seen the political symbolism of the "Tyrannicides." For Xerxes and the Achaemenids who followed, they must have had a different appeal, quite possibly an aesthetic one. Appreciation of Greek art had its place in the culture of the Persian court.

These two works of Hellenic art, we may be certain, were far from the only ones that found their way to the realm of the Great King. Only the accident of survival and discovery preserves them for us. Countless others may well have been on display in palaces or homes of the mighty. Whether they came through exploitation, purchase, or gift, whether they served as tokens of conquest, means of understanding alien cultures, objects of admiration, or mere items of curiosity, they pique the imagination. As Greeks showed a regard for Persian practices, principles, and history, so Persians exhibited an engagement with Hellenic traditions and art—a reciprocity that coexisted with and may have carried more enduring significance than battle encounters and contests for supremacy.

Chapter 2

PERSIA IN THE GREEK PERCEPTION: XENOPHON AND ALEXANDER

CLASHES BETWEEN GREEKS and Persians occurred intermittently and indecisively through much of the fourth century BCE. The record of hostilities can readily be recounted. But that is only part of the story. Rivalry and animosity need not translate into denigration, disparagement, and contempt. Attitudes were far more mixed and ambiguous. Isocrates too often counts as emblematic. It is tempting to cite the rancorous comments of the orator whose *Panegyricus* expressed fierce animosity and pointed to Persian weaknesses and failings.[1] But the context of that oration has to be taken into the reckoning. Isocrates took on a mission to unite Greeks under Athenian leadership for a crusade against Persia. That objective drove his rhetorical flourishes and exaggerated characterization. Depiction of a soft enemy ripe for the taking was a vital element in the portrait. In fact, Isocrates draws as sharp a contrast between Athens and Sparta as he does between Greeks and Persians.[2] His harsh words (only a small part of that long speech) hardly count as representative of widespread Hellenic opinion. A very different work by a contemporary of Isocrates deserves closer attention.

Xenophon's *Cyropaedia*

The most stunning paean to a Persian by a Greek is the remarkable treatise of Xenophon, the *Cyropaedia*. This work, composed probably sometime in the 360s BCE, constitutes a lengthy, extensive, and more than occasionally tiresome encomium to Cyrus the Great, a conqueror of awesome reputation and the man responsible for creating the Persian empire.[3] For Xenophon, Cyrus represents the ideal ruler, indeed emblematic of the

---
[1] Isocr. *Pan.* 150–152, 157–158; cf. Isaac (2004), 282–288.
[2] Isocr. *Pan.* 110–128.
[3] On the date, see Gera (1993), 23–25; Mueller-Goldingen (1995), 45–55, with references to earlier literature. Their discussions disclose just how thin is the evidence for dating this treatise. The comparisons with some Platonic works, themselves not firmly fixed, by Mueller-Goldingen are especially flimsy.

finest qualities desired in one who governs a vast realm comprising disparate peoples and nations. That a Greek military man, historian, and intellectual would single out a Persian monarch as epitomizing the most estimable characteristics of the statesman is a fact of striking significance. It gives the lie to any notion that Hellenic writers perceived the Persians simply as the undesirable and unsavory enemy. How does one account for this startling treatise?

The work itself defies categorization. It combines the characteristics of a romance, a biography, a mirror for princes, a reflection on imperial rule, a military manual, and a treatise on moral and political philosophy. Few will quarrel with the idea that the *Cyropaedia* is largely fiction.[4] Novelistic features recur throughout, a host of tales fashioned or embellished to illustrate Cyrus' sterling qualities. Yet it can hardly be pure fantasy. Much in the work coheres with what can independently be attested about Persian institutions and practices and the achievements of Cyrus. Xenophon had access to a range of sources, and he had considerable personal experience with Persians and the Persian empire.[5] The mix of fiction and fact in the *Cyropaedia* escapes clear determination. But that matters little for our purposes. Xenophon's choice of a Persian monarch as exemplary model of governance remains the item of central consequence.

Cyrus, to be sure, had a favorable reputation, at least in many regards, among Greek writers. Aeschylus in the *Persae* has Darius describe him (by contrast with some other Persian kings) as a man of good fortune whose rule brought peace to all his friends and whose kind disposition won him divine favor.[6] Herodotus gave Cyrus high marks on various counts. Persians regarded him as a kindly father who strove always to benefit them. He rescued his enemy Croesus from the flames and set him up as an adviser. He was a man of acuity, wit, and wisdom. And Herodotus employs him at the very end of his text as exemplifying sage counsel.[7] Ctesias of Cnidus, who became court physician to the Persian king Artaxerxes II at the end of the fifth century BCE, wrote a twenty-three volume *Persica*. Of this, five volumes alone were devoted to the reign of Cyrus, eight times the amount of space that Herodotus allotted to him. Ctesias had a reputation for retailing

---

[4] Cicero alerted his brother to the fact that Xenophon's portrait of Cyrus was not faithful to history but fashioned as a model of just rule; *Ad Q. Fr.* 1.1.23. On the novelistic character of the work, see Tatum (1989), passim; Stadter (1991), 461–491.

[5] Hirsch (1985), 61–85. For possible Persian sources of information, see the discussion of Gera (1993), 13–22. But one needs to be cautious on this matter. Xenophon is unlikely to have done much research on the Persian side. Cf. Briant (1987), 7–8; Tuplin (1990), 17–28. For an extensive, cautious, and judicious study of the relation of the treatise to Persian "reality," see Tuplin (1997), 95–154.

[6] Aesch. *Pers.* 768–772.

[7] Herod. 1.86.6, 1.90, 1.127.1–2, 1.141.1–3, 1.153.1–3, 3.89.3, 9.122.

romantic and sensational stories and for frequently taking issue with Herodotus. The extant fragments indicate that Ctesias produced a version of Cyrus' youth that gave him lowly origins and had him gradually but shrewdly work his way up through the ranks at the Median court from menial tasks to a position of influence and power.[8] Little survives to give a clear sense of Cyrus' character in Ctesias' presentation. But it is unlikely that a court historian would have dwelled at length on the revered creator of the Persian empire only to denounce him. The philosopher and pupil of Socrates, Antisthenes, a contemporary of Xenophon, produced at least two treatises on the subject of Cyrus. The surviving fragments tell us little. But Antisthenes did draw parallels between Heracles and Cyrus in regard to the virtue of hard labor, *ponos*. Other fragments have Cyrus taking wise counsel or giving it. Antisthenes evidently found much to admire in Cyrus. Whether his works influenced or simply complemented Xenophon's *Cyropaedia* cannot be determined.[9] But it is clear that Cyrus represented a figure of note and consequence in Hellenic eyes.

Xenophon's selection of Cyrus as a noble and ideal character therefore creates no great surprise. The choice had some logic. And the historian's own personal experience must have played a role as well. As is well known, he enlisted as a mercenary soldier in the ranks of the younger Cyrus, brother of the Achaemenid monarch Artaxerxes II, in what proved to be a futile expedition into the heart of the Persian empire. The death of Cyrus, the failed challenger to his brother's throne, prompted a glowing encomium by Xenophon in his *Anabasis*. The tribute began, significantly enough, with a comparison to Cyrus the Great. The younger Achaemenid, so Xenophon exclaimed, had the most kingly bearing and was the most worthy of rule of all Persians since the original Cyrus himself.[10] Xenophon proceeds to detail Cyrus the Younger's qualities and virtues, including his self-control, modesty, courage, integrity, trustworthiness, justice, generosity, diplomacy, military achievements, and even horsemanship and hunting skills.[11] The resemblance to characteristics of Cyrus the Great as depicted in the *Cyropaedia* is unmistakable—and hardly accidental.[12] The portrayal

---

[8] For the fragments of Ctesias, see *FGH* 688. And see the discussions of Jacoby (1922), 2032–2073; Drews (1973), 103–116. For the five books on Cyrus, see Ctesias *FGH* 688 F9.8. See now the convenient translation by Llewellyn-Jones and Robson (2010), 159–176.

[9] The relevant fragments are 19–21; cf. 69, in Deceleva Caizzi (1966). See the discussions of Gera (1993), 8–10, and Mueller-Goldingen (1995), 32–44. Determination of the number of Antisthenes' works on Cyrus remains beyond our grasp, a disputed subject; see Mueller-Goldingen (1995), 32–35.

[10] Xen. *Anab.* 1.9.1: ἀνὴρ ὢν Περσῶν τῶν μετὰ Κῦρον τὸν ἀρχαῖον γενομένων βασιλικώτατός τε καὶ ἄρχειν ἀξιώτατος.

[11] Xen. *Anab.* 1.9.

[12] Hirsch (1985), 74–75, 85–86, rightly finds a number of parallels. Cf. also Gera (1993), 10–11. Georges (1994), 212–213, 218, 232–233, regards the *Cyropaedia* as in part a fantasy of

of the latter as prompted by Xenophon's experience with or image of the former seems perfectly plain.

It does not follow, however, that the *Cyropaedia* resolves itself simply into a fanciful biography of an iconic ruler, fashioned by the particular motives of the historian and irrelevant to Hellenic dispositions toward Persia. The scholarly focus on Xenophon's portrait of Cyrus, legitimate though that be, obscures the fact that the work also sets Persian practices and character generally in a most positive light.[13]

Cyrus, after all, received his *paideia* in accordance with the laws of the Persians.[14] Their laws, in Xenophon's presentation, differ markedly from those of most people. They do not give free rein to parents to educate children as they wish or leave adults to their own devices, only subsequently enjoining them not to commit offenses and punishing them when they do. Persian laws aim to inculcate proper behavior from the start and to instill a revulsion for wicked and shameful acts.[15] Whether accurate or not, Xenophon's favorable assessment is clear. Nor is it mere invention on his part. He illustrates the point by affirming that Persians banish all commerce from the center of their city where the royal palace and public buildings are situated, a practice that Xenophon evidently admires.[16] The statement echoes Herodotus' remark (put in the mouth of Cyrus the Great) that berates Spartans for designating a place in the center of their city where men come to violate their oaths and cheat one another. Herodotus interprets the comment as a Persian critique of Greek commercial exchange generally, whereas Persians eschew marketplaces everywhere in their realm.[17] Xenophon's description of the education system contains glowing praise. Persian schools endeavor to instruct their pupils in justice, stressing self-restraint, moderation, and obedience to rulers, with special emphasis on the avoidance of ingratitude, an offense that could lead to every shameful vice.[18] His summary statement on the Persian polity offers comparable accolades. The law prevents no individual from seeking public honors and offices. All Persians have access to the common schools of justice (though not all can afford to send their children there). Those who have had the training in public schools can enter the ephebic ranks, then become part of the office-holding class, and eventually join the elite group of the elders. By

---

what the Persian empire might have been had Cyrus the Younger lived to occupy the throne; cf. also Delebecque (1957), 394.

[13] For Xenophon's views of Persia outside the *Cyropaedia*, see Tuplin (1994), 129–133.
[14] Xen. *Cyr.* 1.2.2: ἐπαιδεύθη γε μὴν ἐν Περσῶν νόμοις.
[15] Xen. *Cyr.* 1.2.3.
[16] Xen. *Cyr.* 1.2.3.
[17] Herod. 1.153.1–2.
[18] Xen. *Cyr.* 1.2.6–8. On Xenophon's account of Persian education in the *Cyropaedia*, see Tuplin (1997), 69–95.

employing this form of governance, in Xenophon's view, Persians judge themselves as capable of being the best.[19] Nor does Xenophon challenge that judgment.

The work constitutes more than an unrelieved laudation of a chimerical Cyrus. Indeed, Xenophon's depiction of the king shows some characteristics that fall short of the absolutely admirable. Cyrus succeeded in governing so vast a realm partly by instilling fear, so as to overawe all his subjects and deter anyone from lifting a hand against him.[20] The art of governance also included artifice. Cyrus, so Xenophon notes, considered it necessary for rulers to distinguish themselves from the ruled not only by being better persons but by beguiling their subjects. He himself chose to put on Median garb and persuaded his companions to do the same, for it would conceal any physical defects and make them appear especially handsome and imposing. They even added lifts to their shoes to give themselves a taller aspect, and, with Cyrus' encouragement, made up their faces and eyes so as to look better than they actually did. These and other devices he designed deliberately so as to make it harder for subjects to disdain them.[21] Cyrus' ardent pursuit of his people's esteem led him to devise schemes that were less than altogether laudable. He contrived contests and prizes that would promote not only competitiveness but rivalry, envy, and strife, thus to assure that all who prevailed would be more attached to him than to one another.[22] Xenophon notes also that the practice of prostration (*proskynesis*) began under Cyrus when the king rose in his chariot, taller even than his tall driver—whether in reality or through whatever means.[23] The historian delivers no overt criticism of his hero on these or any other scores.[24] Clever contrivances to assure secure rule could certainly be justified. But he does

---

[19] Xen. *Cyr.* 1.2.15: ἡ πολιτεία αὕτη, ᾗ οἴονται χρώμενοι βέλτιστοι ἂν εἶναι. Some have found similarities between Xenophon's description of Persian institutions and those of Sparta, at least as presented by Xenophon's own *Res Publica Lacedaemoniorum*; cf. Tigerstedt (1965), 177–189. But the differences are at least as significant as the resemblances. The representation of the Persian system cannot be seen as a mere conscious or subconscious reflection of the Spartan. So, rightly, Higgins (1977), 47–48; Hirsch (1985), 87; Georges (1994), 229; Mueller-Goldingen (1995), 69–75; Nadon (2001), 30–42; and see, most fully, Tuplin (1994), 134–161.
[20] Xen. *Cyr.* 1.1.5.
[21] Xen. *Cyr.* 8.1.40–42.
[22] Xen. *Cyr.* 8.2.26–28.
[23] Xen. *Cyr.* 8.3.14.
[24] It is noteworthy that Xenophon goes out of his way to correct a Greek impression that the Persian ruler dispatched spies, known as the King's Eyes and Ears, to report on any disparaging words or actions by his subjects; Xen. *Cyr.* 8.2.10–12. The passage is correctly interpreted by Hirsch (1985), 101–108. Hirsch's argument (1985), 123–131, that no such institution existed, goes too far. He cannot get around the clear testimony of Xen. *Cyr.* 8.6.16. What matters, however, is Xenophon's firm stance that Cyrus received information voluntarily from his subjects who looked for his favor and generosity, not from paid spies. Whatever the truth of the matter, Xenophon's attitude is plain.

not conceal schemes and machinations that might compromise integrity and trustworthiness.[25] Cyrus appears as an astute and canny ruler, not as a saint. Whatever Cyrus' character, however, Xenophon refrains from any negative judgment on the nation, its character or its people.

With one notable and notorious exception. The last chapter of the last book presents a sudden and stark contrast with almost all that had preceded. Xenophon, having delivered high praise for Cyrus' system, his institutions, and his example, shifts gears dramatically. He asserts that once Cyrus died, things fell apart immediately: his sons engaged in strife with one another, cities and nations rose in revolt, and everything turned for the worse.[26] He then reels off a whole range of areas in which Persian affairs and practices went into a tailspin. Impiety and injustice took over. Oaths were violated, and rulers were untrustworthy and treacherous. Corruption reigned, and enemies could roam unimpeded.[27] The restraint once exercised on personal habits disappeared. Persians indulged in excess and dissipation, giving way to softness and luxury, abandoning the moderation to which their ancestors had been schooled.[28] Their military qualities had eroded; soldierly skills yielded to cowardice, incompetence, and reliance on others (such as Greeks) to fight their battles for them.[29]

How does one account for this jarring about-face? Few readers could have been braced for this concluding chapter. Xenophon's prior narrative had just presented Cyrus' noble deathbed summation of his achievements and advice to his children. And the historian had ostensibly wrapped up the work with an admiring reference to the vast realm that Cyrus governed with grace and wisdom, earning the appellation of "father" from his subjects.[30] And suddenly all is plunged into darkness.

Numerous explanations have endeavored to resolve this conundrum. An attractive and once widely favored one simply excised the offending appendage as non-Xenophontic. An interpolator must have intervened, unhappy with the pro-Persian proclivities of the treatise, and sought to reverse the impression.[31] That solution, however, is too easy, and rightly rejected now by almost all. As was pointed out long ago, the language, style,

---

[25] See the treatment by Gera (1993), 285–299, who sees these and other slightly questionable traits of Cyrus as designed by Xenophon to show that governance of an empire requires an enlightened despotism. Her conclusion, however, that these traits foreshadowed the moral downfall of the regime is unjustified.

[26] Xen. *Cyr.* 8.8.2.

[27] Xen. *Cyr.* 8.8.3–7.

[28] Xen. *Cyr.* 8.8.8–19.

[29] Xen. *Cyr.* 8.8.20–26.

[30] Xen. *Cyr.* 8.8.1.

[31] For discussion of some of the earlier scholarship, see Tatum (1989), 217–225. Among recent treatments, only Hirsch (1985), 91–97, has taken this line. Isaac (2004), 290–293, seems inclined to embrace it but leaves the matter open.

and rhetoric of the last chapter coheres precisely with Xenophon's own mode of presentation elsewhere, even down to the use of particles. An interpolator, had there been one, would almost have had to have access to the interior of Xenophon's mind.[32] Quite apart from the philological argument, a close parallel affirms authenticity. Xenophon's *Res Publica Lacedaemoniorum*, his treatise on Spartan institutions, contains a similar portion that contrasts the degeneration of those institutions with their heyday, which the historian had praised in the bulk of his work.[33]

If the final chapter is genuine, how are we to interpret its flagrant discrepancy with the rest of the text? Or is the discrepancy more apparent than real? One can argue that the epilogue actually reinforces the message of the work as a whole: Cyrus' character and qualities were unique; he and he alone could bring Persia to approximate an ideal society; his departure left the realm in the hands of inferior beings, the whole structure collapsed, and deterioration was inevitable. On this reading, the facts are irrelevant. Xenophon delivered the lesson that a just society required an unusual leader to produce and maintain it. He created a fictitious Cyrus and a utopian Persia that the epilogue highlighted rather than undermined.[34] In a variant of this interpretation, it has been claimed that all depended on the quality of the ruler. The institutions that Cyrus installed did not fail, but a monarchic state and its subjects were only as good as its leaders. Cyrus' successors were not up to the task, and degeneration set in rapidly. The epilogue on this view also followed logically from the implications of what preceded.[35] Such an approach, however, minimizes the harsh and abrupt change of direction that the final chapter represents. It is difficult to imagine readers feeling a smooth transition from the glorification of Persians' virtues under Cyrus to the fierce condemnation of their vices after his death. The contrast stands out the more markedly for Xenophon's having just put a deathbed speech in Cyrus' mouth exhorting his sons to carry on his work and to maintain their loving relationship.[36] If the historian sought to emphasize the major drop in quality between Cyrus and all future rulers of Persia, it is surprising that he avoids making that point in the epilogue.

---

[32] Eichler (1880), passim; cf. Tatum (1989), 223–224. Among other arguments for authenticity, see Delebecque (1957), 405–408; Mueller-Goldingen (1995), 262–271.

[33] Hirsch's effort (1985), 95, to get around this plain parallel by claiming that both "epilogues" are in dispute carries little conviction.

[34] Delebecque (1957), 405–408; Due (1989), 16–20. Cf. also Gera (1993), 299–300, who maintains that Xenophon idealized Cyrus by stressing his important influence on Persian habits during most of the work and by contrasting him with present-day Persians in the epilogue.

[35] Sage (1994), 161–174; Mueller-Goldingen (1995), 264–265, 271; cf. Higgins (1977), 57–58.

[36] Xen. *Cyr*. 8. 7.6–24. The assertion of Nadon (2001), 138–139, that the words "read more as an incitement to fraternal strife than concord," will convince few.

That segment dwells heavily on the degeneracy of Persian morals and the deficiencies of the Persian people but has little to say about Persian kings.[37]

Some recent analyses turn this thesis on its head. Instead of claiming that the antithesis between Cyrus' Persia and the precipitate decline that followed underscored the founder's accomplishment, they find the epilogue bringing to fruition motifs and themes foreshadowed earlier in the text. On this interpretation, Cyrus' machinations as noted above reveal his penchant for political manipulation rather than righteousness. He calculated his generosity and favors to win friends, sow rivalry, and thwart enemies, not out of any sense of justice. He conceived a system wherein to assure his ascendancy, undermine opposition, and exercise surveillance. His contrivances aimed to disarm critics and to engender personal loyalty. Cyrus, in effect, transformed a "republic" into an "empire," largely in the interests of his own security and power. This reconstruction, therefore, sees the epilogue as no break with what preceded. The disintegration of Persia was a mere logical conclusion of Cyrus' own principles and practices.[38] Such a reading of the work has little force. It downplays the overwhelmingly favorable assessment of Cyrus and of Persia that dominates the *Cyropaedia*. And it dismisses the explicit reversals of ancient Persian virtues that the final chapter identifies in the contemporary scene. The entire tenor of the treatise refutes any attempt to find a logical progression from Cyrus' polity to the decay of Persia.[39]

Outside the final chapter, in fact, Xenophon blunts any contrasts between past and present. Indeed he makes numerous references, hardly inadvertent or accidental, to Persian institutions or customs that prevailed in the time of Cyrus and persisted to Xenophon's own day. This holds, for instance, in matters of personal habits and dress. Persians refrained from spitting or blowing their noses in public, just as they avoided passing gas or urinating in the company of others. They regarded such practices as shameful when Cyrus reigned—and they still do.[40] Persians possessed a more modest form of clothing and a more restrained diet than did the Medes in

---

[37] He does refer to the treacherous execution of Greek officers by Artaxerxes (without mentioning his name); *Cyr.* 8.8.3. But it is noteworthy that, according to Xenophon, the officers operated on the assumption that old-line Persian trustworthiness still held—130 years after Cyrus' death. The only explicit mention of Artaxerxes comes with reference to his and his companions' weakness for wine that led them to give up hunting; *Cyr.* 8.8.12. This is hardly a central indictment in the chapter.

[38] For this view, see Too (1998), 288–302; Nadon (2001), passim, esp. 111–146; followed by Ambler (2001), 11–18, in the introduction to his recent translation of the *Cyropaedia*. A similar notion was hinted at but not fully articulated by Higgins (1977), 57–58.

[39] See the criticisms of Nadon by Dillery (2002). To interpret Xenophon largely by what he does not say rather than by what he does is questionable methodology.

[40] Xen. *Cyr.* 1.2.16.

Cyrus' day, habits they continue to honor.[41] They prided themselves on their horsemanship. Cyrus instituted a measure making it demeaning for anyone to whom he gave a horse to be seen traveling by foot. Persians of the upper classes in Xenophon's day, so he points out, still avoid being seen on the road without being on horseback.[42] Cyrus' passion for hunting had more in view than just sport; it served as excellent training. Hence, he regularly took those who needed the training with him on the hunt. The demands in suffering the elements and enduring hunger and thirst afford the best drills for military duty. And, Xenophon notes quite strikingly, the king and his companions even now undergo identical exercises.[43]

Relationships between the ruler and the ruled in Persia show the same continuing characteristics. Members of the Persian elite still report at the gates to offer their services to the king, just as they did in Cyrus' day.[44] Those who did not show up when expected would certainly hear from the king—then as now.[45] Multiple gifts bestowed by Cyrus on his followers started a trend still pursued by present-day kings.[46] Cyrus' practice of honoring his favorites by seating arrangements at dinner, the most favored seated nearest him, and then shifting seats in accordance with the services of the individuals was one that persisted in Xenophon's era.[47] A solemn compact made between the king and the Persian elite to support and protect one another prevails even now, so Xenophon affirmed.[48]

Various aspects of state policy inaugurated by Cyrus retained their force well over a century later, as Xenophon reminds his readers on numerous occasions. Cyrus entered into arrangements with Hyrcanian troops, his allies against the Assyrians, promising them treatment equivalent to that of the Persians and Medes, a compact that held firm through the era of Xenophon.[49] Similarly, Cyrus accorded to his Egyptian allies land grants, even whole cities if Xenophon is to be believed, which their descendants continue to occupy.[50] He introduced scythed chariots, an armament that all subsequent kings adopted.[51] He also established garrisons in various parts of the empire, an institution that still remained to be attested by Xenophon.[52] And supervision of the satraps under a strict system that Cyrus put

[41] Xen. *Cyr.* 1.3.2.
[42] Xen. *Cyr.* 4.3.23.
[43] Xen. *Cyr.* 8.1.36.
[44] Xen. *Cyr.* 8.1.6.
[45] Xen. *Cyr.* 8.1.20.
[46] Xen. *Cyr.* 8.2.7; cf. 8.5.21.
[47] Xen. *Cyr.* 8.4.3–5; cf. 8.6.14.
[48] Xen. *Cyr,* 8.5.25–27.
[49] Xen. *Cyr.* 4.2.8.
[50] Xen. *Cyr.* 7.1.44–45; cf. 8.4.28, 8.6.5.
[51] Xen. *Cyr.* 7.1.47.
[52] Xen. *Cyr.* 8.5.69–70, 8.6.7–9.

in place abided throughout.⁵³ He comported himself in accord with religious prescriptions and cooperated with the religious establishment in a manner that persisted in the court of each king who followed.⁵⁴ Even the processions that accompanied victories in chariot races took a form that was instituted by Cyrus and still practiced in Xenophon's day.⁵⁵ Other instances too could be cited.⁵⁶

The multiple allusions to continuities that linked Cyrus' era to contemporary Persia leave a powerful impression. Xenophon's reiterations were plainly deliberate and purposeful. The historian accentuated the enduring qualities of Cyrus' achievement and their current manifestations. The final chapter, by any comparison, represents a thorough disconnection.

That makes its interpretation all the more difficult. The intrusion of reality on fantasy has seemed to some to explain it. Xenophon's elaborate utopia could not overcome the dismal Persian world that the author himself encountered. Hence, romantic fiction ultimately yielded to historical fact. Xenophon could no longer resist revision and appended the epilogue as his homage to history.⁵⁷ The idea is attractive but ultimately unsatisfying. The defects (if such they were) of contemporary Persia would have been as evident to Xenophon when he first embarked on the *Cyropaedia* as when he reached his conclusion. The notion that he agonized between the confrontation of reality and the escape into fiction can hardly be teased out of a text in which the former is injected as an abrupt and sudden annex that denies all that came before.

The character of that annex deserves closer scrutiny. In all the scholarship on this subject, no one has ever asked whether Xenophon actually believed what he wrote in the epilogue.⁵⁸ Yet he employs there a sardonic and biting tone altogether out of character with everything else in the work. This is no mere matter of the positive replaced by the negative. The historian engages in overstatement that borders on satire and compels attention.

Confiscation of property and wealth, according to Xenophon, has intimidated the innocent and guilty alike, thus discouraging them from support of the royal army. As a consequence, anyone who wishes to make war

---

⁵³ Xen. *Cyr.* 8.6.16.
⁵⁴ Xen. *Cyr.* 8.1.21–24.
⁵⁵ Xen. *Cyr.* 8.3.33–34.
⁵⁶ See the references collected by Due (1989), 34, n. 16; cf. Tuplin (1997), 103. The discussion of these passages by Delebecque (1957), 395–405, concerns itself largely with the historicity of the allusions and their use in reconstructing chronology (most of which is quite speculative).
⁵⁷ Tatum (1989), 215–239. Cf. Higgins (1977), 59.
⁵⁸ The most recent treatment by Isaac (2004), 290–293, like that of everyone else, simply takes for granted that Xenophon (or the author of the epilogue) embraced it in all seriousness.

on the Persians can roam freely in the land without encountering resistance.[59] The logic of that connection is somewhat shaky, and the image of foreign foes wandering wherever they wish in the Persian empire bears little relation to historical reality—as Xenophon well knew.

The historian makes a mockery of Persians' personal habits. They refrained from spitting and blowing their noses, a regimen imposed by Cyrus so as to toughen their bodies through toil and sweat. The practice still continues, Xenophon adds—even though they have given up any strenuous exercise.[60] A parallel case serves him equally well. Persians used to take just a single meal per day, so as to interfere as little as possible with their activities and labor. They still eat just once a day, says Xenophon, but that is because they do so continuously from early morning until the partying ends late at night.[61] The exaggeration is patent. Xenophon did not expect to be taken seriously here. The satirical quality of this segment can hardly be plainer in the next illustration. Xenophon observes that traditional Persian custom prevented the bringing in of vessels to symposia, since they prided themselves on not drinking to excess. The custom still holds, but their drinking habits are such that Persians need to be carried out rather than vessels carried in. The deliberate juxtaposition of εἰσφέρεσθαι and ἐκφέρονται makes the joke clear.[62]

Xenophon does not let up. Persians on the march traditionally refrained from eating, drinking, or being seen while performing natural functions. The practice persists, says Xenophon, but only because the marches are so short that abstinence causes no surprise.[63] Hunting used to be a genuine test of endurance for men and horses; nowadays the king and his companions are too weak from wine to keep up the sport—and they bitterly envy those who do.[64] Xenophon also produces a gratuitous and transparent bit of mischief. He alleges that Persian children once learned to distinguish various plants in order to separate the healthy from the harmful. But now their botanical instruction seems to equip them best for concocting poisonous potions.[65]

Xenophon then plays with the luxury motif. And he does so with tongue in cheek. The old Persian hardness is gone, and only Median softness

---

[59] Xen. *Cyr.* 8.8.6–7.
[60] Xen. *Cyr.* 8.8.8–9; cf. 1.2.16.
[61] Xen. *Cyr.* 8.8.9.
[62] Xen. *Cyr.* 8.8.10.
[63] Xen. *Cyr.* 8.8.11.
[64] Xen. *Cyr.* 8.8.12. This hardly sits well with Xenophon's own statement at 8.1.36 that Persian kings still enjoy the hunt. The historian evidently did not mind the inconsistency—or perhaps expected his readers to notice it and recognize his mischievousness. Due (1989), 37, and Mueller-Goldingen (1995), 267, oddly deny the contradiction.
[65] Xen. *Cyr.* 8.8.14.

remains. Contemporaries require not only delicate sheets and blankets on their beds but also fluffy carpets under their beds to prevent any contact with the floor. They are forever inventing new dishes and sauces for their dinners, and employ persons just for that purpose. They go out in winter with heavy sleeves and gloves, and in summer with servants responsible for providing their shade. They take great pride in putting as many cups on display as possible, unfazed by the fact that they may have been acquired unjustly—or that everyone knows about it. In the old days, Persians were always seen mounted in order to perfect their horsemanship; now they put more blankets on their horses than on their beds, for they prefer the soft seat to the ride.[66] The sardonic character of all this stands out markedly.

Xenophon saves the deterioration of the military for last. This (one might think) should merit more serious treatment. But the historian chose his illustrations to get a laugh. Instead of furnishing hardy cavalry from their estates, Persian grandees produce men who serve as butlers and cooks, specialists who wait on tables, chamberlains who help them get to bed and minister to them in the morning, and attendants who put on their makeup and give them rubdowns.[67] That imagery was deliberately selected. And so was the description of scythed chariots and their drivers in action. Cyrus had introduced these war machines, stressed training for the drivers, and encouraged direct combat. Contemporary drivers, however, often forgo training and, when they close in battle, either jump out or fall out of the chariots, leaving the teams to wreak greater havoc with their friends than with their foes.[68] Xenophon plainly concocted an overblown and nearly farcical scenario.

Why do it? No easy explanations suggest themselves. But one might at least consider the proposition that Xenophon took the opportunity to caricature contemporary stereotypes. The notion of Persian decline and decadence certainly made the rounds in fourth-century Greece. One can find allusions to it in Ctesias, Plato, and Isocrates, as well as later writers who picked up the theme.[69] How seriously they took it cannot readily be demonstrated. Polemical or political motives played a role. Propaganda for a panhellenic crusade against the barbarian had its advocates. Whatever the reality of the situation, however, Xenophon had an inviting target. Disparagement of Persia was in the air. The platitudes about Persian softness and inferiority might be mobilized against his affirmative assessment.

---

[66] Xen. *Cyr.* 8.8.15–19; cf. 4.3.22–23.
[67] Xen. *Cyr.* 8.8.20.
[68] Xen. *Cyr.* 8.8.22–25.
[69] For references, see Briant (2001), 193–210. On Ctesias' role in these stereotypes, see Sancisi-Weerdenburg (1987), 33–44. A more positive verdict on Ctesias can be found now in Llewellyn-Jones and Robson (2010), 24–31, 82–87. Cf. the discussion of Isaac (2004), 283–298.

The historian stole a march on potential critics. He discredited the clichés by exaggerating them with parody and reducing them to absurdity.

The epilogue, in short, does reinforce the text. Not because it underscores a contrast between past and present, and certainly not because it represents a logical culmination of what preceded. The jarring deviation itself captures attention. But it does not disturb the main message. On the contrary, it subjects alternative images to ridicule. The *Cyropaedia* remains powerful testimony to a laudable Persia in the eye of a Greek intellectual who knew the land and its people far better than most.

Alexander and the Persians

For Alexander the Great, Persia embodied the enemy par excellence. He spent much of his short life fighting against the Achaemenid kingdom. His fabled military campaign, occupying a dozen years of tragedy and triumph, defined the era and determined the conqueror's legacy. Yet this titanic clash of Macedonian against Persian, so dramatic and memorable, contains a pointed paradox. Bias against the "barbarian" played no part in the motivation or objectives of Alexander the Great. On this matter the Hellenistic polymath Eratosthenes is quite explicit. Alexander shunned the advice of those who would divide the world into Greeks and barbarians and who advocated treating the first as friends and the second as enemies. The king instead showed favor or disfavor to men in accord with their quality and character.[70] Indeed he went beyond this, according to Plutarch. Alexander dissented from the counsel of Aristotle, who advised that he relate to Greeks as a leader but to barbarians as a master, placing the one in the category of friends and kinsmen, the other in that of animals and plants. The king, by contrast, saw himself as impartial governor of all, mingling lives, customs, marriages, and practices as if in some great loving cup, and distinguishing Greek and barbarian only in terms of virtue and vice.[71]

Those statements stem from intellectuals peering back at Alexander from the distance of generations or centuries. But the impression was powerful, and the assessment by no means without foundation. The Macedonian

---

[70] Strabo 1.4.9 (C66). Strabo himself, in somewhat tortured fashion, interprets Alexander's behavior as ultimately agreeing with his advisers who identified Greeks and barbarians with men of good and bad character respectively. Cf. Dueck (2000), 76; Isaac (2004), 300–301.

[71] Plut. *Mor*. 329 B–D. Plutarch may have had his own designs in mind in constructing this antinomy. And the question of whether he drew here on Eratosthenes cannot be determined— although he cites him shortly thereafter on Alexander's combination of Macedonian and Persian raiment; 329F–330A. Cf. Andreotti (1956), 274–279; Badian (1958), 434–440; Hamilton (1969), xxix–xxxii. But the tradition that Alexander eschewed essentialist distinctions between Greeks and non-Greeks plainly held firm.

monarch's policies and behavior, so far as testimony allows for judgment, bear out the conclusions.

The empire of the Achaemenids represented the target of Alexander's ambitions and the emblem of Hellenic vengeance. But the peoples of the empire, interestingly and meaningfully, did not occupy the role of aliens or irremediable foes. Alexander indeed found them acceptable even as recruits for his own forces as the expedition proceeded eastward. The practice, it appears, began quite early in the campaign. In the letter that Alexander wrote to the Achaemenid monarch Darius after the battle of Issus in 333, he noted that he took responsibility for those who had served with Darius but fled to him and now willingly joined forces with his own army.[72] The letter may owe much to the composition of Arrian three centuries later. But there is no reason to question the enrollment of foreign troops in Alexander's corps, dating already from the time of his initial victories. By 328/327 Bactrians and Sogdians were fighting in his ranks.[73] Various Iranian and Indian contingents served under Alexander during the campaign in India in 327.[74] Most tellingly, the king, probably in 327, ordered thirty thousand young men chosen from all the satrapies of the Persian realm to learn Greek and to be trained in Macedonian weaponry and armament, thereby eventually to enter the ranks of his fighting forces.[75] Whatever the motivation of Alexander, it is plain that he regarded the incorporation of Iranian soldiery into his army to be not only a temporary stopgap but a long-term policy.[76] The training of this younger generation of Persian youth suggests the vision of an enduring multinational army.

Alexander looked to the long run also in the establishment of colonial settlements in the east. The colonies had a multinational character from the start. They would encompass battle-scarred and overage soldiers no longer fit for military service, whether Greek mercenaries or Macedonian veterans, and volunteers, sometimes in substantial numbers, from natives

---

[72] Arrian 2.14.7. It is unclear why Bosworth (1980), 232, assumes that Arrian refers only to Persian nobles here. There is nothing in the text to suggest that. See ὅσοι τῶν μετὰ σοῦ παραταξαμένων.

[73] Arrian 4.17.3. Cf. Bosworth (1995), 119.

[74] Arrian 5.2.2–4, 5.3.6, 5.11.3, 5.12.2; Curt. 9.2.24.

[75] Plut. *Alex*. 47.3; Curt. 8.5.1; cf. Arrian 7.6.1; Diod. 17.108.1–2; Plut. *Alex*. 71.1. Curtius puts the recruitment just prior to the Indian campaign in 327. Plutarch's setting, ostensibly in 330, does not really have chronological connotation. Cf. Hamilton (1969), 128–129. On the recruitment of Asians generally, see Bosworth (1988), 271–273.

[76] Plutarch, *Alex*. 47.3, interprets the action as designed to make indigenous people more familiar with Macedonian customs, leading to a blend and commonality through goodwill, and reinforcing his own security. Curtius, 8.5.1, offers a slightly more cynical interpretation: the young men under training would serve both as soldiers—and as hostages. These, of course, are no more than surmises.

in neighboring regions.[77] Alexander evidently reckoned that communities of mixed ethnic character would be stable and successful entities—and so did those who voluntarily entered into them.[78]

More arresting and more conspicuous was Alexander's adoption of "barbarian" attire. The king obviously meant this to be noticed. He deliberately ran the risk of disgruntlement among his staff and entourage. The matter seemed worthwhile. Our sources differ on just what Alexander wore, when, and how often. But the fact of his dressing in alien apparel is incontrovertible. The king began wearing this garb sometime after the death of Darius, probably in 330 or 329. He put on the diadem of the Persian monarchs, the white robe and belt, and other accoutrements of Achaemenid rule. A hostile tradition brands him as corrupted by eastern luxury, succumbing to debased oriental practices that included the employment of eunuchs, lavish banquets, and a nightly parade of concubines from which he would select his evening's companion.[79] Even the biased testimony, however, indicates that Alexander went about this with caution and in slow steps, embracing some eastern regalia but not all, eschewing the tiara and the trousers, striking a balance between Persian and Median fashions, at first donning such clothing only sparingly and only in formal encounters with Persian representatives or his own Companions.[80] Some Macedonians disapproved, evincing resentment for the "Orientalizing" behavior of their king.[81] But Alexander persisted.[82] And, more significantly, he made a point of displaying that this went beyond a choice of personal attire signifying his own special position. Alexander asked his Companions, the cavalry commanders, and the military officers to don purple-trimmed cloaks—even the horses would wear Persian harnesses.[83]

The king plainly promoted this posture with purposeful forethought. What lay behind it has prompted much speculation. The notion of Alexander enraptured by eastern luxury and opulence is standard rhetorical moralizing, not to be confused with history. Arrian and Plutarch offer a political explanation: Alexander endeavored to show himself accommodating

---

[77] Arrian 4.4.1, 4.22.5, 4.24.7, 5.29.3; Diod. 17.83.2; Curt. 7.3.23.

[78] For a more skeptical view of these settlements, see Fraser (1996), 177–190; Brosius (2003), 178–179. Plutarch's assessment (*Mor.* 328 E) that Alexander saw them as bringing culture and civilization to the barbarian is, of course, far off the mark. See Bosworth (1988), 245–250.

[79] The hostile interpretation surfaces in Arrian 4.7.4, 4.9.9; Diod. 17.77.4–7; Curt. 6.6.1–8; Justin 12.3.8–11. On the timing of Alexander's adoption of Persian dress, see Hamilton (1987), 472–474, as against Bosworth (1980), 5–6.

[80] Diod. 17.77.5; Plut. *Alex.* 45.2, 47.5; Plut. *Mor.* 330 A.

[81] Diod. 17.78.1; Plut. *Alex.* 45.3; Curt. 6.6.9; Justin 12.4.1.

[82] Arrian 4.8.4, 4.14.2, 7.6.3, 7.8.2; Plut. *Alex.* 51.3; Curt. 8.7.12.

[83] Diod. 17.77.5; Curt. 6.6.7. Curtius claimed that the officers were compelled against their will to put on Persian garb but did not dare refuse. That is inference, not testimony.

to native practices, thus to win over the allegiance of the conquered.[84] That makes perfectly good sense. But the political objective could also have been achieved in other ways. Alexander, as is well known, appointed or retained Persians as satraps and administrators in various units of the empire.[85] He installed men of Asian ethnicity as formal attendants in his court and enrolled the most distinguished of them among his ceremonial bodyguards, including Darius' own brother.[86] He associated himself with the founder of the Achaemenid empire, Cyrus the Great.[87] Symbolism played as large a role as politics here. The new regime would encompass Iranian as well as Macedonian emblems, a regime to which all ethnic groups could in principle pledge allegiance. Alexander had come as conqueror of the Persian empire but would preside as representative of all its diverse peoples. Whatever pragmatic motives one might wish to ascribe to the king, and whatever the realities on the ground, the symbolism of a realm that respected indigenous traditions, adopted native accoutrements, and promoted Iranian leaders to positions of eminence delivered a meaningful message. Alexander evidently eschewed any notions of ethnic inferiority among "barbarians."

Most striking and most notorious along these lines was Alexander's effort to introduce *proskynesis* into his court. The practice constituted a conventional gesture whereby Persians paid homage to their king. To Greeks and Macedonians, however, such gestures could only be offered to divinities. To extend them to mortals would cross the line between men and gods and run the risk of being perceived as colossal *hybris* (to Greeks, though not to Persians). Alexander was willing to run the risk. To what end remains a source of continuing controversy. That issue has engendered a repeated barrage of scholarship. For our purposes, Alexander's motives need not be ferreted out. Whether this was an opening wedge to induce acknowledgment of his divinity or a means to provide a uniform court ceremonial can be left aside.

It seems likely, in any case, that some Persians felt discomfort with performing such a ritual while Macedonians were exempt from it—and ridiculed those who practiced it. Two anecdotes underscore the embarrassment. One of Alexander's Companions, Leonnatus, taunted a Persian whose bow was awkward and unseemly, thus stirring the temporary wrath of Alexander.[88] On another occasion (or perhaps an embellished variant of

---

[84] Arrian 7.29.4; Plut. *Alex.* 45.1; Plut. *Mor.* 330 A. Arrian adds that this was also directed at Macedonians, allowing Alexander some refuge from the sharpness of his compatriots' arrogance.

[85] See Hamilton (1987), 468–472. That some of them proved disloyal or incompetent and were subsequently replaced by Macedonians is another matter; cf. Brosius (2003), 188–192.

[86] Diod. 17.77.4; Plut. *Alex.* 43.3; Curt. 6.2.11; cf. Arrian 7.29.4.

[87] Strabo 11.11.4; Arrian 6.29.4–11. Cf. Brosius (2003), 174–175.

[88] Arrian 4.12.2.

the same incident) the Macedonian noble Polyperchon cruelly mocked a Persian who touched his chin to the earth, asking him to perform the act again, this time to give it a good crack on the ground. Alexander (not for the first time) gave vent to his fury and personally threw Polyperchon to the earth, thus to simulate the same act that he had burlesqued.[89] An even more elaborate version has Cassander laugh uproariously at Persians offering *proskynesis* only to have Alexander seize him by the hair and smash his head against a wall.[90] We need not vouch for the historicity of the anecdotes. But they reflect a tense atmosphere in which clashing customs could tread on national sensitivities.

Alexander clearly recognized the problem. If the ritual exacerbated rather than smoothed relations between the peoples, it was not worth pursuing. A different narrative has the king introduce the practice with due caution and care, having it take place at a rigged banquet in which it might appear unobtrusive and pass without resistance, perhaps an experiment to test reaction.[91] The plan did not work. Alexander's own historian Callisthenes objected, declined to go along with the scheme—or reneged on a promise to do so. Alexander evidently was miffed, but Macedonians generally approved Callisthenes' move. The king conceded the point, dropped his effort, and did not again make the attempt.[92] The opposition, however, as our sources represent it, arose not from abhorrence of alien peoples but from resistance to the concept (whatever the reality) that Alexander was grasping after divinity. The fact that he experimented at all with an institution familiar and comfortable to Persians, even if fraught with difficulty for Greeks and Macedonians, carries high significance. Alexander ran the risk, then dropped the idea, lest it undermine rather than promote harmony. It is noteworthy that we hear of no repercussions or even complaints from the Iranians. Perhaps the conduct of the experiment alone assured them of Alexander's goodwill. The gesture sufficed. The king's willingness to adopt even so un-Hellenic a practice illustrates his penchant for crossing conventional boundaries.

Presumed barriers, where they existed at all, fell most dramatically through the embrace of intermarriage. Alexander showed no hesitation on this score. In 327 he married Roxane, the daughter of a Bactrian baron.

---

[89] Curt. 8.5.22–24.
[90] Plut. *Alex.* 74.1–2. Cf. the discussion of these anecdotes in Bosworth (1995), 86–87.
[91] Plut. *Alex.* 54.3–55.1; Arrian 4.1.3–5.
[92] Plut. *Alex.* 54.2; Arrian 4.12.1; Curt. 8.5.20–21; Justin 12.7.3. That Alexander revived the attempt, as is alleged in a speech ascribed to the plotter Hermolaus by Arrian, 4.14.2, is unsupported elsewhere, and most unlikely. We leave aside here the supposed philosophic debate between Callisthenes and Anaxarchus on the acceptability of *proskynesis* as dissolving the line between men and gods; Arrian 4.10.5–12.1; Curt. 8.5.5–24. The debate is very probably fictitious. References to the scholarly discussion can be found in Bosworth (1995), 77–86.

The lady had legendary beauty, so it was said, and Alexander was drawn by a physical passion. But he eschewed the rights of a conqueror and chose a formal wedding ceremony, a decision applauded by Roxane's father and a cause of admiration in our sources.[93] Some of those sources surmise that matters of policy entered into the equation. Plutarch notes that the natives rejoiced in the communion effected by the marriage; in addition to being a love match it also accorded with Alexander's purposes.[94] Curtius expands somewhat on the aim: this wedding would link Persians and Macedonians, stabilizing the empire, and erasing both the pride of the conqueror and the shame of the conquered. He even cites the union of Achilles and Briseis as model![95] No need to doubt that political motives played a role. After two years of heavy warfare in Bactria and Sogdiana, with considerable loss of life and no lack of ruthlessness, Alexander had reason to reconcile the surviving leadership before undertaking his campaign into India.[96] The marriage itself, however, is the central fact. No shock or dissent is recorded. Indeed, Alexander, we are told, persuaded many of his friends to take as wives the daughters of prominent Bactrians and Sogdians.[97] Nothing stands against that testimony. And we have no cause to doubt it. Whatever the political implications of these nuptials, they attest to an absence of ethnic discrimination, at least in the king and many of his officers and friends.

And they were not alone. That large numbers of Macedonians on this expedition married or cohabited with Iranian women is indisputable. These were not one-night stands. Substantial numbers of offspring resulted from the unions, and women and children accompanied the soldiers on service.[98] Of course, sexual partners and continuing companions constituted an essential ingredient for military morale in long campaigns without an obvious terminus. Alexander was sensitive to his soldiers' needs. He had given a furlough to those Macedonians with young wives at home in the winter of 334/333, near the outset of his expedition.[99] Obviously such leaves became increasingly difficult as Alexander's march moved into the interior of Asia. The king, it appears, deliberately encouraged intermarriage or a

[93] Arrian 4.19.5–6, 4.20.4; Curt. 8.4.22–30; Plut. *Alex*. 47.4; Plut. *Mor*. 332 E.

[94] Plut. *Alex*. 47.4. At *Mor*. 338 D, by contrast, Plutarch ascribes the union to passion rather than policy.

[95] Curt. 8.4.25–26: *ad stabiliendum regnum pertinere Persas et Macedones conubio iungi; hoc uno modo et pudorem victis et superbiam victoribus detrahi posse*.

[96] Bosworth (1980), 11, and (1995), 131, oddly sees the act as a demonstration of Alexander's military authority and a cementing of his rule. If this was Alexander's objective, he need not have married a Bactrian princess for the purpose. For Holt (1988), 67–68, Roxane was "as much a bribe as a bride"—a needlessly narrow interpretation. Cf. also Carney (2000), 106–107; Worthington (2004), 139–140.

[97] *Metz Epitome*, 31; Diod. 17, Index λ.

[98] Arrian 6.25.5, 7.4.8; Diod. 17.94.4, 17.110.3; Plut. *Alex*. 42.4, 70.2; Justin 12.4.1–6.

[99] Arrian 1.24.1.

steady cohabitation for his soldiers to prevent homesickness. And, if Justin be believed, he already looked ahead to future soldiers drawn from the offspring of these unions.[100] The practicality of the circumstances certainly had a hand in the policy. But the interracial conjunction notably caused no stir among officers or troops.

The culmination of this development came at Susa in 324. Alexander staged a memorable and conspicuous event that resonated widely from that seat of the Persian monarchs. He took in marriage two princesses of the Achaemenid line: the daughter of Darius and the daughter of his predecessor on the throne, Artaxerxes Ochus. In addition, many of Alexander's Companions wed some of the noblest ladies of the Persian or Bactrian aristocracy. These included another daughter of Darius who became bride of Hephaestion and a niece who married Craterus. Further, Perdiccas, Ptolemy, Eumenes, Nearchus, and Seleucus all took blue-blooded Asian wives. A total of nearly one hundred such marriages graced the elaborate celebration at Susa. All were solemnized in traditional Persian fashion. And the king personally supplied dowries for every couple.[101] The sources here again offer conjectures concerning broader motives that lurk behind the marriages. Plutarch, in the *Life of Alexander*, reports a wedding hymn raised by the king that signified a concord of interests joining the greatest and most powerful of nations.[102] Plutarch's imagery elsewhere of Alexander mingling lives, characteristics, marriages, and customs as if in a great loving cup may allude to this event.[103] Curtius has Alexander announce that he sought by this compact, promising a new generation of mixed offspring, to erase all distinctions between victors and vanquished.[104] Moderns detect a more cynical design: the marriages of Macedonian men and Iranian women—not any Macedonian brides and Persian husbands—would underscore western ascendancy and designate Alexander's Companions as new rulers of a conquered realm.[105] That assessment is harsh. Few Greek or Macedonian women were available at Susa for a reciprocal wedding party. And it would risk offense for the king summarily to summon several dozen aristocratic ladies from Macedon for this purpose. Nor does any

---

[100] Justin 12.4.2–6.
[101] Arrian 7.4.4–8; Diod. 17.107.6; Plut. *Alex.* 70.2; Plut. *Mor.* 329 E; Curt. 10.3.12; Justin 12.10.10; Athenaeus 12.537d–540a; Aelian *VH* 8.7. The numbers are given differently in different narratives. Chares' account, the most authoritative, has 92; *FGH* 125 F 4.
[102] Plut. *Mor.* 329 E: εἰς κοινωνίαν συνιοῦσι τοῖς μεγίστοις καὶ δυνατωτάτοις.
[103] Plut. *Mor.* 329 C. Cf. Andreotti (1956), 278–279; Badian (1958), 438–439.
[104] Curt. 10.3.12. A narrower motive is hypothesized by Justin, who supposes that Alexander acted to alleviate any charge against him by making the event a collaborative one; 12.10.10.
[105] Bosworth (1980), 12; *idem* (1988), 156–157; *idem* (1994), 840; Wiesehöfer (1994), 46; Brosius (2003), 176–177; Worthington (2004), 180–181; Cartledge (2004), 212–214. Carney (2000), 111–112, oddly claims that Alexander's marriage here involved a rejection of Macedonia.

reason exist to see the event at Susa as emblematizing Macedonian supremacy over the empire of the Achaemenids. That is hardly the most obvious conclusion to be drawn from a conspicuous linking of the Macedonian elite with the royalty and nobility of Iran—a linking celebrated in full Persian fashion.[106]

Efforts to read Alexander's mind can be thankfully shelved. The public ceremonial, dramatically shared by the upper crust of both peoples, carries the greatest weight. The Companions put on display their willingness to enter into matrimony with the premier representatives of the Achaemenid realm, and to do so in a manner that placed Persian tradition in the center of the formalities. Did Alexander have to strong-arm his reluctant Companions to perform this gesture? Diodorus says that the king "persuaded" the most eminent of his friends to engage in wedlock.[107] The verb need not imply resistance or recalcitrance. Arrian records a report (without endorsing it) that some of the bridegrooms were displeased with marriages in the Persian style.[108] That may have more to do with the form of the wedding than the ethnicity of the brides. None of the other sources implies any tensions on this score. It is often said that Seleucus alone among the Companions remained married to his Asian wife after the death of Alexander.[109] We do not know this for a fact. Some married again, for a variety of political reasons.[110] But nothing suggests that Asian wives were discarded on ethnic grounds. What then did the ceremony signify? We can avoid sweeping postulates of a blending of the races or a unity of east and west.[111] The celebration exhibited a common concern for the harmony and stability of the realm. A conjugal joining of the elites, whatever the future for individual marriages, represented a powerful gesture that Macedonians rejected ethnic impediments and stereotypes in their relations with the peoples of Iran.

Those weddings involved only the leading houses of the two nations. But Alexander did not stop there. The king arranged a mass celebration to mark the formal registration of all marriages entered into by his soldiers with Asian women, a vast number that Arrian puts at more than ten thousand.[112] Pragmatic purposes doubtless took precedence here, no

---

[106] Hamilton (1987), 484–485, rightly wonders why such a ceremony would be needed to declare the new lords of the empire.

[107] Diod. 17.107.6: ἔπεισε δὲ καὶ τοὺς ἐπιφανεστάτους τῶν φίλων γῆμαι.

[108] Arrian 7.6.2: λέγονται ... τοὺς γάμους ἐν τῷ νόμῳ τῷ Περσικῷ ποιηθέντας οὐ πρὸς θυμοῦ γενέσθαι ... τῶν γημάντων ἔστιν οἷς.

[109] Most recently, Worthington (2004), 181.

[110] See references in Brosius (2003), 176–177. It does not follow that the marriages were mere demonstrations of Macedonian domination, as is claimed by Bosworth (1988), 157; Brosius (2003), 176–177.

[111] For this idea, which no longer needs refutation, see the bibliography in Seibert (1972), 186–192; Bosworth (1980), 1–2.

[112] Arrian 7.4.8; Plut. *Alex*. 70.2; cf. Justin 12.4.2.

grand scheme or vision. The registration simply took official note of the cohabitation or informal unions that soldiers had experienced for some time in the service, a recognition, for the most part, of the status quo. The formalities mattered, however, in terms of legitimizing children and assuring inheritances.[113] Alexander not only provided such assurances but lavished gifts on the troops whose unions were here commemorated. The king made it abundantly clear that the state of matrimony between Macedonians and Asians had his blessing. No one, it appears, raised an issue about racial obstacles.

To be sure, Alexander's policies stirred discontent among the troops. Grumblings about the Macedonian monarch "going native" had surfaced before in the expedition. But objections on that front did not reach serious proportions. Alexander had been careful and prudent, showing an affinity for Persian practices while treading lightly on the sensitivities of Greeks and Macedonians or even stepping back when the tread was too heavy. In the last year of his life, however, grumbling swelled into mutiny. At Susa and then at Opis, the troops grew restive on several grounds. Alexander made the ostensibly generous offer of paying any debts incurred by his soldiers. But they greeted that offer with mistrust, worried that it was a trick to discover which of them had lived beyond his means. An atmosphere of suspicion evidently enveloped their relationship.[114] The arrival in Susa of the *Epigoni*, the thirty thousand Iranian youths whom Alexander had ordered to be instructed in Macedonian arms three years before, exacerbated the tensions. Many Macedonian veterans complained that their ranks were infiltrated by men from the various satrapies of the empire, that they were about to be dispensed with, and that their king would rely increasingly on recruits from the younger generation of Persians.[115] The dissatisfaction spilled over into open insurrection at Opis in 324, an uprising that Alexander repressed with a combination of bluffing, ruthlessness, and generosity.[116] These episodes have been much discussed in the literature and require no further rehearsal here.

Only one relevant question needs to be asked: to what degree did discontent in the ranks reflect hostility to non-Greeks and irritation with Alexander's policy of magnanimity toward them? In fact, there is little evidence to suggest that ethnic animosity provoked the mutinous soldiers. Only Arrian brings this dimension into the reckoning. He comments that

---

[113] Of course, political calculation may have entered into the reckoning; Badian (1985), 483–484; Brosius (2003), 176–177. But it would be wrong to reduce the matter simply to the potential advantages of a new generation of soldiers to be born of mixed marriages.

[114] Arrian 7.5.1–3; Diod. 17.109.2; Curt. 10.2.9–11; Justin 12.11.1–3; cf. Plut. *Alex.* 70.2.

[115] Arrian 7.6.1–5, 7.8.2; Diod. 17.108.3; Plut. *Alex.* 71.1–3; Curt. 10.2.12; Justin 12.11.4–5.

[116] Arrian 7.8.2–7.12.4; Diod. 17.109.2–3; Plut. *Alex.* 71.3–5; Curt. 10.2.13–10.4.3; Justin, 12.11.6–12.12.10.

the Macedonians were already aggrieved that Alexander wore Median garb, encouraged the "Persianizing" of his satrap in Persis, and celebrated the marriages at Susa in Persian style. They then became especially incensed at the incorporation of Iranian units into the army, an indication that Macedonians were becoming supernumeraries.[117] The other sources make nothing of the alleged vexation at Alexander's nativizing tendencies as an element in the mutiny. The anger of the veterans at their prospective discharge and the indignation that Iranian troops might take their place are perfectly intelligible without injecting a supposed ethnic animosity.[118] It is noteworthy that when the insurgency fizzled and the soldiers declared their loyalty once more, Iranian warriors entered the ranks in greater numbers without any difficulty.[119] Even more significant, despite the purported displeasure with Alexander's partiality for Persian ways and Persian auxiliaries, there is no sign that the mutinous soldiers ever proposed to set aside their Persian wives. Alexander asked those veterans who were now to be mustered out and return to Macedon to leave any children born to foreign women behind them so that he could assure their training in Macedonian fashion—and thus have a future supply of recruits.[120] Their mothers would presumably stay with them. But the validity of the mass marriages at Susa remained intact. The authority of that symbolic gesture was not compromised.

The collapse of the mutiny brought about reconciliation between Alexander and his men. To those who complained that Alexander had addressed some Persians as his kinsmen while withholding that designation from the Macedonians, he replied that he regarded them all as his kinsmen.[121] A banquet followed to mark the accommodation. But the personages arrayed at that ceremony went beyond the rank-and-file soldiery. Alexander had a larger symbolism in mind. As Arrian portrays it, the king sat with Macedonians around him, sharing libations from the same bowl. Next to them were Persians, then representatives of other peoples distinguished by rank or virtue. Hellenic seers and eastern magi jointly opened the proceedings. The king then offered a notable prayer that asked, among other benefits, for concord and a common share in rule by Macedonians and Persians.[122] Alexander made sure to identify himself first and foremost

[117] Arrian 7.6.2–5, 7.8.2. On these passages, see Badian (1965), 160–161; Hammond (1983), 139–144.
[118] Worthington's assertion (2004), 183, that Alexander played on the hatred between Macedonians and Asians has no basis in the texts.
[119] Arrian 7.23.1; Diod. 17.110.1–2; Justin 12.12.4.
[120] Arrian 7.12.2; Diod. 17.110.3; cf. Plut. *Alex.* 71.5; Justin 12.4.5–6.
[121] Arrian 7.11.6–7.
[122] Arrian 7.11.9: εὔχετο δὲ τά τε ἄλλα καὶ τὰ ἀγαθὰ καὶ ὁμόνοιάν τε καὶ κοινωνίαν τῆς ἀρχῆς Μακεδόσι καὶ Πέρσαις. There is, of course, nothing here about a "brotherhood of man," as was once argued by Tarn (1948), II, 434–449. See Andreotti (1956), 279–282; Badian (1958), 428–432; C. Thomas (1968), 258–260; Bosworth (1980), 2.

with the Macedonians. But the governance of the realm, so his prayer signified, would be a collaborative one, with Persians on a par with his own people.

Curtius Rufus supplies a speech, placed in Alexander's mouth and delivered to Iranian troops after the mutiny failed. The king recounted his actions in bringing Persian soldiers into the ranks of his army, finding them brave, loyal, and disciplined, and providing them with the same equipment and weaponry that the Macedonians employed. He took note of his own marriages to the daughters of a Bactrian prince and the Achaemenid king. He professed to regard the Iranians as his citizens and soldiers. And he declared the kingdom of Asia and Europe to be a single entity.[123] The speech, of course, is a fiction, unattested by our other sources. But the sentiments accord with the actions of the Macedonian monarch. He did not erase distinctions between east and west. Nor did he evince any interest in "fusing the races." But the commander who avenged the damage inflicted on Greeks, who toppled the Achaemenids and conquered the Persian empire, eschewed racial bias against the "barbarian." Foreigners served in his armies, governed his satrapies, influenced his dress and demeanor, became his wives and the wives of his men, and took a conspicuous place in the ruling circles of his realm.

---

[123] Curt. 10.3.7–14. Note especially 10.3.13: *Asiae et Europae unum atque idem regnum est . . . et cives mei estis et milites.*

Chapter 3

◉ ◉ ◉ ◉ ◉ ◉ ◉ ◉ ◉ ◉ ◉ ◉ ◉ ◉ ◉

EGYPT IN THE CLASSICAL IMAGINATION

THE ANCIENT LAND of Egypt fascinated a host of Hellenic writers and intellectuals. Its antiquity generated awe. And its exotic appeal wove a spell. On the face of it, that mysterious people embodied practices, beliefs, and traditions remote from and even unintelligible to Greek and Roman inquirers. The vast differences themselves sparked intense interest over a remarkable stretch of time. Yet something more remarkable still merits emphasis. The distance between the cultures could be crossed in multiple and intriguing ways that elide the antitheses.

Herodotus

An offhand comment by Herodotus arrests attention. The historian reports that Nechos, king of Egypt, conceived an elaborate design to link the Nile by canal to the Red Sea. But an oracle warned him off: all this work would only benefit the barbarian. The pregnant prophecy (*post eventum*, of course) alludes to the fact that the canal would be completed by Darius of Persia for the benefit of the Persian empire. And Herodotus glosses his expression by asserting that the Egyptians refer to all those who do not speak their tongue as "barbarians."[1] The remark is brief, unelaborated, and rarely discussed.

Yet it may not be altogether innocent. As Herodotus and his readers well knew, Greeks traditionally divided the populated world into Hellenes and "barbarians," the latter identifiable by the fact that their speech was not Greek. The designation need not be pejorative, let alone hostile, nor indeed even an allusion to inferiority. But it did at least provide a signifier of "Otherness." What bears notice here, however, is that Herodotus ascribes that same mode of demarcation between the strange and the familiar to the Egyptians. No Hellenocentrism here. The center shifts to Egypt. But

---

[1] Herod. 2.158: βαρβάρους δὲ πάντας οἱ Αἰγύπτιοι καλέουσι τοὺς μὴ σφίσι ὁμογλώσσους. On this image, see the valuable comments of Lloyd (1988), 157–158; Munson (2005), 65–66.

the analogy turns on a paradox. The Egyptians set themselves apart from other nations who do not share their language (notably the Greeks). Yet the Greeks, employing the identical mode of demarcation, simultaneously disjoin themselves from Egyptians while adopting the same form of disjunction. The historian, one may readily infer, comments as much on his countrymen as upon the "barbarian"—especially as each can represent the latter.

The duplication emblematizes Herodotus' complex perspective on the Egyptians. The historian does not so much relegate that people to the category of the "Other" as he has them relegate others to that category. At the same time, however, he repeatedly problematizes the picture by calling up instances of interplay and overlap.

Herodotus, to be sure, stresses the special character of Egypt and the distinctive characteristics of its people. No reader can miss those aspects. A famous segment of the excursus on Egypt offers a long list of practices and behavior that set Egyptians apart—just as the nature of the Nile stands apart from that of all other rivers. Herodotus contrasts their customs not with those of Greeks as such but with those of all people. In Egypt, among many peculiarities, women do the shopping and sell the wares while men stay home; women urinate standing up, men while sitting; men rather than women serve as priests and devotees of the gods; Egyptians relieve themselves outdoors but eat indoors; they keep animals in their homes, a practice all others shun. In one case only does Herodotus differentiate them from Greeks in particular: Greeks write from left to right, Egyptians the reverse.[2] Indeed Egyptians insist on holding to their own ancestral customs, adding nothing from the outside.[3] They take their separatism very seriously, even to the point of refusing to use implements belonging to Greeks, or eating meat cut by Greek knives, or kissing a Greek who had tasted of the sacred ox.[4] Although Greeks are here mentioned specifically, the prohibition upon handling their objects or fraternizing with them certainly applies to all non-Egyptians.[5] Herodotus makes the point directly when he says that Egyptians reject the customs of Greeks but do not single them out: they reject those of all men everywhere.[6] In such matters, they are nondiscriminatory.

The most notorious of Egyptian peculiarities, without competition, was animal worship. Herodotus goes on at length about it. He asserts even that Egyptians held all animals as sacred (though he acknowledges that some

[2] Herod. 2.35–36.
[3] Herod. 2.79: πατρίοισι δὲ χρεώμενοι νόμοισι ἄλλον οὐδένα ἐπικτῶνται.
[4] Herod. 2.41.
[5] Their unwillingness to sit at meals with Hebrews is mentioned already in the Bible: Gen. 43:32.
[6] Herod. 2.91.

enjoyed this status only in certain parts of the land). The historian proceeds through a lengthy roster of animals and the individual practices associated with them.[7] Nowhere does he issue a direct statement that Egyptian reverence toward creatures puts them at odds with the rest of mankind. He did not need to. The mere recounting of their behavior and attitude sufficed. Egyptians, for example, applied the death penalty to anyone who deliberately killed a sacred animal, and, in the case of certain creatures like the ibis and the hawk, even an unintentional killing resulted in execution.[8] They had special concern for cats: if a fire breaks out, they take greater care in protecting the cats than in quenching the flames. And dead cats were embalmed and buried in caskets like humans.[9] Sacred snakes even have the honor of being buried in the temple of Zeus/Amun.[10] In one district at least the death of a he-goat prompts a decree of mourning for the entire region.[11] These and like descriptions, presented by Herodotus in matter-of-fact fashion, required no commentary to declare their outlandishness. Regarding animals with awe and judging them as holy resembled nothing in the experience of the Greeks. That mental frame was foreign on the face of it.

Herodotus alludes also to a different and not exactly laudable feature of the Egyptian mentality. He observes that after a brief interlude when they enjoyed freedom, following the supposed reign of a priest, the Egyptians reverted again to monarchic rule because they could not endure being without a king for any length of time.[12] That notion receives a footnote of sorts when Herodotus speaks of King Amasis, who took the throne after overthrow of his predecessor and, by shrewdly capitalizing on his rise to power from humble roots, induced the Egyptians "to agree to be his slaves."[13]

No wonder then that recurrent interpretation has Herodotus perceive the Egyptians as a prime example of the "Other."[14] They insisted on their distinctiveness; their habits and beliefs contrasted in every way with those of the Hellenes (and most other people); they resisted adoption of principles and practices that came from elsewhere; they elevated common animals and birds to the status of holiness, an unthinkable notion outside

---

[7] Herod. 2.65–76, with the extensive commentary of Lloyd (1994b), II, 291–330; cf. the briefer treatment by Lloyd (2007), 291.

[8] Herod. 2.65.

[9] Herod. 2.66–67.

[10] Herod. 2.74. See the discussion of Lloyd (1994b), II, 324–325.

[11] Herod. 2.46.

[12] Herod. 2.147: ἐλευθερωθέντες Αἰγύπτιοι μετὰ τὸν ἱρέα τοῦ Ἡφαίστου βασιλεύσαντα, οὐδένα γὰρ χρόνον οἷοί τε ἦσαν ἄνευ βασιλέος διαιτᾶσθαι.

[13] Herod. 2.172: προσηγάγετο τοὺς Αἰγυπτίους ὥστε δικαιοῦν δουλεύειν.

[14] See, e.g., Lateiner (1985), 81–89; idem (1989), 147–152; Cartledge (1993), 56–59; Vasunia (2001), 75–82, 93–109. Cf. also Redfield (1985), 103–110, although his stress is on the contrast between Egypt and Scythia. So also Hartog (1988), 15–19; idem (2002), 214–216. But see R. Thomas (2000), 78–79, 112.

Egypt; and they could not live without subjecting themselves to despotic rule. From that vantage point the picture seems consistent and not especially edifying.

Yet one cannot leave it at that. As is well known, the overall portrait is far from negative. The second book of Herodotus' history abounds in admiring remarks about the land of Egypt and its people. The historian begins by having the Egyptians boast that they are the oldest nation among men.[15] And he later endorses the point in his own voice, asserting that they had existed from the first ages of man.[16] A celebrated anecdote in the history serves to make the point with striking vividness. Herodotus recounts the visit of the historian Hecataeus of Miletus, more than a half century earlier, to the Egyptian priests at Thebes. The Milesian boasted of a genealogy that could be traced back sixteen generations to a god. The priests made mincemeat of that. They showed Hecataeus the interior of their temple, which contained wooden statues of all their high priests, each succeeded by his son, accounting for no fewer than 345 generations—and not a god among them. Hecataeus was firmly put in his place. Gods ruled among Egyptians, so Herodotus reports, but only in the hoary mists of time. The priests had given Herodotus himself the same tour of this impressive array of statuary and the awesome lineage it represented. But he made sure to add that he had not prompted it by flaunting any genealogy of his own.[17] The passage has been endlessly discussed, particularly with regard to Herodotus' dependence on Hecataeus, the accuracy of the narrative, and the degree to which it is pure construction by the historian.[18] These issues need not be settled here. The figures may well be exaggerated, a hereditary succession of high priests is specious, the sly dig at Hecataeus cannot be missed, and the conversation with the priests may be something of a jeu d'esprit. But the anecdote can hardly be dismissed as imaginary.[19] Egyptian priests had sound reasons to claim great antiquity for their nation, the number of generations is reasonable enough (even if Herodotus' calculations of more than eleven thousand years are faulty and fallacious), and indeed large numbers of statues are attested elsewhere in Egyptian shrines.[20] The priests themselves may be responsible for stretching

[15] Herod. 2.2: ἐνόμιζον ἑωυτοὺς πρώτους γενέσθαι πάντων ἀνθρώπων.

[16] Herod. 2.15: δοκέω ... αἰεί τε εἶναι ἐξ οὗ ἀνθρώπων γένος ἐγένετο. On the antiquity of Egypt as an intense interest of Ionian thinkers, see Froidefond (1971), 140–145.

[17] Herod. 2.143–144: ἐποίησαν οἱ ἱρέες τοῦ Διὸς οἷόν τι καὶ ἐμοὶ οὐ γενεηλογήσαντι ἐμεωυτόν.

[18] See, e.g., Fehling (1971), 59–66; S. West (1991), 145–154, with additional bibliography. On Herodotus and Hecataeus more generally, see the remarks of Lloyd (1994b), 127–139; Burstein (1995), 9–12; *idem* (1996), II, 593–597.

[19] As do Fehling (1971), 62–66, and S. West (1991), 145–154. The view of Heidel (1935), 93–97, that Hecataeus himself told the story, which was then maliciously perverted by Herodotus, is implausible in the extreme.

[20] See the cogent analysis of Moyer (2002), 75–82.

80   IMPRESSIONS OF THE "OTHER"

the truth, emphasizing a long, grand history and prompting Herodotus' respect.

Yet Egyptian antiquity is not without ambiguity. Herodotus both promotes and problematizes it. He introduces the subject with a remarkable narrative that actually questions rather than affirms the idea that Egypt predated all other nations—and one that the Egyptians themselves attested to. As the familiar, indeed infamous, account has it, the Egyptian king Psammetichus decided to test the theory that Egypt had chronological priority. He arranged to have two newborn children put in the care of a shepherd who would look after them amidst his flocks and make sure that no human would utter a word in their presence. In this way he could learn what the children themselves would first express without prompting and therefore offer a clue to the original language of mankind. As it happened, the first utterance from both their mouths was "*bekos*," which turned out to be a Phrygian word meaning bread. Psammetichus immediately concluded that Phrygian was the world's first language, and Egyptians thereupon conceded that Phrygians were an older people than they. Herodotus cites the Egyptian priests at the temple of Hephaistos (Ptah) at Memphis as his source.[21]

What does one make of this? The historian does not pronounce a verdict on the validity of the tale. He does, however, dismiss an alternative version that has Psammetichus cut out the tongues of the women charged with rearing the children, lest they allow any words to slip out. Herodotus scorns those Greeks who retail many nonsensical stories of that sort.[22] But he lets the other version stand. The story may very well be Hellenic in origin, trailing as it does the traces of Ionian speculation and Ionian penchant for experimentation to resolve puzzles.[23] Whether Herodotus bought it or not can be debated.[24] The intriguing fact remains that he credits Egyptian priests themselves with a narrative that acknowledges chronological priority for Phrygians over Egyptians.[25] The implications pique interest. If indeed Herodotus heard the tale from (or had it confirmed by) learned Egyptians, it indicates

---

[21] Herod. 2.2.

[22] Herod. 2.2: Ἕλληνες δὲ λέγουσι ἄλλα τε μάταια πολλά. Standard opinion judges that this snide comment refers to Hecataeus, who may have included the version in his history. Cf. How and Wells (1912), 156; Lloyd (1994b), II, 8–11; *idem* (2007), 243. The conjecture is indemonstrable and unnecessary.

[23] Froidefond (1971), 140–141; Lloyd (1994b), II, 9–10.

[24] Froidefond (1971), 141, suggests that he retailed it to critique Hecataeus' belief in Egyptian antiquity. So also Müller (1997), 210–214. An unlikely conjecture.

[25] Heidel (1935), 59–60, dismisses out of hand the possibility that Egyptian priests could have told this tale, and substitutes an altogether hypothetical scenario in which Hecataeus produced a satirical tale naively embraced as fact by Herodotus. The conjecture of A. Salmon (1956), 321–329, that priests spread this story to discredit Psammetichus, whose pro-Hellenic policies they deplored, goes well beyond both evidence and plausibility. Lloyd (1994b), II, 11, surprisingly regards it as possible.

that they did not regard an absolute claim on antiquity to be a vital part of their own identity. Or else Herodotus himself has an even subtler agenda that scholars have ignored. By introducing the entire excursus on Egypt with this fatuous fable and ascribing it to Egyptian informants, he strikes a cynical note on the issue of contested antiquity—a matter of intense curiosity to Greeks, but perhaps not so much so to the detached and secure Egyptians. The historian does not engage here in straight and simplistic reportage.

Herodotus justifies devoting so long a treatment to the Egyptians by referring to the countless wonders that Egypt possesses and the extraordinary works to which no description can do justice.[26] The Egyptians are the most pious of people, even incalculably so—beyond all other nations.[27] They have the reputation, moreover, of being the wisest of all men, a point that the historian does not dispute.[28] Other scattered comments reinforce this glowing image in various ways. Egyptians are by far the most scrupulous of men in maintaining the records of their past.[29] Like no other Greeks but the Spartans they show great respect to their elders, stepping aside for them in the street and yielding seats to them whenever they enter a room.[30] And Herodotus makes a point of refuting the legend of the Egyptian king Busiris, who purportedly sought in vain to sacrifice Herakles. He denounces in robust manner the benighted Greeks who believe this story in ignorance of the fact that Egyptians would not so much as sacrifice dumb animals (with a few exceptions), let alone human beings.[31] This and similar statements roused the indignation of Plutarch half a millennium later, who branded Herodotus as a φιλοβάρβαρος, preferring to criticize his own countrymen rather than to find any fault with aliens.[32]

Plutarch's assessment is well off the mark. Herodotus no more composed his excursus to elevate Egyptians as models for Greeks to emulate than he did to castigate them as bizarre and insular aliens who preferred servility to freedom. The historian saw this unusual people in far more nuanced fashion.

Egyptian "Otherness" resists reductionism. Herodotus' list of practices that single Egyptians out from other nations carries no pejorative con-

---

[26] Herod. 2.35. This does not mean that Herodotus took a naive, tourist-like approach to Egypt. For Froidefond (1971), 118–136, the influence of Ionian science and investigation served as important stimulus.

[27] Herod. 2.37: θεοσεβέες δὲ περισσῶς ἐόντες μάλιστα πάντων ἀνθρώπων. The translation "excessively" for περισσῶς has a negative connotation that would be incongruous with the rest of the passage.

[28] Herod. 2.160: τοὺς σοφωτάτους ἀνθρώπων Αἰγυπτίους.

[29] Herod. 2.77.

[30] Herod. 2.80. See the comment of Lloyd (1994b), II, 340–341; idem (2007), 295.

[31] Herod. 2.45.

[32] Plut. De Malignitate Herodoti 857A. The passage is rightly questioned by Harrison (2003), 151–152.

notations, a notable fact. Writing from right to left, having women as merchants and men as weavers, shaven priests, animals in the house and meals outside, prohibitions (for priests) on eating fish or beans, and comparable customs may be curious but hardly heinous. Herodotus presents the differences but eschews judgment.[33] Even on that most un-Hellenic of observances, the worship of animals, Herodotus recounts the convention with specifics and in detail but nowhere casts aspersion or expresses aversion.[34] With regard to the Egyptians' penchant for monarchy, Herodotus mentions it in a passing remark, not as a reproach, let alone as comparison with free Greeks.[35] He does not deploy the digression on Egypt as a vehicle for political or religious ideology.

That Egypt stands apart from all other nations is plain enough. Herodotus does not disguise the fact that Egyptians hold to their own ways and keep others at arm's length.[36] Whether that is admirable or deplorable is beside the point. Herodotus reports more fully and in more elaborate detail what other Greeks who had any familiarity with Egypt already knew. But he aimed to complicate, even subvert, the very "Otherness" that he identified.

The point emerges clearly and notoriously in Herodotus' insistence on the interlocking character of Egyptian and Greek divinities. Just how he understood that relationship remains murky.[37] He regularly amalgamates comparable deities, a form of syncretism, or simply applies Hellenic names to Egyptian gods. If this is mere *interpretatio Graeca*, however, it is a peculiar form thereof. Herodotus consistently emphasizes Egyptian priority. The historian maintains that the "names" of almost all the gods came from Egypt to Hellas. A few may have been indigenous, he acknowledges, but all the rest have forever been in Egypt.[38] Whether τὰ οὐνόματα actually means "names" in this case (as it should) or characteristics and personalities of the gods need not be decided here.[39] Either way the Greeks have taken their

---

[33] Herod. 2.35–37.

[34] Herod. 2.65–76; cf. Smelik and Hemelrijk (1984), 1879–1881; Munson (2001), 92–96; Hartog (2002), 214. He does describe the coupling of a woman with a goat as a τέρας; 2.46, i.e., a wonder or a portent, but even that was a one-time occurrence and without direct connection to ritual animal worship.

[35] Herod. 2.147. How and Wells (1912), 240, wrongly assert that "H. for once drops his Egyptian sympathies." On Herodotus and Egyptian monarchy, see the sober remarks of Harrison (2003), 149–150.

[36] Herod. 2.41, 2.91.

[37] On Herodotus and Egyptian religion, see the discussions of Wirth (2000), 285–310; Harrison (2000a), 182–189, 208–222.

[38] Herod. 2.50. See also, with regard to Herakles specifically, 2.43.

[39] See the careful and balanced arguments of Lloyd (1994b), II, 203–205, R. Thomas (2000), 274–282, and Harrison (2000a), 251–264, with references to previous discussions. Cf. also Froidefond (1971), 151–152.

models from Egypt and embraced Egyptian conceptions. Herodotus, not surprisingly, cites Egyptian sources for this information. But, unlike other instances where he identifies his sources in order to alert readers to their possible bias, the historian here openly affirms his own agreement with that conceptualization.[40]

Intersections among the divinities plainly excited his interest. As a prime example, Herodotus marshals several arguments (weak and spurious though they may be) for the claim that Herakles (and his parents for that matter) was Egyptian by origin and reckoned by Egyptians as a god, then later adopted by the Greeks, who also have another Herakles as a hero.[41] The Hellenic debt to Egypt gains reaffirmation more than once.[42] It holds also for oracles. The famed oracular centers at Dodona and Siwah both derived from Egypt, at least according to Herodotus' sources, the priests of Thebes. Their story had it that Phoenicians kidnapped two of the Theban priestesses, transporting the one to Dodona, the other to Libya.[43] Herodotus got a different version from the prophetesses at Dodona, and treated it with respect—but not credence. He preferred a rationalistic explanation. Egypt as the source, however, not only for oracular prophecy but also for divination by inspecting sacrificial victims, for sacred festivals, processions, and offerings, was simply taken for granted by Herodotus. For him, the antiquity of Egypt, by contrast with the youthfulness of Greece, sufficed to guarantee it.[44]

Other practices too could be traced to Egypt, according to Herodotus. Its people were the first to prohibit sexual intercourse in temples and even entrance into temples following intercourse, except after washing. They would be offenses against piety. The Greeks adopted the same prohibitions.[45] Additional restrictions held against the bringing of woolen garments into temples or burial in woolen cloaks. Herodotus notes that Orphic and Bacchic rites have similar interdicts but that they really stemmed from Egyptian and Pythagorean rules.[46] Egyptians were not alone in practicing circumcision, but everybody else learned it from

---

[40] Herod. 2.43, 2.50: δοκέω δ' ὦν μάλιστα ἀπ' Αἰγύπτου ἀπῖχθαι.

[41] Herod. 2.43–44.

[42] Herod. 2.4, 2.51. See also the ascription of the Thesmophoria of Demeter (Isis) to the Danaids, who brought them from Egypt; Herod. 2.171. Cf. Lloyd (1988), 209–211. On the identification of Demeter and Isis (Herod. 2.59), see Tobin (1991), 187–200.

[43] Froidefond (1971), 162–163, questions Herodotus' ascription of the story to the Theban priests, without compelling reason.

[44] Herod. 2.54–58: τεκμήριον δέ μοι τούτου τόδε· αἱ μὲν γὰρ φαίνονται ἐκ πολλοῦ τευ χρόνου ποιεύμεναι, αἱ δὲ Ἑλληνικαὶ νεωστὶ ἐποιήθησαν. On the competing tales of kidnapped priestesses, see Lloyd (1994b), II, 251–267.

[45] Herod. 2.64.

[46] Herod. 2.81. See the discussion of Froidefond (1971), 190–192.

them.[47] Nor was Egypt's influence limited to religion and the sacred. The pharaoh Amasis, so Herodotus records, enacted the measure that every Egyptian report the means of his earnings annually to his nomarch (district governor) or risk execution. That law, much praised by the historian, served as the model for one promulgated by the celebrated Athenian lawgiver Solon.[48]

Priority was prized. The older civilization had a head start and could make claims on providing precedents for the younger. Yet that may not be the historian's principal message. The debate about Herakles' derivation deserves another look. Herodotus claims to have many pieces of evidence showing that the name of Herakles came from Egypt to Hellas, rather than the other way round. Herakles, moreover, was one of twelve Egyptian deities who go back seventeen millennia. Herodotus credits Egyptian sources for that information.[49] Those who claimed him for Greece were presumably Greeks. Herodotus does not bother to say so. More importantly, he does not make an issue of rival professions of priority. The notion that chronological precedence confers special distinction on a nation is muted rather than paraded. It would be a mistake to infer that the historian aimed to stress the superiority of the older nation and to humble his fellow Hellenes.[50] One-upmanship did not motivate his agenda. A more significant point merits emphasis: that disputed claims couched themselves in terms of overlaps in the cultures. Whichever people first named or characterized the gods, their recognition by both affirmed that they were, in some sense, shared. The intersection takes precedence.

Nor was it merely a one-way process. What emerges perhaps most interestingly from Herodotus' musings on these matters is a form of cultural entanglement. The connections are multiple, not binary.

Dionysiac rites serve as an example. The festivals of Dionysus, in Herodotus' account, are closely parallel in both Egypt and Greece. Their roots, of course, lay in Egypt. But there was more to it than that. Herodotus identifies the conduit to Greece as the famed prophet and healer Melampus from Pylos.[51] That mythical figure appears already in Homer's *Odyssey*, and subsequent tales of his exploits included the legend that he cured Argive

---

[47] Herod. 2.36.
[48] Herod. 2.177.
[49] Herod. 2.43.
[50] To be sure, he is indignant that some credulous Greeks bought the story of Egyptians practicing human sacrifice; Herod. 2.45. But he is not here making a cultural differentiation between the peoples.
[51] Herod. 2.48–49. Lloyd (1994b), II, 224, maintains that this Dionysus must be different from the Dionysus, son of Semele, mentioned in 2.145–146. But Herodotus does not here make the sort of distinction that he makes between Herakles the god and Herakles the hero.

maidens (for a hefty price) of the madness inflicted on them by Dionysus, whose rites they had spurned.[52] Herodotus does not concern himself here with that part of the myth. The Dionysiac connection leads to a more sweeping conclusion: Melampus' knowledge of the god's name, the mode of sacrifice to him, and the procession at his festival derived from Egypt. The prophet was responsible for transmitting these matters to the Greeks, thus accounting for the close similarities in Dionysiac practices between the two peoples. Herodotus rejects out of hand the idea that transmission might have been the other way round, let alone that it was sheer coincidence. The historian reiterates his insistence that the Egyptians got neither this nor anything else from the Greeks. What merits notice, however, is the further elaboration. Melampus did not get his insight into Dionysus directly from the Egyptians. He learned it primarily from Cadmus the Tyrian and those who came with him from Phoenicia to settle the land of Boeotia.[53] Reference here, of course, is to the fabled founding of Thebes by the Phoenician Cadmus. In Herodotus' exposition, Cadmus must have imbibed Egyptian lore about Dionysus and imparted it to Melampus, who then instructed his fellow Greeks. Since some Hellenic legends have Cadmus as grandfather of Dionysus, Herodotus may have made the connection but muddled the chronology.[54] He has, in any case, complicated the cultural transfer. The Greek diviner drew on Phoenician learning to convey Egyptian rites to Hellas.

The tangled and complex network of stories about Perseus further illustrates the point. That topic receives fuller investigation elsewhere. Suffice it here to point to Herodotus' discussion as part of the Egyptian excursus. It comes interestingly in a segment introduced by his statement that Egyptians shrink from the customs of the Greeks, indeed of nearly all nations. He then swiftly injects an exception. The people of Chemmis possess a temple dedicated to Perseus, part of a sacred precinct that includes a shrine with a cult image of the Hellenic hero. The inhabitants informed Herodotus that they frequently glimpsed Perseus himself in the area and even inside the temple, as attested by the gigantic sandal that he wore. More strikingly still, the Chemmites conduct games and competitions dedicated to Perseus, with prizes—in Greek style.[55] They answered Herodotus' inquiry about this anomaly by tracing Perseus' own genealogy to Egypt

---

[52] Homer *Od.* 11.281–297, 15.225–242; Pherecydes *FGH* 3 F114; Herod. 9.34; Apollodorus 1.9.11–12, 2.1.2. Cf. the remarks of Lloyd (1994b), II, 224–225; Flower and Marincola (2002), 169–170.

[53] Herod. 2.49: πυθέσθαι δέ μοι δοκέει μάλιστα Μελάμπους τὰ περὶ τὸν Διόνυσον παρὰ Κάδμου τε τοῦ Τυρίου καὶ τῶν σὺν αὐτῷ ἐκ Φοινίκης ἀπικομένων ἐς τὴν νῦν Βοιωτίην καλεομένην χώρην.

[54] This does not rule out the possibility that Egyptians may have helped to shape the tradition; cf. Froidefond (1971), 158.

[55] Herod. 2.91: ποιεῦσι δὲ τάδε Ἑλληνικὰ τῷ Περσέϊ.

through the line of Danaus, maintaining even that Perseus had visited Chemmis and there recognized all his kinfolk, and that the games had been instituted on his orders.[56] The Hellenic legend of Perseus was clearly appropriated here by Egyptians, a fact of no small significance. It belies the conventional insularity of the people. The Chemmites did not here convert Perseus into an Egyptian hero but latched onto the Greek story and attached themselves to it. The unabashed celebration of festivities in Hellenic mode underscores the fact.

The practice of circumcision also gave occasion for cross-cultural reflections. Herodotus drew the conclusion that Egyptians and Colchians must come from the same stock since both peoples circumcised their sons, evidently from time immemorial. Nations such as the Phoenicians and the "Syrians who dwell in Palestine" took the custom from the Egyptians, as they themselves acknowledge. Other Syrians assert that they adopted that institution from the Colchians.[57] Further, the historian declines to decide whether Ethiopians followed the lead of Egyptians on circumcision or vice versa, for the practice dates to a very early time for both.[58] Here again it is not the isolation of Egypt but the intercultural connections that come to the fore. The intermingling of cultures could produce the diffusion of traits. Or it could produce their curtailment. Herodotus adds that contacts between Phoenicians and Greeks induced the former to abandon circumcision, which they had picked up from the Egyptians.[59]

An arresting tale provides the best instance of cultural interplay: Herodotus' recounting of the notorious rape of Helen and its repercussions for the fall of Troy. It warrants extended treatment. No legend is more deeply rooted in Hellenic tradition. But Herodotus got a version, so he affirms, from the Egyptian priests at Memphis. In their tale Helen never made it to Troy. After Paris snatched her from the house of Menelaus in Sparta, together with a substantial amount of treasure, he ran into some rough weather and heavy winds at sea, which drove him to the Egyptian coast at the mouth of the Nile. His Trojan attendants deserted him there, seeking refuge in a temple that offered asylum to those who put themselves in the hands of the god. The refugees then proceeded to accuse Paris of wrongful abduction and brought their evidence to the Egyptian official stationed at the mouth of the Nile. He in turn transmitted the charges to the pharaoh Proteus at Memphis, who

---

[56] Herod. 2.91.

[57] Herod. 2.104. Whether Herodotus' "Palestinian Syrians" are Jews has been much debated but need not be decided here. See, e.g., Stern (1974), 3–4. Josephus certainly thought so; *CAp* 1.168–171. But he had his own agenda; cf. Barclay (2007), 99–100. On the identity of the other Syrians, see Lloyd (1988), 23–24.

[58] Herod. 2.104: οὐκ ἔχω εἰπεῖν ὁκότεροι παρὰ τῶν ἑτέρων ἐξέμαθον.

[59] Herod. 2.104: Φοινίκων ὁκόσοι τῇ Ἑλλάδι ἐπιμίσγονται, οὐκέτι Αἰγυπτίους μιμέονται κατὰ τὰ αἰδοῖα.

indignantly ordered that the Trojan prince be arrested and delivered to his presence. An interrogation followed. Paris offered wavering and mendacious answers, easily refuted by his ex-servants. Proteus then gave judgment in exemplary fashion. He would execute no stranger driven to his shores, however justified it might be in this case. Instead, he banished Paris from the land, and he took Helen and the stolen possessions under his authority until such time as they could be returned to their rightful owner.[60]

Herodotus, intrigued by the discrepancies between this narrative and the traditional tale as recounted by the Greeks, probed the priests further. Are the versions reconcilable? The priests had a response ready, claiming that they had inquired themselves and got their information from none other than Menelaus. In their account, the Greek forces that sailed to Troy on Menelaus' behalf first sent representatives, including Menelaus himself, to demand restoration and the stolen treasure, in addition to satisfaction for the injustice, in order to avoid hostilities. The Trojans' reply, that neither Helen nor the treasure had reached them but were lodged in Egypt under the protection of Proteus, produced only incredulity among the Greeks. Talks broke off, the war began, and only after Troy fell and the conquerors entered the fortress did they discover that Helen was indeed nowhere to be found. The story now became credible, and Menelaus went straight to Egypt, where the generous Proteus restored both Helen and the treasure to the Spartan prince. But there was no happy ending. Menelaus, whose departure was delayed by a prolonged period of bad weather, ungraciously and unaccountably sacrificed two Egyptian youths. A fierce reaction forced Menelaus to flee with his ships and drove him to Libya.[61]

With this beguiling variant on the Trojan legend Herodotus seized the opportunity to exhibit his critical and argumentative faculties. He found the Egyptian rendition believable and defensible. And he paraded Homer himself in support. Herodotus cited certain lines of the bard to show that Homer knew the tradition that had Helen and Menelaus in Egypt but chose not to endorse it since it conflicted with the mainstream narrative.[62] He further defended the priestly version as more historically and logically plausible: surely Priam and the Trojans would have surrendered Helen if they had her, rather than to endure or prolong a war that cost them so many lives, including those of Priam's own sons. Hence, Herodotus concludes, Helen really was in Egypt as the priests said, and the Greeks were done in by their own incredulity—an outcome foreordained by the gods determined to punish Troy.[63]

---

[60] Herod. 2.112–115.
[61] Herod. 2.118–119.
[62] Herod. 2.116. The passages he cites are Homer *Il.* 6.289–292; *Od.* 4.227–230, 4.351–352.
[63] Herod. 2.120.

It is easy to find fault with the historian in the particulars of this presentation. The Hellenic character of his exposition stands out, giving reason for some to question the attribution to Egyptian sources. No king Proteus exists in Egyptian king lists, and the name may derive from the minor Greek sea deity famed for changing his shape.[64] The magnanimity of the pharaoh and the deep respect both for hospitality to strangers and for asylum in temples give a decidedly Greek flavor to the narrative. Menelaus' resort to human sacrifice appears totally irrational in the circumstances and may be an echo of his brother Agamemnon's fabled sacrifice of Iphigenia.[65] Further, Herodotus' recourse to Homer for support gains him little. The bard hardly provides compelling corroboration of the Egyptian version. The first passage cited by Herodotus attests only to a stopover in Sidon by Paris when he took Helen to Troy (Herodotus' statement that Phoenicia bordered on Egypt is rather lame). The second and third indicate no more than that Homer placed Helen and Menelaus in Egypt. The poet has no hesitation in alluding to their sojourn in that land.[66] It does not, however, follow that he knew the story attributed by Herodotus to the Egyptian priests. Homer's lines overlap not at all with what the priests transmitted. As for the historian's rationalistic defense of the Egyptian explanation, it falls well short of demonstration. It may seem madness for Priam to sacrifice his sons and people rather than surrender Helen. But it would be equally preposterous for the Greeks to embark on a ten years' siege without at least checking in Egypt on Helen's whereabouts.

Should one then conclude that Herodotus never heard such a fantasy from the Egyptians? Was it a Hellenic concoction foisted by the historian on fictitious Egyptian sources? Not the most obvious conclusion. Cui bono?

Herodotus himself did not invent an Egyptian connection to the tale of Troy. Various versions made the rounds among Greek writers. Homer, as we have seen, put Menelaus and Helen in that land at some point of the legend, possibly after their return from Troy and on their way back to Sparta (where Odysseus encountered them).[67] Hesiod retailed a version that had an image (*eidolon*) of Helen reach Troy but not the person herself.[68] Stesichorus, writing in the early sixth century BCE, also flatly denied that Helen ever went to Troy, and noted that Greeks and Trojans fought over an *eidolon*.[69] But it is unclear where she did go.[70] Menelaus' trip to

[64] How and Wells (1912), 222–223; Lloyd (2007), 322.
[65] So Fehling (1971), 48.
[66] Homer *Od.* 4.125–132.
[67] Homer *Od.* 4.81–85, 4.125–132, 4.227–230, 4.351–352. On the Homeric references to Menelaus and Egypt, see Müller (1997), 203–205.
[68] Hesiod fr. 358 (Merkelbach-West).
[69] Stesichorus fr. 15 (Page *P.Mel.Gr.*); Plato *Republic* 586c.
[70] Fehling (1971), 46–47.

Egypt appears in a fragment of Hecataeus, which does not, however, provide specifics, and nothing suggests that it coincides with Herodotus' version.[71] Hellanicus has Menelaus and Helen depart from Troy together and go to Egypt, where king Thonos attempted to seize Helen and was killed by Menelaus.[72] This bears little resemblance to the other bits and pieces that survive. Diverse stories evidently circulated among Greek intellectuals. The fleshing out of an alternative legend appears in the opening of Euripides' drama *Helen*, roughly contemporary with Herodotus. Helen herself there summarizes her plaintive adventures. Hera frustrated Paris' aims by substituting for the real Helen an *eidolon*, a phantom made to seem alive, which he carted off unknowingly to Troy, thus triggering the horrific conflict. Helen herself in the meantime was swept up by Hermes, on Zeus' orders, and deposited in Egypt, where she came under the protection of Proteus.[73] Menelaus, after the war and years of wandering, found Helen in Egypt, rescued her from an impending marriage with the son of Proteus, and both escaped from Egypt. This plot plainly diverges at great distance from that of Herodotus.

Hellenic fingerprints are all over the story that Herodotus recounts. It does not follow, however, that Egyptians had no hand in it or that Herodotus simply fabricated the fiction that he heard such a tale from priests at Memphis.[74] What would be the point? Did he intend to exhibit superior knowledge to other Hellenic writers by appealing to Egyptian authority for an alternative tradition on the Trojan legend? Few rival authors would have been much impressed by that. Did he come armed with a Greek version that had Helen in Egypt and then ask leading questions of the priests to get the answers he wanted, so as to reweave them into his construct?[75] The conjecture is superfluous and paradoxical. It would have been more straightforward simply to present the version as a Hellenic one, endorse it as his own view, and present confirmation from Egyptian sources. Instead, Herodotus does the reverse. He presents the story itself as an Egyptian

---

[71] Hecataeus *FGH* 1 F307–309.
[72] Hellanicus *FGH* 4 F153.
[73] Eur. *Helen* 1–67.
[74] That is the conclusion of Fehling (1971), 48–50. Cf. Froidefond (1971), 179–182. See the criticisms of Pritchett (1993), 63–71. For Heidel (1935), 75–76, Herodotus was taken in by a parodic treatment composed by Hecataeus and unthinkingly accepted the notion of Egyptian sources. Calame (1998), 81–88, sees the account as part of a larger Herodotean interpretive scheme.
[75] Such is the theory of Lloyd (1988), 46–47; (1994a), II, 109. So also Moyer (2002), 84. Lloyd proposes that Herodotus got the story from Hecataeus, an unnecessary and unsupported hypothesis. He does, however, allow that the Egyptians may have absorbed some Greek material on the subject before Herodotus began his inquiries. Cf. also Froidefond (1971), 181. Neville (1977), 3–12, concerns himself only with Herodotus' attitude toward Homer and ignores the question of Egyptian influence on the tradition.

one, then finds confirmation in Greek tradition (Homer) and constructs arguments to buttress the plausibility of the priests. It is not surprising that Plutarch finds this segment too an example of the historian's "philobarbarism."[76] But that reduces the matter to a slogan and a slander. It hardly accounts for the historian's motivation.

Far easier to take Herodotus at his word. The narrative, doubtless a Greek alternative account already adumbrated by Homer, reshaped and elaborated by Hesiod, Stesichorus, and others, had made its way to Egypt. Priests and intellectuals found it an attractive tale and put their own spin on it. Proteus became the hero of the fable, Menelaus a more dubious character, and both Greeks and Trojans were castigated for fighting a needless war brought on by distrust and incredulity. Herodotus may well have added further Hellenic veneer in reproducing the story. But his repeated insistence on its derivation from priestly sources in Memphis has to be taken seriously. The priests assured him that they had conducted inquiries and that, in any case, they had a secure knowledge of what went on in their own land.[77] Even if Herodotus were taken in (an unlikely assumption), that alone indicates a keen Egyptian interest in propagating the legend.

A telling conclusion follows from this. Egyptians themselves gained familiarity with the Hellenic folklore of the Trojan War, embraced a variant in which they played a role, adapted it to their own purposes, and reshaped it for Greek inquirers. Instead of resisting inclusion, they embellished their own part in Hellas' preeminent myth. Overlap rather than "Otherness" predominates.

Twists and turns mark Herodotus' treatment of Egypt, a layered, not a one-dimensional, exposition. He asserts the Egyptians' priority and antiquity but also has them question it. He underscores their distinctiveness yet draws out their intersections. He points to religious uniqueness and then amalgamates divinities. He sets Egyptians as a contrasting mirror for the Greeks, only to have them adapt Hellenic mythology and insert themselves into it. Herodotus is less concerned with distancing than with connecting.

Diodorus

Four centuries later, the vision of Egypt as shaped by Diodorus of Sicily shows striking similarities to that of Herodotus. Much had transpired in

---

[76] Plut. *De Malignitate Herodoti* 857B—with reference to the story of Menelaus' executing two young Egyptians.

[77] Herod. 2.113: ἔλεγον δέ μοι οἱ ἱρέες; 2.116: ἔλεγον οἱ ἱρέες; 2.118: ἔφασαν πρὸς ταῦτα τάδε ἱστορίῃσι φάμενοι εἰδέναι παρ' αὐτοῦ Μενέλεω; 2.119: τούτων δὲ τὰ μὲν ἱστορίῃσι ἔφασαν ἐπίστασθαι τὰ δὲ παρ' ἑωυτοῖσι γενόμενα ἀτρεκέως ἐπιστάμενοι λέγειν; 2.120: ταῦτα μὲν Αἰγυπτίων οἱ ἱρέες ἔλεγον.

the interim. The Egypt that Diodorus visited and experienced had passed under Hellenic rule in the aftermath of Alexander, had remodeled its character as a Hellenistic kingdom under the Ptolemies, then suffered extended decline as an international power, and now labored under the shadow of Rome, dependent on its favor or indifference, a second-rate presence in the Mediterranean. Diodorus, however, begins his massive "universal history" with Egypt, devoting the whole of his extensive first book to that land (the fullest extant treatment apart from that of Herodotus). And the august Egypt of old—its myths, traditions, religion, pyramids, tombs, other monuments, and the pharaonic legacy—generally prevails. The subsequent, and less estimable, history of Egypt is postponed. The historian announces at the outset that he will deal first with the "antiquities of the barbarians," so as not to interrupt the flow of his historical narrative by inserting this form of ethnographic material later.[78] But it is surely not this pragmatic disclaimer alone that set Egypt at the head of Diodorus' monumental history. The Sicilian historian himself acknowledges that that ancient land has a proper place at the beginning of his work, for mythology designates it as the site where gods had their origins, where the movements of the stars were first observed, and where numerous deeds of great men worthy of record were chronicled.[79]

As in Herodotus, the nation and its practices come in for admiration and praise by Diodorus. That will cause no surprise, since Diodorus regularly refers to Egyptian sources, usually priestly authorities, for his information.[80] But his purpose is not simply to express awe and wonder at Egypt's majestic past. Like Herodotus too, the Sicilian has a more complex cultural agenda. He knew the work of the great Halicarnassan, used it, and shared many of its sentiments.[81] But Diodorus had access to a range of other writers as well, including Manetho and Hecataeus of Abdera. The quest for Diodorus' sources has been the subject of endless and tiresome Quellenforschung, with little unanimity or progress.[82] How much of his book I reproduces Hecataeus, relies on other sources, or represents Diodorus' own assessment cannot be determined and carries small consequence.[83] It provides, in any case, a window on Greek perceptions of Egypt in the mid–first century BCE. And

[78] Diod. 1.4.6: τὰς βαρβαρικάς . . . ἀρχαιολογίας; 1.9.5.

[79] Diod. 1.9.6.

[80] See Diod. 1, passim, and especially 1.69.7. That he visited Egypt personally is mentioned in 1.44.1.

[81] See Chamoux (1995), 37–50.

[82] The debate goes back at least to E. Schwartz (1885), 223–262. See discussion, with citation of the principal scholarship, in A. Burton (1972), 1–34.

[83] The harsh and dismissive comment on Diodorus' use of evidence by Africa (1963), 254, is unjustified. On a more general basis, Sacks (1990), passim, argued cogently and convincingly that Diodorus was no mere slave to his sources.

they bear a remarkable similarity to those of Herodotus.[84] Numerous treatments of Egypt had appeared in the intervening years, extant now only in fragments, if at all. But Diodorus supplies a notable index of continuity.

The antiquity of Egypt and its primacy loom large. As already observed, Diodorus justifies opening his work with that land on the grounds that the gods had their origin there—according to legend.[85] He adopts the line presented by Egyptians themselves that their ancestors invented the art of writing, that they were the first to observe the stars, that they discovered the foundations of geometry and most of the arts, and that they introduced the best laws.[86] The Thebans, in particular, claimed precedence over all other peoples, the first to conceive of philosophy and the precise science of astronomy, the first to establish the calendar, and the first to predict with accuracy both solar and lunar eclipses.[87]

Diodorus maintains that Greeks themselves admired a host of Egyptian institutions.[88] He singles out certain laws that were embraced and adopted by Greeks.[89] The Egyptian legal code, according to the historian, governed the actions of kings as well as all others. They had to render decisions in accord with the law of the land, not by whim or emotion. Egyptian judges reached verdicts with equity, fairness, and adherence to the large corpus of written law. And since kings regularly acted with justice toward their subjects, they earned popular favor in return, cultivating a reputation that would endure well beyond their lifetimes. Their revenues allowed them even to keep taxes at a moderate and modest level for the populace.[90] Egyptian warriors gained inspiration from the deeds of their fathers, whose fearlessness and experience rendered them nearly invincible to their foes.[91]

Even the most dubious of Egyptian practices gains no reproof from Diodorus. He acknowledges that animal worship will strike most as extraordinary but, like Herodotus, proceeds to offer numerous details without passing judgment.[92] One might wish to infer a negative assessment from

---

[84] That he felt it necessary to differentiate himself from Herodotus, who allegedly preferred pretty stories to the truth, is a telltale sign that he made more use of his great predecessor than he was willing to concede; Diod. 1.69.7; cf. A. Burton (1972), 25–29.

[85] Diod. 1.9.6.

[86] Diod. 1.69.5–6.

[87] Diod. 1.50.1–2.

[88] Diod. 1.69.2.

[89] Diod. 1.77.5, 1.77.9, 1.79.3–4. Egyptians also maintained that their laws inspired the sound legislation of Darius of Persia; Diod. 1.95.4–5.

[90] Diod. 1.71.1–5, 1.72.1–6, 1.73.5–6. 1.75.1–3.

[91] Diod. 1.73.9.

[92] Diod. 1.83–89. Smelik and Hemelrijk (1984), 1898–1903, detect a negative undertone in Diodorus' representation of animal worship, but largely on the assumption that he shared Greek feelings generally on that custom. The text itself does not betray that bias, which is what counts. On Egyptian animal worship, see the useful notes of A. Burton (1972), 248–261.

Diodorus' eyewitness account of the Egyptian mob that set upon a Roman envoy who had accidentally killed a cat, or his report that Egyptians resorted to cannibalism during a dire famine rather than slaughter sacred animals for food.[93] He recognizes that readers may be appalled or incredulous, and he describes Egyptian reverence for animals as superstitious, astounding, and beyond belief.[94] But he refrains from condemnation, no innocent omission. In fact, Diodorus goes to some lengths in recounting explanations for the practice that Egyptians themselves provided to him. Three alternative reasons emerged: that the gods themselves initially took on animal shapes, or that images of animals had been carried by units of the army to give order and structure to the military, or that Egyptians appreciated the beneficial services of animals (like the cow who pulls the plow, the dog who helps the hunt, the cat who fends off asps, the ibis who protects against a host of nasty creatures, and even the crocodile who frightens brigands who might otherwise cross the Nile).[95] Diodorus rejects the first explanation as mere fantasy and the product of antique simplicity.[96] Whatever opinion he might have had about the other two, however, he keeps to himself. It was not his purpose to condemn the custom. Moreover, he observes that the priests, as distinct from most Egyptians, offer yet another reason for animal worship—which he is not at liberty to divulge.[97] Diodorus deliberately leaves the matter unresolved, preferring circumspection to censure.

The historian even sets in a positive light a practice that Greeks generally found offensive and distasteful: *proskynesis*. Egyptians (like Persians) bow down before their kings and honor them as if they were truly gods. Diodorus explicitly defends the institution: it derives from an authentic show of gratitude. Egyptians in general, he notes, are regarded as eclipsing all others in display of gratitude for benefactions, and since monarchs are the greatest of benefactors they merit the most distinctive mode of appreciation.[98]

Diodorus did not design the first book of his history as an encomium of Egypt. Praise or blame, favor or disfavor, are equally irrelevant.[99] Nor is the

---

[93] Diod. 1.83.8–84.1.

[94] Diod. 1.83.1: παράδοξον; 1.83.8: δεισιδαιμονία; 1.86.1: θαυμάσια καὶ μείζω πίστεως.

[95] Diod. 1.86–87, 1.89.1–3. There is no good reason to believe that Diodorus got the first explanation from Egyptian sources, the other two from Greek, as do Smelik and Hemelrijk (1984), 1902–1903.

[96] Diod. 1.86.2: τὴν μὲν πρώτην μυθώδη παντελῶς καὶ τῆς ἀρχαικῆς ἁπλότητος οἰκείαν.

[97] Diod. 1.86.2. He later adds yet a fourth explanation offered by "some," that in primitive times, with men warring among themselves, the weaker ones gathered in groups and used images of animals as emblems for their collectives; Diod. 1.90.1–2.

[98] Diod. 1.90.2–3.

[99] The assertion of Smelik and Hemelrijk (1984), 1896, that "this is a highly biased, nationalistic presentation of Egypt . . . at the expense of the rest of the world, especially of Greece," is a serious misreading.

treatment of Egypt a detached and neutral piece of cultural relativism. The historian, writing as a Greek Sicilian in a time of Roman command of the Mediterranean, reckons the land of the Nile very much as a means of reflecting on, comparing, contrasting, and musing about other peoples, notably Greeks. Not that he was setting up Egyptians as either a model or a foil. The juxtapositions are rarely simple or one-dimensional.

Diodorus' allusions to oratory in Egypt have a special resonance. Legal disputes, he maintains, were conducted in court through exchange of written documents. The proceedings did not allow for oral arguments. Diodorus explains that Egyptians followed this practice because they distrusted orators who cast justice in the shade. The techniques of advocates, the "sorcery" of their performance, and the tears of those who were accused induced many to neglect the strictness of the laws and the exactitude of truth.[100] Egyptian judges rule only on pleas presented in writing. Otherwise they might be deflected from sound judgment by the deception, seduction, or appeal to pity exercised through the verbal power of advocates. By limiting themselves to legal briefs in written form, they obviate the possibility that fluid speakers would prevail over the halting, trained over the inexperienced, liars and the brazen over truth lovers and the restrained.[101] The rather strong, even colorful language here, unusual for Diodorus, is notable. One cannot fail to see this as a reflection on the oratorical practices common (or at least stereotyped) in Hellenic (and indeed Roman?) courtrooms. The point is made with explicitness somewhat later in Diodorus' text. In discussing Egyptian burial customs, he describes the judgment scene in which accusers are permitted to level charges against the dead and relatives to refute them and laud the deceased. Whatever the realities of such a scene, the historian slips in a pregnant aside: unlike the Greeks, Egyptian speakers say nothing about the lineage of the departed, for they regard all as equally well born and restrict themselves to the upbringing, piety, righteousness, and self-restraint of the deceased.[102] The virtues that Diodorus lists are all standard Hellenic ones, but the contrast with conventional Greek funeral oratory is pointed.

Diodorus proceeds to elaborate on the point. He notes that Greeks transmit their trust in such matters by fabricated myths and stories about honor for the pious and punishment for the wicked, stories subject to scorn even by lightweight characters. Egyptians take these concerns more seriously, elevating the worthy and penalizing the wicked in truth rather than in myth.[103] The slap at Greek legendary traditions seems almost gratuitous

---

[100] Diod. 1.75.6–76.1: τὴν τῆς ὑποκρίσεως γοητείαν.
[101] Diod. 1.76.2–3.
[102] Diod. 1.92.5.
[103] Diod. 1.93.3–4. Cf. also 1.25.4.

here.[104] Yet Diodorus does not construct Egypt as some artificial utopia to set against the failings of Hellas. Lest there be doubt on that score, he criticizes Egyptian educational practices, which provide little in the way of basic instruction in letters (*grammata*) and nothing at all in wrestling or music.[105] The contrast with Hellenic institutions is implicit but unmistakable—and the Greeks come off the better.

Comparison and contrast, however, play but marginal roles in the text. Diodorus, like Herodotus, has a keener interest in presenting overlap and interconnection. Greek borrowings from Egypt have as prominent a part in his presentation as in Herodotus'. Indeed a steady stream of Greek visitors from the realms of both legend and history made their way to Egypt to imbibe law, science, art, and learning generally from that ancient land and used it to instruct their countrymen. Orpheus went there to immerse himself in the lore of Dionysiac mysteries, Daedalus to hone his architectural talents, Homer to obtain mythical material, Pythagoras to become versed in mathematics and religion, Democritus to gain instruction in astrology, Solon, Lycurgus, and Plato to become acquainted with Egyptian laws, and a number of others on comparable missions.[106] But the historian places less stress on Egypt as source of knowledge and wisdom than on the cultural compatibility between the nations.

This emerges most conspicuously, of course, in the virtual interchangeability of Greek and Egyptian gods. Diodorus' text is riddled with these reciprocal correspondences.[107] His identification of divinities recurs with regularity: Osiris and Dionysus, Isis and Demeter, Zeus and Ammon.[108] Elsewhere he simply employs the Greek designations for Egyptian deities, without need for further explanation.[109] So, in an interesting instance, Diodorus has Osiris, lover of music, dance and, laughter, collect a multitude of musicians, among them nine maidens "whom the Greeks call Muses," as well as their leader Apollo, who thereby received the appellation "Musegetes."[110] The passage evinces a noteworthy absence of self-consciousness. Egyptian institutions are perfectly comprehensible (or, at least presentable) in Greek terms.

---

[104] A comparable jab at Greek myths by contrast with Egyptian facts occurs at Diod. 1.25.4.

[105] Diod. 1.81.7. The statement here is rather at odds with Diodorus' earlier association of (Egyptian) Hermes with invention of the lyre and establishment of a palaestra; Diod. 1.16.1. That passage strikes a more resonant chord with the general tenor of Diodorus' treatment. Cf. A. Burton (1972), 77–79.

[106] Diod. 1.23.2, 1.61.3, 1.69.4, 1.77.5, 1.79.4, 1.92.3, 1.96.1–4, 1.97.4–1.98.6.

[107] See, in general, Diod. 1.13.2–5, 1.25.1–2. For A. Burton (1972), 106–107, this is simple syncretism.

[108] Diod. 1.11.3–4, 1.12.2, 1.13.4, 1.14.3–4, 1.15.3, 1.15.6–7, 1.96.4–5.

[109] E.g., Diod. 1.12.3–4, 1.12.7, 1.13.3, 1.15.9.

[110] Diod. 1.18.4.

There is much more here than syncretism, equivalency, or Hellenic veneer on Egyptian divinity. Diodorus discloses (as Herodotus did before him) the mutual incorporation and appropriation of legend and tradition that entwine the two cultures. The matter merits emphasis. Some quite intriguing instances pique the imagination.

Diodorus records an especially curious Egyptian narrative regarding Prometheus and Herakles. The story has Prometheus as overseer of a certain district in Egypt almost entirely destroyed by a Nile flood that caused him to despair and even to contemplate suicide. Herakles, however, arrived in the nick of time to halt the floodwaters, restore the river to its normal course, and presumably prevent Prometheus from doing away with himself.[111] Diodorus then adds that some Hellenic poets converted that tale into the familiar one (to Greeks) that has Herakles step in to kill the eagle who was chewing on Prometheus' liver.[112] The validity of that inference may not survive scrutiny. What matters is that Diodorus readily presumed that an Egyptian tradition could be transformed without difficulty into a Greek myth. The omnipresent Herakles served both to bridge and to confuse the cultures. Herodotus resolved the confusion by splitting him into two, an Egyptian god and a Hellenic hero. Diodorus adopts (or follows) a similar strategy. His informants claimed Herakles as an Egyptian by birth who at the dawn of antiquity had cleared away wild beasts (thus the club and lion's skin) and brought civilization to the land, a man whose heroic deeds earned him elevation to the status of the gods. That figure was to be distinguished from the Greek hero, son of Alcmene, who lived ten millennia later and whose closely similar accomplishments allowed him to take the same name as his Egyptian model.[113] Diodorus' account thereby reconciles Greek and Egyptian traditions by postulating separate individuals—while at the same time blending their stories.

A more complicated combination occurs with regard to the origin and transference of Dionysiac rites. Diodorus reckons Osiris as identical with Dionysus, the latter simply being the Greek designation applied to the Egyptian god. And he employs the two names interchangeably.[114] In his reconstruction, Greeks adopted the Dionysiac cult mysteries from Egypt, even applying the term "phallus" to the Dionysiac ritual as consequence of the tale of Isis paying homage to the severed genitals of Osiris.[115]

---

[111] Diod. 1.19.2. Diodorus did not invent the tale. It appears also in the work of a certain Agroitas, whose date is unknown but who may have preceded Diodorus; Schol. Apoll. Rhodes 1248. See A. Burton (1972), 11–12.

[112] Diod. 1.19.3.

[113] Diod. 1.24.1–7. Cf. A. Burton (1972), 103–105.

[114] Diod. 1.11.3, 1.13.4, 1.15.6, 1.96.4.

[115] Diod. 1.22.6–7. See the treatment of A. Burton (1972), 96–99.

Diodorus' account of the mysteries' entrance into Hellas serves as an appealing instance of intercultural inventiveness. Egyptian priests got wind of the Greek belief that Dionysus was born to Zeus and Semele in Boeotian Thebes. They sought to set the record straight. In their version, Hellas came to know of Dionysiac practices through Orpheus, the legendary source of Greek poetry and song, through his visit to Egypt. It was there that he encountered the initiatory rites and beliefs of Osiris/Dionysus, then introduced them into Boeotian Thebes and claimed it as the birthplace of the god out of gratitude to the descendants of Cadmus who had paid him high honor in that city. The Theban populace warmly welcomed the idea out of local pride and embraced Dionysiac worship as their own.[116] The priests' tale went further. They claimed Cadmus himself as a native of Egyptian, not Boeotian, Thebes. Cadmus covered up the rape and illegitimate pregnancy of his daughter Semele by alleging divine impregnation, thus producing the germ of the story that Greeks later took to be the birth of Dionysus as offspring of Semele and Zeus. Orpheus proved to be the intermediary. He learned of the tradition in Egypt and transferred it to Boeotian Thebes, where he was entertained generously by the descendants of Cadmus, much to the gratification of the Greeks, who embellished the narrative to their taste and entrenched it forever as a Hellenic one.[117]

The tangles of this tale, quite apart from its implausibilities, do not admit of easy resolution. Confusion between Boeotian and Egyptian Thebes only partially accounts for it. Cadmus, customarily associated with Phoenicia, here seems to be appropriated by both Greeks and Egyptians. And Orpheus' role is duplicated elsewhere in Diodorus' text by Melampus, who visited Egypt and brought back Dionysiac rituals—without any effort by the historian to reconcile the inconsistencies.[118] The complications defy sorting out. They do, however, demonstrate acquaintance with Greek legends in Egypt and efforts to convert them to Egyptian purposes—which implies Egyptian interest in buying into (and transforming) Hellenic legend. Diodorus himself delivers that transformed version (without criticism) as one retransformed by Orpheus for Greeks, who embraced it as their own tradition. The Greek historian appears to take the Egyptian construct at face value. He even employs the Dionysus story as exemplifying Egypt's claim that Greeks have appropriated the most renowned of Egyptian heroes and gods.[119]

---

[116] Diod. 1.23.1–2.
[117] Diod. 1.23.4–8.
[118] Diod. 1.97.4. This version follows that of Herodotus 2.49. See above, pp. 84–85.
[119] Diod. 1.23.8: καθόλου δέ φασι τοὺς Ἕλληνας ἐξιδιάζεσθαι τοὺς ἐπιφανεστάτους ἥρωάς τε καὶ θεούς. Egyptians also claimed their land as the birthplace of Perseus and criticized Greeks for transferring the tale of Io (Isis), the ancestress of Perseus, to Argos; Diod. 1.24.8.

But that is not the whole story. The reverse also holds. Egyptians insinuated themselves into Hellenic tradition and history. Diodorus records a narrative that has Herakles as kinsman of Osiris, who appointed Herakles as general in command of all the land under his authority because of Herakles' reputation for courage and physical strength.[120] This is plainly not Herakles the Egyptian divinity but the Hellenic hero appropriated to enhance Egyptian lore. In comparable fashion, an Egyptian tale, according to Diodorus, has Osiris march into battle accompanied by his two sons, Anubis and Macedon. The former, of course, is a good Egyptian god, and the latter evidently equivalent to his normal companion Wepwawet, the dog-god and wolf-god respectively.[121] But application of the name "Macedon" is hardly inadvertent. Diodorus leaves no question of its significance: Osiris left Macedon as ruler of the land that would acquire its name from him.[122] The claim doubtless takes its origin from Ptolemaic Egypt, whose rulers would profit from the neat reversal that had their homeland of Macedon owe its own origin to Egyptian divinities.[123]

Egyptians indeed usurped a comparable and widespread Hellenic practice to enhance their own cultural pretensions: the fictive foundation tale that had them as forebears of renowned cities and nations. Egyptian colonies, so they alleged, fanned out everywhere. Some settlers, led by "Belus," established themselves on the banks of the Euphrates, bringing from Egypt a knowledge of astrology and science that earned them the appellation of "Chaldeans" by the Babylonians. Other colonists left Egypt under Danaus to found nothing less than Argos, the most renowned city of Hellenic legend. Still others became founders of the nations of the Colchians and of the Jews. As if that were not enough, Egyptians laid claim to Athens itself, asserting that it was settled by colonists from Saïs in Egypt. Its initial rulers, celebrated in Greek legend, Penes, Menestheus, and Erechtheus, were all Egyptians by origin—not to mention the rites of Demeter and the Eleusinian mysteries.[124] But Diodorus, however dutifully he may have followed Egyptian traditions elsewhere, drew the line here. The extravagant claims engendered a forceful disclaimer. He brands such assertions as grasping for renown rather than for truth, the association with Athens in particular being driven by the reputation of that city.[125] And he castigates the practice in

---

[120] Diod. 1.17.3.
[121] Diod. 1.18.1. See A. Burton (1972), 83.
[122] Diod. 1.20.2.
[123] A similar appropriation characterizes the story that Osiris' agricultural expert Maron was left in Thrace to introduce some plants and founded the city of Maroneia, which subsequently bore his name; Diod. 1.20.2.
[124] Diod. 1.28.1–29.4.
[125] Diod. 1.29.5: πολλὰ δὲ καὶ ἄλλα τούτοις παραπλήσια λέγοντες φιλοτιμότερον ἤπερ ἀληθινώτερον, ὥς γ' ἐμοὶ φαίνεται, τῆς ἀποικίας ταύτης ἀμφισβητοῦσι διὰ τὴν δόξαν τῆς πόλεως.

broader terms: Egyptian stories of ubiquitous colonization lack any basis in the evidence, and no historian worth his salt gives them any credence.[126]

The historian faced a complex welter of material and did not expend excessive energy in working out a systematic approach. One might note, for example, that at one point he cites an Egyptian complaint about Greeks usurping title to colonies that were actually sent out by Egypt, and at another he denounces the Egyptians for asserting a fabricated claim on the colonies in the first place.[127] The most potent impression remains that of a give-and-take in which particulars of the cultural overlap could be disputed but interchange, mutual infringement, and appropriation prevail. Diodorus peers through Greek spectacles, and the tales possess an inescapably Hellenic cast. By his own day in the mid–first century BCE, Greeks had been in Egypt for a long time; their tales and their perspective had spread in the land. But the historian's repeated references to Egyptian informants have to be taken seriously. Egyptian priests and intellectuals had imbibed Greek legends and history and fitted them into their own conceptions, just as Greeks had adjusted Egyptian traditions to suit their experience and identity. The fact that each found it useful and rewarding to have a purchase on the other's culture holds the highest significance.

Assorted Assessments

How far the assessments of Herodotus and Diodorus are representative of classical attitudes toward Egypt does not allow of certain conclusion. Their rich and complex mosaics do show that Greek intellectuals took that land and its people seriously over a very long span of time. No other treatments of this fullness survive. But we know that numerous other writers did compose works on the subject—and certainly not works of disparagement or scorn. Hecataeus of Miletus preceded Herodotus in visiting Egypt and incorporating information on Egyptians into his works of history and geography.[128] Hellanicus of Lesbos, a contemporary of Herodotus, produced an *Aegyptiaka* of which a few fragments survive. Almost nothing is known of Aristagoras of Miletus in the mid–fourth century except that he did write something about Egyptian history. Eudoxus of Cnidus, in the first half of the fourth century, gained a greater reputation as a mathematician and astronomer but also produced a work on geography, which included a book devoted to Egyptian religion and culture gleaned from Egyptian priests

---

[126] Diod. 1.29.6: ὑπὲρ ὧν μήτε ἀποδείξεως φερομένης μηδεμιᾶς ἀκριβοῦς μήτε συγγραφέως ἀξιοπίστου μαρτυροῦντος.

[127] Cf. Diod. 1.23.8 with Diod. 1.29.5–6.

[128] There is no longer any need to postulate a full-scale history of Egypt by Hecataeus; see Drews (1973), 11–19; Burstein (1995), 8–11, with further bibliography.

with whom he studied and, among other things, challenged Herodotus' early dating for the land.[129] The topic continued to excite interest. Hecataeus of Abdera composed an influential *Aegyptiaka* at the end of the fourth century that presumably treated Egyptian history, society, traditions, and monuments.[130] Only fragments survive from all these authors, and no confident reconstruction of their views and judgments is possible. But the land of Egypt obviously held continuous fascination for Greek writers from the classical through the Hellenistic period.

Strabo, writing shortly after the Roman annexation of Egypt as a province in 30 BCE, dedicated an entire (and very lengthy) book of his *Geography* to Egypt. It is a sober survey of the terrain, climate, cities, villages, harbors, waterways, countryside, flora, fauna, monuments, temples, and cults, allowing himself little space for digressions on history (apart from a few references to events involving Rome) and almost no comments on Egyptian customs or character.[131] It was not Strabo's purpose to pass judgment on the Egyptian people.[132] He does make reference to prior Egyptian kings, sticklers for self-sufficiency, who resisted foreign imports and slandered all sailors, especially Greeks. But this is no knock on the Egyptians. As Strabo explains, the Greeks had the reputation of plunderers of other people's land since they did not have enough of their own.[133] Indeed he springs to the defense of the Egyptians against the charge of expelling foreigners. He cites Eratosthenes for the comment that all non-Greeks indulge in this and that Egypt is in bad odor only because of the fanciful tale of Busiris (who allegedly sacrificed foreigners), a story altogether falsified for there never was an Egyptian king named Busiris.[134] On the rare occasions when Strabo delivers any evaluation of Egyptians, it is decidedly positive. They live a civilized and praiseworthy life, making worthy use of the naturally favored land in which they dwell; their social and political system is intelligently organized; their priests are steeped in astronomy and philosophy; and geometry originated in that land.[135] Reports had it even that both Plato and Eudoxus spent thirteen years in Egypt studying with the

---

[129] On Hellanicus, see Drews (1973), 99–101; on Aristagoras and Eudoxus, see Burstein (1996), 596–597, with references. On Eudoxus' study with Egyptian priests, see Strabo 17.1.29; Plut. *De Is. et Osir*. 354e.

[130] See Murray (1970), 141–171; Fraser (1972), 496–505; Drews (1973), 122–131; Burstein (1996), 598–599—although the presumption that most of Diodorus' book I on Egypt was drawn from Hecataeus and that Hecataeus' views can therefore be inferred from Diodorus' text is hazardous.

[131] Strabo 17.1, passim.

[132] He restricts himself to criticism of the luxury and licentiousness of the Ptolemaic kings; 17.1.11—a very different matter.

[133] Strabo 17.1.6.

[134] Strabo 7.1.19.

[135] Strabo 17.1.3.

priests because of their expert knowledge of astronomy and calendrical science, which were then imparted to the Greeks.[136] Strabo, stressing his credentials as a reliable witness, explicitly eschewed the dabblings of Herodotus and other predecessors who had disseminated nonsensical fables.[137] His was to be a staid and serious study. The subject merited it. Strabo was sufficiently absorbed with Egypt to devote a substantial portion of his large work to that land and people.

One can lament forever the loss of extensive treatises on Egypt by classical authors and the survival of mere fragments. But the writing of such works itself constitutes the most important fact. Intellectuals saw the subject as one of significance and value, not a target for slander, sneers, and disdain. We may not be able to reconstruct with any security consistent or representative attitudes toward Egypt. But the tendency of modern scholars to collect isolated bits and pieces from writers ranging from Aristophanes to Juvenal and parade them as a sampling of Greek and Roman evaluations of Egypt is not only methodologically flawed but downright misleading.[138] Far better to focus on the sustained extant texts: the thoughtful treatments of Herodotus and Diodorus and the careful survey of Strabo.

Slices and slivers of statements from a range of authors do not far advance a real understanding of ancient assessments of Egypt. They have been taken far too seriously in the past. A survey will be useful to illustrate the point.

Egyptians surface only rarely in Athenian drama. Their most significant appearance comes in Aeschylus' *Suppliants*, for which a fuller discussion can be found below. Suffice it to say here that the play does not aim, as some have thought, to brand Egyptians with infamy. Aeschylus' version of the myth of the Danaids has the daughters of Danaus, with their father, seek refuge in Argos while fleeing from the unwanted marriage of their cousins, sons of Aegyptus. Their pursuers and their representative, the obnoxious herald, villains of the piece, receive decidedly negative depiction. But this is far from sweeping condemnation of Egyptians. The Danaids themselves make no secret of their foreignness and their distinctive ethnicity. But they receive eventual welcome in the city of Argos as distant heirs of a Hellenic lineage. The play does not pit Greek against Egyptian, let alone render the latter contemptible.[139]

---

[136] Strabo 17.1.29.
[137] Strabo 17.1.52.
[138] So, for example, Reinhold (1980), 97–103; K. Berthelot (1999), 191–202; Bohak (2003), 27–43; Isaac (2004), 352–365. It is remarkable that Isaac, an assiduous assembler of fragmentary information, omits any discussion of Herodotus or Diodorus on Egypt! A brief but useful survey of selective examples may be found in Nimis (2004), 34–41.
[139] See below, pp. 230–232, as against Froidefond (1971), 85–102; E. Hall (1989), passim; Vasunia (2001), 40–58; and Isaac (2004), 354.

Euripides' *Helen* is set entirely in Egypt. The playwright dramatizes the version of the Trojan legend that has Helen swept off by Hermes to Egypt while her phantom image is fought over by Achaeans and Trojans at Troy. The tale has Menelaus land in Egypt as a shipwrecked sailor years after Troy's fall to rescue the real Helen (after some problematic mutual recognition) from an undesirable marriage with the Egyptian ruler Theoclymenus and thus preserve her monogamy. No need here to dwell on this complex and fascinating play. It has recently been interpreted as stressing the "Otherness" of Egypt, its exotic and "barbarian" values, its deadly and rapacious people, its sexual aggressors and lustful males set against the chaste Greek female.[140] The drama itself gives little support for so drastic an interpretation. Helen hopes to escape the clutches of Theoclymenus in order to maintain her loyalty to Menelaus, not because he is an Egyptian defiler. She had been protected, in fact, by Theoclymenus' virtuous father Proteus, and her escape facilitated by Theoclymenus' blameless sister Theonoe. Indeed Theoclymenus himself at the conclusion of the play abjures his former quarrel, recognizing the justice of Helen's quest and the nobility of her soul. Egyptians as a people receive no strictures from the poet. Egypt itself carries the character of a fantasy land in which to play out the drama rather than a nation to contrast (favorably or unfavorably) with Hellas.[141]

If Egyptians served themselves up to disparagement by Greeks, one might expect to find them with frequency in Attic comedy. Not so—at least not in the extant texts. References to Egyptians appear only a few times in Aristophanes' plays, asides and throwaway lines, just two or three even faintly pejorative, and altogether insignificant.[142] Three relevant fragments from fourth-century comic dramatists are preserved by Athenaeus through sheer happenstance, for he devoted a portion of his miscellany, the *Deipnosophists*, to eels! Egyptian animal worship supplied ample material for humor and parody. And the eel, whether or not Egyptians held it sacred, was an ideal subject for mockery. Writers of Middle Comedy seem to have leaped to the occasion. Antiphanes jokingly praised Egyptians for their wisdom in elevating the eel to divine status since access to the creature fetched a handsome sum, an allusion both to the Egyptian repute for wisdom and to the absurdity of so unlikely an animal

[140] Vasunia (2001), 58–74.

[141] See the excellent analysis of the play by Segal (1971), 553–614, who rightly finds none of the features in it that Vasunia would see thirty years later. Vasunia's claim (2001), 60, that "barbaros" carries a pejorative connotation whenever it is used by the playwright is not borne out by the text; Eur. *Helen* 224, 295, 666, 863–864, 1100, 1507. The only instance is at 276, where Helen states that among barbarians all are slaves but one—a reference to eastern monarchy in general, not to Egyptian character.

[142] Aristophanes *Peace* 1253; *Birds* 504–507, 1134; *Frogs* 1406; *Thesmophoriazusae* 855–857, 921–922. Cf. Froidefond (1971), 224–228.

for worship.¹⁴³ Anaxandrides went on at greater length in a jocular contrast between the practices of Egyptian and Greek peoples: the one worships the cow, the other sacrifices it; the one reckons eels as divine, the other regards them as the greatest of delicacies; the one refrains from pork, the other relishes it; the one reveres dogs, the other beats them when they snatch food; the one has circumcised priests, the other prefers their priests whole; the one mourns if a cat is ill, the other kills it for its skin; the one is awed by a mouse, the other considers it worthless.¹⁴⁴ And Timocles, in a comic piece titled *The Egyptians*, offered a cynical comment on zoolatry: why expect an ibis or a dog to save you? Since those who commit impieties against the acknowledged gods can do it with impunity, would a cat's altar destroy anyone?¹⁴⁵ The quips are amusing but hardly vitriolic. Herodotus too had juxtaposed Greek and Egyptian customs as reverse reflections of one another without animosity. The cultural difference was most conspicuously marked by Egyptian homage to animals, a matter that lent itself irresistibly to burlesque. That was not tantamount to claims of superiority or diminishment of the "Other." Greeks who beat dogs or skinned cats were hardly more admirable than Egyptians who held them in esteem. These writers engaged in comic lampooning rather than character assassination.

A more serious slander, one might imagine, comes in the allegation of human sacrifice. The slur is embodied in the legendary figure of Busiris, ruler of Egypt in the remote mists of antiquity, whose extreme xenophobia expressed itself in the sacrifice of foreigners who reached Egyptian shores. An oracle had recommended the practice in order to rid Egypt of a nine-year famine. Since the seer who provided this answer was himself a foreigner, Busiris logically made him the first victim. And he continued to pursue this policy until Herakles arrived in the land. Busiris recklessly seized the Greek hero to bring him to the altar, only to have Herakles burst his bonds and turn the victimizer into a victim. The story, in one form or another, made the rounds in Greek and Roman authors from the fifth century BCE to late antiquity.¹⁴⁶ It also appears as a favorite motif for Greek vase painters beginning in the archaic era.¹⁴⁷

Does this represent the "Othering" of Egypt?¹⁴⁸ A hasty inference. Busiris did become emblematic of the cruel tyrant who sacrificed humans, and his

---

¹⁴³ Athenaeus 7.299e.
¹⁴⁴ Athenaeus 7.299f–300a.
¹⁴⁵ Athenaeus 7.300b.
¹⁴⁶ The earliest reference occurs in a fragment of Pherecydes in the early fifth century; *FGH* F3.17. See the assemblage of testimonia in Vasunia (2001), 185–186, and Livingstone (2001), 78–85. The fullest account of the myth can be found in Apollodorus 2.5.11.
¹⁴⁷ The evidence is collected in Laurens (1986), 147–152. See also Miller (2000), 413–442.
¹⁴⁸ That is the conclusion of recent studies by Miller (2000), 413–442, and Vasunia (2001), 183–215. Miller interestingly discerns a shift in the visual depictions of Busiris from the

association with Egypt is consistent throughout. It hardly follows that perpetuation of the tale constitutes a calumny against Egyptians as a whole. The core of the myth involves elimination of the wicked and bloodthirsty monarch by yet another heroic deed of Herakles.[149] Insofar as the Egyptian people are implicated, various Greek writers made it a point to denounce the fiction as a palpable absurdity. Herodotus calls it a silly story, amply refuted by the fact that Egyptians do not even sacrifice animals, with a few exceptions; the idea that they would victimize men was unthinkable.[150] Eratosthenes, cited with favor by Strabo, maintained that the Egyptians' unfortunate reputation for xenophobia stems from the malicious legend of Busiris, even though no such king or tyrant ever existed.[151] Diodorus allows that Egyptian kings had once (before the time of Psammetichus) been inhospitable to foreigners, even to the point of slaying them, and that this supplied the motive for the Busiris legend, a fabricated myth designed to account for Egyptian disregard for conventional practices.[152] Elsewhere he offers a different, etymological, explanation of the Busiris fable, a false connection to the name Osiris and a confused reference to the tradition that red men (non-Egyptians) had once been sacrificed at the tomb of Osiris.[153] The tale retained popularity as an entertaining myth but had little purchase among thoughtful Greeks.

Isocrates in the fourth century composed a whimsical epideictic speech ostensibly designed to rehabilitate the reputation of Busiris. He signals its character at the outset as something not to be taken as a serious effort.[154] It was a rhetorical showpiece. The topsy-turvy speech embellishes and exaggerates Busiris' virtues to transparent excess. Isocrates gives him an obviously fabricated lineage as son of Poseidon and the granddaughter of Zeus.[155] The rhetor then credits Busiris with inaugurating all the institutions, laws, and practices that generate admiration for Egypt. He wisely divided the populace into appropriate classes and categories, some as priests,

---

ethnically Egyptian in the archaic and early classical period to an approximation of the Persian monarch after the mid–fifth century, in either case a mode of representing the "Other." Since we possess only three examples of the latter, however, firm conclusions are hard to come by.

[149] Observe that Herodotus calls it a legend "about Herakles"; 2.45: ὁ μῦθος . . . περὶ τοῦ Ἡρακλέος.

[150] Herod. 2.45.

[151] Strabo 17.1.19.

[152] Diod. 1.67.11; see A. Burton (1972), 204–205.

[153] Diod. 1.88.4–5. Elsewhere Diodorus alludes to the tale of Busiris without bothering to refute it; 4.18.1, 4.27.2–3.

[154] Isocr. *Busiris* 9: οὐ σπουδαίαν. On the genre of the work, see Livingstone (2001), 8–13, 114–121; Vasunia (2001), 193–199.

[155] Isocr. *Busiris* 10.

some as artists, and some as warriors. As a result, Egyptians excel all other artists, possess the best form of government, provide ideal education to the young, and are the most pious of people.[156] Isocrates even offered a novel defense of Egyptian animal worship: Busiris instituted it not because he misapprehended the power of animals but as a test of obedience by subjects to the authorities, to whom they could thus demonstrate their unremitting piety.[157] So great was the Egyptian repute for piety that it induced no less a figure than Pythagoras to visit the land, study its religion, and make it the basis of his teaching, which spread philosophy to the Greeks. And the esteem for Pythagoras reached the point that even now his followers carry more authority by their silence than those with the greatest repute as speakers.[158] The tongue-in-cheek quality of all this is quite clear. If there were any doubt about it, Isocrates puts it to rest by his answer to the putative question of how he justifies ascribing such accomplishments to Busiris. In fact, he offers no answer at all, only rebukes his supposed interlocutor for inventing even more incredible feats for Busiris.[159] In a similar vein, he dismisses the notion of Busiris as responsible for human sacrifice: it is linked to the legend of his slaying by Herakles, and Herakles lived more than three hundred years after Busiris.[160] That particular dodge leaves the story of Busiris as sacrificer of strangers intact![161] Isocrates never expected anyone to take this rhetorical exercise seriously. The fact of its composition and the expectation of a knowledgeable readership, of course, show that the Busiris/Herakles fable continued to have wide currency. But few would have regarded it as a meaningful, let alone plausible, representation of Egypt as the "Other." Isocrates' broad parody of a purported defense of Busiris not only lampooned any ludicrous endeavor along those lines but also ridiculed, by implication, the tale of his dastardly doings and deserved demise.[162] The pronounced silliness of the encomium underscores the equally ludicrous negative portrait on the other side. It draws pointed attention to the double absurdity.

---

[156] Isocr. *Busiris* 15–25. Cf. Livingstone (2001), 133–135. Froidefond (1971), 246–266, sees the *Busiris* as based on a putative Pythagorean treatise that imagined Egyptian priests as embodying religious and philosophical principles that provided the model for a well-organized political and social system. This takes Isocrates' encomium far too seriously.

[157] Isocr. *Busiris* 26–27.

[158] Isocr. *Busiris* 28–29. On this version of Pythagoras' visit to Egypt, see the comments of Livingstone (2001), 155–162.

[159] Isocr. *Busiris* 30–33.

[160] Isocr. *Busiris* 36–37.

[161] This is missed in the commentary of Livingstone (2001), 167–170.

[162] Vasunia (2001), 193–207, quite rightly recognizes the parodic character of the speech but oddly interprets this as a means of reaffirming the hostile tradition on Egypt, a most paradoxical conclusion. A lighthearted mockery of the encomium hardly establishes the veracity of its opposite.

106 IMPRESSIONS OF THE "OTHER"

More revealing and more significant than comic fragments or mock encomiums is an engaging segment of Plato's *Timaeus*. The philosopher, through an interlocutor in the dialogue, links in enticing form the city of Saïs in the Delta and that of Athens itself. The Saïtes, he asserts, claim to be especially enamored of Athenians and reckon themselves in some fashion as akin to them.[163] Plato proceeds to recount the (probably fictitious) visit to Egypt by Solon, allegedly on the statesman's own authority. Solon, much admired by the Egyptians, engaged the priests in discussion regarding traditions on distant antiquity. After hearing the Greek sage expound on ancient Hellenic legends, an aged Egyptian priest put him firmly in his place: "O Solon, Solon, you Greeks are ever children; there is no old Greek."[164] The exchange echoes, in a more whimsical mode, that which Herodotus narrated between Hecataeus and the Egyptian priests, to point out the far greater antiquity of Egypt. Plato continues, however, not only in playful fashion but with a broader message. The elderly priest gently rebukes Solon, among other things, for referring to the Greek version of the flood story while forgetting that numerous deluges took place before it, and he offers scientific explanations for fables like that of Phaeton and the sun.[165] More tellingly, the priest pronounces a novel myth that reverses the chronological order and sets all in a strikingly different light. Athens itself, in this fantasy, preceded Egypt by a millennium, the noblest, bravest, and most artistic of nations, but its people were wiped out in a great flood that caused later descendants from the surviving seed to lose all memory of their glorious past. Athena, patron divinity of both Athens and Saïs, preserved that memory in the sacred records of Egypt. The laws, institutions, social ordering, arts, and sciences thereby took hold in Egypt, a replica of what had once prevailed in Athens.[166] A delicious story. Plato has the venerable priest make sport of the childlike ignorance of Solon but then turn the tables and instruct the Athenian poet-statesman on the even greater venerability of his own city. To see this as part of a debate on the priority of Athens or Saïs is to miss the point.[167] Athena or her Egyptian counterpart

---

[163] Plato *Timaeus* 21E: μάλα δὲ φιλαθήναιοι καί τινα τρόπον οἰκεῖοι τῶνδ' εἶναί φασιν.

[164] Plato *Timaeus* 22B: Ὦ Σόλων, Σόλων, Ἕλληνες, ἀεὶ παῖδές ἐστε, γέρων δὲ Ἕλλην οὐκ ἔστιν.

[165] Plato *Timaeus* 22C–23B. Cf. *Critias* 110A–B, 133A–B.

[166] Plato *Timaeus* 23D–25D. The philosopher here ties this fable to the Atlantis legend, having the ancient Athenians save the world from the rapacious imperialism of the islanders before they were swallowed up by an earthquake. Cf. the remarks of Hartog (2002), 218–220.

[167] As do K. Berthelot (1999), 192–193, Hartog (2002), 218–219, and Vasunia (2001), 231–232. For Froidefond (1971), 285–302, the idealization of Egypt in this fable is a form of *interpretatio Graeca* that draws on Pythagorean ideas, as does Isocrates' *Busiris*, a repeated but unnecessary hypothesis. Vasunia (2001), 216–247, offers a fine and sensitive analysis of the *Timaeus* passage in general, and one well worth reading. But his conclusion that this and comparable tales represent an "anxiety about the other" does not accord with the tone or spirit of the text.

Neith nurtured both nations. Athens' grandeur and nobility may have preceded that of Saïs, but the memory of its achievements remained alive only through the records of Egypt, which then transmitted its knowledge back to Greece. The reciprocity predominates, and the intertwining of the cultures holds central place in this jeu d'esprit.[168]

Snippets from later Greek authors, with offhand allusions to Egypt or Egyptians, shed little light on a comprehensive Hellenic evaluation of the culture of the Nile. So, for example, Aristotle attests to the credit still accorded to Egypt as the birthplace of the mathematical arts, to the flexibility of Egyptian institutions, and to the effectiveness of its social differentiation.[169] His pupil Theophrastus notes with praise that Egyptians are the world's most learned people—and strict vegetarians.[170] By contrast, the orator Hypereides in a courtroom speech disparages his opponent as an Egyptian.[171] And a few stray remarks in Polybius allude to the cruelty of Egyptians when they are angry, to the absence of practical common sense, to dissoluteness, sluggishness, and disinclination to civic life.[172] These do not add up to a systematic "attitude."

A similar assembling of fragmentary bits from miscellaneous Roman writers has kept scholars busy. It is easy enough to cite authors from Cicero to Juvenal, and beyond, to accumulate ostensibly hostile comments about Egypt, and to pile up numbers that seem impressive at first glance.[173] Do they show that Rome seethed with anti-Egyptian prejudice? On closer scrutiny, the significance of these snippets rapidly shrinks.

First of all, a number of the comments conventionally advanced to demonstrate animosity to Egyptians actually refer to Alexandrians. And Alexandria is not Egypt. That city had long been notorious for periodic unrest and upheaval.[174] It contained a combustible mixture of Greeks and Egyptians,

---

[168] Other scattered and isolated remarks by Plato on Egypt are not to the point. He attests to its reputation for keeping foreigners at arms length; *Laws* 953E. And he lumps Egyptians with Phoenicians in regard to tightfistedness (ἀνελευθερία); *Laws* 747B–C. But he also credits the Egyptian god Theuth (Thoth) with the invention of numbers and mathematics, and he has praise for Egyptian rules and practices in educating and training the young; *Phaedrus* 274C–D; *Laws* 656D–E, 799A–B, 819A–D. Cf. Froidefond (1971), 279–284, 309–315. These fragmentary allusions hardly amount to a considered or consistent assessment—nor were they intended to do so. Contra: Froidefond (1971), 337–342.

[169] Aristotle *Met.* 981B; *Pol.* 1286A, 1329B. On Aristotle and Egypt, see Froidefond (1971), 343–353.

[170] Theophrastus *apud* Porphyry *On Abstinence* 2.5.1.

[171] Hypereides *Against Athenogenes* 3.

[172] Polyb. 15.33.10, 27.13.1, 39.7.7; Strabo 17.1.12.

[173] So, e.g., Balsdon (1979), 68–69; Reinhold (1980), 97–103; Smelik and Hemelrijk (1984), 1945–1955; Sonnabend (1986), 49–62, 96–108; K. Berthelot (1999), 196–202; Isaac (2004), 356–369; Nimis (2004), 41–44.

[174] See, most notoriously, Polybius' account of the riots in Alexandria at the end of the third century; Polyb. 15.24–33—which had little to do with *Egyptian* character.

not to mention a mingling of other ethnicities. Cicero's denunciation, for example, of the deceit and trickery associated with Alexandria refers to Greeks rather than Egyptians.[175] The author of the *Bellum Alexandrinum* echoes that notion of the Alexandrians as a race of deceivers.[176] But the stereotype applies to inhabitants of that volatile city, not to Egyptian national character.

A notable portion of the excerpts pounced on by scholars belong to a particular period of Roman history—and a particular political agenda. As is well known, Augustus and those who sided with him or jumped on his bandwagon had pressing motives to brand his opponents Cleopatra and Antony with every form of infamy. It proved serviceable to drape the Macedonian queen and the Roman general in the garb of the alien east and to associate them with the most exotic practices of Egypt.[177] The question of how far this represents a "propaganda" campaign on the part of the regime, discussed ad nauseam, need not detain us here.[178] The consistency of the portrait, in a concentrated burst of time, is clear enough. Vergil's famous lines encapsulate it. For the epic poet Cleopatra is simply Antony's "Egyptian wife," and the battle of Actium pits the Roman divinities Neptune, Venus, and Minerva against "barking Anubis and monstrous gods of every shape."[179] A similar image appears in Propertius. The poet depicts pernicious Alexandria, whose soil breeds deceit, and the harlot queen, who would have barking Anubis oppose Jupiter and the Nile deliver threats to the Tiber.[180] The celebrated "Cleopatra ode" of Horace has the demented queen, together with her polluted gang of shameful followers, plot the destruction of the Capitol and the death of empire.[181] The resonance of the Augustan characterization can still be heard in Lucan's epic two generations later: Cleopatra used her rattle to terrify the Capitol, headed the unwarlike forces of Egypt against Roman armies, and aimed to lead a captive Caesar in Egyptian triumph.[182] The

---

[175] Cic. *Pro Rab. Post.* 34–36.

[176] *BAlex.* 24: *fallacem gentem.*

[177] Sonnabend (1986), 49–62; Maehler (2003), 203–215.

[178] The classic statement is that of Syme (1939), 459–475. Cf. Scott (1933), 7–49. For more nuanced treatments, see Griffin (1984), 189–218; Kennedy (1992), 26–58; White (1993), 95–205; Galinsky (1996), 225–287.

[179] Verg. *Aen.* 8.688: *Aegyptia coniunx*; 8.696–700: *omnigenumque deum monstra*. See also, Ovid *Met.* 185.826: *coniunx Aegyptia.*

[180] Prop. 3.11.33–42: *noxia Alexandria, dolis aptissima tellus . . . ausa Iovi nostro latrantem opponere Anubim, et Tiberim Nili cogere ferre minas.* Cf. also Prop. 2.33a.20: *cum Tiberi Nilo gratia nulla fuit.*

[181] Horace *Carm.* 1.37.6–10. Of course, these lines do not encapsulate Horace's own view of Cleopatra, as the remainder of the poem famously demonstrates. See also *Epode* 9.11–16, which depicts an enslaved Antony bearing arms for a woman and serving wrinkled eunuchs.

[182] Lucan 10.63. Elsewhere he excoriates the luxury–ridden barbarians of Memphis and Canopus, a pack of despicable aliens who murdered his hero Pompey; 8.542–549.

speech that Dio Cassius puts into the mouth of Augustus prior to the battle of Actium, though composed two centuries later, reiterates the calumnies propagated in the Augustan age. The fictitious oration castigates Alexandrians and Egyptians as slaves to a woman and adherents of outrageous rites like animal worship and embalmment, and blasts Antony for paying homage to the queen as if she were some Isis or Selene, to the point where he should be reckoned an Egyptian rather than a Roman.[183] The assessments are harsh caricatures. Romans seem to have reckoned Egyptian foreignness as especially outlandish, thus readily subject to such manipulation. But special circumstances called forth these representations, a portrait tied most closely to a particular time and purpose.

Outside that context most of the observations by Roman authors address the religion, strange customs, and eccentric practices indulged in by Egyptians. They lend themselves to disparagement, incredulity, and scoffing. So Cicero dismisses the omens of Egyptian magi, the delusion of their beliefs, the fickle opinions of the populace drawn from ignorance of the truth.[184] Tacitus refers to the superstition and impudence that makes Egypt a restive Roman province, given to discord and unpredictability, unacquainted with laws and magistrates.[185] Animal worship, of course, served as the most vulnerable target of scorn.[186] Cicero notes that a bull named Apis counts as a god, as do beasts and monsters of every kind.[187] The mentality of the Egyptians is so tainted by such depraved errors that they would submit to any form of torture rather than do violence to a sacred animal.[188] In questioning the grounds on which figures are or are not considered divinities by Romans, Cicero indulges in a reductio ad absurdum by observing that if Roman gods are really divine, we might as well worship Isis and Osiris, or indeed horses, asps, crocodiles, and a host of other animals.[189] But, although Cicero might recoil at the very idea of considering beasts as divine, he tempers his scorn with a dash of cultural relativism. He observes that though Romans may revere their gods, they have not hesitated to despoil shrines and cart off sacred images, whereas no Egyptian would lay hands on a crocodile, ibis, or cat.[190] And, most interestingly, he acknowledges, as did his contemporary Diodorus of Sicily, that the Egyptians, who are

[183] Dio 50.24.6–25.3, 50.27.1.
[184] Cic. *Nat. Deor.* 1.43.
[185] Tac. *Hist.* 1.11.1. The reputation of Egyptians as obstinate, unpredictable, and impudent appears elsewhere among Roman writers of the early Empire; Curtius Rufus 4.1.30; Seneca *Ad Helviam* 19.6; Pliny *Pan.* 31.2–5. Isaac (2004), 361–362, implausibly sees the Pliny passage as reflecting Roman fear of dependence on subject nations.
[186] Cf. Smelik and Hemelrijk (1984), 1955–1997; Sonnabend (1986), 120–124.
[187] Cic. *De Rep.* 3.14.
[188] Cic. *Tusc. Disp.* 5.78.
[189] Cic. *Nat. Deor.* 3.47.
[190] Cic. *Nat. Deor.* 1.81–82.

laughed at by Romans, had their own reasons for deifying animals, like the ibis who kills flying reptiles, namely their utility to society.[191]

There is, to be sure, no tempering in the infamous and vitriolic Fifteenth Satire of Juvenal. In the opening lines, the poet lets loose with abandon, blasting demented Egyptians for revering monstrous deities, a variety of bizarre animals.[192] But how seriously are we to take even this most notoriously venomous text as an instance of deep-seated and general Roman revulsion for Egyptians? Satires contain their own corrective. Juvenal's initial lines possess more flippancy than savagery. He points mockingly to the divinization of the crocodile, the snake-devouring ibis, and the golden image of a long-tailed monkey. He then adds that various districts of Egypt worship cats, river fish, or dogs—but no one reveres Diana. The jarring, even farcical, contrast underscores the satirist's main point. He goes on to further mock outrage. Egyptians abstain from onions and leeks, thus prompting Juvenal to take them too as gods and comment that this must be a holy nation indeed that sports divinities in its gardens.[193]

But a disturbing shift of tone follows. The satirist remarks that no animals of wool can appear on the table and the slaying of young goats is prohibited—but one can feed on human flesh.[194] The charge of cannibalism suggests malice rather than mockery. In fact, the satire itself is generated by a recent event in which a fierce feud between two Egyptian towns resulted in savage violence, punctuated by chopping up and devouring with relish one unfortunate casualty.[195] That vivid and gruesome scene rightly repels the reader. And Juvenal adds that the loathsome deed arose not from famine and desperate hunger but from sheer rage and fury by the worthless and unwarlike mob.[196] The indictment is ferocious. But, whatever the truth of the matter, it is worth observing that Juvenal's conclusion from all this does not focus solely on Egypt; rather it expresses a more general lament about the decline of morals and a nostalgia for an earlier day when men's better nature still prevailed.[197] That nostalgia holds, strikingly enough, even for old Egypt itself. Juvenal contrasts the debased worship of a long-tailed monkey with the glory days of the nation, where once the magic chords of Memnon sounded and ancient Thebes of the hundred gates, now

---

[191] Cic. *Nat. Deor.* 1.101. This is part of the argument against Epicureans, who believe in gods that perform no service whatever.

[192] Juv. 15.1–8.

[193] Juv. 15.10–11: *o sanctas gentes quibus haec nascuntur in hortis numina.*

[194] Juv. 15.13: *carnibus humanis vesci licet.*

[195] Juv. 15.77–92.

[196] Juv. 15.119–131.

[197] Juv. 15. 131–174. See the valuable commentary on the poem by Courtney (1980), 590–612.

a mere ruin, once stood.[198] Egypt provided a dramatic and inviting target for the poet. The canvas, however, was a broader one, the wistfulness for a better age, beyond an assault on this particular nation.[199] A strong strain existed generally in Roman writings on Egypt: admiration for the principles and institutions of its ancient history—by comparison with the inadequacies of its contemporary descendants.[200]

The sum of all this is decidedly smaller than its parts. Romans had no fixation on Egypt and were not preoccupied with deploring the nation. They retailed stereotypes about Egyptian inconstancy, insubordination, and recalcitrance. They found various Egyptian customs alien and outlandish. They scoffed at bizarre rites and found animal worship incomprehensible.[201] But even comments along these lines are dispersed and relatively rare. Some apply to Alexandrians (a hybrid population), some derive from the particular circumstances of the Roman war against Cleopatra, and most express amused disdain by the snobbish. The ferocity of a Juvenal, even if it were serious, stands as the exception rather than the rule. The great popularity of the Isis cult in Rome and increasingly in the empire suffices to show that hostility to Egypt did not pervade the Roman consciousness.[202]

Plutarch

That exemplar of Greco-Roman culture, the learned Greek scholar Plutarch, who thrived in the peace and prosperity of the Roman Empire, provides a more sensitive, balanced, and insightful perspective.[203] His treatise *On Isis and Osiris* serves as a far better witness than the conventional collection of clips from miscellaneous authors. The assiduous researcher dug about in the long Hellenic literature on Egypt and employed it to his

---

[198] Juv 15.4–6.

[199] Juvenal's other incidental remarks on Egyptian matters carry none of this venom; 1.26–29; 6.522–541. Nor is there any special hostility in Martial 7.30.

[200] Sonnabend (1986), 109–118.

[201] Cf. Statius *Silvae* 3.2.113; Lucian *Zeus Trag.* 42.

[202] On the extraordinary spread of the Isis cult, see Witt (1971); Malaise (1972); Takács (1995). Cf. Sonnabend (1986), 128–142.

[203] On Plutarch in his cultural setting, see Swain (1996), 135–186, with bibliography. The extensive studies of the *De Iside et Osiride* by Griffiths (1970) and Hani (1976) are indispensable. One may also consult the more recent commentaries of Cavalli (1985) and Froidefond (1988). A useful bibliography may be found in Richter (2001), 191–216, who offers a different view of Plutarch than is expressed here. See also the brief but valuable summary by Pearce (2007), 259–264. Pearce's recent and thorough examination of Jewish writings, particularly Philo, on Egypt, (2007), passim, obviates the need to consider that subject here. See also Smelik and Hemelrijk (1984), 1906–1920; K. Berthelot (1999), 203–218.

ends.²⁰⁴ But he could supplement it with personal observation. Like Herodotus and Diodorus, Plutarch too had visited Egypt, had conversations with Egyptian priests and others, and drew, at least at second hand, on Egyptian written sources.²⁰⁵ Plutarch sought comprehension, not condemnation, of Egyptian religion—at least comprehension in his own terms. The scholar and philosopher endeavored to find in his subject rational underpinnings. The seeking of "truth" behind rituals and myth would allow the devotee to avoid both superstition and atheism.²⁰⁶ And, where Plutarch encountered unusual rites and practices, he offered interpretations of allegory and symbolism.²⁰⁷

Plutarch's conceptualization reconfirms those of Herodotus and Diodorus, who saw in Egyptian beliefs overlap and intertwining with Hellenic tradition. That feature, of course, became considerably intensified through the cultural dynamics of the Hellenistic and early Roman eras.²⁰⁸ Plutarch's treatise is replete with parallels between Greek and Egyptian myths, divinities, and concepts. He is unconcerned with the origins of the gods or their transference from one culture to another. Plutarch places his focus on the familiarity, even interchangeability, of the gods and their divine functions.²⁰⁹ The gods, he proclaims, belong to a common heritage not peculiar to Egypt. All know and possess Isis and the divinities associated with her.²¹⁰ Different honors, symbols, and appellations might be applied among different peoples, but a single Reason and a single Providence order matters so as to direct intelligence toward the divine.²¹¹

This combination of universalism and pluralism faced a stiff test when confronting the fact of Egyptian animal worship. Plutarch addresses the issue head-on. He acknowledges that veneration of animals has given rise to laughter and derision. Even worse, it has prompted some to fall into religious extremism and others into atheism.²¹² Like his thoughtful

²⁰⁴ On Plutarch's sources, see Griffiths (1970), 75–100; Hani (1976), 12–21.

²⁰⁵ The trip to Egypt is attested in Plut. *Quaest. Conviv.* 5.5.5, 678c. On Plutarch and the Egyptian evidence, see the discussion of Griffiths (1970), 101–110.

²⁰⁶ Plut. *De Is. et Osir*. 352c: ἀλλ' Ἰσιακός ἐστιν ὡς ἀληθῶς ὁ τὰ δεικνύμενα καὶ δρώμενα περὶ τοὺς θεοὺς τούτους, ὅταν νόμῳ παραλάβῃ, λόγῳ ζητῶν καὶ φιλοσοφῶν περὶ τῆς ἐν αὐτοῖς ἀληθείας; 353e, 355c–d.

²⁰⁷ See., e.g., Plut. *De Is. et Osir* 355b, 358e–359a, 362b–d, 363d–364c, 366a–b, 367e–368b, 371a–b, 373a–c, 376f–377a.

²⁰⁸ Stephens (2003).

²⁰⁹ E.g., Plut. *De Is. et Osir*. 356a–b, 360e–f, 361e, 362b, 364d–365a, 374b–d, 375e–376a, 378d–e. Cf. Griffiths (1970), 309–310, 383–386, 390–393, 400–401, 426–428, 517–521, 537–540.

²¹⁰ Plut. *De Is. et Osir*. 377c–d: ἡμῖν τοὺς θεοὺς φυλάττωσι κοινοὺς καὶ μὴ ποιῶσιν Αἰγυπτίων ἰδίους . . . Ἶσιν δὲ καὶ τοὺς περὶ αὐτὴν θεοὺς ἔχουσι καὶ γιγνώσκουσιν ἅπαντες.

²¹¹ Plut. *De Is. et Osir*. 377e–378a

²¹² Plut. *De Is. et Osir*. 379d–e. On Plutarch and the animal cults generally, see the extensive survey of Hani (1976), 381–439. Cf. the comments of Griffiths (1970), 542–544.

predecessors, Herodotus and Diodorus, Plutarch neither dismisses nor embraces the institution. He examines a number of explanations offered for elevating creatures to divine status—and rejects most of them: that gods changed themselves into animals for fear of the evil Typhon; that the souls of the dead are reincarnated as animals; that Osiris separated his troops in various divisions, giving each an individual standard displaying an animal that was subsequently reckoned as divine; that early kings wore animal masks to frighten their enemies on the battlefield; that some cynical and unscrupulous rulers ordered different parts of the population to revere different animals in order to assure that, though unstable and prone to rebellion, they would not act in concert with one another.[213] Plutarch instead, as usual, opts for rational explanations. Some of the animals that enjoy veneration are those which provide benefits to humankind.[214] Other writers too had reached that conclusion on the basis of Egyptian informants.[215] But Plutarch offers an additional reason: some animals are honored on symbolic grounds: cobras, weasels, and scarab beetles because they faintly resemble the power of the god and the crocodile because it lacks a tongue, being thus analogous to the divine *logos*, which has no need of a voice, and because it has a thin membrane covering its eyes so that it can see without (ostensibly) being seen, like the chief god. Still other animals, like the dog and the ibis, are revered on grounds of both utility and symbolism.[216] More notably for our purposes, Plutarch finds cause not only to convey rationalizations for Egyptian practices but to point to comparable institutions in the Greek world: the Lemnians honor larks and the Thessalians honor storks for their actions against locusts and snakes respectively.[217] The interconnections between the worlds remain a major motif. Finally, Plutarch supplies a rationalization of his own: if philosophers like the Pythagoreans can ascribe divine names to certain numbers and abstract figures, surely it is appropriate to apply such designations to sentient creatures. Plutarch shrinks, of course, from endorsing the idea of animals as gods. They should be honored not for themselves but as a reflection of the deity, and as the product of the divine skill that governs all.[218]

The generally sympathetic portrait links Plutarch's learned treatise to the other surviving extended texts on Egypt, those of Herodotus, Diodorus,

---

[213] Plut. *De Is. et Osir.* 379e–380b. Cf. Griffiths (1970), 545–549; Hani (1976), 443–457. These explanations, as we have seen, had already been canvassed by Diodorus 1.86.3–5, 1.89.5.

[214] Plut. *De Is. et Osir.* 380e.

[215] Diod. 1.87; Cic. *Nat. Deor.* 1.101.

[216] Plut. *De Is. et Osir.* 380f–381d. Cf. Griffiths (1970), 554–560; Hani (1976), 458–462.

[217] Plut. *De Is. et Osir.* 380e–f.

[218] Plut. *De Is. et Osir.* 381e–382c: οὐ ταῦτα τιμῶντας, ἀλλὰ διὰ τούτων τὸ θεῖον . . . ὡς ὄργανον ἢ τέχνην δεῖ τοῦ πάντα κοσμοῦντος θεοῦ νομίζειν.

and Strabo. They offer the most reliable window on the outlook of Greeks and Romans who took the land and its people seriously. Those writers were not interested in scoring points, making quips, or retailing stereotypes. Even if some of their information is erroneous and some of their inferences are questionable, they represent our best index of classical views on that strange but fascinating nation. In each instance, they acknowledge the obvious: that Egyptian practices and beliefs have a character quite different from and often at odds with those of the classical world. Yet in each instance they also accentuate the links between the cultures, the comparable institutions, the analogous conceptions, the mutual intersections, and the reciprocal appropriations. Such features (however constructed) deliver the most meaningful message of cultural connectiveness.

Chapter 4

⊙ ⊙ ⊙ ⊙ ⊙ ⊙ ⊙ ⊙ ⊙ ⊙ ⊙ ⊙ ⊙ ⊙ ⊙ ⊙ ⊙

PUNICA FIDES

As prime antagonist of Rome in song and story none could match Carthage. Three Punic wars in the middle Republic seared Roman memory and imagination. The contests with that formidable foe left lasting scars, and the outcomes brought enduring glory. They framed the formative period of Roman imperialism, and they supplied critical landmarks in the shaping of Roman self-consciousness. For Rome, Carthage would seem to qualify as the "Other" par excellence. Hannibal was the bogeyman for generations of Roman children. And the wickedness of the antagonist helped to define the qualities and values that adhered to the Romans' perception of themselves.

A notorious stereotype resonates in the conception of Carthage: *Punica fides*. Carthaginian perfidy served as perfect foil to a hallowed virtue that the Romans held dear (or at least professed to hold dear). The good faith of the Romans, their commitment to the defense and support of allies and friends who depended on their *pistis* or *fides*, stands as a prevailing motif in the history, or rather the historiography, of Roman expansionism in the Mediterranean. The stark contrast with *Punica fides* could therefore serve most advantageously to advance the Romans' self-image as a people who honored their commitments and kept to their word, who protected their allies, and took on the role of *koinoi euergetai* for all.

The construct of *Punica fides* as antithesis to all that Rome stood for could provide a valuable vehicle for projecting that desirable image, and would bring a reassurance of moral superiority. That the Romans propagated such a notion is widely recognized and generally taken for granted.[1] The idea makes sense, and much testimony buttresses it. Yet the picture

---

[1] See, especially, Burck (1943), 297–345; Horsfall (1973–1974), 1–2; Prandi (1979), 90–97; Dubuisson (1983), 159–167; Thiel (1994), 129–131; Devallet (1996), 18–21; Starks (1999), 255–260; Isaac (2004), 324–335. The view is encapsulated, in an otherwise fine article, by Hexter (1992), 345: "The reputation of Carthaginians ... could best be summed up in the phrase *fides Punica*: in Roman eyes, all Carthaginians and Phoenicians were shifty, treacherous, and deceptive." Waldherr (2000), 214–222, recognizes that the portrait has both negative and positive features, without probing the issue. See also Bohak (2005), 223–230.

may be too simple and too monochromatic. Carthaginians do not step easily into the role of cardboard villains, and Punic perfidy does not pervade the multiple impressions that emerge from our texts.

The infamous stereotype, we customarily presume, became proverbial. Or did it? How early and how prevalent? To be sure, writers of the late Republic and beyond allude to the negative characterization that dominates modern discourse. But a closer look suggests ambiguity and complexity rather than consistent slander. The Phoenician image in antiquity did not lend itself readily to denigration and scorn. A look at the broader context is needed. Non-Roman perspectives on that people require scrutiny.[2] They suggest that the Phoenician image was a multivalent one. They were not the most obvious candidates to serve as foils for the Romans or to represent the "Other."[3]

The Hellenic Backdrop

Phoenicians appear in Homer, rarely but interestingly—without a monolithic character.[4] The poet accords them kudos for their seafaring skills, their craftsmanship, and their mercantile success. He introduces them as "noble Phoenicians."[5] They produce handsomely embroidered garments and ceramic ware of great beauty.[6] The king of Sidon had a guest friendship relation, including exchange of expensive gifts, with Menelaus of Sparta.[7] Homer applies to the Phoenicians the epithet "renowned for their ships," and their maritime activities are referred to more than once.[8] To be sure, like other merchants, some of them incline to greed and sharp practice.[9] One particularly knavish Phoenician sought to deceive Odysseus, kept him in Phoenicia for a year, lured him on board ship once again with a pretext,

---

[2] The terms "Phoenician," "Punic," and "Carthaginian," though occasionally distinguishable, are here, for the most part, employed interchangeably. The terminology receives close scrutiny by Prag (2006), 1–37, with different purposes. Franko (1994), 153–158, argued that *Poenus* in early Latin had a negative connotation and *Carthaginiensis* a neutral or positive one. Accepted by Starks (1999), 258. But the distinction is by no means consistent; see Palmer (1997), 74; Prag (2006), 6–7. On the interchangeability of the terms, see Bunnens (1983), 233–238.

[3] Waldherr (2000), 205–209, recognizes that no single portrait prevails but does not pursue or analyze the matter; cf. also Poinsotte (2002), 77–86; Bohak (2005), 223–230.

[4] We are not here concerned with the relationship between the Homeric portrait of Phoenicians and the realities. See the valuable, though somewhat dated, survey by Muhly (1970), 19–64.

[5] Homer *Od.* 13.272.

[6] Homer *Il.* 6.288–295, 23.740–743; cf. *Od.* 4.614–619.

[7] Homer *Od.* 4.614–619.

[8] Homer *Od.* 13.271–284, 14.285–297, 15.415.

[9] Homer *Od.* 13.271, 15.415.

and planned to sell him for a handsome price.[10] Other avaricious Phoenicians kidnapped the boy Eumaeus and his nursemaid, anticipating a lucrative sale.[11] But Homer does not present these figures' penchant as a national trait. Indeed Odysseus tells the tale of Phoenician sailors who rescued him from Crete and, blown off course, landed him on Ithaca itself, where they left him in a deep sleep but made sure to array all his belongings, including substantial treasure, on the sands where he lay. The hero awoke to find nothing missing. That hardly advances the notion of Phoenicians as chronic grubbers for goods, let alone as emblematic of deceit.[12]

In the Hebrew Bible Phoenicians famously emerge as master craftsmen who worked the cedars of Lebanon to adorn the Temple of Solomon. A warm relationship held between Solomon and Hiram, ruler of Tyre, men who treated one another as equals. And another Phoenician, an expert bronze worker, oversaw and helped to fashion the elegant furnishings and accoutrements of the Temple.[13]

Herodotus opens an important window on Hellenic perceptions of Phoenicians in the fifth century. And he strikes no negative note. Phoenicians appear frequently in his pages as merchantmen, shippers, and widespread settlers in the Mediterranean.[14] But we hear nothing of them as wily, avaricious, and deceitful traders. To be sure, Herodotus reports the infamous legend that Phoenicians of remote antiquity were ultimately responsible for the Trojan War. In the course of conducting commercial transactions in Argos, Phoenician traders decided to kidnap Io and a number of other Argive women on the shore, spiriting them away to Egypt and setting in motion a chain of events that culminated in the theft of Helen and the war on Troy.[15] Herodotus, however, does not buy the story. On the

---

[10] Homer *Od.* 14.287–297.

[11] Homer *Od.* 15.415–484. The passage does not imply that Phoenicians generally were notorious for dishonesty and unscrupulousness, as suggested by Mazza (1988), 552; Winter (1995), 249; and Bohak (2005), 223–224.

[12] Homer *Od.* 13.250–286. Winter (1995), 248, finds in this story the implication that Odysseus expected to be robbed by Phoenicians and was surprised to see his goods intact. Nothing in the text suggests this. In fact Odysseus expected to lose his possessions at the hands of Phaeacians; *Od.* 13.200–220. Winter's subtle argument (1995), 256–257, that Homer seeks to contrast the positive wiliness of Odysseus with the negative trickery of the Phoenicians, is perhaps oversubtle. Few auditors or readers would have caught that fine distinction. And it goes well beyond the text to interpret Homer's references to the Phoenicians as constructing the "Other" and conveying "alterity," as does Winter (1995), 261–263.

[13] 1 Kings, 5–7, 9.10–13. Cf. Jos. *Ant.* 8.76. On the Phoenician reputation for craftsmanship, see further Mazza (1988), 553–556.

[14] Herod. 1.1, 3.107, 4.42, 4.44, 4.196, 6.47, 7.90; cf Mavrogiannis (2004), 56–57. Other references to Phoenician seamanship in Mazza (1988), 557–558. The reputation endured. See, e.g., Polyb. 6.52.1. On the material evidence, see Winter (1995), 250–255, with references.

[15] Herod. 1.1. That this was the "zenith" of the Phoenicians' negative image, as asserted by Mazza (1988), 559, is well off the mark.

118 IMPRESSIONS OF THE "OTHER"

contrary, he underscores the fact that this is a Persian narrative and one quite different from what the Phoenicians themselves reported. In their version, Io went voluntarily, having been impregnated by a Phoenician ship captain, and sailed off with the Phoenicians before her parents should discover her indiscretions. Not that Herodotus puts any more faith in the Phoenician legend than in the Persian. He makes a point of identifying the sources in order to alert readers to their possible bias and unreliability, and to get on with what counts as history.[16] A similar conclusion arises from Herodotus' report that Phoenicians were responsible for carrying off two priestesses of Thebes in Egypt, selling the one in Libya and the other in Greece. Each then established religious shrines in her new land. The historian again makes certain to identify his sources and to suggest that axes were being ground: they were the Theban priests of the supreme deity. Herodotus swiftly transmits a different version: the prophetesses of Dodona told him that two black doves from Thebes flew to Libya and Dodona respectively delivering the message that oracular shrines should be installed there. Once more the historian declines to express a preference, but rather offers a rationalistic explanation that takes both traditions into account. He certainly has no interest in blackening the Phoenicians.[17]

One can go further. Two widely separated passages in Herodotus' *History* do have a bearing on the alleged Punic stereotype—but they serve to undermine it. Phoenicians, as we know, provided the principal naval force for the Persian expedition against Greece that forms the climactic subject of Herodotus' whole work.[18] One might expect, in that context, a properly dark portrait of the allies of the Achaemenids. Not so. Herodotus reports, in his own voice, a story about Cambyses, ruler of Persia, who planned aggressive campaigns against Egyptians, Ethiopians, and Carthaginians. In implementing his designs, Cambyses ordered his navy to sail against Carthage. The Phoenicians, however, refused to comply—and since they were the best sailors and fighters in the fleet, Cambyses had to call off the campaign in North Africa. The reason given by the Phoenicians is noteworthy. They were bound by mighty oaths and would not take up arms against their own kinsmen.[19] This act plainly receives Herodotus' approval. The Phoenicians, in short, kept faith with their colonists, an act in accord with *pistis*. The second passage delivers a similar message in a very different context. Herodotus here speaks about the Carthaginians themselves. Among the places where they sail with cargo to conduct business is a site in Libya beyond the Pillars of Herakles. There they set out their wares on the

[16] Herod. 1.2, 1.4–5; cf. Mavrogiannis (2004), 54–56.
[17] Herod. 2.54–57. The absence of negative views in Herodotus is noted also by Barceló (1994), 3–5.
[18] E.g., Herod. 7.89.
[19] Herod. 3.19.

beach, return to their ships, and await the offers of the natives, who leave gold on the shore and withdraw to let the Carthaginians examine it. If the amount seems fair, the business is concluded. If not, the Carthaginians wait again for a larger sum, and the process continues until both sides agree. Herodotus, impressed by this transaction, makes a telling comment. Neither party, he says, plays false with the other. The Carthaginians do not make off with the gold nor the natives with the goods (though each has ample opportunity to do so) until both are satisfied with the equity of the exchange.[20] As reflection on Carthaginian character, it is the very reverse of *Punica fides*.

The repute of the Phoenicians among Greek intellectuals, in fact, was high. They received credit for introducing the alphabet to the Greeks, hitherto unknown to them, a contribution attested and endorsed as early as Herodotus. The historian conveys the tradition that Phoenicians under Cadmus settled in Boeotia, where they taught *grammata* to the Greeks. The latter in turn applied the term Phoenician *grammata* or Cadmean *grammata* to the original alphabet out of proper respect for those who created it.[21] Plainly Phoenicians could not be dismissed as ignorant barbarians. That Cadmus held a firm place in Hellenic legend as founder of the great city of Thebes sends a significant message in itself. Greeks, or some Greeks at least, were content, indeed eager, to associate the origins of Thebes with the land of Lebanon.[22] Herodotus expresses admiration for the extraordinary skill of Phoenicians demonstrated in the construction of a canal—a skill, he remarks, that they possess in a range of activities.[23]

Further, and more telling, Greek political thinkers expressed strong admiration for the institutions of Carthage, reckoning them as characteristic of the balanced and successful form of government. In some circles, Spartans and Carthaginians had the highest reputations for being the best-governed peoples, a renown attested by Isocrates in the early fourth century.[24] Aristotle ranks the Carthaginian system with those of the Spartans and Cretans as laudable efforts to provide a combination of democratic, aristocratic, and monarchical elements. Each, to be sure, has its flaws, according to Aristotle, and none has the balance exactly right. He notes, for instance, the Carthaginian attempt to combine both merit and wealth as criteria for the selection of their leaders, thereby blending oligarchy and aristocracy, but worries that the balance might be tipped toward timocracy. And he

---

[20] Herod. 4.196. The story came to Herodotus from the Carthaginians themselves. But he expresses no skepticism.

[21] Herod. 5.57–59.

[22] On the Cadmus legend in fifth-century Greece, see, e.g., Herod. 2.49; Eur. *Bacch*. 170–172; *Phoen*. 5–6, 638–639.

[23] Herod. 7.23.

[24] Isocr. *Nic*. 24. Plato, *Crito* 52E puts Sparta and Crete in that category.

disapproves the practice of having the same individual hold more than one office simultaneously.[25] But he delivers high praise generally for some features that make the Carthaginian constitution superior even to the Spartan, including the selection of magistrates by merit and the fact that the kingship was not confined to a very restricted number of families.[26] More significantly, Aristotle praises the Carthaginians for the stability of their state, the loyalty of the populace to the system, and the fact that neither civil strife nor tyranny has upset the governance of the realm.[27] Eratosthenes singles out Carthaginians and Romans as those who govern themselves most marvelously.[28] The reckoning of Sparta, Crete, and Carthage as benchmarks for constitutional primacy had become commonplace by the Hellenistic period.[29] Polybius employs Sparta and Carthage in particular as the standards against which to measure the superiority of Rome. For him, Carthage supplies a worthy comparison with Rome, for its institutions too offer a combination of monarchic, aristocratic, and democratic elements, a well-conceived structure, according to the historian.[30] Rome, of course, has the edge for Polybius. The Carthaginian system had already begun to decline by the time of the Hannibalic war while Rome was reaching its peak; Carthage's reliance on mercenary forces contrasted with Rome's citizen army; and the Carthaginian scramble for profit had resulted in candidates for office engaging in undisguised bribery.[31] Polybius' objective, to be sure, was to establish the superiority of Roman practices and institutions. Nonetheless, Carthage, as is clear, supplied the principal criterion by which to measure success.

Greeks acknowledged Phoenician distinction in a whole range of matters related to the life of the mind. Strabo, drawing in part on the Stoic philosopher Posidonius, a Greek from Apamea who subsequently worked and taught in Rhodes, describes a broad realm of Phoenician intellectual activities. Their adventures at sea and their mercantile interests rendered them experts in astronomy and arithmetic, sciences that they transmitted to the Greeks. But they went well beyond. Phoenicians could boast a large number of renowned philosophers. Zeno himself indeed was among them. And Strabo identifies some Tyrians and Sidonians who trained disciples in philosophy in his own day—including himself.[32] Perhaps most impressive, tradition had it that a certain Mochus from Sidon in the distant past, before

---

[25] Aristotle *Pol.* 1273a.
[26] Aristotle *Pol.* 1272b.
[27] Aristotle *Pol.* 1272.b, 1273.b.
[28] Strabo 1.4.9.
[29] Polybius, 6.43.1, includes Mantinea in that company. Cf. Barceló (1994), 7–9.
[30] Polyb. 6.47.9, 6.51.1–2.
[31] Polyb. 6.51–52, 6.56.1–5.
[32] Strabo 16.2.24.

the age of the Trojan War, had been the father of atomic theory. The Phoenicians themselves may have concocted this idea, a source of national pride, and Mochus himself was very probably a fabricated figure, his alleged works translated into Greek, or indeed invented, in the Hellenistic period. What matters, however, is the fact that the learned Posidonius retailed the story. His account reached Strabo whence we have it now. Posidonius felt no need to challenge the Phoenician version. The idea of a Phoenician as the man who accomplished the breakthrough on atomic theory evidently did not trouble Posidonius—a valuable index of the Hellenic perspective on that people.[33]

So far, so good. But the impression of Phoenicians carried some less desirable undertones as well. An aura of chicanery clung to traders, merchantmen, and those engaged in maritime business.[34] Tantalizing hints survive suggesting that the Phoenicians did not altogether escape that stigma. As we have seen, it appears already in Homer. It also surfaces indirectly in Plato's *Republic*. Socrates famously alludes to the "noble lie," the *pseudos gennaion*. And he refers to it quite suggestively as *Phoinikikon ti*, "something Phoenician."[35] That would seem to imply that deception could be expressed as a Phoenician trait, a Phoenician "something." How much to make of this? The linkage may have more to do with Phoenicians as men of commerce than as exemplars of an ethnic character. And the noble lie, in any case, possesses a mixed, not a strictly negative, connotation. An echo of this "Phoenician thing" appears in Polybius, a passage largely unnoticed by moderns. The Greek historian recounts Hannibal's stratagem in preventing plots against his life by his Gallic allies. He contrived a scheme whereby he would put on and take off various wigs fashioned for him as disguises to deceive would-be assassins. Polybius refers to this as "Punic artifice": *Phoinikikon strategema*.[36] Polybius passes no negative judgment on this, simply records it as a clever means of staving off enemies bent on homicide. But the phrase does sound modestly proverbial. Posidonius, writing in the late second or early first century, offers something suggestively similar. Strabo, in recounting various tales regarding the foundation of Gades as prompted by an oracle that directed a colony to the Pillars of Herakles, includes a comment by Posidonius, who opted for one of the stories but called the oracle and multiple missions from Tyre a "Phoenician lie": *pseusma Phoinikikon*.[37]

---

[33] Strabo 16.2.24; Sex. Emp. *Adv. Math.* 9.363. Strabo does express some caution in accepting Posidonius' tale but plainly not on the grounds that it would be unexpected for a Phoenician to accomplish this feat. The notice is embedded in a passage that lists a plethora of Phoenician intellectuals. See further below, p. 138.

[34] Cf. Diod. 5.35.4; Ps. Arist. *De Mir. Ausc.* 135; Capomacchia (1991), 267–269.

[35] Plato *Rep.* 3.414B–C. Cf. Homer *Od.* 13.271, 15.415.

[36] Polyb. 3.78.1. Franko (1994), 158, wrongly sees this as a defamatory phrase.

[37] Strabo 3.5.5.

Is he simply identifying the source of this supposed falsehood or does he employ a proverbial expression? Hard to tell. One might, however, bear in mind that this same Posidonius found entirely plausible the tradition that a legendary Phoenician figure invented atomic theory. His use of the phrase need not imply a dastardly image of the people.

Phoenicians had plural images. Greeks saw them as successful sailors who plowed the sea, enterprising mercantilists, colonizers and settlers all over the Mediterranean. Along with that line of work came some grubbing after profit, acquisitiveness, and cunning.[38] For certain authors, it may have led to some sly playing with phrases that insinuated Phoenician craftiness. But nothing to show that mendaciousness was considered the dominant trait and defining element of the *ethnos*. Greeks in fact gave Phoenicians their due as philosophers, scientists, framers of admirable political institutions, founders of cities (even a great Greek city), and indeed bestowers of the alphabet on the Hellenic world itself. The multiple impressions would not easily provide a basis for the Romans to develop an undeviatingly negative concept of *Punica fides*.

In the Shadow of the Punic Wars

Nor did they do so. Hostile stereotypes of the most virulent form should appeal, if ever, to those who lived in the shadow of the Punic wars. Demonizing of the Carthaginian "Other" ought to have had its heyday in the era of the middle Republic. Is that the case? Our evidence leaves much to be desired. As so often, it is frustratingly fragmentary just when we need it most. The few extant scraps of Naevius' *Bellum Punicum* provide nothing pertinent. Ennius' *Annales* certainly contain fierce animosity, unsurprisingly so in the wake of Hannibal's depredations in Italy and the bitter aftertaste of the Second Punic War.[39] One fragment of his national epic observes that the *Poeni* are wont to sacrifice their little boys to the gods.[40] The legitimacy of that slur need not here be investigated. At the least it reflects a campaign to brand the evildoers with the worst form of wickedness. But where are the stereotypes of duplicity and treachery? Ennius spoke scornfully of the Carthaginians, says Aulus Gellius, as "tunic-clad youth."[41] And

---

[38] Cf. the comic fragment, of unknown authorship, in which a character declares himself a "true Phoenician" because he gives with the one hand and takes with the other; Kassel-Austin fr. 957. Polybius, 9.11.2, regards greed and love of rule as innate Phoenician traits. See also the comment of Diodorus, 5.38.3, on Phoenicians' ability from ancient times to find ways to make profit.

[39] Burck (1943), 301–302.

[40] Ennius *Ann.* 221 V = 214 Sk.

[41] Ennius *Ann.* 325 V = 303 Sk.

elsewhere he describes them as men of *iniqua superbia*.[42] But only one extant allusion hints at a reputation for perfidy. And this refers specifically to Hannibal, not to Carthaginian character in general. Ennius describes the great leader as *dubius*.[43] Not much to go on.

Where does *Punica fides* raise its ugly head? Explanation for war by labeling Carthaginians as breakers of treaties would be a logical place to look. Cato in the *Origines* charged them with violating no fewer than six agreements in two decades.[44] How far this form of demonizing pervaded the Roman imagination is difficult to say. We possess a significant amount of information on Roman/Carthaginian treaties from Polybius, writing in the generation after the Hannibalic war.[45] He provides intriguing access to debates regarding the causes and responsibility for the First and Second Punic Wars. Much of this, unsurprisingly, involved charges of treaty violations—on both sides. The historian records a series of treaties between the two powers, dating back allegedly to the beginning of the Republic, thus a long stretch of cordiality at least on paper. The first charge of treaty breaking of which we are aware, in fact, was an accusation leveled at the Romans! It came from the pen of Philinus, a Sicilian historian who sympathized with Carthage. He maintained that the First Punic War resulted from Rome's crossing to Sicily in violation of a treaty that made Italy off-limits to Carthage and Sicily off-limits to Rome. Polybius denounces Philinus' bias and is at pains to deny the existence of any such document.[46] He had an antidote at his disposal, the work of Fabius Pictor, Rome's earliest historian, a contemporary of the Hannibalic war and one who played a significant diplomatic role in it. Polybius notes his bias also, a writer with as much blind partiality toward Rome as Philinus had toward Carthage.[47] But he cites no charge on Fabius' part regarding Punic perfidy.

Charges flew back and forth regarding treaty violations, however, in the context of preliminaries to the Second Punic War. Polybius cites unnamed writers who blamed Hannibal for initiating the conflict by crossing the Ebro River in contravention of a treaty. The historian's concern here is not to pass judgment on the deed but to beat the drums for his own thesis that such actions at best constitute triggers for war, not genuine causes.[48] Fabius attempted a different sort of explanation, reaching back to the long-term

---

[42] Ennius *Ann.* 286 V = 287 Sk.
[43] Ennius *Ann.* 274–275 V = 474–475 Sk. See Skutsch (1985), 633–634.
[44] Nonius, s.v. "*duodevicesimo*"; Gellius 10.1.10 = Peter, *HRR*, Cato fr. 84. Just what the six breaches were has stirred some unprofitable speculation; see the comments and bibliography in Hoyos (1987), 112–121.
[45] On the treaties, see now Serrati (2006), with bibliography.
[46] Polyb. 3.26. On Philinus' pro-Carthaginian leanings, see Polyb. 1.14–15.
[47] Polyb. 1.14; cf. 1.15.12.
[48] Polyb. 3.6.1–7.

ambitions of Hannibal's uncle Hasdrubal and of Hannibal's own plans devised from boyhood. Polybius finds this wanting for a variety of reasons, but he nowhere suggests that Fabius pointed to the breaking of agreements.[49] Others, however, did at the time. Polybius' report of the exchange is notable. When Hannibal besieged Saguntum, Roman legates protested that by crossing the Ebro he broke the pact concluded at the time of Hasdrubal. Hannibal himself retorted that Rome had initiated hostilities by meddling in Saguntum and executing some of its leading citizens. The Carthaginians, he asserted, very interestingly, would not overlook this form of violating agreements.[50] Whatever the basis for the rhetorical interchange, Polybius has no hesitation in putting a charge of treaty violation in the mouth of a Carthaginian accusing Rome. A subsequent dialogue took place between Roman representatives and the Carthaginian governing body in Carthage. As Polybius presents it, the issue of who broke which treaty seized attention. Romans maintained that crossing the Ebro and attacking Saguntum transgressed the agreement with Hasdrubal; Carthaginians countered by pointing to the treaty of Lutatius that concluded the First Punic War, reading excerpts from it and asserting that it did not encompass Saguntum.[51] The upshot of this is that both Romans and Carthaginians quarreled over which side was responsible for infringing treaty obligations. Of course, one might expect Carthaginian spokesmen to assert their adherence to agreements. What matters is that Polybius, without qualification, presents them as doing so. The sanctity of such obligations was taken for granted on both sides. Polybius' account presupposes that Carthaginians, far from being inveterate treaty breakers, shared the same mind-set with their adversaries.

Pronouncements on the motives and reasons for the Hannibalic war are, of course, irrelevant for our purposes. But if Polybius does reflect, at least in some degree, learned opinion in mid-Republican Rome, as surely he does, the notion of Carthaginians as a treacherous folk who consider treaties as scraps of paper did not prevail in those circles. The historian acknowledged that Carthage had infringed the treaty of Lutatius and that of Hasdrubal. But he also puts into Hannibal's mouth the allegation that Romans had breached an agreement by involving themselves in Saguntum. Both parties disputed the question of which one violated which pact. And Polybius expresses his own view quite unequivocally. The most significant cause of conflict and the real root of the Hannibalic war, he maintains, was the Roman seizure of Sardinia and the tribute "unjustly" imposed as a consequence. In view of those transgressions, he adds, the Carthaginians entered

---

[49] Polyb. 3.8.1–3.9.5.
[50] Polyb. 3.15.5, 3.15.7.
[51] Polyb. 3.21.1–8.

upon war "with good reason."⁵² The matter could hardly be clearer. Breach of trust did not derive from ethnic deficiencies.

On one occasion only did Polybius acknowledge that Hannibal himself violated agreements. He referred there to obligations that the Carthaginian general had undertaken with certain Italian cities and could no longer keep because of deteriorating military circumstances. The historian, however, does not issue a condemnation. Indeed he employs the occasion to justify or at least to account rationally for these actions in light of the loss of Capua and Hannibal's anxieties about defections from other cities.⁵³ That is very far from embracing or even attesting to the notion of inherent Carthaginian wickedness.

In brief, the categorization of Carthaginians as chronic transgressors of treaties had little purchase in mid-Republican Rome. Neither Fabius Pictor, the first of Rome's historians in the late third century and a firm advocate of his nation's cause, nor Polybius, the admiring chronicler of Roman imperialism in the mid–second century, hints that the stereotype of *Punica fides* had been fastened upon Carthage.

In the case of Pictor, one can go further still. He may have found Carthage at fault in recounting the background to two Punic wars. But he would hardly credit the idea of innate character flaws in the people of Carthage. In writing about Rome's legendary past, Pictor observed that the Arcadian hero Evander introduced the alphabet to Rome. And he added that the Greeks themselves had borrowed this invention from the Phoenicians.⁵⁴ The historian evidently found no difficulty in embracing legends that traced Rome's cultural underpinnings to the ancestors of the Carthaginians.

The fierce foe need not be constructed as the moral opposite. Our evidence suggests more mutual respect than fabricated alterity. An anecdote from the middle Republic reinforces that conclusion. It conveys an appealing conversation between Hannibal and his conqueror Scipio Africanus at the court of Antiochus of Syria in Ephesus a decade after the war. The item appears in Livy, drawing at second hand on C. Acilius, a Roman annalist whose history composed in Greek dates to the middle of the second century. Hence the story itself must have surfaced not too long after the supposed event. According to the narrative, Scipio asked his counterpart whom he would rate as the greatest of all military men. Hannibal unhesitatingly named Alexander the Great. Scipio evidently found no fault with that verdict, but then asked Hannibal whom he would put in second place. The

---

⁵² Polyb. 3.10.3–5, 3.15.10, 3.30.4.
⁵³ Polyb. 9.26.1–11. For Polybius' ambivalant judgment of Hannibal, see Polyb. 9.22.8–10, 9.24–26.
⁵⁴ Fabius Pictor fr. 1–2.

Carthaginian named Pyrrhus, supporting his choice with a number of skills and achievements that he attributed to the Epirote ruler. This may have dismayed Scipio, who had reason to expect that he might have been placed at least second to Alexander. But he proceeded to ask for number three. For that slot Hannibal immediately picked himself. That drew some ironic laughter from the Roman general, who reminded Hannibal that he had suffered defeat at his hands. "What would you say," he inquired, "if you had defeated me?" In that event, the Carthaginian replied, he would have set himself ahead of Alexander, Pyrrhus, and all others. Scipio at last got the point. The Roman was much moved by this tribute. For Hannibal had obviously put him in a category by himself, surpassing all the great commanders.[55] The tale, conveyed by a Roman author only a generation or so after Hannibal's death, depicts a remarkable rapport between these erstwhile antagonists. Even more interestingly, Livy, who transmits the anecdote, praises the unexpected twist of Hannibal's retort and describes it as *Punico astu*, Carthaginian cleverness. The Roman historian clearly puts a positive spin on this phrase. He declines to use a term like *calliditas* or something similar that might imply deviousness. Hannibal's wit is shrewd, not insidious. And the pairing with *Punicus* shows that the adjective need not carry a negative connotation.

Fragments and isolated passages, while suggestive, leave much in the dark. But one substantial text, contemporary and revealing, offers a better look at Roman perceptions of Carthage in the age of the Punic wars. Plautus' comedy the *Poenulus*, a rich and provocative work, is, like everything else on this subject, replete with ambiguity.

The timing itself is significant. Plautus produced the play about a decade after the end of the Hannibalic war, Rome's most trying travail, a contest that nearly put an end to Roman history as we know it. Animosity toward the Punic "Other" ought to have been at its peak at this point. And indeed the comedy is often interpreted as reinforcing Roman prejudices about Carthaginian values and character.[56]

On the face of it, *Poenulus* does contain allusions to slurs on Punic traits. The title alone, "The Little Carthaginian," might hint at a derogatory attitude—though his size plays no role in the drama itself.[57] The prologue introduces Hanno the Carthaginian, the play's central character, as one who knows all languages but pretends not to know: *dissimulat*. He is therefore a "Carthaginian indeed," says Plautus, "no need to say more": *Poenus plane*

---

[55] Livy 35.14.5–12. The anecdote is given in a slightly different version by Appian *Syr.* 10; Leigh (2004), 29–37.

[56] Mazza (1988), 560; Prandi (1979), 90; Franko (1994), 155–156; *idem* (1996), 425–452; Maurice (2004), 267–290.

[57] It appears only indirectly as one of the exaggerated insults hurled by the *miles gloriosus*; Plaut. *Poen.* 1309–1310.

est. quid verbis opust.[58] The speaker evidently refers to a shared understanding with the audience: pretense and dissembling are only to be expected of a Carthaginian. Hanno's mode of searching for his daughters is described as clever and shrewd.[59] And Hanno, in the course of the drama, duly does hide for a time the fact that he can understand Latin, thus generating a scene of considerable amusement.[60] Further, the *servus callidus* Milphio mocks Hanno's clothing, likening him to a colored bird, and remarks sarcastically on the appearance of his attendants, who carry rings in their ears instead of on their fingers.[61] The *miles gloriosus* also comments on the exotic attire of Hanno and issues a stream of invective that brands him with effeminacy, low-class background, ill-smelling body, and generally alien peculiarities.[62] All this provides grist to the mill of those who see the play as reflecting stereotypes of the Punic trickster and unwelcome outsider, catering to the biases of a Roman audience still scarred by the wounds of the dreadful Hannibalic conflict.

The matter is not so simple. A Greek play, of course, served as model for Plautus' composition, and we cannot readily discern how much the Punic image owes to that now-lost predecessor. No point in pursuing that avenue. But, whatever the character of the earlier play, it was Plautus' decision to produce a drama that featured a Carthaginian as its principal figure in the aftermath of a deadly conflict with his nation. That can hardly be an accident.

It may very well be true that the *Poenulus* alludes to contemporary stereotypes of the alien. If so, however, Plautus subverts rather than endorses those stereotypes. It is surely no coincidence that the persons who deliver the hostile aspersions on Hanno are the least admirable characters in the play: the scheming slave and the swaggering soldier. Hanno, in fact, defies the caricatures; he is a man of erudition, understanding, and forgiveness whose determined search for his kidnapped daughters culminates in success, the comeuppance of the wicked, and a happy ending. Not only does Hanno surmount the Punic stereotype, he surmounts the comic stereotype; he is a worthy and respected figure, not the standard comic *senex*.

Hanno, to be sure, enters the stage speaking unintelligible Punic—or some comic form of it—and concealing at that point that he knows Latin. Is that confirmation of the proverbial Punic, the devious alien? Not likely. The pose serves only to undermine the guileful slave (the real *dissimulator*) whose pretense at offering a Latin translation makes him all the more ludicrous.

---

[58] Plaut. *Poen.* 112–113.
[59] Plaut. *Poen.* 111: *docte atque astu*.
[60] Plaut. *Poen.* 990–1034.
[61] Plaut. *Poen.* 975–981.
[62] Plaut. *Poen.* 1298–1318.

Hanno the Carthaginian has the upper hand in strategy, character, and smarts. Even more striking, Hanno is four times associated in the play with *pietas*, that quintessentially Roman quality.[63] Indeed one might note that Hanno makes reference to a still more quintessential Roman term, none other than *fides* itself.[64] If a Carthaginian can exemplify Roman values, Plautus surely sends a pointed message. The dramatist plainly plays with inversion here, as so often in comedy. He may upset the expectations of the prejudiced, but he evidently anticipated a sympathetic audience for his thrusts. Hanno in the end is a complex, even paradoxical character, a bundle of mixed characteristics, ranging from the estimable to the questionable.[65] But the fact that Plautus could toy whimsically with such a figure, parodying purported Punic practices while puncturing Roman prejudices, within just a decade of the Hannibalic war, constitutes the most striking and perhaps most meaningful feature of the play.[66]

That Hanno commands both Punic and Latin deserves note. It possesses implications well outside the *Poenulus* or comic drama—or even the Punic "Other." It bears on Roman culture and self-consciousness in the Mediterranean world of the middle Republic. Bilingualism has ambiguous repute, a double-edged quality. When Hanno reveals that he knows Latin as well as Punic, thus having rendered the wily slave Milphio ridiculous, Milphio

---

[63] Plaut. *Poen.* 1137, 1190, 1255, 1277. Cf. Hanson (1959), 87–95; Palmer (1997), 33–34. Franko (1996), 437–443, raises the possibility that ascription of *pietas* to Hanno was simply a sardonic joke, at odds with the Carthaginian's character and behavior. In fact, however, it conforms to that character and behavior as the play presents them, the father's determined search to recover his daughters and save them from a life of prostitution. Franko (1995), 250–252, and (1996), 444–445, interprets lines 1298–1311 as indicating that Hanno approached his daughters with embraces that suggested sexual fondling. Cf. Leigh (2004), 30. But the inference is quite unjustifiable. The girls, in fact, once they learned of the relationship, took the initiative in embracing their father; 1259–1261, 1292–1294; cf. Zehnacker (2000), 428–429. Even if the lines carried the implication that Franko supposes, they are set in the mouth of the boastful soldier, amidst a flurry of abuse, simply reflecting his hopeless misunderstanding of the situation. Cf. Maurice (2004), 286–287. It is true that the prologue, 104–111, has Hanno begin his search in each city by seeking out its prostitutes, spending the night with them, and then asking afterward of their origin. Franko (1996), 429–430, makes much of this. So also Maurice (2004), 279. But it is sheer comic travesty, altogether at odds with Hanno's deportment in the play.

[64] Plaut. *Poen.* 967.

[65] Starks' balanced treatment, (2000), 163–186, recognizes the complexity of the character and the manipulation of stereotypes. So also, in briefer fashion, Faller (2004), 168–170; Syed (2005a), 366–370. The recent study by Maurice (2004), 167–290, offers a more one-sided view. She stresses deception as the central characteristic of Hanno and sees it as corresponding to the Carthaginian trait expected by a Roman audience.

[66] Cf. the remarks of Cassola (1983), 57–58; Palmer (1997), 31–34; Waldherr (2000), 210–211; Zehnacker (2000), 430; Faller (2004), 168–170. Henderson (1999), 3–37, stresses the special disorderliness of the play, with its multiple and deliberate allusions and confusions, but does not address the issues of concern here.

turns on him with ferocity: "you have a forked tongue, like a serpent."[67] The motif recurs in later texts. In book I of the *Aeneid*, Venus, wary of the Phoenicians and their cunning queen Dido, refers to them as "bilingual Tyrians."[68] That is plainly not an endearing phrase. Similar phraseology appears a century later in the work of another epic poet, Silius Italicus. He too appears to equate Punic bilingualism with deception, the forked tongue. The poet has Scipio, in negotiations with Masinissa the Numidian, urge him to dismiss from mind his Punic bilingual allies.[69] The people of Carthage, for good or ill, had the reputation of bilingualism.

But there is something odd about all this. The Romans did not in fact disparage that skill. They shunned neither the concept nor the practice. As is well known, Roman intellectuals of the mid-Republic were frequently bilingual in Greek and Latin, from Fabius Pictor to Scipio Aemilianus. That included Cato the Elder, who professed scorn for Greeks but mastered the language. The level of accomplishment and the numbers of those fluent in Greek and conversant with Hellenic culture only expanded in the later Republic.[70] Bilingualism proved to be a valuable tool for Rome. It not only facilitated diplomatic dealings and cultural intercourse with the Hellenistic east but gave Romans the advantage in such encounters. The Greeks did not learn Latin. The Romans employed that advantage to underscore their superiority.[71]

Would this hold for Punic? Greek, one might argue, occupied a special place in the cultural world of the Mediterranean. Would association with Punic be more an embarrassment than a boast, a descent from Hellenism to barbarism? Not so. A remarkable episode illustrates Roman regard for intellectual accomplishment in Punic. A massive treatise on agriculture, composed in twenty-eight volumes by the Carthaginian writer Mago, came to Roman notice in the mid–second century BCE. The Senate of Rome itself ordered its translation into Latin—and this despite the fact that no less a figure than Cato had already composed (a rather shorter) work on the same subject. The commission went to D. Silanus, who, according to Pliny, was the Roman most accomplished in the Punic language. Obviously he was not alone in control of the tongue.[72] This event demonstrates not only

---

[67] Plaut. *Poen.* 1034: *bisulci lingua quasi proserpens bestia.*

[68] Verg. *Aen.* 1.661: *quippe domum timet ambiguam Tyriosque bilinguis.*

[69] Sil. Ital. 156–157: *dimitte bilingues ex animo socios.*

[70] See the discussion in Gruen (1992), 227–271, with bibliography cited there. On Cato, see Gruen (1992), 52–83. On the late Republic, see Rawson (1985). The study of Kaimio (1979) is essential. And see the wider surveys of Petrochilos (1974) and Wardman (1976).

[71] See examples collected in Gruen (1992), 235–241.

[72] Pliny *NH* 18.5.22: *peritisque Punicae dandum negotium, in quo praecessit omnes . . . D. Silanus.* See also Columella *De Re Rust.* 1.1.13. Varro, *De Re Rust.* 1.1.10, offers a different version, in which Mago's volumes were translated into Greek by Cassius Dionysius and dedicated to the

Roman respect for Carthaginian knowledge in this area (Mago's work exercised considerable influence on Varro and Columella), but, equally important, it discloses the fact that some members of the Roman aristocracy were fully conversant with the Punic language. In short, Roman acquaintance with languages, at least in certain cases, extended not just to Greek but to Punic. The stereotype of the forked tongue had more to do with literary convention than with authentic reflection of Roman sentiments on the *Punica fides* of their adversary.

When did the portrayal take on darker hues? The crushing of Carthage in 146 might seem to qualify as a pivotal time. That act carried significant reverberations. To most outside viewers the attack on Carthage must have seemed baffling and unnecessary. The annihilation of the city was even more inexplicable and, for some indeed, indefensible, certainly not redounding to the credit of Rome. Nor did it require an outside viewer to take that position. As is well known, sharp division occurred in Rome during the period leading to hostilities with Carthage. Cato the Elder's forceful advocacy of war ran into sharp opposition from Scipio Nasica and others who found cogent reasons for restraint.[73] This is not the place to assess those arguments, let alone to debate the real causes of the Third Punic War. But there is no reason to doubt that strong opinions questioned the legitimacy and rationale for an assault on Carthage, which by then had become a third-rate power on the international scene. It is arresting, however, that the Carthaginian reputation for duplicitous dealing does not appear to have played a role, so far as we can tell, in manufacturing reasons for war. We know only that Cato, in the fourth book of his *Origines*, claimed that Carthaginians six times breached a treaty with Rome in the twenty-two (or eighteen) years after the First Punic War.[74] The allegation may have helped to justify Rome's war on Hannibal in retrospect. Whether Cato said anything comparable in his campaign for a prospective third war with Carthage, however, goes unreported.[75] Cato's thunderings directed themselves against a potential Carthaginian threat, not against Carthaginian character. In any event, charges of treaty violations, a regular feature of rationales for war, are quite different from accusations of an ethnic propensity for perfidy.

---

praetor Sextilius. The two accounts are not incompatible. And even Varro's version shows the Roman interest in Punic learning on agriculture.

[73] On the debates, see Plut. *Cato* 26–27; Appian *Pun.* 69. Cf. the analysis of Cassola (1983), 41–51.

[74] See above, p. 123.

[75] The author of the rhetorical treatise *Ad Herennium*, 4.20, imagines an argument in which Carthaginians are represented as having frequently broken treaties; cf. Quint. 9.3.31. But the conjecture that this comes from a speech of Cato lacks any corroborating testimony.

The questioning of Roman motives became much graver after the eradication of Carthage. One notes with real surprise, therefore, the absence of references to fierce animosity toward Carthaginians based on ethnic traits or character deficiencies. Polybius famously reports a range of opinions among Greeks in the aftermath of the war, some approving Rome's action, others condemning it. Two sets of clashing verdicts receive description in his text. In the first, Rome's defenders took the pragmatic line that Carthage represented a long-standing potential menace, and a decision to eliminate that threat derived from prudent foresight. The skeptics in response claimed that Carthage had taken no hostile steps and had complied with Roman requests only to suffer harsh and irremediable treatment, a sure sign of decline in the moral stature of Rome. In the second set of opinions, supporters of Rome relied on a legalistic argument, alleging that Carthaginian surrender gave the Romans carte blanche to act in any way they saw fit; in destroying Carthage, therefore, the Romans violated no laws, agreements, or divine injunctions. In the eyes of their detractors, however, the Romans, who had once conducted war only on noble principles, here employed devious tactics and rendered impious decisions.[76] Almost nowhere in this welter of assessments is there resort to Carthaginian treachery as a motive or rationale for war and destruction.[77] Perfidy, insofar as it has a place in the debate, attaches to Rome.

How closely these verdicts correspond to attitudes actually expressed among Greeks in the aftermath of Carthage's destruction remains unknowable. Polybius may have had his own agenda in framing the debate in such a fashion. But whatever the historicity of his presentation, no grounds exist to question the fact of discussions, divisions, and speculation about Rome's decision to wipe out a woefully inferior city. Even if the particular arguments were fabricated, Polybius, a contemporary of the events and a man who had access not only to Greek ruminations on the matter but also to Roman thinking at the highest policy levels, must reflect in some fashion current reactions and considerations. Hence it is remarkable that, at a time when Romans needed to produce an argument to justify actions of so shocking and brutal a nature, they did not put Carthaginian character or *Punica fides* on center stage. Two generations later, Cicero explained the destruction of Carthage on political, military, and economic grounds.[78] Not a word about inveterate hatred or a fundamental difference of values.

---

[76] Polyb. 36.9.

[77] The sole exception is a claim by defenders of the Romans that they violated no oaths or agreements but accused the Carthaginians of doing so; Polyb. 36.9.16. This, however, comes in the context of rebutting charges made against *Romans* for impiety and injustice, and it makes no allusion to Carthaginian national character.

[78] Cic. *De Leg. Agrar.* 2.87.

The absence of recourse to the perfidious stereotype at a time when Romans could most profitably use it gives cause for serious rethinking. Did the construct of *Punica fides* in fact testify by contrast to that prime Roman virtue of spreading benevolence and protection over the *orbis terrarum*, eventually to be enshrined by Vergil as *parcere subiectis* and *debellare superbos*?[79] Did Romans in fact erect an oppositional model to highlight their integrity in the world of international politics and diplomacy?

The Manipulation of the Image

The phrase *Punica fides* occurs in explicit form no earlier than Sallust among extant texts. And there it is applied not to a Carthaginian at all but to the wily Moorish king Bocchus. Sallust, in recounting Bocchus' wavering maneuvers between Rome and Jugurtha, suggests that he acted more in *Punica fides* than on the basis of public protestations, thus leading both sides on while he pondered which way to move.[80] The label plainly indicates a trope of some kind, already familiar in Sallust's day. But it bears notice that one need not be Punic to engage in *Punica fides*. The phrase lacked a strictly ethnic connotation.

Sallust, of course, did not invent the idea. Carthaginian repute for treachery could serve as an exercise in the rhetorical schools.[81] Cicero, whose penchant for ethnic slurs tainted various folk (whenever it suited his purposes), also branded Carthaginians with untrustworthiness. They were "breakers of treaties."[82] He asserts in a speech that the Phoenicians of old, as attested by memorials and histories, were the most duplicitous of all peoples, and their descendants, the Carthaginians, notorious as violators and breakers of treaties, showed themselves to be true heirs of their forefathers.[83] Consistency, however, was not the orator's strong suit. The motif appears again in another Ciceronian speech, but this time with a very different significance. Carthaginians are deceivers and liars to be sure, but this has nothing to do with their race, rather with their location on the sea, where harbors and commercial exchanges lend themselves to mendacity.[84] The orator also had conflicted views about Hannibal, by no means a mere villain. His *calliditas*, in fact, was

---

[79] Verg. *Aen.* 6.853. Cf. Livy 30.42.17; Appian *Pun.* 250.

[80] Sallust *Iug.* 108.3: *magis Punica fide quam ob ea quae praedicabat*. See further Burck (1943), 311–315.

[81] E.g., Cic. *De Inv.* 1.71; *Ad Her.* 4.20, cf. 4.66.

[82] Cic. *De Off.* 1.38: *foedifragi*.

[83] Cic. *Scaur.* 42: *fallacissimum genus esse Phoenicum . . . ab his orti Poeni . . . multis violatis fractisque foederibus nihil se degenerasse docuerunt*. Additional Ciceronian references and discussion in Burck (1943), 304–311.

[84] Cic. *Leg. Agrar.* 2.95: *non genere sed natura loci*.

in the same category as that of Fabius Maximus.[85] Moreover, Cicero can refer to Carthaginians as exemplary of *calliditas* in a surprisingly positive context: the Romans do not surpass them in cunning, any more than they surpass Gauls in strength, Greeks in art, or Italians in sensibility.[86]

In the age of Augustus, the concept of Punic perfidy clearly had some force—but not with unequivocal consistency. It recurs in Livy, more than once.[87] Most pointedly, he describes the treachery of Hannibal as "even more than Punic."[88] Carthaginian behavior evidently constituted a benchmark for condemnation. Elsewhere the historian alludes, with more than a touch of sarcasm, to Hannibal's violation of a pledge as reverential observance of *Punica fides*.[89] And Livy can employ the motif explicitly as contrast with Roman character. He has the Spartan tyrant Nabis describe Romans as men who hold *fides* as most sacred, while Carthaginians, at least in repute, pay it no heed. Yet there is a notable irony in the context. Nabis in effect throws this in the teeth of Romans who had chosen to attack him in violation (from his vantage point) of *Roman* treaty obligations.[90] Elsewhere Livy distinguishes Roman conscientiousness from Punic craftiness and Greek cunning. But the phraseology here, which employs *calliditas* for Greeks and makes no mention of *fides*, suggests that the expression *Punica fides* is not exactly an acknowledged stock phrase.[91] Livy interestingly does put that phrase in the mouth of Hannibal himself, offering surrender after Zama. The Carthaginian concedes that *Punica fides* may have recently become suspect in Roman eyes, thereby implying that the concept itself need not carry negative overtones.[92] Horace refers to Hannibal as *perfidus* and Carthaginians as *perfidi hostes* (in the context of executing Regulus) but offers no blanket condemnation of the people as an ethnic or racial group.[93]

---

[85] Cic. *De Off.* 1.108. Additional passages cited in Burck (1943), 309. Nepos, *Hann.* 9.2, indeed praises Hannibal as *callidissimus*.

[86] Cic. *Har. Resp.* 19: *nec robore Gallos nec calliditate Poenos nec artibus Graecos nec . . . sensu Italos ipsos . . . superavimus*; 4.66. Cf. also Livy 22.22.15, where Punic *calliditas* has a positive connotation.

[87] See the passages collected by Burck (1943), 317–336.

[88] Livy 21.4.9: *perfidia plus quam Punica*.

[89] Livy 22.6.12: *Punica religione servata fides*. See his allusions also to *Punica fraus*; 22.48.1, 30.22.6. Cf. 28.44.4: *infidis sociis*. He describes a Carthaginian artifice as *Punico ingenio*; 34.61.13.

[90] Livy 34.31.2–4.

[91] Livy 42.47.7: *religionis haec Romanae esse, non versutiarum Punicarum neque calliditatis Graecae*. Cf. Paladino (1991), 179–185. The context is a discussion of dubious Roman policy in outwitting Perseus of Macedon. A very similar pronouncement on this matter appears in Diod. 30.7.1 which contrasts Roman virtue with Phoenician connivance.

[92] Livy 30.30.27. Livy has both admiration for and animosity toward Hannibal; 21.4.5–9. A thoroughly positive portrait of Hannibal occurs in the biography by Livy's near contemporary Cornelius Nepos. Cf. Burck (1943), 315–317.

[93] Horace *Carm.* 3.5.33, 4.4.49.

There is, in short, ambivalence and pluralism, hardly consistent character assassination.

The most resonant voice of the era leaves the most enduring mark. Vergil's *Aeneid* deserves pride of place here. The great epic sang of Rome's origins and its destiny. A central part of that destiny, of course, was the titanic clash with Carthage that would determine the rule of the western Mediterranean and the future of the Roman Empire. Vergil signals that momentous rivalry in a moving and memorable tale that emblematized the coming struggle long before the founding of the city itself: the narrative of Aeneas and Dido. At the very outset of the poem, Vergil juxtaposes Rome and Carthage, sets them in geographic and political contrast, foreshadowing the great and grim contests that would one day grip the two powers and bring glorious triumph to Rome.[94] Dido, the Phoenician queen of Carthage, and Aeneas, the Trojan hero whose line would bring Rome into being, serve as symbols of the two nations, and the bitter termination of their union, punctuated by Dido's suicide, presaged the future conflict. Dido herself proclaims it by vowing vengeance and a relentless pursuit of Aeneas even after death.[95] And, on the brink of suicide, she delivers a mighty curse, not only on Aeneas but on all his race to come, enjoining the Carthaginians to wreak ferocious retaliation on the Trojans and their heirs.[96]

Fierce rivalry and violent encounters, however, need not entail ethnic disdain or disparagement. The *Aeneid* indeed suggests precisely the reverse. Insofar as Dido represents the values of the Phoenician nation, Vergil's epic holds them up to admiration and respect. Even the clash between the powers need never have happened but for the jealousy of the goddesses and the inexorability of fate. Dido, prompted by Mercury, offers gracious hospitality to the Trojans.[97] The Temple of Juno, dedicated by Dido, contains images of the Trojan War, thus bringing painful memories to the awestruck Aeneas but demonstrating the Phoenicians' connections to the legends of Troy and its heroes.[98] When the Trojan spokesman Ilioneus laments the initial resistance to the landing of Trojans on Carthaginian shores, Dido offers apology, reassurance, and hospitality. More tellingly, she asks them to consider her city their own. If they wish to settle, Trojan and Tyrian would be on the same level.[99] In her banquet for the visitors, the queen's toast

---

[94] Verg. *Aen.* 1.12–22; cf. 10.11–14. It is not clear why Reed (2007), 73, interprets this as ethnic allegory.
[95] Verg. *Aen.* 4.381–387.
[96] Verg. *Aen.* 4.609–629.
[97] Verg. *Aen.* 1.297–304.
[98] Verg. *Aen.* 1.441–519; cf. 1.613–629.
[99] Verg. *Aen.* 1.561–578, esp. 1.573–574: *urbem quam statuo vestra est . . . Tros Tyriusque mihi nullo discrimine agetur.* Horsfall (1973/1974), 4–5, presumes, on the basis of future Roman/

linked the two people in joy and friendship.[100] When her sister Anna urges a union with Aeneas, she puts it in terms of a joint realm and collaboration by the nations.[101] One might note even that the negotiations between Juno and Venus, though each had her own cynical agenda, expressed, however deviously, mutual desire for peace, unity, and a mingling of the peoples.[102] That outcome, of course, would not come to pass. But Vergil retained the vision. The ruined city of Carthage in fact was resurrected with Roman colonists in the era of Vergil himself. The poet's sense of a peaceful blend perhaps took its cue from that event.[103]

Dido herself is a compelling figure—and an admirable one. She escaped the city of Tyre after the murder of her husband and seizure of the realm by her brother. She took the lead in gathering wealth and resources for a major settlement abroad. Her shrewdness allowed the new colonists of Carthage to purchase enough land for a great city, to establish laws, and to install a government.[104] Dido cut an impressive figure as ruler of the realm, issuing directives and distributing tasks in fair and equal fashion.[105] Even as she resolved to end her life, she took pride in the achievements of avenging her husband and building a celebrated city.[106] And Vergil's judgment upon her death is moving: she perished before her time, taken neither by fate nor by a deserved death.[107]

If Dido is symbol of Carthage, the poet's construct is far from hostile. And where is *Punica fides*? The answer is striking and important. Insofar as perfidy enters the story, the label fits Aeneas, not Dido. Venus' plans for Aeneas require the goddess to entrap Dido with guile and deceit.[108] And it is the hero's betrayal of his lover, of course, that triggers her suicide and forecasts the clash between the nations. Dido, quite properly, twice hurls the epithet *perfide* at her erstwhile consort—and once brands him as *perfidus* to another.[109] The queen denounces Aeneas' treachery and laments

---

Carthaginian hostility, that Dido must be disingenuous here. Vicenzi (1985), 98–99, more plausibly, takes it as a serious offer. Cf. also Reed (2007), 88–90.

[100] Verg. *Aen.* 1.731–735.

[101] Verg. *Aen.* 4.47–49.

[102] Verg. *Aen.* 4.90–114. See the analysis of Reed (2007), 94–95.

[103] Cf. Vicenzi (1985), 103–106; Hexter (1992), 352.

[104] Verg. *Aen.* 1.357–369: *dux femina facti*. The story of how Dido cunningly acquired an extensive amount of land for the city of Carthage receives a negative connotation in later authors. But Vergil sets it in a decidedly positive context. See Starks (1999), 268–271.

[105] Verg, *Aen.* 1.503–508.

[106] Verg. *Aen.* 4.652–662.

[107] Verg. *Aen.* 4.696–697: *nam quia nec fato, merita nec morte peribat, sed misera ante diem*.

[108] Verg. *Aen.* 1.673: *dolis*; 1.682: *dolos*. See also 4.95: *una dolo divum si femina victa duorum est* and 4.296: *dolos* (with regard to Aeneas). See Starks (1999), 274–276.

[109] Verg. *Aen.* 4.305, 366, 421.

that *fides* is nowhere safe.[110] Most tellingly, she castigates the whole race of Trojans as violators of oaths.[111] She resorts, in fact, to some sardonic mockery in summing up Aeneas' *fides* as transfer of his *penates* and bearing his father on his shoulders.[112] Dido alludes to her own bad faith just once. And there she refers to breaking *fides* with her murdered husband by not keeping herself chaste thereafter.[113] The unspoken reason for that, of course, is her own betrayal at the hands of Venus and Aeneas, The legendary emblems of Rome were the real source of the perfidy. Insofar as *Punica fides* had entered the Roman imagination, Vergil turned it on its head. Like Plautus he subverted the stereotype and provided a broad-minded vision that better reflected Roman sensibilities and understanding.[114]

To be sure, the stigma had footing in the early Empire. Valerius Maximus describes Punic *calliditas* as known the world over and juxtaposes it to Roman *prudentia*.[115] Silius Italicus characterizes Carthaginian soldiers as trained in deception and never slow to entrap their foes.[116] The image of Carthaginians as inveterate breakers of treaties held sway, as Appian attests in the mid–second century CE.[117]

The dark repute of Carthage persisted, indeed expanded.[118] Yet a notable fact, easily overlooked because too obvious, needs emphasis. References to *Punica fides* or comparable characterizations occur well after the ancient Carthaginians themselves, the most awesome of Roman enemies, had been eradicated. The destruction of Carthage by Rome in 146 BCE had put a definitive end to any threat that could be mustered from that source. The

---

[110] Verg. *Aen.* 4.373: *nusquam tuta fides*.

[111] Verg. *Aen.* 4.541–542: *necdum Laomedonteae sentis periuria gentis?*

[112] Verg. *Aen.* 4.597–598.

[113] Verg. *Aen.* 4.550–552. Horsfall's claim, (1973/1974), 6, that Vergil here censures Dido's moral lapse, has little to commend it. See the comments of Vicenzi (1985), 99–100, and Starks (1999), 276–277.

[114] See, for example, Ovid's sympathetic portrait of Dido. He quotes her epitaph that blames Aeneas for bringing about her death; *Fasti* 3.545–550; *Her.* 7.195–196. And he composed a fictitious letter of Dido to Aeneas that repeatedly reminded the Trojan of his violation of *fides*; *Her.* 7.7–8, 7.18, 7.30, 7.57, 7.81–82. Horsfall (1973/1974), 1–13, takes *Punica fides* for granted as an underlying motif and hence interprets Dido's every action in that light, reckoning Vergil's portrait of Dido as a harsh condemnation of her violence, greed, duplicity, and hatred. But the motif does not appear in the text, and Horsfall's use of it as a touchstone is questionable methodology. He is followed, with subtle modifications, by Syed (2005b), 143–162. Starks (1999), 255–283, considerably exaggerates the prevalence of negative Punic stereotypes among Roman writers, but he rightly exempts Vergil from that group. Similarly, Vicenzi (1985), 97–106.

[115] Val. Max. 7.4.4: *illa toto terrarum orbe infamis Punica calliditas, Romana elusa prudentia*; cf. 9.6.ext.1: *verum ut ipsum fontem perfidiae*; 2.9.8, 7.3.ext.8, 7.4.ext.2. This does not, however, prevent him from bestowing high praise on Hannibal; 5.1.ext.6.

[116] Sil. Ital. 3.231–234. On Silius and *fides*, see Vessey (1975), 391–405; Burck (1988), 49–60.

[117] Appian *Pun.* 53, 62–64.

[118] See, e.g., Plut. *Mor.* 799 D, who does not, however, speak of deception or treachery.

concept of Punic perfidy emerges in the generation after that cataclysmic event. Perhaps it could serve to justify the dastardly deed and to deflect criticism, internal and external. And the Carthaginians no longer existed as an entity to challenge the construct. Yet even here, as we have seen, ambivalence rather than uniform censure prevailed. Roman depictions were more admiring than adverse.

The Enhancement of the Image

Carthaginian achievements on the intellectual front indeed earned high esteem in the cultivated circles of Greeks and Romans alike. One might note, for example, that the Carthaginian explorer Hanno in the fifth century BCE composed a *Periplus* that described or at least claimed to describe an expedition along the West African coast. The work, whether as genuine exploration or as fanciful wonder-tale, received translation into Greek, perhaps in the Hellenistic period, and gained wide circulation, cited also by Roman geographers.[119] The learned Hasdrubal in the mid–second century BCE took on a Greek persona himself, adopting the name Clitomachus, moving to Athens to study with Carneades, acquiring a command of Platonic, Aristotelian, and Stoic tenets, and succeeding Carneades as head of his school.[120] Yet he had not abandoned his Carthaginian identity. Hasdrubal taught philosophy in Punic to his compatriots. And, among other works, he composed a *Consolatio* to the Carthaginians for the destruction of their city. Nor did this estrange him from Rome. Hasdrubal moved freely in Roman circles, dedicating compositions to the senator L. Censorinus and the satirist Lucilius. Roman appreciation for Carthaginian achievement eclipsed any nasty stereotypes.

And there is more. We know of a certain Laetus, either a Greek or a Roman writing in Greek, probably in the second century BCE, though cited only by Christian authors like Clement, Tatian, and Eusebius. Laetus, we are told, undertook to translate the works of certain Phoenician historians into Greek. Their writings, steeped in both Greek and Jewish legends, included tales of the rape of Europa, the arrival of Menelaus in Phoenicia, and the relations of Hiram of Tyre with King Solomon of Judah.[121] This obviously attests to Greek rather than Roman interest in Phoenician literature. But the circulation of these works among the intelligentsia of an increasingly Roman Mediterranean probably reached the elite of Rome. They would certainly not have discouraged it.

---

[119] *GGM* 1.1–14; Pliny *NH* 2.169; Mela 3.90.
[120] Diog. Laert. 4.67. Cf. Momigliano (1975), 4–5.
[121] Stern (1974), I, 129.

Two other obscure Hellenistic authors, Dius and Menander, known to us only through Josephus, bear notice in this connection. Josephus identifies them as historians who conscientiously transcribed the archives of Tyre, turning the Punic into Greek for the purpose of composing histories of the Phoenicians.[122] The endeavors demonstrate a keen Hellenic curiosity about Phoenician institutions and history. They also reveal that the Tyrians at least kept records scrupulously and made them available to researchers. Josephus himself claims to have consulted the Tyrian archives, which he praises as preserving with care the chronicles of Phoenician history.[123] Once again, this gives no direct attestation of Roman interest. But Josephus evidently expected that his plaudits to Phoenicians would be plausible and acceptable to Roman readers.

Direct attestation occurs elsewhere. Sallust demonstrates the attraction to Roman researchers of Punic records. The historian affirms that he drew on material translated from the *Punici libri* of king Hiempsal of Numidia, apparently a translation from Punic into Latin commissioned upon Sallust's own request.[124]

Phoenicians justifiably took pride in their scientific accomplishments. And they proceeded to trumpet them in the age of the Roman Empire. The astrological poem of Dorotheus of Sidon in the first century CE claimed the origin of astronomy for his own people, a claim bought by Roman writers like Strabo, Propertius, and Pliny.[125] If Posidonius could accept the Phoenicians' insistence that atomic theory originated with them, Roman writers had no difficulty in acknowledging Phoenician origins for astronomy. The geographer Pomponius Mela, from Roman Spain and writing in Latin in the first century CE, put the matter quite pointedly. He asserted that the Phoenicians are accomplished in both war and peace, skilled in literature and the arts, no mere sailors but rulers over nations.[126] The tribute was echoed by Pliny, who accords Phoenicians the *magna gloria* of inventing the alphabet and the arts of astronomy, navigation, and military science.[127] For Florus, the Carthaginians were simply a *nobilis populus*.[128] And nearly three centuries later Augustine could still cite learned men who pointed to the great wisdom stored in "Punic books."[129]

[122] Jos. *Ant.* 8.144–149, 9.283; *CAp.* 1.12–120. See the comments of Troiani (1991), 215–216.

[123] Jos. *Ant.* 8.55; *CAp.* 1.106–107. Whether Josephus, in fact, consulted them may be questioned. But this does not mean that the existence of the archives is in doubt, as implied by Mazza (1988), 549.

[124] Sallust *Iug.* 17.7.

[125] Strabo 16.2.24; Prop. 2.27.1–4; Pliny *NH* 5.13.67.

[126] Mela 1.65. On Punic literary accomplishment, see Garbini (1991), 489–494; Bohak (2005), 229–230.

[127] Pliny *NH* 5.67.

[128] Florus 1.22.2.

[129] Aug. *Epist.* 17.2.

To conclude. In the age of the Punic wars, the Romans did not require a construct of Carthaginians as barbarous, wicked, and faithless to bolster their self-esteem or exhibit their superiority. Stereotypes circulated about Punic merchantmen with an eye for gain and a penchant for double-dealing, a reputation that naturally adhered to commercial seafarers. But they did not define Carthage in the Roman imagination. Indeed the stereotypes could be mocked, undermined, and inverted, as in Plautus' *Poenulus* and Vergil's *Aeneid*. Despite three devastating and memorable wars, Romans never embraced the idea that ethnicity and character molded Carthaginians into treacherous violators of compacts, the reverse of Roman moral steadfastness.

The concept of *Punica fides* in Roman thinking emerged late, after the destruction of Carthage, and the phrase itself later still (at least in our extant sources). Insofar as it had value for Roman self-perception, this may have come once Carthage had been wiped off the map and Romans felt a need to explain (at least to themselves) why such an act made sense. Eradication of the Carthaginian people as an entity also allowed them the more easily to be shaped and reshaped as a concept. They were not around any longer to object. But even then the negative image of Carthage did not dominate Roman sensibility or pervade Roman consciousness. Vergil's nuanced, complex, and largely sympathetic treatment of Dido at the legendary origins of discord between the powers suffices to demonstrate that. Romans respected and profited from Carthaginian learning. Some indeed knew Punic, a source of pride, not embarrassment. The fierce adversarial relationship on the battlefield coexisted with a more fundamental mutual regard that eclipsed slurs and slander.

One last celebrated episode merits mention here. Scipio Aemilianus, conqueror of Carthage in the Third Punic War, burst into tears when he witnessed flames rising over the city whose destruction he had ordered. That scene was not a fictive invention. Polybius witnessed it and recorded it.[130] In an important sense, the event encapsulates the entangled relationship between the nations. Rome could take pride in defeat of the great adversary. But elimination of the ancient city also struck a somewhat different chord, powerful feelings of respect for a long-standing and highly accomplished rival. Romans' sentiments transcended ethnic labeling and reductive alterity.

The tension that we postulate may not have had such intensity for the protagonists. Without paradox, Romans could both differentiate themselves from and incorporate the foreigner. The Punic Hanno in the *Poenulus* dressed, spoke, and behaved differently from the Greek, that is, Roman, characters in the play. But he could also exemplify Roman virtues. Hannibal

---

[130] Polyb. 38.21.22. On Scipio's tears, see Astin (1967), 282–287; Momigliano (1975), 22–23.

was the quintessential and most formidable antagonist. But he could be represented, without contradiction, as a worthy and generous admirer of Scipio Africanus. Carthaginians might, in some circles, carry the stigma of treaty breakers. But for thoughtful intellectuals in Rome and in Greece, they were regarded less as the transgressors than as the transgressed. Romans who commanded the language rendered Punic agricultural treatises and historical works into Latin. There is no inconsistency in any of this. As Romans expanded their authority in the Mediterranean, east and west, they developed a self-assurance and a conviction of superiority that did not require repeated denigration of the *Poeni*. Instead, they appropriated Carthaginian achievements and manipulated Carthaginian images in complex and shifting ways that produced a multidimensional construct—one that may indeed have approximated the truth.

Chapter 5

CAESAR ON THE GAULS

Julius Caesar fought for nearly a decade in Gaul. And he wrote seven books of commentaries on the wars. That corpus offers an invaluable entrance to a critical subject: the mode of representing to a Roman readership a foe with a long history of hostility and one that had recently claimed many Roman lives while straining the manpower and resources of the nation for several bloody years.

Caesar the general had little prior experience with the people against whom he would wage war. But Caesar the author could draw on prior descriptions, either knowledgeable or fanciful. How far he did so remains controversial and perhaps in the end, for our purposes, unimportant.[1] What we have in the *De Bello Gallico* is what the author chose to compose and convey. And it discloses what a Roman readership could be expected to find palatable and credible.

Prior Portraits

Prior accounts, however, provide a necessary setting. Gallic stereotypes had certainly circulated well before Caesar sat down to write. Gauls were allegedly tall and muscular, immoderate drinkers, greedy, fickle, and untrustworthy, internally divided, and, though frightening in their initial attack, incapable of maintaining the offensive. All this already appeared in Polybius and much of it in Posidonius, if one can judge from the comments of Diodorus and Strabo. The authors had their own agendas. And ethnographic writings generally tended to pick out the traits that would appeal to readers interested in the striking rather than the subtle.

Caesar may well have been familiar with some of this. It would be surprising if a cultivated Roman intellectual who included an ethnographic

---

[1] Useful summaries of the ethnographic tradition that would have been familiar to Caesar can be found in Tierney (1960), 189–197; Riggsby (2006), 47–59.

excursus on the Gauls did not avail himself of material on the subject.[2] How assiduous he was in this matter remains beyond our grasp. And what might he have found? Those writing from the vantage point of Rome were hardly inclined to paint a rosy portrait. Gauls or Celts represented inveterate adversaries of Rome. The Gallic sack of Rome in the early fourth century BCE remained a blot on the city's history. Repeated battles engaged Romans with Celts in northern Italy during the third and second centuries. One might anticipate a dark image. Yet, perhaps surprisingly, even if Caesar did his homework with some thoroughness, he would not have found a consistently hostile or disparaging portrait of the Celts in his sources.

The Achaean historian Polybius, writing in Rome under Roman patronage in the later second century BCE, took up the subject. He dealt with the wars of Rome against the Celts. And his comments reflect attitudes of ambivalence that mingled contempt with fear and respect. The contests were still fresh in Roman memory, indeed not yet obviously ended. Polybius had reason to detail Gallic faults, perhaps to reassure Roman readers or possibly to make them wary. Celts had a general reputation for greed and untrustworthiness, so the historian maintains, perfectly capable of appropriating the property of neighbors or allies.[3] They were excessive drinkers and notoriously fickle and unpredictable in their behavior.[4] Moreover, though their opening assault might be fierce, they did not have the capacity to sustain it.[5] The negative characteristics stand out.[6]

But that is not the end of the matter. Polybius also shows begrudging admiration. The Celts' hostility to Rome was deep.[7] And they could strike terror into their foes.[8] Polybius sketches those qualities that made Gauls worthy adversaries for Rome. They were men of size and beauty, and they displayed boldness and daring on the battlefield.[9] Polybius praised the good order of their military formation.[10] And he provides a telling comment on

[2] The Gallic ethnography appears in Caes. *BG* 6.11–29. See the discussion of Kremer (1994), 202–218, with bibliographical references. On what information and opinions might have been available, see the fine discussion of Williams (2001), 18–69. The valuable observations of Woolf (1998), 48–76, on Roman attitudes toward the Gauls, are largely drawn from later sources.

[3] Polyb. 2.7.5–6, 2.19.3–4.

[4] Polyb. 2.19.4, 2.32.7–8, 3.70.4, 3.78.2.

[5] Polyb. 2.33.2–3, 2.35.6.

[6] Williams (2001), 79–88, stresses the negative in Polybius' account, to the exclusion of all else, a somewhat reductive analysis. He puts excessive emphasis on Polyb. 2.17.9–12, which describes Celts as relatively primitive peoples, largely absorbed in war and agriculture, leading nomadic lives, and deficient in art and culture. But even in this passage Polybius speaks of their simplicity of life, not of flaws in character or nature.

[7] Polyb. 3.34.2, 3.78.5.

[8] Polyb. 2.18.1–2, 2.31.7.

[9] Polyb. 2.15.7, 2.18.1–2, 2.35.2, 3.34.2.

[10] Polyb. 2.29.5.

the motivation for their renewed struggle against Rome in the early third century: they resisted Roman encroachment, which threatened wholesale expulsion and destruction.[11] Even in the hands of Polybius, who did not take kindly to Gauls, they hardly emerge as cardboard figures. The historian eschewed mere clichés and stereotypes.

Polybius supplied no ethnographic study of the Celts. Posidonius, writing in the next generation, certainly did. The work unfortunately is lost, but parts of it evidently found their way to Diodorus and Strabo. Whether they reflect the opinions of Posidonius requires no investigation here. They surely worked with material familiar to and conveyed by Posidonius, even if filtered through their own vantage points in the late first century BCE.[12]

Diodorus took an interest in ethnography. He devoted seven chapters in his history to a digression on the Celts. Much of it followed the standard lines of climate, geography, natural resources, appearance, clothing, customs, and beliefs. Comments are generally bland and descriptive. But they give a sense of the impressions of Gauls that circulated among Greek writers contemporaneous with Caesar.[13] The fondness for wine reappears here—the unmixed variety, taken to excess and often inducing a stupor or mad behavior—a great boon for Italian wine merchants.[14] Diodorus also notes the avarice conventionally ascribed to Gauls, although he tempers it with the observation that they never touch the vast amounts of gold deposited in the temples as dedications to the gods.[15] Like Polybius, he comments on their tall stature, white and muscular bodies, and blond hair, with a touch of bleach to enhance it. Diodorus has some fun with this, as he does with Gallic moustaches that serve as a sieve through which their beverages pass.[16] The historian passes no negative judgment here, and certainly does not seek to project an image of the alien. Indeed, when he records the Gallic practice of rewarding the men whom they admire with the prime cuts of meat at the table, he compares Homer's verses on the similar awards bestowed on Ajax after his contest with Hector.[17] He comments further on their hospitality, a readiness to host strangers and to inquire of their business only after providing a meal.[18] The Gauls' penchant for challenges among themselves to individual combat, even over insignificant disputes,

[11] Polyb. 2.21.9.
[12] See the careful discussion of Malitz (1993), 169–198.
[13] On the use of Posidonius by Diodorus and Strabo, see Tierney (1960), 203–211. Kremer (1994), 266–272, treats Diodorus' excursus but confines himself largely to summary rather than analysis. Cf. the trenchant remarks on Posidonius and the Celts by Momigliano (1975), 67–72.
[14] Diod. 5.26.3.
[15] Diod. 5.27.4.
[16] Diod. 5.28.1–3.
[17] Diod. 5.28.4.
[18] Diod. 5.28.5.

may not be admirable. But Diodorus explains it as stemming from their belief in the transmigration of souls—a view, so he remarks, that they share with the Pythagoreans.[19] We might cringe from the description of severed heads mounted on the necks of horses as a signal of victory or the pickling and preserving of heads to put on display.[20] But Diodorus allows himself just a single judgmental comment: to retain furor against men of the same race even after death is akin to bestial behavior.[21] In general Diodorus avoids polemic. He prefers the posture of the neutral ethnographer.

Insofar as Diodorus offers assessments, they are a mixed bag. The Gauls are fearsome in appearance, harsh and deceptive in conversation, boastful and threatening, disparaging others, and overblown in their language.[22] At the same time, Diodorus gives them high marks for sharpness of wit, not by any means lacking in erudition. Their numbers include philosophers, lyric poets whom they designate as bards, theologians whom they call druids, and diviners to whom they pay high honor.[23] The practice of human sacrifice, unmentioned by Polybius, does receive notice in this context. Diodorus finds it especially peculiar and incredible, even offering a rather graphic description of the process. Yet he stops short of condemnation. It was a means of divination, always presided over by a philosopher, a link between men and gods.[24] Distinctions among these religious and/or secular leaders seem confused in Diodorus' presentation. It is unclear where, if at all, lines are to be drawn among bards, philosophers, diviners, and druids. But the historian plainly has respect for these holy men, even claiming that they can halt warring armies in their tracks, as if by magic, thus causing Ares to yield to the Muses.[25] Only in the final chapter of his excursus does Diodorus vent criticism and suggest barbarism. The most distant Celts are reputed (he does not endorse the notion) to be cannibals. The ferocity of the people is notorious, Diodorus asserts, from their sack of Rome, plunder of Delphi, overrunning of parts of Europe and Asia Minor, and sacrificing prisoners and criminals to the gods.[26] And he adds, almost as a gratuitous appendix, that Gauls prefer homosexual trysts to their wives, offering their bodies without hesitation and without shame.[27] Just what one is to make of this mishmash is difficult to say. It certainly provides some fodder for those

---

[19] Diod. 5.28.5–6. The Gauls preferred individual combat on the battlefield against foreign foes as well; 5.29.2.
[20] Diod. 5.29.4–5.
[21] Diod. 5.29.5.
[22] Diod. 5.31.1.
[23] Diod. 5.31.1–3.
[24] Diod. 5.31.3–4.
[25] Diod. 5.31.5.
[26] Diod. 5.32.3–6.
[27] Diod. 5.32.7. The Gauls' reputation of fondness for homosexuality was not an invention of Diodorus—or of Posidonius for that matter. It appears already in Aristotle *Pol.* 1269b.

who might wish to find reasons for condemnation. On the whole, however, Diodorus conveys information that is more respectful than damning, a collection of curiosities rather than censures, a delineation of differences but a sense, even on the intellectual and cultural levels, of a certain familiarity.

Parallel comments can be found in Strabo of Amasia, writing in the age of Augustus. He remarks on the Celts' bellicosity, their large physique, their spiritual and intellectual leadership from bards, diviners, and druids who are learned in natural science and moral philosophy, their belief in the immortality of souls, their boastfulness and fondness for ornamentation, their fastening of enemies' heads on the necks of their horses and the embalmming of them to put on display, and human sacrifice for purpose of divination supervised by the druids.[28] Strabo explicitly cites Posidonius for the Celtic practice of displaying severed heads.[29] One may reasonably infer that he and Diodorus both drew on the Posidonian ethnography—although it does not follow that they adopted it wholesale. Each author supplies some information not to be found in the other and perhaps derived from elsewhere. And Strabo had the advantage of Caesar's *De Bello Gallico* to consult as well.[30]

Strabo's presentation, however, noticeably refrains from judgment or criticism. He comments on the Gauls' eagerness for battle but adds that they are otherwise simple and honorable. Their military tactics are straightforward and uncomplicated, owing more to forcefulness and daring than to calculation, thus making them vulnerable to stratagems. But they can come together when they believe that their neighbors have been wronged. Strabo further notes, as did Diodorus, that Gauls are interested in education (*paideia*) and learning.[31] On Gallic customs, Strabo sticks almost entirely to descriptive and neutral statements. The sole exception is his characterization of the display of severed heads on horses' necks as barbarous and alien. Yet it is interesting that even here Strabo comments that Posidonius at first found the practice hateful but, with greater familiarity, took it calmly.[32] That may well describe his own reaction. The digression is certainly not a diatribe.[33]

---

[28] Strabo 4.4.2–5. Kremer (1994), 304–320, offers a useful perspective on Strabo's Celtic digression, noting his emphasis on the differences between the Gauls' practices and character prior to Caesar's conquest (on which he focuses) and their behavior after the submission to Rome; Strabo 4.4.2.

[29] Strabo 4.4.5.

[30] So, for instance, Strabo's discussion of the Belgae in 4.3 clearly stems from Caes. *BG* 2.4. It is unnecessary to hypothesize, as some have done, that Strabo used Timagenes as an intermediary. So, rightly, Kremer (1994), 301–302, 310–311, 318–319. Similarly, Dueck (2000), 94–95, 182–183. Kremer (1994), 304–320, makes a good case in general for Strabo's independence of judgment, not being a writer slavishly reliant on his sources.

[31] Strabo 4.4.2. See also 4.1.5 on the Gauls' eagerness to school themselves in Greek.

[32] Strabo 4.4.5.

[33] Cf. the sympathetic treatment by Sherwin-White (1967), 1–13.

Such are our best, if only fragmentary, glimpses of the perspectives on Gauls that might have held the field in the age of Caesar. Greek writers seem to have taken a greater interest in them than did Latin authors prior to the Roman invasion. Cato the Elder, a contemporary of Polybius, was an exception. He had observed Celts at first hand in the Hannibalic war and in Spain. His *Origines* treated Italian peoples and cities, including the Gauls of northern Italy. How much detail he provided cannot be known, for this important historical work survives only in small fragments. But one of those fragments has notable relevance for our purposes. Cato made the sweeping statement that most of Gaul pursues two things most assiduously: the art of war and speaking with wit.[34] The comment, brief though it be, evidently represents a general judgment, and by no means a hostile one.[35] More significantly perhaps, it corresponds closely with Greek impressions, as conveyed by Diodorus and Strabo, and probably to be found in Posidonius. The warlike tendencies of the Celts appear in every treatment, obvious and unsurprising. Less obvious, hence particularly noteworthy, was their interest in education and literature, a point that appears in both Diodorus and Strabo.[36] One might note also that Cicero was acquainted with Divitiacus, an eminent druid, whom he describes as a lover of learning and one who predicts the future through a combination of augury and conjecture.[37] The image of the Gauls in late Republican Rome had a complex character, generating mixed reactions of curiosity, distress, and admiration.

The most hostile portrait, in fact, occurs in a speech of Cicero dating to 69 BCE. The orator spoke, in his customarily uninhibited and uncompromising style, on behalf of M. Fonteius, accused of extortion and oppression of the Gauls during his three-year governorship of Gallia Transalpina.[38] The prosecutors, as was common in such cases, brought provincial witnesses to testify against the defendant, and Cicero in typical fashion did his best to discredit them. In this instance, he pulled out all the stops, including ancient history, to remind jurors of the Gallic sack of Rome and the assault on Delphi, events rather remote both in time and in relevance. But the orator did not hold back. He represented the Gauls as inveterate enemies of

---

[34] Cato *Orig.* F2.3, Beck and Walter: *pleraque Gallia duas res industriosissime persequitur, rem militarem et argute loqui.* See Momigliano (1975), 65; Williams (2001), 79–80.

[35] One might observe also that Cato accepted the legend, perpetrated by Greeks, that the Veneti of northern Italy possessed Trojan origins; *Orig.* F2.12, Beck and Walter. Although he distinguishes Veneti from Galli, he was plainly willing to have non-Roman settlers in the north share in the legendary past of the classical world. Cf. Williams (2001), 72–79, who, however, may overstress Cato's distinction between Gauls and Veneti.

[36] Diod. 5.31.1; Strabo 4.1.5, 4.4.2.

[37] Cic. *De Div.* 1.90.

[38] On Cicero's representations of the Gauls in this speech, see the discussion of Kremer (1994), 85–104. Cf. Clavel-Lévêque (1983), 613–618.

Rome, the most hostile and most cruel of foes.[39] He even conjures up the specter of a new Gallic war or imagines one already under way.[40] He does what he can to blacken the witnesses against Fonteius, particularly Indutiomarus, leader of the Allobroges. In the process, he takes the defamation to a broader level, claiming that even the most distinguished native of Gaul does not bear comparison with the lowliest of Romans. The evidence of their testimony is worthless since they care naught for oaths and have no respect for divine authority. They do not wage war on behalf of their own religion; they conduct assaults on all religions. Indeed they take up arms against the immortal gods themselves.[41] And, worst of all, they practice human sacrifice, that most cruel and barbaric of customs.[42] A rather hefty charge sheet. But the exaggeration is patent. As is notorious, the same Allobroges whom Cicero defames as faithless witnesses here, he employs only a few years later as trustworthy witnesses against the Catilinarians, and they were generously rewarded for their testimony by the Senate.[43] The overblown rhetoric falls properly within the conventions of the criminal courtroom, but it hardly reflects the authentic convictions of contemporaries.[44] The *metus gallicus* was a convenient ploy, often slung about in Latin writings but hard to reckon as a deep-seated fear in Roman consciousness.[45] Few Romans would have taken seriously the prospect of a Gallic invasion or uprising. Cicero's wildly distorted picture of the Celts' war on all religions and all gods must have been understood as a concoction for rhetorical purposes. And the practice of human sacrifice by Gauls had long been familiar to the Romans, without stirring repulsion or horror.[46] Cicero utilized some popular negative images, ancient memories, and twisted stereotypes. The forensic context encouraged them. And the conventions were seen for what they were—far from a faithful representation of general sentiment.

The Caesarian Rendering

Julius Caesar took up his pen under very different circumstances. His experience with Gauls was direct and extensive. He did not mindlessly parrot Posidonius or convey a stream of clichés. Caesar's diplomatic dealings with

---

[39] Cic. *Pro Font.* 13, 30, 32–33, 35, 41, 43.
[40] Cic. *Pro Font.* 44, 46, 49.
[41] Cic. *Pro Font.* 29–30; cf. 12, 23, 26.
[42] Cic. *Pro Font.* 31: *illam immanem ac barbaram consuetudinem hominum immolandorum.*
[43] Cic. *Cat.* 4.5, 4.10; Sallust *Cat.* 50.1, 52.36.
[44] Contra Woolf (1998), 61–62, who takes the rhetoric as speaking to ingrained prejudices and anxieties in Rome.
[45] On the *metus gallicus*, see Bellen (1985), who exaggerates its potency. Cf. Kremer (1994), 99–103, who also puts more weight on this feature than it deserves.
[46] Cf. Livy 38.47.12.

148 IMPRESSIONS OF THE "OTHER"

Gallic leaders and envoys, his encounters with generals, chieftains, and the rank and file on the battlefield gave him insights and understandings unavailable to ethnographers. It does not, of course, follow that his observations are accurate, dispassionate, or reliable. How closely they relate to the realities of Gallic behavior or belief cannot be ascertained with any confidence. But they do allow us to penetrate somewhat into the mentality of the man and to gain a sense of the portrait that he expected to resonate with his readership.

Some of the stereotypes resurface. The *De Bello Gallico* contains occasional allusions to the capriciousness and instability of the Gauls. They act on impulse and they are restless, ever ready for change.[47] The allegation, already present in Polybius, that Gauls are swift and anxious for combat at the outset of a campaign but lose heart upon defeat and have no staying power reappears in Caesar.[48] The historian brands them with recklessness or impetuosity, a characteristic seemingly inherent in the nation.[49] He even has one of their own leaders reproach them for *temeritas*—throwing in foolishness and weakness of will on top of it.[50] Nor are the Celts trustworthy. Caesar more than once alludes to perfidious behavior on the part of the Gauls—or rather some Gauls.[51] Isolated comments also occur in the text suggesting heedlessness, avarice, susceptibility to bribery, or cruelty.[52] But a large majority of such comments refer to particular tribes or particular circumstances. Caesar rarely levels them as sweeping accusations applicable to all Gauls, or as characteristics that constitute national traits.[53] Taken together as a collective, they amount to a very small proportion of the text, fragmented and scattered through the work—hardly conspicuous or central. Caesar had no agenda to construct a villainous or deficient race with which to place in relief the virtues and advantages of the Romans.[54]

---

[47] Caes. *BG* 2.1.3: *mobilitate et levitate animi novis imperiis studebant*; 3.8.3: *sunt Gallorum subita et repentina consilia*; 4.5.1, 4.13.3; cf. 3.10; cf. Rambaud (1966), 326; Kremer (1994), 161–165, 172–175.

[48] Caes. *BG* 3.19.6: *nam ut ad bella suscipienda Gallorum alacer ac promptus est animus, sic mollis ac minime resistens ad calamitates perferendas mens eorum est.*

[49] Caes. *BG* 7.42.2: *temeritas, quae maxime illi hominum generi est innata*; cf. 6.7.2.

[50] Caes. *BG* 7.77.9.

[51] Caes. *BG* 4.13.1, 7.17.7, 7.54.2.

[52] Caes. *BG* 3.17, 5.56.2, 7.17, 7.37, 7.42, 7.43, 7.77. See also references to Gallic cruelty collected by Riggsby (2006), 231, n. 45; 236, n. 74.

[53] The long article of Heubner (1974), 103–182, despite its promising title, *Das Feindbild in Caesars Bellum Gallicum*, confines itself to Caesar's characterization of certain enemy leaders in book I, picking out the negative comments and reading them reductively as a means of justifying Roman imperial expansion.

[54] Burns (2003), 119–123, 131, mistakenly judges Caesar's overall theme to be one of "a clash of cultures." For Dauge (1981), 105–111, Caesar concerns himself only with the barbarity of the Gauls. Riggsby (2006), 73–105, gives a more accurate and subtle account of the

He may indeed resort to the reverse. Gallic attributes, as has long been recognized, can be made to serve the purpose of shedding an unflattering light on the Romans. The opening chapter of the *Gallic War* signals the direction. Caesar identifies the Belgae as bravest of all the Gallic peoples. And he offers two reasons for it. They are closest to the Germans dwelling across the Rhine, against whom they wage perpetual war. And they stand at the greatest distance from the cultivated civilization of the Roman province, thus experiencing the least traffic of commercial goods that feminize the spirit.[55] Among the Belgae themselves, the Nervii were accounted the most ferocious, for they dwelled at the farthest distance.[56] The Nervii, moreover, took intense pride in remaining impervious to temptation. They kept merchants at a safe distance; they permitted no wine or similar products to be brought into their communities, for they saw such imports as sapping their spirits and weakening their resolve.[57] Caesar carries this motif further in his ethnographic digression, speaking of the Celts in general and offering a near lament for the decline in Gallic valor. Once upon a time, so he ruminates, Gauls exceeded Germans in *virtus*, initiated wars with them, encroached on their territory, and confiscated their lands. But no more. The proximity of Roman provinces, which afford access to ample goods and luxury items from overseas, has enervated them, bringing a string of military defeats, with the result that their *virtus* can no longer compare with that of the Germans.[58] In short, hardy Gauls, in contact with Roman comforts, have gone soft. Use of this motif, the standard trope that luxury enervates the tough, here points a finger at Rome. The seductions of Roman prosperity have caused Gallic valor to crumble. Association with the more "civilized" people made Gauls inferior to their enemies and vulnerable to decay.[59]

Caesar's analysis, however, goes well beyond conventional cliché. It will not do to view his construct simply as corruption of the noble savage through the lures of a cultivated society. Caesar had more in mind than elevating the life of the unrefined and the uncivilized as an ideal attained by ancient Romans and lost by contemporary ones. If Celts succumbed to the

---

similarities between the peoples as presented by Caesar, although his argument that this involved a gradual assimilation by Gauls of Roman values is less plausible.

[55] Caes. *BG* 1.1: *a cultu atque humanitate provinciae longissime absunt, minimeque ad eos mercatores saepe commeant atque ea quae ad effeminandos animos pertinent important.*
[56] Caes. *BG* 2.4.
[57] Caes. *BG* 2.15.3–5, 2.27.5.
[58] Caes. *BG* 6.24.1, 6.24.5–6: *Gallis autem provinciarum propinquitas et transmarinarum rerum notitia multa ad copiam atque usus largitur, paulatim adsuefacti superari multisque victi proeliis ne se quidem ipsi cum illis virtute comparant.*
[59] On Caesar's use of traditional ideas here, see Isaac (2004), 414–416; Schadee (2008), 163–165. For Riggsby (2006), 59–71, Caesar both adapts and subtly deviates from the ethnographic tradition on the Gauls.

enervating effects of Roman affluence, the fault lay at least as much with the Celts as with the Romans. Both sides of the coin count. Caesar does not take sides. Why then appropriate the trope at all?

The intertwining of qualities and the mutual reflections stimulate the writer. Caesar's interest in the Gauls goes beyond depiction of the foe or shaping of the "Other." And the ethnography, at best, takes second place. Caesar calls attention to contexts and characteristics whereby the societies shed light each on the other.[60]

For Rome, *virtus* stands as a value of the highest esteem. It manifests itself most obviously as bravery on the battlefield. No surprise that it appears with great frequency in Caesar's commentaries on the Gallic wars. Perhaps more surprising, and quite striking, is the fact that Gauls can lay claim to it at least as often as Romans. To be more precise, Caesar ascribes it thirty-one times to Gauls and twenty-eight times to Romans (not to mention five times to Germans).[61] That is more than evenhandedness.[62] The author signals that possession of this quality and aspirations toward this objective unite the nations at a fundamental level.[63]

Caesar equates the two in notable fashion. Prior to combat with Ambiorix and the Eburones in 54 BCE, he observes that the combating forces were equal in *virtus* and in zeal for fighting.[64] And much the same statement occurs during the climactic contest at Alesia in 52. According to Caesar, desire for praise and fear of ignominy spurred both sides to *virtus*.[65] Setting Celts and Romans on a level plane in a concept of such centrality for the victor is a matter of serious significance.[66]

The concept comes into play in the very first chapter of the work—and, remarkably, it applies there to Gauls. Caesar introduces the Helvetii as men who stand first among Gauls in *virtus*.[67] He reinforces that judgment a little later by referring to the ancient *virtus* of the Helvetii and

---

[60] Cf. the remarks of Riggsby (2006), 118–132—with different objectives.

[61] McDonnell (2006), 302, n. 28. A slightly different count in Rawlings (1998), 188, n. 30.

[62] Note the pointed comment put into the mouth of the German leader Ariovistus; Caes. BG 1.36.7.

[63] The fact that Caesar applies the term to Gauls right at the start of his work and then repeatedly thereafter weakens the argument of Riggsby (2006), 96–105, that the author sees Gauls gradually adapting to the Roman concept.

[64] Caes. BG 5.34.2: *erant et virtute et studio pugnandi pares*.

[65] Caes. BG 7.80: *utrosque et laudis cupiditas et timor ignominiae ad virtutem excitabant*.

[66] In one instance only, with regard to the battle against the Veneti, does Caesar assert that Roman troops easily exceeded the enemy in *virtus*; BG 3.14.8. This contest is interestingly analyzed by Erickson (2002), 602–618. But Caesar's assertion is quite exceptional, far from typical. Nor does he deny *virtus* even to the Veneti. By contrast note the words of Vercingetorix, who claims that Romans owed a victory not to *virtus* but to artifice and siege warfare; BG 7.29.2; cf. 1.13.6.

[67] Caes. BG 1.1: *Helvetii quoque reliquos Gallos virtute praecedunt*.

affirming that the Helvetii had absorbed the lessons of their fathers and ancestors, who taught them to battle their foes with *virtus* rather than with trickery and to eschew deception.[68] The reference to the *maiores* of the Helvetii as the fount of their values and behavior clearly echoes Roman conceptualization.

Helvetii had no monopoly on this quality. Far from it. Caesar had great admiration for the Belgae in general. And among them he singles out the Bellovaci as preeminent in *virtus*, authority, and numbers.[69] But not they alone. In a single paragraph on the Nervii, Caesar employs the term three times. That hardy folk, in his estimation, allowed no access to merchants, banned the import of wine and everything else that might be conducive to the slackening of their spirit or the diminution of their *virtus*. They were fierce men of great *virtus*, indeed highly critical and accusatory of other Belgae who had surrendered to Rome and had thus cast away their native *virtus*.[70] The author here plainly employs *virtus* as more than courage on the battlefield. It represents an ingrained value tenaciously clung to by Nervii even when abandoned by fellow Belgae. Caesar had his hands full with that formidable foe. In a climactic battle against the Romans, the Nervii, with all hope of victory or survival gone, nevertheless fought with exemplary *virtus* and displayed a greatness of spirit that Caesar could not but admire.[71] The Nervii stood out. But others shared their values. Caesar makes much the same comments about the Aduatuci, allies of the Nervii and the Romans' next target. Incapable of withstanding Roman siege engines, the Aduatuci sued for terms, surrendering most of their weaponry, and were spared. But a minority of the people concealed their arms, fashioned makeshift shields, and attacked Caesar's forces in a sudden sally—though with little hope of success. The author could have branded them with temerity and reckless foolishness. Instead, he depicted them as brave warriors in a desperate fight who placed all hope of success in their *virtus* alone.[72]

Virtus has resonance beyond fortitude in fighting.[73] Caesar, in fact, employs the phrase *virtus belli*, courage in war, with reference to the Senones,

---

[68] Caes. *BG* 1.13.6: *pristinae virtutis Helvetiorum . . . se ita a patribus maioribusque suis didicisse, ut magis virtute quam dolo contenderent aut insidiis niterentur.*

[69] Caes. *BG* 2.4.

[70] Caes. *BG* 2.15: *nullum aditum esse ad eos mercatoribus; nihil pati vini reliquarumque rerum inferri, quod eis rebus relanguescere animos eorum et remitti virtutem existimarent; esse homines feros magnaeque virtutis; increpitare atque incusare reliquos Belgas, qui se populo Romano dedidissent patriamque virtutem proiecissent.*

[71] Caes. *BG* 2.27: *At hostes etiam in extrema spe salutis tantam virtutem praestiterunt . . . ut non nequiquam tantae virtutis homines iudicari deberet . . . animi magnitudo.* For Caesar's treatment of the Nervii, see Kremer (1994), 147–151, with bibliography.

[72] Caes. *BG* 2.33.4: *in una virtute omnis spes salutis consisteret.*

[73] McDonnell (2006), 301, quite misleadingly asserts that *virtus* in Caesar's commentaries almost always denotes martial courage. The misconception is compounded by his claim that

thereby implying that other *virtutes* also existed—for Gauls as for Romans.[74] They existed for Germans too. The Germanic leader Ariovistus expounded at length on his *virtutes*.[75] A more general comparison between Gauls and Germans gained expression in this form as well. Caesar pauses at one point in his narrative to make an observation about the shifting fortunes of the peoples. The Gauls had once exceeded Germans in *virtus*, but the proximity of the Roman province and the availability of luxury goods had engendered so steep a decline that their *virtus* could no longer bear comparison to that of the Germans.[76] The historian refers specifically to military defeats here. But the implications had deeper significance for Gallic character. *Virtus* is, in any case, the Roman measuring rod. Caesar utilizes it readily as a quality once possessed, now compromised, by the Gauls.

A special twist on the term is placed in the mouth of a Gallic chieftain himself. Critognatus, an eminent figure among the Arverni, delivered a powerful speech to an assemblage of Gauls besieged in Alesia, the climactic event of the long war. He dismissed with scorn and derision those who contemplated surrender: they were unworthy even of attending the conclave. He directed his attention instead to those who argued for an assault on the besiegers. Their view appeared to have a consensus, so Critognatus asserted, because a memory of ancient *virtus* still lingered amidst the gathering. His reaction, however, was to turn it upside down. A swift finish is no *virtus* at all, rather the reverse: *mollitia* (softness). It is easier to rush to a sure death than to endure with patience the suffering required to hold out while there is still hope of rescue.[77] A precipitous plunge meant not only destruction for those besieged but a calamitous loss for the Gallic nation as a whole.[78] Caesar here gives voice to a fundamentally Roman conception that prizes *virtus* as something other than, indeed quite different from, warrior impulse. It possesses deeper substance, a sense of inner confidence and commitment to a collective purpose. There can be little doubt that

---

Caesar usually associates *virtus* with his own supporters; 308. That would hardly apply to men like Ariovistus and Critognatus—to whom Caesar assigns the most elaborate speeches. Riggsby (2006), 83–96, offers a more nuanced analysis of *virtus* in Caesar as a matter of mental toughness, discipline, and participation in a collective endeavor. But he too confines the discussion essentially to *virtus* as a military quality.

[74] Caes. *BG* 5.54: *qui virtute belli omnibus gentibus praeferebantur.*

[75] Caes. *BG* 1.44.1. Cf. also, with regard to Germans, 1.36.7. McDonnell (2006), 302, wrongly sees Ariovistus' *virtutes* as solely military qualities.

[76] Caes. *BG* 6.24. On the differences between Gauls and Germans, as depicted by Caesar, see now Schadee (2008), 175–178—with different purposes.

[77] Caes. *BG* 7.77.4–5: *omnium vestrum consensu pristinae residere virtutis memoria videtur; animi est ista mollitia, non virtus, paulisper inopiam ferre non posse; qui se ultro morti offerant facilius reperiuntur quam qui dolorem patienter ferant.* Cf. Riggsby (2006), 89–91.

[78] Caes. *BG* 7.77.9. A similar sentiment in Tac. *Agr.* 42. The best treatment of Critognatus' speech is Riggsby (2006), 107–118.

Caesar shared that sentiment. That makes all the more remarkable the fact that he chose to put it in the mouth of a Gaul. This need not signify that Gauls were coming round to an appreciation of Roman values. Critognatus' audience, after all, concurred with his view only if all else failed.[79] But Caesar's use of a Gallic spokesperson to deliver the most cogent expression of this line suggests that for him the Gauls (at least the wiser among them) shared principles held dear by Rome.

As is well known, Caesar freely acknowledged the struggle of his foes to resist Roman rule and to make a strike for liberty. That acknowledgment constitutes more than just conventional projection, an ascription to any people of a desire to live free of foreign domination. Caesar's narrative betrays genuine admiration. And something beyond: that Gauls had a deep-seated commitment to *libertas* ingrained in the national character.

To be sure, the author affirms that all men by nature have zeal for liberty and despise the condition of servitude. Hence he could expect that nearly all Gauls would be eager to overthrow Roman authority.[80] But he ascribes to the Gallic temperament a more fundamental bent on this score, no mere trait shared with the rest of humanity. Their *libertas*, as he has them present it, is deeply rooted in the traditions of the people. The Veneti, for instance, rallied resistance to Rome by reminding their compatriots that they owed their *libertas* to their ancestors and urged them to cling to that legacy rather than to endure servitude imposed by the Romans.[81] The long years of war and the numerous defeats at the hands of Caesar's forces did not diminish the tenacity of the Gauls in this regard. In 52 BCE turmoil in Rome raised hopes that Caesar would be preoccupied by political events and might delay his return to Gaul. Gallic chieftains seized the occasion to stir up patriotic sentiments, calling on their countrymen to restore *libertas* to Gaul. Whatever the risk, it was better to fall in battle than fail to recover the *libertas* that they had received as a legacy from their ancestors.[82] Caesar's ascription to Gauls of a passion for freedom makes a powerful statement, no mere conventional trope.[83]

Internal divisions notoriously divided the Gauls. Caesar's account is riddled with Gallic rivalries, divided loyalties, and shifting allegiances that the Roman commander could exploit to his advantage. Nonetheless, appeals to unity continued to have powerful resonance. The slogan of a common

---

[79] Caes. *BG* 7.78.
[80] Caes. *BG* 3.10.3.
[81] Caes. *BG* 3.8.4: *ut in ea libertate quam a maioribus acceperint permanere quam Romanorum servitutem perferre mallent.*
[82] Caes. *BG* 7.1.5–8: *Galliam in libertatem vindicent … in acie praestare interfici quam non veterem belli gloriam libertatemque quam a maioribus acceperint recuperare;* cf. 7.64.3.
[83] On Caesar and Gallic liberty, see Sherwin-White (1967), 23–25, though his idea that this represents Roman self-criticism is flawed. So, rightly, Seager (2003), 22–26.

interest by Gauls in the principle of liberty for the whole nation recurs frequently in the text. Ambiorix, a leader of the Eburones, had been a beneficiary of Caesar, but his real loyalties lay elsewhere. He built on a consensus of Gallic opinion that held they had entered upon the conflict for the purpose of regaining freedom for all.[84] The phrase *communis libertas* in one form or other reappears with regularity. Vercingetorix, leader of the Arverni, gathered widespread and enthusiastic support by proclaiming the need to take up arms on behalf of a common freedom.[85] The Aeduan Litaviccus echoed those words, reminding his compatriots that they were born free men and that, whatever benefits he owed to Caesar, his greater responsibility was to *communis libertas*.[86] The Roman commander's efforts to split Gallic opposition and gain allies by according advantages to individual tribes or leaders could often prove effective. But he knew the deeper truth and acknowledged it tellingly: so great was the unanimity of Gaul in pressing for *libertas* and recovering their ancient renown in war that no number of Roman benefits or recollection of Roman friendship could budge them.[87] Critognatus appealed powerfully to that sentiment by calling on his compatriots to resist even in dire straits, lest all of Gaul be made victim to perpetual slavery.[88] After the Gauls had yielded to the superior might of Rome at the critical siege of Alesia, concluding book 7 of the *De Bello Gallico*, the last one Caesar composed, Vercingetorix offered his fellow soldiers the option of his death or his surrender to Rome. But he defended to the end his fateful decision to undertake the fight, for it had come on behalf of *communis libertas*.[89] These are among the last words of the extant text. They plainly carried significance for Caesar.

The Gallic commitment to *libertas* was resolute, neither irrational nor precipitous but fundamental. Even the Aedui, allies of Rome, the people who had summoned Caesar to their aid against the Helvetii, felt its force.

---

[84] Caes. *BG* 5.27.6: *Galliae commune consilium ... cum de recuperanda communi libertate consilium initum videretur*. Caesar's critical evaluation of Ambiorix elsewhere does not devalue the commitment to a communal liberty, despite Barlow (1998), 149–151; cf. Kremer (1994), 156–160.

[85] Caes. *BG* 7.4: *hortatur ut communis libertatis causa arma capiant*. Cf. 7.71.3. Barlow (1998), 152–153, dismisses this as rhetoric. But the fact that Vercingetorix summoned the poor and the ruined to his assistance hardly subverts the force of that rhetoric. Cf. also *BG* 7.1.5: *misereantur communem Galliae fortunam ... deposcunt qui ... Galliam in libertatem vindicent*. Caesar's depiction of Vercingetorix is explored by Kremer (1994), 181–191.

[86] Caes. *BG* 7.37.4: *hortaturque ut se liberos et imperio natos meminerint ... plus communi libertati tribuere*.

[87] Caes. *BG* 7.76: *tanta universae Galliae consensio fuit libertatis vindicandae et pristinae belli laudis recuperandae, ut neque beneficiis neque amicitiae memoria moverentur*.

[88] Caes. *BG* 7.77.9. Riggsby (2006), 114, surprisingly sees Critognatus as articulating this Gallic unity for the first time.

[89] Caes. *BG* 7.89: *communis libertatis causa*.

They did not provide the grain that had been expected for Roman soldiers and were rather lukewarm in support of Caesar's endeavor, drawing severe reprimand from the general. An Aeduan spokesman supplied explanation: some among them, including very influential persons, felt that if they could not achieve primacy in Gaul, it was better to subordinate themselves to other Gauls than to Romans, for the latter were determined to deprive them and everyone else of *libertas*.[90] A similar sentiment came later from the Aeduan leader Dumnorix. In resisting Rome, he trumpeted the fact that he was a free man in a free state.[91] And Critognatus, in his extended and compelling speech at Alesia, called to mind the forefathers of his people who had maintained a tenacious resistance to German invaders (though they needed to sustain themselves through cannibalism), thus setting an example for their descendants. Even had there been no precedent, Critognatus adds, he would urge the setting of one, for it would be in the service of *libertas* and a model for posterity.[92] This reiteration of the *exempla* of the *maiores* carries a quintessentially Roman message. That Caesar put it in the mouth of a Gaul can hardly be incidental. A respect for common values trumps the notion of "Otherness."

If one sought means of distinguishing the alien, religion might be the most likely place to look. Caesar gives some space to Gallic religious practices in his ethnographic excursus, most of it devoted to the druids. His readership might well have expected it. That body of priests drew considerable attention from classical authors. Aristotle had included them among the philosophers of non-Greek peoples, on a par with Persian magi, Babylonian

---

[90] Caes. *BG* 1.17.4: *si iam principatum Galliae obtinere non possint, Gallorum quam Romanorum imperia praeferre. Neque dubitare quin, si Helvetios superaverint Romani, una cum reliqua Gallia, Aeduis libertatem sint erupturi.*

[91] Caes. *BG* 5.7.8: *saepe clamitans liberum se liberaeque esse civitatis*. Barlow (1998), 141–144, observes that Caesar elsewhere points to various flaws in Dumnorix's character. But this does not diminish or compromise his championship of Gallic freedom, for which he fought to the end. On Caesar's defamation of Dumnorix, perhaps to justify the execution of the Gallic leader, see Rambaud (1966), 317–321. The lengthy discussion of Heubner (1974), 132–149, on Caesar's treatment of Dumnorix adds little and concludes only that Dumnorix's appeal to *libertas* was an anachronism.

[92] Caes. *BG* 7.77: *facere quod nostri maiores . . . fecerunt . . . cuius rei si exemplum non haberemus, tamen libertatis causa institui et posteris prodi pulcherrimum iudicarem*. The analysis of Schieffer (1972), 480–494, that the speech is a Caesarian rhetorical set piece designed to showcase Gallic cruelty and barbarism and the perils posed by Gallic unity, thus to justify Caesar's war for culture and civilization, is far too one-sided. Somewhat comparable analyses by Rasmussen (1963), 47–54; Kremer (1994), 191–195. Di Lorenzo (1993), 553–575, offers a more balanced interpretation. He acknowledges the ferocity and barbarism, punctuated by cannibalism, that Caesar sets in Critognatus' mouth but sees the Gallic leader's tenacious adherence to *libertas* as a reflection of Caesar's own sensitivity to an indomitable Gallic spirit. Cf. also Lieberg (1998), 155–160; Riggsby (2006), 116–118. On Caesar's representation of the Gallic menace more generally, see Gardner (1983), 181–189.

Chaldeans, and Indian gymnosophists. The idea of druids as philosophers reappears in a number of authors.[93] Caesar's contemporary Diodorus Siculus reckons them not only as philosophers but as bards, as diviners who use the innards of human victims to probe the future, a somewhat unsavory mode of divination, and even as men with occult power who can halt contending armies.[94] A comparable description appears in Strabo, who describes the druids as students of both natural and moral philosophy, as arbiters of private and public disputes, and as possessing the ability to stop armies dead in their tracks.[95] The work of the first-century BCE historian Timagenes also emphasized the learning of the druids, seeing them as a clique of philosophers who investigated arcane and esoteric matters, including the immortality of the soul, while looking down on all matters human.[96] A number of other writers make brief mention of druids in passing, noting their role as diviners and seers, their knowledge of the heavens and of natural science, their prophetic wisdom, and their practice of magic.[97] They fell afoul of official Roman policy in the Julio-Claudian era. Augustus forbade Roman citizens from embracing the religion, Tiberius banished the druids for practicing magic, and Claudius acted to suppress the religion branded as dread and inhuman.[98] How serious the emperors were about crushing the cult and what effect their decrees had can be questioned.[99] The actions may have had more to do with public relations than with concern for any threat that druids could have posed. Even on that supposition, however, the priests must have had at least a dubious reputation so that the Julio-Claudians might benefit from taking steps against them.

Julius Caesar could, in principle, have used that reputation to set the druidic religion as alien, undesirable, and a foil for proper relations with the gods as practiced by Rome. In fact, nothing of the kind appears in the text. His description is straightforward and respectful. Two classes hold sway over the Gauls, a secular and a religious establishment, the first referred to as *equites*, the second as druids.[100] Caesar gives little space to the former but dwells at some length on the latter. Druids supervise sacrifices,

---

[93] Diog. Laert. 1.1; Cyril of Alexandria *Contra Jul.* 4, citing Alexander Polyhistor; Clement of Alexandria *Strom.* 6.3.33.2. For a convenient listing of sources on druids, see Webster (1999), 2–4.

[94] Diod. 5.33.2–5.

[95] Strabo 4.4.4.

[96] Timagenes *apud* Amm. Marc. 15.9.8.

[97] Sources in Webster (1999), 2–4.

[98] Pliny *NH* 29.52, 30.4; Suet. *Claud.* 25.

[99] Cf. King (1990), 233. Webster (1999), 11–12, speculatively and unconvincingly sees these actions as response to a perceived, even genuine, druidic threat of resistance to imperial rule. Similarly, Kremer (1994), 217.

[100] Caes. *BG* 6.13.1.

public and private. They interpret matters of religion. Youths flock to them in great number to gain instruction and hold them in high esteem. They arbitrate almost all private and public disputes, passing judgment on civil and criminal offenses, and they enforce their decisions by banning offenders from sacrifices, a social stigma of the most grievous sort. Druids gather once a year at a sacred site reckoned as the very center of Gaul, there to exercise judgments and render decisions.[101] The historian proceeds to offer more detail on the kind of training that young men receive at the hands of the druids, a serious discipline that for some lasts for twenty years. They are drilled in rigorous memorization so as to reduce reliance on writing to a minimum. Teachers school the youth in astrology and cosmology, in the nature of the universe, the power of the immortal gods, and the doctrine of transmigration of souls.[102] All this accords well with the representations of druids in other sources, although Caesar adds other data and offers a more elaborate exposition.[103] Whether Caesar drew much of his account from the lost Celtic ethnography of Posidonius, which may lie behind the comments of Diodorus, Timagenes, and Strabo, remains controversial and need not be decided here.[104] The Roman commander had opportunities of his own to gain information about the druids and perhaps even to encounter them. The significant point is that his text gives little indication of an effort to disparage or blacken the druids, let alone to underscore their "Otherness." Indeed Caesar omits the more dubious attribution attested elsewhere, that druids practiced magic. As learned men, teachers, and disciplinarians, they cut admirable figures.

The religious activities of the Gauls generally gain only brief attention. The institution of human sacrifice, perhaps surprisingly, receives comment but not condemnation. Caesar offers some graphic portrayal. In situations of serious crisis, whether suffering from grave illness or embroiled in perilous warfare, Gauls offer up human sacrifices or vow to do so, employing druids to officiate at the ritual. They even erect huge structures made of twigs in which they place men to be incinerated alive. The victims include those convicted of theft, brigandage, or other offenses whose punishment would be welcomed by the gods. In the view of the Gauls, according to Caesar, appeasement of the gods requires the giving of a life to compensate for one lost. And when the supply of criminals runs out, they even resort to

---

[101] Caes. *BG* 6.13.
[102] Caes. *BG* 6.14.
[103] Webster (1999), 8–10, claims to find discrepancies between the treatment of Caesar and those of his Greek predecessors, but her own tables show more overlap than differences.
[104] The argument that Caesar was almost wholly dependent on Posidonius was made by Tierney (1960), 211–218, 222–224; adopted, e.g., by Momigliano (1975), 68–72. But little of the argument survives the assault of Nash (1976), 112–136; Rawlings (1998), 172–173; Webster (1999), 7–8; Isaac (2004), 413–414.

executing the innocent.[105] Caesar, of course, does not condone the practice. But he refrains from explicit denunciation. One might argue that the description alone serves as harsh censure.[106] Perhaps. But Romans too had indulged on occasion in human sacrifice.[107] And Caesar's bare-bones account lacks any sign of indignation or outrage.

More important, Caesar proceeds immediately to a discussion of Gallic gods that places them squarely in the context of Roman beliefs. He names Mercury as the god to whom they are most devoted. They set up images to him in large numbers, regarding him as the creator of all arts, the guide of highways and byways, and the overseer with greatest influence on commerce and monetary exchange.[108] In addition, they pay homage to Apollo as averting diseases, Minerva as providing the origin of arts and crafts, Jupiter as holding sway over the heavens, and Mars as governing war. In such beliefs, says Caesar, they largely share the opinions of all other peoples.[109] That assessment plainly reflects an *interpretatio Romana*. Caesar did not likely spend much time investigating the particulars of Gallic rituals or the nuances in their characterizations of the gods. But the fact that he chose to underscore their similarities to Roman beliefs (and, by extension, to those of all other peoples) is significant. The author minimizes, rather than accentuates, the differences.[110]

The Gauls may be enemies on the battlefield. But they are not alien creatures, with values altogether incommensurable with those of Rome, antithetical to Roman practices and character, and averse to the principles of their antagonists. Caesar portrays them, in clear-eyed and unsentimental fashion, with all their flaws, as a valorous people, fiercely devoted to liberty, and adherents of moral and religious values remarkably akin to those of Rome.

[105] Caes. *BG* 6.16.

[106] Sherwin-White (1967), 27, goes well beyond the text in claiming that Caesar was appalled by these practices and that he reproved the Gauls here. Cf. also Kremer (1994), 216–217. Rambaud (1966), 330, by contrast, implausibly proposes that Caesar deliberately played down human sacrifice among the Gauls in order to calm Roman fears.

[107] Livy 22.57; Plut. *Marc.* 3.4.

[108] Caes. *BG* 6.17. The suggestion of Rambaud (1966), 333, that this is a Caesarian construct to reassure *mercatores* and encourage future Gallo–Romans is far-fetched.

[109] Caes. *BG* 6.17: *de his eandem fere, quam reliquae gentes, habent opinionem*.

[110] It is noteworthy that the only items Caesar mentions, apart from druids, as differentiating the Gauls from all other peoples are rather marginal and insignificant: that they reckon time by number of nights, not days, and that they do not allow their sons to appear with them in public until they reach military age; *BG* 6.18.

Chapter 6

TACITUS ON THE GERMANS

THE *GERMANIA* OF Tacitus holds a unique place among extant texts from antiquity. It stands as the sole surviving full-scale monograph by a classical author on an alien people. Not that he was the first or only to produce such a work. We possess ethnographic excursuses composed as parts of larger works, even some quite lengthy ones like those of Herodotus and Diodorus on Egyptians, Caesar on Gauls, and Sallust on African nations. The Germans themselves received treatment in digressions by Caesar and by Pliny.[1] And predecessors of Tacitus did produce self-standing monographs on foreign folk, as did Hellanicus on Egyptians, Xanthus on Lydians, and Megasthenes on Indians.[2] But none of them survived the passage of time and the vagaries of fashion. We have good reason to be grateful for the durability of the *Germania*. On the face of it, Tacitus' investigation of the Germans ought to supply our most comprehensive literary portrayal of the "Other."[3]

Germans and Romans

But the portrayal is far from straightforward and neat. Tacitus masterfully eludes reductive categorization. As practically all commentators have in-

---

[1] Pliny's account no longer survives. Cf. Tac. *Ann.* 1.69. And the German "ethnography" of Caesar is confined to a very few remarks designed primarily to distinguish Germans from Gauls—in plainly artificial fashion for Caesar's own particular purposes; Caes. *BG* 6. 21–24; cf. 4.1–2, on the Suebi. The fullest discussion is Walser (1956), 52–77. See also Rambaud (1966), 334–339; Sherwin-White (1967), 29–32; Lund (1996), 12–33; Seager (2003), 30–34; Riggsby (2006), 59–71. A short digression on the Germans appears even in Seneca, *De Ira*, 1.11.34. On its possible relation to Tacitus, see Krebs (2007), 429–434.

[2] Hellanicus *FGH* 4 FF53–55, 173–176; Xanthus *FGH* 765; Megasthenes *FGH* 715.

[3] A brief but serviceable summary of earlier scholarship on the *Germania* appears in Benario (1983), 209–230. The extensively annotated bibliography of Lund (1991b), 1989–2222, provides a rich resource for research. The principal commentaries are Much (1937), J. Anderson (1938), Lund (1988), Perl (1990), and Rives (1999). On the structure and organization of the work, see the lucid treatment of Urban (1989), 80–105.

sisted, he is as much, if not more, interested in the Romans as in the Germans.[4] The treatise, in one way or another, constitutes a reflection on his countrymen. How then is the alien represented? For many, the historian creates a contrived and idiosyncratic portrait, painting Germans as ideal primitives, noble savages, in contrast to self-satisfied, listless, and degenerate Romans. On this analysis, the Germans represent values of simplicity, hardiness, and self-restraint once exemplified by Romans but long since abandoned or betrayed.[5] That picture proved attractive to some modern Germans who took it as authentic depiction of reality.[6] Recent and sober analyses find greater nuance and complexity. Historical reality might occasionally be discerned or presumed, but Tacitus' treatise was more construct than description.[7] And the construct itself cannot be reduced to a simplistic contrast of the virtuous Germans and the reprobate Romans. As many have noted, the historian's characterization of Germanic peoples points to flaws as well as virtues, objectionable traits as well as admirable ones.[8] It misconceives Tacitus' design to interpret it as mere elevation of the barbarian in order to disparage the Roman. There is much else going on here. Nor will it do to catalogue the work simply as an ethnographic treatise.[9] Tacitus had more in mind than recounting the origins, customs, institutions, dress, and beliefs of the Germans. Insofar as the *Germania* presents the alien, it does so in sophisticated and calculated fashion—certainly not

[4] See, e.g., Perl (1988), 25: "die 'Germania' enthalte implizit zugleich auch eine 'Romania'"; O'Gorman (1993), 135: "The *Germania* ... is about Rome"; Dauge (1981), 250–254; Krebs (2005), 34–37.

[5] The classic statement is in Wolff (1934), 121–164. Cf. J. Anderson (1938), xvi–xix; Beare (1964), 69–73; Isaac (2004), 433, 436. A similar but more nuanced view in O'Gorman (1993), 147–149; Krebs (2005), 41–43.

[6] On the *Germania* in early modern Europe, see Kelley (1993), 152–167. As an example in the 1930s, see Naumann (1934), 21–33. Considerable scholarly value still resides in the learned commentary of Much (1937), despite the inferences one might be tempted to draw from the date of its publication.

[7] The degree to which the *Germania* approximates German reality cannot here be investigated. Among the many discussions of this topic, see Anderson (1938), xxvii–xxxvii; Lund (1984), 205–210; *idem* (1991a), 1951–1954, with bibliography; Perl (1983), 79–89; *idem* (1990), 42–45; Rives (1999), 56–66; also the collection of articles in Neumann and Seemann (1992).

[8] So, e.g., Anderson (1938), ix–x; Lund (1999), 62–72; Rives (1999), 50–51; Krebs (2005), 81–85. See the succinct and pointed summary of German traits in the *Germania* by Urban (1989), 94. Further bibliography in Krebs (2005), 82.

[9] The fundamental study of this aspect is Norden (1923). Cf. the critique of Norden on ethnographic topoi by Bringmann (1989), 59–78. Emphasis on the ethnographic traditions and clichés as background for the *Germania* can be found also in Anderson (1938), xii–xv; Drexler (1952), 54–58; Flach (1989), 45–56; Städele (1990), 157–163; Rives (1999), 11–27; von See (1994), 31–51; Lund (1988), 56–69; *idem* (1991a), 1862–1870; Perl (1990), 28–38. Timpe (1989), 106–127, argues vigorously against conventional ethnography as shaping Tacitus' work and finds contemporary political circumstances as the stimulus. The negative argumentation is cogent but the reconstruction operates on a rather narrow basis.

as mindless stereotype. Our purpose here is to discern just what image Tacitus does construct of the German and what this tells us about perceptions of the "Other."

Germans, it is often presumed, were in Roman eyes the quintessential "barbarians." If so, Tacitus certainly does not perpetuate the stereotype. The term "barbarian" itself is nearly absent in the *Germania*, appearing but three times in the text—and without intent to vilify. The first instance carries no pejorative overtones, quite the contrary. Tacitus asserts that Germans were almost alone among *barbari* in being monogamous, a trait that he finds most laudable.[10] A darker vision surfaces when he reports the practice of human sacrifice, described as a "barbarian rite." But Tacitus speaks here of the Semnones, not of Germans generally, and couples it with a report that has the Semnones as the oldest and noblest of Suebian tribes.[11] He evidently did not employ the phrase to stigmatize the Semnones, let alone Germans as a whole. The last occurrence of the term, near the very end of the *Germania*, does carry a tone of disparagement. Tacitus sneers at the Aestii, who collected amber but had no idea of its value. Like the *barbari* that they are, they neither inquired nor learned of its character.[12] Here too a particular tribe is singled out, not the German folk as a collective. German ethnicity, in fact, is irrelevant. Tacitus sets the Aestii in the wider category of the stereotypically rude foreigner. The *Germania* nowhere tars Germans as a body with that broad brush.

Praise and blame can be found—or, at least, what looks superficially like approbation or condemnation. Yet these judgments, if such they be, are more often modern inferences than explicit assessments. And the descriptions frequently come with qualifications, paradoxical statements, or cynical comments. Tacitus' text rarely delivers unambiguous appraisals—which is hardly an accident. That fact itself may carry greater significance and bring better understanding than efforts to elicit the realities of German experience or the prejudices of the historian.

Irony is a Tacitean stock in trade.[13] The *Germania* has a rich vein of it. The very first paragraph, ostensibly a conventional opening for ethnographic treatises, begins with geography. But Tacitus turns it in idiosyncratic fashion. It need not be geography alone that separates Germans from Sarmatians and Dacians. The author adds politics to topography, and does so with conspicuous alliteration: mutual menace or mountains divide the

---

[10] Tac. *Germ.* 18.1.

[11] Tac. *Germ.* 39.1: *vetustissimos nobilissimosque Sueborum Semnones memorant . . . celebrant barbari ritus horrenda primordia.*

[12] Tac. *Germ.* 45.4: *nec quae natura quaeve ratio gignat, ut barbaris, quaesitum compertumve.*

[13] So, Syme (1958), 206: "Irony is all-pervasive." On irony in Tacitus elsewhere, see Robin (1973); O'Gorman (2000). The study of Köhnken (1973), 32–50, has a narrower focus but broader implications.

people.[14] The touch is typically Tacitean. Enmity and fear could be as potent a partition as terrain. The historian communicates at the outset that this will be more than standard ethnography.

Tacitus injects similar mischief in moving to another ethnographic topos: an inquiry into the origins of the people. The author proposes that Germans were autochthonous, indigenous to the land, barely if at all mixed with peoples who arrived from elsewhere. The Germans resemble no one—except themselves.[15] Among the purported explanations for this, one stands out as arresting and (not incidentally) sardonic: who would have left Asia, Africa, or Italy to seek Germany with its untamed landscape, its harsh weather, and its gloomy aspect—unless it was his native land?[16] Tacitus does not go in for bland reporting. The opening chapters already signal that the work possesses a special character of its own.

The body of the text regales the reader with complexities and ambiguities. If Tacitus' Germans are designed to throw Roman practices and institutions into relief by contrast, they do so only in shifting and problematic ways. The historian has no consistent agenda either to elevate or to denigrate the foreigner.

Simplicity, forbearance, and restraint ostensibly count as praiseworthy qualities. As applied to Germans, so it is frequently inferred, they provide indirect commentary on the absence of such virtues among contemporary Romans. Yet Tacitus does not provide (nor perhaps intend) so blunt a juxtaposition. The historian prefers mixed messages and incongruity.

To be sure, one can readily discover German traits paraded by Tacitus as implicit (and preferable) inversions of Roman practices. One might note, for instance, his comments on morals and temperance. German women, he claims, have the good fortune of not being corrupted by the enticements of spectacles or the stimulations of lavish banquets—not to mention that both men and women are innocent of clandestine (love) letters, and that society enjoys a near absence of adultery.[17] Lest anyone miss the point, Tacitus adds that no German belittles vices or calls corruption a mere sign of the times.[18]

---

[14] Tac. *Germ.* 1.1: *mutuo metu aut montibus*. As is well known, much of the opening section of the work parallels the wording of Caesar's *Bellum Gallicum*. But there is no corresponding phrase to this one. Tacitus, of course, knew the *BG* and admired it; Tac. *Germ.* 28.1. On parallels generally between the two works, see Thielscher (1962), 12–25. Devillers (1989), 845–853, stresses Tacitus' manipulation rather than adoption of Caesar's text.

[15] Tac. *Germ.* 2.1, 4.1: *tantum sui similem gentem*. For background of the phrase, see Much (1937), 66–68; cf. Lund (1999), 57–62.

[16] Tac. *Germ.* 2.1. See the somewhat comparable statement by Thucydides, 1.2.4, commenting on Athenian autochthony: the poverty of Attic soil discouraged immigrants.

[17] Tac. *Germ.* 19.1: *nullis spectaculorum inlecebris, nullis conviviorum irritationibus corruptae; litterarum secreta viri pariter ac feminae ignorant; paucissima in tam numerosa gente adulteria*.

[18] Tac. *Germ.* 19.1: *nemo enim illic vitia ridet, nec corrumpere et corrumpi saeculum vocatur*.

A snide comment follows that surely has Rome in its sights. In calling attention to the German refusal to limit numbers of children or to countenance infanticide, Tacitus observes that good morals (as among the Germans) have greater effect than good laws elsewhere.[19] That remark doubtless alludes to Roman legislation such as Augustus' laws on marriage and childbearing, which were honored more in the breach than in the observance.[20] A less direct but no less pointed comment in the *Germania* reflects on the upbringing of the young. Tacitus states that master and slave in German households receive the same training. One could not tell them apart on this score, for the children of the master class receive no petty privileges to distinguish them.[21] The sneer directs itself against the pampering of spoiled offspring of the Roman aristocracy.

This implicit contrast arises again in the treatment of German burial customs. Their funerals avoid display or extravagance. The only distinction enjoyed by the illustrious is burial with special types of wood. They pile no garments or spices on the pyre, simply the weapons of the deceased and perhaps some flesh of his horse. The tomb is a mere mound of turf; heavy monuments would only be a burden to the dead.[22] All these are but thinly disguised comments on the indulgences of Tacitus' Roman contemporaries.

Politics lies not far from the surface. And Tacitus manipulates material to bring it forth. The Germans revere women, he observes, even finding in them the gift of prophecy and a kind of holiness—but they do not descend to adulation and make them into goddesses.[23] Few readers could have missed here the allusion to the Roman deification of females in the imperial household, an institution for which Tacitus had little but contempt. The historian remarks on freedmen in German society, by no means an idle or innocent remark. He observes that they rank only slightly above slaves; they rarely carry authority in the household and never in the state.[24] That comment transparently calls attention to the often powerful role played by *liberti* in the palace and policy of the emperors, a matter that regularly aroused Tacitus' resentment. He allows for exceptions among those Germanic tribes ruled by kings—yet again probably a sly hit at the governance of his own land.[25] Equally telling is Tacitus' statement that the Batavi, allies of Rome on the Lower Rhine, enjoy exemption from tribute

---

[19] Tac. *Germ.* 19.2: *plusque ibi boni mores valent quam alibi bonae leges*.

[20] Cf. Perl (1990), 187; Rives (1999), 205. Cf. also Tac *Ann.* 3.27: *corruptissima re publica plurimae leges*.

[21] Tac. *Germ.* 20.1: *dominum ac servum nullis educationis deliciis dignoscas*.

[22] Tac. *Germ.* 27.1.

[23] Tac. *Germ.* 8.2: *non adulatione nec tamquam facerent deas*. Cf. Rives (1999), 155–156.

[24] Tac. *Germ.* 25.2. See the note of Perl (1990), 198–199.

[25] Tac. *Germ.* 25.2: *exceptis dumtaxat iis gentibus quae regnantur*.

and escape the oppressions of the tax collector.[26] Whatever this might mean with regard to the status of the Batavi, it allows Tacitus to sneer at Roman *publicani*. More pointedly, the historian delivers an innuendo that had special contemporary resonance. After providing a condensed history of Roman wars with the Germans over the previous two centuries, Tacitus concludes by saying that, in most recent times, they have been more triumphed over than conquered.[27] That can only be a reference to the triumph celebrated by the emperor Domitian over the Chatti in 83 CE, a feat elsewhere disparaged by the historian and others.[28]

Yet it will not do to reduce the *Germania* to a tract that opposes the virtuous primitive to the debased sophisticate. Tacitus' shafts strike all targets. He depicts Germans as abstemious in their diet, restricting themselves to wild fruit, game brought from the hunt, and curdled milk. They avoid elaborate preparation or fancy seasonings.[29] Is this implicit contrast with Roman lavishness and self-indulgence?[30] More directly and more strikingly it contrasts with the Germans themselves in Tacitus' own text just two paragraphs earlier. There, he affirms that no people indulges more liberally in feasting and hospitality. Their doors are open to all, and when resources are exhausted they pass guests on to a neighboring home where they enjoy similar generosity.[31] Quite admirable, no doubt—but hardly compatible with a people who shun all but the most simple fare.

Tacitus proceeds further to deconstruct their hardiness. They are formidable on the battlefield—but only on offense.[32] They react poorly to adversity, and they shrink from exertion. Germans have no patience with hard labor. They prefer war to agriculture; the rewards are quicker and greater. Why acquire by sweat what you can obtain by bloodshed?[33] Long periods of peace and leisure cause restlessness and prompt young men to enlist in the battles of other tribes. When there are no foes to fight, however, they sink into idleness; even the fiercest and bravest among them do little but eat and sleep, leaving domestic duties to women, the elderly, and the infirm.

---

[26] Tac. *Germ.* 29.1: *nec tributis contemnuntur nec publicanus atterit.*

[27] Tac. *Germ.* 37.5: *proximis temporibus triumphati magis quam victi sunt.*

[28] Cf. Tac. *Agr.* 39.1; Pliny *Pan.* 16; Dio 67.4.1. See Perl (1990), 229; Rives (1999), 281–282. On Tacitus' disparagement of Domitian's achievements here, see Nesselhauf (1952), 234–245.

[29] Tac. *Germ.* 23.1. A similar formulation in Caes. *BG* 6.22.

[30] So, e.g., Much (1937), 222–223; Perl (1990), 194–195.

[31] Tac. *Germ.* 21.2: *convictibus et hospitiis non alia gens effusius indulget.* Caesar, *BG* 6.23.9, also stresses German commitment to hospitality, but, unlike Tacitus, leaves no impression of lavishness or indulgence.

[32] Tac. *Germ.* 4.1: *magna corpora et tantum ad impetum valida.* Cf. Perl (1990), 142, with citations of comparable passages.

[33] Tac. *Germ.* 4.1, 14.2–3.

Tacitus relishes the paradox, as he usually does: the very same men who despise peace also love sloth.³⁴

Indolence supplies a recurring theme, as does fondness for drink, not endearing qualities in Tacitus' repertoire. The Germans are slow even to gather in their political assemblies, usually wasting two or three days in dillydallying before getting down to business.³⁵ Tacitus compounds that gratuitous remark with another somewhat later: Germans prolong their sleep until well into the day. And when they awake, they are as likely to proceed to revelry as to industry. Indeed their drinking can stretch night into day without anyone suffering opprobrium.³⁶ The Germans may restrict their diet to simple necessities but they do not skimp on drink. Tacitus even adds that, if one were to indulge their drinking habits by offering as much as they wish, the Germans could as easily be vanquished by their vices as by force of arms.³⁷ The historian subsequently twists the knife with special sarcasm. He has the Treveri and the Nervii show particular enthusiasm for claiming a German origin, evidently a most desirable affiliation. Why? On Tacitus' tendentious interpretation it was as if they thought that the glory of such a bloodline would hold them apart from any suggestion of similarity with the inertia of the Gauls.³⁸ In view of what he had already said, more than once, about *German* inertia, the sentence fairly drips with irony.

Tacitus, to be sure, pays tribute to the virtues of certain Germanic tribes—but often only to contrast them with Germans in general. He singles out the Chatti for their hard bodies, sinewy limbs, fierce facial expressions, and, most notably, their mental acuity. He then appends to that statement a characteristic innuendo: they have much reasoning power and shrewdness—at least for Germans.³⁹ Tacitus has high regard for the Chauci. He reckons them as the noblest of German peoples, a nation that prefers to preserve its greatness through the exercise of justice. The Chauci provoke no wars, send no raiders, and engage in no pillage or plunder. They possess martial skills to be used if needed, but they rest their reputation on maintaining peace.⁴⁰ The historian plainly admires those qualities, but his

---

³⁴ Tac. *Germ.* 15.1: *idem homines sic ament inertiam et oderint quietem.* Cf. 26.3, 45.3. Devillers (1989), 850, sees the passage as an example of Tacitean moralizing, which misplaces the emphasis.

³⁵ Tac. *Germ.* 11.1.

³⁶ Tac. *Germ.* 22.1.

³⁷ Tac. *Germ.* 23.1: *haud minus facile vitiis quam armis vincentur.* Cf. Tac. *Agr.* 21.

³⁸ Tac. *Germ.* 28.4: *tamquam per hanc gloriam sanguinis a similitudine et inertia Gallorum separentur.* The irony is missed by Much (1937), 265–266, and brushed over by Perl (1990), 207. Cf. also the double-edged remark about the Ubii, who, though they prefer the designation of Agippinenses, thus exhibiting their status as a Roman colony, nevertheless do not blush to acknowledge their German origin; Tac. *Germ.* 28.4: *ne Ubii quidem . . . origine erubescunt.*

³⁹ Tac. *Germ.* 30.2: *multum, ut inter Germanos rationis ac sollertiae.*

⁴⁰ Tac. *Germ.* 35.1–2.

readers knew well, without having to be told again, that they contrast sharply with the aggressive, bellicose, and truculent character of most other Germans. Moreover, the blessings of peace have their underside. Tacitus singles out the Cherusci for having long escaped attack and nourished an excessively enervating peace. The policy was more enjoyable than safe. As Tacitus reminds his audience, the Cherusci seem to have forgotten that they dwell among peoples who understand only force and for whom moderation and integrity are mere names for the stronger. Hence the Cherusci, once regarded as worthy and equitable, are now considered lazy and foolish.[41] Tacitus has some faint praise for the Aestii, but solely to point up comparisons with other Germans. They work patiently at cultivating grain and other products of the earth, rather more patiently indeed than is customary given the usual inertia of Germans.[42] Approbation for the exception simply accentuates the failings of the norm. In fact, some German tribes even fall below the norm. The Sitones are distinguished from their neighbors by having a woman as ruler. In this regard, says the historian, they recede not only from freedom but even from slavery.[43] Tacitus does not hold a brief for Teutonic values.

The *Germania*, however, goes well beyond cavils for Germans. The intricate and interweaving threads between Romans and Germans interest Tacitus more—especially when they reveal paradox and provoke irony. Tacitean innuendos can assimilate as well as counterpose the traits of the nations.

Germans care naught for precious objects; gold and silver count for no more than earthenware, according to Tacitus. The coins they employ are of the old, familiar, and unremarkable sort, suitable for purchases of the least expensive items, since they are unimpressed by luxury or ornament.[44] They shun the practice of putting out loans at interest and then charging exorbitant rates. No legislation is necessary to enforce that prescription. The Germans observe it of their own volition more stringently than any law on the books.[45] The noble savage? Perhaps so, but only up to a point. Since they possess no precious specie to begin with, they hardly deserve credit for failing to lend it out. Tacitus engages in some mischief here. And there is more. The tribes of the interior fit the mold of a simpler and older commerce with little need for currency. Those Germans dwelling more closely to the Roman sphere of influence, however, become accustomed to coinage

---

[41] Tac. *Germ.* 36.1.

[42] Tac. *Germ.* 45.3: *frumenta ceterosque fructus patientius quam pro solita Germanorum inertia laborant.*

[43] Tac. *Germ.* 45.6: *in tantum non modo a libertate sed etiam a servitute degenerant.* This comment too reflects more irony than conviction. Cf. Tacitus' remark on Boudicca, whom the Britons had as queen: they make no distinctions of gender among their rulers; *Agr.* 16.

[44] Tac. *Germ.* 5.2–3.

[45] Tac. *Germ.* 26.1.

and put a higher value on silver and gold.[46] There is little to suggest that this bears any relation to reality.[47] The historian here may well be taking a back-handed swipe at his own cultural compatriots: the nearer Germans come to the realm of Rome, the more likely they are to become infected by the commercialization of the "civilized" nation.[48] Tacitus' wry wit is rarely missing for long. He opens this segment of his work by ascribing to the gods the decision to deny Germans gold and silver and adds, with tongue in cheek, "whether in kindness or anger can be questioned."[49] But, though the paragraph may contain an indirect skewering of Romans (always a favorite pastime of Tacitus), it also compromises the putative integrity of Germans. Their introduction to precious metals by the Romans soon dissolved antique abstinence.

The same cynicism on a similar topic surfaces in another passage. Tacitus notes that tribal leaders have long received gifts from neighboring communities, whether of horses, weaponry, or various ornaments. It took the Romans to teach them to accept cash.[50] The coin of the realm could also be useful to bolster martial success. In speaking of the Marcomani and the Quadi beyond the Danube, Tacitus remarks that their power rests on the authority of Rome, occasionally through armed assistance—more often through cash subsidies.[51] This double-edged representation occurs once again near the end of the treatise. Tacitus reports that the Aestii on the Baltic gather up amber in the shallows and on the shore, but they have no idea of its value and had long let it lie until Roman *luxuria* gave it a name. And now they are astonished at what price it brings.[52] Astonished or not, however, they evidently took the money. The historian's irony applies as much to the *Germani* as to the *Romani*.

The Germans are hardy warriors, inured indeed to war, which tests the mettle of their manhood. A leader strives to excel in martial prowess, and his entourage to emulate his courage. Abandonment of the leader defines prime disgrace.[53] To flee from the contest, leaving one's shield on the

---

[46] Tac. *Germ.* 5.3: *quamquam proximi ob usum commerciorum aurum et argentum in pretio habent formasque quasdam nostrae pecuniae agnoscunt atque eligunt.* The sentiment appears famously already in Caes. *BG* 1.1.

[47] Cf. Lund (1988), 128; Perl (1990), 145–147; Rives (1999), 133–135.

[48] Cf. O'Gorman (1993), 140–141.

[49] Tac. *Germ.* 5.2: *argentum et aurum propitiine an irati di negaverint dubito.* Krebs (2005), 89–99, rightly recognizes some of the ambiguities and inversions in Tacitus' accounts of Germanic "simplicity." But he oddly believes that the statement above has more a tone of resignation than of irony; 98–99.

[50] Tac. *Germ.* 15.2: *iam et pecuniam accipere docuimus.* References to similar passages in Much (1937), 171.

[51] Tac. *Germ.* 42.2: *raro armis nostris, saepius pecunia iuvantur.*

[52] Tac. *Germ.* 45.4: *pretiumque mirantes accipiunt.*

[53] Tac. *Germ.* 14.1.

battlefield, exhibits craven cowardice, strips the perpetrator of civic privileges, and brings public ignominy often culminating in suicide.[54] The dropped shield symbolizing spinelessness is, of course, a cliché in both Greek and Latin literature, doubtless a familiar commonplace to Tacitus' readers.[55] But the historian, by setting Germans into this classical context, notably diminishes their "Otherness."

The fondness for paradox recurs with some frequency. Tacitus notes that Germans have an unequivocal duty not only to honor their fathers' friendships but also to pursue their enmities. Continuation of the family feud was a matter of necessity—though not to the point of implacability. Even in the case of homicide, settlements could be arranged with an appropriate compensation of cattle or sheep. Unfettered animosities were too perilous for the community. The public welfare counted for more than private feuds.[56] The restraint exercised here surely earned Tacitus' approbation. But what he gives with the one hand, he often takes with the other. Only a few lines later the historian describes the drunken brawls in which Germans regularly indulge and which rarely limit themselves to verbal abuse but more commonly issue in murder and bloodshed.[57] So much for a general policy of avoiding mayhem for the public good.

The pattern of inversion emerges elsewhere. Tacitus expressly lauds the marriage practices of the Germans. They take the institution most seriously. Germans are among the only foreigners who restrict themselves to just one wife. Some tribes indeed insist on chastity before the wedding vows, and the bride pledges to stay with her man, remarriages are frowned upon, enduring loyalty celebrated. And mothers nurse their children, no wet nurses or even day-care personnel permitted.[58] Tacitus plainly approves: none of their practices is more praiseworthy than the adherence to monogamy.[59] And there can be little doubt that this form of marital and familial morality serves to throw an indirect and not very flattering light on contrasting Roman practices. But there is more to it than that. The historian savors a put-down of both societies. The language employed to characterize the chastity of German women is notable, less a matter of volition than restriction: "fenced-in modesty."[60] Tacitus unobtrusively slips in a sly judgment to color what follows. Further, having just asserted that Germans, almost alone among barbarians, restrict themselves to a single partner, he then inserts an exception: there are some Germans who are sought out for

[54] Tac. *Germ.* 6.4.
[55] References in Perl (1990), 152; Rives (1999), 144.
[56] Tac. *Germ.* 21.1.
[57] Tac. *Germ.* 22.1.
[58] Tac. *Germ.* 18.1, 19.2, 20.1.
[59] Tac. *Germ.* 18.1: *nec ullam morum partem magis laudaveris.*
[60] Tac. *Germ.* 19.1: *saepta pudicitia.*

multiple marriages, not because of lust (he swiftly adds), but because of their eminence.[61] That is to say, social and political considerations could dilute or compromise moral prescriptions. On this score, far from contrasting Germans and Romans, Tacitus sets them on the same plane.

Interpretatio Romana?

The *Germania* does as much to blur as to sharpen distinctions between Romans and "Others." Much sets the Germans apart. But on matters of real interest to the historian, the boundaries are curiously fluid. The concept of *libertas*, for instance, looms large, a matter of preeminent importance in Roman thinking—but also of keen significance to Germans. Did the two peoples view it in contrasting ways? That inference has many advocates. But the matter is not so simple. Ambiguity rather than consistency marks Tacitus' account, as so often it does.

The term first appears in the *Germania* with a negative connotation. Tacitus offers a disparaging assessment of German sluggishness in gathering for political assemblies: they sometimes drag their heels for two or three days before public discussion gets under way. And the cynical author ascribes this vice to their *libertas*.[62] Freedom here comes close to license, a release from authority and regularity. Hence moderns take it as a touchstone for Tacitus' contrast between Germanic irresponsibility and Roman temperance.[63] The idea receives reinforcement in a subsequent passage that refers to family feuds among Germans. The perpetrators do not allow them to get out of hand, according to Tacitus, for private quarrels become the more dangerous when juxtaposed to *libertas*.[64] The term here once again approximates irresponsibility. "Freedom" seems a matter of reproach rather than approbation. One might note, however, that insofar as Germanic *libertas* renders enmities more perilous, the Germans themselves set the restraints that curb those very hostilities. Even when employing "liberty" with a negative significance, Tacitus duly complicates rather than darkens the image of the Germans.

The term can also have a very different connotation. Its most striking use in the *Germania* comes at a crucial moment in that text. Tacitus casts off any pretense of conventional ethnography and moves back briefly to history. His treatment of the Cimbri gives him occasion to summarize the record of Roman wars against Germans over the past two centuries. And he

---

[61] Tac. *Germ*. 18.1: *exceptis admodum paucis, qui non libidine, sed ob nobilitatem pluribus nuptiis ambiuntur*.
[62] Tac. *Germ*. 11.1: *illud ex libertate vitium*.
[63] E.g., Lund (1999), 67–70.
[64] Tac. *Germ*. 21.1: *quia periculosiores sunt inimicitiae iuxta libertatem*.

begins with a telling phrase: for so long has Germany been in the course of conquest.[65] The idea that Tacitus speaks here as advocate of Roman imperialism misses the main point.[66] His reference to a seemingly endless contest, marked, as he goes on to say, by numerous defeats on both sides, delivers the customary Tacitean cynicism, a slap at the claims of many Romans to have brought that land to subjection. He notes, among other things, the Cimbric victories in the time of Marius, the grave hardships inflicted by Germans on Julius Caesar, Drusus, Tiberius, and Germanicus, the great disaster suffered by Varus, the empty threats of Caligula that issued in farce, and the upheavals in Germany during the Roman civil war. He concludes, as we have seen, with indirect allusion to the fruitless campaigns of Domitian that brought triumphs without conquest.[67] This is no clarion call for resuming Roman militarism but a caustic reminder of foolish and often fatal shortcomings in the face of redoubtable Germans. They have been more formidable, he notes, than Samnites, Carthaginians, Spaniards, Gauls, and Parthians. And the historian is quite explicit about the source of their power: the *libertas* of the Germans makes them fiercer than those who live under the despotism of a Parthian.[68] Tacitus' objective (as usual) is more subtle than obvious. The conjecture that he needs to remind his countrymen of how tough Germans are, thereby to prepare them (or to encourage Trajan) for another contest to come, misperceives the historian's project.[69] Tacitus puts stress on *libertas* here, no negative notion but a reservoir of

[65] Tac. *Germ.* 37.2: *tam diu Germania vincitur*.
[66] As, e.g., Drexler (1952), 61–66; Timpe (1989), 81–85. In this connection most of the debate has centered on whether to discern a positive or negative meaning in Tac. *Germ.* 33. 2: *urgentibus imperii fatis*. See the useful surveys of scholarship by Benario (1968), 37–50, and Lund (1991b), 2127–2147. Cf. also the comments of Krebs (2005), 75–81. The matter need not be decided here.
[67] Tac. *Germ.* 37.3–5. See Much (1937), 325–326; Lund (1988), 207; Perl (1990), 226–229. For treatments of *Germ.* 37 in terms of Tacitean ideology, see Paratore (1977), 152–166; Ternes (1980), 165–176; Savino (1989/1990), 99–104; additional bibliography in Lund (1991b), 2151–2157. Much discussion has focused on the implications of *Germ.* 37.4–5: *at Germani Carbone et Cassio et Scauro Aurelio et Servilio Caepione Maximoque Mallio fusis vel captis quinque simul consulares exercitus populo Romano, Varum trisque cum eo legiones etiam Caesari abstulerunt; nec impune C. Marius in Italia, divus Iulius in Gallia, Drusus ac Nero et Germanicus in suis eos sedibus perculerunt; mox ingentes Gai Caesaris minae in ludibrium versae . . . proximis temporibus triumphati magis quam victi sunt*. The relevant bibliography is registered by Beck (1995), 97–132. Beck ingeniously and at undue length seeks to deny the negative connotation of this passage, by repunctuating a crucial part: instead of *abstulerunt; nec impune C. Marius . . .* he proposes *abstulerunt nec impune; C. Marius . . .* But this reverses the entire tenor of the passage from beginning to end. Even when Tacitus is ostensibly evenhanded, he speaks not of successes on both sides but of mutual losses; *Germ.* 37.3: *multa in vicem damna*. That is no accident.
[68] Tac. *Germ.* 37.3: *quippe regno Arsacis acrior est Germanorum libertas*.
[69] For this notion, see, e.g., Thielscher (1962), 15; Dauge (1981), 251–253; Isaac (2004), 436–437.

strength and will that has sustained a people for more than two centuries. The explicit contrast is with eastern despotism rather than with Rome. But the context is that of long-standing contests between Romans and Germans in which the latter's successes are ascribed to *libertas*. Tacitus' readers could draw their own inferences. *Libertas*, far from unrestrained license, has given energy and authority to Germans—and, perhaps, a rebuke to Romans.

The reflection on Rome becomes unmistakable in Tacitus' caustic comment on freedmen, already noted above. The author lauds Germans for keeping *libertini* at the lowest rung of the social ladder, barely above slaves, and for never letting them meddle in public affairs. As all commentators recognize, Tacitus here aims a jab at Roman emperors who elevated freedmen to positions of responsibility and authority, a matter of supreme distaste for the historian. But the language is noteworthy. *Libertini* clamber above not only the freeborn but even the nobility in states ruled by kings. Everywhere else, he claims, proper hierarchy prevails and freedmen know their place—testimony to *libertas*.[70] The term has yet another meaning here, quite different from freedom, let alone license. *Libertas* denotes a society lacking a king but possessing an ordered social structure in which each class has its appropriate station. German communities hold to it; Roman emperors violate it.

Once again, however, a bald contrast misconceives the matter. Many German peoples, on Tacitus' own showing, were in fact subject to royal authority. They had no consistent access to *libertas*—any more than Romans did.

On occasion, the German commitment to *libertas* can overcome even the strictures of autocracy. Tacitus describes the Gotones as a people ruled by kings, somewhat more rigidly so than other German tribes but (he adds) not so rigidly as to repress *libertas*.[71] Even despotic rulers could not always suppress *libertas*. The historian admires it here, sneers at it elsewhere.[72] Consistency is not his object. Fluidity of the concept corresponds to the complicated relationships that both Germans and Romans had with it.

Those relationships, in the historian's presentation, carried additional convoluted complications. As we have seen, Tacitus more than once insinuates that contact with Rome can have a deleterious effect on Germans. Their indifference to precious metals, to commerce, and to cash became

---

[70] Tac. *Germ.* 25.2: *apud ceteros impares libertini libertatis argumentum sunt.* For similar phraseology, see Tac. *Ann.* 14.39.2.

[71] Tac. *Germ.* 44.1: *Gotones regnantur, paulo iam adductius quam ceterae Germanorum gentes, nondum tamen supra libertatem.* For Lund (1988), 228, the contrast is not with all other Germans but with those who have kings.

[72] A clearly positive significance for *libertas* occurs also at *Germ.* 28.3: *quia pari olim inopia ac libertate eadem utriusque ripae bona malaque erant.* Whatever *libertas* signifies here, it is among the *bona*, as *inopia* is among the *mala*.

compromised when the proximity of Romans taught them the value of commodities and bolstered their military resolve with monetary subsidies. One might imagine then that more remote tribes, less subject to Roman influence, would maintain their traditions with greater tenacity and enjoy fuller access to *libertas*. But Tacitus characteristically upsets expectations. The Batavi, for instance, on the Lower Rhine and the North Sea, enjoy the privileges of exemption from Roman tribute and the absence of the tax-farmer. Yet none would apply to them the term *libertas*. They fought for Romans. As Tacitus puts it, they were set apart for use only in battles, reserved for warfare—like weapons and arms.[73] The Batavi would become part of the *imperium Romanum*.[74] The Marcomani and Quadi on the Danube, once governed by their own rulers, now endure the overlordship of foreign kings, and those kings in turn are backed by Roman authority.[75] Distance from Rome evidently does not bring greater freedom of action. The Gotones, as already noted, hail from the remote Baltic but suffer under the most stringent monarchy, even if it has not yet altogether suppressed *libertas*.[76] Things get worse when Tacitus moves farther geographically. He characterizes the Rigii and Lemovii as notably subservient to their kings.[77] Among the Suiones, the ruler's authority has no restrictions, and the claim on obedience is unequivocal.[78] When he comes to the Sitones, at the outer end of Suebia, Tacitus reckons them as so far from *libertas* that they have even dropped below servitude because they are ruled by a woman.[79] Distance from Rome, therefore, does not allow Germans to breathe a freer air, rather the reverse.[80] As so often, the historian disdains simplistic dichotomies. *Libertas* no more defines Germans than it defines Romans. Germans might enjoy *libertas*, but they can also take it to excess or indeed fall short of it. Romans may aspire to it but too often betray it. Tacitus plays with the concept, but applies it in complex and elusive ways to both societies.

Nor does Tacitus hesitate to assign that quintessential Roman term, *virtus*, to the Germans. It crops up regularly in describing their aims, values, and character. Germans may choose their rulers for reasons of genealogy, but they pick their military leaders for their *virtus*.[81] On the battlefield, honor demands that a *princeps* allow no one to exceed him in *virtus*, and a

---

[73] Tac. *Germ.* 29.1: *tantum in usum proeliorum sepositi, velut tela atque arma, bellis reservantur.*
[74] Tac. *Germ.* 29.1: *pars Romani imperii fierent.*
[75] Tac. *Germ.* 42.2.
[76] Tac. *Germ.* 44.1.
[77] Tac. *Germ.* 44.1.
[78] Tac. *Germ.* 44.3.
[79] Tac. *Germ.* 45.6. See above, n. 43.
[80] Cf. the remarks of Rives (1999), 310.
[81] Tac. *Germ.* 7.1: *reges ex nobilitate, duces ex virtute sumunt.* On Tacitus' use of *reges* and *duces*, see Much (1937), 104–107; Perl (1990), 154; Rives (1999), 144–146. On Tacitus' depiction of

similar drive motivates his retinue to equal his *virtus*.[82] The battle cry of the Germans, as Tacitus presents it, seems not so much the sound of voices as a convergence of *virtus*.[83] That phraseology implies that *virtus* was a central ingredient embedded in their military being, acknowledged, even endorsed, by Tacitus, a signal of values parallel to those of Romans. Comparable assessments appear when Tacitus treats certain individual tribes. In singling out the Batavi for praise, Tacitus designates them as preeminent among neighboring tribes for *virtus*.[84] The Chatti, another Germanic people whom Tacitus admires for their martial success, disdain reliance on fortune as too questionable but bank on *virtus* as a solid foundation.[85] Their warriors, in fact, remain vigorous and active until old age renders them unequal to the harsh demands of *virtus*.[86] And the historian, most interestingly, adds that the Chatti, rare among Germans, put faith in their leader rather than in the rank and file—a trait otherwise reserved for Roman discipline.[87] Hence he juxtaposes his praise for the Chatti as holding *virtus* as a goal with his likening of their military discipline to that of Rome. Tacitus can identify overlapping traits as well as contrasts. *Virtus* links rather than divides the peoples.

Virtus does not confine itself to courage in battle or martial prowess.[88] In fact, it can even signal a successful policy of peace. Tacitus gives plaudits to the Chauci as most noble of German tribes who prefer to preserve their realm through justice rather than arms, who provoke no wars, and who refrain from rapine and plunder. This may be unusual among Germans. But it constitutes, for Tacitus, the best proof of their strength—and of their *virtus*.[89] He associates the alien unhesitatingly, whether in war or in peace, with a *virtus* readily recognizable to Romans.

German political and social institutions more generally, see Timpe (1988), 502–525; Lund (1988), 35–43.

[82] Tac. *Germ.* 14.1. See also 13.2.

[83] Tac. *Germ.* 3.2: *nec tam voces illae quam virtuti concentus videntur.* The manuscript reading should be retained here. The emendation of *vocis . . . videtur* has little to recommend it, despite Much (1937), 53; Anderson (1938), 49. Lund (1988), 119–120, prefers to emend with *audiuntur*, for which there is no good justification. Perl (1990), 82, rightly prints the manuscript reading. The translation of Rives (1999), 78, follows it, although he seems unaware of the problem.

[84] Tac. *Germ.* 29.1.

[85] Tac. *Germ.* 30.2: *fortunam inter dubia, virtutem inter certa numerare.*

[86] Tac. *Germ.* 31.3. See the long note by Much (1937), 295–298.

[87] Tac. *Germ.* 30.2: *quoque rarissimum nec nisi Romanae disciplinae concessum, plus reponere in duce quam in exercitu.* Some manuscripts have the alternate reading, *ratione* for *Romanae*. The former is preferred by Lund (1988), 194–195, but this requires emendation to *rationi*, and his argument for abandoning *Romanae* is weak.

[88] Städele (1990), 162–163, wrongly sees it restricted to a military meaning.

[89] Tac. *Germ.* 35.2: *id praecipuum virtutis ac virium argumentum est.*

The Roman concept of "manliness" had still wider connotations.[90] And Tacitus shows no difficulty in bringing Germans within that broader concept. He employs the term in a more abstract sense when speaking on one of his favorite themes: the importance of distinctions in the social hierarchy. He notes the German penchant for providing the same schooling and circumstances to the offspring of both servants and masters. But not for long. When the proper time comes, *virtus* will distinguish the freeborn from the lowborn.[91] The personification of *virtus* is common in Roman conceptualizing. For Tacitus it transfers readily to the German. Among the Chatti, the real coming of age for the warrior youth is demonstrated by the slaying of his first enemy, an event celebrated by removal of hair and beard that had been vowed and committed to *virtus*.[92] Here again a personified *virtus*, indeed one to whom vows were made, appears on the German scene. Whether Tacitus means to suggest a literal performance of a vow to an image or employs a metaphor for rhetorical purposes matters little.[93] The abstraction itself has both a place in the German context and resonance for Rome, a pointed allusion to overlap in the cultures.

Parallels and intersections become more complicated when Tacitus chooses to remark on religion.[94] Gods and heroes in the text appear in forms familiar to the Greco-Roman world. The historian reports legends that bring Herakles and Ulysses to Germany; he names Mercury as chief god of the Germans, Mars, Hercules, and Isis among those to whom they make sacrifice, Castor and Pollux whom they venerate, and the mother of the gods whom they worship.[95] How best to understand this? Customary interpretation sees the nomenclature as nothing more than *interpretatio Romana*, an imposition of Roman names on Teutonic deities, an artificial coupling of divinities that may have had little of substance in common, even a form of Roman cultural imperialism.[96] Perhaps so. But there is more to be said.

[90] See the far-ranging study of McDonnell (2006), who, however, may place too much stress on the military and aggressive aspects of this concept.

[91] Tac. *Germ.* 20.1: *donec aetas separet ingenuos, virtus adgnoscat*.

[92] Tac. *Germ.* 31.1: *nec nisi hoste caeso exuere votivum obligatumque virtuti oris habitum*.

[93] On this see the discussions of Much (1937), 292; Anderson (1938), 155; Perl (1990), 114; Rives (1999), 250.

[94] It is outside the scope of this study to investigate the realities of cults and worship in Germany. Among numerous treatments of this topic, see Spickermann (2001), 94–106. The sober and cautionary study of Timpe (1992), 434–485, argues for a limited and selective interest in German religious practices on Tacitus' part—and none in any abstract notion of "religion."

[95] Tac. *Germ.* 3.1, 9.1, 43.3, 45.2; cf. *Ann.* 2.12.1.

[96] The standard interpretation goes back to Wissowa (1916–1919), 1–49. That it was a feature of Roman cultural imperialism is claimed, among others, by Krebs (2005), 50–53. For Timpe (1992), 448–455, Tacitus' notion of *interpretatio Romana* has a more abstract connotation, rather than suggesting a substantive correspondence with Roman deities. Ando (2005), 41–51, rightly questions the idea that *interpretatio Romana* signifies nothing more than the

Cicero supplies the classic statement to this point: the gods have as many names as there are human languages.[97] And the expression *interpretatio Romana* comes from Tacitus himself, indeed from the *Germania*, the sole example of its use. He speaks of a rather distant and somewhat obscure German tribe, the Nahanarvali. They caught his attention as practicing an ancient ritual in a grove, presided over by a priest in female garb and honoring two divinities, young men and brothers. For Tacitus this was bound to evoke Castor and Pollux, hence an *interpretatio Romana* as he calls it here.[98] The author provides an explicitness and self-consciousness that does not normally characterize his work. The parallel was striking, and Tacitus rightly pointed it out. But he did not subsume the German ritual to the Roman cult, nor did he dissolve the differences. The "force of the divine spirit" reminded him of the Dioscuri; the German name for them was the "Alci."[99] The German rites, however, were strictly their own, with no alien intrusion.[100] When Tacitus elsewhere refers to the Teutonic worship of Mercury, Mars, and Herakles, he evidently detected (or found in his sources) similarities in some German gods that evoked those familiar deities.[101] Yet he does not regard them, despite common perception, as identical figures who are merely accorded different names by different cultures, a rather bland *interpretatio Romana*. Tacitus is alive to the distinctions and keeps readers aware of them. Germans on certain days even offer human sacrifice to Mercury, a practice that Tacitus mentions in passing and on which he avoids judgment—but it would have escaped no one that the institution was reprehensible to his countrymen.[102] Further, a few German divinities appear in his writings for which he provides no Roman equivalents. The *Germania* records an earth goddess named Nerthus, worshipped in common by several tribes, with a ritual that perceives her as riding among the people in a chariot drawn by cows.[103] Elsewhere Tacitus mentions

---

imposition of Roman names on foreign gods. But just how he does understand its meaning remains obscure.

[97] Cic. *Nat. Deor.* 1.83–84: *quot hominum linguae, tot nomina deorum.*

[98] Tac. *Germ.* 43.3: *apud Nahanarvalos antiquae religionis lucus ostenditur; praesidet sacerdos muliebri ornatu, sed deos interpretatione Romana Castorem Pollucemque memorant.*

[99] Tac. *Germ.* 43.3: *ea vis numini, nomen Alcis.*

[100] Tac. *Germ.* 43.3: *nullum peregrinae superstitionis.*

[101] Tac. *Germ.* 9.1. Tacitus' remark about Mercury as being the god most favored with worship by the Germans echoes an identical statement by Caesar about the Gauls; *BG* 6.17.1. And Herodotus much earlier had identified Hermes as chief god of the Thracians; 5.17. But this is more than a literary topos. Interactions between Gauls and Germans in the vicinity of the Rhine, plus the influence of Roman soldiers and settlers, could well have shaped worship of a divinity that suggested Mercury to Roman observers. Cf. Much (1937), 120–124; Perl (1990), 158–159; Rives (1999), 156–158.

[102] Tac. *Germ.* 9.1. Other references to human sacrifice in Perl (1990), 159.

[103] Tac. *Germ.* 40.2–3.

briefly and without explanation the shrines of Tanfana and of Baduhenna.[104] And he registers Teutonic foundation legends with their mythical gods that correspond to the origins of the nations.[105] Tacitus has no agenda to transform alien gods into classical deities.

More strikingly, the historian can shift his vantage point with notable implications. Far from applying a superficial *interpretatio Romana*, he permits a perspective from the inside out. In the case of the Suebi, Tacitus affirms that a segment of that people offers sacrifice to the goddess Isis, a cult well known in Rome and spread widely through the Roman Empire. He specifically designates it, however, as a "foreign cult" whose worship is imported.[106] Of course, Isis is an Egyptian divinity and could be said to have been imported to Rome as well (though she had now been part of the Roman scene at home and abroad for a very long time). But Tacitus is not here peering through Roman lenses. Isis has come as outsider to indigenous German religion. He would make the same point with regard to reverence of the Alci. *Interpretatio Romana* may assimilate them to Castor and Pollux, but, Tacitus insists, the ritual has not a trace of "foreign superstition."[107] The distinctions matter.

In fact, Tacitus takes note of a particularly important distinction. The Germans, so he maintains, were firmly aniconic. They do not shut their gods inside walls and they do not liken them to any form of a human face.[108] He reinforces this statement with regard to the Nahanarvali: they have no images of deities and, as just noted, no sign of alien religion.[109] The blanket statement, to be sure, has its exceptions. Tacitus, as is his wont, subtly qualifies or even undermines his own representation in different contexts. German warriors, in his account, believe that divinity accompanies them when waging war and thus bring with them images and statues from their sacred groves into battle.[110] That takes the form of a general statement. In a concrete instance, the worshippers of Nerthus, the mother earth deity, have a priest who ministers to her and accompanies her chariot ride amidst the people, and then brings her back to her "temple," after which the deity (presumably an image thereof) is bathed in a hidden lake.[111] The description

---

[104] Tac. *Ann.* 1.51.1, 4.73.4.

[105] Tac. *Germ.* 2.2. See the informative notes of Perl (1990), 132–133 and Rives (1999), 108–117. Cf. also the unnamed god of the Semnones, described as *regnator omnium deus*; *Germ.* 39.2.

[106] Tac. *Germ* 9.1: *pars Sueborum et Isidi sacrificat . . . peregrino sacro . . . advectam religionem.*

[107] Tac. *Germ.* 43.3: *nullum peregrinae superstitionis vestigium.* Cf. Much (1937), 381–382.

[108] Tac. *Germ.* 9.2: *nec cohibere parietibus deos neque in ullam humani oris speciem adsimulare.*

[109] Tac. *Germ.* 43.3: *nulla simulacra, nullum peregrinae superstitionis vestigium.*

[110] Tac. *Germ.* 7.2–3: *velut deo imperante, quem adesse bellantibus credunt; effigiesque et signa quaedam detracta lucis in proelium ferunt.*

[111] Tac. *Germ.* 40.3.

would appear to be at odds both with supposed German aniconism and with their rejection of any enclosure to house deities. Scholars have scrambled to explain away the inconsistency: perhaps *templum* refers only to the inner recesses of the sacred grove or another sacred place and the image to some rude and unformed symbol.[112] The efforts are implausible and unnecessary. When Tacitus speaks of a *templum*, he means a building—as he does when speaking of the *templum* of the German goddess Tanfana in the *Annals*.[113] Inconsistencies rarely worried our author.[114] These specifics have the effect of questioning and diminishing the proud claims of Germans to resist artificial images or constructed dwellings of divinity. Once again Tacitean mischief rather than mishap may be in play here. Whatever he may have thought of aniconism as a principle, he let it be known that the Germans themselves, despite their protestations, did not practice it with rigid uniformity.

Tacitus' intentions evade reductionism. His comments on German religion refrain from both praise and disparagement. Nor do they constitute an effort to represent it as some form of primitive worship, rude and unsophisticated but pure, by contrast with the more advanced (for good or ill) forms of Roman worship.[115] Tacitus accounts for the Germans' commitment to eschew temples and images on the grounds that they find them inadequate to express the majesty of heavenly beings.[116] That is no unsophisticated notion. In fact, it accords with the attitude that Varro ascribes to the early Romans, who, allegedly, also avoided divine images because they reckoned them as inadequate to capture the nature of the gods.[117] Similarities and differences weave in and out of the Tacitean account in intricate ways.

The lines of overlap play as important a role as the examples of difference. Legendary deeds of Herakles were not out of place in Teutonic regions, and the wanderings of Ulysses could also be imagined in the lands of the Germans.[118] Tacitus both illustrates contrasting religious practices and

---

[112] So, e.g., Much (1937), 359; Anderson (1938), 190; Lund (1988), 219; Rives (1999), 294–295. Timpe (1989), 87–88, accounts for the discrepancy by seeing the reference to German aniconism as an ethnographic topos; cf. also Perl (1990), 160.

[113] Tac. *Ann.* 1.51.1.

[114] For a sampling of his inconsistencies, see Krebs (2005), 39, n. 23.

[115] So, Cancik (2001), 51–59, 62–63; Krebs (2005), 48–50. In the view of Timpe (1992), 455–485, Tacitus' comments derived from a combination of scattered traditions and isolated reports, which he shaped in accord with his own interests; he had no inclination for a sustained and systematic study.

[116] Tac. *Germ.* 9.2: *neque in ullam humani oris speciem adsimulare ex magnitudine caelestium arbitrantur.*

[117] Varro *apud* Aug. *CD* 4.31. It does not follow that Tacitus alludes to Varro's comment or employs a German analogy as critique of the degeneracy of Roman worship.

[118] Tac. *Germ.* 3. Tacitus does not commit himself to the authenticity of these legends.

finds connection between German and Roman deities. The use of classical names for Teutonic divinities is no mere *interpretatio Romana*, nor is it a syncretistic blending of the gods. Rather it signals that, even with all the differences in practice and belief, the one culture can still be understood in terms applicable to the other.

The *Germania* remains an ambivalent and slippery text. Tacitus neither branded the German as "Other" nor propped him up as inspired primitive to contrast with the degenerate Roman. The historian's nuanced, clever, and often sardonic text had other ends in view. He could point to the foibles of Germans as he did to those of Romans, employing each to reflect on the other. German restraint might contrast with Roman indulgence, but Roman discipline contrasted with German impatience. Roman subsidies to German warriors put in question the martial traditions of both nations. When Tacitus singles out individual German tribes for praise, he casts indirect aspersion not only on Romans but on other Germans. Compromise of principle occurs indiscriminately on both sides of the divide. Prime values associated with Rome, like *libertas* and *virtus*, apply equally to Germans, take a variety of forms and meaning in each society—and experience betrayal in both. Ostensible similarities in modes of worship and characteristics of divinities coexist with a strong sense of distinctiveness felt by both and subtly undermined by Tacitus for each. Germans and Romans alike provide grist to his mill in overlaid fashion. The historian serves up innuendos and imputations with balanced roguery. He aims not to underscore the "Otherness" of the Germans but to dissect and deconstruct it, to complicate and confuse it. For Tacitus, irony regularly trumps ideology.

Chapter 7

◉ ◉ ◉ ◉ ◉ ◉ ◉ ◉ ◉ ◉ ◉ ◉ ◉ ◉ ◉ ◉ ◉

TACITUS AND THE DEFAMATION OF THE JEWS

Jews do not fare very well at the hands of Cornelius Tacitus. The great consular historian devoted thirteen chapters to them at the beginning of book 5 of his *Histories*. Those chapters constituted a digression from his main text, but a remarkably extensive one. Tacitus sets it at the point where he intends to embark on the narrative of the Roman siege of Jerusalem in 70 CE. The reason, as he puts it, is that, since he is about to relate the demise of a famous city, he thought it appropriate to say something about its origins.[1] The opening sends its own signal. Tacitus employs the phrase *famosa urbs*, a characteristically Tacitean touch, that is, "infamous" or "notorious" city rather than "renowned" or "celebrated." And matters seem to go downhill from that point on.

This excursus is the longest extant discussion of the Jews by any Greek or Latin author—or rather by any pagan author. Hence it merits a spotlight for the treatment of ancient attitudes toward Jews. And it does so on more than one count. The digression ostensibly contains some of the most hostile comments on record regarding that people.[2] Among other remarks, Tacitus brands the Jews as a race of men hated by the gods.[3] They regard as profane everything that we (Romans) hold as sacred—and vice versa.[4] Their practices are base and wicked, and prevail through their own depravity.[5] They are a people most especially inclined to lust. Although they will not sleep with gentiles, among themselves there is nothing they will not do (*nihil inlicitum*). Those who cross over to their ways scorn the gods, abandon their own nation, and hold their parents, siblings, and children cheap.[6]

---

[1] Tac. *Hist.* 5.2.1: *sed quoniam famosae urbis supremum diem tradituri sumus congruens videtur primordia eius aperire.*
[2] On the harsh and unusual language employed, see Rosen (1996), 107–108; Bloch (2002), 75–79.
[3] Tac. *Hist.* 5.3.1.
[4] Tac. *Hist.* 5.4.1.
[5] Tac. *Hist.* 5.5.1.
[6] Tac. *Hist.* 5.5.2. Cf. Juv. *Sat.* 14.96–106.

Jewish rites are sordid and ridiculous.[7] Jews throughout their history were the most despised of subject peoples and the basest of nations.[8]

That is pretty strong stuff. One should hardly be surprised that Tacitus has been reckoned as the quintessential pagan anti-Semite, the Jew baiter, a representative of fierce Roman animosity toward Jews, indeed of its most virulent strain. That view prevails almost without dissent.[9] Even those who have found some favorable allusions to Jews in this dark text ascribe them to Tacitus' sources rather than to Tacitus himself.[10] An odd conclusion. If so, did Tacitus transmit those favorable views inadvertently? That historian almost never did anything inadvertently. Modern scholars have without exception taken the digression on the Jews as authentic reflection of Tacitean animosity.[11]

The Question

An immediate question arises. Just why should Tacitus have expressed such offensive opinions about the Jews? The question has important bearing on our understanding of the historian himself. Although his remarks have often been taken as exemplary of Roman reactions in general and hence a window on broader attitudes toward alien religions, they do not, in fact, fit neatly into such a picture.

The vast majority of preserved comments about Jews by Roman writers and intellectuals in the early and high Empire deliver a rather different impression. A brief summary only is required here. More extensive discussions can be found elsewhere.[12] Roman intellectuals, to be sure, were not

[7] Tac. *Hist.* 5.5.5.

[8] Tac. *Hist.* 5.8.2.

[9] So, e.g., I. Levy (1946), 339–340; Wardy (1979), 613, 633–635; Gager (1985), 63–64, 83; Y. Lewy (1989), 15–46; Feldman (1991), 336–339; Mellor (1993), 38, 49, 109; Yavetz (1993), 17; (1998), 90–98; Rosen (1996), 108–126; Barclay (1996), 314–315, 362–363; Schäfer (1997), 31–33, 74–75. See the valuable review of scholarship by Bloch (2002), 17–26. Although he shares the view that Tacitus' portrait is a hostile one, he offers a more nuanced and complex analysis that sets the author apart from simplistic anti-Semites; (2002), 159–176.

[10] Feldman (1991), 336–339, 359–360; (1993), 192–194. See also Rokeah (1995), 293–295, for whom Tacitus embraced earlier Greek denunciations of the Jews but transmitted some favorable traditions as well. Yavetz (1998), 83, acknowledges only hostile Greek sources. None gives much credit to Tacitus' own shaping of the portrait.

[11] The greatest of Tacitean scholars, Sir Ronald Syme, surprisingly evinced almost no interest in the matter. The more than 800 pages of his magisterial two-volume work on the historian devote only a few lines to the subject of Tacitus on the Jews. The opinion expressed, however, takes the standard line: "Tacitus appears to nourish in hypertrophy all the prejudices of an imperial race. His anger bears most heavily upon the Greeks and the Jews." Jews are "beyond the pale"; Syme (1958), 530.

[12] See Gruen (2002b), 27–42; (2002a), 41–52, with bibliography. See now also, with similar views, Goodman (2007), 366–376. The issue of whether any of the expressed Roman judgments

great advocates or admirers of Jews. But their remarks, on the whole, do not fall into the category of intense antipathy. They were generally dismissive or scornful rather than vituperative.

Roman attitudes toward the Jews hardly lend themselves to confident reconstruction. Scattered observations and occasional notices among a range of authors from the late Republic through the high Empire may or may not be representative. At best, they provide a glimpse into the perceptions or misperceptions that Romans held about Jewish character, principles, and practices. Did Jews give the masters of the universe any reason for concern?

Jews were monotheists. For some scholars, Romans may have reckoned this as a challenge to the proper religious order, disrespect for the divinities who guaranteed the security of the Roman empire.[13] But the dichotomy of "monotheism" and "polytheism" has a decidedly anachronistic ring. It owes more to modern conceptualization than to ancient understanding. Neither term would be meaningful to Romans.[14] And there is nothing to suggest that Jewish worship of Yahweh, to the exclusion of other gods, struck the Romans as dangerous or threatening. Indeed the great Roman polymath Varro, writing at the end of the first century BCE, equated the god of the Jews with Jupiter, there being no difference between them other than the name.[15] Varro indeed even gave the Jews high marks for their aniconism, comparing it to the admirable practice of ancient Romans—before they resorted to images that only cheapened piety.[16]

Romans seem untroubled by Jewish religion. They did apply to it the term *superstitio* or *deisidaimonia*, a less than flattering designation.[17] That reflects a supercilious attitude toward alien cults and benighted beliefs. But it betrays no sense of anxiety.[18]

Seneca went further and described the Jews as a pernicious people (*sceleratissima gens*).[19] The expression has become a locus classicus for the thesis that Romans harbored hostility to Jews and reckoned them as criminals. But how characteristic a view was this—even for Seneca? One might observe that the philosopher's vast and varied extant corpus contains no other

---

constituted "anti-Semitism," an endlessly discussed topic, needs no additional rumination. See the useful recent summary of opinions by Isaac (2004), 440–446.

[13] E.g., Feldman (1993), 149–153; *idem* (1997), 44, 51–52; Schäfer (1997), 183–192.

[14] Cf. Beard, North, and Price (1998), I, 212, 286–287, 312. Even the notion of Jewish monotheism is problematic; Hayman (1991), 1–15.

[15] Varro *apud* Augustine *De Consensu Evangelistarum* 1.30; cf. 1.31, 1.42.

[16] Varro *apud* Augustine *CD* 4.31.

[17] E.g., Cic. *Pro Flacco* 67; Seneca *apud* Augustine *CD* 6.11; Plut. *De Stoic.Rep* 38; *De Superst.* 69C; Quintilian 3.7.21; Tac. *Hist.* 2.4, 5.8.2–3, 5.13.1; *Ann.* 2.85. Cf. Horace *Sat.* 1.5.97–101, who alludes to the Jewish penchant for credulity.

[18] On *superstitio*, see Beard, North, and Price (1998), I, 214–227.

[19] Seneca *apud* Augustine *CD* 6.11.

direct mention of Jews at all.[20] And this passage itself comes secondhand from Augustine's *City of God*. The context for the remark and the intentions of Seneca remain indecipherable. It falls well short of evidence for general Roman apprehension about the Jews.[21]

Juvenal might appear to signal a deeper disquiet about the Jewish menace. He maintains that Jews are wont to despise Roman enactments, preferring instead to learn, obey, and fear Jewish law, which Moses handed down in some secret tome.[22] But it is hazardous to place too serious an interpretation on Juvenal's sardonic wit. These comments occur in the midst of Juvenal's broader mockery of the Jews' peculiar practices, all of them, in Juvenal's eyes, more laughable than dangerous. His contrast of Roman *leges* and Jewish *ius* does not denote genuinely competing institutions or legal systems, but the satirist's derision of idiosyncratic Jewish customs.

Those customs provided fodder for caricature. Most prominent was the Jews' penchant (or reputation) for holding to their own kind. Adherence to tradition seemed for many to require separatism and detachment, a wariness of too much intermingling. Greeks noticed this well before the Romans, labeling the Jews as antisocial, even misanthropic.[23] Juvenal characteristically found a way to make fun. He observed that Jews are so exclusive in keeping their own company that they decline even to give directions in the street to those who are not circumcised—quite a feat since men were not in the habit of going about unclothed.[24] The exaggeration is patent. Jews, to be sure, preferred their own communities. But that tendency would not give Romans any concern.

There was, to be sure, concern about converts. Tacitus, as we shall see below, makes reference to converts who abandoned ancestral gods and traditions. Juvenal's snide remark about people embracing Mosaic law and scrapping Roman *leges* also applies essentially to converts. Does this indicate a Roman wariness of Jewish proselytism that threatened to corrode allegiance to the deities who protected the state? The case for Jewish missionary activity of any sort is weak and unpersuasive.[25] The comments of Tacitus

---

[20] Interestingly, Quintilian also calls them a *perniciosa gens* on one occasion (3.7.2)—and never mentions them again.

[21] Cf. Goodman (2007), 373–374.

[22] Juv. *Sat.* 14.100–102: *Romanas autem soliti contemnere leges / Iudaicum ediscunt et servant ac metuunt ius / tradidit arcano quodcumque volumine Moyses*. Schäfer (1997), 185, takes this as suggesting Jewish rejection of the Roman system and embrace of an alternative authority.

[23] So, e.g., Hecataeus of Abdera *apud* Diod. 40.3.4; Manetho *apud* Jos. *CAp.* 1.239; Posidonius *apud* Diod. 34/5.1–3; Apollonius Molon *apud* Jos. *CAp.* 2.148.

[24] Juv. *Sat.* 14.104.

[25] No need here to rehash the arguments about whether or not the Jews proselytized. The negative case is made most persuasively by Goodman (1992), 53–78; *idem* (1994), 60–90. For other bibliography on both sides, see Gruen (2002a), 274–275, n. 206.

and Juvenal, though they complain about those who leave the fold, give no hint of aggressive Jewish activity to solicit them. Seneca, however, makes an ostensibly more ominous remark: the Jewish way of life prevails so widely that it permeates all the lands of the world—so much so that the vanquished impose their laws on the victors.[26] How seriously to take it?[27] The meaning and implications of that peculiar statement are difficult to assess. Once again we do not have access to Seneca's words at first hand but only through the intermediary of St. Augustine. Insofar as a context is provided, the comment follows on the heels of the philosopher's mockery of Jews' idleness on the Sabbath, a disparagement of their general lethargy.[28] Emphasis on Jewish lethargy hardly advances the notion that zealous missionaries undermined (or were thought to undermine) the Roman religious establishment.[29]

What did Romans have to fear from Jews? Their economic power? Jews did pay an annual tribute to Jerusalem, and the Temple (before its destruction) was the repository of some wealth. But the stereotype of the greedy and unscrupulous financial predator who preys on Gentiles is altogether anachronistic—and for the ancient period quite absurd. Roman satirists like Martial and Juvenal, in fact, far from representing the Jews of Rome as plutocrats tended to bracket them with beggars.[30]

By far the heaviest proportion of Roman remarks on Jews have a common character. They consist of allusions to quaint and curious Jewish traits, practices, and customs that attracted attention precisely because they seemed outlandish—but not because they represented any reason for alarm.

Romans puzzled over the observance of the Sabbath, they found monotheism foolish, they wondered why anyone would exclude pork from his diet, and they regarded circumcision as mutilation of the genitals. So, for instance, Seneca made the crack that, by observing the Sabbath, Jews use up one-seventh of their lives in idleness.[31] Pliny the Elder indeed claims to know of a river in Judaea that dries up every Sabbath. One should presumably infer that even Jewish rivers take one day a week off.[32]

---

[26] Seneca *apud* Augustine *CD* 6.11: *cum interim usque eo sceleratissimae gentis consuetudo convaluit, ut per omnes iam terras recepta sit; victi victoribus leges dederunt.*

[27] Isaac (2004), 458–459, 479–480, inclines to think that this does reflect genuine Roman concern about the threats that converts posed.

[28] Seneca *apud* Augustine *CD* 6.11: *multa in tempore urgentia non agendo laedantur.*

[29] Horace's lines in *Sat.* 1.4.139–143 have often been taken to suggest Jewish proselytism. See bibliography in Gruen (2002a), 275, n. 208. Add now Isaac (2004), 455. But the poet says only that "we [the band of poets], like the Jews, will compel you to defer to this throng" (*ac veluti te Iudaei cogemus in hanc concedere turbam*). This need have nothing to do with conversion. Jews never engaged (or were even accused of engaging) in compulsion to gain converts.

[30] Martial 12.57.13; Juv. 3.10–16, 3.296, 6.542–547; cf. Isaac (2004), 464–465. On Jewish economic circumstances, see Sevenster (1975), 575–588; Applebaum (1976), 631–700.

[31] Seneca *apud* Augustine *CD* 6.11.

[32] Pliny *NH* 31.24.

Abstention from pork struck the Romans as especially bizarre. Petronius concluded that since Jews do not touch pork, they must worship a pig-god (*porcinum numen*).[33] Juvenal observed that Judaea is the one place in the world where pigs must be happiest, for they can live to a ripe old age.[34] Plutarch went to the lengths of inventing a wholesale dialogue in which the interlocutors debated whether Jews shrank from pork out of reverence for the hog or abhorrence of that creature. It is not easy to take the arguments on either side as entirely serious. The spokesman who maintained that Jews honored the animal suggested that pigs first dug up the soil with their projecting snouts, thereby prompting men to conceive the idea of inventing the plow, from which Jews learned to farm the soil. And the interlocutor on the other side offered as one explanation for Jewish distaste for pork that pigs' eyes are so twisted and pointed downward that they can never see anything above them unless they are carried upside down.[35] That hardly seems a compelling reason for refraining from swine's flesh. One may well suspect that Plutarch was having his own little joke in this fictitious after-dinner debate.

Circumcision provoked a similar combination of perplexity, misinformation, and amused disdain. For Horace, "circumcised Jews" was a natural expression.[36] Petronius remarks about a talented Jewish slave who possesses many skills that he has but two faults: he is circumcised and he snores—never mind that he is also cross-eyed.[37] Martial's poems included one to the notorious nymphomaniac Caelia, who gave her favors even to the genitals of circumcised Jews, and another that referred to a circumcised poet who indulged in both plagiarism and pederasty.[38] As Philo noted, circumcision regularly drew ridicule from non-Jews.[39]

In short, most Romans writing in the early and high Empire who deigned to take notice of this alien people contented themselves with superficial appearances and impressions. As a consequence, they retailed shallow, half-baked, and misinformed opinions. They were either indifferent to Jews or derided them with mockery.

Why should Tacitus be any different? Did he carry a bitterness and anger that set him apart? Some scholars have indeed detected a deep-seated antagonism and proposed reasons for it. A number of explanations have made the rounds. Tacitus sought, so it is claimed, to justify Rome's destruction of the Temple in Jerusalem and thus felt a pressing need to

---

[33] Petronius fr. 37.
[34] Juv. *Sat.* 6.159–160; cf. 14.98–99.
[35] Plut. *Quaest. Conv.* 4.4–5.
[36] Horace *Sat.* 1.9.70: *curtis Iudaeis*.
[37] Mart. *Sat.* 6.8.8; cf. 102.14.
[38] Martial 7.30.5, 11.94.
[39] Philo *Spec. Leg.* 1.1–2.

blacken Jews, their beliefs, and their practices as forcefully as possible.[40] On a different view, Jewish proselytism enraged Tacitus. The historian was furious that this defeated people should still be in Rome and elsewhere converting good gentiles to their wicked creed and undermining Roman morals.[41] Or else his intense aversion represented anxiety about this rebellious folk who continued to multiply, rejected Roman deities, grew in strength, and threatened Roman values.[42] The digression has elsewhere simply been dismissed as a product of anti-Semitism, ignorance, and silliness.[43]

None of these suggestions compels assent. The idea that the Jewish nation, so devastatingly crushed in the failed revolt of 66–73 CE, represented any sort of threat to Rome or was even perceived to do so stretches the imagination. Tacitus composed his *Histories* in the period from roughly 105 to 110 CE, long after the Jewish revolt and in a period of Jewish quiescence. To be sure, new outbreaks of rebellion would occur near the end of Trajan's reign, several years after publication of the *Histories*. But unless we confer on Tacitus the mantle of a prophet, he can have had no inkling of that.[44] The Jews of Rome itself, it is worth noting, did not participate in either uprising. Their circumstances, so far as we can tell, were no different in Tacitus' time than they had been before. If they engaged in any vigorous proselytism, for which there is in fact little or no evidence, they seem to have carried it on without interference—and without any concern on the part of Roman authorities.

What of the purported need to justify the destruction of the Temple? No hint exists that Tacitus or any other Roman felt the urgency to manufacture an apologia by ascribing moral failings or religious perniciousness to the Jews. The practices of the Jews had been familiar to dwellers in Rome for at least two centuries. They may have found them bizarre, but hardly menacing. Nothing in monotheism gave cause for anxiety, and Romans had long tolerated Jewish unwillingness to participate in the imperial cult. Destruction of the Temple followed a lengthy and tenacious rebellion. The Jews, as the conqueror and future emperor Titus put it in

[40] Lewy (1989), 28–34; Yavetz (1998), 94; S. Cohen (2006), 49. Rightly questioned by Bloch (2002), 167–168.
[41] Yavetz (1993), 17; (1997), 47–48; (1998), 97–98; Barclay (1996), 315, 409–410.
[42] Wardy (1979), 633–635; Gager (1985), 63–64; Lewy (1989), 31–42; Rosen (1996), 110–111; Schäfer (1997), 185–192. For Bloch (2002), 102–107, Tacitus emphasizes the rebelliousness of the Jews.
[43] Chilver (1985), 90.
[44] Rosen (1996), 119–126, actually attributes foresight of this sort to Tacitus on the grounds of Jewish apocalyptic literature of which he might have had at least indirect knowledge—a far-fetched hypothesis. Bloch (2002), 132, is rightly skeptical. References to scholarly discussions in Heubner and Fauth (1982), 151–155. Some even find source material for Tacitus in the Dead Sea Scrolls; Griffiths (1970), 363–378; (1979), 99–100; Barrett (1976), 366.

the account of Josephus, had been ingrates, turned against their Roman benefactors, and bit the hand that fed them.[45] Romans required no further justification.

How then does one account for Tacitus' rage and bitterness? To begin, it is important to note that the historian's excursus on the Jews by no means constitutes a consistently anti-Jewish tract. A number of remarks imply a rather positive assessment, even admiration of Jewish character or actions. So, for example, among the stories that Tacitus retails regarding the origin of the Jews is one that identifies them with the Solymoi, celebrated in the Homeric poems, whence they got the name Hierosolyma (Jerusalem) for their central city—a most distinguished lineage, says Tacitus.[46] In recounting a version of the Israelite exodus from Egypt, Tacitus ascribes to Moses a speech affirming self-reliance and determination to his people.[47] The historian, in his own voice, pays a comparable compliment, asserting that the inhabitants of Judaea were men of healthy constitution and capable of enduring fatigue.[48] Indeed, they proved themselves durable in other ways. Tacitus elsewhere affirms that the Jews patiently suffered the oppression of Roman procurators until the arrival of Gessius Florus, when they could not take it any longer.[49] Jews then readied themselves for the onslaught of Roman power. They had, according to Tacitus, made every provision, well in advance, for a lengthy siege.[50] When the assault came, everyone who could take up arms did so, indeed more than their numbers would ever have suggested.[51] Men and women exhibited tenacious resolve, reckoning death preferable to loss of their country.[52] This was unmistakably admirable behavior. And not for the first time. Tacitus reports that when Gaius Caligula proposed to set up his image in the Temple in Jerusalem, the Jews preferred to take up arms rather than to acquiesce.[53] Further, Tacitus notes, Jews may not be eager to mix with gentiles, but among themselves they show a fierce loyalty and a ready compassion.[54] They regard it as evil to slay any late-born child, they consider all souls lost in battle or by execution to be immortal, and they thus have no fear of death.[55] In all these

---

[45] Jos. *BJ* 6.333–336.
[46] Tac. *Hist.* 5.2.2.
[47] Tac. *Hist.* 5.3.1. See the notes on this passage by Heubner and Fauth (1982), 33–38.
[48] Tac. *Hist.* 5.6.1.
[49] Tac. *Hist.* 5.10.1. Bloch (2002), 106–107, unjustifiably puts a negative interpretation on this.
[50] Tac. *Hist.* 5.12.2; cf. 2.4.3.
[51] Tac. *Hist.* 5.13.3: *arma cunctis, qui ferre possent, et plures quam pro numero audebant.*
[52] Tac. *Hist.* 5.13.3: *obstinatio viris feminisque par; ac si transferre sedis cogerentur, maior vitae metus quam mortis.* Bloch (2002), 112, 150–157, here too sees this as an unfavorable verdict.
[53] Tac. *Hist.* 5.9.2.
[54] Tac. *Hist.* 5.5.1.
[55] Tac. *Hist.* 5.5.3. See the commentary of Heubner and Fauth (1982), 74–76.

statements Tacitus takes a decidedly admiring line on Jewish traits, values, and behavior.

What do we make of this paradox? Is this schizophrenia on the part of Tacitus? One does not readily discern such a characteristic in that crafty and calculating historian. Did he get the favorable bits from his sources and transmit them, even though inconsistent with his own assessment? If so, this can only be by design, not through inattention. Did he underscore Jewish courage and determination in order to alert Romans to the possible menace that Jews represented? Hardly a plausible scenario for a people whose rebellion, for all its doggedness, had ended in abject failure. Have we then reached a dead end? Should one regard the Tacitean account a mere muddle, a mass of confusion? Few will take that route.

Tacitean Irony

A different approach may be salutary. Whatever else may be said about Tacitus, one aspect of his work holds primacy. Tacitus is the consummate ironist. None questions the fact, which is obvious on almost every page of the historian's work.[56] Paradox and inconsistency abound, juxtaposed statements and explanations undermine one another, suggestions are put forward, then turned upside down, plausible versions emerge only to be compromised by subtle hints, bitter jibes, or cynical analysis. None of this is innocent, none of it is inadvertent. The wit is sharp, and the humor is dark. One thinks immediately, of course, of the biting barbs aimed at the Julio-Claudians in the *Annals*. But Tacitus' caustic wit was already there in the *Histories*. None can forget the concentrated contempt in his assessment of Galba: *capax imperii—nisi imperasset*.[57] Equally devastating is the historian's remark on the exchange of letters between Otho and Vitellius, each accusing the other of shamelessness and felonies: they were both right (*neuter falso*).[58]

A fresh look at the excursus on the Jews in this light offers provocative possibilities. Previous interpretations have tended to play it straight. They have taken the anti-Jewish statements as read, a symptom of Tacitean prejudices and animosity, even of a broader Roman malice. The ostensibly favorable comments are then explained away as conveying the opinions of others, not Tacitus' own, or as a means of alerting Romans to the dangers of Jewish strengths and accomplishments. All this

---

[56] See Robin (1973), 1–24, 245–323, and passim; O'Gorman (2000), 10–22, 176–183, and passim.
[57] Tac. *Hist*. 1.49.
[58] Tac. *Hist*. 1.74.

misses the irony and black humor for which Tacitus is otherwise justly renowned.[59]

Perhaps the most conspicuous paradox occurs in relation to a matter that speaks directly to Jewish religious sensibilities: images in the Temple. Tacitus asserts flatly, without ascribing the report to other authors, gossip, or rumor, that the Jews dedicated an image (plainly a statue) of an ass in the inner sanctum of their sacred shrine. That animal, he had earlier noted, this time on the authority of other writers, had directed Israelite wandering in the wilderness to a watering hole, thus preventing them from perishing of thirst.[60] The image of an ass in the Temple? Is this evidence for anti-Semitic propaganda retailed by our historian? That would be a hasty inference. In a subsequent paragraph, Tacitus, without referring to his previous statement, refutes it unequivocally. He asserts that the Jewish conception of the deity is a purely mental construct, and that Jews condemn as profane those who set up images of gods in the form of men.[61] Moreover, he adds, they erect no statues in their cities, let alone in their temples.[62] Tacitus reinforces this affirmation a bit later in the text when he records the entrance into the Temple of the conquering Pompey, who found the shrine empty, devoid of any representation of the gods.[63]

Where did the statue go? Interpreters have scrambled to explain away this starkly discordant note.[64] Was Tacitus perhaps only transmitting other writers' accounts of the ass story? Not very likely. He alludes to no other authors here. Does the "image," *effigies*, refer only to a dedication, not a sacred object, that is, an *anathema* rather than an *agalma*? In the context of his statement, which involves a direct contrast of Jewish and Egyptian *worship* of divinities, that is a most implausible interpretation.[65] Was Tacitus

---

[59] Bloch (2002), the best study of the excursus, does recognize ironic elements in it, 174–176, but sees them in the service of Tacitus' broader purpose, a dark portrait of the Jews. The fine treatment of Tacitean irony by O'Gorman (2000) confines itself to the *Annales*. Robin (1973) takes a much broader sweep. But the excursus on the Jews receives only one brief paragraph in his extensive work; 303. Plass's useful monograph (1988) has much of value to say about wit, parody, and incongruity in Tacitus but also gives less than a paragraph to the Jewish excursus; 55.

[60] Tac. *Hist*. 5.4.2: *effigiem animalis, quo monstrante errorem sitimque depulerant, penetrali sacravere*; cf. 5.3.2: *grex asinorum*.

[61] Tac. *Hist*. 5.5.4: *Iudaei mente sola unumque numen intellegunt; profanos qui deum imagines mortalibus materiis in species hominum effingant*.

[62] Tac. *Hist*. 5.5.4: *igitur nulla simulacra urbibus suis, nedum templis sistunt*.

[63] Tac. *Hist*. 5.9.1.

[64] Efforts to wriggle out of the inconsistency are conveniently assembled by Bloch (2002), 66. See also Sevenster (1975), 120–121. They point to the paradox but provide no real resolution. Bloch's view that Tacitus did not worry about inconsistencies so long as they left his general picture unaffected is unsatisfactory; 65–67, 159–160.

[65] The sharp contrast with Egyptian animal worship seriously undermines the argument of Heinen (1992), 124–149, that Tacitus' excursus on the Jews was drawn largely from anti-Jewish Egyptian sources.

simply nodding the first time, then correcting himself, without having the mettle to admit the earlier mistake? That too has been suggested. In such an event, however, the historian could simply have erased the offending lines. And it is always hazardous to ascribe inattention to the ever-vigilant Tacitus.

Leaving the two inconsistent assertions in place and unreconciled must be deliberate. The story of Jewish adherence to a cult of the ass was in circulation. In one form or another, it had appeared in Diodorus, in Apion, and in Josephus (who, of course, rejected it).[66] Without explicitly refuting it, a heavy-handedness that would not accord with Tacitus' normal style, he presents it in a matter-of-fact fashion—and then, in similar fashion, reports Jewish aniconism as well known and long established. The implication was subtle and suggestive: no need for argument, let alone for reconciling contradiction. The irony exposed the fatuousness of those who imagined an Eselkult among a people who scorned both images and animals.

A comparable example emerges from close scrutiny of another item in the text. Tacitus ostensibly reacts with *ira* and *studium* against the converts to Judaism: they despise the gods, turn their backs on their *patria*, and hold their own parents, children, and siblings in contempt.[67] The language is harsh, suspiciously so, perhaps consciously hyperbolic. Tacitus' outburst here, unsurprisingly, has caused many to infer that Jewish proselytism had deeply infiltrated Roman society and undermined Roman values.[68] Commentators, however, have overlooked a rather intriguing incongruity in the Tacitean presentation on this point. Only a few lines earlier, he had depicted in sardonic fashion the Jews' observance of the Sabbath. The Jews, in his account, adopted the practice of taking leisure every seventh day because, so they say (*ferunt*), it represents an end to their labors.[69] This, of course, had been observed by a number of Latin writers such as Seneca, who, as we saw, derided the Jews for wasting one-seventh of their lives in idleness.[70] But Tacitus went him one better, adding that they enjoyed the delights of indolence so much that they created the Sabbatical year in order to prolong their sloth.[71] That delivers a characteristically Tacitean insinuation. But a more interesting implication lies therein. A proclivity to idleness is hardly compatible with a policy of energetic proselytism. Once again, this surely represents no innocent conjunction by

---

[66] On the "ass-libel," see Bar-Kochva (1996), 310–326; *idem* (2010), 206–249.

[67] Tac. *Hist.* 5.5.2: *transgressi in morem eorum idem usurpant, nec quicquam prius imbuuntur quam contemnere deos, exuere patriam, parentes liberos fratres vilia habere.*

[68] See the works cited by Heubner and Fauth (1982), 70–73. Add also Feldman (1993), 300; Barclay (1996), 315, 410; Schäfer (1997), 32.

[69] Tac. *Hist.* 5.4.3: *septimo die otium placuisse ferunt, quia is finem laborum tulerit.*

[70] Seneca *apud* Augustine *CD* 6.11. Other references in Heubner and Fauth (1982), 54–57.

[71] Tac. *Hist.* 5.4.3: *dein blandiente inertia septimum quoque annum ignaviae datum.*

Tacitus. In the directly preceding passage, which contains his remarks about converts to Judaism who were indoctrinated to despise their own gods, country, and families, Tacitus provided a noteworthy account of Jewish practices. The Jews, he claims, keep themselves apart from all other peoples, even exhibit an undeviating detestation of them. They emphasized their distinction from all gentiles.[72] The paradox is stark. How does one gain converts among gentiles while insisting on dissimilitude and distance from them? The juxtaposition of two incompatible ideas, once more, is unlikely to be an accident. The historian deftly discloses the incongruity of holding both those opinions simultaneously. This is less a statement of Tacitus' own attitude toward Jews than a sardonic comment on simplistic stereotypes.

At the outset of his Jewish excursus, Tacitus lists no fewer than six different—and largely incompatible—versions of where the Jews came from. They have received much discussion.[73] For our purposes it is unnecessary to dwell on them at length. Most of the debate has centered on the issue of which of these versions Tacitus actually believed—or wanted his readers to believe. That may be precisely the wrong question to ask. Scholars have pored over the different tales, finding some favorable, some neutral, and at least one downright hostile. General agreement has it that Tacitus opted for the last, the most negative portrait, one drawn from Egyptian sources that conveyed a dark tale of the Exodus as an expulsion of Jews for having brought a plague upon the land.[74] On the face of it, that appears to make sense. Tacitus saves the story for the end, he ascribes to it a consensus of most authorities, and he devotes more space to it than to all the other versions combined. Presumably, then, this is what he wanted his readers to remember, without having committed himself to it—a familiar Tacitean technique. One need mention only the famous account of Augustus' character and motivations as perceived by two opposing groups of interpreters at his funeral in the beginning of the *Annals*.[75] The debunking interpretation comes last, has greater length, and is more memorable. On that analogy, Tacitus here too opts for the most hostile tale, further evidence for his animosity toward the Jews.

The conclusion seems obvious. But the obvious solution is not always the correct one. Strong reasons call for reconsideration. First, the allegedly

---

[72] Tac. *Hist.* 5.5.1–2: *adversus omnis alios hostile odium; separati epulis, discreti cubilibus . . . circumcidere genitalia instituerunt ut diversitate noscantur.*

[73] See, e.g., I. Levy (1946), 331–340; Feldman (1991), 339–360; (1993), 184–196; Yavetz (1998), 91–94; Bloch (2002), 84–90. See also the valuable assemblage of references in Heubner and Fauth (1982), 20–43.

[74] Tac. *Hist.* 5.3.1; Heubner and Fauth (1982), 30; Rosen (1996), 111–112; Schäfer (1997), 31; Yavetz (1998), 91–94.

[75] Tac. *Ann.* 1.9–10; cf. Yavetz (1998), 93.

negative narrative, saved for the end and given at some length, is not all that negative. The story identifies the Jews as deriving from Egypt, blamed for a plague that infected the country and expelled by the king on the advice of the oracle of Ammon.[76] Hence began the Exodus, a wandering in the wilderness under the leadership of Moses, the discovery of an oasis through the arrival of a herd of wild asses, and a march of six days. On the seventh, they seized the Promised Land, drove out the inhabitants, and then founded a city in which they dedicated their Temple.[77] Comparable stories, with variants, can be found in several earlier authors, from the time of Manetho in the early third century BCE. Tacitus did not invent the material, but he did put his own spin on it. The earlier narratives, from Manetho to Apion, contained far harsher assessments of the Hebrews as lepers and villains. Tacitus omits most of that and even holds Moses in some esteem for his leadership in bringing his people to eventual triumph.[78] To be sure, he calls them "a race of men hateful to the gods" (*genus hominum invisum deis*). But it is essential to stress that Tacitus does not here deliver his own judgment. He conveys the characterization applied to Jews by the Egyptian king, and the gods in question are the Egyptian gods—a vital distinction. These are not divinities whom Tacitus embraced (the Egyptians, after all, worshipped animals). And the last part of the passage is particularly noteworthy. The Hebrews wandered for just six days and accomplished their purpose on the seventh. The figure of six days for the time spent in the wilderness plainly served others as an etiological explanation for the Sabbath.[79] But Tacitus takes it to a whole new level. He has them not only arrive in the Promised Land on the seventh day but expel all the indigenous dwellers and occupy the whole country in which they founded Jerusalem and built the Temple![80] To debate the degree to which this account is favorable or unfavorable seems singularly irrelevant. Its main characteristic is absurdity. And one would be hard-pressed to imagine that Tacitus expected anyone to believe it. As a vehicle for blackening Jews, this would hardly do the job.

Furthermore, the other stories of Jewish origins that Tacitus retails more briefly and ascribes to unnamed sources claim no greater credibility. Some of them assigned the Jews' beginnings to the island of Crete at the time when Saturn lost his throne to Jupiter. The explanation for this theory, according to Tacitus, lay in the existence of Mount Ida in Crete, which led

---

[76] Tac. *Hist.* 5.3.1.
[77] Tac. *Hist.* 5.3.1–2.
[78] Cf. Heubner and Fauth (1982), 30–33; Feldman (1991), 354–357; (1993), 192–194.
[79] Justin 36.2.14; Apion *apud* Jos. *CAp.* 2.21; Plut. *Isis and Osiris* 31.
[80] Tac. *Hist.* 5.3.2: *et continuum sex dierum iter emensi septimo pulsis cultoribus obtinuere terras, in quis urbs et templum dicata.* The phraseology, probably intentional, leaves the impression that the city and Temple were founded in Moses' lifetime. Cf. Heubner and Fauth (1982), 42.

some to identify the Idaei of Mount Ida with the Iudaei of Judaea.[81] Such a notion stands neither to the advantage nor to the disadvantage of the Jews.[82] Rather it serves to discredit the story. The alternative versions reach similar levels of implausibility. One has the Jews migrate from Egypt at the time of Isis, also in the distant mists of legendary antiquity.[83] Another has them stem from Ethiopia, driven by fear and hatred to seek new lands in the reign of King Cepheus, father of Andromeda, once more shrouded in myth and beyond chronology.[84] Still another makes them Assyrian by origin, a striking contrast with the biblical narrative in which Assyrians are the fiercest foes of the Israelites. In Tacitus' account they lacked sufficient land in Assyria, packed their bags, conquered part of Egypt, and planted their own cities in the Hebrew country adjoining Syria.[85] Further, he records the apparently flattering tale that identifies Jews with the Solymoi, a Lycian people renowned in the Homeric epics for their toughness as fighters. But flattery is not Tacitus' prime objective. The root of this fiction counts for more. The name of Jerusalem, Hierosolyma, suggested to some a connection with the Solymoi, thereby generating the conjecture.[86] Once again the issue of whether or not the yarn compliments the Jews misses the point. Tacitus in this entire segment simply plays with a farrago of legends that foolish authors have transmitted and credulous readers have bought. We hear the voice of the sardonic historian, not the Jew hater.

The digression reinforces this analysis at several junctures. Comments frequently serve Tacitus' purpose less as reflections on the Jews than as indirect jabs against others. So, for instance, he refers to Jewish sacrifices of rams and oxen. Why make this seemingly innocuous point? Tacitus leaves his readers in little doubt. Jews sacrifice the ram, he explains, as if to deliver a deliberate insult to Egyptian reverence for the ram-god Ammon. And they slay the ox as a further affront to the Egyptians, worshippers of the Apis bull.[87] Tacitus, we may venture to assume, knew full well that the ancient Israelites led a variety of animals to the sacrifice—as did the Greeks and the Romans. That he should single out these particular motives for

---

[81] Tac. *Hist.* 5.2.1. See Feldman (1991), 339–346; (1993), 184–188, for whom this represents a most positive assessment of Jews.

[82] The claim of Bloch (2002), 84–86, that Tacitus here delivers a negative judgment, presenting the Jews as a *Randvolk*, is implausible.

[83] Tac. *Hist.* 5.2.2; cf. Plut. *Isis* 31. Bloch (2002), 86–87, sees this as a hostile report.

[84] Tac. *Hist.* 5.2.2. On this legend, see the discussions of I. Levy (1946), 332–334; Heubner and Fauth (1982), 25–26.

[85] Tac. *Hist.* 5.2.3.

[86] Tac. *Hist.* 5.2.3; cf. Jos. *Ant.* 7.67; *CAp.* 1.172–174. See I. Levy (1946), 334–339; Feldman (1991), 351–354; (1993), 190–192.

[87] Tac. *Hist.* 5.4.2: *caeso ariete velut in contumeliam Hammonis; bos quoque immolatur, quoniam Aegyptii Apin colunt.* On Egyptian practices here, see the scholarship cited by Heubner and Fauth (1982), 48–51.

sacrificing the ram and the ox and cast them as derisive of Egyptian religion suggests recourse to some black humor. The remarks serve more as a snide commentary on Egyptian homage to animals than on the customs of the Jews.

Nor does Tacitus miss a chance to take an indirect swipe at the Caesars. The Jews, he says, refuse to set up images in their cities or temples. They pay no such flattery to their kings, nor such honor to the emperors.[88] Some have taken this as a Tacitean criticism of the Jews for failing to pay due allegiance to Rome.[89] Not very likely. Tacitus had little enthusiasm for emperor worship himself. One might recall his nasty remark about Augustus' aggressive push to have his own priests and flamens, and to promote reverence of his sacred images in temples. The historian adds that there would be nothing left by which to honor the gods.[90] A similarly caustic comment surfaces when Tacitus reports a proposal to build a temple to the divine Nero. Some interpreted it, so he notes with relish, as a sign of Nero's impending death.[91] One may be quite confident that when the historian narrates the Jews' refusal to accept a statue of Caligula in their Temple, he was making no brief for Caligula.[92] In short, the mention of Jewish aversion to divine honors for the Caesars constitutes a sneer at the imperial cult, rather than at the Jews. Tacitus further takes a gratuitous slap at Claudius in this excursus. He speaks of the Jews as having bought the privilege of constructing walls in peacetime as if they were going to war, thus availing themselves of Roman avarice in the age of Claudius.[93] Even one of Tacitus' supposedly favorite *principes* comes in for a cutting put-down. Titus preferred to assault Jerusalem rather than wait for its surrender. Why? Tacitus offers his own elucidation: Titus already envisioned the wealth and pleasures he could enjoy in Rome, and, unless Jerusalem fell swiftly, he would have to delay his delights.[94] The cynical historian injects a characteristic analysis—and he has the Roman leader, not the Jews, as his victim.

Jewish history also afforded Tacitus an opportunity to skewer one of his favorite targets: the imperial freedman. He maintains that Claudius converted Judaea into a Roman province and entrusted it to *equites* or to freedmen. That happens to be inaccurate, but no matter. Tacitus' objective was to heap further abuse on Antonius Felix. That individual was, in fact, the

---

[88] Tac. *Hist.* 5.5.4: *nulla simulacra urbibus suis, nedum templis sistunt; non regibus haec adulatio, non Caesaribus honor.*
[89] Bloch (2002), 95–96.
[90] Tac. *Ann.* 1.10.
[91] Tac. *Ann.* 15.74.
[92] Tac. *Hist.* 5.9.2.
[93] Tac. *Hist.* 5.12.2: *per avaritiam Claudianorum temporum.*
[94] Tac. *Hist.* 5.11.2: *ipsi Tito Roma et opes voluptatesque ante oculos; ac ni statim Hierosolyma conciderent, morari videbantur.*

only *libertus* to serve as procurator of Judaea, an appointee of Claudius, a man who had insinuated himself into the imperial household and family, and one who behaved with monarchical savagery and licentiousness in his procuratorial capacity.[95] Tacitus' strictures, of course, did not arise out of compassion for the Jews but from malevolence toward ex-slaves appointed to the imperial service. The digression on the Jews served a variety of purposes for the acerbic historian.

Finally, the matter of religion. The excursus concludes with a chapter on prodigies that flared up at the time of the Jewish rebellion against Rome. Arms were spotted contending in battle in the skies, the fiery gleam of weapons flashed, and suddenly the Temple itself lit up with a flame from the clouds.[96] Tacitus remarks that the Jews misconceived and fatally misunderstood those omens. As a people inclined to *superstitio* and hostile to *religio*, they rejected as improper any expiation of prodigies by sacrifice or vows.[97] Instead, they relied on their own messianic prophecies that promised world rule by men who set forth from Judaea. The Jewish commons, blinded by ambition, insisted on interpreting those predictions in their own favor and refusing, even in adversity, to see the truth. For the truth was, according to Tacitus, that the ambiguous prophecy pointed to the future universal power of Vespasian and Titus, not to any supremacy by Jews.[98]

On the face of it, that interpretation appears to be a decisive rebuke of Jewish belief, practice, and trust in the divine. And so it is always read. Yet one might well ask just how much faith Tacitus himself put in prodigies— *quindecemvir de sacris faciundis* though he was.[99] The historian, of course, rarely wears his heart on his sleeve on such matters, or indeed any matters. In this connection, however, it is worth considering his comment at the beginning of the *Histories*. Tacitus takes note of warning prodigies in heaven and earth, whether equivocal or obvious (*ambigua manifesta*). He then adds that the gods do not trouble themselves about our well-being, only about our punishment.[100] Even more telling, later in the *Histories*, he records a whole series of bizarre omens, almost in the style of Livy, that spread terror at the time of Otho's preparations against Vitellius. The canny Tacitus does not commit himself to their authenticity. Men took as omen or prodigy, he says, what actually came by chance or nature.[101] The historian was even

---

[95] Tac. *Hist.* 5.9.3.
[96] Tac. *Hist.* 5.13.1.
[97] Tac. *Hist.* 5.13.1: *evenerant prodigia, quae neque hostiis neque votis piare fas habet gens superstitioni obnoxia, religionibus adversa.*
[98] Tac. *Hist.* 5.13.2.
[99] On his priesthood, see Tac. *Ann.* 11.11.
[100] Tac. *Hist.* 1.3: *non esse curae deis securitatem nostram, esse ultionem.*
[101] Tac. *Hist.* 1.86: *a fortuitis vel naturalibus causis.*

more direct in recording a torrent of portents that followed the assassination of Agrippina the Younger. They came with frequency, he observes—and without meaning (*prodigia crebra et inrita*). Indeed they exhibited only the indifference of the gods (*sine cura deum*).[102]

In view of these passages, the vigilant reader could put into perspective Tacitus' sneer about Jewish proclivity to read omens to their own advantage. Romans were as prone to misinterpret prodigies as the Jews—or anyone else. As Tacitus notes, it was a general human inclination (*mos humanae cupidinis*). Moreover, as he put it elsewhere, the gods treat instances of virtue and vice with perfect impartiality.[103] In short, at the close of the excursus we still hear the caustic tone of the master of irony.

Tacitus is not quite finished on this subject. He includes one other striking omen among those forecasting the doom of the Jewish rebellion. He remarks that the doors of the Temple suddenly flew open and a superhuman voice was heard to exclaim that the gods were exiting the sacred shrine.[104] That sort of portent, that is, divine abandonment of a city or shrine thereby signaling its imminent demise, is a common convention, a means of reassuring the warriors or justifying their victory. But why "gods" in the plural? The Jews had only one deity who could abandon them, as he had done so many times in the past. Was this a slip by Tacitus, an unconscious use of customary language, or an *interpretatio Romana*?[105] Not a likely solution. The historian had made a point of underscoring Jewish monotheism, contrasting Jews here not with Romans, interestingly enough, but with the Egyptians, who worship a multitude of bestial and composite divinities.[106] Tacitus once again, it would be reasonable to infer, plays with paradox, testing his readers. Are they alert? Do they recognize the dissonance? What will they make of it? The narrative teases as much as it informs.

A summary is in order. Tacitus' aversion to Jews could hardly be plainer. The text contains a number of offensive statements that cannot easily be dismissed or explained away. Tacitus undoubtedly shared the preconceptions and misgivings of many Romans before, during, and after his time toward the practices of alien peoples that they found outlandish and did

---

[102] Tac. *Ann.* 14.12.

[103] Tac. *Ann.* 16.33: *aequitate deum erga bona malaque documenta*.

[104] Tac. *Hist.* 5.13.1: *apertae repente delubri fores et audita maior humana vox, excedere deos*.

[105] Bloch (2002), 111–112, presumes that Tacitus thinks purely in Roman terms, offering Verg. *Aen.* 2.351–352 as parallel. Similarly, Heubner and Fauth (1982), 150. But Josephus, *BJ* 6.300, also uses the plural here, presumably not as an *interpretatio Romana*. Whether this indicates that Josephus and Tacitus drew on the same source is a question that can be left aside. We may, in any case, be confident that Tacitus did not mindlessly adopt a phraseology inconsistent with assertions about Jewish monotheism.

[106] Tac. *Hist.* 5.5.4.

not bother to understand properly. But he did not compose the excursus on the Jews to effect a denunciation and intellectual demolition of that people. Tacitus acts here neither as polemicist nor as advocate. This segment of the *Histories* has for too long been taken too straightforwardly. It goes well beyond ethnographical diversion.[107] What we find instead is the familiar Tacitus, the historian fond of paradox and antinomies, prone to irony and incongruity, who challenges his readers, forces them to pick apart the opinions and images set before them, offering solutions and then snatching them away, forever eluding their grasp. The digression on the Jews served to put on display the skills of the cunning and cynical writer, who professed to inform his readers but in fact teased and toyed with them.

[107] Bloch (2002), 143–166, usefully compares the excursus with Tacitus' treatments of Germans and Britons, finding both parallels and illuminating differences that give the discussion of the Jews a special character. His stress on the negative side of the Jewish excursus is somewhat unbalanced. But he rightly observes that none of the excursuses is pure ethnography for its own sake. Cf. also Bloch (2000), 38–54.

Chapter 8

PEOPLE OF COLOR

The ancients were not color-blind. Greek and Latin authors observed with curiosity and interest persons of black skin. They remarked on that color, wondered about it; some had discomfort with it, even occasionally mocked and caricatured it. Are we here in the realm of ethnic bigotry or animosity?

Textual Images

Classical writers associated blacks most commonly with the regions of Africa located to the south of Egypt, beyond the First Cataract, and, to a lesser degree, with parts of northwest Africa. Neither geography nor terminology was particularly precise.[1] The land of Nubia appears as Kush in Egyptian and biblical texts, more often as Ethiopia in Greek and Latin works.[2] The term *Aithiops*, signifying "sunburnt face," became the regular designation, thus indicating that color represented the most conspicuous and defining feature.[3] Unsurprisingly so. The observation of difference hardly amounts to racial stereotyping, let alone racism. Too much of the scholarship has concerned itself with that issue. The distinctive physical characteristics of "Ethiopians" gain repeated mention by classical authors. And moderns have quarreled over the degree to which Greeks and Romans possessed racial prejudice or resisted it. But "race" may be an altogether

---

[1] For geographical confusion among classical authors regarding "Ethiopia," see Nadeau (1970), 339–349; (1977), 75–78; Bourgeois (1971), 30–39; Gardner (1977), 185–193; Lonis (1981), 69–70, 75. Cf., e.g., Herod. 7.70; Strabo 2.3.8.

[2] The evidence on knowledge of the Ethiopians by classical writers is conveniently collected by Snowden (1970), 101–120. Bourgeois (1971), 30–80, discusses the testimony of Greek authors more fully. His principal aim, to show that their information was reasonably accurate, does not always persuade. But that issue is marginal to the question of ancient attitudes.

[3] Thompson (1989), 57–62, 70–73, properly points out that the term could be used in more than one sense, whether ethnographic, geographic, or somatic. But the most common designation referred to black Africans.

misleading and erroneous category. There is little to suggest that the ancients ascribed moral, intellectual, or cultural deficiencies to persons on the basis of their color. Nor did they assume that such physical characteristics were inherited traits, fixed across the generations.[4]

Ethiopians, in fact, enjoyed high repute in classical literature. Whatever the realities, they entered early into the realm of Greek mythology. Homer characterizes them as "blameless Ethiopians." Zeus enjoyed a repast at their table, and all the gods joined him in partaking of Ethiopian hospitality.[5] Iris too looked forward to their banquets, an exhibit of their unusual piety.[6] Even when other Olympians assembled in the dwelling of Zeus, Poseidon took himself off to the Ethiopians in their remote location, where he could indulge their festive generosity marked by a hecatomb of bulls and rams.[7] Heroes also visited their land, notably Menelaus, who made a detour there on the way home after the fall of Troy.[8] Ethiopia's legendary hospitality and devotion to the deities became fixed in the tradition, still taken as proverbial by Lucian.[9] It was repeated and enlarged by Diodorus Siculus. The first-century BCE historian quotes Homer to that effect and represents the Ethiopians as the very first who learned to honor the gods with sacrifices, processions, and celebrations, and whose offerings were especially pleasing to divine power, thus earning them the favor of heaven. Such connections with the powers above, according to Diodorus, who cites unnamed sources, enabled the Ethiopians to escape foreign rule and to live perpetually in freedom and internal concord. Many an invader attacked them, but none succeeded.[10] The piety of the Ethiopians withstood even Herakles and Dionysus, the greatest of legendary conquerors, who gave up the attempt.[11]

Ethiopians' reverence, moreover, had an expansive and embracing character. They reckoned the sun, the moon, and the entire cosmos as eternal

---

[4] Beardsley (1929) provided the first extensive treatment of the artistic evidence, raising the issue of racial prejudice in ancient attitudes toward blacks, although she gave short shrift to the Roman period. The important work of Snowden, in a series of articles and books, stressed the wide range of sources that offer positive evaluations or favorable assessments; e.g., Snowden (1947), (1948), (1960), (1970), (1983), (1997). Thompson rightly observed that the notion of "race" is irrelevant and misguided, and offers a useful survey of earlier scholarship, although he makes the point at excessive length, with some gratuitous criticisms of Snowden; Thompson (1983), 1–21; (1989), 1–56 and passim. Snowden's hostile review of Thompson, in turn (1990) 543–557, tends to be one-sided and exaggerated. The two reach more conclusions in common than either was willing to acknowledge. For more restrained reservations about Snowden's thesis, see Desanges (1975), 408–411; Goldenberg (2009), 89–90.
[5] Homer *Il.* 1.423–425.
[6] Homer *Il.* 23.205–207.
[7] Homer *Od.* 1.22–25, 5.282–287.
[8] Homer *Od.* 4.81–85.
[9] Lucian *Sacr.* 2; *Jup. Trag.* 37. Cf. also Statius *Theb.* 5.426–428.
[10] Diod. 3.2.2–4.
[11] Diod. 3.3.1.

deities. But they saw others, in euhemeristic fashion, as former mortals elevated to divine status, like Zeus, Herakles, Isis, and Pan, an eclectic assemblage, through their benefactions to mankind.[12] The wisdom of the nation was renowned, according to Lucian. Ethiopians were wiser than all others, experts in astrology, a knowledge of the heavens that they transmitted to the Egyptians.[13] Heliodorus' romantic tale, the *Aethiopica*, similarly ascribes astrological learning to the Ethiopians, whence other nations derived their understanding of the celestial universe.[14] The romance also depicts that people as a utopian nation, favored by, indeed descended from, gods and heroes.[15] Their ruler plays an ambiguous but fundamentally noble role in this complex novel. Ethiopians are good fighters, though not bloodthirsty, and their king generally prefers to spare rather than to slaughter his enemies.[16] The blackness of the Ethiopians is noted, but only briefly in passing, and without a hint of negative connotation.[17] The people, in Heliodorus' fiction, to be sure, practiced human sacrifice. The author, however, problematizes its role, by no means a direct, or even indirect, reflection on Ethiopian character. It is limited strictly to initial captives in war, as firstfruits for the gods and the virgins (men and women).[18] And, more importantly, the narrative presents the king as deeply conflicted regarding implementation of the practice, and the populace as ready to scrap it.[19] The author shows a fundamental sympathy and admiration, no critique of the nation. An altogether comparably rosy portrait appears in the *Alexander Romance*, which turns Ethiopia into a fantasy kingdom.[20] One might, of course, legitimately question how far the imaginary constructs of the Ethiopians may have affected public opinion generally among dwellers in the Roman Empire.[21] But the romances of Pseudo-Callisthenes and Heliodorus at least will have circulated beyond a narrow elite. And the fact that creative writers found Ethiopia to be an appropriate setting for utopian fancies delivers a significant message about the image of that land and its people.

More notable still, Ethiopians stood among the few peoples to whom Greeks accorded the status of autochthony. Herodotus reckons them and the Libyans as original dwellers in Africa, the Phoenicians and Greeks as

---

[12] Diod. 3.9.1–2. Cf. Strabo 17.2.3.
[13] Lucian *Astr.* 3–5.
[14] Heliod. *Aeth*. 4.12.
[15] Heliod. *Aeth*. 10.4, 10.6.
[16] Heliod. *Aeth*. 8.1, 8.16–17, 9.5–6, 9.13, 9.20–23, 9.26.
[17] Heliod. *Aeth*. 4.8, 8.16.
[18] Heliod. *Aeth*. 9.1, 9.24–26, 10.7.
[19] Heliod. *Aeth*. 10.7, 10.9, 10.16–17.
[20] Ps. Callisth. 3.21–23 (Kroll). On the depiction of Ethiopians in these romances, see Lonis (1981), 81–84.
[21] As does Thompson (1989), 88–93.

latecomers.[22] Diodorus goes much further. He drew on sources who maintained that Ethiopians preceded all other peoples and thus were the only ones who genuinely merit the label "autochthonous." Those who dwelled in lands nearest to the sun logically emerged first when solar warmth dried the earth to permit human life.[23] Ethiopians, so report had it, had colonized Egypt itself, that most ancient of lands, with none other than Osiris as leader of the colony![24] Ethiopians possessed the most venerable of pedigrees.[25]

Legend also accorded a prominent role to the hero Memnon, king of the Ethiopians, so labeled already by Hesiod and doubtless even earlier amidst the lost works of the Trojan Cycle.[26] Memnon, the son of Dawn, had a distinguished role as ally of Priam in the war over Troy; slain by Achilles after a valiant resistance, he was then elevated among the immortals.[27] His provenance, it is true, was disputed.[28] Various tales had him come from the east, associated with Susa, where a great structure carried his name, the Memnonion. But the Ethiopians claimed him as their own, pointing to a Memnonion in their land, a version that eventually gained primacy.[29] For Pausanias, Memnon was king of the Ethiopians but came to Troy via Susa, having conquered the peoples of the east.[30] Another version had him rule Ethiopia for five generations but never get to Troy.[31] The African connection held firm. Alexander the Great had a burning desire to see Memnon's celebrated palace in Ethiopia.[32] Vergil notably describes him as "black Memnon."[33] And writers of the Roman period regularly have Memnon as an Ethiopian.[34]

Another celebrated Greek tradition set its central tale in the African kingdom. A prominent version of Andromeda's rescue by Perseus identified the realm of her father Cepheus as Ethiopia.[35] Ovid, among others, retails

[22] Herod. 4.197.
[23] Diod. 3.2.1.
[24] Diod. 3.3.2.
[25] On the tradition of Ethiopian autochthony, see the discussion of Billault (2001), 347–355.
[26] Hesiod *Theog.* 985–986.
[27] See, e.g., Dio Chrys. 11.14; Paus. 10.31.7; Quint. Smyrn. 2.30–32, 2.100–161, 2.211–647.
[28] Drews (1969), 191–192.
[29] The competing traditions appear in Diod. 2.22.1–5. Herodotus knows only the Memnonion in Susa; 5.53–54, 7.151. Strabo locates Memnonia in Susa and in Egypt; 15.3.2, 17.1.42, 17.1.46.
[30] Paus. 10.31.7.
[31] Philostratus *Vita Apoll.* 6.4.1–3.
[32] Curt. Ruf. 4.8.3.
[33] Verg. *Aen.* 1.489: *nigri Memnonis arma*. Cf. Quint. Smyrn. 2.30–32. The blackness of Memnon appears already in Pindar *Ol.* 2.92.
[34] See references in Snowden (1970), 151–153, 308–309.
[35] Pliny *NH* 6.182; Ovid *Met.* 4.669, 4.764, 5.1; Propertius 4.6.78; Apollodorus *Bib.* 2.4.3; cf. Tac. *Hist.* 5.2.

that version and describes Andromeda herself as black.[36] The mythology of Argos famously included the strife of the brothers Danaus and Aegyptus, and the flight of the Danaids from Egypt to Argos. Aeschylus' *Suppliants*, the most memorable rendition of the tale, describes both the sons of Aegyptus and the daughters of Danaus as swarthy and dark skinned, evidently alluding to black Africans, and doing so without rancor or prejudice.[37] Ethiopia thus had a place in the fabled past of heroic legend.[38]

When Ethiopia emerges from fable to history, Greek narratives continue to hold its people in high esteem. As Pliny strikingly put it, who would ever have believed the Ethiopians existed before actually seeing them?[39] Herodotus affirms that Ethiopians are the tallest and most attractive of all men.[40] When the historian recounts the conquest of Egypt by the Ethiopian ruler Sabakos (Shabaka) in the eighth century BCE, his treatment is decidedly favorable to the new king and his reign. In Herodotus' narrative, Sabakos refused to execute Egyptian miscreants but sentenced them to construction work in their native communities, each in accordance with the gravity of his offense, a great boon to the towns and an instance of exemplary justice.[41] The king reigned for half a century, according to Herodotus (a considerable exaggeration), then yielded his power voluntarily, having received a vision in his dream that advised him to gather all the priests in Egypt and cut them in two. Rather than commit so heinous and sacrilegious an act, Sabakos terminated his rule and departed from Egypt.[42] The tale itself, a pronouncedly pro-Ethiopian fable, may carry little value for history, although the reign of Shabaka (a much shorter one) is historical.[43] But Herodotus' readiness to adopt and transmit the story offers a revealing glimpse of Ethiopian rule over Egypt in Hellenic eyes. Diodorus adapts the Herodotean tale, giving still more credit to the Ethiopian Sabakos, whom he regards as far superior in piety and integrity to all his predecessors on the Egyptian throne. In Diodorus' account, the king also substitutes hard labor for execution of criminals, with salutary results for the

---

[36] Ovid *Ars Amat.* 1.53, 3.191. Cf. Ovid *Met.* 4.668–681, with no indication of color. Philostratus, *Imagines* 1.29, places the Andromeda story in Ethiopia but insists that she was herself white.

[37] Aesch. *Suppl.* 154–155, 719–720; cf. *Prom. Bound* 851. A different but complementary tradition had Danaus marry an Ethiopian woman who gave birth to his daughters; Apoll. *Bibl.* 2.1.5. Aeschylus elsewhere refers to a black race dwelling near the "river Aethiops" and "Ethiopians" dwelling where Ocean refreshes the steeds of the sun; *Prom. Bound* 808–809; Strabo 1.2.27.

[38] Cf. Beardsley (1929), 1–9; Bourgeois (1971), 20–29; Lonis (1981), 74–78.

[39] Pliny *NH* 7.6: *quis enim Aethiopas antequam cerneret credidit?*

[40] Herod. 3.20.

[41] Herod. 2.137.

[42] Herod. 2.139.

[43] See the comments of Lloyd in Asheri et al. (2007), 339–342.

welfare of Egyptian villages, and later withdraws from power, despite a divine vision, to avoid the hideous impiety of slaughtering Egyptian priests.[44] This image of the righteous Ethiopian monarch who shrank from the execution of his enemies, championing restraint and justice, reappears in Heliodorus' novel *Aethiopica*.[45]

The Ethiopians come off well also in Herodotus' account of the Persian Cambyses' effort to take over their kingdom. The Ethiopian ruler resisted his blandishments, exposed Cambyses' representatives as spies rather than well-wishers, and exhibited the superiority of Ethiopian character, customs, authority, and wisdom.[46] The narrative, more folktale than history, concludes with Cambyses' reckless and ill-prepared invasion of Ethiopia, terminating in failure and withdrawal.[47] Seneca picked up the tale for his own purposes, having the Ethiopians reject Cambyses' offers, thwart the arrogant king's objectives, and trigger the anger that led ultimately to his ignominious retreat.[48] The inhabitants of the land, in any case, emerge in a glowing light.[49]

The elevated praise of Ethiopians did not bypass or ignore their color. On the contrary. It went hand in hand with repeated references to their conspicuous pigmentation. Ethiopians became virtually synonymous with blackness, the classic representative of it.[50] In proverbial contrasts between white and black, Ethiopians were the obvious candidates to be cited as exemplifying the latter. The contraposition appears, for instance, in Varro and Juvenal.[51] Petronius makes the point clearly. He has a character mock

---

[44] Diod. 1.65.2–8. A somewhat comparable story appears in Diod. 1.60.2–5, with regard to a different Ethiopian king, Actisanes, who gained control of Egypt and meted out punishment to criminals in stern but fair-minded and judicious fashion. The ruler is otherwise unknown, and this may be a confused doublet of the Sabakos story. But it attests further to the favorable image of Ethiopians in Greek tradition. The theme of the Ethiopian monarch unwilling to execute any of his subjects reappears in different form in Diod. 3.5.2–3. It is interesting and ironic that, according to Diodorus, the Ethiopian king who broke with this admirable practice in the Hellenistic period and actually ordered the execution of priests was one who had a Greek education and was a student of Greek philosophy! Diod. 3.6.3–4.

[45] Heliod. *Aeth.* 9–10.

[46] Herod. 3.19–24, with the valuable commentary of Asheri, in Asheri et al. (2007), 418–423.

[47] Herod. 3.25; Asheri, in Asheri et al. (2007), 423–425.

[48] Seneca *De Ira* 3.20.2–4.

[49] On the favorable portrait of Ethiopia in classical writers generally, see the discussion of Snowden (1983), 46–59. So also P. Salmon (1994), 283–302—with some reservations.

[50] So, e.g., Manilius 4.723–724; Arrian 5.4.4.; Cf. also Plaut. *Poen.* 1289–1291, naming the *Aegyptini* as the standard for blackness—by which he must refer to Ethiopians. See further the texts conveniently assembled by Snowden (1947), 273–280.

[51] Varro *LL* 8.41: *aut unus albus et alter Aethiops*; 9.42: *si alter Aethiops, alter albus*; cf. 8.38; Juv. 2.23. The claim of Thompson (1989), 65–67, 72–74, 77, 105–106, that *albus* signifies some general (and preferable) Mediterranean color midway between the pale northerner and the black southerner has no warrant in the texts. Nothing indicates that *albus* represented the

the suggestion of a compatriot that they use blackface disguise to pass as Ethiopians. His sharp retort asserts that they might as well use circumcision to pass as Jews, ear piercing to pass as Arabians, or whiteface to pass as Gauls.[52] The parallels evoke stereotypes but carry no negative implications. Ancients (or most of them) ascribed the Ethiopian skin color to the sun's rays, a conventional, if not particularly scientific, inference. Scythians and Ethiopians became the conventional instances of extreme coloration because they sat at the northernmost and southernmost locations respectively.[53] Herodotus explains the blackness of the Ethiopians as a consequence of solar heat, a passing remark without pejorative overtones.[54] The same surmise surfaces, more than once, in Strabo and in Pliny's *Natural History*.[55] The latter also tells the interesting story of the celebrated boxer Nicaeus from Byzantium, whose mother was the product of an adulterous affair with an Ethiopian yet showed no signs of it in her skin color. The dark pigmentation evidently skipped a generation, for Nicaeus himself turned out to look like his grandfather.[56] Pliny includes the tale out of curiosity, as an instance of inherited resemblances—and certainly not as a reflection on the character of Nicaeus.

Nor was it color alone that made the Ethiopians stand out. Classical authors took note of characteristics like curly hair, snub noses, and fleshy lips as representative markers of that people.[57] The sixth-century Ionian philosopher Xenophanes famously observed that different nations tended to ascribe to the gods features that accorded with their own. As examples he could cite Thracians, who depicted their gods with blue eyes and red hair, and Ethiopians, who reckoned theirs as having black faces and flat noses.[58] That illustration of cultural relativity could still be cited centuries later when Sextus Empiricus contrasted Ethiopians with Persians, the former considering as most admirable their own features of blackness and flat noses.[59] Herodotus comments on the Ethiopians who served with the Persian forces that invaded Greece under Xerxes: they looked like everybody else except for their hair. Those from the east had straight hair; the others

---

preferable and superior pigment of Greeks and Romans. So, rightly, Dee (2003–2004), 157–167.

[52] Petronius *Sat.* 102. Cf. also Plaut. *Poen.* 1289–1291.

[53] Herod. 2.22; Aristotle *De Gen. Anim.* 5.3.782b; Strabo 1.1.13; Ptolemy *Tetrabib.* 2.2; cf. Menander fr. 612 (Koerte). See Snowden (1960), 22–32.

[54] Herod. 2.22.

[55] Strabo 1.2.27, 15.1.40; Pliny *NH* 2.189, 6.70. Further references in Snowden (1970), 258, n. 6.

[56] Pliny *NH* 7.51. Cf. Thompson (1983), 9–14; (1989), 73–78. A similar phenomenon appears in Aristotle *Gen. Anim.* 1.722a.

[57] Cf. Snowden (1947), 268–271, 281–282.

[58] Xenophanes fr. 16 (Diels).

[59] Sex. Emp. *Adv. Math.* 11.43.

were the most curly haired of all peoples. Here again the historian passes no adverse judgment, indeed even ignores the color of their skin.[60] These were not matters of import. Aristotle too drew the conclusion that Ethiopian hair was frizzy because of the dry climate, in a passage of scientific neutrality.[61] Diodorus notes the wooly hair, the black color, and the snub noses as characteristic of most Ethiopians. Although he has criticisms to make of practices among certain Ethiopians, he draws no negative inferences from their physical features.[62] The hair and complexion of Ethiopians did, in fact, become an issue of dispute, but only among intellectuals who debated their origins. Strabo records arguments between the Hellenistic writers Onescritus and Theodectes as to whether nearness of the sun or the nature of the water produced those features.[63] The author of the *Moretum*, included in the *Appendix Vergiliana*, does describe an African woman, sole helpmate of a rustic farmer, with characteristics he claims as altogether typical of her native land: wooly hair, puffy lips, dark color, a broad chest with pendulous breasts, a narrow middle, thin legs, and wide feet.[64] The description need not have hostile overtones. Certainly the first three items, the only ones commonly associated with Ethiopians, possess none.[65] Those characteristics occur with frequency in the pages of Greek and Latin writers but without adverse or disdainful significance.[66]

Ethnographers, or writers who indulged in ethnographic excursuses, naturally found the Ethiopians an object of curiosity.[67] Herodotus unfortunately devotes almost no space to them. He provides only a couple of sentences on the Trogodutai, a subset of the Ethiopians, who were the swiftest of men (fortunately, because the Garamantes chased them in chariots), lived on reptiles, and had squeaky voices like bats.[68] Diodorus, however, offered an expansive ethnography.[69] The Sicilian historian, as we have seen,

[60] Herod. 7.70. So also Martial *De Spect.* 3.10. Pliny, *NH* 2.189, mentions both dark skin and curly hair and beard.

[61] Aristotle *Gen Anim.* 5.3.782b.

[62] Diod. 3.8.1–2.

[63] Strabo 15.1.24; cf. Vitruvius 6.1.4.

[64] *Moretum* 31–35: *Afra genus, tota patriam testante figura.*

[65] The only other reference to large breasts among the women of Meroe appears in the satirical comment of Juvenal 13.163.

[66] For additional references, see Snowden (1970), 2–11.

[67] See the extensive treatment of the ethnographic writings by Bourgeois (1971), 30–80, who concludes that Greek researchers did a serious job of collecting information from a great variety of sources and did not limit themselves to superficial treatments or amateurish curiosity—even if the results are not always reliable.

[68] Herod. 4.183. The correct reading is "Trogodytes," not "Troglodytes" (cave dwellers) as the Loeb has it. See Corcella, in Asheri et al. (2007), 706–707. Cf. Diod. 3.14.6, 3.32–33; Strabo 16.4.17; Pliny *NH* 6.189.

[69] On Diodorus and his sources for the remarks on Ethiopians, see Desanges (1993) 525–537.

found much to admire among the Ethiopians, particularly their piety, their hospitality, their devotion to freedom, and their venerable pedigree.[70] He had reservations, to be sure, about the habits and practices of at least certain Ethiopians. Diodorus noted their shrillness of voice, primitive and uncivilized, even bestial, behavior, a willingness to live nearly unclothed, and their survival as hunters and gatherers as well as shepherds.[71] But he proceeds to outline religious beliefs, burial rites, and the choosing of leaders, all of which suggest a rationally ordered society.[72] Comparable ethnographic remarks come in the pages of Strabo, who supplies information on social, religious, and eating habits.[73] The few comments of Pausanias merely describe the location of the Ethiopians but add that those who dwell in Meroe are the most righteous of all.[74] Treatment of the remote and distant tribes allowed writers like Diodorus and Pliny, drawing on earlier ethnographers like Agatharchides of Cnidus and Artemidorus of Ephesus, to describe more exotic, indeed often largely fanciful, practices.[75] The practices may have had little in common with Greek conventions. But Hellenic writers did not aim generally at condemnation or disparagement of Ethiopians on the basis of color or appearance.[76] The Pseudo-Aristotelian treatise *Physiognomica*, it is true, maintained that people who were black and curly haired (the author includes both Egyptians and Ethiopians in that category) were generally cowardly. He says the same, however, of those who were especially fair in color as well, presumably peoples of the north. Those whose coloring falls into neither category (evidently the author's own Mediterranean folk) have a pigment that signifies courage.[77] The sweeping statement goes well beyond a targeting of Ethiopians. And it is highly exceptional. For most Greek intellectuals, color carried no inherent quality. The second-century BCE historian and ethnographer Agatharchides of Cnidus gave clear expression to the point. The blackness of the Ethiopians, he observed, and the oddity of their appearance might frighten Greek infants, for whom it would have been an inexplicable novelty. But such concerns swiftly evaporate with childhood. Decisions on matters of substance and importance depend on courage and experience, not the color of one's skin.[78] A similar sentiment appears in the fragment of a Greek comedy. The

[70] See above, p. 198.
[71] Diod. 3.8.2–6.
[72] Diod. 3.9.1–4.
[73] Strabo 17.2.1–3.
[74] Paus. 1.33.4.
[75] Diodorus 3.10–33; Pliny *NH* 5.43–46, 6.187–195. Cf. Lonis (1981), 78–80.
[76] Pliny *NH* 6.190, records just one remote and obscure tribe whose members felt shame at their black color and tried to obscure it by smearing red all over their bodies.
[77] Ps. Aristotle *Physiognomica* 6.812a–b.
[78] Agatharchides *Mar. Erythr.* 16. See the treatment of this passage by Snowden (1983), 74–75, as against Dihle (1962b), 214–215.

comic poet affirms that one who is naturally inclined to the good should be regarded as nobly born, even if he be an Ethiopian—or a Scythian.[79] In short, Black Africans though lacking high social status. But they ought to be judged by their character, not by their birth.[80] As Aristotle pointedly put it: with regard to their place in the human species, no difference exists between a black man and a white man.[81]

To be sure, the contrast of white and black, conjuring up images of light and dark, day and night, had symbolic connotation for Greeks and Romans. The former had positive value, the latter negative, associated with the underworld, with evil omens, and with death. The antithesis holds in most societies, well beyond antiquity.[82] That some felt the need to address and to neutralize the perception, would not be surprising. A moving verse inscription from Antinoe in Egypt, dated to the third century CE, gives voice to a deceased Ethiopian slave who declares (or perhaps his master declared for him) that he was deep black in life, as if burnt by the rays of the sun, but his soul, ever covered with white flowers, gained the benevolence of his wise master, for beauty is secondary to a good soul which thus crowned his black form.[83] The epitaph suggests that some would consider his color as a superficial drawback and needed to be disabused. But it hardly follows that blackness was reckoned a serious liability that had to be surmounted.[84] The affirmation expressed by the verse epitaph speaks more eloquently. Hadrumetum in North Africa, recorded in the *Anthologia Latina*, delivers a sneering comment on the "dregs of the Garamantes" and the scary visage of a black slave who looks as if he should be a guard at the gates of Hell. But it also allows that the slave, homegrown as he is, took pride in his pitch-black body.[85] Comparable sentiments appear in the *Alexander Romance*. The beautiful Candace, queen of Meroe, asserted in a fictitious letter to Alexander that the righteous Ethiopians are not to be judged by the color of their skin but by the whiteness of their souls, more splendid than those of the best of Greeks.[86]

---

[79] Ascribed to Menander fr. 612 (Koerte), but to Epicharmes in Stobaeus 86, 493.

[80] See Snowden (1948) 38–39.

[81] Aristotle *Met.* 10.105ba–b. Goldenberg (2009), 88–108, rightly recognizes that the ancient focus on the skin color of blacks does not entail corresponding attitudes about innate character and behavior. But, somewhat paradoxically, he does presume that all references to black skin color are negative and hostile.

[82] Cracco Ruggini (1979), 108–133; Snowden (1983), 82–85; Thompson (1989), 110–113; Goldenberg (2009), 93–97.

[83] Peek (1955), 341–342, #1167.

[84] As Lonis (1981), 83–84; P. Salmon (1994), 301. A better understanding by Snowden (1970), 177–178; Cracco Ruggini (1979), 108–112.

[85] *Anth. Lat.* #183: *et piceo gaudet corpore verna niger*. Cf. also *Anth. Lat.* # 182. See Desanges (1976), 257; Thompson (1989), 36–38; P. Salmon (1994), 301—with negative interpretations.

[86] Ps. Callisth. 3.18.6. Cf. Cracco Ruggini (1979), 110–112.

The texts disclose the lingering presence of prejudice—but also its rejection and dismissal.

Blacks, of course, were not immune from caricature or mockery. The author of the *Moretum*, as we have seen, described a maidservant with frizzy hair, thick lips, a dark complexion, low-hanging breasts, a small belly, thin legs, and big feet. The poet plainly engaged in some burlesque here. Yet the woman was hardly a discreditable figure, the sole helpmate of her peasant master, with whom she shared hardships and close relations.[87] Petronius certainly does indulge in parody when a character in the *Satyricon* proposes to his comrade that they disguise themselves as Ethiopian slaves by dyeing themselves black. His partner, as we have seen, shoots back that color alone would not do it. To pass as blacks they would need to swell their lips to exaggerated proportions, curl their hair, scar their foreheads, walk bow-legged, and trim their beards in foreign fashion.[88] Are these ethnic slurs? The character also suggests that it would be comparably difficult to pass as Jews, Gauls, or Arabs, since each would require comparable physical changes. Petronius satirizes rather than stigmatizes.[89] Much the same can be said of Martial, who makes sport of a cuckolded husband by claiming that none of the seven children in his household was his own. One is described as a Moor, identified by curly hair, and another with a flat nose and swollen lips is unmistakably a son of Pannychus the wrestler.[90] The joke, however, is on the cuckolded husband, not on the paramours or children. Martial utilizes familiar ethnic stereotypes but disparagement of blacks is not his point.[91]

Satirists must have their due. They skewer targets with cynicism and dark humor, a familiar function. One need not conclude that their parodic ethnic jabs represent widespread public prejudice. Juvenal's jibes regularly serve scholars as evidence for seething Roman hostility against blacks. The testimony needs to be reassessed.

In satire 2 Juvenal twits hypocrites who criticize others for failings that they also share, a group of pots calling kettles black. In illustration of who might properly level criticisms, he cites the upright walker who mocks the limper and the white man who mocks the *Aethiopes*.[92] It would be excessive

---

[87] *Moretum* 31–35. See Thompson (1989), 30–31, 159–160. His claim that the passage suggests a distaste for the black physiognomy, however, is unjustified.

[88] Petronius *Sat.* 102.

[89] Thompson (1989), 63–66, makes more of the passage than is warranted.

[90] Martial 6.39.1–9: *hic qui retorto crine Maurus incedit . . . at ille sima nare, turgidis labris ipsa est imago Pannychi palaestritae.*

[91] Pace Thompson (1989), 26–27, who regards these as mocking and derogatory comments. Nor is it obvious that Martial alludes to the threat posed to social hierarchy by adultery with men of the lower classes; so Thompson (1989), 78–79.

[92] Juv. 2.20–28: *loripedem rectus derideat, Aethiopem albus.* Cf. Martial 3.34.

to infer from this that whites regularly derided blacks.[93] Another passage has been comparably distorted. In Juvenal's famous poem contrasting the lavishness of the patron's dinner table with the slim pickings of the invited client, he alludes to an African servant. The client, instead of being served by the high-priced and beautiful cupbearer from Asia, must receive his cup from a "Gaetulian" groom or the bony hand of a black Moor whom one would not wish to meet in a dark alley. Juvenal cleverly labels him as a "Gaetulian Ganymede."[94] The contrast between the effeminate Asian boy and the swarthy African, however, delivers a satirical hit at both. Juvenal underscores the inequity of the patron being catered to by a costly and delicate youth who scorns the lowly client and the (presumably inexpensive) black servant on whom the task devolves. The satirist blasts the social gap between the powerful and the dependent. To see this as a slur against Africans badly misses the point.

The theme of the cuckolded husband, a natural topic for satirists, appears also in Juvenal. He observes that lower-class women have little choice but to go through the labors of childbirth and nursing, whereas abortifacients are available for the wealthy. Good thing too, Juvenal reminds his addressee: otherwise you might wake to find yourself the father of an "Ethiopian," an heir of the wrong color who will monopolize your will and whom you would prefer not to see by light of day.[95] That the putative child is imagined as black need not signify that that color is especially heinous, only that it is inescapably conspicuous. Juvenal targets adultery more than ethnicity.[96] One may go further. No hint exists that miscegenation itself is deplorable or even unusual. Certainly neither Greeks nor Romans had laws

[93] The conclusion of Wiesen (1970), 138–139, that this entitles the white man to "sneer at his natural inferior" is a distortion. Thompson (1989), 33–35, rightly dissents from Wiesen. But he concurs (1989), 45–46, that blacks, like cripples, were objects of mockery. On derision of the disabled, see Garland (1995), 73–86.

[94] Juv. 5.49–64. Wiesen (1970), 139–141, wrongly interprets this as deliberate demeaning of the black man. He proceeds even to see him as portrayed as an "uppity" black man. But that may misread lines 60–65. The sneering servant more probably refers to the Asian boy, not to the African groom: *nescit tot milibus emptus pauperibus miscere puer, sed forma, sed aetas digna supercilio . . . quippe indignatur veteri parere clienti.* Others share that misreading: J. A. Hall (1983), 108; Thompson (1989), 38–40. Thompson's view that the master recruited the black groom to protect his youthful Ganymede from the advances of his guests is hard to take seriously. Graft-Hanson (1978), 180, surprisingly states that "the overall impression we get of Juvenal's attitude towards Africans is that he despised and hated them." This conclusion rests almost exclusively on Juvenal's fierce hostility toward Crispinus—who was an Egyptian; Juv. 1.26–30, 4.1–33, 4.108–109.

[95] Juv. 6.592–601.

[96] Wiesen (1970), 141–143, of course, offers a more negative interpretation. But, as he acknowledges, the subject under scrutiny is adultery, not miscegenation. So also Watts (1976), 86, though he wrongly sees this as Juvenal thinking "in racial types." Use of the term *decolor* need signal no more than "nonwhite," not in itself a stigma—except for the cuckolded husband.

on the books that would prohibit interracial marriage. We lack evidence as to the frequency of such relationships. But they never provided occasion for controversy nor even fodder for satirists.[97] As late as the third or fourth century CE, an interracial couple had themselves proudly displayed in adjoining panels of a mosaic from Tunisia, reclining in leisure and enjoying the pleasures of their own funerary banquet.[98]

Humorous nicknames too could call attention to characteristics, even with an ironic twist by suggesting the opposite. Juvenal lists a few examples: the dwarf called "Atlas," the deficient and misshapen girl called "Europa," the lazy and mangy dog called "Leopard," "Tiger," or "Lion"—and the Ethiopian called "swan."[99] The sobriquets may owe something to warped humor. But Juvenal's list hardly suggests that blackness itself was opprobrious.[100]

Satirists traffic in stereotypes. A passage in Juvenal notes that what might seem surprising to outsiders could be perfectly normal in its own context. As examples he names pygmies snatched up by birds, goiters in the Alps, Germans with blue eyes and blond, greasy, twisted hair—and women with very large breasts in Meroe.[101] The images may be amusing, based on conventional notions or stereotypes. But they do not require animosity toward the subjects, including blacks.[102] The distinct color of the Ethiopians lent itself to jokes, parody, and dark humor—a matter quite different from ethnic bigotry or abhorrence of the nation.

How blacks fared in day-to-day encounters with others lies beyond our knowledge. Their degree of assimilation into the society of Greeks and Romans remains a matter of guesswork. Greeks encountered "Ethiopians" primarily as mercenaries or auxiliaries in the armies of their foes or through the tales of travelers and merchants. Acquaintance expanded in the Hellenistic era, particularly in the land of the Ptolemies, where commerce, warfare, and the researches of explorers and geographers increased knowledge and created connections. That era of fluidity and interaction certainly attracted Ethiopians to Alexandria or to Cyrene, and probably a number elsewhere in the Greek world as the evidence of artistic representations

---

Thompson (1989), 28, unconvincingly takes it as "derogation of negritude." And Snowden (1970), 4, needlessly regards it as reference to a "mulatto."

[97] On miscegenation, see Snowden (1970), 192–195.
[98] Snowden (1983), 92 and #56.
[99] Juv. 8.30–39.
[100] Wiesen (1970), 143–144, has no justification in claiming that Juvenal classified blacks with "other freaks."
[101] Juv. 13.162–173.
[102] Contra: Wiesen (1970), 144–146. A similar point is made by Seneca, *De Ira* 3.26.3, who says that one should not consider the color of Ethiopians or the red hair of Germans as unusual or disgraceful for they are not so considered among their own people.

suggests.[103] Others may have come as victims of war in adverse circumstances. Evidence, however, is too slim to allow conjectures, let alone draw conclusions, about how they may have managed. The once-prevalent notion that blacks portrayed in Greek vase paintings or on plastic vessels must have been slaves cannot be sustained. No textual evidence supports the claim, and few artistic representations indicate servile status.[104] The number of Ethiopians who entered the social world of Greek cities prior to the Hellenistic era may have been quite modest.

Immigration stepped up in earnest, however, with the coming of Rome, a notable influx into the municipalities of Italy and Sicily, especially into the capital of the Empire itself. Most immigrants arrived in servitude, whether as war captives or through the mart. But it is essential to emphasize that slavery and blackness had no intrinsic connection. The vast majority of slaves in the Roman world were white. The society with which black slaves engaged most intimately was that of white slaves. They formed no separate associations or communities of their own. And a Roman institution of high significance needs special stress here: the admission of freed slaves to the citizenry of Rome. This remarkable practice, a matter of astonishment to Greeks, allowed a gradual process of assimilation to a limited degree in the first generation, increasingly thereafter. The ready entrance of freedmen into the citizen body signified a level of comfort with foreigners that was unmatched elsewhere in the classical world. One need not ascribe it to altruism or generosity. Romans profited from the loyalty and industry of slaves looking ahead to manumission and from the continued allegiance of those who had been freed and formed part of the clientage of the aristocracy. Nevertheless, Romans had no fears of diluting the purity of the stock by admitting aliens to the citizenry.[105] And manumission applied to all races and ethnicities alike. Nothing suggests that black freedmen suffered any liability by virtue of their skin.

To be sure, the status of most blacks, even after emancipation, kept them in the humbler ranks of society. But the material evidence shows them in a wide range of occupations, in the theater, the entertainment world generally, as athletes, jockeys, charioteers, cooks, construction workers, and as

---

[103] Bourgeois (1971), 86–88, is much too optimistic in seeing the "realism" of Greek portraiture of Negroes as proof that many blacks must have resided in Greece itself.

[104] See the cogent arguments of Bourgeois (1971), 88–109.

[105] On manumission and Roman citizenship, see Treggiari (1969), 11–20; Bradley (1984), 81–85; Wiedemann (1985), 162–175; Gardner (1993), 7–38; Bradley (1994), 158–165. According to Suetonius, *Aug.* 40.3, Augustan restrictions on manumission aimed to keep Romans free of foreign or servile blood. But the *princeps*' measures, in fact, were designed only to control and slow down the process, thereby securing the socialization of ex-slaves. There were no racial overtones; Cogrossi (1979), 158–177; Bradley (1984), 87–95; Gardner (1993), 39–41.

soldiers.[106] Further, one can readily imagine that within two or three generations after manumission and several intermarriages, former black slaves moved more readily into higher echelons (and become less distinguishable in the material record). A few certainly reached positions of some eminence, like Memnon, the highly educated pupil of Herodes Atticus in the mid-second century CE, who treated him as a son.[107] Skin color itself carried no handicap to further mobility. In at least one area, blacks held positions of some importance. The cult of Isis spread around the Mediterranean, with Meroe as one of its principal centers, and made considerable headway in Rome itself. In that context Ethiopians played a major role as ministers to the cult, their expertise in the ritual in demand and respected.[108] In short, testimony on the treatment of blacks and their position within Greco-Roman society is frustratingly thin. But enough exists to indicate that no notions of innate inferiority barred the doors to integration.

Visual Images

Blacks appear in the material record with some frequency. Here one need not rely on just a few scraps of evidence. That record proves quite telling and informative. Representations of blacks place them in a remarkably wide range of activities and set them in contexts both historical and mythological. They held strong attraction for vase painters, for makers of bronze, marble, mosaics, and terra-cotta. They show up as figures on wall painting, as statues, as busts, as lamps, as terra-cotta figurines, in every medium. Although their features are generally recognizable without difficulty, they form no collective stereotype, they are rarely subject to caricature, and they are not singled out as a separate species—let alone a marginalized species.

A thorough survey of the material evidence would be quite superfluous. That job has already been undertaken.[109] But certain representative examples can help to make the point. Depictions of blacks present them conducting a notable variety of tasks, particularly in the Hellenistic period, when the evidence jumps substantially. Some, to be sure, count as rather menial jobs or as services performed for others. Even those, however, generally require a certain degree of skill and training. An especially handsome bronze statuette, for example, treats with sensitivity and favorable regard a

---

[106] Snowden (1970), 161–168, 187–188; (1983), 88–91. And see below, pp. 211–212.

[107] Philostratus *Vita Apoll.* 3.1; *Vita soph.* 2.588. He might be the imposing African depicted on a Pentelic marble bust; Snowden (1970), #73; (1976), #336–338. See also the equally impressive black head from Egypt from this same period; Snowden (1970), #71.

[108] Snowden (1970), 189–190; (1983), 97–99; Leclant (1976), 282–285.

[109] See the extensive collection of images in Snowden (1976). A somewhat smaller number in Snowden (1970), and a yet smaller but still quite useful selection in Snowden (1983).

212 IMPRESSIONS OF THE "OTHER"

young musician.[110] Others show dancers, jugglers, or acrobats, performing no doubt for the powerful but nonetheless as competent artists and entertainers.[111] A famous Hellenistic bronze from Artemision has a youthful black as a jockey, while a marble relief from Herculaneum in the early imperial period has one as a charioteer.[112] Elsewhere they appear as athletes, whether boxers or wrestlers, from widely scattered periods.[113] More significantly, blacks turn up as warriors. One can find them on vase paintings at least as early as the fifth century BCE.[114] A different and more imaginary portrayal, the Nilotic landscape on the mosaic at Praeneste, has them as hunters, well proportioned and impressive figures.[115] A third-century CE mosaic depicts a group of animal fighters resting and drinking after their labors, one of whom is black, not otherwise set apart from his comrades.[116] Familiar artistic subjects, like a boy with a goose or a youth pulling a thorn from his foot, could as easily represent blacks as anyone else (fig. 5).[117] Terra-cotta masks, a frequent form of representation, generally fashioned for decorative purposes, also employed faces with black features.[118] They appear too, with some regularity, as head vases, that is, ceramic ware of various kinds—bowls, beakers, or jugs—in the shape of a human head, in these cases with distinctive negroid features like black color, curly hair, large lips, and flat noses.[119] The owners and commissioners of such wares had no qualms about employing or displaying drinking vessels and containers in the form of heads that evoked Ethiopians. More remarkable still are the handsome head vases of blacks wearing laurel wreaths and impressively decorated caps.[120] Far from disparaging portraits, these images elevate their subjects into the admirable and enviable. Indeed, blacks appear even on the coinage of Athens and Delphi in the fifth and fourth centuries.[121] However one may interpret them, representations on state issues can hardly have been a source of embarrassment. In an altogether different genre, wall

---

[110] Bourgeois (1971), 114–118; Snowden (1970), #60; (1976), #253–255; (1983), #48.

[111] Dancers: Snowden (1970), #103–104; jugglers: Snowden (1970), #101; (1976), #266; acrobats: Snowden (1970), #51, 107; (1976), #205, 299.

[112] Jockey: Snowden (1970), #63; (1976), 275, and see now Hemingway (2004), esp. 111–112; charioteer: Snowden (1970), #50.

[113] Snowden (1970), #106; (1976), #228; (1983), #54.

[114] Snowden (1970), #16–17, 80–81; (1976), #158, 164; (1983), #46.

[115] Snowden (1976), #234. Cf. Clarke (2007), 89.

[116] Snowden (1983), # 26.

[117] Snowden (1970), #38, 45; (1976), #226, 268; (1983), #44.

[118] Snowden (1970), #7, 98–99; (1976), #161–163, 181–183.

[119] Snowden (1970), #9, 27–32; (1976), #153–154, 208–210; (1983), 16. Other examples in Croissant (1973), 205–225. See the discussion of this genre by Beardsley (1929), 30–39. On its origins, a matter of speculation, see Biers (1983), 119–126, with bibliography. Cf. Lissarague (1995), 4–9. See also A. Cohen (forthcoming).

[120] Bourgeois (1971), 92–96; Snowden (1970), #31; (1976), #208–209.

[121] Bourgeois (1971), 109–114; Snowden (1976), #187–192.

paintings from Herculaneum portray priests and worshippers of Isis, blacks as well as others in both capacities.[122] There is little to suggest that blacks held interest only for being exotic, bizarre, or outlandish. They fitted with surprising ease into an extraordinary range of motifs, scenes, and designs.

Visual representations can, of course, be ambiguous and difficult to interpret. Did artists or patrons of art find blacks convenient figures to caricature and burlesque?[123] Some images, to be sure, fall into that category. The female figure on a fourth-century Apulian vase, for example, appears as a nude dancer with prominent breasts amidst a group of maenads and satyrs, in an unflattering pose.[124] Bronze lamps, vases, bowls in the form of heads with negroid features, even a herm topped by a negroid head, suggest playful whimsy or even sardonic mockery (fig. 5).[125] Persons depicted with negroid comic masks appear on vase paintings evidently as objects of humor.[126] Macrophallic Ethiopians, performing outrageous acts, can be found on a Pompeian frieze, plainly designed to prompt laughter.[127] Even scenes from mythology in comic mode, like representations of Circe and Odysseus with negroid features and a negroid Nike driving the chariot of Herakles, indicate a form of capriciousness to amuse the viewer.[128] A striking image, appearing in several examples, in which the base of a drinking cup comes in the shape of a youthful black writhing in the grasp of a crocodile, defies clear explanation.[129] Is it a comic allusion, a parody of something like the celebrated Laocoön group?[130] If so, the black youth, in any case, is not the object of ridicule. Indeed none of these scenes or portrayals implies animosity toward people of color per se. One might note that nonblacks also appear, with still greater frequency, in comic scenes, mocked, parodied, or satirized depending on the genre or purpose of the depiction.[131] Ethnic prejudice has little relevance here.

Two figures of special note from mythology have Ethiopian roots: Memnon, king of the Ethiopians, who fought nobly at Troy and fell at the hands of Achilles, and Andromeda, a princess of the land, rescued from disaster by the hero Perseus. Legend gave each of them associations with other regions as well, notably in the east. But the Ethiopian connection looms large

[122] Snowden (1983), #60–61. Cf. Snowden (1976), #329–330, although the priests here do not have obviously negroid features.
[123] Cf. Winkes (1973), 908–911.
[124] Snowden (1970), #2, 94; (1976), #220.
[125] Snowden (1976), #312–316.
[126] Snowden (1970),#7, 98–99; (1976), #161–163, 181–183.
[127] Clarke (2007), 91–94, wtih figures 38 and 39.
[128] Snowden (1970), #36, 88; (1976), #184–185; (1983), #42–43.
[129] Snowden (1970), #33; (1976), #165, 213–214.
[130] So Beardsley (1929), 37–38. Snowden (1976), 150, sees the representation as a poignant one.
[131] So, rightly, Snowden (1976), 245.

Figure 5. Bronze herm with negroid head, Roman period. Ashmolean Museum (inv. no. Fortnum B 50).

in the tradition. The visual portrayals of these personages, however, exhibit a noteworthy feature. Although their attendants may be black, neither Memnon nor Andromeda appears with any negroid characteristics.[132] Does this indicate that painters shrank with distaste from the idea of associating heroic characters with blackness, an indirect disparagement of the Negro? Not a necessary conclusion. For Greek and Roman artists and audiences, divinities or heroes could take no other form than the conventional one.

[132] Memnon: Snowden (1970), #15, 18–19; (1976), 155–156; see also Beardsley (1929), 42–54, on possible representations of the Memnon myth. Images of Memnon are catalogued by Kossatz-Deissmann (1992), 448–461. Andromeda: Snowden (1970), #26, 90; (1976), #174–175; (1983), #17, 59; Schauenburg (1981), 774–790. A vase of the later fifth century from Capua depicts what may be a scene from Euripides' *Andromeda*, and a female figure with slightly negroid features depicted there has been interpreted as a personification of Ethiopia; Bieber (1961), 31–32. Snowden (1976), #176; (1983), #21, regards her as a "mulatto." No need to press the conjecture. But the woman cuts an impressive figure.

Anything else would be incongruous or incomprehensible.[133] Which is not at all the same as repugnance or aversion to blacks.[134]

A still more arresting phenomenon needs comment: the juxtaposition of black and white faces on a variety of plastic vases. Examples date as early as the seventh or sixth century BCE on a perfume vase from Cyprus that has a bearded man back-to-back with one of negroid features.[135] Numbers increase in the early Classical period. The Janus vases conjoin heads of black and white women (fig. 6),[136] a white woman and a bearded black man,[137] a double black head,[138] and even a negro and a head of Herakles.[139] The combinations include two juxtaposed heads made from the same mold, identical except that one is painted black with wooly hair, the other white. The features are satyr-like, but plainly they can be applied to persons of either color (fig. 7).[140] What are we to infer from these Janiform juxtapositions? Did artists play to prejudices by contrasting the acceptable norm with the inferior alien? Did these vases represent a jarring pastiche to reinforce standard stereotypes? The images themselves lend little support to such suppositions. Back-to-back placements of black-and-white women display no caricature nor suggest any effort to elevate the one over the other. The bearded black man paired with a white woman depicts the former neither as menacing nor as subordinate.[141] Setting a black head with that of Herakles bears particular notice. The lowly servant as attendant to the hero? The kantharos has them both on a level. And duplication of black and white heads from the same mold would hardly buttress racial or ethnic bias. The vessels were poured from or drunk from by the same individuals who surely

---

[133] Bérard (2000), 402–406, rightly states that artists could not conceive of a prestigious heroic figure with negroid features. But his inference that this is a form of cultural racism has no justification.

[134] To be sure, mythology also included an antihero with African associations, the notorious king Bousiris, who made it a practice to sacrifice foreigners until he ran into Herakles, who reversed matters and turned Bousiris into a sacrificial victim. Some artistic representations of the tale have Bousiris' attendants portrayed with negroid features, and even Bousiris seems to show comparable characteristics; Snowden (1970), #4, 20, 91–92; (1976), #150–151, 170–172; (1983), #19–20. For Bousiris himself, see Snowden (1970), #91; (1976), #170–172; Laurens (1986), 147–152. But Bousiris, as both the legend and artistic depictions emphasize, was an Egyptian king. If he has any African attributes, they are designed to intensify his differences from the Hellenic hero; Miller (2000), 413–442. The hint of negroid features (by no means common in portraiture of Bousiris) does not itself render him a "black" villain.

[135] Snowden (1970), #11; (1976), #149; (1983), #15.

[136] Snowden (1970), #12–13; (1976), #159–160, 193.

[137] Snowden (1976), #178–179. There is no reason to see the male here as a satyr; Bérard (2000), 409.

[138] Snowden (1976), #199; (1983), #27a.

[139] Snowden (1970), #14.

[140] Snowden (1970), #93.

[141] So, rightly, Bérard (2000), 409–411.

Figure 6. Kantharos in form of conjoined heads, white and Negro, late sixth century BCE. Museum of Fine Arts, Boston (inv. no. 98.926).

did not shrink with disdain from one side of the container. Elements of exoticism may have a role here, a fascination with the unusual and the distinctive, an intriguing contrast of types without the imposition of a preference. And there is certainly playfulness, a sense of amusement connecting like with unlike, catching the fancy of those who use the vessels, particularly

Figure 7. Terra-cotta vase with Janiform heads, fourth century BCE. Metropolitan Museum of Art, New York (inv. no. 06.1021.204). Photograph courtesy of Art Resource, New York.

Figure 8. Kantharos with Janiform heads, early fifth century BCE. Archaeological Museum, Thessaloniki (inv. no. I.ΔΥ.8). Photograph courtesy of the Getty Museum, Los Angeles.

at symposiastic gatherings where inversions and incongruities were the order of the day.[142] But the jugs convey no cruel jokes.

A particular instance brings the matter into sharper focus. A recently discovered kantharos of the early fifth century BCE, from the necropolis of Akanthos and now in the Archaeological Museum of Thessalonika, provides guidance with a rare inscription.[143] The Janus vase depicts a white woman's head on the one side, a black head with mustache and trim beard on the other (fig. 8). A tag inscribed on the mouth of the jar above the woman's head reads "I am the most beautiful Eronossa" and another above the man's head reads "Timyllos is beautiful like this face." The graffito has an obviously ironic quality, good-natured joking suitable for symposiastic bantering, not a matter of sneering derision.[144] It would be hazardous and unjustifiable to infer that African features themselves were reckoned as unsightly or disagreeable.[145] The evidence in general stands overwhelmingly against such an inference.

Textual and material testimonies cohere. Blacks impinged conspicuously on the classical consciousness. Their color and their physiognomy captured

[142] See A. Cohen (forthcoming).
[143] Rhomiopoulou (1987), 723–728.
[144] Cf. Voutiras (2001), 32–33.
[145] Lissarague (2002), 109–110, sees the representation of the black man as a caricature since the artist shows him with prominent teeth. Perhaps so. But it is worth noting that that feature appears elsewhere in portrayals of Africans, more a matter of convention than a sign of animosity. See the more nuanced treatment of this vessel by A. Cohen (forthcoming).

notice, causing comment and speculation, and generating a host of visual representations. The impression, however, was far from negative or unsavory. Hellenic legends set Ethiopians in a favorable light, according them integrity, wisdom, piety, and antiquity. References to the pigmentation, unusual hair, facial or other bodily features of contemporary Africans abound in the writings of Greeks and Romans. Ethnographic researchers found them intriguing, and assiduously collected information both trustworthy and dubious. The appearance of blacks could, of course, lend itself to skewering by satirists for whose mill all was grist. And some persons may well have had aversion to the dissimilar and the uncommon. Yet visual portrayals suggest that blacks who migrated to the communities of the eastern and western Mediterranean held a remarkable range of occupations and vocations with which they mingled freely in society. We have no way to gauge the extent of integration. But there is little trace of discrimination or marginalization. If the occasional image of blacks verged on the comic, the vast majority treated them with respect rather than with distaste. This was not a matter of tolerance or indulgence. Acknowledgment of anomalous features, even good-humored mockery, went hand in hand with mundane and comfortable conjuncture. The familiar Janiform vases that juxtaposed black and white heads, without diminution of either, suitably symbolize the untroubled intersection.

PART II

Connections with the "Other"

Chapter 9

FOUNDATION LEGENDS

Group identities in antiquity did not possess a pure and unadulterated character. Nor were they meant to do so. Communities and peoples, rather than considering themselves as hermetically sealed entities, regularly proclaimed ties to other societies, even inserting themselves into their history and traditions. By setting their patriarchs and legendary heroes into the folklore of other folks, they could attach themselves to the other peoples' experience and take credit for their qualities and achievements—a form of "identity theft."

The Greeks had a special flair for this. The Jewish historian Josephus captured the Hellenic mentality nicely on that score. Having recounted the tale of the Tower of Babel, he notes that the diversity of languages scattered nations, spurring the foundation of colonies everywhere and the establishment of new lands as each people settled in the region that God accorded them. In some cases, nations still retain the names provided by their founders; others have changed their names; still others recast their names in such a way as to make them more intelligible to those who dwelled among them. Greeks, says Josephus, have principal responsibility for these shifts. When they became powerful, they took the ancient glories for themselves, adorning the nations with names that they would understand and describing thier shape of government as if they were people descended from their own stock.[1] Josephus had them dead to rights. Greeks did regularly reconceptualize other people by according them a past that fit with Hellenic traditions or providing them with an ancestry that stemmed from Hellenic heroes. Egyptians indeed complained about that tendency. They charged Greeks with expropriating Egypt's most celebrated heroes and gods, even claiming as their own the colonial foundations actually sent out by Egyptians.[2] The Greeks were certainly guilty as charged. But they were by no means alone.

---

[1] Jos. *Ant.* 1.121: καλλωπίσαντες τὰ ἔθνη τοῖς ὀνόμασι πρὸς τὸ συνετὸν αὑτοῖς καὶ κόσμον θέμενοι πολιτείας ὡς ἀφ' αὑτῶν γεγονόσιν.

[2] Diod. 1.23.8: καθόλου δέ φασι τοὺς Ἕλληνας ἐξιδιάζεσθαι τοὺς ἐπιφανεστάτους ἥρωάς τε καὶ θεούς, ἔτι δ' ἀποικίας τὰς παρ' ἑαυτῶν.

Egyptians indulged in this same thievery. So did Phoenicians, Jews, Romans, and others. The practice permeated the Mediterranean.

Foundation Tales as Cultural Thievery

This convention expressed itself most flagrantly in foundation tales, a convenient conveyance of such usurpation. Celebrated characters from legend could serve as founders of foreign nations. Or, more inventively, fictive tales ascribed names derived from extant peoples to fabricated figures who became those peoples' progenitors. The Hellenic penchant for peering through parochial spectacles is well known. Alien nations became transformed and familiar when fitted into Greek traditions.

That held true even for the supposed archenemy, Persia. According to Herodotus, the Hellenic hero Perseus wed his rescued damsel Andromeda whose son by him was named Perses. And from him the Persians took their own name.[3] So Herodotus (or rather his sources). The story is a noteworthy one. The most inveterate foe of Hellas thus came within the Hellenic embrace. Greeks slipped one of their most celebrated legendary figures into a fictitious narrative of Persian history, thus to account for the very name of the people.

That fable, in its many manifestations, will be pursued in detail later. It may be the most dramatic instance of identity theft. But far from the only one. Another tradition took this maneuver a step further. The ruling house of Persia carried the designation of Achaemenids. That played nicely into the hands of Greek fashioners of legend. They concocted an Achaemenes as founder of the dynasty, made him a son of Perseus, and explained his name as derived from his grandfather, who came from Achaea in the Peloponnese.[4] So even the prime villains of the Greek master narrative, the Achaemenid clan and the Persian empire, turn out to be Greek in origin. That is appropriation indeed.

If Persians could be hellenized, anyone was fair game. Greek tentacles extended to Armenia. Its forefather, one naturally presumed, must have been a certain Armenus. That fictive character was conveniently imported into the legend of Jason and the Argonauts, becoming an officer in Jason's entourage, his own name derived from his hometown of Armenium in Thessaly. After the hero's death, Armenus gathered together the remnants of his forces and installed them in the region henceforth to be known as

---

[3] Herod. 7.61; cf. Hellanicus 4 fr. 59–60.
[4] Nic. Dam. 90 fr. 6.

Armenia.⁵ In similar fashion Greeks could take credit for the great kingdom of the Medes, the mighty power that once held sway over the Persians. Standard logic dictated that the founder of Media had to have the name of Medus. And Medus could readily be discovered in Greek mythology. He was, in fact, Jason's stepson, son of his wife Medea and her former husband, the king of Athens.⁶ So the Medes, precursors of the Persians as lords of the east, took their origins from an Athenian. Even the barbarous Scythians were brought into the Hellenic orbit. Herodotus reports a tale told him by the Greeks of Pontus about the origins of the Scythian monarchy. It derived from the union of Herakles and a composite creature, half woman and half snake. They produced three sons, only the third of whom performed the tasks that Herakles had instructed the sons' mother to monitor. That third son, of course, was Scythes, who gave his name to the royal line of Scythian kings.⁷ Greeks therefore staked a claim on the origins of Medes, Achaemenids, Persians, Armenians, and Scythians. Instead of shrinking from association with the barbarians, they proclaimed themselves as their progenitors.

But the Greeks had no monopoly on this sort of "identity theft." Egyptians employed the same form of imaginary lineage that attached foreign cultures to themselves. Egyptian mythology that made its way to Diodorus of Sicily included a tale of the wanderings of Osiris, most venerable and sacred of the nation's deities. The story has Osiris venture across the Hellespont to Thrace and beyond. In the course of his travels he left behind a son named Macedon as ruler of a land that was henceforth to be known as Macedonia. And, for good measure, he left behind another son, now aged, who would oversee the cultivation of plants in Thrace and found a city there, duly to be designated as Maroneia.⁸ The invention doubtless surfaced in the Hellenistic era, in Ptolemaic Egypt, where Greek stories of fictive founders who gave their names to celebrated cities and states circulated. The Egyptians evidently could give as good as they got. Macedonians may have installed an alien dynasty on the Egyptians' land. But, on this concoction, Macedonia itself owed its origin to an Egyptian dynasty.

---

⁵ Strabo 11.14.12 (C 530); Justin 42.2.7–10, 42.3.8.

⁶ Diod. 4.56.1, 10.27; Justin 42.3.6. Herodotus, 7.62.1, offers a slightly different version in which Media adopted its name as consequence of a visit to the land by Medea. Cf. Hecataeus 1 fr. 286. Medus appears also in Hesiod *Theog.* 1000–1001; Aesch. *Pers.* 765.

⁷ Herod. 4.8–10. The Scythians naturally offered a different version of their origins. But they too ascribed them to a son of Zeus, a certain Targitaus; Herod. 4.5. Hence the Scythians themselves bought into Greek mythology. A different version appears in Diod. 2.43.3, according to which Scythes was son of Zeus and the serpent woman and gave his name to the people. On the legend, see the analysis of Hartog (1988), 22–27.

⁸ Diod. 1.18.1, 1.20.1–3.

This form of national usurpation, as practiced by Egyptians, goes back at least to the very beginnings of Hellenic rule in Egypt, and perhaps even earlier. Hecataeus of Abdera, writing in the time of Ptolemy I, attests to it already in the late fourth century BCE. Erudite and clever Egyptians imposed their heroes on the origins of other august nations (even when those heroes had themselves to be converted first into Egyptians). Egyptian colonial foundations, so they maintained, fanned out everywhere. Belus, for example (plainly a form of Baal but here claimed as an Egyptian), led a group of settlers to the Euphrates, where he installed a colony at Babylon and appointed priests on the Egyptian model whom the Babylonians thereafter called Chaldeans. Hence the Chaldean skills in astrology owed their origins to Egyptian immigrants and followed the practices of the Egyptian priesthood.[9] National pride did not stop there. Egyptians boasted that one of their number, Danaus, was founder of the ancient and renowned Greek city of Argos, and that another, Cadmus, headed a group that also established themselves in Hellas, evidently in the ancient citadel of Thebes.[10] Never mind that Cadmus normally counted as a Phoenician. Egyptians were happy to claim him as their own. Nor did that suffice. Egyptians claimed Moses too. The version reported by Hecataeus has Moses, who was noted for his intelligence and his bravery, instructed to leave Egypt, like Cadmus and Danaus, and to settle Egyptians elsewhere. In this case he planted them in the land between Arabia and Syria, where he founded Jerusalem and inaugurated a wholesale set of admirable institutions.[11] Hecataeus' informants were certainly not shy about Egyptianizing foreign settlements. They added even the Colchians in Pontus as a colony of Egyptians. Their juxtaposition with colonists to Judaea neatly served to explain the custom of circumcision, found among Colchians and Jews alike. It was simply an Egyptian import.[12]

Imaginative annexation of alien lands and lore to bolster the cultural credentials of the usurper makes perfectly good sense. The self-esteem of nations could be augmented by appropriating the reputation and prestige of others. No surprise there. But a more intriguing and more arresting phenomenon warrants notice: the readiness of the ancients to embrace or even to fabricate foreign founders who represented the dawn of their own history.

This holds even, perhaps foremost, for the Greeks. For all their propensity toward cultural usurpation, they showed no shyness in telling similar

---

[9] Diod. 1.28.1.

[10] Diod. 1.28.2, 40.3.2. Thebes itself is not explicitly mentioned. But mention of Cadmus as leader of settlers to Greece can have no other referent.

[11] Diod. 40.3.3; cf. 1.28.2–3.

[12] Diod. 1.28.2–3. Note also the allusion in Josephus to the Egyptian pretense of kinship with the Jews; *CAp*. 2.28–31.

tales on themselves. The idea that mythical figures from abroad stood at the origins of Greek lands and peoples obviously did not rock Hellenic self-esteem—especially as the myths themselves were Hellenic concoctions.[13] We focus here on the most celebrated individuals whose legends had them immigrate to bring Hellenic communities into being: Pelops, Danaus, and Cadmus.

Pelops

Pelops stands out as exemplary of this process. Favorite of the god Poseidon and legendary ancestor of the house of Atreus and the Mycenaean/Argive dynasty, he gave his name to the whole of the Peloponnesus.[14] Yet Pelops came from Asia, a Phrygian or Lydian, possibly even a Paphlagonian. The connection of an easterner with that venerated land demands attention.

As with most legends, variants and divergences marked the tales attached to heroes of the remote past. The earliest references we possess to Pelops give little or no hint of his ethnic origins. In Homer he is simply forefather of Agamemnon, a conveyer of the scepter of the gods that would pass to that ruling dynasty.[15] In the verses of the seventh-century Spartan poet Tyrtaeus, Pelops is already associated with the whole of the Peloponnesus, "the broad island of Pelops," but his own origins are not specified.[16] Sons of Pelops, in subsequent stories, were associated with the founding of key cities in the Peloponnesus like Troizen, Sikyon, Kleonai, Corinth, and Epidaurus.[17] By the fifth century, at least, this namesake of the Peloponnesians was regularly perceived as an easterner. Pindar, who has Pelops as originator of that quintessential Hellenic institution, the Olympic Games, describes him as a Lydian.[18] That tradition is sharpened by the association of Pelops with Mount Sipylus, which is in Lydia north of Smyrna.[19] Pindar's contemporary Bacchylides calls him a Phrygian, as does Sophocles.[20]

---

[13] Erskine (2005), 121–136, stresses the Hellenocentric mentality in the transmission of Greek tales to other societies but overlooks Hellenic willingness to embrace the idea of their own foreign connections.

[14] On the legend of Pelops and its various forms, see Lacroix (1976), 327–334, with references to earlier literature. The main line of the legend appears in Apollod. *Epit.* 2.3–9.

[15] Homer *Il.* 2.100–108.

[16] Tyrtaeus fr. 2 (Diehl).

[17] Paus. 2.6.5, 2.15.1, 2.26.2, 2.30.8, 5.8.2; Strabo 8.6.14; Plut. *Thes.* 3.1; Schol. Eur. *Or.* 4.

[18] Pindar *Ol.* 1.24, 1.93, 9.9. Cf. Paus. 5.8.2.

[19] Pindar *Ol.* 1.36–38; Nic. Dam. *FGH* 90 F10; Paus. 2.22.2–3.

[20] Bacchylides 8.31 (Snell); Sophocles *Ajax* 1292; cf. *Ant.* 824–825, with reference to Pelops' sister Niobe. M. West (1985), 157–159, argues for an origin of the legend in Asiatic Aeolia. But see Lacroix (1976), 329–330.

The historians concur. Hecataeus of Miletus affirms that barbarians occupied the Peloponnesus prior to the coming of the Greeks, and Pelops, who brought Phrygians into the land henceforth to take its name from him, serves as prime example.[21] Pherecyides, the Athenian historian of the mid–fifth century, confirms the connection with Mount Sipylus.[22] Herodotus puts into the mouth of Xerxes a jingoistic speech that exhorts the Persian nobility to back a war against Greece, affirming, among other things, that the Phrygian Pelops, though no more than a slave (like everyone else) of the Persian kings, had subjugated the whole of the Peloponnesus, whose land and people now bore his name.[23] Thucydides, most tellingly, reports that he learned from those who were most knowledgeable about Peloponnesian traditions that Pelops came from Asia, took control of the land, and, though a foreigner, gave his name to the land.[24] The fable was firmly fixed and transmitted by those steeped in the heritage of the Peloponnesians themselves. A later version, recorded by Apollonius of Rhodes, has Pelops as a Paphlagonian.[25] That tradition appears also in Diodorus.[26] Pelops' origins seem to have floated about in western Anatolia. But the Asiatic roots predominate.[27]

Did this carry a stigma? There is little in the evidence to suggest it. The absence of explicit reference to Pelops as a foreigner prior to the early fifth century has much to do with the thinness of our testimony for the archaic period. It would be rash to infer that Pelops became orientalized after the Persian wars as part of a negative characterization of the foreigner. To be sure, certain strands of the Pelops legend show dubious features. The hero resorted to questionable means in wooing Hippodameia, the daughter of Oinomaos, and then disposed of the charioteer Myrtilos, who had helped him achieve his end. But however problematic Pelops' character may have been, our authors do not tie this to his immigrant status. It is noteworthy that Pindar, in the first half of the fifth century, endeavors to clean up some aspects of the legend and represents Pelops in the most positive terms but does not hesitate to identify him as a Lydian.[28] Xerxes cites Pelops as a

[21] Hecataeus *apud* Strabo 7.7.1. Even if the example is Strabo's addition (he includes other examples as well), it is hard to imagine that Hecataeus had anyone else in mind.

[22] Pherecydes *FGH* 3 fr. 38.

[23] Herod. 7.8.g.1, 7.11.4.

[24] Thuc. 1.9.2: λέγουσι δὲ καὶ οἱ τὰ σαφέστατα Πελοποννησίων μνήμῃ παρὰ τῶν πρότερον δεδεγμένοι Πέλοπά... ἦλθεν ἐκ τῆς Ἀσίας... δύναμιν περιποιησάμενον τὴν ἐπωνυμίαν τῆς χώρας ἔπηλυν ὄντα ὅμως σχεῖν.

[25] Apoll. Rhod. 2.357–359, 2.790.

[26] Diod. 4.73.6–4.74.1

[27] This is not necessarily inconsistent with traditions that have Pelops accompanied by Boeotians or peopling the Peloponnesus with Phthiotic Achaeans; Strabo 8.4.4, 8.5.5; cf. Schol. Pindar *Ol.* 1.35.

[28] Pindar *Ol.* 1.35–94. Miller (2005), 72–75, 86–87, notes that Pelops appears consistently in eastern garb on vase painting after the mid–fifth century and suggests that this may allude to

precedent in Herodotus' portrait in order to underscore eastern success in occupation of western lands—not to associate the hero with wickedness.[29] The sole passage that does deploy Pelops for harshly negative purposes comes in Sophocles' *Ajax*, when Teucer throws in Agamemnon's teeth the fact that his grandfather was a barbarian, and Phrygian to boot.[30] A nasty slur? Perhaps, but not necessarily an ethnic libel. Agamemnon had characterized Teucer precisely thus: son of a captive woman and speaking in a barbarian tongue.[31] Teucer, born of the Trojan princess Hesione, did not shun the characterization but reveled in it. He had stood shoulder to shoulder with his half brother Ajax, slave and son of a barbarian mother though he was.[32] Teucer pointedly reminded Agamemnon that he too came of barbarian stock. He did not denigrate Pelops' ethnicity.

What counts is that the Greeks of the Peloponnese embraced the idea that their *Stammvater* was an Asian. Thucydides' testimony on this holds primary authority. He cites those who knew best the traditions of the Peloponnese—and they affirmed that Pelops the foreigner from Asia took power in their land and gave them his name.[33] No hint of embarrassment or awkwardness there. Eastern origins played an integral part in Peloponnesian self-perception.

Danaus

A comparable position in legend belongs to Danaus. He is bracketed more than once with Pelops and with Cadmus as immigrants from abroad who came to rule Greeks.[34] Danaus arrived in Argos as a fugitive from Egypt together with his fifty daughters, who fled the aggressive desires of their fifty cousins, sons of Aegyptus, and their dastardly designs on marriage. In circumstances only fuzzily known from the preserved fragments of the

---

the dubious moral quality of his tactics. But there are too few examples to draw any confident conclusions, and the connection is quite indirect. The literary sources, in any case, neither condemn Pelops' actions nor associate them with foreignness.

[29] Herod. 7.8.g.1, 7.11.4.

[30] Sophocles *Ajax* 1291–1292: οἶ κ οἶσθα σοῦ πατρὸς μὲν ὃς προύφυ πατὴρ ἀρχαῖον ὄντα Πέλοπα βάρβαρον Φρύγα. E. Hall (1989), 176, reckons this "one of the most extraordinary arguments in any tragic *agon*." But why?

[31] Sophocles *Ajax* 1228, 1262–1263.

[32] Sophocles *Ajax* 1288–1289.

[33] Thuc. 1.9.2. See above, n. 24. There is no compelling reason to believe that Thucydides relies here on Hellanicus of Lesbos; cf. Hornblower (1991), 32. The fact that Pelops does not appear in oriental fashion in works from the Peloponnese carries little significance in view of the paucity of examples, as Miller (2005), 75, rightly observes. On the artistic representations of Pelops, see also Lacroix (1976), 334–341; Triantis (1994), 282–287.

[34] Hecataeus *apud* Strabo 7.7.1; Plato *Menex.* 245 C–D; Isocr. *Helen* 68; *Panath.* 80.

saga, Danaus succeeded in attaining the throne of Argos, the city that looms so large in Hellenic legend.[35] The term "Danaoi" already in Homer—who knows nothing of this story—was equivalent to Greeks in general, used interchangeably with "Achaeans" and "Argives." Homeric usage may have helped inspire later formulations of the fable that had Danaus order the name Danaoi to supplant that of Argives and indeed to apply to all inhabitants of Hellas—or their earlier incarnation as Pelasgians.[36] And Danaus' own Egyptian origins became assimilated to Hellenic lineage by making him descendant of the Argive princess Io, who was driven from Greece by the machinations of Hera and eventually impregnated by Zeus in Egypt.[37] Danaus thus possessed four generations of Egyptian ancestors—but ultimately an Argive foremother (not to mention a divine forefather).[38] Egyptians claimed him as one of their own.[39] But Greeks had framed the story to have him return to his Argive roots.

The double identity of Danaus and especially his daughters the Danaids emerges in full ambiguity in Aeschylus' *Suppliants*, performed probably in the 460s BCE.[40] The drama is evidently the first of a trilogy, the second and third plays no longer extant, and an attempt to reconstruct them has little point. The *Suppliants* depicts the arrival in Argos of Danaus and his daughters, who seek protection and assistance from the Argive king, notably named Pelasgus (an allusion to indigenous origins?). Although reluctant and uncertain at first, Pelasgus' will is steeled by backing of the Argive populace; he faces down the boorish and blustering herald of Aegyptus and his sons, and champions the cause of the Danaids. The play concludes with the young maidens prepared to settle in Argos, having left behind the land of the Nile.

Danaus might trace his ancestry back to an Argive princess, but his assimilation in Egypt had been thorough. The drama ostensibly depicts Danaus and his daughters as unqualified Egyptians. The chorus of maidens present themselves as speaking a barbarian tongue.[41] Upon first

---

[35] See, e.g., Apollodorus 2.1.4; Paus. 2.16.1, 2.19.3–4, 10.10.4.

[36] Apollodorus 2.1.4; Strabo 5.2.4, 8.6.9.

[37] This was the prevailing form of the myth as it appears in Aeschylus' *Suppliants* in the first half of the fifth century—and thereafter. Another, perhaps earlier, version has Io impregnated in Euboea; Hesiod fr. 296 (Merkelbach-West). An epic poem, the *Danais*, treated the myth, perhaps in the sixth century, but is now lost. It did, however, identify Danaus as an Egyptian king. Other elements in the saga are not relevant here. See the summary of testimony in Friis Johansen and Whittle (1980), I, 44–55; Sandin (2005), 4–8. On possible Near Eastern parallels or influences on the myth, see M. West (1997), 442–447.

[38] Aesch. *Prom.* 787–856; Apollodorus 2.1.3–4.

[39] Herod. 2.91.5; Diod. 1.28.2, 40.3.2.

[40] Friis Johansen and Whittle (1980), I, 21–29. Scullion (2002), 87–101, has recently argued for a date in the 470s. But see Sandin (2005), 1–4. On the double identity of the Danaids, see Kurke (1999), 320–322; Vasunia (2001), 40–43; Mitchell (2006), 210–218; (2007), 124–126.

[41] Aesch. *Suppl.* 119, 130. Note also the reference to their dark skin color; 154–155; cf. 70–71; Sandin (2005), 86.

encountering them, the king of Argos is taken aback by their barbarian robes and luxurious garb, unlike anything that would be worn by Argive women, or indeed by anyone in Greece.[42] For Pelasgus they are as foreign as they can be. He guesses at their origins: they seem like Libyan women, or perhaps from the land of the Nile, possibly even Indian nomads bordering on Ethiopia; indeed they might have been thought Amazons had they carried bows—certainly nothing like Argives.[43] Danaus himself draws the ethnic distinction: his appearance is quite different; the Nile nourishes a race dissimilar to that of Inachos (Io's Argive father).[44] Both Danaus and his daughters acknowledge that as aliens they are subject to censure and calumny.[45] In referring to their lustful suitors, the Danaids brand them as the raging race of Aegyptus, insatiable in war.[46] The king's harsh exchange with the Egyptian herald points most sharply at the contrast between the barbarian invaders and the land of "Pelasgian men": do they think they have come to a city of women?[47] Indeed they will have to contend with real men—not those who drink their wine made from barley (beer)![48]

Does the drama then reflect Greek (or at least Athenian) prejudice and hostility toward the alien?[49] It might be hasty to make that inference. The harshest comments leveled at Egyptians direct themselves not to the nation in general but to the insatiably lustful progeny of Aegyptus, the villains of the piece.[50] And the herald, their representative, constitutes the play's principal target. His arrogant bullying and threats, and his pitting of Egyptian deities against Greek gods, carry no weight with the king of Argos, who holds fast to his determined stance, backed by the authority of the populace, to protect the Egyptian suppliants.[51] Aeschylus does indeed portray Danaus and the Danaids (and they portray themselves) as thoroughly Egyptian, a distinct contrast with Hellenic language, garb, and appearance.[52] But not with Hellenic character. The dramatist is altogether

---

[42] Aesch. *Suppl.* 234–237. On the text here, see Friis Johansen and Whittle (1980), II, 191–192; Sandin (2005), 142; Mitchell (2006), 212.
[43] Aesch. *Suppl.* 279–289.
[44] Aesch. *Suppl.* 496–498.
[45] Aesch. *Suppl.* 972–974, 994–995.
[46] Aesch. *Suppl.* 741–742, 817–821.
[47] Aesch. *Suppl.* 911–914.
[48] Aesch. *Suppl.* 952–953. Cf. Friis Johansen and Whittle (1980), III, 255.
[49] So E. Hall (1989), 118–119 and passim; Vasunia (2001), 33–74. By contrast, Bernal (1987), I, 88–98, endeavors to draw out the Egyptian elements in the play; see the criticisms of E. Hall (1996), 338–339. A more balanced judgment by Mitchell (2006), 205–223.
[50] Aesch. *Suppl.* 741: ἐξῶλές ἐστι μάργον Αἰγύπτου γένος; 817–818.
[51] Aesch. *Suppl.* 836–965. It is noteworthy that, although the herald scorns the Hellenic gods, Pelasgus voices no criticism of Egyptian divinities.
[52] Cf. E. Hall (1989), 118, 136, 172–173.

sympathetic to the plight of the fugitive women and to the modest demeanor of their father.[53] Solid rapport between the Greek king and the Egyptian suppliants emerges unmistakably in the drama.[54] As for the contrast between the nations, the Danaids' exchange with Pelasgus dissolved it. The maidens, in recounting the tale of Io and delineating their own genealogy, demonstrated precisely that Pelasgus' dynasty and the house of Danaus are linked in the most fundamental sense: they derive from the royal lineage of Argos.[55] And the king acknowledged the force of their tale. As he conceded, "you do seem to me to share this land of old."[56]

We cannot reconstruct the particulars of the trilogy's other plays. But Danaus, as Aeschylus' audience knew, would soon occupy the throne of Argos itself, representing a blend of Greek and Egyptian, the establishment of an alien ruler in the hallowed land of the Argives but one who represented their own ancient traditions. The play does not conceal the Danaids' foreignness, indeed emphasizes it—thereby to underscore the message that the outsider could revive and enhance the antique values of the nation.

The tale of Danaus and the Danaids as Egyptians with Greek genealogy who settled in Argos had taken firm root by the early fifth century. It appears in Pherecydes and Herodotus as well as Aeschylus.[57] Danaus as hybrid figure who fused Hellenic heritage with four generations of Egyptian ancestry then became founder of a new dynasty in Argos.[58] Artistic representation

---

[53] The interpretation of E. Hall (1989), 123, that Danaus' advice to his daughters to maintain a modest decorum (*Suppl.* 176–203) was a form of "Egyptian cunning," is implausible. Does Pelasgus' advice to Danaus as to how to address the assembly (*Suppl.* 517–519) count as "Greek cunning"? Hall (1989), 125, oddly seeks to soften any distinction between the deplorable fierceness of the herald and the restraint of the Danaids. And her claim, 202–203, followed by Vasunia (2001), 54–56, that Aeschylus depicts the women as rejecting the institution of marriage is difficult to sustain. They want to avoid a forced and bad marriage; *Suppl.* 393–395, 798–799, 1031–1032, 1052–1053, 1062–1064; cf. *Prom.* 858.

[54] Aesch. *Suppl.* 954–965. To be sure, Pelasgus appears irresolute at first and hesitates to promise the Danaids security, maintaining that he required the approval of the Argive populace; *Suppl.* 365–369, 397–401. And it is striking that the Danaids actually argue that the king is the state and should exercise his own autocratic power; *Suppl.* 370–375: σύ τοι πόλις, σὺ δὲ τὸ δήμιον. Cf. E. Hall (1989), 192–193, 199; Vasunia (2001), 70–71, 143–145. It does not follow, however, that Aeschylus is here condemning an Egyptian commitment to autocracy while commending the Argive (Athenian?) devotion to democracy. The Danaids simply marshaled their best argument for a swift and successful resolution. And Pelasgus appears much more as fretful, anxious, and vacillating than as a champion of democracy.

[55] Aesch. *Suppl.* 291–326, and, especially, 274–275: Ἀργεῖαι γένος ἐξευχόμεσθα, σπέρματ' εὐτέκνου βοός.

[56] Aesch. *Suppl.* 325–326: δοκεῖτε (δή) μοι τῆσδε κοινωνεῖν χθονὸς τἀρχαῖον. This generous expression undermines the notion that Aeschylus sought to stress the anteriority of the Greeks; as Vasunia (2001), 37.

[57] Pherecydes *FGH* 3 F21; Herod. 2.91.5, 2.171.3, 2.182.2, 7.94; Aesch. *Prom.* 787–869.

[58] Aesch. *Prom.* 869: αὕτη κατ' Ἄργος βασιλικὸν τέξει γένος (with reference to the daughter of Danaus).

echoed the ambiguity of the ethnic combination, with a mixture of Greek and oriental imagery.[59] But nowhere is the installation by the immigrant of a ruling house in that ancient city, so redolent with myth and history, portrayed as the injection of the unwanted or degenerate east. The Argives had made it a part of their own venerated tradition.

Cadmus

Another city rich in legend and saga also had a purported foreign founder. The Phoenician Cadmus, as the tale (at least in its full-blown form) had it, was *ktistes* of Thebes—and Greeks were quite comfortable and unembarrassed about those origins.

In the most familiar version of the tale Cadmus came from Phoenicia, whether Tyre or Sidon, went in search of his sister (or niece) Europa, and asked help from the oracle at Delphi. There he was told to follow a cow and to found a city wherever that cow should collapse of weariness. The cow, as it happened, ended its journey in Boeotia on the site that would become Thebes. Cadmus first had to confront a fierce dragon, slay it, and then sow the dragon's teeth, on the advice of Athena. Once this was accomplished, armed men, the Spartoi, sprang from the ground and fought fiercely among themselves until Cadmus hurled stones at them, provoking still more violent quarrels that resulted in the slaughter of all but five. There followed the founding of Thebes and the wedding of Cadmus with Harmonia, daughter of Ares and Aphrodite. A host of stories about subsequent generations are not relevant here.[60]

Much ink has been spilled on just when different parts of the myth came into being, how far back the Phoenician connection goes, and whether a historical kernel can be extracted from the encrustation of legend.[61] No decisive resolution lies within our power on any of these matters. A few methodological points should be underscored here. Given the piecemeal and scattered state of our evidence, the first appearance of the saga or an element thereof may have little bearing on the actual time of its invention.[62] Inferences about the growth and development of a story that

---

[59] Miller (2005), 75–79.

[60] Many of the key elements of the tale can be found in Apollodorus 3.1.1, 3.4.1–2. Cf. Ovid *Met.* 3.1–137. These and other features, together with the ancient testimony, are summarized in Edwards (1979), 19–34.

[61] For a valuable résumé of the scholarship, see Edwards (1979), 50–64. See further the briefer but more recent summary by Mitchell (2007), 182–184.

[62] Gomme's lengthy and incisive article (1913), 53–72, 223–245, makes the classic case for Phoenician origins as a late addition to the tale, emerging only with the fifth-century logographers. Vian (1963), 51–69, follows much the same line, although he allows that Cadmus

had so many variants rest on very shaky foundations. And legends can carry significance for self-perception and identity that skirts any arguments about historicity.[63] What requires emphasis is the fact that Cadmus' foreign origins, while not always explicitly attested in the fragmentary testimony we possess, are nowhere denied or challenged. The celebrated city of Thebes, in popular imagination, owed its existence to a hero from abroad.

Cadmus plays no role in the Homeric epics, mentioned but once as father of Ino.[64] "Cadmeians," on the other hand, gain repeated mention as the inhabitants of Thebes, clear attestation that Cadmus was already reckoned as the city's founder.[65] His origins go unmentioned, irrelevant to the epics. But the poet does identify one of Zeus' conquests (the mother of Minos and Rhadamanthys, thus plainly Europa) as "daughter of far-famed Phoenix."[66] This need not make her a Phoenician (Phoenix can simply be a proper name without ethnic connotation). But in the context of these legendary figures, the name is certainly suggestive.[67] Fragments of the epic cycle, Hesiod, the Hesiodic *Catalogue of Women*, and archaic poetry fail to get us any further. Europa reappears as daughter of Phoenix, but no explicit reference links her to Cadmus or identifies either one of them as Phoenician.[68] That testimony, limited and lacunose, remains inconclusive. The

---

might have been turned into a Phoenician in the late seventh or sixth centuries. Tourraix (2000), 98–99, sees the shift as a political manipulation of the myth in the fifth century. Similarly, Kühr (2006), 101. But cui bono? The idea that it represented anti–Theban propaganda after the Persian wars is narrow and reductive; cf. Buxton (1994), 184–193. Edwards (1979), 65–86, offers a more balanced judgment and leaves open the possibility that the Phoenician legend goes much further back. The argument from silence is especially weak given the state of the surviving evidence on this subject Cf. Kühr (2006), 97. The very substantial record in the fifth century and later is unanimous on Cadmus' foreignness. And nothing in the earlier evidence denies it. An acute article by Berman (2004), 1–22, judges the Cadmus tale to be later than another Theban foundation story, that of the twins Amphion and Zethos, and sees the legend of Cadmus as product of the era of colonization. On this aspect of the myth, see Kühr (2006), 118–132. On the connection between Greek colonization and the shaping of the legend, see also Tourraix (2000), 105–106. Whether that connection existed or not, the fact that the "colonizer" is a barbarian rather than a Greek remains the most arresting feature.

[63] Edwards (1979), 115–207, seeks to make a cautious case for some substratum of history in the legend. Vian (1963), 51–75 and passim, takes a skeptical line. So also Kühr (2006), 87–91, 96–100.

[64] Homer *Od.* 5.333.

[65] E.g., Homer *Il.* 4.376–409, 10.285–289, 23.677–680; *Od.* 11.271–276.

[66] Homer *Il.* 14.321–322. The connection of Cadmus and Europa may go back at least to Eumelus, the eighth century Corinthian epic poet; see M. West (1985), 82–83.

[67] For some, the name Phoenix has no ethnic significance; e.g. Gomme (1913), 54–55; Vian (1963), 56; Mitchell (2007), 183. Others put more weight on it; e.g., Edwards (1979), 68–69; Bernal (1987), 85–86. See E. Hall's criticisms of Bernal (1992), 185–187, with Bernal's reply (1992), 206.

[68] See references to the texts in Gomme (1913), 55–60.

point at which Cadmus' foreignness entered the tradition is beyond our grasp. Yet it is there, unequivocally, by the fifth century. And it is unlikely to have sprung from nowhere. For all we know, it was there from the beginning.

The foreignness fluctuates. Bacchylides gives Cadmus' lineage as Egyptian, while identifying Europa (elsewhere) as Phoenician.[69] Pherecydes has Cadmus as brother of Phoenix but as grandson of the Nile, thus reaffirming an Egyptian connection.[70] In early Ptolemaic Egypt, the Egyptians certainly claimed Cadmus as one of their own.[71] Association with Egypt was not reckoned as incompatible with Phoenician ethnicity. Most of our sources have Cadmus as descendant of Io while at the same time identifying him as Phoenician.[72] And later authorities have him as both Egyptian and Phoenician.[73] But none makes him a Greek.

For Herodotus, the Phoenician origins of Cadmus and the Cadmeians who peopled Thebes are uncontroversial. His opening tongue-in-cheek chapters, with their reciprocal snatching of damsels from east to west and vice versa, identify Europa as daughter of the king of Tyre.[74] And a more sober passage confirms her as a Tyrian who commenced her wanderings from Phoenicia.[75] Cadmus too came from Tyre and brought Phoenicians with him who settled the land of Boeotia.[76] Moreover, they transmitted a number of cultural advantages to Greece, foremost among them the art of writing.[77] Herodotus evinces no doubts.[78]

---

[69] Cadmus: Bacchylides 18.39–48 (Snell); Europa: 16.53–54. Pindar, despite references to various features of the Cadmus tale, does not touch on his ethnicity.

[70] Pherecydes *FGH* I 3 F21. According to a fragment attributed to Hellanicus (*FGH* IA 4 F51), Cadmus was himself son of Phoenix. Cf. Vian (1963), 21–26.

[71] Hecataeus of Abdera *apud* Diod. 40.3.2. See also Diod. 1.28.4; Tzetzes on Lycophron 1206 (Scheer).

[72] Cf. Bacchylides 18.39–48.

[73] See references in Edwards (1979), 47–48; Kühr (2006), 91.

[74] Herod. 1.2.1. Note also his allusion to Io, purloined from Argos by Phoenicians and brought to Egypt, according to the Persians; 1.1.1–3.

[75] Herod. 4.45.4–5.

[76] Herod. 2.49.3. Cf. 4.147.4.

[77] Herod. 5.57–61. The motif of Cadmus as purveyor of "Phoenician letters" to Greece recurs regularly in subsequent authors; see references in Edwards (1979), 23, and the discussion of Kühr (2006), 103–105.

[78] The claim of Demand (1982), 52–53, that Herodotus, reflecting Athenian attitudes, conveyed the legend as an anti-Theban portrait to call attention to the barbarism of Thebes has no support in the texts and nothing to recommend it. Miller (2005), 79–84, points out quite tellingly that Cadmus is nowhere depicted in barbarian attire or guise on the vase paintings. But her proposal that the frequent depiction of Cadmus in the company of Athena suggests an Athenian effort to trump the Thebans by making Athens' patron deity assist at the foundation of Thebes rather than have it done by a "barbarian" is far-fetched. On the visual representations of the legend, see also Vian (1963), 35–50; Tiverios (1990), 863–882.

The tradition was firm and fixed by the late fifth century when Euripides produced his *Phoenissae*. The play can take for granted that Cadmus stemmed from Phoenicia and arrived on Greek shores to establish the city of Thebes.[79] The legend appears also in straightforward form in the prologue to Euripides' lost *Phrixus*.[80] Other elements of the myth appear elsewhere in Euripides.[81] After the fifth century the Phoenician/Theban connection recurs in a plethora of writers extending from late classical Greece to the Byzantine period.[82] Scarcely a hint of discomfort surfaces anywhere.[83]

A noteworthy conclusion follows. Rather than "Othering" the alien, many Greeks quite contentedly traced their lineage to him. But what of Athens? Did not that great city vigorously assert its resistance to foreign genealogy?

Athenians and Pelasgians

The Athenians famously claimed autochthony. They had always occupied the soil on which they dwelled, the most ancient of the Greeks.[84] That boast came to be repeated with regularity, even monotony. How others might have reacted to it escapes notice. It would be unwise to assume irritation or resentment. More likely indifference—if they knew of it at all. The Athenians, so we are told, went even further. They vaunted their distinctiveness in Hellas on that score. They and they alone were pure Greeks, without any barbarian admixture in their bloodlines. The claim is direct and potent. On the face of it, the Athenian posture would seem to express, as clearly as one might wish, a recoiling from the taint of foreign adulteration.

That may be hasty and erroneous judgment. The locus classicus for this posture occurs in Plato's devious dialogue the *Menexenus*. Socrates, in the midst of a concocted funeral oration, ostensibly not of his own composition, asserts that Athenians come from unalloyed stock, free of barbarian

---

[79] Eur. *Phoen.* 4–6, 216–219, 244–248, 280–282, 291, 638–648.

[80] Eur. *Phrixus* fr. 819 (Nauk); cf. also *Bacch.* 170–172.

[81] See Gomme (1913), 68–69.

[82] The citations are conveniently collected in Edwards (1979), 45–47.

[83] To be sure, the standard genealogy has Cadmus derive ultimately from the Argive princess Io. But this can hardly be seen as an effort to reclaim Cadmus as a Greek; so, e.g., Mitchell (2007), 183–184. Io's associations are as strong with Egypt as with Greece. And the Hellenic heritage nowhere in our texts compromises Cadmus' Phoenician ethnicity. So, rightly, Edwards (1979), 49–50.

[84] E.g., Herod. 7.161.3; Eurip. *Ion.* 589–592; *Erechth. apud* Lyc. *Leok.* 100; Aristoph. *Vesp.* 1075–1080; Thuc. 1.2.5, 2.36.1; Lysias *Epitaph.* 17; Isoc. *Paneg.* 24; *Panath.* 124; *Peace* 49; Demosth. *Epitaph.* 4. On the Athenians and autochthony generally, see Montanari (1981); E. Cohen (2000), 91–103; Loraux (2000), 13–27; Isaac (2004), 114–124. Cf. also Rosivach (1987), 294–306; J. Hall (1997), 51–56; and E. Cohen (2000), 82–88, who argue that the claim to autochthony did not precede the fifth century. But see Shapiro (1998), 130–133.

hybridization. In this they stood apart from other celebrated Greek cities or regions, which, though Hellenic in practice, were barbarians by nature. For they were contaminated by founders from abroad like Pelops, Cadmus, Aegyptus, or Danaus.[85] Plato's contemporary, Isocrates, as befits his purpose, raised the contrast from the level of Athens to that of all Greece. Hellas itself, he proclaimed in two separate, widely spaced, orations, has turned its back on an ancient time when its lands had been occupied by foreigners—the Peloponnesus by Pelops, Argos by Danaus, Thebes by Cadmus—to retaliate through seizure of the cities and territories of the barbarian.[86]

Embrace of these statements as representing a general Hellenic abhorrence of the "barbarian" would be a serious misapprehension. Their context needs consideration. Plato's *Menexenus* is a parodic dialogue, and the funerary oration that occupies most of it cannot readily be taken as a serious exercise. The dialogue opens with a mischievous, tongue-in-cheek exchange in which Socrates' praise for the emotional uplift provided by speeches on fallen warriors is transparently overblown and comically extravagant.[87] Menexenus recognized instantly that Socrates was making sport of Athenian orators—and nothing that his interlocutor said in response denied it. Socrates, in fact, insisted that such speeches can be produced instantaneously; orators have them at the ready, evidently a collection of clichés. Socrates had one to offer on the spot. He had heard it just yesterday, a speech of Aspasia rehearsed in his presence, and he could deliver it word for word![88] With such an introduction, readers could hardly expect an earnest speech. And the funeral eulogy itself, in addition to bromides, contains various historical errors—not to mention the fact that it records events that were to occur well after the deaths of both Aspasia and Socrates. Although the speech itself is ostensibly sober and serious, the conclusion of the dialogue reverts to the lighthearted interchange of the opening. The impressionable Menexenus hails the oration and pronounces himself especially impressed with the blissful Aspasia—if indeed a woman could produce a speech like that. The final exchange is replete with playful irony.[89] In this context, the proclamation that Athens had not a drop of foreign blood and despised barbaric peoples, especially the founders of the Peloponnese, Argos, and Thebes, most plausibly carries the same overtone

---

[85] Plato *Menex.* 245 C–D: ἐστι καὶ φύσει μισοβάρβαρον, διὰ τὸ εἰλικρινῶς εἶναι Ἕλληνες καὶ ἀμιγεῖς βαρβάρων. οὐ γὰρ Πέλοπες οὐδὲ Κάδμοι οὐδὲ Αἴγυπτοί τε καὶ Δαναοὶ οὐδὲ ἄλλοι πολλοὶ φύσει μὲν βάρβαροι ὄντες, νόμῳ δὲ Ἕλληνες, συνοικοῦσιν ἡμῖν, ἀλλ' αὐτοὶ Ἕλληνες, οὐ μιξοβάρβαροι οἰκοῦμεν.
[86] Isoc. *Helen* 68; *Panath.* 80.
[87] Plato *Menex.* 234C–235C.
[88] Plato *Menex.* 235C–236D.
[89] Plato *Menex.* 249 D–E.

of mockery. The implication is underscored by the conceit that has the speech composed not only by a woman but a foreign woman at that![90] As cornerstone of the argument that Athenians deplored the injection of foreign elements in Hellenic lands, it would be markedly paradoxical.

Nor do Isocrates' statements carry any more weight. The orator says much the same in both passages, harking back in each to the mythological era that preceded the Trojan War. The first passage, contained in Isocrates' sportive encomium to Helen, affirms that it was due to her that the Greeks first united their forces in harmony against the barbarian. Prior to the Trojan War, Greece suffered the embarrassing misfortune of being occupied by alien rulers like Danaus in Argos, Pelops in the Peloponnesus, and Cadmus in Thebes.[91] One ought not confuse this rhetorical ploy with an authentic reference to fourth-century attitudes toward non-Greeks. The same can be said for the second passage from the *Panathenaicus*. In that work, a composition of Isocrates' old age, the orator delivered an encomium to Athens, largely to the detriment of Sparta, but paused for an excursus on the Trojan War. Here he gave accolades to Agamemnon for his merger of squabbling Greek leaders and states in a conflict ostensibly to rescue Helen, in fact to unite Hellas so that she need not again have to endure the ignominy of her cities taken and ruled by barbarians like Pelops, Danaus, and Cadmus.[92] Once again this hardly qualifies as insight into Attic aversion to foreigners. It would be hazardous indeed to extrapolate from these mythological allusions a sober analysis of xenophobia.

If indeed Athenian snobbery toward the foreign founders of other states did receive authentic expression in these passages, a significant inference would follow. While Athens boasted of a freedom from barbarian elements in its lineage and history, others had no comparable qualms. The boast itself, regardless of its legitimacy, strikes a notable chord. It implies that Greek states generally (Athens being the exception) acknowledged, evidently without difficulty, their roots in non-Hellenic peoples.

In fact, the Athenian claim itself is by no means uniform and monolithic. A tangled tradition had it that the original Athenians were not even Greek

---

[90] Scholars have divided over the years on the seriousness of the speech (none contests the parody in the opening and conclusion of the dialogue). For references to earlier literature, see Tsitsiridis (1998), 63–64. The ironic elements were discerned long ago in the dissertation of Berndt (1888). For a more recent treatment of the *Menexenus* as parody, see Loraux (1986), 312–327; cf. E. Cohen (2000), 100–102; J. Hall (2002), 214–217. The long discussion of Tsitsiridis (1998), 63–92, bent on seeing both sides, reaches no clear conclusion and labels the work a "pastiche." The ingenious but highly speculative interpretation of Kahn (1963), 220–234, that the *Menexenus*, though it contained some satiric features, was a serious political pamphlet criticizing Athenian policy and appealing to earlier panhellenic sentiments, has won little following.

[91] Isoc. *Helen* 68.

[92] Isoc. *Panath*. 80.

or Greek speakers. They descended from Pelasgians. Those quintessential mystery people continue to baffle researchers. Just who were the Pelasgians—or indeed whether they ever existed outside the imaginations of mythmakers—exceeds the boundaries of this inquiry.[93] But their image as *Urvolk* who preceded or generated Greeks carries important implications.

The key text, alas, is a tortured and nearly impenetrable one.[94] Herodotus maintains that when Croesus inquired about the most powerful of Greek states, he learned that Spartans were preeminent among Dorians, Athenians among Ionians. The former were Hellenic by origin, the latter Pelasgian. Herodotus acknowledges that the Hellenes wandered widely while the Pelasgians stayed at home (evidently an allusion to the Athenian myth of autochthony). Then matters get more complicated. Herodotus refrains from pronouncing on the Pelasgian language, but he is quite confident that it was not Greek. He bases that judgment on the language spoken in his own day by people whom he takes to be remnants of the ancient Pelasgians, some in the vicinity of the Tyrrhenians in Italy, others in two cities of the Hellespont, and still others in settlements originally Pelasgian that subsequently changed their names. On that evidence, Herodotus asserts unequivocally that Pelasgians spoke a barbarian tongue.[95] And, since this was true of all Pelasgians, the Athenians, being Pelasgian, must have changed their language when they became Greeks. Herodotus' account then becomes even more convoluted. The Hellenic people, so it seemed to him, had always used the same language. But when they split off from the Pelasgians, they grew in strength and were augmented by a multitude of people, especially the Pelasgians and many other barbarian folk. The Pelasgian *ethnos*, he concludes, being a barbarian people, had experienced no great increase.[96]

Parsing this text is no easy matter. Confusion and inconsistency clearly mark the presentation.[97] But certain key elements merit stress. Athenians, according to Herodotus, were originally Pelasgians, and Pelasgians were non-Greeks who spoke a barbarian tongue (and still do). Whatever else one makes of the account, it derives Athenians from a non-Greek people—however fictitious, fabricated, and problematic they may be.[98] It is tempting to interpret Herodotus here as twitting the Athenians, mischievously turning

---

[93] For the texts and various opinions, see Sakellariou (1977), 81–100. Sourvinou-Inwood (2003), 103–104, rightly eschews an investigation of historicity.

[94] Herod. 1.56–58.

[95] Herod. 1.57.2: ἦσαν οἱ Πελασγοὶ βάρβαρον γλῶσσαν ἱέντες.

[96] Herod. 1.58: τὸ Πελασγικὸν ἔθνος, ἐὸν βάρβαρον, οὐδαμὰ μεγάλως αὐξηθῆναι.

[97] See the philological analysis of McNeal (1985), 11–21, who rightly argues against emendation but does not clear up the confusion. His attempt to take τὸ Ἑλληνικὸν as partitive, i.e., the Greek (non-Pelasgian) part of the Athenians, is unconvincing. See R. Thomas (2000), 120.

[98] See also Herod. 8.44.2: Ἀθηναῖοι δὲ ἐπὶ μὲν Πελασγῶν ἐχόντων τὴν νῦν Ἑλλάδα καλεομένην ἦσαν Πελασγοί; cf. 2.56.1.

their myth of autochthony upside down and transforming them into a barbaric people who only later became Greek.[99] But no polemical overtones characterize the text. The passage contains more muddle than malice. Indeed Herodotus' inconsistencies on the Pelasgians are sprinkled throughout his work. This particular segment is free of prejudice and program. Herodotus, in fact, does not dispute the Athenians' claim to continuous habitation of their land but confirms it: the Greek *ethnos* is repeatedly on the move; the Pelasgian stays where it is.[100] And, most telling, the historian finds the admixture of barbarian people, including Pelasgians, to be a source of strength.[101]

The idea of "Pelasgians" as the prehistoric incumbents of Hellas persisted. It can be traced at least as early as Hecataeus of Miletus in the late sixth century.[102] Herodotus endorsed it: Greece was once called Pelasgia.[103] Assorted variants turn up in other versions. Ephorus in the fourth century places them originally in Arcadia but has them spread widely and apply their name all over Greece and beyond.[104] Diodorus of Sicily quotes the Hellenistic writer Dionysius Skytobrachion, who names Pelasgians as the first to make use of "Phoenician letters" brought by Cadmus to the Hellenic world.[105] Strabo offers a number of traditions. One has the Pelasgians as a people occupying the whole of Greece, with special ties to the Aeolians of Thessaly. Another makes them just one of numerous foreign peoples who settled Greece in its earliest era. Yet another connects them initially with Argos, where their name became transformed as Argives, Danaoi, and eventually equivalent to all Greeks.[106]

None of this precluded Strabo from transmitting a very different story. He has Pelasgians as a particular group driven out of Boeotia to Athens, where they gave their name to a part of the city.[107] Pelasgians as an individual people rather than an overall term for prior inhabitants of Hellas can be

---

[99] So R. Thomas (2000), 120–122; (2001), 222–225; Mitchell (2007), 86–87. Georges (1994), 130–138, sees the text as betraying Herodotus' own Dorian ethnicity, expressing a position plainly offensive to Athenian sensitivities. Munson (2005), 7–9, regards the passage as polemic against Athenian hegemonic propaganda as expressed in Herod. 6.137–140.

[100] Herod. 1.56.2: τὸ μὲν οὐδαμῇ κω ἐξεχώρησε, τὸ δὲ πολυπλάνητον κάρτα.

[101] Herod. 1.58: τὸ δὲ Ἑλληνικὸν ... ἀπὸ σμικροῦ τεο τὴν ἀρχὴν ὁρμώμενον αὔξηται ἐς πλῆθος τῶν ἐθνέων, Πελασγῶν μάλιστα προσκεχωρηκότων αὐτῷ καὶ ἄλλων ἐθνέων βαρβάρων συχνῶν.

[102] Hecataeus *apud* Strabo 7.7.1: σχεδὸν δέ τι καὶ ἡ σύμπασα Ἑλλὰς κατοικία βαρβάρων ὑπῆρξε τὸ παλαιόν.

[103] Herod. 2.56.1. Cf. Thuc. 1.3.2, who has the Pelasgians as the dominant *ethnos* in Greece prior to the coming of Hellen.

[104] Ephorus *apud* Strabo 5.2.4.

[105] Diod. 3.67.1.

[106] Aeolians of Thessaly: Strabo 5.2.4; one among various barbarian settlers: Strabo 7.7.1; Danaoi and Argives: Strabo 8.6.9. A fragment of a lost Euripidean play had Danaus, after he had come to Argos, declare that Pelasgians would henceforth be called Danaoi; Strabo 5.2.4. Further references in Sakellariou (1977), 157–158.

[107] Strabo 9.2.3; cf. Dion. Hal. 1.28.4; Paus. 1.28.3.

found as early as the work of the fifth-century mythographer, historian, and ethnographer Hellanicus of Lesbos, who reports that they were driven out of Greece and settled in Italy, where they became known as Tyrrhenoi.[108] An association with the Tyrrhenoi is attested indeed by Thucydides, who identifies Pelasgians as Tyrrhenoi among the foreign peoples speaking mixed tongues now located in the peninsula of Acte who formerly lived in Lemnos and Athens.[109] And a Sophoclean fragment identifies the mythical Argive ancestor Inachus as king of the Tyrrhenian Pelasgians.[110] A particular connection with Arcadia, alluded to by Herodotus, reappears in Pausanias, derived from Arcadian informants who honored a "Pelasgus" as first inhabitant and ruler of the region, initially called Pelasgia, only later altered to Arcadia.[111]

Pelasgians flit in and out of our sources in bewildering fashion. They obviously served as a flexible and elastic nation with no fixed geographic station or ethnic identity. In the *Iliad*, Pelasgians appear on both sides of the Trojan War, located at one point in "Pelasgian Argos" (evidently in Thessaly), at another in Larissa (evidently in Asia). In the *Odyssey* they are among the inhabitants of Crete.[112] And Homer even labeled the great oracle of Zeus at Dodona in Epirus as "Pelasgian."[113] Hesiod echoed that line.[114] Other locations for Pelasgians also occur in the texts, depending on the agendas of the authors. Aeschylus, in his *Suppliant Women*, perhaps taking a cue from the *Iliad*, has the king of Argos as Pelasgus, ruler over extensive territory, his Argives identified as Pelasgians—but a thoroughly Hellenic folk.[115] The Argive mythographer Acusilaus, a contemporary of Hecataeus, enhanced still further his own city's association with this legendary past by making Argos and Pelasgus brothers, both sons of Zeus.[116]

But Pelasgians could not be pinned down to one city. In Herodotus' work alone, they come in a variety of guises that defy consistency or coherence.[117] In addition to seeing them as primordial dwellers in Hellas, he

---

[108] Hellanicus *apud* Dion. Hal. 1.28.3.
[109] Thuc. 4.109.4. Cf. Herod. 1.57.1, 4.145.2, 6.137.
[110] Soph. fr. 270 (Jebb/Pearson).
[111] Paus. 8.1.4–6, 8.4.1; cf. Herod. 1.146.1. Pausanias elsewhere finds Pelasgians also in Athens, Laconia, and Messenia; 1.28.3, 3.20.5, 4.36.1. On the identification of Pelasgians with individual peoples, see the texts collected and treated by Sourvinou-Inwood (2003), 113–117.
[112] Homer *Il.* 2.681, 2.840–841; *Od.* 19.177. Cf. Strabo 5.2.4; Diod. 5.80.1.
[113] Homer *Il.* 16.233–234. Cf. Herod. 2.52.1; Strabo 5.2.4.
[114] Strabo 7.7.10. That the oracle was founded by Pelasgians is affirmed by Ephorus; Strabo 7.7.10. For the Pelasgians in Homer, see Sakellariou (1977), 150–157; on Larissa, 133–136.
[115] Aesch. *Suppl.* 236–237, 250–259, 911–914. Cf. E. Hall (1989), 170–172.
[116] Acusilaus *FGH* 2 F25a; Apollodorus 2.1.1.
[117] Sourvinou-Inwood (2003), 121–131, 140–144, struggles to find design and purpose in Herodotus' multiple constructs of the Pelasgians. Cf. Pelling (2009), 480–481.

elsewhere identifies them as "Arcadian Pelasgians," or as inhabitants of Samothrace who subsequently moved to Athens at about the time that the Athenians were becoming Greek and taught them certain religious rites, or as occupants of Lemnos whence they repaired after being expelled by the Athenians only to take revenge by kidnapping Athenian women who were celebrating the festival of Artemis at Brauron.[118] Even the roster of Xerxes' allies who mustered for the invasion of Greece included Ionians whose ancestors had come from Achaea in the Peloponnese, where they had been known as Pelasgians, islanders once identified with Pelasgians, later with Ionians, and Aeolians also called Pelasgians of old.[119] These loose and overlapping strands cannot readily be woven together. Nor is there any point in attempting to do so. The term "Pelasgian" served a variety of purposes in divergent traditions concocted or conveyed in manifold forms.[120]

Were there real Pelasgians who originated in Arcadia, Epirus, or Thessaly and who became the basis for the expansive fictions and fabrications that transmuted them into mythical forebears of the Hellenic populace? Conjectures are possible, and reconstructions have been frequent.[121] But a decision on the historical kernel (if there be any) need not detain us. The fictions hold greater interest. The malleable and mercurial Pelasgians played multiple roles, either as ancestors of particular nations, as individual peoples extending into historical times, or, most significantly, as primordial precursors of the Greeks. Numerous places claimed some association with Pelasgian roots in the distant and mythical past. And the concept of "Pelasgian" came to represent an aboriginal folk who preceded and, in some sense, served as forerunners of the Greeks.

A key element demands stress here. Pelasgians are commonly conceived as "barbarians," that is, non-Greeks who spoke a non-Greek language.[122] Yet the designation nowhere carries a pejorative or negative connotation. The idea that Greeks, even Athenians, evolved from an indigenous or primeval people who were pre-Hellenic did not send shivers up the spines of those who listened to legends or heard the recounting of Herodotus' *Histories*. And Plato's parody of a funeral oration that contrasted Athenian pu-

---

[118] Arcadia: Herod. 1.146.1; Samothrace: Herod. 2.51; Lemnos: Herod. 4.145.2, 6.137–140; cf. 5.26. Cf. Sakellariou (1977), 182–188. Herodotus even knows of a Pelasgian town in the Troad; 7.42.

[119] Herod. 7.94–95.

[120] For various sites, testimony, and discussion, see Sakellariou (1977), 158–230; Sourvinou-Inwood (2003), 107–121. On their malleability, cf. J. Hall (2002), 33–35. For Munson (2005), 10–13, Herodotus reckoned Pelasgians as hybrids who alternately spoke Greek or a barbarian tongue.

[121] E.g., How and Wells (1912), I, 442–446; Lloyd (1994b), II, 232–234; Bernal (1987), 75–83.

[122] Hecataeus *FGH* 1 F119; Herod. 1.57–58, 2.51.2; Thuc. 4.109.4; Strabo 7.7.1. This is the predominant Pelasgian image in early Greek literature; Sourvinou-Inwood (2003), 107–115.

rity of lineage with other states' embrace of foreign founders only underscored the ubiquity—and comfort—of the latter.

Rome, Troy, and Arcadia

The most celebrated and familiar case of fictitious foreign kinships must surely be that of Troy and Rome. Readers of Vergil from antiquity to the present have the tale of Rome's linkage to the survivors of the Trojan War as a fixture in their consciousness. Roman roots, or at least a vital component thereof, lay in Asia Minor, as conveyed by the mainstream narrative of the city's mythic history. The fact, normally taken for granted, has telling significance. A prime source of the nation's greatness (in its own estimation) originated abroad.

The Romans themselves did not invent the tale. Nor is the Aeneas saga the only construct of Rome's origins. Greek writers took the initiative, seeking to impose a Hellenic genealogy on Rome. Various versions circulated long before Vergil placed his distinctive stamp on them. A swirl of stories associated Rome's ancestry with legends of the Trojan War and its aftermath. Hesiod already included Italy among the wanderings of Odysseus.[123] When Rome itself captured Greek notice, perhaps through Campania or Sicily, the tales proliferated. Some traditions traced links to Odysseus or his sons, to descendants of Herakles, to the Arcadian Evander, or to a fictive Trojan captive named Rhome who gave her name to the city. The diverse threads overlapped, entangled themselves, and formed no coherent picture. But by the fourth century BCE, Heracleides Ponticus could already refer to Rome as a Greek city *tout court*.[124]

Once Aeneas was added to the mix, the entanglements multiplied—and the cultural implications became still more meaningful. There is no need to traverse this well-traveled ground at any length.[125] In the canonical version Troy's celebrated hero Aeneas, a son of Aphrodite, escaped the fall of his city, migrated to the west where his wanderings brought him to Italy, and spawned a lineage whose members ultimately founded Rome itself. That version, however, was a long time in coming. A bewildering variety of inventive concoctions circulated in the Hellenistic world, many of them claiming Greek migrants as responsible for peopling Latium and even founding Rome. In diverse tales Achaean settlers gained the credit as often as, or more often than, Trojan refugees. Odysseus and his descendants

---

[123] [Hesiod] *Theog.* 1011–1016.
[124] Plut. *Cam.* 22.2.
[125] For a summary of the legends and much of the bibliography, see Gruen (1992), 8–21. Among more recent contributions, see Cornell (1995), 63–68; Moatti (1997), 258–266; Erskine (2001), 15–43.

played a prominent role, as wanderers par excellence. At least one strand of these bewildering traditions had Odysseus and Aeneas reach Italy together and collaborate in the founding of Rome.[126] The tales derive largely from Greek imagination. Their thrust, as is plain, was not to distance Hellas from the barbarian but to embrace, incorporate, and appropriate him. As a form of Hellenic cultural imperialism, this causes no surprise.[127] But there is more to it than that. The very overlap of Greek and Trojan genealogies shows that cultural amalgam rather than disjunction prevailed. And, most significant, the Roman engagement in adapting and refashioning these legends implies an active interchange and reciprocity, not a one-way street.

Rome had its own indigenous traditions, most notably that of the twins Romulus and Remus who were adjudged responsible for the founding of the city. Hellenic intellectuals managed to weave the web of their tales to encompass and appropriate those stories, rendering the twins, in diverse tales, as distant descendants of Aeneas.[128] The Roman reaction, however, holds special interest. The miscellany of tales registered a plethora of connections with Hellenic and Trojan forebears. But we have no sign of Roman resistance to foreign roots or insistence on native beginnings. The reverse holds. Historians and poets welcomed that association with the eastern Mediterranean, reshaped and perpetuated it.

The first Roman historian, in fact, wrote in Greek. Fabius Pictor composed his history near the end of the third century BCE. Only fragments survive, but some revealing ones. Pictor endorsed the tale of Aeneas as forefather of Rome, or at least a version of that tale that has Aeneas' son Ascanius found Alba Longa, the mother city of Rome.[129] Even more interesting, he conveyed stories of still earlier migrations from the Greek world: Herakles himself landed in Italy, and the Arcadian hero Evander, who planted a colony on the Palatine Hill, introduced the alphabet, an invention that the Greeks had actually borrowed from the Phoenicians.[130] The Roman historian, steeped in Hellenic lore, unequivocally embraced legends that postulated Greek ancestry for Rome, indeed acknowledged that cultural underpinnings went back to the Phoenicians. Far from shunning alien associations, he proudly proclaimed them.

When historians began to write in Latin, one might expect a sharper turn to homegrown legends. But the enmeshing of traditions had already resisted untangling by the second century BCE. Cato the Elder stands out as stereotypical standard-bearer for nativism. Numerous accounts have

[126] Dion. Hal. 1.72.2.
[127] Bickermann (1952), 65–81.
[128] On this, see, inter alia, Cornell (1975), 1–32; Gruen (1992) 8–21; Wiseman (1995); Erskine (2001), 15–43.
[129] Diod. Sic. 7.5.4–5; Dion. Hal. 1.74.1; Plut. *Rom.* 3.1–3.
[130] Pictor F1–2 (Beck and Walter).

him inveigh against Hellenic influence in Roman society. Among other things, Cato took pride in composing his history in Latin, breaking with the traditions of Greek historiography. Much of this was posturing rather than authentic.[131] The fact remains that Cato adapted and transmitted Hellenic myths on Trojan figures at the dawn of Roman history. A complex combination of legends gains expression in the surviving fragments of Cato's *Origines*. They include the narrative of Aeneas' arrival in Italy, contests between Trojans and Latins, a reconciliation marked by the wedding of Aeneas and Lavinia, daughter of the indigenous king Latinus, and the founding by Aeneas' son Ascanius of Alba Longa, which became the mother city of Rome.[132] Cato, like Fabius Pictor, traced Roman roots back further still into Hellenic mists. He accepted the notion that aborigines in Italy from whom the Romans descended were, in fact, Greek.[133] Nor did he stop there. Cato perpetuated a tradition in which Arcadians under Evander disseminated the Aeolic dialect among Italians, a tongue adopted by none other than Romulus himself.[134] In short, that most Roman of writers (at least professedly so) had no hesitation in associating his ancestors with peoples of the Hellenic east.

Poets complied as readily as historians. Both Naevius in the late third century and Ennius in the early second century subscribed to the traditions of Rome's foreign pedigree. They conveniently simplified the lineage by making Aeneas' daughter the mother of Romulus, sweeping aside the long generations that separated them in other traditions and ignoring the saga of Alba Longa and its intervening kings. Aeneas' ancestry would be close and direct, the Trojan connection a more immediate one.[135] The traditions took multiple forms, and variations in detail proliferated. But the idea that Rome's lineage could be traced to foreign forefathers had a firm footing long before Vergil underwrote the canonical version.[136]

One can sharpen the picture by focusing on a particular and noteworthy element in this multiplicity of constructs: the affiliation of Rome with Arcadia. The origin of that tradition eludes our grasp. But versions certainly circulated in the Hellenistic era as attested by Dionysius of Halicarnassus. They derived the Romans from aborigines many generations prior to the Trojan War itself. In Dionysius' account, some claimed the aborigines as an autochthonous people, but others as migrants from Arcadia in the central

---

[131] For this view of Cato, see Gruen (1992), 52–83; cf. Henrichs (1995), 244–250.
[132] Cato F1.4–15 (Beck and Walter).
[133] Dion. Hal. 1.11.1, 1.13.2. See below.
[134] Cato F1.19; cf. 2.26 (Beck and Walter).
[135] Serv. *Ad Aen.* 1.273.
[136] Erskine (2001), 15–43; *idem* (2005), 124–125, endeavors to minimize pre-Vergilian references to the Trojan myth and sees it as largely a product of the Augustan era, an extreme position. See the criticisms of Rose (2003), 479–481.

Peloponnese. Dionysius, who advocates the latter version, cites sources as early as the fifth century in support. Whether the identification is theirs or Dionysius' own interpretation, the association suited the fancy of Greek writers, like Dionysius, who insisted on the Hellenic character of Rome.[137] That notion goes back at least to the fourth century BCE when, as we have seen, Heracleides Ponticus declared Rome simply "a Greek city."[138]

Aborigines as Arcadians in the most remote past, however, were too fuzzy and had less than impressive pedigrees. The Arcadian roots therefore gained further elaboration when mythmakers summoned a more attractive figure, the hero Evander, son of Hermes by an Arcadian nymph. That accorded impressive credentials. The tale that took shape had Evander lead a number of Arcadians to Italy where they planted a colony on an inviting hill near the Tiber, which they named Pallantion after their own hometown—a site later adopted by the Romans as the Palatine.[139] Additional elaborations connected the tale to the adventures of Herakles. A variant brought the great hero, fresh from conquest in Spain, with a band of Greeks including Arcadians to a settlement on the Capitoline Hill in Rome. Herakles subsequently reinforced the Arcadian affiliation by marrying the daughter of Evander and generating offspring who would leave an Arcadian stamp on Rome.[140] The legend finds echo in no less a historian than Polybius. One might expect the rigorous Polybius, fiercely scornful of credulous predecessors, to reject or ignore such tall tales. But it is useful to recall that he himself was an Arcadian. Hence it causes little surprise that Polybius should find the legends of Evander at the origins of Rome so enticing. He gives the Arcadian connection still greater luster by having the colony named after young Pallas, son of Herakles and grandson of Evander.[141] Greek writers, even a scrupulous historian, took satisfaction in the purported Arcadian underpinnings of the western power.

But not Greeks alone. More strikingly, Roman intellectuals took up the tale with comparable relish. Fabius Pictor in the late third century not only recorded the arrival of Herakles in Italy but also credited Evander with bringing the alphabet, earlier taught to Greeks by Phoenicians, and thus giving double cultural authority to the Latin language.[142] Fabius, to be sure, wrote in Greek, being a noted philhellene and well conversant with Hellenic legends. But the idea had wider appeal among Romans. Cato the Elder

---

[137] Dion. Hal. 1.10–13, 1.89.1–2. J. Hall (2005), 265–271, considers this as little more than an invention on Dionysius' part.
[138] Plut. *Cam.* 22.2.
[139] Dion. Hal. 1.31, 1.89.2; Strabo 5.3.3.
[140] Dion. Hal. 1.34.1, 1.41–44.
[141] Polyb. *apud* Dion. Hal. 1.32.1.
[142] Pictor F2 (Beck and Walter).

himself, who did not parade his Hellenism, took a comfortably comparable line. He accepted the proposition that aborigines in Italy from whom the Romans descended, were, in fact Greek.[143] Further, as we have noted, Cato propagated, perhaps even expanded, a tradition in which the Arcadians under Evander introduced the Aeolic dialect to Italians, whence it extended even to Romulus.[144] The reciprocal playing with legends augmented the ties that intertwined Greeks with Romans.

The process became the more entangled when Aeneas and the Trojans entered the picture. Trojan origins for Rome had become increasingly orthodox doctrine, at least among Romans, by the late Hellenistic period. That need not, however, preclude the Hellenic ingredient. Inventive ingenuity would see to it. A tradition emerged that traced Aeneas' roots to Greece itself—indeed to Arcadia. The tale claimed Atlas as first king of Arcadia in the distant mists of antiquity, with a glorious lineage to follow that embraced Zeus himself and his Arcadian son Dardanus, the ancestor of Aeneas. On this story Dardanus led out an Arcadian expedition, after floods had devastated his native land, to settle in the Troad. Hence Aeneas, the quintessential Trojan, was in fact of Arcadian heritage.[145] Arcadian intellectuals welcomed and embellished the idea. Some had Aeneas settle in Arcadia after his departure from Troy and live out his days there. Others, however, combined the traditions and completed the circle: Aeneas, the Trojan of Arcadian heritage, moved from Troy to Arcadia, and then to Italy—where he bore a son named Romulus![146] The Troy-Arcadia-Rome line thus gained full expression. Greek writers obviously filled out the fictions. But eminent Romans happily embraced them. The great scholar and polymath Varro gave his weighty endorsement to the tale of Aeneas' Arcadian origins.[147] It had become an integral part of Roman tradition.

The interplay of legend making evades any simple formula. Greek authors converted the sagas of Troy to bring Romans within the matrix of Hellenic traditions. And Romans in turn spun those stories to their own taste, embracing a Trojan lineage that gave them a character distinct from that of Greeks but solidly within the Greek construct. This was no linear

---

[143] Dion. Hal. 1.11.1, 1.13.2.

[144] Cato F1.19 (Beck and Walter): ὥς φασιν ὅ τε Κάτων . . . Εὐάνδρου καὶ τῶν ἄλλων Ἀρκάδων εἰς Ἰταλίαν ἐλθόντων ποτὲ καὶ τὴν Αἰολίδα τοῖς βαρβάροις ἐνσπειράντων φωνήν; cf. F2.26 (Beck and Walter).

[145] Dion. Hal. 1.60–62.

[146] Dion. Hal. 1.49.1–2; Strabo 13.1.53; Erskine (2001), 119–121.

[147] Serv. *Ad Aen.* 3.167, 7.207. No need here to pursue the legend as reframed in different ways by Vergil and Ovid. See on this the valuable remarks of Fabre-Serris (2008), 13–30, who, however, unnecessarily conjectures that the emergence of the Evander tale was designed to compensate for the negative association of Troy with eastern luxury.

development but an intricate overlapping in which Romans defined themselves as a constituent element in a broader cultural network.

The sense of genealogical connectedness permeates the fictive constructs. And they go beyond Rome itself. Cato's great historical work, the *Origines*, encompassed other cities and peoples of Italy. On this front too he transmitted tales that assigned foreign founders to various parts of the peninsula. A particularly notable one deserves mention. Cato, we are told, reported that the robust Sabines of central Italy derived from a Spartan founder named, unsurprisingly, Sabus. The etymological play may be transparent fiction. But the underlying message had significance for Roman self-perception. The Romans, according to Cato, developed their hardy traits from imitation of the Sabines, and the latter in turn had derived that admirable toughness from the toughest of tough peoples, the Spartans. Cato in short traced the very genesis of Roman ruggedness to the Lacedaemonians, that epitome of Hellenic hardiness. Nor was this a Catonian idiosyncracy. A later second-century historian, Cn. Gellius, took the same line. The notion held respectability among Roman intellectuals.[148] A separate tradition, drawn from local Sabine sources, had Spartan colonists depart from the homeland at the time of Lycurgus; some settled among the Sabines and imparted to them their warlike, frugal, and uncompromising habits.[149] The idea of Sabines owing their origins to Spartans recurs among subsequent writers.[150] Sabines came to embody the austerity and moral virtue that Romans held dear.[151] That this could be credited to Hellenic heritage is noteworthy indeed.

And not to Hellenic heritage alone. An intriguing legend, transmitted by Hyginus, the learned freedman of Augustus, appointed by him to head the Palatine library, makes Sabus a Persian! But the Spartan connection,

---

[148] Cato F2.22 (Beck and Walter): *Cato autem et Gellius a Sabo Lacedaemonio trahere eos originem referunt. Porro Lacedaemonios durissimos fuisse omnis lectio docet* = Serv. Auct. *Ad Aen.* 8.638. Dion. Hal. 2.49.2 reports Cato as saying that Sabines took their name from Sabinus, son of a local deity, thus leading some to deny the evidence of Servius that Cato gave Sabus a Spartan origin; see Poucet (1963), 157–169; Letta (1985), 29–34. Musti (1988), 253–257, attempts to reconcile the versions. Cato's authority is accepted by Dench (1995), 86–87, and Farney (2007), 101. In any case, Gellius' adoption of the tale is unquestioned, and its circulation in second-century Rome seems plain. Various Roman aristocratic families also traced their lineage through the Sabines to the Spartans; see Farney (2007), 102–104.

[149] Dion. Hal. 2.49.4–5.

[150] Ovid *Fasti* 1.260; Plut. *Rom.* 16.1; *Numa* 1.3; Justin 20.1.14–15.

[151] Cato F2.22: *Sabinorum etiam mores populum Romanum secutum idem Cato dicit; merito ergo 'severis', qui et a duris parentibus orti sunt et quorum disciplinam victores Romani in multis secuti sunt.* This image of the Sabines, to be sure, was not universal among Roman writers; see the discussions of Dench (1995), 87–94, and Farney (2007), 105–111, both of whom attribute it to Cato himself.

obviously firmly entrenched by that time, could not be evaded. So Hyginus has Sabus pass through Sparta on the way to Italy, evidently taking Spartans with him, who then settled the territory that became Sabine.[152] The engaging twists and turns of these tales, however remote from reality, reaffirm Roman readiness to attribute Spartan qualities to the rugged Sabines—and ultimately to themselves.

Cato found additional foreign connections among Italian communities. The *Origines* incorporated a number of such traditions that Cato showed no discomfort in repeating. So, Argos was the mother city of Falerii in southern Etruria; Greek-speaking peoples founded Pisa; the community of Politorium, just south of Rome, took its name from Polites, son of the Trojan king Priam; a town called Thebes existed among the Lucanians; and Tibur (Tivoli) was planted by an Arcadian who headed the fleet of Evander.[153] An impressive array of associations with Hellenic legends. The *Origines*, unfortunately, exists only in fragments. Just how Cato or his sources fleshed out these stories cannot be ascertained. But the fact that Cato the Censor, that self-professed champion of native chauvinism, embraced legends linking Italian cities to forebears from abroad opens an important window on the Roman mentality.

That mentality merits one final illustration. The emperor Claudius looked back on the early history of the city and observed that Roman kings came from elsewhere than Rome. Tarquinius Priscus in fact, so Claudius declared in a public inscription, was born of an Etruscan mother and a Corinthian father.[154] Greek blood therefore flowed in the veins of Roman monarchs. The emperor proudly pronounced that lineage. The fashioning of a national image did not require disassociation or distance from others.

The idea of autochthony or indigenous origins never made much headway in Rome. Legends and fables, bewildering in their variety though they be, consistently portrayed the nation as deriving from the cultures of the east. The Trojan lineage gained primacy in the tradition, but Roman writers found it perfectly compatible with Hellenic connections and even paid homage to more distant Phoenician contributions. Roman identity was from the start deeply entangled with others. Romans represented themselves without embarrassment as a composite people who belonged intimately to the broader Mediterranean world.

---

[152] Serv. *Ad Aen.* 8.638. A variant on this in Sil. Ital. 8.414–415, who connects the Sabine city of Caseria with the Bactrians. The discussion of Poucet (1963), 203–213, is illuminating but contains excessive speculation.

[153] Cato F2.15, 2.24, 2.26, 3.2 (Beck and Walter). See also the list of Italian cities with legendary Greek founders collected in Justin 20.4–16.

[154] *ILS* 212.

Israel's Fictive Founders

The Israelites were not an autochthonous people even by their own lights. Abraham's family, after all, came from Ur of the Chaldees, and then settled in Haran in Mesopotamia before moving to the land of Canaan.[155] The very origins of the nation, therefore, derived from external migration. Far from reckoning this an embarrassment, association with Chaldeans or Babylonians remained a source of pride. Philo does not hesitate to call Moses a Chaldean by race, though born and raised in Egypt. And he refers to the language of the Bible itself as "Chaldean."[156] Josephus still gave voice to this affiliation at the end of the first century CE. He asserted unabashedly that the Chaldeans were the progenitors of the Jewish people and possessed a blood relationship with them.[157] In a different version circulating in the Hellenistic period Abraham ruled in Damascus, having come from the Chaldeans, thus giving rise to the idea that Jews themselves had their origins in Damascus.[158] The idea very likely derived from Jewish sources. Pagans had no reason to make it up.[159]

Other tales of Jewish origins made the rounds. Tacitus gathered no fewer than six of them—without, alas, naming his sources or indicating how far back they go. Most rest on flimsy conjecture or fabricated fiction. Nor can one be confident about which of them might have been welcomed or propagated by Jews themselves. It is noteworthy, however, that all involve connecting the Jews from their beginnings with other peoples or places.

One speculation had it that the nation began in Crete and then moved to the most distant parts of Libya at the time when Saturn had been deposed by Jupiter.[160] This was sheer conjecture, as Tacitus himself notes: an inference from the superficial similarity of the term *Iudaei* and the *Idaei* who dwelled on Mount Ida in Crete. Jews might not have drawn that inference. But they could well have bought into it. And they would certainly find it gratifying to be set into the most remote antiquity of Greek mythology.[161] Even better was the report that identified Jews with the Solymoi, an illustrious people who fought bravely in the Trojan War and were celebrated by Homer. This connection too had an etymological basis: the ostensible similarity of the name Hierosolyma, the city of the Solymoi, to

---

[155] Gen. 11.27–12.1.

[156] Philo *Mos.* 2.31, 2.40; *Legat.* 4.

[157] Jos. *CAp.* 1.71.

[158] The claim that Abraham ruled in Damascus comes from Nicolas of Damascus; Jos. *Ant.* 1.159–160. For Jews as originally Damascenes, see Pompeius Trogus in Just. 36.2.1.

[159] Cf. Gager (1972), 52; Feldman (2000), 59–60.

[160] Tac. *Hist.* 5.2.1.

[161] Cf. the useful discussion of Feldman (1991), 339–346. Bloch (2002), 84–86, oddly sees this as an account hostile to Jews.

Jerusalem.[162] Here again Jews are unlikely to have invented this link themselves, but they would not have been averse to spreading it.[163]

Other hypotheses about Jewish beginnings transmitted by Tacitus have them as Ethiopians, Assyrians, or Egyptians.[164] One tale has Jews as of Ethiopian stock driven from the land out of fear and hatred in the reign of the legendary king Cepheus (elsewhere known as father-in-law of the hero Perseus). The narrative is hardly favorable to Jews. But it is not irrelevant that they are set in the hallowed era of Greek mythology and allotted the ethnicity of a folk highly regarded in the classical tradition.[165] The version that labels Jews as Assyrians has them migrate in search of arable land, take control of part of Egypt, and eventually plant their own cities in the regions of the Hebrews bordering on Syria. That variant may owe something to biblical traditions themselves. And the notice that Jews actually seized control of part of Egypt may well draw on a Jewish embellishment, giving them greater authority in that ancient land than anything to be found in the books of Genesis or Exodus. The report that Jews came initially from Egypt had the assent of most authors, according to Tacitus, and it involved the tangled tale of expulsion in the time of a plague, a saga that had already gone through many versions before it reached the Roman historian.[166]

The diverse traditions defy efforts to sort them out. They rest on surmise, hasty deduction, or simplistic fitting together of disparate testimony. But they have in common a consistent derivation of Jews from other peoples or amalgamation with them. The stories, whatever their origins, presuppose that the nation is to be understood in terms of familiar entities in the Greek or Near Eastern worlds, that it does not exist in a vacuum, and that it constitutes no unique folk. Jews could thus fit into the matrix of Greek mythology, the legends of migrations, and the interconnections of Mediterranean peoples. These cannot simply be *interpretationes Graecae*. They must reflect in no small degree Jewish self-representation.

---

[162] Tac. *Hist.* 5.2.3. Cf. Homer *Il.* 6.184; *Od.* 5.283. The association of Jews with Solymoi who fought in Persian ranks in Xerxes' invasion of Greece goes back to the fifth-century poet Choerilus of Samos, according to Josephus, *CAp.* 1.172–175. But that is Josephus' own inference, not necessarily Choerilus', as he himself acknowledges. Cf. also Jos. *CAp.* 1.248; *Ant.* 7.67.

[163] I. Lévy (1946), 334–339, sees the tale's origin in Jewish exegesis. Feldman (1993), 520, n. 55, is properly skeptical, but his reason, that Jews would not have altered the biblical account, is hardly adequate. Jewish postbiblical writers did so with regularity.

[164] Tac. *Hist.* 5.2.1–5.3.1.

[165] See above, pp. 198–201.

[166] See the discussions of Lévy (1946), 331–340; Feldman (1991), 331–360; *idem* (1993), 184–196; Bloch (2002), 84–90. Heinen (1992), 128–140, implausibly sees all this as owed to Egyptian sources hostile to the Jews. For Tacitus on the Jews, see above, pp. 190–192. For the vicissitudes of the Exodus story in pagan literature, cf. the interpretation of Gruen (1998), 41–72.

252 CONNECTIONS WITH THE "OTHER"

The legends explored here provide a sample rather than a survey. But the sample is neither random nor peripheral. It includes some of the central figures and narratives with which Greeks, Romans, and Jews fashioned the inception of their history. Foreign founders play critical roles: Pelops, Cadmus, Danaus, Aeneas, Abraham. And the yarns spun about them repeatedly enmesh the origins of communities and people with migrations from abroad: Egyptians, Phoenicians, Pelasgians, Trojans, Assyrians, and others, a nod to the intermingling of cultures everywhere in the Mediterranean.

Chapter 10

FICTITIOUS KINSHIPS: GREEKS AND OTHERS

The ancient Mediterranean was a multicultural world. A remarkable number of peoples, nations, tribes, groups, and cities clustered about that pond. The ebb and flow of military, commercial, and cultural contact blurred boundaries, brought linguistic fluidity, and engendered ethnic complexity. In that polyglot and entangled universe a sense of distinctiveness by groups and peoples was an ongoing process, a series of constructs that shifted and modulated with time and circumstances, and expressed itself in a bewildering variety of ways. The constructs did not always (or usually) take the form of separate and singular entities. Cross-cultural connectiveness played a conspicuous role, modifying, complicating, and augmenting discrete group identities.

We pursue here a particularly promising avenue of investigation: the phenomenon of kinship relations among peoples—whether embellished, imagined, or simply invented. To determine whether such relations might represent some distant memory of or bear resemblance to historical reality is not the purpose.[1] The phenomenon itself illuminates a powerful ancient tendency: to stress affiliation rather than disjunction. A number of telling instances merit treatment.

Perseus as Multiculturalist

The legend of Perseus holds special interest. The vicissitudes and varieties of that myth defy ready reduction. They follow no straight path but meander messily around the Mediterranean and beyond. Neither the origins nor the direction of divergent versions can be satisfactorily sorted out. But the diversity itself carries significance. The hero's adventures could be exploited

[1] Cf. the controversy, once raging and now simmered down, over Martin Bernal's *Black Athena* (1987, 1991). A battery of responses is assembled by Lefkowitz and Rogers (1996). Our focus is on the implications of the constructs rather than their relation to reality. Nor do we deal here with purported kinships as a mode of ancient diplomacy, a subject already productively investigated by Curty (1995) and Jones (1999).

in different ways by different peoples, transformed and reshaped to suit multiple interests. The process, though resistant to precise reconstruction, illustrates the tangled manner in which societies could blur distinctions and link themselves to defining figures that arose from dissimilar traditions. The figure of Perseus served over time to stimulate a complex of cross-cultural representations.

Perseus was Hellenic in conception and character. The central narrative appears in fullest form in the indispensable *Bibliotheca* of Apollodorus, who, at some unknown date but probably in the high Roman Empire, compiled a vast array of stories from Greek mythological and legendary lore. The high points of the Perseus legend can be briefly summarized.[2]

Acrisius, ruler of Argos, sought oracular prediction on whether he would have male issue. The oracle responded by telling him that his daughter Danae would give birth to a male child but that this child would kill his grandfather. Danae was indeed impregnated not by a mortal but by Zeus in the form of a golden shower, and produced a child, Perseus. Acrisius, fearful of the oracle's foreboding, had both Danae and Perseus locked up in a chest and cast into the sea. The chest, however, washed up on the island of Seriphos, where its occupants were rescued and Perseus raised by the kindly Dictys. The king of Seriphos, Polydectes, the not so kindly brother of Dictys, lusted after Danae but had to contend with the now-grown Perseus. Polydectes expected to thwart Perseus by demanding that he bring the Gorgon's head as price for preserving his mother's purity. The hero received the assistance of Hermes and Athena, obtaining winged sandals, a pouch, and the cap of Hades, which rendered him invisible. These accoutrements, together with divine aid, allowed him to cut off the head of Medusa, the one mortal among the deadly Gorgons, drop it into his pouch, and head off (surprisingly) to Ethiopia.

A new and unrelated adventure awaited him there. The ruler of that land, Cepheus, had the misfortune of having married the vain and talkative Cassiopeia, who boasted of exceeding the Nereids in beauty. That stirred the wrath of Poseidon, who sent a flood and a sea monster to devastate the land. Cepheus had just one way of averting disaster, according to the prophecy of the god Ammon: to chain his daughter Andromeda to a rock and leave her as prey to the leviathan. And so he did. Perseus, however, arrived in the nick of time, fell in love with Andromeda, and promised Cepheus to slay the monster if he could have the hand of the king's daughter in marriage. The bargain was struck, Perseus killed the savage beast, released the damsel, and used the Gorgon's head to turn into stone Andromeda's

---

[2] On the myth in general, see now Ogden (2008), passim. Its fundamentally Hellenic character does not, of course, rule out Near Eastern precedents. For some suggestions along those lines, see Morenz (1962), 307–309.

conspiratorial former fiancé. Only then did he head back for Argos—with yet another detour on the way. The hero stopped in Seriphos, turned Polydectes and his entourage into stone by showing Medusa's head, and made his foster father Dictys king of the realm. Finally, Perseus returned to Argos, with both mother and bride in tow. His grandfather Acrisius fled at the news and hoped to remain safe and secret at Larissa. The oracle, however, would not be cheated. Perseus turned up at Larissa to compete in athletic games there. His perfectly innocent toss of the discus struck Acrisius and killed him instantly. Fulfillment of the oracle brought Perseus no pleasure or sense of triumph. He buried his grandfather and declined to accept the heritage of rule over Argos—but he was happy enough to trade that legacy for the realm of Tiryns.[3]

Such is the main line of the tale. It made the rounds early, in one form or another, in Greek literature. Apollodorus' narrative rests largely on the account in Pherecydes, the Athenian mythographer of the mid–fifth century BCE, when the legend was already in full flower.[4] But the story, or parts of it, was much older. Homer attests to the union of Zeus and Danae from which sprang Perseus (though he omits the detail of a golden shower).[5] Hesiod knows the tale of Perseus' decapitation of the Gorgon Medusa.[6] Images of Perseus and the Gorgon go back to the seventh century.[7] They become increasingly popular in various visual forms from that time on. Representations of Andromeda's rescue by Perseus begin to appear in the sixth century and become regular portrayals on ceramic ware and other objects thereafter.[8] The divine and heroic genealogy of Perseus gains mention in the Pseudo-Hesiodic *Catalogue of Women*, probably of the sixth century.[9] Pindar, at the beginning of the fifth century, could take for granted that his readers would be familiar with the myth. He made reference to Perseus' birth via the golden shower, to the slaying of Medusa, and to the hero's turning his foes on Seriphos into stone.[10] Athenian tragic dramatists adapted the tale in various versions in the fifth century, none of which, unfortunately, is extant. We know that Aeschylus produced a trilogy on the theme, in addition to a satyr play focusing on the rescue of Perseus and Danae on Seriphos by Dictys, a scene that also inspired vase painters. Sophocles

---

[3] The above is a paraphrase of Apollodorus *Bib.* 2.4.1–4.
[4] Pherecydes *FGH* 3 fr. 26; Fowler (2000), fr. 10–12.
[5] Homer *Il.* 14.319–320.
[6] Hesiod *Theog.* 274–281. It is referred to also in the pseudo-Hesiodic *Shield of Heracles*, 216–237.
[7] Dahlinger (1988), 290; Roccos (1994), #117. Cf. Schauenburg (1960), 19–20.
[8] Schauenburg (1981), #1–30; Roccos (1994), #175–216; Schauenburg (1960), 55–77, with plates 23–29. See the valuable surveys of visual representations of the myth generally by Schauenburg (1960), passim, and Phillips (1968), 1–23, with plates 1–20.
[9] Ps. Hesiod *Cat.* fr. 129 and 135.
[10] Pindar *Pyth.* 10.44–48; 12.6–16.

followed with three plays, titled *Acrisius*, *Danae*, and *Larissaeans*, obviously drawn from elements of the myth. And Euripides composed a *Danae* and an *Andromeda* of his own. Titles and a few fragments show that comic dramatists also found this story to provide rich material for their own genre. The fantasy of Zeus transformed into gold rain dripping through a roof for purposes of sex had evidently showed up in several tragedies, enough to be alluded to as a tragic motif in Menander's comedy *Samia*.[11] And images on Athenian pottery of diverse scenes from the legend proliferate.[12]

Perseus is a quintessentially Hellenic hero. Yet the myth proved susceptible to massaging that reached across the Mediterranean and intimated bonds with peoples of the Near East. Testimony surfaces already in 472 BCE in a pregnant passage of Aeschylus' *Persae*. The chorus of Persian elders, in recounting the vast array of their nation's forces, added that this grand troop is headed by a king who is himself an equal of the gods—for he is the scion of a race of gold.[13] The allusion must be to the tale of Perseus born to Danae through Zeus' metamorphosis into an impregnating golden shower. The fact that this myth could be referred to by Aeschylus without explanation or elaboration has striking significance. It implies that a notable feature of the legend had already gained assent in early fifth-century Athens, namely that the rulers of Persia were descendants of the Greek hero Perseus.

The fable appears in fuller form in Herodotus' *History*. The Persians had more than one designation in antiquity, so reports the Greek historian. But the one that stuck derived from the Perseus myth. The hero, son of Zeus and Danae, had taken to wife Andromeda, daughter of Cepheus, who gave birth to a son named Perses. Since Cepheus lacked male heirs, the considerate Perseus left his own son behind in the land of his father-in-law. And from him the Persians took their appellation.[14] Herodotus' tale presupposes that Cepheus ruled in Persia. The historian Hellanicus of Lesbos, a contemporary of Herodotus, has a variant version: the Chaldeans, previously called Cephenians, from king Cepheus, set out from Babylon and occupied the land that would be called Persia from Cepheus' grandson Perses.[15] That variant, however, preserves the kernel, namely that the Persian realm took its origin from the Hellenic hero.[16]

The origin of the association between Perseus and Persia cannot be pinned down. That it had become an accepted tradition in Athens by the

---

[11] Menander *Sam.* 589–591. A convenient collection of references to the use of the theme in Athenian drama may be found in Ogden (2008), 13–17, 40–41, 69–70.

[12] See above, n. 7; also Ogden (2008), 35–37, 43–47, 77–79.

[13] Aesch. *Pers.* 79–80: χρυσογόνου γενεᾶς ἰσόθεος φώς.

[14] Herod. 7.61.

[15] Hellanicus *FGH* 4 fr. 59–60.

[16] So also Deinias *FGH* 306 fr. 7 (third century BCE); Lycophron *Alex.* 1413–1414.

early fifth century, however, carries heavy weight. It signifies the imposition of a Hellenic genealogy even on the most notorious enemy of Hellas. Greeks took the initiative in acknowledging a fundamental kinship relation between the peoples. But it need not have been a strictly one-sided proposition. Herodotus' account of the Persian War includes a memorable narrative that bears emphasis. Prior to marching his army upon Greece, the Achaemenid king Xerxes sent an envoy to Argos to seek the neutrality of that city in the coming conflict. Xerxes' plea rested on that legendary connection embraced by Hellas. He pointed out that Perses, ancestor and namesake of the Persians, was son not only of Andromeda, the daughter of Cepheus, but of Perseus, son of Danae, and hence from the nation of the Argives. A blood bond therefore linked the Achaemenid house to Argos and should preclude hostilities between them. The Argives accepted the proposition and (for their own reasons) remained neutral in the war. The kinship itself was unquestioned.[17] Herodotus reports that he heard this account in Greece, which is perfectly plausible. But it does not preclude the possibility that the Persians found the supposed connection convenient and turned it helpfully to their own ends.[18] The matter was mutually advantageous. Both Argives and Persians were perfectly comfortable with it. The idea that the nations had a common ancestor transcends conflict and warfare, and challenges the concept of "Otherness."

Perseus as Persian progenitor, however, is only part of the intercultural story. The hero had Egyptian roots. The royal house of Argos possessed strong migratory bonds with Egypt. The myth of Io lurks behind it, the Argive princess in the hoary mists of antiquity who caught Zeus' eye and became yet another of the insatiable god's sexual conquests. This time, however, Hera discovered the deed, and Io was victimized once more, transformed by Zeus (or alternatively by Hera) into a white cow doomed to wander across half the world at the prodding of a gadfly inflicted by the vengeful Hera. The princess leaves Argos forever and eventually ends in Egypt, where Zeus restored her to her original form and fathered a new line by her. The mournful myth appears, with slight variations, primarily in Aeschylus, Apollodorus, and Ovid.[19] Herodotus supplies a different version, indeed two of them, leaving the gods out of account and centering on mortals. At the beginning of his *History*, he records (with some mischief) the competing accounts of where blame lies for the origins of the Trojan War. A Persian *logos* claimed that Phoenicians started it all by kidnapping Io from Argos and depositing her in Egypt. The Phoenicians, for their part,

---

[17] Herod. 7.150.
[18] See the cogent arguments of Georges (1994), 66–71.
[19] Aesch., *Prom. Bound* 561–886; Ovid *Met.* 583–750; Apollodorus *Bib.* 2.1.3.

denied responsibility, retailing the story that Io got herself pregnant by a ship captain (no Zeus involved) and, out of embarrassment, boarded a Phoenician vessel voluntarily (not kidnapped) and landed in Egypt of her own accord.[20] Either way, the legend places her firmly in Egypt, where she would wed the ruler of the land, in which her descendants would dwell and in which she would be identified with Isis herself.[21]

Egypt now became the homeland. The Argive connection, however, loomed ever in the background and would be resumed four legendary generations later. In the famous tale, descendants of Io, the twins Danaus and Aegyptus, entered into a deadly quarrel over ascendancy in the kingdom, a quarrel aggravated by the fifty sons of Aegyptus who sought to wed the fifty daughters of Danaus. The would-be brides were not enamored of their cousins, fled the scene together with their father, and headed for the ancestral soil of Argos. No need to follow the story, which Apollodorus recounts in specifics and which forms the centerpiece of Aeschylus' *Suppliants*.[22] What matters is that the Danaids, Egyptians by birth and appearance, revived their Argive lineage and Danaus recovered the authority of his ancestors over the Hellenic city. The legend enmeshed Egypt and Argos. And four generations later the line of Danaus produced the celebrated damsel Danae, whose impregnation by the golden emission of Zeus resulted in the birth of Perseus.[23]

Matters would soon come full circle when the hero headed for the continent of Africa. It was in Libya that he encountered the Gorgons and slew Medusa.[24] And from there that he moved to Ethiopia. By contrast with the tale preserved by Herodotus, the more common version of Perseus' adventures with Cepheus and his daughter in distress has Cepheus not as ruling in Persia but as king of Ethiopia. Euripides' play *Andromeda* was set in Ethiopia, indicating that that location was already fixed by the late fifth century, and it appears with regularity thereafter both in literary texts and in the visual representations of Andromeda with black retainers.[25] The third-century BCE historian Deinias, perhaps grappling with the inconsistencies, went to some length to bring the disparate traditions together. He has the hero start from Argos of course (Deinias was an Argive), then go to Ethiopia, where he liberated the daughter of Cepheus, and then to Persia,

[20] Herod. 1.1–2, 1.5.
[21] Apollodorus *Bib*. 2.1.3; Ovid *Met*. 1.747; cf. Herod. 2.41.
[22] Aesch. *Suppl*. passim; *Prom. Bound* 853–869; Apollodorus *Bib*. 2.1.4–5. See the discussion of the *Suppliants* in Vasunia (2001), 40–58; and see above, pp. 230–232.
[23] Apollodorus *Bib*. 2.2.1–2.
[24] Herod. 2.91; Paus. 3.17.3.
[25] Euripides fr. 145, 147; see Kannicht (2004), with testimonia on p. 234. For later references, see, e.g., Apollodorus *Bib*. 2.4.3; Strabo 1.2.35; Ovid *Met*. 4.669; Pliny *NH* 6.182; Philostratus *Imagines* 1.29; and the images in Schauenberg (1981), #2–6.

where the land took its name from Perses.[26] A satisfying combination. Whence the connection with Ethiopia arose remains beyond our grasp. It did, however, provide a convenient link that could be exploited and expanded on in Egypt.

Herodotus provides a telling account. The historian's visit to Egypt brought him, among other places, to the site of Chemmis in the Thebaid. There he found nothing less than a square temple to Perseus in a sacred enclosure, including a shrine that held a cult image of the hero. The inhabitants of Chemmis informed Herodotus that they often catch sight of Perseus in the area and even within the temple, and occasionally find his giant sandal, a sign of prosperity for all Egypt. They honor the hero in Greek fashion, with games, contests, and prizes. When Herodotus inquired further of why the Chemmitans alone among Egyptians celebrate games in Greek style, he received an intriguing response. His informants pointed out that Perseus' lineage can be traced to Chemmis for it was the hometown of Danaus before he set out for Argos and the hometown of Lynceus, who became Danaus' son-in-law and direct ancestor of Perseus. They added also that Perseus, after taking the Gorgon's head in Libya, came to Egypt and made a special visit to Chemmis, where he recognized all his kinfolk, confirming what he had heard about the city from his mother. The gymnasium-style games were then instituted on his instructions.[27]

The narrative carries real significance. The inhabitants of Chemmis very likely identified Perseus with an Egyptian divinity, probably Horus.[28] But the institution of Greek games to honor the god is especially noteworthy. This is no mere *interpretatio Graeca*. The Chemmitans took the initiative here, adapting Hellenic modes of paying tribute to a Greek hero whom they claimed as their own by virtue of his Egyptian lineage. Nor were they alone. Herodotus makes mention of the "Watchtower of Perseus," which he locates in the Delta, a site placed elsewhere by Strabo but in any case an Egyptian monument referring to the Hellenic hero.[29] The legend of Perseus doubtless reached Egypt through Greeks.[30] But the fact that the Egyptians fastened on it is especially revealing. They reinterpreted the legend as emblematic of kinship ties between the peoples, they assimilated the Greek hero to an Egyptian deity, they embraced the Hellenic mode of paying homage, and they appropriated Greek lore to create a combined and overlapping construct.

[26] Deinias *FGH* 306 fr. 7.
[27] Herod. 2.91.
[28] So Lloyd (1969), 84; (1994b), 367–369; Stephens (2003), 25–26, 133.
[29] Herod. 2.91; Strabo 17.1.18. It appears also in Euripides *Helen* 769.
[30] Lloyd (1969) 85–86, proposes that it was the product of a mixed Greek/Egyptian enclave in Chemmis, an unnecessary hypothesis.

Perseus' cultural interconnections did not stop there. We catch hints of additional variations that extended and complicated the nexus. A Mesopotamian affiliation surfaces in our texts, mingled in diverse ways with other nations. Herodotus, as we have seen, reported the Argive/Persian kinship that made Perseus forerunner of the Persians, a claim embraced (or perhaps initiated) by Persians. But the Persians (or some of them) put their own spin on it. They questioned Perseus' Greek credentials, claiming that he was an Assyrian by origin, only subsequently becoming a Greek. And they pressed the legendary lineage to its logical conclusion: Acrisius, king of Argos and grandfather of Perseus, actually descended from Egyptians, a genealogy for which the Persians (rightly) cited the Greeks themselves. They then drew the interesting, if somewhat anomalous, conclusion that the line of Acrisius was Egyptian while that of Perseus was Assyrian, thereby denying the kinship between the ancestors of the two men.[31] But the Persians did not deny their own connection to Perseus. Such a concoction plainly has something in common with the recital of Hellanicus that Cepheus came from Chaldea and his countrymen invaded and occupied the land that took its name from Perses, son of Perseus and Andromeda.[32] Just how these entangled variations worked themselves out we cannot say. But it appears that Persian fictions, drawing on but reshaping Hellenic legend, connected their own history in diverse ways with Assyrians, Greeks, and even Egyptians, a genuinely multicultural mix.

A still more remarkable variant, perhaps the most remarkable, demands notice. It transferred Perseus' legendary feat to none other than the land of the Jews. At some stage Cepheus' realm, the site of Perseus' heroic rescue of Andromeda, underwent startling transformation. The whole narrative received a Levantine setting. Cepheus now took on a Phoenician identity. The binding of Andromeda and her exposure to the sea monster in fact gained a precise location: the harbor city of Jaffa or Joppa. Perseus' liberation of the princess took place in the city associated with Phoenicia but eventually to become a chief port of the Jews. Jewish appropriation of the classical myth turns out to be perhaps the most fascinating element of the hero's vicissitudes.[33]

The first extant reference to this version appears in a Greek geographical work attributed to Scylax but actually composed in the mid–fourth century BCE.[34] The geographer, in summarizing the towns along the Palestinian coast, includes "the city of Joppa where they say that Andromeda was

---

[31] Herod. 6.54.

[32] Hellanicus 4 fr. 59–60.

[33] The best treatment of the Joppa story is Harvey (1994), 3–12. See also Schürer (1979), 33–34; Stern (1980), 193–194; Flusser (1987), 1080–1083; Ogden (2008), 84, 116–118.

[34] Ps. Scylax, 104 = Müller *GGM* 1.79 = Stern (1984), #558: For the date, see Gutschmidt (1854), 141–146; Fabre (1965), 353–366.

exposed to the monster."[35] Phoenician mythographers may have intervened here to put their own spin on the Perseus legend and locate the center of the drama within their cultural (if not political) sphere. After Joppa came under Jewish control in the era of Hasmonean expansion in the second century BCE, however, the tale was evidently promoted and propagated by Jews who found it attractive to buy into that hallowed Hellenic tradition.[36]

Strabo attests to the familiarity of this version in his own day in the late first century BCE. For some, he says, Joppa had replaced the older setting of Ethiopia for the dramatic rescue of Andromeda. Strabo, somewhat cynically (though doubtless accurately), regards this transfer as a concoction, produced not out of geographical ignorance but desire for a good story.[37] The concocters at least, so Strabo notes, had a good idea, for Joppa has a high elevation, a perfect place for Andromeda to be set up on a rock and spied by the leviathan.[38]

The story had by that time made the rounds sufficiently so as even to prompt rationalization. A younger contemporary of Strabo, Conon, who composed diverse and diverting fictions, extant now only in summaries by the Byzantine scholar Photius, produced one on the subject of Perseus and Andromeda. But he offered an ingenious rendition that stripped it of mythological flavor. In Conon's invention, the events do indeed take place in Joppa (later named Phoenicia), the kingdom of Cepheus. But it is a story of human frailty. The trouble began with two rival suitors for the hand of Andromeda, one of whom was Cepheus' brother. The king wished to bestow her on the other but did not wish to offend his brother. Hence he hatched a scheme whereby the other suitor would take her away by ship, as if in a kidnapping (hence Cepheus would be in the clear). The vessel, by no coincidence, happened to be called "Sea-Monster." But the damsel would not cooperate, bemoaning her abduction and crying out for help. Perseus just happened to be sailing in the vicinity, fell in love at first sight, rescued Andromeda in the nick of time, destroyed the good ship "Sea-Monster," and when the crew was petrified by fright, killed them all. So, says Conon with great self-satisfaction, those are the facts from which grew the supernatural tales of Perseus' slaying a sea monster and turning his enemies into

---

[35] Ps. Scylax 104: [Ἰόππη πόλις ἐκτε]θῆναί φασιν ἐνταῦθα τὴν Ἀνδρομ[έδαν τῷ κήτει]. Although much here is restored, including the city of Joppa, the restorations are nearly certain in view of Strabo 16.2.28. See Stern (1984), 10–12.

[36] Harvey (1994), 6, speculates that the Joppa story arose through Greek visitors to the city who learned that Jonah set out from that port and associated his leviathan with the sea monster of Andromeda, an inventive but undemonstrable hypothesis.

[37] Strabo 1.2.35: τὰ περὶ τὴν Ἀνδρομέδαν ἐν Ἰόπῃ συμβῆναί φασιν, οὐ δήπου κατ' ἄγνοιαν τοπικὴν καὶ τούτων λεγομένων, ἀλλ' ἐν μύθου μᾶλλον σχήματι. Strabo's evidence stands against the assertion by Flusser (1987), 1080–1081, that the original version of the legend had Joppa as the location.

[38] Strabo 16.2.28.

stone.[39] Of course, the rationalized narrative has no more claim on authority than the myth. But it attests quite eloquently to the popularity of the Joppa version by the turn of the millennium.

In fact, the legend served even to promote Joppa as a tourist attraction. Its inhabitants were able to argue that the city was the seat of Cepheus' kingdom on the grounds that certain ancient altars existed there, held in highest reverence and inscribed with the titles of Cepheus and his brother.[40] We hear even that a shrine had been erected in honor of the storied leviathan.[41] Visitors to the site might be shown the red water that appeared in a spring near Joppa, and would learn from their guides that Perseus, having disposed of the sea creature, washed the blood off his hands in that spring, thereby staining the waters forever.[42] Further, the very marks of the chains that had bound the unfortunate Andromeda could be seen on a rock that jutted from Joppa.[43] And for those who might still be skeptical, the locals put on display the gigantic bones of the sea monster itself, proof positive that Perseus' rescue of Andromeda occurred in that hallowed spot.[44] One prominent Roman certainly bought the story—or professed to do so for his own purposes. M. Aemilius Scaurus, who had served with Pompey in the conquest of Judaea in 63 and was left in charge of Syria and Palestine, took full advantage. He carted off the colossal bones of the monster and brought them to Rome, where he would proudly exhibit them as part of the garishly ostentatious entertainments he sponsored in his aedileship of 58. The skeleton measured forty feet, its height exceeded that of Indian elephants, and its spine alone was a foot and a half thick.[45] This made for quite a show in Rome, gaining Scaurus a deserved reputation for outlandish excess. But it also gave wider exposure to the Perseus legend as a Palestinian event.

The Jews plainly had a hand in nurturing the narrative that associated themselves with one of the most celebrated sagas in Hellenic lore. Turning Joppa into a tourist attraction attests decisively to that. Josephus confirms it, if confirmation be needed. He describes the steep cliffs and jutting rocks of the city where the impressions left by the chains of Andromeda can still

---

[39] Conon in Photius *FGH* I 26 fr. 1 = Stern (1974) #145.

[40] Pomponius Mela *Chor.* I 11 62–64 = Stern (1974), #152: *quod titulum eius fratrisque Phinei veteres quaedam arae cum religione plurima retinent.*

[41] Pliny *NH* 5.69: *colitur illic fabulosa Ceto.* "Ceto" is clearly a transcription of the Greek *ketos*, the term regularly used for the sea monster. Pliny can hardly mean that the creature was worshipped at Joppa, as Harvey (1994), 7–8, but rather that its legend was honored there. Similarly, the altars dedicated to Cepheus, as noted by Mela (see previous note) represented homage to the myth, not a shrine to the mythological figure.

[42] Paus. 4.35.9. Cf. Philostratus, *Imagines* 1.29, who puts this in Ethiopia.

[43] Pliny *NH* 5.69; cf. 5.128.

[44] Pomponius Mela *Chor.* I 11 62–64 = Stern (1974), #152.

[45] Pliny *NH* 9.11; cf. Amm. Marc. 22.15.24.

be seen, thus demonstrating the antiquity of the myth. The historian does not question it.[46] In fact, three hundred years later tourists still gawked at the rock of Andromeda in Joppa, thereby drawing the scorn of Saint Jerome.[47]

Discrepant strains in the tradition are not readily sorted out. Cepheus appears as ruler of Ethiopia in the mainstream narrative but as ruler of Phoenicia/Palestine at Joppa in a tributary. Some evidently made efforts to fit the discordant strands together. As Strabo notes, certain writers sought to transfer Ethiopia to Phoenicia in order to set the story of Andromeda in Joppa.[48] Pliny attests to the linkage by citing the legend of Andromeda as evidence for Ethiopia's control of Syria in the age of King Cepheus.[49] Tacitus, more tellingly, preserves what appears to be a distorted echo of that mixture. In his summary of diverse proposals as to the origin of the Jews, he registers one as propounded by many, that Jews were a people of Ethiopian descent whom fear and hatred forced to migrate in the reign of Cepheus.[50] Where Tacitus got that bit of misinformation we cannot say. It carries no small whiff of hostility to Jews, yet another variant on the tales that have Jews exiled rather than depart voluntarily for their eventual homeland.[51] But that may very well indicate a manipulation of the Cepheus/Andromeda/Perseus saga that the Jews themselves endorsed. And it provides indirect testimony to the prevalence of the purported links between Joppa and Ethiopia and between the Hellenic legend and the Jews.[52]

The willingness of Jews to advance this fictive association is noteworthy. They did not in this instance, as often elsewhere, take impetus from a Greek genre to retell a Jewish tale. Here they simply adopted a Hellenic legend and transferred it (or endorsed its transference) to Jewish soil. The

---

[46] Jos. *BJ* 3.420.

[47] Jerome *Comm. In Ionam.* 1.3; *In Rufinum* 3.22; *Ep.* 108.8.

[48] Strabo 1.2.35: εἰσὶ δ᾽ οἳ καὶ τὴν Αἰθιοπίαν εἰς τὴν καθ᾽ ἡμᾶς Φοινίκην μετάγουσι, καὶ τὰ περὶ τὴν Ἀνδρομέδαν ἐν Ἰόπῃ συμβῆναί φασιν.

[49] Pliny *NH* 6.182: *et Syriae imperitasse eam* [i.e., Ethiopia] *nostroque litori aetate regis Cephei patet Andromedae fabulis.*

[50] Tac. *Hist.* 5.2.2: *plerique Aethiopum prolem, quos rege Cepheo metus atque odium mutare sedis perpulerit.*

[51] On this passage, see the valuable collection of testimony and bibliography by Heubner and Fauth (1982), 25–26. See also the discussions of Stern (1980), 34, 193–194; Feldman (1991), 348–350; Harvey (1994), 7; Ogden (2008), 84, 116–118. Flusser (1987), 1082–1083, speculatively suggests that Tacitus' sources placed Ethiopians in Joppa, who broke with Cepheus when he prepared to sacrifice his daughter and moved into the interior, thus explaining the origin of the Jews.

[52] The compilation of Stephanus of Byzantium, the sixth-century CE grammarian, included an entry for Joppa (s.v. Ἰόπη), which sought to explain the connection on grounds of the similarity of the names Ἰόπη and Αἰθιόπη, a far-fetched conjecture. Ogden (2008), 84, considers it possible.

refashioning of the tale implies a readiness both to espouse a relationship with Greek tradition and to adapt it to a Jewish setting.

The manifold mixture is quite arresting. Tradition embraced Perseus as the quintessential Hellenic hero, among other things tracing the Doric kings back to him as *Urvater*.[53] At the same time, Greeks acknowledged that his mother Danae, from the royal house of Argos, had deeper roots in Egypt, thus making the Dorian chieftains ultimately Egyptians. No discomfort, it seems, troubled the purveyors of those genealogies. Egyptians picked up on the inventions, erected a shrine to Perseus, and appropriated him for their own. Persians supplied their own versions. They were happy enough to accept Perseus as a forebear, in accord with Hellenic folklore, but they tampered with his ancestry, reckoning him an Assyrian who only later became Greek. Yet they had no hesitation in accepting the tradition that the ancestors of Perseus' mother Danae were Egyptians. Legend makers among Phoenicians and Jews showed equal ingenuity in shifting the location of the tale in order to attach it to their own history. And Jews transformed it into a showcase for their association with Hellenic legend. This remarkable genealogical stew illuminates the ancient propensity to multiply and entangle lineages that cross ethnic boundaries. The juggling of Perseus allowed Persians to link parts of their heritage to Mesopotamia and to Egypt, as well as to Greece. Egyptians could interpret the hero as incarnation of one of their own deities, while honoring him in the fashion of the Greeks. Jews attached themselves to the multicultural blend by advertising part of the saga as having occurred on their shores. And all the information reaches us through stories recycled by the Greeks. The intercultural bonds stretched across the classical and Near Eastern worlds.[54]

Alexander the Great claimed Perseus as an ancestor.[55] So did the Ptolemies.[56] Linkage with a celebrated mythological figure from the Greek past had obvious advantages for Hellenistic rulers. But we can now appreciate the special attraction of Perseus to Alexander and the Ptolemies. He was

---

[53] Herod. 6.53.

[54] They could even extend to Italy. A quite independent tradition had Perseus' mother Danae reach Italian shores in the boat on which Acrisius had shipped her off. There she married a Latin prince with whom she founded Ardea and became an ancestor of Aeneas' chief rival Turnus; Verg. *Aen.* 7.372, with Servius *ad loc.* Cf. Ogden (2008), 119. The standard Perseus saga was sufficiently well known in Rome to be mocked in a Horatian poem. Horace turns the impregnation of Danae by a golden shower into a cynical and amusing escapade whereby Zeus bribes her guards with gold in order to have his sexual pleasure; Horace *Odes* 3.16.1–11. For some later manifestations of the legend, see the summary by Ogden (2008), 131–143. Note, for example, the use made of Perseus in Lycia; Borchhardt and Mader (1972), 3–16; and in Cilicia; Ziegler (2005), 85–105.

[55] Arrian *Anab.* 3.3.2; Pliny *NH* 15.46.

[56] Callimachus fr. 655 (Pfeiffer); Isidorus *Etym.* 17.7.7; see Pfeiffer (1949), 435.

more than a Hellenic hero. He carried wider cultural connotations of a cross-Mediterranean character.

That the ancients manipulated, molded, embellished, twisted, distorted, remodeled, and transformed legends with regularity is not news. The saga of Perseus, however, presents an especially engaging illustration of how nations framed a tradition in multiple modes to connote connections rather than discern divergence among cultures.

Athens and Egypt

Imaginative compositions found numerous ways to forge links between societies and cultures. An especially appealing one held between the proud city of Athens and the venerable land of Egypt. The connection appears in various forms in different (mostly lost) authors, and the tangled threads cannot readily be sorted out, nor the evolution of the tales reconstructed with any confidence. But the overlap of traditions shows that the ties between the celebrated Greek city and the ancient kingdom were vigorously discussed in the fourth century and the Hellenistic period. An affiliation appears already, though vaguely formulated, in Plato's *Timaeus*. An interlocutor in the dialogue draws attention to the city of Saïs in the Delta, seat of the Saïte dynasty that ruled the land from the mid–seventh through the later sixth century BCE. The inhabitants of that city, so he claimed, were admirers of Athenians and were, in an unspecified way, related to them.[57] That remark took sharper form in writings of fourth-century Greek historians, in the generation after Plato. The Attidographer Phanodemus and the Alexander historian Callisthenes both maintained that the people of Saïs were actually descendants of the Athenians—presumably as consequence of the city's foundation by Athenian settlers.[58] This served as a characteristic piece of cultural imperialism by Greek writers. Egyptian intellectuals, however, did not leave it at that. They turned the tale on its head. Diodorus, drawing on Hecataeus of Abdera, reports a tradition that reversed the process. Athens, instead of the colonizer, became the colonized. Saïs had sent out the settlers, and the kinship worked in the other direction. The creative concoction used an etymological argument comparable to that customarily employed by Greeks. Since Athenians uniquely applied the term *asty* to their city, they must have borrowed the term from the like-named city in Egypt, thus proving their Egyptian origin.[59] The inventiveness did

---

[57] Plato *Tim*. 21E: μάλα δὲ φιλαθήναιοι καί τινα τρόπον οἰκεῖοι τῶνδ' εἶναί φασιν. See above.

[58] The citations of Phanodemus and Callisthenes come from Proclus on Plato *Timaeus* 21E; *FGH* 124 F 51 = 325 F 25. So also Diod. 5.57.5: Athenian colonists founded the city of Saïs.

[59] Diod. 1.28.4.

not stop there. Hellenized writers turned legendary Athenian figures into Egyptians as well. The father of Menestheus, leader of the Athenian host that joined the expedition against Troy, came from Egypt and only later acquired citizenship in Athens. And the hero Erechtheus too was Egyptian by birth and subsequently became king of Athens, a claim that rested on his access to grain from Egypt during a great drought.[60] These and other stories irritated Diodorus, who asserted that Egyptians spread them in order to attach themselves to the great reputation of Athens, a matter of self-glorification rather than any connection with the truth.[61] Doubtless so. But the process parallels precisely the identity theft engaged in by Hellenes themselves.

One can readily reckon this as rivalry, competing claims on priority, Saïs as Athenian colony or Athens as Saïte colony, depending on nationalist proclivities.[62] But that may not be the proper angle of perception. Proclus' commentary on Plato's *Timaeus*, while citing Phanodemus and Callisthenes as Greek authors who had Saïs founded by Athens, also mentions another Greek author, identified as "Theopompus" who reversed the sequence: Saïtes colonized Athens.[63] That version, doubtless derived from Egyptian conceptualizing, was transmitted by "Theopompus" as well as by Hecataeus of Abdera, Greek intellectuals both. Cultural competition, in short, is not the principal ingredient here. More to the point, both peoples found significance and value in postulating kinship connections with the other. The genealogical links could go in either direction—less a matter of conflicting claims than of reciprocal appropriation.

Who borrowed what from whom could not always be ascertained. And it might make little difference anyway. An Egyptian tradition recorded by Diodorus has Osiris as head of a great military force that roamed the entire earth and brought civilization, particularly in the form of cultivating the land, to savage peoples everywhere. This estimable feat naturally evokes comparable services performed by the Hellenic hero Herakles. And, sure enough, the story adds Herakles to its narrative, only now he is a subordinate of Osiris. The god set up Herakles as general over all the realm, for he was not only remarkable for courage and physical strength

---

[60] Diod. 1.28.6–29.1.
[61] Diod. 1.29.5: πολλὰ δὲ καὶ ἄλλα τούτοις παραπλήσια λέγοντες φιλοτιμότερον ἤπερ ἀληθινώτερον, ὥς γ' ἐμοὶ φαίνεται, τῆς ἀποικίας ταύτης ἀμφισβητοῦσι διὰ τὴν δόξαν τῆς πόλεως. A similar rebuke of Egyptian appropriation appears in Diod. 5.57.4–5. See above, pp. 98–99.
[62] So Vasunia (2001), 230–232.
[63] Proclus on Plato *Timaeus* 21E = *FGH* 72 F20b. The identification may well be erroneous, a confusion between the Athenian historian Theopompus and another fourth-century historian, Anaximenes of Lampsacus, who composed a work using the pseudonym of his more famous contemporary. See Vasunia (2001), 231. Either way, the Saïte origin of Athens is here transmitted by a Greek.

but also a relative of Osiris. The postulate of kinship relations once again characterizes the connection. And framers of the tale injected a still more intriguing twist. Osiris, in addition to installing Herakles as overseer of his empire, also appointed Busiris to govern that part of Egypt neighboring on Phoenicia and Antaeus to supervise the regions bordering on Ethiopia and Libya.[64] That supplement can be no innocent conjunction. As a knowledgeable audience would be well aware, Herakles, in other and independent legends, famously overcame the savagery and barbarism of Busiris and Antaeus. And Herakles was firmly claimed as an Egyptian.[65] A combination of Hellenic tales were here usurped and transformed for Egyptian ends. The scramble for Herakles' heritage indeed began quite early. Herodotus himself insisted that Herakles had not been appropriated by Egyptians from Greeks, but rather the other way round. He was a deity in the Egyptian pantheon, then adapted by Greeks, who turned him into a mortal son of Amphitryon, evidently to be distinguished from the Herakles whom legend had as son of Zeus. In fact, both of Herakles' mortal parents, according to Herodotus' Egyptian informants, were themselves Egyptians![66] The tangle of diverse traditions once more reflects not so much heated rivalry over precedence but overlapping re-creations with a consistent element of common kinship claims.

The Legend of Nectanebos

Greeks, of course, ruled Egypt in the age of the Ptolemies. The land had come under Hellenic authority after the arrival of Alexander the Great, whether as occupation or liberation—depending on one's perspective. Egyptians were sensitive about the matter. And the Ptolemies who ruled the nation had from the start to address the question of the legitimacy of a Greco-Macedonian ruling class in that land whose traditions long predated their own history. Both peoples struggled to work out the relationship to mutual satisfaction—or at least to represent it in a fashion that both would find palatable. That difficult and intricate process cannot be pursued here. But one absorbing tale allows entrance into the mental mechanism.[67]

The so-called *Alexander Romance* constitutes a bewildering welter of folktales, novelistic fiction, historical embellishments and distortions, and inventive creation, shaped and reshaped over a period of centuries. It survives in three main recensions, the earliest of which was composed around

[64] Diod. 1.17.1–3.
[65] Diod. 1.24.1–7.
[66] Herod. 2.43. See above, pp. 83–84.
[67] Discussion of the Nectanebos legend can be found also in Gruen (2006a), 308–312.

300 CE, but utilizing material that must go back to the early Hellenistic period.[68]

The opening portion of the text holds particular interest. The tale centers on Nectanebos II, the last pharaoh of Egypt, ousted from power in 342 by a second Persian conquest of Egypt, driven to the south, and ending in obscurity. But he looms large in legend. The Persian dynasty that succeeded him did not last long, defeated and removed forever by the invasion of Alexander. The image or construct of the last Egyptian ruler took on particular importance in the decades after establishment of Ptolemaic authority. Egyptian national consciousness and the legitimacy of the new order were both at stake. In this milieu the saga of Nectanebos in the *Alexander Romance* took shape.

A résumé of the narrative, or its relevant parts, is in order.[69] The author introduces Nectanebos not only as the last pharaoh but as a man especially skilled in the magical arts. Through reasoning power he could bring all the elements of the universe to do his bidding. If war threatened, he did not bother with arms, weaponry, or military machines. He simply defeated enemies on land and sea with incantations, model ships and soldiers floated in a cauldron, and appeals to the god Ammon. This worked like a charm for a long time. But when one massive invasion took place, the cauldron delivered some alarming news: Egyptian gods were piloting the little wax boats of the enemy! Nectanebos got the message. He put on disguise, gathered what treasure he could stuff into his clothes, and fled the country. After wandering through a number of nations, he landed in Pella, seat of the Macedonian monarchy, the ruling capital of Philip II. There the resourceful Nectanebos presented himself as an Egyptian seer and astrologer.[70]

The Egyptians themselves, bereft of their king after his mysterious vanishing act, sought guidance from the ancestor of the gods, who sent a reassuring oracle. The prediction affirmed that the monarch may have fled as an old man but would return to Egypt as a youth and subject the enemies of his countrymen. No one quite grasped the significance of the oracle at the time, but the Egyptians ordered it inscribed on Nectanebos' statue, hoping that some day it might be fulfilled.[71]

Nectanebos soon made quite a reputation in Macedon as an eminent seer, a reputation that reached the ears of the alluring queen Olympias, who summoned him to the palace. Her husband Philip was conveniently away at war—as was his wont. Nectanebos took full advantage, flattering

---

[68] For summaries of the complex strands of the *Alexander Romance* and its evolution, see recently Stoneman (1991), 8–17; (2008), 230–245; Fraser (1996), 205–226.
[69] See the valuable discussion of the story in Stoneman (2008), 13–24, who sets it in the context of similar tales and traditions but does not treat the matters at issue here.
[70] *Alex. Rom.* 1.1–3.3.
[71] *Alex. Rom.* 1.3.4–6.

the queen and boasting of his skills as dream interpreter, caster of horoscopes, and master of the magical arts. He then prophesied a future separation from Philip, who would marry another, but offered a far better compensation: Olympias would sleep with a god, none other than the Libyan ram-headed deity Ammon, with whom she would conceive a son, a future avenger of Philip's misdeeds. Nectanebos had hatched a dastardly erotic scheme. Alerting Olympias to the fact that she would first dream of intercourse with the god and would subsequently experience it, he exerted all his magical powers to induce precisely the right dream, thus persuading the queen of his prophetic gifts. Nectanebos now had Olympias where he wanted her. He forecast that the god would appear to her in the guise of a serpent, then in Ammon's own form, followed by that of Herakles and of Dionysos in turn, and finally (not surprisingly) taking the shape of Nectanebos himself. Olympias eagerly welcomed the prediction, proclaimed that if the forecast were fulfilled she would announce him as father of the child, and duly submitted herself to the mantic cloaked as multiple divinity. The queen rapidly became pregnant, her womb housing a child whom Nectanebos presciently prophesied to be invincible and dominant.[72]

There was, of course, still the problem of Philip. He returned to Macedon to discover a pregnant wife—whom he had obviously not impregnated. But Nectanebos' mantic powers managed to persuade the king that Olympias had been visited by a deity, no mere human adulterer. Philip was readily gulled. Olympias appropriately delivered a child amidst lightning flashes, rolling thunder, and earthquakes. None could doubt that the father must have been divine. The boy, Alexander, who bore no resemblance to Philip or Olympias, had a great future in store.[73]

Young Alexander assimilated the martial prowess and fierce ambition of Philip, his early years consumed in rivalry with the king. Nectanebos continued to hang about the court, evidently enjoying the frequent absences of Philip. Alexander probed the prophetic powers of the seer and sought to benefit from his astrological knowledge. But in a stunning turnabout, the impetuous prince hurled Nectanebos against a rock, smashing his head and exclaiming that he had no business investigating the mysteries of heaven when he could not command the earthly realm. The dying Nectanebos revealed to Alexander that he was Alexander's father, the consequence of his devious deception of Olympias. Alexander then felt both remorse and betrayal. He regretted the murder of his father but blamed him for never disclosing the deed until the end. Alexander informed his mother, and a proper burial followed.[74]

---

[72] *Alex. Rom.* 1.4–7.
[73] *Alex. Rom.* 1.8–12.
[74] *Alex. Rom.* 1.13–15.

When the all-conquering Alexander eventually reached Egypt, the prognostications came to fruition. Priests and prophets hailed him as the new pharaoh, his enthronement occurring in the ancient seat of Memphis. And Alexander noticed the statue of Nectanebos with its inscription that forecast the return of the king, not as elderly monarch but as a young man who would subdue the dreaded Persians. Alexander immediately embraced the statue, publicly proclaimed Nectanebos as his father, and declared the fulfillment of the oracle.[75]

Such is the gist of the tale. How to interpret it? Egyptian conceptualization must lie at its core. The element of divine fatherhood for the ruler of the land holds a central place in the legend. This can hardly be anything but an allusion to the standard myth of Amon-Re as fathering the pharaoh through a nocturnal visit to the queen in the guise of her husband.[76] Nectanebos' choice of divinity is hardly accidental. The attachment of this lofty lineage to Alexander brought the Macedonian king into line with Egyptian tradition, thus asserting a critical continuity between pharaonic rule and Greco-Macedonian overlordship. The Egyptian element in this construct is fundamental.[77] In this fashion the Egyptians could claim the accomplishments of Alexander for themselves. The overthrow of the Persian empire and the occupation of Egypt, therefore, came not at the hands of an alien conqueror but through the son of Pharaoh and under the aegis of Ammon. It would not be the first time that such a connection was concocted to camouflage the succumbing of Egypt to external power. A closely comparable story had assuaged the sensitivities of Egyptians after conquest of the land by the Persian king Cambyses in the sixth century. They transformed Cambyses into the son of Cyrus and an Egyptian princess, thus laying claim on the heritage of Cyrus the Great.[78] The parallel is nearly precise. This represents more than the ascription of divine sonship to Alexander. It constitutes Egyptian expropriation of the Macedonian achievement to their own purposes.

It would be a mistake to see this as "nationalist propaganda" with an anti-Macedonian bent.[79] The contrary holds. The thrust of the Egyptian construct was to subsume and transform the Hellenic overlord, not to reject or undermine him. Egyptian appropriation of celebrated Greek figures possessed a solid history. Reports had it that the most eminent of Greeks, like Orpheus, Homer, Pythagoras, Solon, and Plato, all gained their learning from visits to Egypt.[80] Alexander fit suitably in that company.

---

[75] *Alex. Rom.* 1.34.
[76] Brunner (1964).
[77] Cf. Lloyd (1982), 46–50; Huss (1994), 129–133; Stephens (2003), 67–73.
[78] Herod. 3.1–2.
[79] As do, e.g., Lloyd (1982), 46–50; Huss (1994), 129–133.
[80] Diod. 1.96–98.

But that is not the whole story. This narrative had undergone more than one transmutation before attaining the form in which it has reached us. The Greek text has a strongly Greek flavor. A reworking at Hellenic hands needs to be taken into account. Sardonic and satirical elements inhere in the yarn. Of course, such elements were not foreign to Egyptian writings, even occasionally in mockery of their own rulers.[81] But an intriguing ambiguity, suggesting a give-and-take representation, characterizes the text and accords it a special quality. Nectanebos appears as hero of the story, providing Alexander with an Egyptian lineage. Yet the hero is flawed and suspect. Nectanebos is certainly no warrior (a stark contrast with Philip). He wins his battles with toy ships and necromancy. When a serious enemy appears on the horizon, he collects his goods, dons disguise, and flees for his life. His seduction of Olympias succeeds through trickery and skullduggery. Nor is Olympias a mere passive instrument in the fugitive Egyptian's lecherous scheme. She summoned him to the court in the first place. In a subtle touch, unnoticed by critics, the text hints that she knew precisely what was happening. When told that a succession of gods would arrive in her bedroom, Olympias responded to her would-be seducer by saying that once a child was born she would proclaim him the son of Nectanebos.[82] One might well wonder whether the queen was manipulating the situation to have back at Philip.

Nectanebos, in any case, hardly cuts an admirable figure. He comes to an early death in ridiculous fashion by being tossed on a jutting rock by the youthful Alexander. And it is noteworthy that Alexander, once he learns that Nectanebos is indeed his father, blames him for sealing his own fate by neglecting to mention that salient fact. Alexander takes full advantage of the situation when he encounters the inscribed oracle in Memphis, laying claim to pharaonic heritage and accepting the forecast of conquering Persia as avenger of Egypt. But as the narrative makes clear, Alexander had inherited the qualities of Philip, not of Nectanebos.

The text, however, no more presents an anti-Egyptian message than an anti-Macedonian one. Olympias may have collaborated with or even engineered the scheme of Nectanebos. But the fugitive king managed to provide the Egyptian lineage that enabled his countrymen to associate themselves with the conqueror rather than the conquered. Alexander had eclipsed and even eliminated his flawed father. But he accepted the Egyptian connection and made it the rallying cry of his campaign against Persia.

How much of this narrative stems from Egyptian and how much from Greek reflection cannot be known. The date of composition remains elusive, and a quest for it probably unhelpful. Nor does it much matter. In a

---

[81] Silverman (1995), 49–61; Stephens (2003), 71.
[82] *Alex. Rom.* 1.6.3–4.

text reworked many times, the strands naturally intertwine. And any specific date, even it could be known, would carry little meaning for the complex composition. One may presume that the narrative arose in the circumstances of Ptolemaic Egypt, in its initial form probably relatively early in the history of that regime. The Egyptians had reason to seek a reassuring accommodation to Hellenic rule. And the Ptolemies had reason to seek legitimacy in Egyptian eyes for their own usurpation. More than one constituency benefited from this elaborate tale. An aspect of high significance, however, needs emphasis. Neither Greeks nor Egyptians relegated the other to the status of barbarian.[83] On the contrary. Each found cause for associating themselves with the achievements or traditions of the other.

Numidians and the Near East

Legendary genealogies that connect diverse peoples come in various forms—and occasionally quite surprising ones. A most peculiar and unexpected tale surfaces fortuitously in Sallust's monograph on the Jugurthine War, composed circa 40 BCE. The Roman historian paused in his narrative to indulge in an excursus on the origins of African peoples with whom Rome engaged or clashed. Sallust opens the digression by citing his source, the sole occasion in which he does so. He drew his material, so he maintains, from the "Punic books" that were said to be of King Hiempsal and written in accord with the beliefs of the indigenous dwellers. Sallust warns his readers that this account, which was translated for him, differs from the (probably Greek) tradition that many people subscribe to, and he does not vouch for its accuracy.[84] The historian wisely covered his flanks. But historicity is not our concern. The tale, in any case, circulated in North Africa and was conveyed by the Numidian prince, composed in Punic, and congruent with native belief.[85]

The legend is unusual and intriguing. According to Sallust's report, the initial inhabitants of Africa were Gaetulians and Libyans whom he describes

---

[83] The people labeled as "barbarians" in the narrative are the enemies of Egypt, specified as including almost any people one could imagine in the east, ranging from Skythians to Euonimitai—but no Greeks; *Alex. Rom.* 1.2.2, 1.3.1.

[84] Sallust *Iug.* 17.7.

[85] Some have argued that Sallust actually relied on a Greek source and that the *libri Punici* were simply a disguised Hellenistic text that claimed indigenous authority and the authorship of Hiempsal. See Oniga (1995), 51–68, with bibliography. Paul (1984), 74, equivocates on this. But there is no good reason to question Sallust's statement about his source or his commissioning of a translation. He served as proconsul of Africa Nova in 46 BCE. We know independently that *libri Punici* were later consulted by the learned Juba II; Solinus 32.2; Amm. Marc. 22.15.8. See the convincing arguments of Morstein-Marx (2001), 195–197. On Juba, see now the full-scale treatment by Roller (2003).

as rough and uncultivated people, governed by no law or authority, rootless wanderers without settled communities. But, as the Africans believe, when the hero Herakles died in Spain, his mercenary troops dispersed, and contingents of Persians, Medes, and Armenians found their way to Africa. The Persians intermarried with Gaetulians and gradually amalgamated with them. They picked up nomadic ways, called themselves Nomads, and became progenitors of the Numidians.[86] The Libyans, for their part, united themselves to the Medes and Armenians and led a more civilized life, soon dwelling in towns and exchanging commerce with Spaniards, by contrast with the Gaetulians, who lived in the interior, farther to the south and away from the coast. The Libyans and their barbarous tongue were responsible for corrupting the name "Medes" into "Mauri," thus the ancestors of the Moors.[87] It was the Persians, however, whose power soon increased, and, in the next generation, under the name of Numidians, a segment of them split from their parents and occupied the place nearest to Carthage that is now called Numidia. The collaboration of former Persians and Gaetulians, more warlike than the Libyans, brought much of the neighboring territory under their rule, gained them glory and renown, and eventually they controlled most of North Africa, which became the land of the Numidians.[88]

Such is the gist of Sallust's report. The historian, to be sure, had his own agenda in recounting this tradition, selecting or elaborating as seemed useful. His portrait of the hardy and warlike Gaetulians, toughened by their nomadic existence in the less hospitable parts of Africa, contrasted with that of the Libyans, whose dwelling on the coast and contacts with city life express familiar stereotypes. Environmental and social factors, geographic and ethnographic elements, help to determine character and divide the weak from the strong. In the context of Sallust's monograph, the excursus plainly evokes the contrast between the powerful and ambitious Jugurtha and the compliant and ineffective Adherbal, rivals for the Numidian throne. The emergence of the Numidians from the combined forces of Persians and Gaetulians sets up and symbolizes the future clash between Rome and Numidia. The historian manipulates the legend to serve the purposes of his construct.[89]

But Sallust did not invent the tradition that linked the peoples of North Africa with migrants of Persian, Median, and Armenian stock who had fought in Spain under the redoubtable Herakles. The *libri Punici* were his source, a work ascribed to the Numidian ruler Hiempsal II, writing in the

---

[86] Sallust *Iug.* 18.1–8.
[87] Sallust *Iug.* 18.9–10.
[88] Sallust *Iug.* 18.11–12.
[89] See the illuminating analyses of Green (1993), 185–197, and Morstein-Marx (2001), 179–188.

first half of the first century BCE.⁹⁰ That the king would compose his work in Punic need not surprise us. That language held sway in North Africa in this era. And *libri Punici* later provided material for the scholarly monarch Juba II.⁹¹ The Numidian royal house had an attachment to Greek as well as to Punic learning, an attachment that goes back at least to the time of Micipsa in the mid–second century BCE.⁹² A mixture of Greek and Punic elements in these books can be expected. A separate and quite different tale had Herakles as mythical forefather of the Numidian royal line.⁹³ The ethnic linkage in the tradition conveyed by Sallust, however, does not come directly (or perhaps even indirectly) from Hellenic legend. The Phoenicians, as is well known, had long since adapted Herakles for their own rites and rituals and identified him with the native deity Melqart. The Herakles who perished in Spain in the story transmitted by Sallust is plainly Herakles-Melqart. The Carthaginians commemorated his final resting place and established a celebrated shrine that supposedly contained his bones in Gades, a shrine subsequently honored by Romans as well.⁹⁴ The tale found by Sallust had a distinctively Punic flavor and had been embraced, as he says, by "Africans." It may have been conceived by intellectuals, whether Carthaginian or Numidian, but it had resonance for the natives, quite distinct from Hellenic speculation or Roman adaptation.

A linkage to the great nations of the east obviously had appeal to those who dwelled in North Africa. And it can be traced to a time well before Sallust. A peculiar notice in a Livian epitome (the only source for this) gives the name of a general of Numidian forces that had entered Carthaginian territory before the outbreak of the Third Punic War: a certain Arcobarzanes, grandson of Syphax.⁹⁵ Nothing more is known. But the name Arcobarzanes (or, better, Ariobarzanes) is plainly Iranian, found among Medes and Cappadocians. A Numidian leader or chieftain had taken it as his own, evidently an allusion to that Iranian heritage that Sallust found in the *libri Punici*.⁹⁶ Traces of this connection can be discerned elsewhere. Pomponius Mela and Pliny the Elder make reference to the Pharusii as

---

⁹⁰ Reference is surely to Hiempsal II, grandfather of Juba II, not to Hiempsal I, who ruled only briefly a half century earlier. Cf. Matthews (1972), 331–332; Kontorini *AC* (1975), 94; Morstein-Marx (2001), 196. Matthews (1972), 331–334, canvasses the idea that *libris Punicis, qui regis Hiempsalis dicebantur* refers to works owned by, rather than composed by, Hiempsal; cf. Pliny *NH* 18.22. Not very plausible; see Ritter (1978), 315–316. A decision would, in any case, not affect the main point here.

⁹¹ Solinus 32.2; Amm. Marc. 22.15.8.

⁹² Diod. 34/5.35; cf. Strabo 17.3.13.

⁹³ Plut. *Sert.* 9.4–5; see Oniga (1995), 65.

⁹⁴ Pomponius Mela 3.46. Further sources and discussion in Oniga (1995), 67–68.

⁹⁵ Livy *Per.* 48.

⁹⁶ This was rightly pointed to by Ritter (1978), 313–317. Morstein-Marx (2001), 197, oddly and unjustifiably dismisses it as "a product of textual corruption."

accompanying Herakles when he moved to the west. And Pliny helpfully adds that Pharusii, now located in Africa, were Persians in origin.[97] This may only be an etymological guess. But the suggestive association is no coincidence.[98] The evidence is frustratingly fragmentary, yet tantalizingly tempting. The connection held between North Africans and peoples who originated in the lands of the Achaemenid empire—at least in the minds of the former. Sallust encountered it and embellished it. But the tradition plainly precedes the last generation of the Roman Republic. Why else would a Numidian prince of the mid-second century BCE acquire the name of Ariobarzanes?

Just what significance this link carried admits of no easy answer.[99] The image of the Persians as imperial conquerors, as possessors of holdings that extended from Ionia to Afghanistan, must have held allure. The Medes had a similar image, predecessors of Persians, eclipsed by them but still an integral part of their rule in its heyday. The place of Armenians in this picture is harder to account for. Perhaps the reputation of that tough and mountainous region, with its skilled horsemen and hardy warriors, whose ruling dynasty retained authority through the Achaemenid and Seleucid periods, held a fascination that could attract legendary lineages.[100] One might, in any case, bear in mind that the shape of the tale as transmitted by Sallust has Persians come out on top, transformed into Numidians, whose power expands and territory increases, while the Libyans, blended with Medes and Armenians, have to take a secondary role. Numidians had cause to mold the tradition. Yet national pride does not tell the whole tale. Learned scholars played with Greek and Punic traditions, researched the wanderings of Herakles, knew the Phoenician versions of Melqart in Spain, and added the ingredient of eastern peoples with a glorious past to help forge the folks of North Africa. One need not search out special circumstances or

---

[97] Pomponius Mela 3.103; Pliny *NH* 5.46: *Pharusi, quondam Persi, comites fuisse dicuntur Herculis ad Hesperidas tendentis*. So also Solinus 31.6. Cf. Oniga (1995), 83–84. Note further a fragment of Sallust, whose placement is uncertain, referring to the Mauri who claimed that the Antipodes who dwelled beyond Ethiopia lived in accordance with the admirable customs of the Persians; Sallust *Fragmenta dubia vel falsa* 3 (Maur). See the discussion of Oniga (1995), 117–131—though his placement of the fragment is speculative. This is further testimony, however dubious, for belief in a Persian/African connection.

[98] Cf. Ritter (1978), 314–315. An intriguing passage of Strabo, 17.3.7, may be relevant here. He reports a theory that the Maurusians (Mauretanians) were Indians in origin and came west with Herakles. Some have emended Μαυρούσιοι to Φαρούσιοι, whom Strabo also mentions in this segment. That is tempting but unprovable, as is Ritter's preference for Μήδους instead of Ἰνδούς; (1978), 315. See Oniga (1995), 84–85.

[99] That the impetus came largely from a desire to find etymological connections, as Oniga (1995), 86–92, proposes, is not very plausible.

[100] On the Armenians, see Sherwin-White and Kuhrt (1993), 15–17, 190–197; Briant (2002), 741–743.

particular events that prompted this narrative—which may well have taken form over an extended stretch of time.[101] The link itself remains most compelling. Hellenic and Phoenician traditions were recast to incorporate mighty nations of the east into the mythical history of North Africa. That process corresponds strikingly to the parallel practices of Egyptians, Jews, Greeks, and Romans. Numidians were no more bashful in tracing their roots to distant peoples and legendary ancestors.

Claims on cultural mixtures crossed the Mediterranean. An assemblage of nations traded on the myth of Perseus, Greeks and Egyptians adapted one another's traditions, and even Numidians found links to peoples of the Near East through the intermediaries of Greek and Punic inventions. The practice holds real significance for the self-perception of groups in antiquity. Concocted kinships declared composite identities.

[101] The stimulating analysis of Morstein-Marx (2001), 189–192, seeing "Persians" as surrogates for Parthians and thus evoking Rome's principal foe in the time of Sallust, may place too much emphasis on the Roman perspective.

Chapter 11

FICTITIOUS KINSHIPS: JEWS AND OTHERS

The ancient Jews notoriously preferred their own company to that of anyone else. A famous prayer, stemming from rabbinic traditions and found already in the Mishnah, sums it up nicely. The Jewish worshipper offers a prayer of thanksgiving: "thank you, O Lord, for not making me a slave, for not making me a woman, — and for not making me a goy!" Better not to have any truck with the goyim. On that score, one might say, the Jews have an "attitude." Of course, they were not alone. The Greeks had their own version of this phraseology. A well-known saying, ascribed both to Thales and to Socrates, put the sentiment in comparably pointed form. It gave thanks to the gods "that I was born a human not an animal, a man not a woman, and a Greek not a barbarian."[1] The Jews, however, developed a special reputation for sticking to their own kind, keeping non-Jews at arm's length, and maintaining their own traditions unsullied by contact with others. How defining was that characteristic?

The Separatist Impression

Pagan writers noticed Jewish separatism and made a point of remarking on it. The earliest Greek who wrote anything substantial about the Jews, Hecataeus of Abdera in the late fourth century BCE, observed that the laws of Moses prescribed a rather antisocial and inhospitable lifestyle.[2] The comment came in an extended passage that also contained many positive reflections on Jewish history and practices. Hecataeus did not go in for slander. But the image of the Jew already possessed the character of one who kept to his own kind. Hecataeus' near contemporary, the Hellenized Egyptian intellectual Manetho (or perhaps Pseudo-Manetho) asserted that a Mosaic law forbade Jews from contact with anyone but their

---

[1] Diog. Laert. 1.3.
[2] Hecataeus *apud* Diod. Sic. 40.3.4. See the discussion, with extensive bibliography, by Berthelot (2003), 80–94.

own coreligionists.[3] That perception persisted. A Greek rhetorician and intellectual of the first century BCE, Apollonius Molon, branded the Jews as atheists and misanthropes.[4] A little later, in a tale reported by the Sicilian historian Diodorus, the Jews were characterized as the only nation who shunned relationships with other people and regarded them all as their enemies.[5]

The stigma held firm in the Roman period. Pompeius Trogus, a Gallic intellectual writing in Latin, maintained that Jews held themselves apart from all gentiles—though he notes that this stemmed from the time when they were expelled from Egypt on the charge of carrying contagious diseases. It was a means to avoid further odium.[6] The Alexandrian writer Apion declared that Jews swear by their god to avoid cordiality with any non-Jews, especially Greeks.[7] That most formidable of historians, Tacitus, weighed in with a caustic comment: Jews show intense loyalty and compassion toward one another but have fierce hostility toward all others; they will not eat with gentiles, they will not sleep with them—but there is no depravity that they will not commit with one another.[8] The satirist Juvenal went so far as to write that the Jews of Rome will not even give directions in the street to anyone who is not circumcised![9] That is plainly comic hyperbole. But it testifies to the enduring reputation of separatism and misanthropy. One can readily cite numerous additional passages expressing similar sentiments.[10]

The charges did not arise from a void. Nor do they come only from alleged Jew baiters or anti-Semites. Jews themselves readily put into the mouths of gentiles remarks that stigmatized the Israelite nation as one unassimilated and apart from all other peoples.[11] In the Greco-Roman period they did not shrink from underscoring their distinctiveness and celebrating their differences from pagans. One might take as a striking instance the Jewish-Hellenistic composition *The Letter of Aristeas*, which recounts the tale of the translation of Hebrew scriptures into Greek. That treatise is normally understood as exemplary of harmonious interchange between Jew and Greek. And so it is. But there are limits to togetherness. The Jewish author makes that point quite unambiguously. He puts into the mouth

---

[3] Manetho *apud* Jos. *CAp*. 1.239. Cf. Berthelot (2003), 94–101.
[4] Apollonius *apud* Jos. *CAp*. 2.148, 2.258.
[5] Diod. Sic. 34/5.1.1–4; cf. Jos. *Ant*. 13.245.
[6] Trogus *apud* Justin 36.2.15. Cf. Bloch (2002), 54–63; Berthelot (2003), 156–160.
[7] Apion *apud* Jos. *CAp*. 2.121.
[8] Tac. *Hist*. 5.5.1–2.
[9] Juv. 14.103–104.
[10] See references in Sevenster (1975), 89–96; Feldman (1993), 125–131; Schäfer (1997), 167–179; Berthelot (2003), 80–171.
[11] E.g., Esther 3.8; 3 Macc. 3.4.

of the High Priest Eleazer as forthright a statement as one could wish on this score. Eleazer is pleased to collaborate with the Greeks who seek a translation of the Torah, providing men and gifts to facilitate the project. But he disabuses those who imagine that Jewish beliefs can be folded into Hellenic practices. The High Priest mocks and denounces the idolatry indulged in by Greeks, reaffirming the special character of Mosaic law. He insists indeed that Moses had equipped his people with impenetrable fences and iron walls, so that they would stand apart from all other nations and mingle with none, keeping body and soul free of empty delusions and devoting themselves to their sole god.[12] The very work that emblematizes concord between the cultures also trumpets Jewish uniqueness and superiority. That sense of separateness carried a powerful image for Jews in the Greco-Roman era.[13]

Nor should this surprise us in any way. The idea of the Israelites as God's chosen people permeates the Pentateuch.[14] And the future of Israel depends on a commitment to Yahweh, who alone can bring success against all other nations determined to resist or corrupt these chosen people. Jewish identity derives from distinguishing the clan from its neighbors and asserting its own special quality. To serve that end, it was useful to engage in demonizing the "Other."[15] Preeminent among such peoples, of course, are the Canaanites. They serve from the outset as the quintessential "Other."[16] The memorable tale of Noah's three sons, Shem, Ham, and Japheth, exemplifies it. Ham observed his father in a drunken sleep and naked in his tent but failed to cover his nakedness. He informed his brothers instead, who took a cloak, walked backward into the tent so that they would not see their father in this state, and covered his body without looking at him. As a consequence, Noah, when he woke and learned what had happened, delivered a mighty curse not on Ham, as one might expect, but on Ham's son Canaan: "Cursed be Canaan, the lowliest slave shall he be to his brothers."[17] Displacement of this curse on the apparently innocent Canaan can have

---

[12] *LetArist.* 131–139. Cf. Holladay (1992), 147–149; Barclay (1996), 143–145; Gruen (1998), 215–216.

[13] Cf. 2 Macc. 14.3, 14.38; Esther Add. B.3–5; 2 Baruch 48.20–23; Mattogno (2002), 103–132.

[14] E.g., Gen. 12.1–3; Exod. 6.7, 33.16; Lev. 20.26; Num. 23.7–10; Deut. 7.6, 10.15, 14.2; Bertholet (1896), 79–90. The motif could receive even more forceful expression in some post-biblical literature; cf. II Esdras 6.53–59; Assumption of Moses 1.12–13.

[15] It would be quite impossible to catalogue the limitless bibliography on this topic. One might consult the incisive, though one-sided, recent monograph on the subject by Benbessa and Attias (2004). See also the articles collected in Silberstein and Cohn (1994). The standard line is reasserted now in the useful summary by Wills (2008), 1–12. Cf. the remarks of R. Schwartz (1997), 120–142. A more balanced statement in Spina (2005), 1–13.

[16] See Cohn (1994), 74–90.

[17] Gen. 9.18–27. The translation is Alter's (1996), 41.

but one purpose: to foreshadow and justify the eventual Israelite subjugation of the Canaanite land. Abraham already gave voice to the need to keep the nations distinct. He instructed his servant to find a wife for his son Isaac among the peoples of his own homeland—and under no account allow him to wed a daughter of the Canaanites.[18] Yahweh's subsequent covenant with Moses assured expulsion of the Canaanites, among other peoples, from the land in which they dwelled and authorized the Israelites to smash their altars, their idols, and their sacred objects. Moreover, the Lord forbade any agreements with these nations, and prohibited all intermarriage lest his chosen people abandon their god and embrace the deities of others.[19]

A comparable biblical pronouncement held against Moabites and Ammonites. The book of Deuteronomy includes a ban on those nations, forbidding them from entering the congregation of the Lord. Edomites and Egyptians had a similar liability, but only to the third generation. For Moabites and Ammonites the interdiction would hold forever.[20] An infamous legend in Genesis provided grounds for this prohibition—or was shaped to account for it. God had spared Lot after the destruction of Sodom and Gomorrah, but the only other members of his family who survived were two virgin daughters, now lodged with their father in an isolated cave. Desperate to perpetuate the existence of their line, and having no other recourse, the sisters twice led Lot into a deep slumber induced by wine and had sexual relations with him in turn—unbeknownst to their father. From those unions two sons were born, each given a name that alluded to the incest, Moab and Ben-Ammi, who proved to be the progenitors of the Moabites and Ammonites respectively.[21] The legend does not condemn the acts. Lot himself was innocent and unaware, and the daughters sought to keep the family lineage alive in the only way that seemed left to them. But the names of the sons, an obvious accretion, plainly aimed to taint the peoples later branded as enemies of the Israelites.[22] Just what is meant by a ban on "entering the congregation of the Lord," whether a prohibition on intermarriage or conversion or, more literally, entering the assemblies of the Israelites, remains unclear, a source of much dispute among later Jewish and Christian authors.[23] But the rejection of contact with those nations and the assertion of Israelite segregation emerge unmistakably.[24]

---

[18] Gen. 24.3–4, 24.37.

[19] Exod. 23.23–28, 34.11–16; Deut. 7.1–6. See, most recently, Wills (2008), 29–34.

[20] Deut. 23.4–9.

[21] Gen. 19.30–38.

[22] Cf. von Rad (1972), 218–219; Westermann (1985), 314–315; Wills (2008), 24.

[23] S. Cohen (1999), 248–252.

[24] They remain among the emblematic foes of Israel in, e.g., the War Scroll from Qumran; 1 QM 1.1–2: Edomites, Moabites, Ammonites, and Philistines.

The shunning of exogamous marriages becomes a recurrent theme in biblical and postbiblical literature. It surfaces most starkly in the Ezra-Nehemiah composition. The text presents Ezra, Israelite priest, emissary of the Persian court, and representative of those restored to Judah after the Babylonian Exile, as shocked by the discovery of intermarriage between the former exiles and the peoples who continued to dwell in the land. He learned that Israelites of all levels, even priests, Levites, and other community leaders had engaged in this forbidden practice, uniting with the daughters of various nations, including Canaanites, Ammonites, and Moabites. The distraught Ezra reacted with outrage and even hysteria. He tore his clothes, pulled hair from his head and beard, and sat in horror—shocking behavior by one of priestly rank.[25] That caught people's attention. Ezra echoed biblical pronouncements against mixed marriages, wept, and prostrated himself before the Temple. He then obtained the response he sought. Large numbers of men gathered with vows to expel all foreign wives and the offspring that resulted from their unions. And Ezra extracted a promise that they would segregate themselves from the locals of the land and from any alien women.[26]

The issue, however, would not die. Nehemiah, an Israelite courtier of the Persian monarch, according to the text, made two trips to Judah to implement the rebuilding of the walls and to oversee the new order. The text introduces his second visit with a reading from the Torah that reiterated the ban on Moabites and Ammonites, who were prohibited admission to the congregation of the Lord for all time.[27] Nehemiah then confronted the same problem that Ezra had encountered: the community of former exiles had married women from Moab, Ammon, and Ashdod, and their children could no longer speak Hebrew. Nehemiah reacted even more strongly than Ezra. Instead of tearing out his own hair, he tore out the hair of those men who had offended against the marriage proscriptions! He reinstituted the injunction in still stronger terms and purged the priesthood of all foreign elements.[28] The real conflicts at this time were complex and entangled, involving struggles between Israelites who remained in the land during the Exile and those who had returned, struggles among local and regional leaders, and contests over land, property, legal rights, political ascendancy, and relationship of Israel to Persian suzerainty.[29] But the authors of Ezra-Nehemiah chose to underscore the conflict over intermarriage, to

---

[25] Ezra 9.1–3. Cf. Williamson (1985), 129–133; Blenkinsopp (1988), 174–178; Wills (2008), 64–70.
[26] Ezra 10.1–12; Neh. 10.29–31.
[27] Neh. 13.1–3; cf. Deut. 23.4.
[28] Neh. 13.23–30.
[29] See M. Smith (1971), 75–112; Grabbe (1998), 123–197; Smith-Christopher (1994), 243–265; *idem* (2002), 150–162; Wills (2008), 70–74.

represent or misrepresent an indigenous population as Moabites, Ammonites, and other foreigners, and take a firm line against assimilation.[30] The children of Israel in this construct had to maintain a separatist identity.

The *Book of Jubilees*, composed probably in the second century BCE, constitutes a rewriting of the early portions of the Hebrew Bible. The author retells, with additions, substitutions, or omissions, the narratives in Genesis and the first part of Exodus through the escape from Egypt and the institution of the Passover festival.[31] And the work makes no bones about its affirmation of Jewish exclusivity. The author puts in Abraham's mouth a farewell speech to his children and grandchildren with a variety of admonitions, a scene that has no counterpart in Genesis. The final words of the patriarch contain some harsh pronouncements against sexual transgressions, including an insistence that his descendants take no wife from among the Canaanites—for the seed of Canaan will be removed from the land.[32] Abraham delivers a separate speech to Jacob, enjoining him to isolate himself from the gentiles, to refrain from eating at their tables and associating with them, for their ways are contaminated, unclean, and defiled. And he adds that Jacob (as progenitor of the house of Israel) forbear from wedding any daughter of Canaan, whose seed must be rooted out of the earth.[33]

The author further reinforces that line in retelling the story of Jacob being sent to the house of Laban in order to avoid the mistake of his brother Esau, who married two Hittite (also called Canaanite) wives. In Genesis, the marriages bitterly disappointed his parents Isaac and Rebecca, and Isaac firmly warned Jacob off any Canaanite women in sending him away to the family of his mother.[34] The author of *Jubilees* elaborates on the tale, placing more extensive emphasis on the issue of exogamy. He creates a full-scale dialogue between Rebecca and Jacob in which the mother plays a role not paralleled in the Genesis version, denouncing in fiercest terms the transgressions of the Canaanites and exhorting Jacob to do his mother's will in keeping to his own kind. Jacob loyally replies that it never crossed his mind to disobey the instructions of Abraham—and he would certainly adhere to the wishes of his mother.[35] Shunning contact with Canaanites constitutes the main message.

---

[30] For Fishbane (1985), 115–121, the authors employed an exegetical blend of Deut. 7.1–3 with Deut. 23.4–9, thereby to bring Moabites and Ammonites, contemporaries of the postexilic community, under the same proscriptions that applied to Canaanites. Cf. Wills (2008), 74–80.
[31] On the date, see VanderKam (2001), 17–22.
[32] *Jub*. 20.4.
[33] *Jub*. 22.16–20.
[34] Gen. 26.34–35, 27.46–28.2, 36.2.
[35] *Jub*. 25.1–10; cf. 27.8–10. See the analysis of Endres (1987), 73–77.

The shift from the biblical account to place the spotlight on exogamy is clearer still in *Jubilee*'s version of the rape of Dinah. Genesis has the young daughter of Jacob raped by an impetuous citizen of Shechem, son of the leader of that community. The offender, however, fell in love with Dinah and ardently sought her in marriage. Arrangements were made for a wholesale marriage alliance between the children of both houses, for which the Shechemites agreed even to have themselves circumcised on the insistence of Jacob's sons, the brothers of Dinah. But it was all a ruse. When the Shechemite men had undergone their surgery, rendering themselves sore and vulnerable, they were massacred by Levi and Simeon, sons of Jacob, who proceeded to loot the city of Shechem and carry off the women and children of the city. For that deed they earned the enduring hostility of their father.[36] *Jubilees* recasts the story with notable variation. Genesis had placed its focus on the rape of the girl and on vengeance exercised by her brothers for that foul deed. *Jubilees* condenses the narrative, omitting the negotiations for the agreement, the willingness of the Shechemites to undergo adult circumcision, and the anger of Jacob for the deception and ruthlessness of his sons. Instead the author sets the issue of exogamy to the fore. He has Dinah snatched away not by a single individual but by the Shechemites generally, thus implicating the entire community in the crime. That is a telling change. Then, having completed his abbreviated narrative, he draws the lessons in his own fashion. The rape of Dinah fades into the background, and the central message becomes that of avoiding intermarriage with the outsider. The text forecasts dire consequences for any Israelite who gives daughter or sister to the gentiles and foreshadows a Mosaic prohibition on such defilement for sons or daughters, a violation of which would bring plagues and curses on Israel.[37] The necessity of keeping the nation free of the pollution that crossbreeding would bring commands principal attention for the author of *Jubilees*.

The message reappears elsewhere in Second Temple texts. The *Testament of Levi* gives the supposed deathbed advice of Levi to his sons, which includes recommendations on marital partners: in addition to seeking wives who are blameless and pure, they are to avoid any who come from alien nations.[38] And the *Testament of Job*, an altogether separate composition, not part of the *Testaments of the Twelve Patriarchs*, nevertheless delivers the parallel pronouncement. Job's dying words to his children, in addition to exhortations to do good works, also add that they must take no wives from alien peoples.[39] The refrain recurs.

---

[36] Gen. 34, 49.5-7.
[37] *Jub.* 30.1-17. See Endres (1987), 120–139; VanderKam (2001), 67–69.
[38] *T. Levi* 9.10; cf. 14.6.
[39] *T. Job* 45.1-3.

Another text of the Hellenistic era draws the bonds of internality even tighter. The *Book of Tobit* trains its sights on kinship within clan and tribe. It may have taken its cue from the Torah where Moses, on instructions from Yahweh, declared that inheritance passes through the tribe and directed that marriages remain within the clan.[40] *Tobit*, however, takes the matter to another level. The work's hero introduces himself as having married a woman from the seed of his own family, a source of pride and a leitmotif throughout.[41] Two separate story lines drive the novel, eventually converging for a happy ending. One involves Tobit's son Tobias, dispatched on a mission by his dying father; the other features the luckless Sarah, whose efforts at marriage, terrorized by a demon, sent seven consecutive suitors to their doom on their wedding nights. All seven had been kinsmen, and Sarah laments that she has run out of kin—the only appropriate husbands to maintain the household of her father.[42] Tobit's advice to his son includes the admonition to wed only one from his own tribe, as did the patriarchs of old, and to shun all alien wives. Endogamy had thus become very taut indeed. Never mind Moabites or Ammonites. For the author of *Tobit*, "alien wife" had now been reinterpreted to mean anyone outside the clan.[43] Tobias had the good fortune to be steered to the house of Raguel, father of Sarah, by the angel Raphael, who forecast his future wedding. Indeed a wedding to Sarah, according to Raphael, is not only desirable but inevitable. Tobias proved to be her nearest of kin, hence the appropriate husband with other relatives now dead, a bond enjoined by Mosaic law.[44] Here was a marriage truly made in heaven, as the text indicates: Sarah and Tobias had been destined for one another from the beginning of time.[45]

The meaning of all this may lie beneath the surface. So intimate are the familial bonds in this novel that practically every character in the story, far-flung though they might be, is a relative of Tobit. The individuals, with numbing repetition (no fewer than sixty-six times!), greet one another as "brother" and "sister"—no matter what their actual relationship to one another.[46] The only personage of note in the tale who is not a relative is the angel Raphael. And even he (arriving in disguise) has to establish his credentials to Tobit by claiming to be the son of his kinsman.[47] This is a tight

---

[40] Num. 36.
[41] *Tobit* 1.9.
[42] *Tobit* 3.15.
[43] *Tobit* 4.12–13. Cf. Moore (1996), 168–169.
[44] *Tobit* 6.11–13; Moore (1996), 203–205; Fitzmyer (2003), 210–214. On Hebrew levirate law (Deut. 25.5–10), which may govern inheritance rights in cases of this sort, see Davies (1981), 138–144, 257–268.
[45] *Tobit* 6.16–18., 7.10–12. Cf. Fitzmyer (2003), 230–234.
[46] Wills (1995), 78; Gruen (2002a), 157.
[47] *Tobit* 5.11–13.

circle indeed, endogamy with a vengeance. Perhaps too tight. One need not take the portrait seriously. *Tobit* contains more parody than earnestness.[48] But it was plainly parodying something. The principle of endogamy still had force in the society of Hellenistic Judaism.

Marriages of the patriarchs could be an embarrassment in this connection. Joseph, according to a few very brief notices in Genesis, was wed to a certain Aseneth, daughter of the Egyptian priest Potiphar, who bore him two children.[49] That was awkward for those who promoted the precepts of endogamy. A new and original tale emerged probably in the Hellenistic or early Roman periods, bowing, of course, to the testimony of Genesis but placing a wholly new spin on the union of the Hebrew patriarch and the Egyptian woman.[50] The story, *Joseph and Aseneth*, a Greek composition produced in Jewish circles, reinterprets the marriage as consequence of a thoroughgoing, humbling, even abject embrace by Aseneth of the religion of Joseph. The young Egyptian wept and wailed, renounced her former heresies, smashed all her idols to pieces, put on sackcloth and ashes, refrained from any food and drink, pulled hairs from her head, repeatedly beat herself around the head and breasts, denounced herself unremittingly for devotion to false gods, and pleaded desperately for compassion from the Lord.[51] The debasement seems a bit excessive. But even that did not suffice. It took a visit from an angelic figure to advise Aseneth on how to behave and dress, a full-scale remake of the maid, plus a mysterious ceremony to prepare her fully for the nuptials to come.[52] Only then did Joseph accept her as his bride, an acceptance culminated by Aseneth's washing the feet of the man whom she now acknowledged as her lord. And it is noteworthy that the young woman's accreditation did not come until Joseph's kisses infused her with the spirit of life, wisdom, and truth.[53]

The narrative plainly portrays a total transformation on the part of Aseneth. She had to divest herself of foreignness in order to enter the world of Joseph. This nicely circumvents the problem of alien marriage. The novel had already made a strong statement about irreconcilable differences between Jew and Egyptian. When Joseph entered the house of Aseneth's father (called Pentephres in the novel), he refused to eat at the

---

[48] Gruen (2002a), 148–158.

[49] Genesis 41.45, 41.50–52, 46.20.

[50] The date is much disputed. See, among others, the diverse conclusions of Burchard (1965), 143–151; Philonenko (1968), 108–109; S. West (1974), 79–81; Sänger (1985), 90–104; Chesnutt (1995), 80–85; Standhartinger (1995), 16–20; Kraemer (1998), 225–244.

[51] *Jos. As.* 9–13.

[52] *Jos. As.* 14–17. The meaning of the mystifying actions of the heavenly figure remains as mystifying as ever. See the ingenious, but highly speculative, conjectures of Bohak (1996), 1–18.

[53] *Jos. As.* 19–20.

same table with Egyptians, which he reckoned as abhorrent—thus turning upside down their own horror at sharing a meal with Israelites.[54] And when Aseneth approached Joseph for the first time, offering him a kiss on her father's prompting, Joseph rebuffed her unceremoniously. He physically pushed her away, declaring that no man who worships the living God can bestow a kiss on an alien woman whose mouth has blessed deaf and dumb idols; nor would he eat and drink from a table defiled by their contamination. The same prohibition holds for any contact between a God-fearing woman and a foreigner.[55] Association with a foreigner, as Jacob had warned Joseph, can bring only corruption and destruction.[56] Aseneth had to undergo a proper metamorphosis. The novel had indirectly forecast it from the outset, when the young virgin was described as similar in no way to the maids of Egypt but fully reminiscent of Sarah, Rebecca, and Rachel.[57]

The dichotomy seems stark. The gulf between Jew and gentile can be surmounted only by unequivocal renunciation by the latter and embrace by the former. *Joseph and Aseneth* therefore appears to restate the fundamental antithesis and to reinforce the contrast between the cultures.[58] That message certainly stands out in the text, and the attitude must reflect some external reality. Yet, as in the case of *Tobit*, the author subtly undermines and subverts it. The terms "Jew" and "gentile" appear nowhere in the novel. The "conversion" of Aseneth in any theological sense meant simply the abandonment of idolatry. Joseph's own creed gains no definition beyond worship of a single god. Most notably, the wedding of Joseph and Aseneth had as attendants all the nobility and leadership of Egypt, and took place under the auspices of the pharaoh himself, the very embodiment of the Egyptian kingdom—who had undergone no form of conversion.[59] The gentile ruler sanctioned the union of the Hebrew patriarch and the daughter of an Egyptian priest. Antagonism between the nations is thus softened and compromised. *Joseph and Aseneth* is a complex work, not readily subject to reductionism.

The ambiguity of texts like *Tobit* and *Joseph and Aseneth* causes some misgivings, and should prompt some rethinking. How committed were Jews to keeping gentiles at arm's length? How vital was the sense of separateness to the construct of Jewish identity? How firm was the principle—let alone the practice—of shunning intermarriage?

[54] *Jos. As.* 7.1; cf. Gen. 43.32.
[55] *Jos. As.* 8.4–7.
[56] *Jos. As.* 7.5.
[57] *Jos. As.* 1.5.
[58] So Philonenko (1968), 48–52; Sänger (1985), 96–100; Chesnutt (1995), 97–108; Barclay (1996), 204–216.
[59] *Jos. As.* 20.6–21.8. Cf. Goldenberg (1997), 75–78; Gruen (1998), 94–96.

The Bible's Other Side

Some of the Bible's most central figures hardly qualified as ideal advertisements for endogamy. Abraham may have wanted a hometown girl for Isaac. But he himself had taken as wife Hagar, the Egyptian maidservant of Sarah, for purposes of procreation.[60] A later wife, Keturah, may well have been a non-Israelite also.[61] Joseph dodged the desires of Potiphar's wife but married an Egyptian anyway, daughter of a different Potiphar.[62] Other sons of Jacob also wed gentile women, according to *Jubilees*. Simeon and Judah married Canaanites, and Naphtali a Mesopotamian. Simeon later changed his mind—but only to marry a Mesopotamian.[63] Moses received as wife the daughter of a Midianite priest, bestowing on his son by her a name that signified his status as alien in a foreign land. Yet he neither shrank from the marriage nor regretted it. That union was defended by God himself.[64] Later, Gideon, Israel's great general and conqueror of the Midianites, took a Shechemite as a secondary wife, and the hero Samson became involved with a series of Philistines, at least one of whom he wed.[65] The outcomes may have been undesirable, but there is no suggestion that the unions in any way transgressed fundamental prohibitions.[66] The same holds for David's marriage to a daughter of the king of Geshur—and indeed to Bathsheba, widow of Uriah the Hittite, and very possibly a Hittite herself.[67] Most notoriously, Solomon's voracious appetite for women brought hundreds of royal wives to his bed, including not only the daughter of the pharaoh but Moabites, Ammonites, Edomites, Sidonians, and Hittites. Yahweh, of course, was mightily displeased. But the displeasure stemmed from Solomon's temptation toward the gods of his foreign wives, rather than from the crossbreeding itself.[68] Gentile women can be seductive and dangerous. Yet strict segregation need not be the answer.

The drive for separatism was far from absolute. Biblical texts supply substantial testimony to that effect. The people of Israel could be quite comfortable with mingling and mixture. An important illustration serves to make this point with some force: the very origins of the nation as conceived

---

[60] Gen. 16.1–3.
[61] Gen. 25.1. Cf. Westermann (1985), 395–396.
[62] Gen. 41.45.
[63] *Jub.* 34.20; on Simeon, see also Gen. 46.10.
[64] Exod. 2.16–22; Num. 12.1–8.
[65] Judg. 8.30–31, 14–16.
[66] Samson's parents wondered why he chose the daughter of uncircumcised Philistines when there were so many Israelite women available, but they cited no formal ban; Judg. 14.3.
[67] 2 Samuel 3.3, 11.2–3, 11.27.
[68] 1 Kings 11.1–11.

in the book of Exodus. When the Israelites departed from Egypt, they were accompanied by a "mixed multitude."[69] That is no inadvertent notice. Reference to non-Israelites who were part of the Exodus recurs more than once in the Bible—and even in Hellenistic Egyptian writers, recasting the tale for their own purposes.[70] Just who these foreigners were has been the subject of much speculation but need not detain us.[71] What matters is that Jews themselves conceived the shaping of their nation in combination with gentiles. The inauguration of the Passover ceremony followed shortly thereafter. As mark of Israelite distinctiveness, its commemoration takes a central place. Yet there is a noteworthy ambivalence between inclusion and exclusion in this vital matter. The Lord declared to Moses and Aaron that the whole community of Israel must partake of the Passover but that no foreigner may do so, nor any stranger or hired servant. This unequivocal assertion of Israelite identity, however, is immediately qualified. A purchased slave can participate once he is circumcised. So also can any resident alien, provided that all members of his household undergo circumcision. He will then enjoy the same status as a native-born. Indeed, so Yahweh concluded, there will be but one law for the native and the resident alien.[72] The ambiguous language and peculiar sequence of thought in this segment on the "Pesach rule" leaves much room for dispute on interpretation.[73] But it merits emphasis that circumcision, rather than ethnic origin, determines eligibility for belonging to the Israelite community.[74] Rigid rules hold, but entrance into that community is available to the gentile. In the defining moment for Israel, this is a token of the utmost importance.

Biblical texts reinforce this principle with some frequency. Openness to the alien gains recurrent expression. The fact that foreigners dwelled amidst the Israelites is implicit—and taken for granted—in repeated divine pronouncements. They adjure the children of Israel not to wrong or oppress aliens who live among them, a reminder that they were once themselves aliens in the land of Egypt.[75] That admonition takes a more precise form in the passage that prohibits Ammonites and Moabites from joining the congregation of Yahweh. For the singling out of those nations contrasts sharply with the exhortation to welcome others. The Lord asserts that Edomites and Egyptians are admissible after the third generation: Edomites

---

[69] Exod. 12.37–38.
[70] Num. 11.4; Deut. 29.10; Josh. 8.35; Jos. *CAp.* 1.234, 1.290.
[71] Propp (1999), 414–415.
[72] Exod. 12.43–49; Num. 9.14, 15.15–16.
[73] See the treatment, with bibliography, of Propp (1999), 416–421.
[74] Cf. S. Cohen (1999), 123–125.
[75] Exod. 22.21, 23.9; Lev. 19.33–34; Deut. 5.14–15, 10.19, 16.11–12, 24.18–22, 27.19.

should be treated as brothers and Egyptians respected, for Israelites were once strangers in that land.[76]

The prophet conventionally labeled as "Third-Isaiah" makes a telling declaration on this score. He delivers the words of Yahweh on the reception of outsiders. No foreigner who has joined himself to the Lord will be excluded from his people. Nor will eunuchs be rejected if they observe the Sabbath and keep to the Covenant. The sacrifices and offerings of the foreigner will be acceptable on the Lord's altar. God's house will be known as a house of prayer for all peoples.[77] The gentile might not have welcomed bracketing with the eunuch. But the sentiment is noble and comprehensive.

The idea of Yahweh as god of all nations, no mere parochial deity, surfaces, albeit rarely, in the prophetic material. The lofty manifesto of Third-Isaiah coheres with a dictum of Malachi, who proclaims Yahweh as honored from farthest east to farthest west, his name great among the nations.[78] Amos puts the point more forcefully in conveying Yahweh's anger at the Israelites. They are in the same category as other peoples whom the Lord has also accorded his favor: "Are you Israelites not the same to me as the Kushites? Did I not bring Israel from Egypt, the Philistines from Caphtor, and the Arameans from Kir?"[79] And Ezekiel conjures up a vision of the future in which the heritage of Israel will be distributed not only to the tribes but to those foreigners who dwell among them.[80]

Diverse strands complicate the picture. A piecemeal pastiche of passages will not readily settle the matter. But certain stories, spun as separate narratives, have a life of their own and provide a more telling commentary on the Jewish perception of non-Jews.

First, the tale of Judah and Tamar. The engaging narrative occurs somewhat awkwardly in the midst of the Joseph story, whether as an intrusive insertion or as a subtle linkage of parts.[81] Judah, fourth son of Jacob, was instrumental in persuading his brothers to spare Joseph's life but also in prompting his sale as a slave. The Genesis account has Judah wed a Canaanite woman who bore him three sons. As wife for Er, his firstborn, Judah

---

[76] Deut. 23.8–9.

[77] Isa. 56.3–7, 60.7, 66.18–22; cf. 1 Kings 8.41–43. This is a noteworthy shift from Deut. 23.1, where eunuchs are excluded from the community of the Covenant. On the acceptance of sacrifices by gentiles, see further Lev. 17.8–16, 22.17–25; Num. 15.13–16. A different view is expressed in Ezek. 44.5–9, which represents Yahweh as angry at the admission of aliens to the Temple cult.

[78] Mal. 1.11. This is somewhat at odds with his earlier remarks at 1.2–4, which denounce the Edomites.

[79] Amos, 9.7. Cf. Hendel (2002), 67–69.

[80] Ezek. 47.22–23, with Bertholet (1896), 110–113. On the prophets and "universalism" generally, see Bertholet (1896), 91–104.

[81] For the latter view, against the bulk of scholarship, see Alter (1981), 3–12.

found a certain Tamar. But the marriage ended abruptly when Yahweh, offended by something that Er had done, ended his life. Judah then arranged that Tamar marry his second son, Onan, in expectation that he would do his proper duty, namely, produce a son who would carry on the line of his brother. But Onan would not go along with the plan. Irritated that any progeny of his would simply be proxy for his dead brother's stock, he decided to practice *coitus interruptus*, spilling his seed on the ground as Genesis puts it. How often he got away with this we are not told. But Yahweh would have none of this wastage of good semen, and eradicated Onan too. Judah was down to one son—and was understandably nervous about his possible fate. This youth too was promised to Tamar in order to keep the line intact. But Judah was in no hurry to have the arrangement implemented. Tamar could wait until young Shelah grew up. In the meantime she was ordered to go back and live with her father. Judah, it appears, had no intention of going through with the bargain, lest the boy end up like his brothers.[82]

Much time passed. It evidently dawned on Tamar that she might have to wait forever. Shelah had grown up, and nothing happened. Judah himself was now available, having lost his wife and gone through the period of mourning. Tamar then decided to take matters into her own hands. When she learned that Judah planned to be in her vicinity to have his sheep sheared, she developed a scheme to ensnare him. She disguised herself, covering her face with a veil, and sat down at an entrance gate. Judah, who encountered her there, took her for a prostitute (as she evidently intended), and did not hesitate to ask for her sexual favors. Tamar replied by bargaining for the night's events. Judah pledged to send a kid from the flock as payment, and the bargain was struck—but only after Tamar extracted from him certain tokens to serve as promissory notes: his personal seal, cord, and staff, unmistakable markers of identity. The arrangement was made, a night of passion followed, and Tamar became pregnant.[83]

The plot now thickens. Judah sent a friend with the promised kid in order to recover his identity tokens. But the purported prostitute was nowhere to be found, and inhabitants of the area denied that any such person existed. Judah's friend returned empty-handed and baffled. This put the old man in a pretty fix. It would be rather embarrassing to conduct a wholesale search for a tart, thereby to make a laughingstock of himself. Better to let her keep the insignia (he had at least made an effort) and forget the whole thing.[84]

Tamar in the meantime began showing. Word got out to Judah that his daughter-in-law had played the whore and had conceived a child in her

[82] Gen. 38.1–11.
[83] Gen. 38.12–19.
[84] Gen. 38.20–23.

waywardness. Judah ordered Tamar to be hauled off and burned alive. But she had hatched her scheme shrewdly. Tamar produced the tokens, announcing that their owner had made her pregnant. The scales fell from Judah's eyes; he acknowledged the objects as his own and had to admit that Tamar was more righteous than he—for he had not carried out his promise to wed her to his son Shelah. The chastened Judah refrained from further intercourse with his daughter-in-law. But the story is not quite over. Tamar gave birth to twins. And quite an interesting birth it was. The first child to emerge from the womb stuck out a hand, and the alert midwife immediately tied a crimson thread around it, so as to be sure to identify the twin who had the rights of the firstborn. As it happened, however, this one withdrew his hand again, and his brother successfully scrambled to get out ahead of him, leaving the baby with the crimson thread to emerge a close second. The first was then aptly named Perez, meaning "breach."[85] The narrative ends there. But the knowledgeable reader would know what a pregnant event this indeed was. Perez turned out to be the direct ancestor of King David himself—and ultimately, according to the constructed genealogy, of none other than Jesus Christ.[86]

Such is the story, entertaining and memorable. Not perhaps quite as familiar as many of the other Genesis legends, for it is a bit too raunchy to become standard fare in the Sunday school curriculum. But it holds compelling interest for our purposes. Maintenance of the line of Judah, with priority to the firstborn, forms a central element of the yarn. Yet Tamar was evidently more committed to keeping the tight household intact than was Judah himself. Who was Tamar, and where did she come from? The narrator is remarkably reticent on this key point. But he leaves some hints and clues that she was no Israelite. Judah had gone to settle in Adullam, where he found a Canaanite wife and presumably where he gave Tamar as wife for his first son—at least there is no indication that he had to send home for a wife.[87] Tamar's family dwells in the vicinity of Timnah, evidently in Canaan.[88] And she receives no Israelite pedigree in the text. Later writers drew what seemed to be logical conclusions from this silence. *Jubilees* identifies Tamar as among the daughters of Aram, thus perhaps an Aramean.[89] In the *Testament of Judah*, she is brought from Mesopotamia to be the bride of Judah's firstborn.[90] Philo takes the assumption to yet a further level: Tamar

---

[85] Gen. 38.24–30.
[86] Ruth, 4.12–22; 1 Chron. 2.4–15; Matt. 1.3–16.
[87] Gen. 38.1–6.
[88] Gen. 38.11–14. On the location, see Emerton (1975), 343–346.
[89] *Jub.* 41; cf. VanderKam (2001), 79.
[90] *Test. Judah* 10.1. For Emerton (1976), 90–93, the authors of *Jubilees* and the *Testament of Judah* found the idea of Tamar as Canaanite unacceptable and hence sought a different origin for her.

stemmed from Syria, an idol worshipper who honored a multitude of gods but became the quintessential proselyte to the life of piety.[91]

Why the silence in Genesis? Some suggest that the text reflects the reality of a mixed ethnic population in the region of Judah that encompassed Canaanites as well as Israelites, even perhaps the reworking of a Canaanite tale.[92] If so, the absence of any explicit reference to Tamar's ethnicity would seem to dilute the thesis. Others take the reverse line: the text deliberately suppresses Tamar's non-Israelite origins, thus to skirt the problem of prohibition against intermarriage.[93] But the most striking fact surely is that the issue of ethnicity simply does not arise. It becomes a matter of concern, to be sure, for the author of *Jubilees*, who has Judah's son wish to honor his mother's nation and marry a Canaanite, then be forbidden to do so by Judah.[94] The *Testament of Judah* goes further. It has Judah apologize for his marriage to a Canaanite by blaming it on youthful passion and strong drink—adding indeed that the later dalliance with Tamar was brought about by a similar condition. Ironically enough, the drive for endogamy in this text is ascribed not to Judah or to Tamar but to the insistent Canaanite mother who sought to keep her sons within the bloodlines of Canaan![95]

None of this, however, appears in Genesis. The author of the tale shows not the slightest worry about ethnic mixture. Judah's marriage to a Canaanite passes without comment. And Tamar's genealogy, though evidently non-Israelite, causes no misgivings among the characters. It is the Israelite patriarch who comes off badly in the narrative. His espousal of levirate marriage as a means of continuing his line falls short of Tamar's own commitment to that principle.[96] His little fling with a supposed harlot lands him in comic chagrin, and his misjudgment of his daughter-in-law requires him to eat humble pie.[97] Tamar, not a member of the clan, emerges as the more clever, successful, and admirable figure. She shrewdly entraps and manipulates Judah, she gains her objective of becoming a mother, and she manages personally to perpetuate the line of the patriarch. And all this was

---

[91] Philo *Virt.* 21

[92] Speiser (1964), 300; von Rad (1972), 357; Emerton (1979), 410–414; Westermann (1986), 50.

[93] Cf. Menn (1997), 54–55.

[94] *Jubilees*, 41.1–2.

[95] *Test. Judah* 10–11. Menn's idea that this is a means of demonstrating Yahweh's universalism, (1997), 146–147, is hard to credit.

[96] On levirate marriage, see Deut. 25.5–10. The institution itself was evidently questionable, and marriage to a brother-in-law is expressly forbidden in Lev. 18.16, 20.21. But perhaps procreation, rather than marriage, was the principal issue. Cf. Thompson and Thompson (1968), 88–96; Coats (1972), 461–466.

[97] Judah had also (though unwittingly) violated the biblical proscription against having intercourse with one's daughter-in-law; Lev. 18.15. On some comedic aspects of the tale, see Whedbee (1998), 108–111; Spencer (2003), 13–15; Shields (2003), 31–51.

accomplished without divine assistance. God makes no appearance in the narrative; Tamar handled the matter on her own.[98]

The tale, attractive and appealing on a number of fronts, should not, however, be mistaken for a feminist tract (even if that term were applicable). Tamar's accomplishment certainly earned the author's praise. But the praise derived in no small part from Tamar's success in assuring continuity of the patriarchal clan—far more successful on that front than the patriarch himself.[99] And the long-term consequences need to be underscored: Tamar's progeny, with non-Israelite blood, eventually issued in the house of David.

That startling fact has significant echoes elsewhere. The book of Ruth develops the message in fruitful and fascinating ways. The endearing tale has long been a favorite, and justly so. It is set in the days of the Judges, when a famine hit the land of Judah. Elimelech, his wife Naomi, and their two sons pulled up stakes from their home in Bethlehem and settled in Moab. The two sons both married Moabite women. Our text describes the event without consternation or commentary. No suggestion that Moab was dangerous territory or that law and custom forbade unions with Moabites.[100] The relocation, however, proved in the long run not to be propitious. Elimelech died, and after another decade both sons were dead as well. Naomi was left alone without male protection and no near of kin apart from her daughters-in-law, both of them now widows. Naomi decided to return to her ancestral home, her daughters-in-law eager to accompany her. She did her best to persuade them to stay, insisting that she was too old for remarriage and certainly too old to produce more sons for them to marry. Even if she could, the young women could hardly be expected to hold themselves in readiness while the boys grew up. After much weeping and wailing, Naomi's entreaties succeeded with one of the daughters-in-law but got nowhere with the other. Ruth clung to Naomi and delivered the moving and memorable sentiments forever associated with her: "whither you go, I will go; wherever you dwell, I will dwell; your people are my people, and your gods my gods." Ruth's resolve was unswerving, and Naomi yielded. The two women made their way to Bethlehem in dire straits, with no obvious means of livelihood and an ostensibly bleak future.[101]

After resettlement in Bethlehem, Ruth received Naomi's permission to glean in the barley fields, an ancient Israelite practice allowing the landless poor to gather the remaining crops that were not harvested by the proprietors.[102] The Moabite woman had the good fortune of choosing for her

---

[98] For a different view, see, most recently, Sawyer (2002), 58–64, who perceives an overriding theology in these events.
[99] For a similar analysis, see Spina (2005), 35–51.
[100] Ruth 1.1–4; cf. Spina (2005), 120–121.
[101] Ruth 1.5–22. For *elohim* as a genuine plural here, see Goldenberg (1997), 16.
[102] Cf. Lev. 19.9–10, 23.22; Deut. 24.19–22.

task the land of Boaz, who happened to be a kinsman of Naomi's late husband—and also a man of great generosity and goodwill. This is presented as a stroke of luck, not an act of God. But matters now, at last, took a more favorable turn. When Boaz learned of Ruth's identity, he insisted that she do all her gleaning in his fields, he asked her to follow closely in the footsteps of his own female laborers, and he instructed his men to keep their hands off her. Ruth, overwhelmed with this unexpected magnanimity, asked what she had done to earn such favor. Boaz knew her story by then. He praised her for the great loyalty she showed to Naomi, abandoning her own parents and home, entering a strange land, and looking only to the interests of her mother-in-law. He provided her with food, permitted her to glean to her heart's content, and made it possible for her to bring a substantial haul back home. Naomi, once she learned whose barley fields Ruth had stumbled upon, greeted the news with joy and informed her of Boaz's relationship to the family (he had not identified himself to Ruth). Ruth proceeded to glean regularly until the harvest season was over.[103]

Now things begin to get really interesting. Naomi realized that the yield from the harvest, welcome though it was, would provide no permanent solution. Boaz had been kind and generous. But the whole harvest season had passed, and he had made no pass at Ruth. Naomi came up with a more promising scheme. Boaz, as she knew, was hard at work winnowing the grain on the threshing floor. That labor, followed by a hearty meal and drink, would induce a good sleep. Naomi advised Ruth to pretty herself up, go to the threshing floor, and stay out of sight until Boaz dropped off to sleep. Then she should lie at his feet and uncover.[104] Just what is to be uncovered is a matter of considerable controversy and stimulating speculation. The words employed refer to feet. But uncovering Boaz's feet is rather a tame act. "Feet," however, can sometimes stand for "legs," which gets more interesting. Or indeed as a euphemism for genitals, rather more interesting still.[105] And who is being exposed here? Boaz or Ruth? That too is disputed, and one cannot presume to pronounce definitively on the question. But there can be little doubt that this is a seduction scene of some sort. Ruth was not just playing footsy. Why else would Naomi suggest that Ruth doll herself up, sneak surreptitiously into Boaz's slumber, and then engage in a bit of disrobing? This may not have been, as one commentator suggests, a midnight striptease. But it was hardly an innocent sleepover. Naomi's last words to Ruth before she went off were "Boaz will tell you what to do." That puts the point quite bluntly.

[103] Ruth 2.1–18.
[104] Ruth 3.1–4.
[105] See Campbell (1975), 121, 131–132; Nielsen (1997), 67–70; van Wolde (1997), 443–445; Zakovitch (1999), 137; Spencer (2003), 18–19; LaCocque (2004), 84–85, 91–92.

Ruth acted dutifully in accord with her mother-in-law's suggestion. She uncovered whatever it was that she uncovered. Boaz awoke with a start and groped about, finding to his surprise that there was a woman lying at his feet. He did not seem displeased. Ruth, having identified herself, asked Boaz to spread his garment over her since he is her "redeemer."[106] The meaning here again is contested. Ruth's gesture may be a symbolic form of requesting protection and indeed proposing marriage. Or perhaps it simply asked Boaz to bring them both under the covers, thus to allow matters to take their course.[107] The sexual implications, in any case, can hardly be denied. Boaz expresses pleasure that Ruth came to him rather than going after younger men. He asks her to stay the night. And, most tellingly, he made sure that she left before anyone saw her. No one was supposed to know, he said, that a woman had come down to the threshing floor.[108] There is not much ambiguity there.

The night's escapade had its desired result. Boaz now proclaimed his readiness to undertake the duty of "redeemer." This involved in some way his responsibility as near of kin to redeem Naomi's property. But one other man had a better claim on next of kin, and had to be offered his chance first. A bargain took place before a selection of the town's elders at the gate of Bethlehem. The anonymous next of kin proved willing to accept the role of redeemer so far as acquisition of property was concerned. But when Boaz added that the redeemer would also acquire Ruth, with the obligation to perpetuate the line and the inheritance of her dead husband, he demurred. He had no intention of jeopardizing his own inheritance. That left the field clear for Boaz. He would now take on the task of redeemer. He would purchase the estate that had once belonged to Elimelech and then to his two sons, and claim the right to marry Ruth, thereby to continue the family name into subsequent generations. The company at the gate bore witness to the transaction, and the deal was struck.[109]

The legal aspects of this exchange need not concern us here. They involve ambiguities and complexities that may not ultimately be subject to resolution. The obligation of next of kin to provide a means of continuing the family name when a widow was childless clearly has affinities with the story of Tamar. Whether this counts as a "levirate marriage" as prescribed in Deuteronomy, however, is more problematic. No brother-in-law is involved here. Boaz indeed intends an enduring marriage, not just the fulfillment of the next of kin's duty to supply a son, as did Judah, who subsequently forbore to have intercourse with Tamar. And the relationship

---

[106] Ruth 3.5–9.
[107] See discussions by Campbell (1975), 123; Nielsen (1997), 72–74; Pressler (2002), 289–290; LaCocque (2004), 86–87, 94–97.
[108] Ruth 3.10–14.
[109] Ruth 4.1–11.

between this responsibility and the "redeemer's" charge to reclaim land belonging to the next of kin remains obscure.[110] These matters can be set aside. Boaz, in any case, claimed Ruth as his bride, to maintain the house of Elimelech, while witnesses gave their blessing and expressed their favor toward the union. Indeed they called on Yahweh to make it fruitful on the model of Rachel and Leah, the wives of Jacob who between them built the house of Israel. And they made explicit reference to the house of Perez, the firstborn of Tamar and Judah—or at least the one who first pushed himself out of the womb, shoving his brother back in to gain priority.[111]

The connection gains further emphasis at the conclusion of the tale. Boaz wed Ruth, who shortly thereafter conceived and give birth to a boy. The child, intended as sustainer of the house of Elimelech, was, in fact, given to Naomi to nurture, the future mainstay of her old age. And the women of the neighborhood proclaimed him as the long-awaited son of Naomi.[112] The text provides a genealogy at its close, a final linkage of the chain that goes back to Tamar and looks ahead to David. The child received the name Obed. He would be the sire of Jesse, father of David. The line in fact began with Perez and produced in the tenth generation, as we learn for the first time, none other than Boaz.[113]

The significance of this lineage can hardly be overstated. The text lists only the male members of Perez's line. But the stories of Tamar and Ruth have already disclosed their pivotal and indispensable roles in providing the continuity of that line, the one perhaps a Canaanite and the other a Moabite. The implications carry real importance.

Some have tried to explain them away. The genealogy, it can be argued, is detachable from the story of Ruth, affixed later by supporters of the house of David or by those who sought to refurbish his reputation.[114] On this view, David's Moabite ancestry was a historical fact that could not be swept under the rug. And a connection to Moabites continued to carry a severe stigma. Opponents of David or of his line could use it, presumably had used it, to discredit him. One way to counter the propaganda, since the ancestry could not be denied, was to tie the lineage to an edifying tale in

---

[110] The key text on levirate law is Deut. 25.5–10. On redemption of property, see Lev. 25.23–25; Jer. 32.6–12. For treatment of the legal issues, cf. Thompson and Thompson (1968), 79–99; Beattie (1974), 251–267; Campbell (1975), 132–137, 157–161; Carmichael (1977), 321–336; Sasson (1989), 125–129; Nielsen (1997), 74–76, 84–89, with additional bibliography; LaCocque (2004), 108–118.

[111] Ruth 4.11–12.

[112] Ruth 4.13–17.

[113] Ruth 4.17–18. The lineage appears also in 1 Chron. 2.3–5, 2.9–15.

[114] Hubbard (1988), 293–301. For Sasson (1989) 178–183, 232–240, the genealogy was an integral part of the book from the start, designed to bolster David's claim to the throne. For a different view, see Zakovitch (1999), 172–173. That the genealogy is an integral part of the work is argued recently by LaCocque (2004), 148–150.

which the Moabite heroine sets a shining example.[115] That idea operates on a questionable premise: that Moabite descent constituted a blemish that had to be whitewashed or wiped away. But to take that assumption as starting point is to beg the question. What reason is there to presume the historicity of David's Moabite blood? Because no one would have invented it? Another tradition includes the Canaanite prostitute Rahab among David's foremothers. Few would reckon that as a fact of history.[116] Further, Ruth's ethnicity is nowhere concealed. The text identifies her as a Moabite on several occasions.[117] In none of those instances is ethnicity an issue. Elimelech brought his family to Moab unhesitatingly when a famine hit Judah, both sons married women from that land, and Ruth's origins never gave Boaz any pause. If David required defense against charges that his great-grandmother was a Moabite, the tale of Ruth would hardly mollify the critics.[118] The attachment of David's lineage as an annex to the novella, or indeed the invention of the story to give the lineage respectability, seems a real stretch. What reader would come away from this text feeling that David had been cleared of Moabite taint? Far easier to believe that associations between the peoples raised no problem. Ruth, after all, is not portrayed as the "good Moabite," in contradistinction to her compatriots. They had readily accepted the family of Elimelech in Moab—and they were equally acceptable in Judah.

On a different analysis, the book of Ruth represents a broadside against the advocates of exclusionism, as represented by Ezra, Nehemiah, and their followers.[119] Their rigorous insistence on endogamous marriages, part of the campaign to establish ascendancy against rivals after the Exile, then provoked a reaction by the more liberal-minded. The Ruth tale thus exemplifies the "universalist" trend as against the narrow parochialism that prevailed. The dichotomy, however, is simplistic. And the book of Ruth reads like anything but a polemical tract.[120] No villains appear in the piece. And the propriety of intermarriage is simply taken for granted. The tale lacks any hint of a battleground.

Is this a story of "assimilation"? Ruth the Moabitess clings to Naomi. Most famously she vows not only to make Naomi's home her own but to

---

[115] Campbell (1975), 169; A. Anderson (1978), 171–183; LaCocque (1990), 84–116; Nielsen (1997), 21–28, 96–99. Friendly relations between David and Moab appear in 1 Sam. 22.3–4, but no genealogical connection.

[116] Matt. 1.1–6. See the appropriate skepticism of LaCocque (1990), 89–90.

[117] Ruth 1.4, 1.22, 2.2, 2.6, 2.21, 4.5, 4.10.

[118] In the view of LaCocque (2004), 11–12, 19–21, the genealogy could have been composed only when David's reputation was no longer in dispute.

[119] Cf. LaCocque (1990), 99–100; Goulder (1993), 307–319; Zakovitch (1999), 38–41; Pressler (2002), 266; LaCocque (2004), 2, 18–28.

[120] So rightly Campbell (1975), 26–27.

make Naomi's gods her own.[121] The novella, on this analysis, lauds not so much Israelite openness and broad-mindedness toward the "Other," as the decision of the Moabite woman to abandon her idols and embrace Yahweh. In short, it represents a conversion narrative.[122] That interpretation too, however, misses the point. The pledge to Naomi was a personal pledge, not a religious decision. It is no accident that the text repeatedly refers to Ruth as a Moabite, well after she had implemented her commitment to Naomi. One might observe that all the invocations of Yahweh that occur in the work are uttered by characters other than Ruth. The only exception comes in Ruth's initial vow to stick with Naomi through thick and thin. And here, far from calling on Yahweh as her new safeguard and champion, she asserts that, no matter what Yahweh may do to her, only death will part her from Naomi.[123] If this is a conversion story, it is rather weak stuff. Indeed Yahweh barely has an impact in the narrative. Characters appeal to his name. But Yahweh in fact appears only twice. Naomi decides to return to Judah when she learns that the famine had ended and Yahweh had brought food back to his people.[124] And, near the end of the tale, Yahweh made Ruth conceive, and she gave birth to a son.[125] So Yahweh can bring bread and babies. Beyond that there is little discernible theology in the novella.[126] Individuals make the decisions and take the decisive steps. Ruth overcomes Naomi's objections and moves to Bethlehem with her. Naomi hatches the scheme to bring Ruth together with Boaz. And Boaz conducts the negotiations that carry the scheme to fruition. God enters the picture only to make sure that Ruth will deliver a boy. Religion does not stand front and center. And the tale does not push for conversion. Ruth made an independent choice without theological overtones.[127]

None of this turns Ruth into a feminist heroine. Apart from the initial decision to accompany Naomi, her role is a relatively passive one. Naomi instructs her on how to carry out the seduction—and adds that Boaz will tell her what to do! Ruth dutifully caries out the instructions. She is a

[121] Ruth 1.16–17.
[122] Ozick (1994), 211–232.
[123] Ruth 1.17. Cf. Zakovitch (1999), 98.
[124] Ruth 1.6.
[125] Ruth 4.13.
[126] Cf. Larkin (1996), 50–52; Zakovitch (1999), 22–24; Pressler (2002), 268–269. Contra: Sawyer (2002), 80–86.
[127] Honig (1999), 62–64, rightly has reservations about the idea of a conversion. But her proposal that Ruth's claim to embrace Naomi's god was simply a reassurance that she would be no trouble to her host at home trivializes the scene. Brenner (1999), 158–162, goes further still, comparing Ruth to a foreign worker who had no choice in the matter, performed a verbal contract to care for her patroness, received only the privileges that her employer accorded her, and had no right even to reclaim her baby who was taken by Naomi. This scenario departs wholesale from the text. A more balanced view in Campbell (1975), 80–82.

mere pawn in the transactions that take place between Boaz and Naomi's next of kin. And, after giving birth to her child, she disappears from the scene. Naomi and the women of Bethlehem take over. As in the case of Tamar (though she is a more active participant in her story), the patriarchal needs hold prime of place. Ruth serves as an instrument to assure the continuity of Elimelech's heritage and to give Boaz a place in the lineage that would culminate in David. The story pivots on the interests of the Israelites. But it is no small matter that a Moabitess provides the critical link in this chain—and one who did not have to shirk a tainted ethnicity to do so.

The book of Ruth resolves itself into neither pro-Davidic propaganda nor polemic against endogamy nor advocacy of conversion. The entrancing tale of personal fidelity, subtle seduction, legal contrivances, and clan continuity holds enduring appeal in its own right. But it also underscores that strong strain in Jewish thinking that embraces rather than resists the foreigner.[128]

Ishmaelites and Arabs

The Jews could also bring Arabs into their extended family. The famed tale of Ishmael in Genesis stands at the foundation of this nexus.[129] As is well known, Abram's wife Sarai could not conceive and generously offered to have her Egyptian slave-girl Hagar share her husband's bed in hopes of producing an heir. Abram duly complied, and Hagar became pregnant. Sarai's generosity, however, swiftly reached its limit, and she had Hagar put to flight. The tale then took a sharp turn when Hagar, wandering in the wilderness, encountered a messenger of the Lord, who directed her to return to Sarai but promised her the birth of a son, to be called Ishmael, a son who would be like a wild ass in a struggle against all, emblematic, it appears, of fierce independence and nomadic life. Hagar complied, returned to Abram and Sarai, and gave birth to Ishmael.[130] The previously barren Sarai (renamed Sarah by God) soon conceived and produced Isaac, a source of joy to Abram (renamed Abraham by God) but a potential strain for the household. Sarah once again insisted on the expulsion of Hagar together with her son. The reluctant Abraham acceded to his wife's wishes, buoyed by the voice of God, which promised that Abraham's seed would be perpetuated through Isaac—but adding that the house of Ishmael too would issue in a

---

[128] Cf. the remarks of Spina (2005), 133–136.

[129] On the diverse strands and sources for this tale in Genesis, see the discussions in Knauf (1985), 16–45, and Retsö (2003), 222–229.

[130] Gen. 16.1–16.

nation to carry on Abraham's heritage.[131] Hagar's second trip to the wilderness almost resulted in disaster when she could no longer nourish her son and gave him up to die. But God's messenger once again reassured the woman, provided sustenance for the child, and proclaimed that God would make him into a great nation.[132] Ishmael subsequently thrived, lived to a ripe old age, and produced twelve sons who would become chiefs of their tribes.[133]

Nothing in this narrative makes reference to Arabs. Nor are Arabs identified with the descendants of Ishmael anywhere in the Bible.[134] But later Jewish writers did indeed make the connection. The *Book of Jubilees*, composed in Hebrew sometime in the second century BCE, may be the earliest attestation of it.[135] The text supplies a deathbed scene for Abraham in which the patriarch summoned Ishmael and his twelve children, as well as Isaac and his two sons, plus Abraham's other children and grandchildren by his second wife Keturah. After delivering his final pronouncements, Abraham bestowed his possessions on Isaac but gave gifts also to Ishmael and his sons, and to the sons of Keturah, sending all the sons away from those lands occupied by the house of Isaac. Their families went to dwell in the territory that stretched from the entrance to Babylon all the way to Faramon, perhaps Pelusium in the northeasternmost part of the Nile Delta. And the author concludes the segment, quite significantly, by stating that these people mingled with each other and were called Arabs and Ishmaelites.[136] By the second century BCE, in short, Jews (or some at least) associated Arabs with the posterity of Ishmael and thus with the house of Abraham.

That link appears too in the work of the Jewish-Hellenistic author Artapanus, writing in the second century BCE as well. The few fragments of his work, quoted by Alexander Polyhistor and preserved by Eusebius, include a section on Joseph. Artapanus' version of the quarrel between Joseph and his brothers has him appeal to neighboring Arabs to convey him to Egypt. They proved willing to comply with Joseph's wishes, so reports Artapanus, because the kings of the Arabs were descendants of Ishmael, the son of Abraham and brother of Isaac.[137] The construct that has Arabs as Ishmaelites

---

[131] Gen. 21.8–13. For the change of names, connected with God's grant of the Covenant, see Gen. 17.1–5, 17.15.

[132] Gen. 21.14–21.

[133] Gen. 25.12–17. The subsequent verse, 18, appears to echo the initial prediction for Ishmael, that he would clash with his kinsmen, 16.12, but its meaning is less than obvious; cf. Speiser (1964), 188; Westermann (1985), 399.

[134] See the discussion of Eph'al (1976), 225–231.

[135] On the date of *Jubilees*, see, most recently, VanderKam (2001), 17–21.

[136] *Jub*. 20.1, 20.11–13. On the geography, see Retsö (2003), 338.

[137] Euseb. *PE* 9.23.1. The text itself reads ἀπογόνους Ἰσραήλ υἱοὺς τοῦ Ἀβραάμ, Ἰσαὰκ δὲ ἀδελφούς. The emendation Ἰσραήλ υἱοῦ readily suggests itself. See the apparatus in Holladay

thus appears in second-century texts from both Palestine and the diaspora. That connection, it seems, had gained acceptance well beyond the whims of idiosyncratic writers.

The fact is strikingly confirmed by reference to the tradition in a non-Jewish author. The first-century BCE rhetorician Apollonius Molon of Rhodes obviously knew it. Molon, whose work on the Jews was not a sympathetic one, nonetheless transmits a version of the Ishmael story (without the name) that he must have picked up from a Jewish source or sources that had already modified the biblical narrative. In Molon's presentation, Abraham took two wives, one a kinswoman and neighbor, the other an Egyptian servant. He had twelve sons by the Egyptian woman, who settled in Arabia and became the first kings of those who dwelled in the land. From that time on, the Arabs always have twelve kings whose names derive from them.[138] The confusion about who fathered the twelve sons (Abraham rather than Ishmael) is a minor matter. Molon's testimony demonstrates quite compellingly that the link between Ishmaelites and Arabs had become a widespread notion among Hellenistic Jews.

By the time Josephus composed his *Antiquities*, a century and a half later, this was well-established tradition. The biblical account formed the basis of his narrative, but the Arab/Ishmaelite connection had now become a firm part of that expanded narrative.[139] Josephus repeats the Genesis listing of the sons of Ishmael, in its Septuagintal version, and then adds that they occupied all the land that stretched from the Euphrates to the Red Sea, naming it Nabatene, and giving their names to the nation of the Arabs and to the tribes that stemmed from them, thus signaling their own virtue and the distinction of Abraham.[140] As the Jewish historian has God later remind Amram the father of Moses, Abraham bestowed Arabia on Ishmael and his descendants.[141] Josephus explicitly identifies the traders to whom Joseph was sold by his brothers as "Arabs from the race of the Ishmaelites."[142] And he affirms the continued connection in his own day with reference to circumcision: Jews circumcise their sons in the eighth day, as Abraham did for Isaac, and Arabs wait for the thirteenth year, when Abraham circumcised Ishmael.[143] Jewish

---

(1983), 206; also Holladay's note at 228—although he himself opts for the manuscript reading. Even without emendation, however, the connection between Arabs and the house of Abraham is clear, whether or not presented in confused form by Artapanus.

[138] Euseb. *PE* 9.19.1–2.

[139] The valuable article of Millar (1993), 23–45, gives too much credit to Josephus for originality on this score.

[140] Jos. *Ant.* 1.220–221: οἳ τὸ τῶν Ἀράβων ἔθνος καὶ τὰς φυλὰς ἀφ' αὐτῶν καλοῦσι διά τε τὴν ἀρετὴν αὐτῶν καὶ τὸ Ἀβράμου ἀξίωμα.

[141] Jos. *Ant.* 2.213; cf. 1.239.

[142] Jos. *Ant.* 2.32: ἐμπόρους ἰδὼν Ἄραβας τοῦ Ἰσμαηλιτῶν γένους. Cf. Feldman (2000), 140.

[143] Jos. *Ant.* 1.214; cf. 1.191–193.

writers had plainly planted their identity on Arabs by making them offspring of the house of Abraham.

Did the identification of Arabs as Ishmaelites associate them with outsiders, the marginalized children of the marginalized Hagar, run out of Israel so as not to compete with the heritage of Isaac and the patriarchs? Genesis, as already noted, does indeed liken Ishmael to a wild ass who will act in defiance of his kinsmen.[144] And Ishmaelites do appear in the Joseph story as nomadic tribes.[145] But the portrayal is no negative one, even in Genesis.[146] Ishmael represents a different lifestyle, the hardy survivor of adverse circumstances, the brother who does not require the support of his kin to make a success of existence outside the conventional bounds of agricultural society. God himself, after all, reassured Abraham, with regard to Hagar and Ishmael being sent out to the desert, that this son too would be progenitor of a great nation.[147] And so indeed he did become, in the Genesis narrative itself.[148] The postbiblical re-creations all present Ishmael in a positive light. Even the Genesis prognostication of a defiant life in the wilderness disappears in the later treatments.[149] Ishmael moves out of Canaan to become founder of a new race and to transmit the seed of Abraham to his progeny elsewhere. The literary appropriation of Arabs for Abraham's line in the Hellenistic period further illustrates that powerful propensity of mediterranean peoples for incorporating the outsider by making him a kinsman.

Jews and Greeks as Kinsmen

Jewish horizons expanded dramatically in the decades and generations that followed Alexander the Great's conquests in the Near East. The Greek presence made itself felt in the land of the Jews. Greek migrations, the founding of new cities or the addition of Hellenic layers to the old ones, notably widened the experience of Jews, large numbers of whom moved and settled in the wake of the Greeks in various parts of the Mediterranean. The Hellenistic diaspora was not (for the most part) the consequence of a forced emigration but was itself an attraction for the adventurous and the enterprising. Not that Jews had never moved abroad before. But the pace quickened and the numbers multiplied in the Greek era. And even those

---

[144] Gen. 16.12; cf. 25.18. On the ambiguity of this phraseology, see Bakhos (2006), 14–16.
[145] Gen. 37.25. On other references to Ishmaelites in the Bible, see Knauf (1985), 10–16.
[146] Of course, they do turn up occasionally among the enemies of the Israelites; e.g., Judg. 8.24; Ps. 83.4–8—but not identified as Arabs. Cf. Eph'al (1976), 225–226.
[147] Gen. 21.13, 21.18. Cf. *Jub.* 15.20.
[148] Gen. 25.12–18.
[149] Cf. Jos. *Ant.* 1,189–190.

who remained in Palestine found Hellenic culture close and conspicuous. Numerous Greek or Greco-Phoenician communities stood on the Mediterranean coast or in the lower Galilee. Hellenic culture penetrated to Judaea itself in a wide variety of forms.[150] The importance of redefining and articulating Jewish identity in the circumstances of this new world, with Jews frequently living cheek by jowl with gentiles, took on greater urgency. This did not entail a choice between absorption or isolation—let alone syncretism. But it certainly required some introspection, and some novel ways of self-presentation.

Biblical traditions remained potent, undiminished in the Hellenistic era. As we have seen, strong elements in those traditions attest to receptiveness to outsiders, diminution of differences, and even intermingling that led to a hybrid ruling house of Israel. Jewish-Hellenistic writers built on those foundations but produced structures of even greater inventiveness and creativity.

A striking story can serve as illustration. It stems from an otherwise unknown writer named Cleodemus Malchus, and it involves a mishmash of biblical genealogy, Greek legend, and Jewish fiction. Genesis reports that Abraham married a second time, and his new wife Keturah bore him a number of sons who produced a great progeny of descendants.[151] Cleodemus reproduced this tradition in garbled form. He combined it with one of the countless legends of the Greek hero Herakles. The latter story, also in different versions, has Herakles in one of his travels enter Libya, where he wrestled the giant Antaeus into submission, thereby allowing Herakles to bring civilization to the wild and barbarous land of Africa. He then proceeded to a union with Antaeus' wife, the fruit of which became the rulers of North Africa.[152] Cleodemus refashioned the Hellenic tales and produced a new concoction that linked them miraculously to Abraham. In Cleodemus' fantasy, two sons of Abraham and Keturah, named Apher and Aphran, fought together with Herakles in bringing Antaeus to subjection. Herakles' new bride, in this narrative, was not the wife of Antaeus but a daughter of Apher, granddaughter of Abraham, and through her derived the line of African rulers. Indeed, Abraham's progeny had an even more illustrious future, according to Cleodemus. The African city of Aphra took its name from Apher, and the whole of Africa had Aphran as its forebear. And, as if that were not enough, Cleodemus adds that a third son of Keturah, Assouri, became the namesake of Assyria.[153]

[150] See, especially, the classic work of Hengel (1974), passim; also Schürer (1979), II, 29–80. On the Hellenistic cities in Palestine, see Schürer (1979), II, 85–183.

[151] Gen. 25.1–4.

[152] Apollod. *Bib.* 2.5.11; Diod. Sic. 4.17.4–5; Plut. *Sert.* 9.3–5.

[153] The sole extant fragment of Cleodemus to give this reconstruction was transmitted by the first-century BCE Greek scholar Alexander Polyhistor, preserved in turn by Josephus, *Ant.* 1.239–241, and by Eusebius, *PE* 9.20.2–4. The best treatment of the literary background

Scholars have disputed the origins of the mysterious Cleodemus. But the fabrication of a tale that has Abraham's sons provide muscle for Herakles' victory and become the forefathers of nations must be an *interpretatio Judaica*, whether Cleodemus invented it or got it from elsewhere. The new narrative represents a usurpation of Hellenic legend to advance the Hebrew patriarch's reputation. His sons had brought Herakles into the family, and his reach now extended to Africa and Assyria.[154]

The implications of the story need to be underscored. It does not constitute a Jewish effort at assimilation. The labors of Herakles and the African succession are brought into line for the heritage of Abraham. No Greek would have bought this for a moment. The fable doubtless circulated among Hellenistic Jews in the second or first century BCE. It demonstrates an expropriation of Greek legend rather than an adaptation to it. And it has a wider significance as well. The narrative that Cleodemus created or conveyed discloses a Jewish inclination to incorporate Hellenic tradition into the Jews' own national story. The outsider is brought inside. The new tale blends the traditions and entwines the families to spawn a lineage that rules nations.

This form of ingenuity emerges in another intriguing construct. Report had it that communications took place between the Judaean High Priest Onias and the Spartan king Areus, evidently in the early third century BCE. The king wrote with considerable pleasure to announce that he had come upon a written text recording a kinship between Spartans and Jews: they both stemmed from the stock of Abraham. Areus greatly welcomed this discovery, wished the Jews well, and asserted that their goods and property should be considered as joint possessions.[155] Onias' reply is unrecorded. But there were further exchanges in the mid–second century. The Hasmonean High Priest Jonathan addressed the Spartans as "brothers," acknowledged Areus' letter of long ago, and asked for renewal of the friendship and alliance that held between the two peoples. The Spartan reply arrived after Jonathan's death, when his brother Simon had succeeded him. (No one seems in a particular hurry to answer his mail in this correspondence.) But it too contained warm greetings and an eagerness to keep the close relationship alive.[156] So, Spartans and Jews not only collaborated in the Hellenistic age; they enjoyed a joint ancestor in Abraham, and were thus bound in blood.

Are we to trust the authenticity of these communications? They appear in ostensible documents supplied by historical narrative, not in a piece of

---

is that of Gutman (1963), II, 137–143 (Hebrew). See also Freudenthal (1874–1875), 130–136; Holladay (1983), I, 245–259; Doran (1985a), 883–887; Schürer (1986), III.1, 526–529.

[154] Cf. Gruen (1998), 151–153.

[155] 1 Macc. 12.20–23; Jos. *Ant.* 12.225–227.

[156] 1 Macc. 12.6–18, 14.16–23; Jos. *Ant.* 12.225–227, 13.164–170; cf. 2 Macc. 5.6–10.

romantic fiction. And diplomatic correspondence between states in the Hellenistic period frequently expressed itself in terms of kinship relations.[157] A long and large scholarly literature has debated the genuineness of the letters, and a substantial number of commentators take them seriously. Indeed, they should be taken seriously. But hardly as history. That debate, however, need not be rehearsed here.[158] What matters is the character of the correspondence and the image of Jewish identity that it projects. For there can be little doubt that the letters, as they have come down to us, are Jewish compositions. Abraham, after all, is the forefather in the fictive genealogy, not Herakles or some legendary Lacedaemonian figure. The idea of Spartans creating or accepting a lineage that traces their origin to a Hebrew patriarch beggars the imagination. The language of Areus' supposed letter gives the case away. He announced, in good biblical phraseology, that "your cattle and goods are ours, and ours are yours."[159] No Spartan would have been caught dead speaking like that. And Jonathan's purported letter equally betrays its artificiality. He makes mention of the alliance between the peoples and offers to renew it in friendly fashion. But not before he observes that Jews do not actually need such alliances. They have all the support they require in their holy books, they have successfully prevailed over their foes with the aid of Heaven, and they have done all this without troubling the Spartans or any of their other allies and friends. Jonathan further claims that Jews have at every opportunity remembered Sparta in their sacrifices and their prayers. He does not, in short, petition the Spartans for assistance but presents a patronizing position in which Jews have the upper hand as benefactors for their presumably grateful beneficiaries.[160] One can imagine the reaction of proud Spartans if such a letter had actually been sent!

Whatever the validity of the diplomatic communication, the genealogical link between these two nations is transparent fiction. What called it forth? Hellenistic Jews, or at least some of them, found the repute of Sparta appealing. The Spartan system had long been a source of admiration among Hellenes for its inculcation of military prowess, the premium it placed on rigorous training, loyalty, and tolerance of suffering, its adherence to ancestral laws, and the endurance of its political institutions.[161] Josephus later still used Spartans as the benchmark for judging the virtues and successes

---

[157] See the collection of testimonia in Curty (1995), passim, and the discussion of Jones (1999), passim.
[158] See the skeptical treatment of Gruen (1996), 254–269, with extensive bibliography. Add Jones (1999), 75–79. Momigliano (1975), 113–114, gives the correspondence greater credence.
[159] 1 Macc. 12.23. Cf. 1 Kings 22.4; 2 Kings 3.7.
[160] 1 Macc. 12.9–15; cf. Jos. Ant. 13.167–168.
[161] Cf. Ollier (1933–1943); Tigerstedt (1965, 1974, 1978); Kennell (1995).

of other communities—although he made it clear that Jews had surpassed them in all matters in which the Spartans had once claimed superiority.[162] The value of an association with Sparta for Jewish self-esteem in a Greek world is plain enough.

Its implications deserve emphasis. Jews were not here attempting to fit themselves into a Hellenic social scene, adjusting their sights to some form of accommodation to the dominant culture—let alone hoping for political or diplomatic advantage. The supposed connection underlines Jewish precedence. The Hebrew patriarch is progenitor of the two clans. Jews could borrow some of the aura of the Spartan mystique and set themselves in the pattern of a people renowned for authority, stability, self-sacrifice, and adherence to law (even if the reputation no longer matched reality in the Hellenistic period). But the constructed correspondence exhibits the superiority of Jewish institutions and faith. The fact that the linkage was conceived and broadcast, however, remains fundamental. Whether or not any Spartan ever acknowledged the concocted kinship, Jews had calculatingly fashioned an affiliation with a gentile people that enhanced their own self-image.

The sociability of Israel holds a central place in the nation's tradition and history. That strand in the story rarely receives the prominence that it merits. The record, to be sure, contains many instances of alienation, self-absorption, hostility, and xenophobia. They cannot be denied or explained away. Harsh circumstances, inner conflict, or clashing ambitions could engender and exacerbate them. But openness to the alien remained a cardinal characteristic throughout. The elevating exhortations of Second-Isaiah ring out with resonance. The prophet famously declared that Yahweh had called on his servant to be a covenant for the people and a light to the nations. It was not enough, so Yahweh spoke, to establish the tribes of Jacob and restore the remnants of Israel. The servant of God is appointed to be a light to the nations and to extend salvation to the ends of the earth.[163] The all-encompassing sentiments expressed there still possessed power centuries later. They recur in a different form in the voice of a very different Jewish author. The philosopher Philo maintains that Mosaic law enjoined Jews to place high value on foreigners who have abandoned their homeland, customs, shrines, and idols, and to embrace them not only as friends and kinsfolk but as their very selves in body and soul.[164] That note is not one sounded as a cry in the wilderness. It expresses a vital principle in the long chronicle of Israel.

---

[162] Jos. *CAp.* 2.225–235.

[163] Isai. 42.1–6, 49.1-6, 51.4.

[164] Philo *Virt.* 102–103; *Spec. Leg.* 1.51–53, 1.308–309, 4.177–178. Cf. *Quaest*, in Exod. 2.2. A noteworthy phrase by Pseudo-Phocylides, a Hellenistic Jewish author who took the pseudonym of a renowned sixth-century Greek poet, is relevant here; 39: "foreigners should be held in equal honor as citizens."

To conclude. The subject treated here is not the overcoming of particularism by universalism, a dichotomy often noted by scholars.[165] One can as easily detect universalist tones in Jewish tradition, whether in the covenant with Noah or the book of Isaiah or through much of Wisdom literature, as one can discern particularism in the frequent references to Israelites as the Chosen People of Yahweh. Nor is the issue that of the openness of Jews to conversion or to "God-fearers" and others who might be sympathetic to the tenets and practices of Judaism. A different feature captures attention here—neither universalism in which Yahweh embraces all people nor a call to conversion to bring as many as possible within the fold of Judaism. It is both less than this and more than this. Jews issued a claim on kinship relations between and among nations—or at least some nations. This carried no loss of distinctive identity. It involved a construct of family ties with other peoples of Palestine, the invention of common ancestry with Assyrians, Arabs, or Spartans, and an assertion of origins that connected with Babylonian tradition or Greek mythology. Jewish identity did not reduce itself to a separatist singularity. Jews could also visualize themselves as part of a broader cultural heritage, discover or fabricate links with other societies, and reckon the intermingling of bloodlines not as a compromise but as an enrichment of their self-esteem.

[165] For a recent discussion, see Levenson (1996), 143–169.

Chapter 12

CULTURAL INTERLOCKINGS AND OVERLAPPINGS

Linkages among cultures in the Mediterranean crop up regularly in creative fiction and symbolic action. The phenomenon is neither exceptional nor marginal. A plethora of texts speak to affinity rather than estrangement. The treatment here cannot claim to be exhaustive. But several probes in different contexts can bring the concept into sharp focus. Some matters receive consideration at length, others a briefer discussion. All, however, relate to the theme of interconnection and incorporation. They include the reciprocal appropriation by Jews and Greeks of common philosophical traditions, a range of imaginative representations of gentiles by Jewish intellectuals, mutual perceptions of Phoenicians and Hellenes, and a variety of Roman adaptations of alien cultures. As a body they provide a perspective quite different from one that seeks to distance the "Other."

Jews and Greeks as Philosophers

The classic contrast between "Judaism" and "Hellenism" long held sway in analysis of the Jewish relation to Greco-Roman culture. The metaphor stressed polarity, antithesis, and incompatibility. Scholarship in the past generation, however, has moved toward a more complex conceptualization. Distinctions mattered, but they were more fluid than previously assumed. Tertullian's notorious challenge, "What has Athens to do with Jerusalem?" is no longer unanswerable. A scholarly shift has taken hold.[1] The notion that Jews could have regarded Greeks as the "Other" at a time when they were enmeshed in Hellenic culture and part of Hellenic society seems singularly off the mark. Jews and Greeks did indeed view each other through their own peculiar lenses. But they did not do so with the presupposition that the object of their gaze was an alien people whose idiosyncratic characteristics

---

[1] See the valuable review of scholarship, stemming from the classic work of Hengel (1974), by Aitken (2004), 331–341. Among recent works, see Barclay (1996); Gruen (1998); Levine (1998); Rajak (2001); J. Collins (2000); *idem* (2005).

served only to set off and underscore the distinctiveness of the superior culture.

A noteworthy and fascinating instance of interconnectedness deserves exploration: the interest that both peoples exhibited in the concept of philosophy. The issue here is not that of the influence of Greek philosophy on Jewish thinking. That Hellenic philosophical tenets made their way into Jewish writings from Kohelet to Philo does not need to be argued here.[2] A rather different topic claims attention: the reciprocal set of perceptions (or constructs) in which Greeks understood Jews as philosophers and Jews viewed Greek philosophers as dependent on Jewish lore. This double lens, however distorted its refractions, suggests something very different from "Otherness."

A fragment of Theophrastus, the most celebrated pupil of Aristotle and his successor as head of the Peripatetics, demands notice in this connection. Writing as he did in the late fourth and early third centuries, Theophrastus belongs to the very beginning of the Hellenistic period and is thus unlikely to have had much (if any) acquaintance with Jews, their customs, or their principles. And his comments on Jewish sacrificial practices reflect that lack of comprehension. The fragment comes from Theophrastus' *Peri Eusebeias*, as transmitted by Porphyry, and reflects his hostility to the institution of animal sacrifice. Jews are mentioned in this connection as a people among the Syrians who sacrifice animals in a way repellent to Greeks, for they do not eat the victims but burn them whole, pouring honey and wine on them so that the deed is finished quickly and at night lest this terrible thing be witnessed under the sun. And they proceed to fast on intervening days. Theophrastus goes on to claim that Jews were the first to conduct human as well as animal sacrifices.[3]

A puzzling passage. Just what it was that Theophrastus found objectionable in nighttime holocausts remains obscure. Holocausts were not uncommon in antiquity, and were often done at night. References to honey, wine, refraining from meat, and fasting evidently derive from erroneous or confused information. As for human sacrifice, Theophrastus is more concerned to excuse than to condemn: the Jews did this, according to him, out of compulsion rather than zeal. Nor does he suggest that they maintain this practice in his own day.

The segment has given rise to tortured and ingenious interpretations. Most of them focus on the question of whether Theophrastus had a positive or a negative impression of Jews.[4] That issue has occupied too much

---

[2] See the survey and bibliography in Schürer (1986), 567–593; (1987), 871–889. Cf. also the discussion of Boccacini (1991), 77–205.

[3] Porphyry *de Abstinentia* 2.26 = Stern (1974), I, 10.

[4] E.g., Stern (1974), I, 8; Mélèze-Modrzejewski (1990), 107–110; Feldman (1993), 7–8, 203–204; Bar-Kochva (2010), 15–39.

scholarly energy. It is not likely to be resolved, it appears irrelevant to Theophrastus' objectives, and it bears only marginally on our purpose. The passage demonstrates little more than that the author retailed misinformation, had only marginal familiarity with Judaism, and was prepared to embrace unreliable reports. Ignorance rather than ideology seems paramount.

More to the point are Theophrastus' remarks elsewhere in that fragment. He calls the Jews "a nation of philosophers" who converse with one another about God, gaze at the stars and speculate about them, and summon the divinity through their prayers.[5] Here again Theophrastus' knowledge of the Jews has distinct limitations. The description as stargazers appears to equate them with astrologers, an attribution that he would not have drawn from a knowledgeable source. That they discuss God among themselves and call on him with prayers suggests priestly responsibilities, as if all Jews were priests, a characterization that could hardly be based on serious research. Theophrastus relied on surmise and inference rather than trustworthy authorities (or perhaps any authorities).

That does not, however, render the surmise any less significant. How did Theophrastus reach the conclusion that Jews were a nation of philosophers? A number of possibilities have been proposed, none of them exclusive of the others. Perhaps Theophrastus knew of Jews as monotheists and inferred that those who speculated about a solitary divinity must be philosophers by nature.[6] Or he was impressed by Jewish aniconism, which he associated with a strong Greek philosophical tradition rejecting anthropomorphic representations of the divinity.[7] Or he reckoned Jews as a philosophic caste within the Syrians.[8] Or he confused the priestly class in Judaea with the people as a whole.[9] Embrace of any of these propositions has to come with considerable caution. Nothing in the passage alludes to monotheism or aniconism. The denotation of the Jews as a people of the Syrians refers to their sacrificial customs, not to their philosophic character.[10] And the conclusion that Theophrastus might have conflated Jewish priests with Jews as a whole, turning them into philosophers as well, is hardly an obvious one.

---

[5] Porphyry *de Abstinentia* 2.26 = Stern (1974), I, 10: ἅτε φιλόσοφοι τὸ γένος ὄντες, περὶ τοῦ θείου μὲν ἀλλήλοις λαλοῦσι, τῆς δὲ νυκτὸς τῶν ἄστρων ποιοῦνται τὴν θεωρίαν, βλέποντες εἰς αὐτὰ καὶ διὰ τῶν εὐχῶν θεοκλυτοῦντες.

[6] Jaeger (1938), 131–134; Stern (1974), I, 11; Gabba (1989), 619; Mélèze-Modrzejewski (1990), 107–108.

[7] Satlow (2008), 15–19.

[8] So Bernays (1866), 111, in the classic work on Theophrastus. Similarly, Stern (1974), 10; Feldman (1993), 525; Bar-Kochva (2010), 34, 81, who prefers the term "community" to "caste."

[9] Satlow (2008), 13–14.

[10] Bar-Kochva (2010), 34–36, combines these and has Theophrastus regard the Jews as a community of philosopher-priests among the Syrians.

The root of Theophrastus' tangled description cannot be recovered. On any reckoning, however, he regarded Jews as a nation of philosophers, a people whose conception of divinity involved them in rational discussions among themselves, thus plainly seeing them in the light of Greek philosophical tradition. It is pointless and immaterial to argue about whether this puts Theophrastus into the camp of those who viewed Jews positively.[11] In all probability, he, like his younger contemporaries Clearchus and Megasthenes (see below), viewed them as among eastern nations whose wise men presided over practices and beliefs that seemed akin to Greek philosophical inquiry. Later Hellenic writers regularly cast legendary or semilegendary religious figures of the east together in comparative schemata. Moses thus found his place with Orpheus, Musaeus, Amphiaraus, the Magi in Persia, and the gymnosophists in India.[12] Theophrastus may have been among the first to set Jews on a plane with other eastern nations to whom Greek writers imputed an "oriental wisdom" that they found to resonate with Greek philosophy.

A fragment from yet another pupil of Aristotle belongs in this category. Clearchus, from the Cyprian city of Soli, produced a work (now lost) titled *On Sleep*, from which Josephus quoted a choice item.[13] The Jewish historian utilizes the passage as part of his lengthy argument that Greek writers knew of Jews from an early period and found much to admire. Clearchus' text (or Josephus' extract from it) served this purpose very conveniently.[14] Clearchus described a chance encounter in Asia Minor between his master Aristotle and an unnamed Jew from Coele-Syria. He puts the narrative into the mouth of Aristotle, although the tale itself may have been a concoction of the pupil.[15] Whether fictitious or not, it offers a striking instance of a Greek intellectual's depiction of a learned Jew. According to the anecdote, the Jew mightily impressed Aristotle. He admired in particular the man's remarkable endurance and self-restraint. He describes him as a Jew τὸ γένος from Coele-Syria.[16] The Jews, evidently unfamiliar to Clearchus'

---

[11] Bar-Kochva (2010), 24–30, 36–39, maintains that the identification of Jews as philosophers does not outweigh the critical character of his comments on their sacrificial practices. Satlow (2008), 1–2, rightly questions the value of categorizing Greek thinkers in terms of their supposedly positive or negative opinions of Jews.

[12] See, e.g., Strabo 16.2.39; cf. 16.1.68, 16.1.70. Cf. Lewy (1938), 216–221; Momigliano (1975), 85–86; Gabba (1989), 618–624; Feldman (1993), 7–9. In the view of Satlow (2008), 10–11, Greeks blurred the line between eastern philosophers and ritual experts.

[13] On Clearchus' work and career, the evidence is assembled by Wehrli (1948). See also the discussions by Lewy (1938), 205–235, and now, most importantly, Bar-Kochva (2010), 40–89, with extensive bibliography.

[14] Jos. *CAp.* 1.176–183; cf. Clem. Alex. *Strom.* 1.15.70.2.

[15] Whether the anecdote is historical has properly been doubted by Jaeger (1938), 130–131; Bar-Kochva (2010), 47–49.

[16] Jos. *CAp.* 1.179. The term τὸ γένος employed twice by Clearchus and also by Theophrastus in reference to Jews as philosophers τὸ γένος, does not readily lend itself to precise translation.

presumed readership, then receive a fuller description. They are descendants of philosophers in India, men called Calanoi by the Indians but Jews by the Syrians. This particular individual, so notes Clearchus in the voice of Aristotle, was a frequent guest among many Greeks in Asia on his visits from the highlands to the coastal places, for he was Greek not only in his speech but in his very soul.[17] When he encountered Aristotle and other scholars in Asia, he tested their wisdom and, in view of his having dwelled with many people of παιδεία, he was rather able to impart something of his own.[18] "Aristotle" went on to recount in detail the Jew's great and astounding endurance and the self-restraint he exhibited in the conduct of his life, but Josephus chose not to repeat all of that, encouraging his readers to look up Clearchus' book themselves.[19] Such is the account.

Here again, the question of whether Clearchus sought to deliver a favorable assessment of Jews misses the point. He had his own agenda. And his portrait plainly imposes an *interpretatio Graeca*. For Clearchus, the skills of the cultivated Jew came not from being steeped in biblical texts but from his time spent in the company of numerous learned Greeks, the men of παιδεία. The esteem felt for him expresses itself as praise for his Greekness. The ability to hold his own in philosophical dialogue exhibited the Hellenic soul. The "Greek" qualities serve as the measuring rod. Nevertheless, characterization of the Jew in those terms is a telling fact. Clearchus elevates him by making him a philosopher.[20]

But more than "Greekness" is involved here. Clearchus has Aristotle bring in Indian wise men. And not incidentally. He introduces Jews themselves as a people descended from philosophers in India. Indeed they are

---

Here it appears to mean something like "by origin." So Bar-Kochva (2010), 46. Barclay (2007), 104, prefers "by ancestry" or "by descent." But since Clearchus proceeds to speak of Jews as descendants of Indian philosophers, this seems inappropriate. Satlow (2008), 13–14, chooses "race" for Clearchus but leans toward "caste" for Theophrastus, which would be a highly unusual rendering.

[17] Jos. *CAp.* 1.180: Ἑλληνικὸς ἦν οὐ τῇ διαλέκτῳ μόνον, ἀλλὰ καὶ τῇ ψυχῇ.

[18] Jos. *CAp.* 1.181: ἐντυγχάνει ἡμῖν τε καί τισιν ἑτέροις τῶν σχολαστικῶν πειρώμενος αὐτῶν τῆς σοφίας. ὡς δὲ πολλοῖς τῶν ἐν παιδείᾳ συνῳκείωτο, παρεδίδου τι μᾶλλον ὧν εἶχεν. On the meaning of μᾶλλον here, not "more" but "rather," see Barclay (2007), 105; Bar-Kochva (2010), 49–53.

[19] Just why Josephus elected to omit the rest has been the subject of much fruitless speculation. For Stern (1974), I, 52, Josephus did not have access to Clearchus' text but only a later compilation that included parts of it. Bar-Kochva (2010), 75–79. suggests that, by ascribing the virtues of καρτερία and σωφροσύνη to the Jews, he really transferred to them characteristics of the Indian gymnosophists, the principal focus of his attention, and Josephus omitted the details because he recognized them as inapplicable to Jews. The idea is ingenious but unpersuasive. Josephus was not averse to ascribing καρτερία and σωφροσύνη to Jews; *CAp.* 2.146, 2.170; see Barclay (2007), 106.

[20] Nothing in the text supports the interpretation of Bar-Kochva (2010), 53, that praise for the Jew signified primarily surprise that a member of a "barbarian" nation had managed to acquire Greek speech and learning.

philosophers in their own right, called Jews among Syrians on a par with those called Calanoi among Indians.²¹ Clearchus evidently reckons Jews as a philosophic sect. They hold that place among Syrians, as Calanoi do among Indians. Confusion, as well as invention, permeates this text. Calanoi, as such, do not exist. Clearchus has simply and erroneously extrapolated from the figure of Calanus, the celebrated Indian gymnosophist noted for his sparring with Alexander the Great.²² But the connections he evokes are significant. Clearchus elsewhere in his corpus claims that Indian gymnosophists descended from Persian magi. And others conjectured that Jews themselves had magi as ancestors.²³ As the philosophic elite of Persia, magi stood with Chaldeans in Babylon and gymnosophists in India.²⁴ Clearchus placed the Jews in that category. These speculative fantasies, however remote from reality, offer insight into what passed as plausible perceptions of Jews in the early Hellenistic period. They belonged to the wise men of the east. Characterization as philosophers allowed them to combine eastern wisdom with Hellenic παιδεία. The associations counted for more than any "Otherness."

The notion of Jews as philosophers certainly went beyond the school of Aristotle. The erudite Megasthenes served as envoy of Seleucus I at the court of the Indian ruler Chandragupta on one or more occasions and dwelled in India for a number of years, whether on several visits or an extended one. At some point, perhaps in the 290s, he composed a major study of that land and its people, the *Indica*, cited and quoted by several later Greek and Roman writers, evidently a classic work on the subject. Only one preserved fragment refers to the Jews, but it is a most intriguing one, particularly in light of the comments of Theophrastus and Clearchus, his slightly earlier but near contemporaries. The passage appears in the *Stromateis* of Clement of Alexandria, who was eager to find parallels between Greek philosophy and eastern learning, and thereby to establish that Hellenic precepts were derivative from the older wisdom of the east. To that end Clement quotes Megasthenes as witness to the antiquity of Jewish philosophy, its priority to and influence over the Greeks. In the segment quoted, Megasthenes asserted that everything said about nature by the ancient Greeks can also be found among those outside Greece who philosophize, some of the views held by the Brahmans in India, some by those called Jews in Syria.²⁵

---

²¹ Jos. *CAp*. 1.179: οὗτοι δ' εἰσιν ἀπόγονοι τῶν ἐν Ἰνδοῖς φιλοσόφων, καλοῦνται δέ, ὥς φασιν, οἱ φιλόσοφοι παρὰ μὲν Ἰνδοῖς Καλανοί, παρὰ δὲ Σύροις Ἰουδαῖοι.
²² On Calanus, see Arrian *Anab*. 7.2–3; Strabo 15.1.61–68; Plut. *Alex*. 65, 69.
²³ Diog. Laert. 1.9.
²⁴ Diog. Laert. 1.1; Clem. Alex. *Strom*. 1.15.71.4. Cf. the discussion of Parker (2008), 264–272.
²⁵ Clem. Alex. *Strom*. 1.15.72.5 = Stern (1974), I, 46: ἅπαντα μέντοι τὰ περὶ φύσεως εἰρημένα παρὰ τοῖς ἀρχαίοις λέγεται καὶ παρὰ τοῖς ἔξω τῆς Ἑλλάδος φιλοσοφοῦσι, τὰ μὲν παρ' Ἰνδοῖς ὑπὸ

The passage is often misconstrued. It does not show that Megasthenes himself gave priority to Jewish learning (or to Indian learning) over that of the Greeks—even though Clement used it to that purpose. Megasthenes seems in fact to employ Greek views as the touchstone of the argument, with the others seen by comparison with it. Strabo quotes Megasthenes at greater length on the Brahmans and the parallels he found with Hellenic opinions about nature. The quotation significantly contains Megasthenes' remark that some of the Brahmans' ideas rest on myths and suffer from simplicity because Brahmans are better at deeds than words. That would hardly qualify them as sages from whom Greeks drew their philosophy.[26] The approach once again suggests an *interpretatio Graeca*. The Hellenic vantage point is paramount. How far Megasthenes may have researched or written about Jewish beliefs is beyond our knowledge. What parallels he discerned, if any, with the Brahmans also elude conjecture. The sole surviving passage implies that Jewish and Brahman beliefs, at least in some respects, diverged.[27] More importantly, however, both overlapped with Greek ideas and both engaged in philosophizing, the central point of Megasthenes' text. He refrains from making a genealogical connection, as does Clearchus. But Jews are once again bracketed with Indian wise men and their opinions associated with Greek philosophers. The juxtaposition carries meaning. Hellenic thinkers seemed quite comfortable in ascribing to Jews conceptualizations that coincided with their own and reckoning them as part of Greek philosophical tradition.

This was not, however, a one-sided proposition. Hellenistic Jews who had drunk deep (or even shallow) at the springs of Greek philosophy could turn the relationship around to their own advantage. The celebrated *Letter of Aristeas*, a Jewish composition, is a striking case at point. Its narrative has significant implications for the place of Jewish intellectuals in the culture of Hellenism.[28]

Familiarity with Greek philosophy pervades the text. The Jewish author has Demetrius of Phaleron, Athenian philosopher and statesman, now counselor to Ptolemy II of Egypt, advise the king to commission the translation of the Hebrew Bible into Greek. In doing so, Demetrius commends the legislation contained in the scriptures for its particularly philosophical character.[29] Hellenic virtues like justice, piety, self-restraint, and philanthropy

---

τῶν Βραχμάνων, τὰ δὲ ἐν τῇ Συρίᾳ ὑπὸ τῶν καλουμένων Ἰουδαίων. On the work of Megasthenes, see Parker (2008), 42–48, with bibliography.

[26] Strabo 15.1.59 . See the valuable discussion of Bar-Kochva (2010), 146–156.

[27] So, rightly, Bar-Kochva (2010), 156–157. See Clem. Alex. *Strom*. 1.15.72.5 = Stern (1974), I, 46: τὰ μὲν . . . ὑπὸ τῶν Βραχμάνων . . . τὰ δὲ . . . ὑπὸ τῶν καλουμένων Ἰουδαίων.

[28] On the *Letter of Aristeas* more generally, see further below, pp. 333–337.

[29] *LetArist*. 31: φιλοσοφωτέραν.

gain repeated mention as Jewish qualities.³⁰ The High Priest in Jerusalem, in recounting the significance of Jewish dietary prescriptions, explains them in good Greek style either as having a rational basis or as requiring allegorical interpretation.³¹ Jewish legislation on food and drink, as he puts it, is an expression of "right reason."³²

The central exhibit on this score is the extended symposium recorded by the *Letter of Aristeas*. In this scenario the king interrogates each of the seventy-two Jewish sages who had come from Jerusalem to Alexandria for the task of rendering the Bible into Greek.³³ The episode occupies fully one-third of the whole work, something to which the author evidently sought to call attention.³⁴ The banquet with intellectual exchange is a quintessentially Greek institution, familiar from Plato's *Symposium*, and the format of a king asking questions of sages appears in Plutarch's *Symposium of the Seven Wise Men*. Ptolemy, over a period of a week, asks each of the Jewish elders in turn a question, receives a reply, and (without fail) praises the speaker. A large proportion of the questions involve the proper means for a monarch to govern his realm, thus putting this segment in a genre similar to that of Hellenistic treatises on kingship. And a substantial number of the responses depend on Greek philosophy or political theory, each one, however, punctuated by reference to God as ultimate authority. But the divinity often appears in mechanical, even irrelevant, fashion. The context is strictly philosophical rather than theological. To the question of what constitutes the strongest form of rule, for instance, the Jewish interlocutor replies "to control oneself and not be carried away by passions"— standard Stoic ideology.³⁵ Ptolemy's queries to the Jews included the Socratic one of whether wisdom can be taught, though the term τὸ φρονεῖν refers to practical wisdom rather than theoretical wisdom. The response looks like a clever side step: if the soul's receptivity to all that is good is guided by divine power, this would hardly amount to being taught.³⁶ To one guest Ptolemy actually poses the direct question of "what is philosophy?"—indicating that the answer would best come from a Jew. The response was little different from those delivered several times in various forms by the guests: to deliberate with reason and resist passions, a perfectly good Stoic formulation in the mouth of the Jew.³⁷

---

[30] E.g., *LetArist*. 2, 131, 147, 189, 208, 209, 237, 292.
[31] *LetArist*. 128–171.
[32] *LetArist*. 161: σημείωσιν ὀρθοῦ λόγου. See also *LetArist*. 244.
[33] On the banquet scene, see O. Murray (1967), 344–361; Fraser (1972), 701–703; Parente (1972), 549–563.
[34] *LetArist*. 184–296.
[35] *LetArist*. 222; cf. 211.
[36] *LetArist*. 236.
[37] *LetArist*. 256.

The relationship with Greek philosophy, however, takes a more complex and ambiguous turn. The author of the *Letter of Aristeas* has a mischievous side. Greek philosophers appear directly in the narrative, appointees of the king and members of the court, playing a supportive role that sets off the wisdom of the Jews by comparison and contrast. When Ptolemy completed his first round of questioning and hailed each of the Jewish scholars for the acuity of their answers, he turned to his own sages asking for confirmation of his opinion. Their spokesman Menedemus of Eretria, who gained repute as a significant thinker in the early third century BCE, responded appropriately, endorsing the king's assessment and praising the Jewish guests for their focus on God.[38] Menedemus' approbation of the Jews, solicited by Ptolemy, and Ptolemy's immediate assent to his remarks in turn imply a staged event, an implication that the author perhaps offers with a wink and a nod. At the conclusion of the next day's interrogation, the king, having once more commended every answer, however banal or commonplace, looked again to his entourage for assent. All responded on cue and joined in the approbation—especially the philosophers.[39] The author surely did not inject this item fortuitously. His portrait of Greek intellectuals, prompted by the king, acknowledging their own inferiority through what were doubtless clenched teeth, has to be deliberate whimsy. And he underscores the point by adding in his own voice that the Jewish wise men, in their conduct and speech, far outpaced the philosophers.[40] At the end of the seven-day banquet, "Aristeas" gives high marks to the Jewish scholars who had supplied such prompt, careful, and acute answers to difficult questions that should have required lengthy deliberation. He concludes the section by reiterating his earlier message: everyone admired the Jews' replies, especially the philosophers.[41] The repetition here gives a satiric edge to the author's treatment. Jewish sages, though fresh from Jerusalem, had fully absorbed the tenets of Greek philosophy, topping the Greek professionals themselves. The playful character of the exchange is hard to miss.[42] The oblique mockery does not represent a challenge to the caliber of Hellenic learning. But it reminds the readership that Jewish thinkers had assimilated it, shaped it to their own purposes, and even improved on it. Once again,

---

[38] *LetArist.* 200–201. Menedemus served at the court of Antigonus Gonatas; Diog. Laert. 2.125–144. Both his dates and his service with the Macedonian king make it improbable that he would become a confidant of Ptolemy II in Alexandria. "Aristeas" may have imported Menedemus into the text simply as a philosopher whose name might be known to his readership.

[39] *LetArist.* 235: μάλιστα δὲ τῶν φιλοσόφων.

[40] *LetArist.* 235: ταῖς ἀγωγαῖς καὶ τῷ λόγῳ πολὺ προέχοντες αὐτῶν ἦσαν.

[41] *LetArist.* 295–296.

[42] For this interpretation of the *Letter of Aristeas* more generally, see Gruen (1998), 206–222; (2008), 134–156.

and this time from the Jewish side, the links take precedence over any sense of alienation.

Other Hellenistic Jews took the matter further and on a different track. They made Greek philosophers dependent on Jewish text and tradition. First and foremost among perpetrators of that endeavor was the gifted and inventive intellectual Aristobulus, probably an Alexandrian of the second century BCE.[43] Like the author of the *Letter of Aristeas*, a treatise perhaps contemporary or nearly so, Aristobulus offered an engagingly imaginative presentation of Jewish involvement with Greek philosophy.[44] He had or at least was purported to have had philosophical credentials. Clement of Alexandria and Eusebius, who preserve the extant fragments of his work, designate him a Peripatetic.[45] The characterization need not, strictly speaking, mean that he was a follower of the Aristotelian school. It signifies more general philosophical interests or even wider intellectual leanings. He certainly had a familiarity with a range of Greek philosophical traditions.[46] Aristobulus, purportedly a tutor to Ptolemy VI of Egypt, produced an extensive composition, either a commentary on or a substantial exegesis of the Torah, of which only a few fragments survive.[47] They suffice, however, to disclose a notable agenda. Aristobulus undertook the task of establishing that the Hebrew Bible lay behind some of the best of Greek philosophical thought.

The author reached back to a famed and fabled figure: Pythagoras of Samos, the sixth-century philosopher, scientist, and religious thinker around whom legends collected and a pseudonymous literature accumulated. In Aristobulus' formulation, Pythagoras borrowed heavily from the books of Moses and incorporated them into his own doctrines.[48] Whether he had actually read any Pythagoras may be doubted. But the aura of Pythagoras' mystique invited a fictive association—especially one in which Jews got the credit. Aristobulus pressed the point with regard to an even

---

[43] Specific provenance and date remain somewhat disputed. But few will challenge the conclusion that Aristobulus was a Jewish intellectual of the mid-Hellenistic period. The essential study remains that of Walter (1964), 13–123. See also the important work by Gutman (1958), I, 186–220 (Hebrew). The edition of Aristobulus' fragments, with translation, commentary, and bibliography by Holladay (1995), is indispensable. On the lengthy debate, see the valuable summary of Holladay (1995), 49–75. Further bibliography in Gruen (2002a), 337, n. 55.

[44] The relative dates of Aristobulus and the *Letter of Aristeas* and the question of who influenced whom have long been debated, with no consensus; see, e.g., Walter (1964), 88–103; Holladay (1995), 64–65, 86, n. 90, with bibliography. Each could easily have drawn on the same tradition.

[45] Clem. Alex. *Strom*. 1.15.72.4; Euseb. *PE* 9.6.6; 13.11.3.

[46] See Walter (1964), 10–13.

[47] Euseb. *PE* 7.13.7, 7.32.16; Euseb. *Chron*. Ol.151; Clem. Alex. *Strom*. 5.14.97.7; cf. Holladay (1995), 74, 92–94.

[48] Clem. Alex. *Strom*. 1.22.150.3; Euseb. *PE* 9.6.8, 13.12.1.

more celebrated figure, Plato, who, in his view, followed the precepts of the Jewish lawgiver and worked assiduously through every detail of the laws.[49] He added Socrates too to that lineup, alluding to his famous "divine voice" and putting him in the company of Pythagoras and Plato (who claimed that they heard the voice of God when they observed the form of the universe so meticulously created and sustained by him), and Aristobulus used Moses' words to affirm the fact.[50] Nor did he stop with the ancient philosophers. He saw fit also to cite the Hellenistic poet Aratus of Soli, who had studied with the Stoic master Zeno and whose astronomical poem, the *Phaenomena*, suffused with Stoicism, served his purposes nicely. Aristobulus seized on the opening lines of the poem, in which Aratus offered a pantheistic vision of God not only as father of all but as permeating every corner of the universe. By the simple device of altering Aratus' terminology from Δὶς or Ζεύς to θεός, he underlined the debt owed by the Stoic poet to Jewish ideas.[51] In case anyone missed the point, Aristobulus added a still more sweeping statement that a consensus holds among all (Greek) philosophers about the necessity of maintaining reverent attitudes toward God. And that conviction, he notes, is most prominently promoted in the Jewish school of philosophy.[52] Indeed, Mosaic law enshrines the principles of piety, justice (righteousness), self-restraint, and all other qualities that are genuinely good.[53] It is hardly an accident that Aristobulus cites those virtues that became standard traits in Greek philosophical thought. The creative writer had no hesitation in framing Hellenic philosophy as an expression of Jewish tradition.

Indeed he needed to be creative. Pythagoras, Socrates, and Plato lived long before the composition of the Septuagint. Unless they miraculously gained a command of Hebrew, they could hardly have had access to the laws of Moses. Aristobulus did not resort to conjuring up miracles, but he did the next best thing. He got around the problem by compounding the fiction: Greek translations of at least parts of the Bible, he claimed, had been available some centuries before the compiling of the Septuagint. So Pythagoras, Plato, and others could have studied the scriptures in an accessible language to their heart's content.[54] The idea, of course, is preposterous. How many people might actually have believed it can be left to the

---

[49] Clem. Alex. *Strom.* 1.22.150.1; Euseb. *PE* 13.12.1.
[50] Clem. Alex. *Strom.* 5.14.99.3; Euseb. *PE* 13.12.4. Cf. Gutman (1958), I, 192–194 (Hebrew), who sees the proposition as a plausible one.
[51] Clem. Alex. *Strom.* 5.14.101.4b; Euseb. *PE* 13.12.6–7; Gutman (1958), I, 195–196 (Hebrew).
[52] Euseb. *PE* 13.12.8: ὃ μάλιστα παρακελεύεται καλῶς ἡ καθ' ἡμᾶς αἵρεσις. Use of αἵρεσις here is noteworthy, for the term regularly denotes a Greek philosophical school.
[53] Euseb. *PE* 13.12.8.
[54] Clem. Alex. *Strom.* 1.22.150.2; Euseb. *PE* 13.12.1.

imagination. One might indeed suggest that Aristobulus concocted the idea with tongue largely in cheek. A certain playfulness exists in his whole contrived scenario not only of Greek philosophers poring over biblical texts but also of numerous Greek poets and dramatists reproducing the lessons of the Bible.[55] But whether serious or not, Aristobulus' imaginative fabrications set Greek philosophy into the framework of the Jewish intellectual and religious achievement—the reverse of "Othering."

Aristobulus' work heralded a long tradition of Jewish claims to the priority of their teachings and the indebtedness of Hellenic philosophers. This edifying inference found its way into the works of the great Jewish philosopher and exegete Philo of Alexandria, where it appears in various forms and in numerous scattered places of his vast corpus. Philo, like Aristobulus, traced the effects of Jewish learning back to the pre-Socratics. Greeks had claimed that Heraclitus first hatched the idea that only the contemplation of opposites leads to understanding of the whole. Philo dismissed that claim: Moses had propounded the notion long before Heraclitus.[56] Even Heraclitus' famous statement regarding the soul's death as entombment in the body and its release to life when the body dies merely follows the teaching of Moses.[57] Philo duly acknowledges the persuasiveness of Plato's cosmology, which sees the world as created and indestructible. But, although some ascribe the origin of this view to Hesiod, Philo asserts that one can find it already in *Genesis*, thus to the credit of Moses.[58] The Jewish philosopher also paraphrases with approbation Plato's famous dictum that states can reach their potential only if kings become philosophers or philosophers become kings. But he points out that Moses had long since blended both kingship and philosophy in his own person—not to mention his roles as lawgiver, priest, and prophet.[59] So the scriptures again supplied precedent for Plato.

Hellenistic philosophy, for Philo, owes a similarly heavy debt to the teachings of the scriptures. He cites with high praise the thesis of Zeno the Stoic with regard to the necessity of subjecting the intemperate to the wise, but adds the conjecture that he must have got this idea from Isaac's command in Genesis that Esau serve his brother Jacob.[60] Stoic doctrine held that the wise man alone, no matter his material circumstances, is true ruler

---

[55] For this interpretation, see Gruen (1998), 246–251; (2002a), 221–224. Other scholars take Aristobulus' endeavor as an altogether serious enterprise. E.g., Gutman (1958), I, 186–220 (Hebrew); Walter (1964), passim; Hengel (1974), 163–169; Schürer (1986), 579–587; Barclay (1996), 150–158; J. Collins (2000), 186–190.
[56] Philo *Her.* 207–214.
[57] Philo *Leg. All.* 1.105–108.
[58] Philo *Aet.* 13–19.
[59] Philo *Mos.* 2; cf. Plato *Rep.* 5.473D.
[60] Philo *Prob.* 53–57; cf. Gen. 27.40.

and king and that virtue has unassailable authority. Philo, however, finds this principle already enshrined in a passage of Genesis wherein the Hittites (Canaanites) hail Abraham as a Prince of God among them.[61] Philo elsewhere allows himself a rather gratuitous bit of one-upmanship. He notes that Greek philosophers regarded those who first applied names to things as sages. But Moses had the better of them on that, for he had the distinction of naming Adam![62] Philo rarely shows flashes of humor. But this just might be an instance of it. And one can perhaps find another in his arresting claim that Socrates' thoughts about God's fashioning of body parts that perform excretory functions drew on Moses![63] Philo's powers of invention were not negligible. In re-creating the education of Moses, he performs a neat and surprising twist on the interpenetration of Greek and Jewish learning. Philo has Moses not only learn arithmetic, geometry, music, and hieroglyphics from erudite Egyptians but progress through the rest of the curriculum, presumably rhetoric, literature, and philosophy, with Greek teachers.[64] Just where Moses might have found itinerant Greek schoolmasters in late Bronze Age Egypt Philo leaves to the imagination. This too may have been no more than a half-serious flight of fancy. But it attests to a continuing byplay of *interpretationes Graecae* and *interpretationes Iudaicae*.

A generation after Philo, the idea that Greek philosophers hewed closely to the concept of God obtained from acquaintance with the books of Moses still made the rounds. The Jewish historian Josephus retailed the notion in his last—and most contrived—treatise, the *Contra Apionem*.[65] Josephus interestingly forbears, as he puts it, to make the case that the wisest of the Greeks learned their doctrines about God from the formulations of Moses. The idea could by that time be taken for granted. He affirms indeed that Greek philosophers have long since testified to the excellence and suitability of Jewish formulations with regard to the nature and glory of God. He cites Pythagoras, Anaxagoras, Plato, and the Stoics as witnesses to the fact. But why stop there? Josephus extends the point to encompass nearly all philosophers, since they hold similar views about the nature of God. And he gives the advantage to Moses on more than just priority. The Greeks philosophized to a small circle; Moses spoke with both actions and words not only to his contemporaries but to all future generations.[66] The historian makes a similar point elsewhere: the first imitators of Mosaic laws were

---

[61] Philo *Mut.* 152; *Somn.* 2.244; cf. Gen. 23.6.
[62] Philo *Leg. All.* 2.15.
[63] Philo *Q. Gen.* 2.6.
[64] Philo *Mos.* 1.23.
[65] On the contrived character of the work, see Gruen (2005), 31–51.
[66] Jos. *CAp.* 2.168–169. Josephus refers to Pythagoras' knowledge of Jewish matters also at *CAp.* 1.162.

Greek philosophers who, although ostensibly observing the practices of their native lands, actually in their deeds and their philosophizing followed the precepts of Moses.[67] Josephus can also become more specific. He cites two principles of Plato, that citizens should study their laws assiduously with precision and that they should restrict the introduction of foreigners so as to limit the state to those who adhere to its laws. On both those counts, he maintains, Plato took his cue from Moses.[68] For the Jewish readership of Josephus, like that of Philo, such claims were evidently uncontroversial, part of a long-standing application of Jewish tradition to Hellenic thought.

How long-standing? As we have seen, Greek writers had already made connection between Jewish sages and Greek philosophy in the late fourth century BCE. The assertion that Greeks owed philosophical doctrines to the Jews, on the other hand, appears, as one might expect, in Jewish texts, beginning at least with Aristobulus in the mid–second century BCE. This pattern, however, is crossed by a fascinating passage from a Hellenic author with no obvious Jewish axes to grind, one who precedes any extant Jewish texts on the matter. Hermippus of Smyrna, a pupil of Callimachus in Alexandria, composed a wide range of works, including a biography of Pythagoras, sometime in the late third or early second century BCE.[69] This puts him approximately half a century earlier than Aristobulus. Yet Hermippus included the arresting statement that Pythagoras imitated and adapted the views of Jews and Thracians. Coming from a Greek at so early a date, this striking remark demands attention.

The quotation comes from Josephus' *Contra Apionem*, which has as one of its chief aims a demonstration that Jews were held in esteem by eminent Greeks familiar with their writings. Josephus indeed has an ax to grind. But that does not itself cast suspicion on the accuracy with which he conveys Hermippus' remarks. A curious story about Pythagoras appeared in the first book of Hermippus' biography, as reported by Josephus. Pythagoras spoke about the death of one of his followers, Calliphon of Croton, whose soul then accompanied him day and night. He urged that one ought not to cross a spot where an ass sank to its knees, one ought to avoid any thirst-producing water, and one ought to refrain from all blasphemy.[70] An odd combination of precepts. To this point, Josephus appears to be paraphrasing Hermippus. He then quotes him directly as saying that Pythagoras acted on

---

[67] Jos. *CAp.* 2.281: πρῶτοι μὲν γὰρ οἱ παρὰ τοῖς Ἕλλησι φιλοσοφήσαντες τῷ μὲν δοκεῖν τὰ πάτρια διεφύλαττον, ἐν δὲ τοῖς πράγμασι καὶ τῷ φιλοσοφεῖν ἐκείνῳ κατηκολούθησαν; cf. 1.175.

[68] Jos. *CAp.* 2.257: Πλάτων μεμίμηται τὸν ἡμέτερον νομοθέτην.

[69] On the life and works of Hermippus, see the discussion, with testimony and bibliography, by Bollansée (1999), 1–20; also Bar-Kochva (2010), 167–173.

[70] Jos. *CAp.* 1.164. Whether the advice comes from Pythagoras or from the soul of Calliphon is ambiguous in the text. See Bar-Kochva (2010), 184. A decision is not required for our purposes.

and spoke about such matters by imitating and adapting to himself the views of Jews and Thracians.[71] And in his own voice Josephus adds that Pythagoras is rightly said to have brought into his philosophy many of the precepts found among the Jews.[72]

The passage is noteworthy. One will not be surprised to learn that some scholars have seized on this information to argue that Hermippus falls into the category of those Greek intellectuals who had a positive appreciation of the Jews and that he embraced the idea of a Jewish influence on Greek philosophy even before the Jews did.[73] But, as usual, the matter is not so simple. Hermippus' writings gained popularity—enough to warrant epitomes of them for a wider readership already in the second century BCE by Heraclides Lembus.[74] But the popularity did not arise from sober, scholarly monographs. Hermippus earned the reputation of a lively storyteller, noted for parody, fantasy, and rather caustic comments on the subjects of his works.[75] His depiction of Pythagoras falls into that category. It was no laudatory one. Fragments of the biography suggest sarcasm, innuendo, and mockery.[76] Nor was Hermippus the first. Pythagoras was a controversial figure who drew considerable criticism from philosophers and others.[77] That puts a very different slant on the passage conveyed by Josephus.

The particulars ascribed to Pythagoras appear, under this lens, to border on the ludicrous. The story of Calliphon's spirit dwelling night and day with the philosopher looks like an ironic comment on his doctrine of the immortality of the soul.[78] And the three prohibitions that he prescribed hardly suggest earnest guidance to his followers. Avoidance of a spot where an ass sank to his knees and refraining from salty or sugary water recall a host of Pythagorean pronouncements that few outside the sect (or perhaps even within) would take seriously.[79] The ban on blasphemy looks more solemn. But it is one so widely shared among creeds and sects that it might have been included for its banality rather than its solemnity.[80] Hermippus

---

[71] Jos. *CAp*. 1.165: ταῦτα δὲ ἔπραττε καὶ ἔλεγε τὰς Ἰουδαίων καὶ Θρακῶν δόξας μιμούμενος καὶ μεταφέρων εἰς ἑαυτόν.

[72] Jos. *CAp*. 1.165.

[73] E.g., Gabba (1989), 623–624; Feldman (1993), 201–202.

[74] On the subsequent reputation of Hermippus, see Bollansée (1999), 104–116.

[75] See Bollansée (1999), 118–153, and Bar-Kochva (2010), 171–173.

[76] Examples in Bar-Kochva (2010), 173–181. See, e.g., Diog. Laert. 8.41. Cf. Bollansée (1999), 44–52, who, however, takes far too generous a view of Hermippus' bias.

[77] E.g., Diog. Laert. 5.1, 8.7, 8.36, 9.1, with the discussion of Bar-Kochva (2010), 181–182.

[78] Cf. Diog. Laert. 8.32; Barclay (2007), 96; Bar-Kochva (2010), 184.

[79] Jacobson (1976), 145–149, makes a laudable but ultimately unsuccessful attempt to find biblical prescriptions behind Hermippus' statements. Similarly, Gorman (1983), 33–36. See the criticisms of Bar-Kochva (2010), 190–193.

[80] Bar-Kochva (2010), 187–189, goes further to argue that Greeks did not worry about blasphemy anyway except at a sacred shrine—an extreme position.

was having some fun with the superstitions and ritual taboos associated with Pythagoreanism.

What then are we to make of Hermippus' statement (here in a direct quote by Josephus) that Pythagoras both asserted and practiced these precepts in imitation of Jewish and Thracian doctrines? It certainly constituted no compliment to Jews or Thracians. A search for Jewish parallels for the three prohibitions leads nowhere, let alone guesswork as to which may have been Thracian and which Jewish.[81] On the other hand, it does not follow that Hermippus was denigrating Jews and Thracians together with Pythagoras. The philosopher was said to have been conversant with and influenced by various eastern traditions, including those of Egyptians, Chaldeans, and magi.[82] It would be logical enough to add Jews to that company. As for Thracians, a people usually regarded as on the periphery of civilization, one might be tempted to infer that Hermippus inserted them as yet another sardonic jab at Pythagoras. He did not, however, invent the connection. Biographical references to the sage include one that has his slave bring Pythagorean teachings to the Thracians.[83] More important perhaps is the association of Pythagoras with Orphism.[84] Since legend has Orpheus, the father of Hellenic song and poetry, as a Thracian, the suggestion of influence from Thrace on Pythagoras need not itself be a hostile one. But it is easy enough to imagine that Hermippus might have turned the relationship to his own purpose in comic fashion.

Josephus' own comments go well beyond what might be inferred from the Hermippus fragment. The historian introduces the subject by stating that Pythagoras, a figure of great antiquity, preeminent among philosophers in wisdom and piety, not only knew about Jewish matters but was a most eager emulator of them.[85] And he closes the segment by affirming that Pythagoras is correctly said to have imported many Jewish precepts into his own philosophy.[86] This plainly embellishes and enhances the information in Hermippus. It is picked up and further amplified by Origen, who cites Hermippus for the view that Pythagoras transferred his own philosophy from Jews to Greeks.[87] Those sweeping assertions have more to do with the objectives of Josephus and Origen than with the more cynical intent of Hermippus.

---

[81] So, rightly, Barclay (2007), 97–98; Bar-Kochva (2010), 190–193.
[82] Diog. Laert. 8.3; Porphyry *Vita Pyth.* 6, 11–12.
[83] Herod. 4.95; Strabo 7.3.5; Iamblichus *Vita Pyth.* 14–15.
[84] Cf. Iamblichus *Vita Pyth.* 146; Barclay (2007), 97.
[85] Jos. *CAp.* 1.162: σοφίᾳ δὲ καὶ τῇ περὶ τὸ θεῖον εὐσεβείᾳ πάντων ὑπειλημμένος διενεγκεῖν, τῶν φιλοσοφησάντων, οὐ μόνον ἐγνωκὼς τὰ παρ' ἡμῖν δῆλός ἐστιν, ἀλλὰ καὶ ζηλωτὴς αὐτῶν ἐκ πλείστου γεγενημένος.
[86] Jos. *CAp.* 1.165: λέγεται γὰρ ὡς ἀληθῶς ὁ ἀνὴρ ἐκεῖνος πολλὰ τῶν παρὰ Ἰουδαίοις νομίμων εἰς τὴν αὑτοῦ μετενεγκεῖν φιλοσοφίαν.
[87] Origen *CCelsum* 1.15.334. Cf. also Porphyry *Vita Pyth.* 11.

This does not, however, obviate the main point. There is no reason to doubt that the association of Pythagoras with Jewish ideas and traditions was already current in the time of Hermippus. Even if he alluded to the presumed connection only in order to mock Pythagoras, he attests to its existence. It matters not whether Josephus had access to Hermippus' text, to an epitome of it, or even a reference to it in a Jewish author. Hermippus' affirmation that Pythagoras was influenced by Jewish beliefs can hardly be sheer invention.[88] It reflects both the Hellenic conceptualization that links eastern wisdom with Greek philosophy and the Jewish construct that has Greek philosophers derive their ideas from Jewish learning. The overlap and interconnection leave a deep impression.[89]

The reciprocation has a long history. Two striking passages provide a coda to underscore it. Philo in the mid–first century CE comments that the world contains multitudes of rich, eminent, and pleasure-seeking individuals but very few who are wise, just, and virtuous. He then specifies important examples of the latter category: the seven sages of Greece, the Persian magi, the Indian gymnosophists, and the Jewish Essenes.[90] The Jewish philosopher, therefore, echoes a linkage between Hellenic savants and eastern wise men (including Jews) that goes back more than three centuries to Greek thinkers like Megasthenes, Clearchus, and Hermippus.[91] And as late as the second half of the second century CE, the Platonist philosopher Numenius of Apamea (whom some referred to as a Pythagorean) reiterated the affinities of Plato and Pythagoras with the teachings of Brahmans, Egyptians, magi, and Jews.[92] Numenius has the signal distinction of uttering the

---

[88] Bar-Kochva (2010), 196–202, whose dissection of the text is decidedly superior to other treatments, nevertheless takes a minimalist approach. His conclusion that Hermippus made no allusion to Jews except for the three precepts actually recorded by Josephus is implausible. A similar view in Schürer (1986), 696. Gorman (1983), 32–33, Barclay (2007), 98, and Bar-Kochva (2010), 196–198, propose that Josephus based his broader statement about Jewish influence on Pythagoras strictly or largely on Aristobulus (Euseb. *PE* 13.12.1). The language is indeed similar (though not identical). But many Jewish writers, now lost, may have conveyed parallel information. Josephus nowhere cites Aristobulus. To infer that he simply adopted Aristobulus' formulation about Jewish impact on Pythagoras and ascribed it to Hermippus without any basis except the three precepts is highly questionable. Bar-Kochva's view that Origen's statement is a mere paraphrase of Josephus also stands on shaky ground. Whereas Josephus cites Hermippus' *Life of Pythagoras*, Origen drew his information from Hermippus' work *On Lawgivers*; *CCelsum* 1.15.334. Bar-Kochva's conclusion that the information simply passed from Aristobulus to Josephus to Origen, denying any role to Hermippus, is too reductive.

[89] Note also the comment of Josephus that Essenes borrowed their way of life from Pythagoras! *Ant.* 15.371.

[90] Philo *Prob.* 72–75.

[91] The presumed parallels were still very much alive among Greek thinkers in the time of Strabo; see 16.1.39.

[92] Euseb. *PE* 9.7.1.

most celebrated remark in this entire subject: "For what is Plato, but Moses speaking in good Attic Greek?"[93] As Philo the Jew mirrors the constructed interconnections first formulated by Greeks, so Numenius the Greek mirrors the conceit of Jewish origins for Greek philosophy first formulated by Jews. Alterity and otherness take a backseat. The mutual appropriations suggest that Jews and Greeks found a cross-cultural association to be not a diminution of their identity but an enhancement of it.

Jewish Presentations of Gentiles

A range of imaginative writings, whether recastings of biblical stories, adaptations of Greek genres, or creations of historical novels, attest to the Jewish construction of links to the non-Jewish world. Some pertinent examples offer illumination.

The most fascinating author under this heading is a relatively obscure figure named Artapanus. That at least is the name that has come down to us, a Persian name, perhaps a pseudonym, belonging to a writer known only from a few fragments quoted by Alexander Polyhistor and preserved for us by Eusebius. Of his life and time we are ignorant, except to say that he lived sometime between the mid-third and early first centuries BCE, between the composition of the Septuagint and the *floruit* of Alexander Polyhistor.[94] He composed his work in Greek, and he was almost certainly a Jew.[95] Artapanus undertook to re-create biblical stories and to rewrite

---

[93] Euseb. *PE* 9.6.9: τί γὰρ ἐστι Πλάτων ἢ Μωσῆς ἀττικίζων. Other references in Stern (1980), II, 210.

[94] The fragments are conveniently collected, translated, and commented on by Holladay (1983), I, 189–243, with extensive bibliography. A lengthy bibliography on Artapanus' dates and provenance existed already when summarized by Holladay (1977), 199–204; subsequent references to the scholarship in Sterling (1992), 167–169; Gruen (1998), 150–153; Collins (2000), 38–39. Artapanus has drawn increased attention in recent years; see Flusser and Amorai-Stark (1993–1994), 217–233; Koskenniemi (2002), 17–31; Johnson (2004), 95–108; Kugler (2005), 67–80; Jacobson (2006), 219–221. Zellentin (2008), 7–8, rightly points out that the assumption of Artapanus' dependence on the Septuagint is not watertight—but it remains most plausible. Zellentin's efforts (2008), 27–39, to find a more precise date for Artapanus by having his work respond directly to a Ptolemaic decree of 118 BCE are ingenious but highly speculative. How many readers would have the knowledge and acuity to draw the inferences required by this theory?

[95] The point was argued with force and cogency long ago by Freudenthal (1874–1875), 147–174, who added, more dubiously, the suggestion that Artapanus was masquerading as a pagan; rightly questioned by Sterling (1992), 167–168. A cautious doubt about Artapanus' Jewishness was injected by Fraser (1972), I, 706; II, 985, and by Feldman (1993), 208, and has recently received more serious challenge by Jacobson (2006), 210–221. Jacobson is quite right that a favorable attitude toward the Hebrew patriarchs and Moses does not establish Artapanus as a Jew. But he obviously belonged to a circle thoroughly conversant with biblical

Israelite history. How far his work, titled *On the Jews*, went is beyond our grasp. The extant fragments consist of two short excerpts from his treatment of Abraham and Joseph and a somewhat lengthier treatment of Moses. They exhibit an inventive mind and an idiosyncratic manipulation of his material. But they also provide an arresting example of a Jewish intellectual's conception of interrelationships between Israelite traditions and other cultures of the ancient world.[96]

Artapanus' aims are regularly misconstrued. Scholars generally see his work as a counterattack against pagan critics of biblical figures like Moses.[97] But to whom would such a counterattack be directed? Few gentiles would be likely to encounter, let alone read, a reconstruction of biblical tales embellishing the deeds of the patriarchs. The audience must have been largely Jews, who alone would appreciate the whimsical liberties Artapanus took with the scriptures. Nothing in the fragments indicates polemics.[98] Artapanus had broader objectives. The name alone may be suggestive. "Artapanus" need not indicate actual Persian ancestry. Ascription of that name or pseudonym to the author could signify the very outreach that his work embodies.

The figure of Abraham, even in the short fragment that we possess, exemplifies the approach.[99] Artapanus presents the patriarch as coming to Egypt with his entire household, there to instruct the pharaoh in astrology. That particular notice both alludes to Abraham's Babylonian origins and makes him a contributor to Egyptian learning. And Artapanus adds another element. The same fragment includes a peculiar notice assigning the name "Hermiouth" to the Jews as a Greek translation. Whatever this might mean, it hints at a connection with the Greek god Hermes, a name elsewhere employed by Artapanus as an alternative designation for Moses. Abraham thus does quadruple duty as forerunner of the Jews, conveyer of Chaldean traditions, mentor of Pharaoh, and link to the Hellenic world.

The fragment on Joseph yields little for our purpose. But a scrap or two may be relevant. Artapanus molds the Genesis story to his own taste, leaving out most of it and shaping the rest as it suits him.[100] The biblical version has Joseph sold to the Ishmaelites who took him to Egypt.[101] In Artapanus,

---

traditions on these figures and in a position to catch the author's witty twists on and deviations from the standard version. A knowledgeable and discerning readership for such a work would include few gentiles.

[96] What follows is an adaptation and abbreviation of the fuller treatment, providing bibliography, in Gruen (2002a), 201–211, with a slightly different objective. A parallel adaptation in Gruen (forthcoming).

[97] See the long list of modern works who take this line in Gruen (2002a), 332, n. 83.

[98] Zellentin (2008), 21–24, reaches a similar conclusion.

[99] Euseb. *PE* 9.18.1.

[100] Euseb. *PE* 9.23.1–4.

[101] Gen. 37.28.

they become "Arabs," a perfectly reasonable designation from a Hellenistic vantage point. But they are no longer slave traders, rather neighboring peoples whom Joseph on his own initiative asked to bring him to Egypt—which, in friendly fashion, they did. Artapanus adds the explanation that the rulers of the Arabs, as sons of Abraham and brothers of Isaac, were descendants of "Israel." There is obvious confusion here, the name "Israel" perhaps garbled in transmission. But Artapanus plainly evokes the tradition that has Arabs descended from Ishmael, thus from the house of Abraham. Further, among the deeds of Joseph in Egypt singled out by our author (in addition to organizing the economy and introducing Egyptians to weights and measures) was his wedding to Aseneth, the daughter of a Heliopolite priest. The stress on ethnic connections can hardly be accidental.

Artapanus takes still greater liberties in his rewrite of the Moses story. He employs the book of Exodus as no more than a frame to construct his own adventure tales that make Moses a foiler of plots and assassinations, military hero, inventor, author of Egyptian institutions, and prime benefactor of humanity. And he made sure to associate Moses with a variety of cultures. In Artapanus' re-creation, Moses was named Mousaios by the Greeks and became the teacher of Orpheus, the legendary singer and father of Hellenic poetry.[102] The Egyptian priests for their part called Moses Hermes because he was able to interpret hieroglyphics.[103] This fanciful brew gives a revealing glimpse into Artapanus' mentality. The Greeks identified Moses with Mousaios, seizing on the similarity of names, according to Artapanus. But he goes them one better: Moses was teacher of Orpheus rather than the other way around, as Hellenic legend had it. This was a playful one-upmanship. And the Egyptian priests who dubbed him Hermes, in Artapanus' construct, had more in mind than the Greek divinity. They associated Moses with the Egyptian version of Hermes, Thoth, who, like Moses, possessed the skills of craftsmen and the ability to interpret sacred writings.[104] By having Greeks and Egyptians make the identifications and the ascriptions, Artapanus gives Moses a central place in both cultures, the amalgam that was Ptolemaic Egypt.

The creativity of Artapanus is breathtaking. There was little in Egyptian society or experience that could not be traced to Moses. The Hebrew hero was responsible for inventing ships and weapons, for hydraulic and building devices, and for the introduction of philosophy. He divided the land into the nomes that became the basis of political organization, he set aside property for the priests, he apportioned divinities to each nome, and he

---

[102] Euseb. *PE* 9.27.3–4.
[103] Euseb. *PE* 9.27.6.
[104] See the valuable discussions of Gutman (1963), II, 120–122, and Mussies (1982), 97–108.

even introduced animal worship to the people.[105] Nor was that all. When Moses buried his mother Merris, he named the river and the site Meroe after her, thus establishing that designation for the greatest city of Ethiopia. He founded the city of Hermopolis, named after him (Hermes), and made the ibis sacred there. It was Moses too who introduced Ethiopians to the practice of circumcision. His magical rod so impressed the Egyptians that they installed rods in all their temples and associated them with the worship of Isis. Moses' manipulation of the Nile in order to intimidate Pharaoh into releasing his people became the origin of the river's annual inundation. And his advice on the best oxen to till the land turned out to inspire the consecration of the sacred bull Apis, a central element of Egyptian worship.[106]

Mischief abounds in this work. Artapanus toys with traditions and delights in surprise twists. He repeatedly upsets the expectations of readers familiar with the Exodus and invents scenes never even hinted at in the Bible. They include Moses' conduct of a military campaign on the scale of the Trojan War, his personal duel with a knife-wielding assailant, his escape from prison when the gates miraculously swung open, and his felling of Pharaoh by whispering the Lord's name in his ear.[107] The puckish quality of all this is plain. And the idea that the Hebrew lawgiver actually brought Egyptian institutions into being (no mention is made of Moses giving laws to the Israelites) and endorsed, even introduced, animal worship could only invite amusement.

But there is more than jocularity here. The theme, repeated in an ingenious variety of ways, of interconnections between the founder of the Israelite nation and other peoples and cultures pervades the text. Artapanus also brings Arabs into the mix. He alters the biblical narrative that has Moses wed the daughter of a Midianite priest, describing the union more broadly as marriage into the leading house of Arabia.[108] Egyptians saw him as Thoth, Greeks as Mousaios; he brought hieroglyphics to Egypt and circumcision to Ethiopia; and his family could trace its bloodline to Arabia. The work qualifies as a prime document of cultural integration. Not that

---

[105] Euseb. *PE* 9.27.4–5. For most scholars, Moses' responsibility for Egyptian religious institutions, especially animal worship, is hard to swallow, thus leading to the conclusion that Artapanus must have been a polytheist, a syncretist, a half Jew, or a pagan—or a shrewd legislator patronizing inferior Egyptians without buying into their beliefs. See the summary of views by Koskenniemi (2002), 26–31 (who adopts the last solution), and Jacobson (2006), 215–216 (who reckons Artapanus a non-Jew). It does not help much to label Artapanus as a "henotheist" or as one who believes in "monolatry" rather than "monotheism." Almost all scholars overlook the playful and whimsical character of the text. See Gruen (2002a), 201–211; endorsed now by Zellentin (2008), 6–7.

[106] Euseb. *PE* 9.27.9–10, 9.27.12, 9.27.16, 9.27.28, 9.27.32.

[107] Euseb. *PE* 9.27.7–8, 9.27.18, 9.27.23–25.

[108] Euseb. *PE* 9.27.19.

Artapanus championed syncretism or synthesis. Jewish identity remained at the center of the enterprise. Moses indeed usurped the achievements accredited to other nations' heroes and divinities, becoming mentor, founder, and originator of institutions for a whole range of peoples. Artapanus' capricious but learned book exemplifies the self-perception of Jews who reckoned insight into other cultures as an enrichment of their own.

Artapanus was not alone in fitting figures of the biblical past into a cultural amalgam. An extended fragment attributed to a certain Eupolemus by Alexander Polyhistor and transmitted to us by Eusebius discloses a similar approach. The author rewrote parts of the Abraham story in Genesis and added elements that derived from both Babylonian and Greek legendary material.[109] Polyhistor's attribution may or may not be accurate. Given the widespread convention, it will be convenient to use the designation "Pseudo-Eupolemus." Whether our author is identical with the Jewish historian Eupolemus, himself usually identified with a Maccabean supporter of the mid–second century, remains controversial and need not be discussed here.[110] What matters is the text. And it shows remarkable similarity to the mind-set of Artapanus.

The fragment uses a portion of Genesis as springboard but leaps well beyond it. The initial focus is on Babylon, first built by those who survived the Flood, according to Pseudo-Eupolemus. He proceeds then to assign the building of the Tower of Babel to giants who were subsequently scattered over the earth after God destroyed the structure.[111] The report has echoes of Greek myths on the Gigantomachia, here imported onto the biblical exegesis. The author next introduces Abraham, the chief figure of the fragment, as one who excelled all in nobility and wisdom and who discovered astrology and Chaldean craft. The phraseology is reminiscent of a line from the Babylonian historian Berossus, who wrote in Greek, thus suggesting that our author dabbled in Babylonian as well as Hellenic sources.[112] Certainly he has Abraham impart his Mesopotamian knowledge to other Near Eastern peoples. The patriarch, according to Pseudo-Eupolemus, taught the cycles of the sun and moon, and much else besides, to the Phoenicians (here perhaps equivalent to Canaanites), ingratiating himself with

---

[109] Euseb. *PE* 9.17.1–9. For what follows, see Gruen (1998), 146–150, with bibliography.

[110] The case for the author of this fragment as a "Pseudo-Eupolemus" rather than Eupolemus, as Polyhistor thought, was made long ago by Freudenthal (1874–1875), 82–103, and followed by most scholars thereafter. See discussion and bibliography in Sterling (1992), 187–200. But it is not definitive. See the arguments of Doran (1985b), II, 873–878; cf. Gruen (1998), 147–148. Collins (2000), 47–49, retains the standard view. That the historian Eupolemus himself is identical with the Maccabean supporter should not be taken for granted—although almost no one has questioned it. See Gruen (1998), 139–141.

[111] Euseb. *PE* 9.17.2–3.

[112] Euseb. *PE* 9.17.3. See, especially, Gutman (1963), II, 97–99 (Hebrew). The line of Berossus is preserved by Josephus *Ant.* 1.158, who took it as reference to Abraham.

the Phoenician king. And, later, when he moved to Egypt, Abraham became mentor to Egyptian priests, teaching them astrology and a range of other matters.[113] This cross-cultural mix becomes still more explicit in the author's gloss on Abraham's explanation to the Egyptians of the origins of astrology. The patriarch ascribed the discovery to Enoch. Pseudo-Eupolemus then went on to recount a mythical genealogy stemming from Kronos, also known as Belos (Baal) by the Babylonians, one of whose descendants, Canaan, became ancestor of the Phoenicians (Canaanites); another, Kush, became forefather of the Ethiopians; and still another, Mizraim, sired the Egyptians. The connection of all this with Enoch is unclear. But the author adds that Greeks acknowledge Enoch as the discoverer of astrology, although they call him Atlas. And through the line of Enoch knowledge has come down through the ages to "us" (presumably the Jews).[114]

The jumbled genealogy defies sorting out. But the author has clearly dug about in Babylonian, Israelite, and Greek lore and swept into its vortex Ethiopians and Egyptians as well, all this connected, however awkwardly, with the narrative of Abraham. What did Pseudo-Eupolemus have in mind with this conglomerate? It is misguided to interpret the intention as verifying Jewish tradition by finding external confirmation, let alone as elevating that tradition against pagan or polytheistic versions. Pseudo-Eupolemus wove together diverse strands drawn from Hellenic and Near Eastern legends into the Jewish fabric to produce a new—though hardly seamless—tapestry. The Abraham narrative in Genesis became altogether transformed; the patriarch was associated even with the legendary figure of Enoch, whose story had been inflated and embellished by Hellenistic Jews.[115] The Hebrew patriarch stands in the midst of this extraordinary intercultural web. He is both progenitor of Israelites and purveyor of culture to other peoples of the Mediterranean, both national hero and world-historical figure. This imaginative network engineered by Pseudo-Eupolemus reinforces the idea of reciprocal advantage among the nations—not a parting of the ways.[116]

The interconnections could be displayed in a slightly different but equally appealing fashion. A favored fiction among certain Hellenistic Jewish writers was the derivation of Hellenic ideas from Jewish roots. Prime of

---

[113] Euseb. *PE* 9.17.4, 9.17.8.

[114] Euseb. *PE* 9.17.8–9. See Gutman (1963), II, 100–101 (Hebrew); Wacholder (1963), 89–99.

[115] On the complex Enochic traditions, see now Nickelsburg (2001), passim.

[116] Alexander Polyhistor quotes another brief but closely related fragment that he attributes to an anonymous author; Euseb. *PE* 9.18.2. The passage has Abraham trace his ancestry to the giants who dwelled in Babylonia, gain familiarity with astrology, and teach the subject first to Phoenicians, then to Egyptians. Although some scholars take this as product of a different writer, the fact that it reproduces the principal themes in Pseudo-Eupolemus' fragment makes it easier to presume that the one is a garbled summary of the other.

place in this regard, as we have seen, belongs to Aristobulus, a Jew probably of the mid-second century BCE familiar with Greek philosophy and literature, and determined to demonstrate that much of it owed its origins to the teachings of Moses. His work was substantial, and its character is discernible even from the few remains preserved by Clement of Alexandria and Eusebius.[117]

Mosaic law constitutes a repeated reference point in Aristobulus' construct. Greek philosophers recurred to it regularly to frame their own positions. Pythagoras, if one believes Aristobulus, adapted much of what he found in Hebrew teachings and embedded it in his intellectual system. And Plato followed suit, even poring over the particulars of Moses' legislation in working out his thoughts. The chronological difficulty, that the Septuagint did not come into being for well over a century after Plato, and nearly three centuries after Pythagoras, neither of whom could read Hebrew, was, as noted above, neatly skirted. Aristobulus simply postulated that parts of the Pentateuch, those dealing with the Exodus, the conquest of Canaan, and all the legislative details, had already been rendered into Greek long before the composition of the Septuagint.[118] The transparent fabrication came in a good cause: to bring the teachings of Greek philosophy under the umbrella of Jewish law.

Aristobulus advances that project elsewhere in his writing. All philosophers, he says, concur on the need to hold pious convictions about God—and that point is no better made than in the school of Judaism itself, preeminent for its doctrines on piety, justice, self-control, and all other genuinely good qualities.[119] In short, all that was admirable in Greek philosophy coincided with precepts long ago articulated by the Torah.

Aristobulus could appropriate Greek literature as well. The legendary Orpheus, wellspring of Hellenic poetry, speaks of all things being in the hand of God, a sign, for Aristobulus, that Orpheus paralleled the teachings of the scriptures. Aristobulus—or someone—even went to the trouble of composing or adapting a full-scale poem, ascribed to Orpheus and directed to his son Mousaios, that espoused a moving monotheism.[120] This composition, whether or not from the pen of Aristobulus, certainly represents a significant aspect of Hellenistic-Jewish thinking. By assigning to the ancestor of pagan poets a poem with a lofty monotheistic vision of the deity, the author has associated the inspiration for Greek literature with the doctrines

---

[117] On Aristobulus, see above, pp. 317–319. The remarks here are adapted from Gruen (1998), 246–253. See, more recently, Collins (2000), 186–190.
[118] Euseb. *PE* 13.12.1; Clem. *Strom.* 1.22.150.1–3. See above.
[119] Euseb. *PE* 13.12.8; cf. Gutman (1958), I, 192–199 (Hebrew).
[120] Euseb. 13.12.5. On the vexed questions of different versions of this poem and the relationships among them, see Holladay (1996), IV, passim, who devoted an entire volume to the subject.

of Judaism. And, lest there be any uncertainty about it, the hymn proclaims that even Orpheus could witness God only through a cloud, in a fuzzy way, while all others had their vision blocked by ten layers of obscurity. The sole exception was a certain man who came of Chaldean stock and who was expert in the movement of the sun and that of the earth around its axis. That can hardly be any other than Abraham.[121] Thus Orpheus himself, the very source of Hellenic poetry, pays homage to the Hebrew patriarch—at least in the conception of the inventive Jewish author.

Aristobulus' ingenuity stretched further still. He identified the sanctification of the Sabbath with a veritable law of nature that gave a special resonance to the number seven, already widely used in Greek philosophical circles.[122] Aristobulus proceeded to parade verses of Homer and Hesiod (whether authentic or spurious), whose allusions to the "seventh day" he took as echoes of the Hebrew scriptures—even when he had to resort to emendations of the text![123] Aristobulus was not above assigning invented lines to the mythical poet Linus, who came down in the tradition either as son of Apollo or music teacher of Herakles. He has Linus assert that all was made complete on the seventh morning, a perfect number that signified also the creation of the seven heavenly bodies (planets) set shining in their revolving orbits.[124] Nor did Aristobulus limit himself to poets of distant antiquity or mythology. He neatly turned the astronomical poem of the Hellenistic writer Aratus of Soli to his own purposes. By substituting "God" for "Zeus," Aristobulus reinterpreted Aratus' pantheism as an acknowledgment of the Jewish deity.[125]

The canny contrivances of Aristobulus have parallels in other, anonymous, Jewish authors who showed comparable craft. They searched through the texts of Greek tragic and comic drama to dig out verses that might resonate with Jewish precepts. And when they failed to find them, they did not hesitate to make them up.[126] These included supposed verses by Aeschylus, who hailed the awesome power of "God most high," an epithet frequently employed by Hellenistic Jews—and hence readily taken as a paean to Yahweh.[127] Sophocles (or at least purported lines of Sophocles) served the purpose as well. He blasted idolatry, criticized the philanderings of Zeus, proclaimed the unity and uniqueness of God, and forecast

---

[121] He is explicitly identified as such by Clement, *Strom.* 5.14.123.

[122] Euseb. *PE* 13.12.12. On the philosophical background, see Gutman (1958), I, 203–210 (Hebrew); Walter (1964), 68–81; Holladay (1996), IV, 230–231.

[123] Euseb. *PE* 13.12.13–15; Clem. *Strom.* 5.14.107.1–3. Cf. Walter (1964), 150–158.

[124] Euseb. 13.12.16. A good discussion by Walter (1964), 158–166.

[125] Euseb. *PE* 13.12.6–7; cf. Clem. *Strom.* 5.14.101.4b.

[126] The relevant passages are collected by Denis (1970), 161–174. See translations and notes by Attridge (1985), II, 824–830.

[127] Ps. Justin *De Monarch.* 2; Clem. *Strom.* 5.14.131.2–3; Euseb. *PE* 13.13.60.

the destruction of the universe with the salvation of the righteous.[128] Those phrases proved most convenient for Jewish intellectuals—and equally so for the Church Fathers who preserved them. Two lines of Euripides suited these ends as well. They spoke of an all-seeing god invisible to mortals and asserted the principle that no dwelling fashioned by human hands can contain the spirit of God.[129] Helpful verses were also ascribed to comic dramatists like Philinus, Diphilus, and Menander attesting to God's justice, to the punishment of the wicked, and to the need to honor the one god who is father for all time, inventor and creator of every good.[130]

All these ostensible conjunctions indeed seem too good to be true. But that makes them all the more interesting. The very lengths to which Jewish writers would go to discover or manufacture links between their traditions and Greek philosophy and literature are quite extraordinary. The endeavor itself carries weighty meaning. Aristobulus and others ransacked Greek classics to find formulations and sentiments that evoked scriptural lessons. And they made a veritable industry of shaping, interpreting, or inventing passages from Hellenic poets and philosophers that called to mind precepts of the Jews. The precedence of Jewish learning constitutes a consistent theme. As Abraham was responsible for the astronomical skills of the Phoenicians in Pseudo-Eupolemus and Moses for Egyptian hieroglyphics in Artapanus, so the Torah lies behind the most sublime teachings of Greek philosophers and the powerful messages of Greek drama in Aristobulus and those Jewish intellectuals of like mind. The fabrications are clever, arresting, indeed often amusing, in many instances never intended to be taken seriously. They surely did not represent sober efforts to persuade pagans of Jewish respectability (how many pagans would be persuaded by these transparent concoctions?). Nor would they advance any cause of assimilation (Greeks could hardly be expected to swallow reconstructions that had their leading intellectual heroes dependent on the precepts of the Torah). These creative constructs must have circulated largely among Jews themselves. And they demonstrate the premium their authors placed on viewing Hebraic traditions through Hellenic lenses—and vice versa.

The classic text for the blending of Greek and Jewish ideas, and the collaboration of the peoples, is the celebrated *Letter of Aristeas*. That work, composed most likely in the second or early first century BCE by a Hellenized Jew probably from Alexandria, has received voluminous scholarly

---

[128] Ps. Justin *De Monarch*. 2–3; Clem. *Strom*. 5.14.111.4–6, 5.14.113.2, 5.114.121.4–122.1; Euseb. *PE* 13.13.38, 13.13.40, 13.30.48.

[129] Clem. *Protr*. 6.68.3; *Strom*. 5.11.75.1; cf. Ps. Justin *De Monarch*. 2.

[130] Ps. Justin *De Monarch*. 2–5; Clem. *Strom*. 5.14.119.2, 5.14.121.1–3, 5.14.133.3; Euseb. *PE* 13.13.45–47, 13.13.62.

scrutiny—and the volumes have only increased in recent years.[131] It purports to narrate the circumstances surrounding the translation of the Torah into Greek in Alexandria during the reign of Ptolemy II Philadelphus. Only selected highlights need to be noted here.

The narrator, "Aristeas," presented as a prominent figure at the court of Ptolemy Philadelphus, sets forth the events in a communication to his brother "Philocrates." The Jewish author in short employs a Greek pseudonym and Greek persona—not to deceive his readers but as a literary device the better to convey his portrait of harmonious interchange between the peoples. According to the narrative, the idea for a translation of the Pentateuch came from Demetrius of Phalerum, head of the great library in Alexandria. It would be an invaluable addition to the shelves. Ptolemy was happy to endorse the suggestion and arranged with Eleazer, High Priest in Jerusalem, for the dispatch of seventy-two distinguished scholars from Jerusalem, as knowledgeable in Greek as in Hebrew, to prepare the translation in Alexandria.[132] The narrator presents himself as one of the Ptolemaic envoys to Jerusalem, where he listened with rapt attention and awe to the High Priest Eleazer's disquisition on the religious beliefs and dietary prescriptions of the Jews.[133] Just why the Jewish scholars needed to travel to Egypt for this purpose is not indicated, but it allowed Ptolemy to entertain them handsomely, display his generous hospitality, and underscore his friendly regard for the nation of the Jews. Among other things, as we have seen, the king entertained his visitors in a seven-day symposium, each dinner strictly kosher, and each evening punctuated by a question-and-answer session in which the king asked his guests for their views on the proper conduct of government and of life. The Jews' responses in each session demonstrated their great aplomb. The seventy-two sages, comfortably ensconced in a mansion on the island of Pharos, then proceeded to produce their translation in precisely seventy-two days. The culmination of the process came when the Jews of Alexandria (who presumably knew little or no Hebrew) assembled to hear the books of Moses read out to them in Greek and erupted in applause. Ptolemy himself lavished praise on the Jewish lawgiver, treated the newly translated texts with great respect, and loaded gifts on the Jewish scholars, who now returned to Jerusalem.[134]

No wonder that the tale generally ranks as the locus classicus for the blending of Hellenic and Hebraic ideology. We are not here concerned with how much (or how little) of this text can count as history. Some form

---

[131] See the bibliographic references in Schürer (1986), 679–684; Gruen (1998), 206–222; add also Collins (2000), 97–103, 191–195; Honigman (2003), 13–91; Wasserstein and Wasserstein (2006), 19–26; Gruen (2008), 134–156; Rajak (2008), 176–193; (2009), 24–63.
[132] *LetArist*. 1–11, 28–41, 120–123.
[133] *LetArist*. 128–170.
[134] *LetArist*. 301–312, 317–321.

of what we now know as the Septuagint was doubtless composed in Alexandria with the assistance of Jews from Jerusalem.[135] But the bulk of the text, on any reckoning, is embellishment or invention, an entertaining legend. For that very reason it gives welcome insight into the mode whereby Jewish intellectuals conceived their relationship to Hellenic culture and the reaction of gentiles to Hebraic tradition.

The *Letter of Aristeas*, composed by a Jew in the guise of a Greek, is heavily Hellenic in character. Eminent Greeks, literary and philosophical figures, make an appearance or are referred to in the text. The Jewish High Priest Eleazer receives description in terms that evoke a cultivated Hellenic aristocrat.[136] The scholars whom he sent to Alexandria not only command Greek as well as Jewish learning but express the noblest Hellenic ideal of striving for the "middle way."[137] In the symposium, a standard Greek setting, the sages provide answers drawn from the intellectual arsenal of Greek philosophy or political theory.[138] Even the High Priest, in offering allegorical interpretation of Jewish dietary restrictions, speaks like a Greek philosopher.[139] On the face of it, this work seems the prime document of cultural convergence.

Does this then represent assimilation or "acculturation" of the Jews to the world of the Greeks? Those terms, often applied, may be misleading in thrust and direction. Eleazer the High Priest was unequivocal in drawing distinctions on fundamental matters. Moses' pronouncements, so Eleazer insisted, had asserted God's unity and omnipresence, and affirmed that all other peoples worshipped multiple deities, paying homage to fatuous images of wood and stone, the Greeks in particular reckoning as their wisest men those who simply fabricated myths.[140] More pointedly still, the High Priest asserted that Moses set unbreakable fences and iron walls between his people and those of other nations, thus to keep body and soul free of empty doctrines and to maintain focus on the one and mighty God.[141]

Further, the text repeatedly affirms or implies the superiority of Jewish learning, traditions, and institutions. Hecataeus of Abdera stated, according to the *Letter*, that Greek historians, poets, and intellectuals held the Hebrew books in awe for they possess a certain sacred and holy character.[142]

---

[135] For a skeptical analysis, see Gruen (1998), 208–210. Rajak (2009), 38–43, 55–63, 86–91, has now argued for a more moderate position, making a defensible case for Ptolemaic involvement in the enterprise.
[136] *LetArist*. 3.
[137] *LetArist*. 122.
[138] E.g. *LetArist*. 209, 211, 222–223, 256, 292. See above, pp. 315–317.
[139] *LetArist*. 128–170.
[140] *LetArist*. 131–137.
[141] *LetArist*. 139, 142.
[142] *LetArist*. 31.

The king, who was deeply affected by the majesty of the newly translated scriptures, asked his librarian Demetrius why no gentile writer had ever made reference to them. Demetrius explained that the power of the Bible was God-given and those who ventured to exploit it ran into unexpected divine afflictions. Theopompus declared that when he once quoted carelessly from the scriptures, his mind became unhinged for a month. And the tragic poet Theodectus testified that his attempt to use a biblical passage in his play caused him to suffer from cataracts.[143] Even the Egyptians conceded Jewish uniqueness: their chief priests named the Jews "men of God," a designation accorded only to those who worship the true God.[144]

The best demonstration of Jewish superior accomplishment comes in the table talk of the symposium. As we have seen, Ptolemy fired off a different question to each of the seventy-two sages over the course of a week. He got a brief, pointed answer from each, usually employing standard Hellenic formulations, often hardly more than clichés, adding only a reference to God on every occasion. The replies contained little profundity, only an exhibit that Jewish scholars could play easily with Greek ideas. But the author, with more than a hint of tongue in cheek, has Ptolemy react to each answer with concurrence, commendation, and compliments, struck by the novelty and insights of the speakers. And not him alone. As noted above, the Greek philosophers present at the exchange conceded that they could not match wits with the Jewish elders, led the applause in congratulating them, and acknowledged that they themselves were far outstripped by men who recognized God as the source of beauty and power in discourse.[145] It is not easy to imagine Hellenic intellectuals subsidized by the court confessing their inferiority to Jewish visitors, a more elaborate and no less comic rendition of Moses outdoing Pharaoh's magicians prior to the Exodus. The author makes clear that, though mutual regard prevailed, the learning and traditions of the Jews remained the benchmark whereby to assess authentic wisdom. The scholars from Jerusalem had mastered Hellenic learning—better than the Greeks.

Insofar as the *Letter of Aristeas* might be advertisement for assimilation, it would be the other way around. The compatibility of Hebraic and Hellenic concepts emerges most strikingly in a celebrated passage often quoted as exemplary of a "universalism" that dissolves barriers and blends cultures. "Aristeas" counsels the king on appropriate actions toward the Jews. He observes that the god who sustains the kingdom of Egypt is also the god who generated the law of the Jews. Indeed, he adds, the god who is worshipped by Jews as supervisor and creator of all things is the god whom we all worship,

---

[143] *LetArist.* 312–316.
[144] *LetArist.* 140.
[145] *LetArist.* 200–201, 235, 296.

though we refer to him differently as Zeus or Dis.[146] The statement carries real significance—but not quite as indication of the interchangeability of cultures. The words are put into the mouth of a gentile speaker, a fact that does not diminish its value in the least.[147] Quite the contrary. The Jewish author represents a pagan propounding the principle that the god of the Jews can readily be embraced by Greeks, who simply know him by another name. This is not to be confused with proselytism. Nor is it directed only to sophisticated Greeks who preferred monotheism to the polytheism of the populace.[148] Whether the *Letter* had a Greek readership in mind at all is controversial and, on balance, unlikely.[149] The work, in any case, delivers a powerful message for the self-representation of Jews in the Hellenistic era. They hold firmly to the special quality and the precedence of their teachings, which they can express as effectively through Hellenic formulations and the Greek language as in their traditional tongue. But those teachings have relevance also to gentiles who recognize their force and enter into their spirit. Moses' iron walls exclude idolators and animal worshippers. They remain open to those who perceive the overlap of precepts and principles through which Hellenic culture can be subsumed under Hebrew doctrine.

Jewish adoption of a gentile persona has perhaps its most pronounced manifestation in the Sibylline oracles. Commandeering the voice of the Sibyl certainly arrested attention. The prophecies of the divinely inspired Sibyl or Sibyls held a prominent place in pagan tradition. Ringing pronouncements on the wickedness of humanity and the coming doom of evildoers marked the Sibyl's utterances, reckoned as divinely inspired and unequivocal. A shadowy female figure assigned to distant antiquity and located in a variety of sites, she specialized in dire and doleful predictions for individuals, nations, and peoples. Collections of the Sibylline oracles, duly edited, expanded, or invented, had wide circulation in the Greco-Roman world—long before Jewish writers exploited them for their own purposes. The gentile originals have largely been lost, surviving only in fragments or reconstructions.[150] The extant corpus of Sibylline books, drawing on but refashioning those models, derive from Jewish and Christian compilers, who had their own agenda to promote.[151]

[146] *LetArist.* 15–16.

[147] As is suggested by Barclay (1996), 143, and Gruen (1998), 215–216. See Collins (2000), 192, who somewhat misinterprets Barclay on this.

[148] So, Collins (2000), 192–193.

[149] See, especially, Tcherikover (1958), 59–85. Cf., with additional bibliography, Gruen (1998), 221.

[150] On the Sibyls and Sibylline oracles, see Alexandre (1856), II, 1–101; Rzach (1923), 2073–2183; Parke (1988), 1–50; Potter (1994), 71–93; Buitenwerf (2003), 92–123; Lightfoot (2007), 3–23, 51–70.

[151] The history of scholarship on these texts is conveniently summarized now by Buitenwerf (2003), 5–64; on the assemblage of the collection in antiquity, 72–91.

Appropriation of this particular genre would seem at the very opposite remove from texts that suggested common ground and communion between Jew and gentile. The Sibyl's fierce forecasts blast the wicked and anticipate the catastrophes that will befall them. The Third Sibylline Oracle constitutes the principal document here, almost entirely a Jewish compilation, showering vitriol on pagans and auguring a glorious conclusion for the Jewish faithful in an apocalyptic future. Yet, even in this most divisive of texts, an undercurrent hints at a more fundamental convergence.

The dating of the Third Sibyl remains controversial, and the structure of the whole has baffled inquirers for two centuries. Those scholarly disputes can here be happily set aside. Allusions in the text refer to scattered historical events mostly of the second and first centuries BCE but are (in the manner of the genre) unsystematic and without logical sequence. Whether these derive from a core text with accretions or represent a conglomerate of oracles pieced together over an extended period of time or actually form a unity owing to redactional composition at a particular time need not here be decided.[152] The character of the work and its implications for Jewish perception of the "Other" occupy attention.

Tension and conflict dominate the Sibyl's prophecies. She twice gives a roll call of kingdoms that will rise and fall. The first begins with nothing less than the Titans and runs through the Egyptians, Persians, Medes, Ethiopians, Babylonians, Macedonians, Egyptians again, and Romans. The second uses Solomon's kingdom as starting point, together with Phoenicians, Pamphylians, Persians, and a group of Asia Minor principalities (a bizarre assemblage), to be followed in turn by Greeks, Macedonians, and Romans, the last two in particular wreaking disaster all over the earth.[153] Other oracles condemn (in suitably obscure verses) the afflictions that Alexander, his successors, and their descendants will bring on all nations.[154] The Sibyl further delivers even more virulent assaults on Romans, denouncing the expansion and imperialism that will devastate Asia, and predicts the dreadful consequences in store for Rome in the course of civil

---

[152] The argument for a core text composed probably in the second century BCE goes back to the early nineteenth century, based largely on three references to a seventh king of Egypt identified with Ptolemy Philometor of the mid–second century. It received the most vigorous defense, on several different occasions by Collins, most recently in Collins (2000), 83–97. This view, which commanded the assent of most scholars in the past generation, has encountered growing criticism in recent years. See, e.g., Nikiprowetsky (1970), 195–225; Barclay (1996), 216–228; Gruen (1998), 268–285; Buitenwerf (2003), 124–134; Lightfoot (2007), 95–97. Buitenwerf's view that the text does have a literary unity and was composed sometime between 80 and 31 BCE depends on an allusion to the Third Sibyl in Alexander Polyhistor preserved by Eusebius, *Chron.* I, 23 (Schoene). But this does not take into account certain passages that clearly must post-date 31; cf. Gruen (1998), 271.
[153] *Sib. Or.* 3.156–190.
[154] *Sib. Or.* 3.381–400.

war.[155] She roams beyond this too, referring to a time when Rome will rule Egypt (after 31 BCE) and again evidently to the reign of Nero beyond that, with a comparable prediction of disaster for the city and its people.[156] Jews will be the ultimate beneficiaries of all this destruction. They will endure much suffering at the hands of the wicked. But their devotion to righteousness and virtue, their rejection of idolatry and sorcery, and their adherence to the law guarantee that they will gain glory in the end when the terrible might of divine justice descends.[157]

This apocalyptic vision, setting good against evil and proclaiming desolation for all peoples while sparing the Jews, would seem an unimpeachable document for alienation of the chosen people from the rest of humanity. But that judgment may be hasty and the interpretation inadequate. One ought to observe, first of all, the choice of genre by the Jewish author. By cloaking himself in the garb of the Sibyl, he has adopted a Hellenic persona and embraced a mode of expression with resonance in the Greco-Roman world. The thunderous pronouncements of the Lord, conventionally delivered through biblical prophets, here issue forth in the mouth of the pagan Sibyl—in epic hexameters. That itself carries a significant validation of the alien prophetess.

The Sibyl, in this text, can peer into the mysteries of Near Eastern, biblical, and classical lore alike. She recounts the tale of the Tower of Babel, then connects it directly with the era of Kronos and Titan, proceeding to give a version of Hesiod's *Theogony* on the myths associated with the birth of Zeus and the struggles of pagan gods and Titans.[158] She is well versed in the outlines of Israelite history, including the Moses story, the destruction of Solomon's Temple, and the restoration under Persian rule.[159] She knows the poems of Homer (and has much to criticize about them).[160] She forecasts both the fall of Troy and the Exodus from Egypt.[161] And she possesses close familiarity with selected events and developments in Roman Republican history.[162] The author sets her into the hoary mists of antiquity, encompassing a range of peoples and cultures. The Sibyl appears as relative of Noah, of the same blood as the man who survived the Flood. She came

---

[155] *Sib. Or.* 3.175–195, 350–380, 464–473, 484–488, 520–544.

[156] *Sib. Or.* 3.46–74. These lines, to be sure, do not belong to Third Sibyl proper but were subsequently bracketed with it.

[157] *Sib. Or.* 3.218–294, 573–600, 702–731.

[158] *Sib. Or.* 3.97–155. See the comments of Nikiprowetsky (1970), 112–126, and Buitenwerf (2003), 167–177. One might note, as a particularly striking illustration, the transformation of the three sons of Noah (Shem, Ham, and Japheth) into Kronos, Titan, and Japetos, sons of Gaia and Ouranos; *Sib. Or.* 3.110–115; cf. Gen. 9.18–19.

[159] *Sib. Or.* 3.248–294.

[160] *Sib. Or.* 3.419–432.

[161] *Sib, Or.* 3.248–256, 3.414–418.

[162] Cf. *Sib. Or.* 3.175–190, 464–473, 484–488.

from Babylon, then dispatched to Greece where, in her mantic trance, she could deliver fiery prophesies that conveyed the messages of God in divine riddles to all men. Her origins, so she claimed, were assigned by different persons to different places, including Erythrae, seat of the most renowned Sibyl, and her pronouncements reckoned as mad falsehoods, but she was the authentic prophetess of the great God.[163] She thus asserts the most ancient lineage embodying Hebrew traditions, Near Eastern legends, and Hellenic myths, all integral parts of the persona.

Even more telling, the glories of the eschaton need not be confined to the chosen people alone. Evildoers will certainly get their just deserts—Romans in particular, the scourge of the world, especially the oppressors of Hellas.[164] But the hand of the Lord reaches out to the Greeks. The Sibyl exhorts the inhabitants of the Hellenic world to repentance, urging acknowledgment of the true God and offering hope of salvation. Oracular verses expose the folly of trust in mortal leaders and resort to idolatry, proclaiming instead the need to recognize the great God, thereby to escape the woes that will fall upon Hellas.[165] The appeal to repentance gains further vividness with prescriptions for sacrifices, prayers, and righteous behavior to earn divine favor.[166] In a later passage, the Sibyl repeats her appeal to unhappy Greece to abandon haughtiness and embrace the true God—which will bring a share in the blissful peace to come.[167] Insofar as the Third Sibyl contains negative aspersions on Greeks, it includes them among wayward peoples whose failure to see the truth has led them into arrogance, impiety, and immorality, thus provoking divine retaliation.[168] But the prophetess eagerly invites Greeks to enter the fold of the true believers.[169]

This magnanimous exhortation should not be confused with a call for conversion—whatever conversion may have meant in this era. The book would have had little appeal for Greeks—especially as it maligned Homer, denounced Hellenic beliefs as idolatry, and even branded the Macedonian conquest of Persia as destructive savagery. Its principal readership was surely Hellenized Jews.[170] This was no effort at proselytism.

But the oracle offered a wider vision of Judaism itself. The Third Sibyl simultaneously possessed Hellenic literary form and content and resonated

---

[163] *Sib. Or.* 3.809–829.
[164] *Sib. Or.* 3.350–380, 464–488.
[165] *Sib. Or.* 3.545–572.
[166] *Sib. Or.* 3.624–634.
[167] *Sib. Or.* 3.732–761.
[168] *Sib. Or.* 3.196–210, 295–365, 594–600. The more dire anti-Macedonian forecast of lines 381–400 directs itself to the aggressions of royal imperialists, not to the Hellenic people as such.
[169] Cf. Gruen (1998), 287; Collins (2000), 160–161.
[170] Cf. Walter (1994), 153–154; Buitenwerf (2003), 370–376.

powerfully with Jewish apocalyptic writings like I Enoch, Daniel, and the Qumran documents. It evoked an image of the alien that transcended conflict and alienation, expressing a promise of divine deliverance to those who shared common values. The Sibylline declarations, in short, expressed the mind-set that could contemplate an accommodation of gentiles into the world of the Jews.

Phoenicians and Greeks

Contention over priority and precedence was common currency among Mediterranean peoples. Greeks had a passion for establishing their responsibility for the cultural contributions of other nations—and vice versa. That much is well known. Less well known is the fact that Greeks also had little difficulty in acknowledging the claims of others and building them into their own cultural personality.

The Phoenicians represent a revealing instance.[171] Hellenic attitudes toward that people diverged and splintered. One can find numerous snide comments about Phoenicians as crafty merchants, profiteers, deceitful characters, given to fraud, and altogether untrustworthy.[172] Yet popular legend, widely disseminated among Greeks, had it that Cadmus the Phoenician was founder of the great city of Thebes.[173] Some Greeks at least felt no qualms about associating their origins with the land of Lebanon. And Phoenicians themselves took the cue and exploited it. A Hellenistic inscription from Sidon reveals that the city honored one of its own citizens for winning an athletic competition at the Nemean Games in Argos and exclaims that "Kadmeian Thebes" also rejoices in the victory of its mother city in Phoenicia.[174]

The association with Phoenicia went beyond Thebes. It turns up in some surprising places. The Spartan Theras, a member of the Lacedaemonian royal family, uncle to two kings, and regent during their childhood, came, so says Herodotus, from the stock of Cadmus. And he never shunned the connection. When the boys matured and took up their royal station, Theras balked at his newly subordinate position and decided to sail off to his kinsfolk in the island of Thera. For Cadmus, we are told, had stopped at Thera in the course of his travels and left several of his companions, including a family member, to inhabitant the island. Their descendants still dwelled

---

[171] A briefer version of this in Gruen (2006a), 306–308.
[172] Mazza (1988). But see above, pp. 116–122.
[173] E.g., Herod. 2.49, 5.57; Euripides *Bacch*. 170–172; *Phoen*. 5–6, 638–639; see Edwards (1979), Kühr (2006), and see above, pp. 233–236.
[174] Moretti (1953), 41.

there eight generations later. Hence Theras simply rejoined his kinsmen and took pride in his Phoenician heritage.[175]

Equally noteworthy is the clan to which Athens' celebrated tyrannicides, Harmodius and Aristogeiton, belonged—at least in one version. As Herodotus reports, that Gephyraioi clan claimed to originate in Eretria in Euboea. But the historian had done his own research and discovered that the Gephyraioi were actually Phoenicians, descendants of those who had come with Cadmus to occupy the land of Boeotia. When the Boeotians rose up to expel them, the Gephyraioi found refuge in Athens, where the Athenians accorded them certain civic privileges.[176] Hence the tyrant slayers, who helped to lay the groundwork for Athenian democracy, had Phoenician roots. That was clearly a positive virtue in the mind of Herodotus, who proceeds to laud the Phoenicians for introducing the alphabet to Greece.[177] The Gephyraioi may have preferred to assert a different background lest they compromise their Athenian privileges. But the story that Herodotus found more reliable, presumably also an Athenian one, linked Athens' icons of resistance to tyranny with the legacy of Phoenicia.

Cultural competition, however, offers an even more interesting angle. Philo of Byblus, a thoroughly Hellenized Phoenician writing in the early second century CE, reflects it. Philo produced an erudite work on Phoenician history, culture, and religion, drawing on Sanchuniathon, a writer who allegedly lived before the Trojan War. The material transmitted by Philo, however, almost certainly reflects Hellenistic speculation, wrapping itself in the name of Sanchuniathon in order to give the aura of distant antiquity.[178] Among other things, he made a point of asserting Phoenician priority in the invention and transmission of ancient tales regarding the origins of the gods and the universe. In particular, Philo preserves a Phoenician version of the Kronos legend that corresponds in part to the account in Hesiod's *Theogony* but differs in most essentials—including the introduction of a Euhemeristic analysis that has the gods originate as men. And the learned Phoenician proceeds to assert that Hesiod and other Greek poets simply appropriated the tales from Phoenician writings, embellished, expanded, and embroidered with gigantomachies, titanomachies, and castration fantasies of their own.[179]

---

[175] Herod. 4.147.1–148.1. One might, of course, argue that Theras is a renegade, a somewhat dubious figure, and thus not a particularly good advertisement for Phoenician origins. But it is more telling that the narrative has an individual of Phoenician descent in the Spartan royal family at all.

[176] Herod. 5.57.

[177] Herod. 5.58.

[178] Baumgarten (1981), 48–51, 57; Attridge and Oden (1980), 3–9. This does not mean that the material itself may not represent authentic Near Eastern traditions that date back to the Bronze Age, as almost certainly they do; M.West (1966), 18–31.

[179] Philo of Byblos in Euseb. *PE* 1.10.40.

Philo takes aim as well at Pherecydes, the sixth-century Greek writer on the birth of the gods and the cosmos. In Philo's view, Pherecydes too got his information from Phoenician sources.[180] The whole Hellenic concept of cosmogony is thus derivative.

If there was a Greek response to these Phoenician claims, we do not have it. Hellenic writers preferred to cite Hesiod and let it go at that. What we do have, however, suggests that Greek intellectuals, or some of them at least, far from engaging in contentious rivalry with Phoenicia, could readily acknowledge Phoenician cultural precedence on certain fronts. A notable instance concerns the origins of atomic theory. Here too Phoenicians had claimed one of their own as its father, a certain Mochus also identified as dating to a time prior to the Trojan War, whose works were subsequently translated (perhaps fabricated) by the Hellenistic writer Laitos. Such a claim could be expected. What is more remarkable is the recording of that construct by the eminent Greek historian, philosopher, and scientific thinker Posidonius in the first century BCE. Posidonius did not refute or dispute it. He presents the testimony of "Mochus" as given. Although some might credit Democritus or Epicurus with first reckoning atoms as the basic units of matter, Posidonius evidently awarded that distinction to the Phoenician Mochus of Sidon.[181] The remarks of the erudite Stoic philosopher open an important window on the mentality of the Hellenistic elite. The willingness of Posidonius to accept the priority of Near Eastern wisdom on a critical item of scientific theory counts for a lot. He preferred to embrace the association with Phoenician learning rather than to trump it.

Roman Adaptation and Appropriation

Evidence abounds, of course, on Roman impressions of the alien. A negative slant exists and regularly receives prominence. Scholars have found it enticing to pounce on sneers, stereotypes, caustic judgments, and ascriptions of inferiority. An array of such assessments can readily be assembled. On the face of it, they declare Roman distinctiveness and superiority. A wider perspective, however, is warranted. It can redress the balance.[182]

Cato the Elder gave voice to a celebrated antithesis: "the words of the Greeks issue from their lips; those of the Romans come from the heart."[183] Cicero later sharpened the contrast, juxtaposing Greek *levitas* with Roman

---

[180] Philo of Byblus in Euseb. *PE* 1.10.50.
[181] Posidonius in Strabo 16.2.24; Sext. Emp. *Adv. Mathematicos* 9.359–364.
[182] The subsequent segment follows closely, with additions and omissions, the treatment in Gruen (2006b), 459–460, 463–468.
[183] Plut. *Cat. Mai.* 12.5.

gravitas.[184] In assessing those who dwelled farther east, the Roman orator could become progressively more caustic. He ascribed to the Greeks themselves slurs against Asians that he gleefully transmitted (or invented). Stereotypes, so Cicero alleged, reached the status of proverbs: the best way to improve a Phrygian was to whip him; the ultimate insult was to label an individual the worst of the Mysians; as for Carians, they are so worthless as to be fit only for human experiments.[185] Cappadocians became emblematic for stupidity, tastelessness, and being a low form of humanity.[186] Syrians and Jews are peoples born for servitude.[187] Livy delivers the same denunciation of the servile character of Syrians, and even lumps Asiatic Greeks into that category.[188] And Cicero targets Jews directly as addicted to a "barbarian superstition."[189] Sardinians came from Phoenician stock, but they had been rejected by the Phoenicians themselves and abandoned on that disagreeable island.[190] Elsewhere Cicero lumps Gauls, Spaniards, and Africans together: they are all monstrous and barbarian nations.[191] Catullus' vulgar joke about a particular Spaniard even has him generalize that all Spaniards brush their teeth in urine.[192] Blending of east and west brought still greater degeneracy, so Livy would have it. The Gauls at least used to be fierce fighters, terrifying their foes, though Roman virtue always surpassed Gallic ravings. But once Gauls moved east and mingled with Hellenic folk, they became infected with Greek decadence, a mixed bag of "Gallo-Grecians," just like the Macedonians, who came as conquerors of the Near East and then deteriorated into Syrians, Parthians, and Egyptians.[193]

Comparable statements can also be found.[194] What is one to infer from them? That Romans regularly disparaged non-Romans, found aliens offensive or degenerate, and felt the need to express superiority over other peoples of the Mediterranean in order to articulate the qualities that helped define their own identity? The inference would be imprudent and off the mark. We have seen already the hazards of seizing on scattered bits of information or fragments taken out of context. Fuller scrutiny of extended texts places a very different face on Roman understanding of peoples like Gauls, Germans, Phoenicians, and Egyptians. One can go further. Roman

[184] Cic. *Sest.* 141.
[185] Cic. *Flacc.* 65.
[186] Cic. *Red. Sen.* 14.
[187] Cic. *Prov. Cons.* 10.
[188] Livy 35.49.8, 36.17.4–5.
[189] Cic. *Flacc.* 67.
[190] Cic. *Scaur.* 42.
[191] Cic. *Q Fr.* 1.1.27.
[192] Catull. 37.20, 39.17–21.
[193] Livy 38.17.5–11.
[194] See the collection of testimony by Balsdon (1979), 30–34, 59–70; Dauge (1981), 57–131. Cf. Burns (2003), 7–8, 12–24; Isaac (2004), 381–405.

traditions claimed no purity of lineage. Distinctiveness of blood or heritage never took hold as part of the Roman self-conception. Indeed, the Romans lacked a term for non-Roman. They had to borrow the Greek notion of "barbarian," a particular irony since it signified in origin non-Greek speakers—a category into which the Romans themselves fell. Mixed ancestry, in fact, was part of the Roman image from its inception. Instead of an embarrassment, it served as a source of pride.[195]

That outlook issued in a more complex approach to external cultures, an approach that manifested itself in manifold ways. Attraction and appeal, rather than aversion, proved to be more characteristic. Some revealing illustrations can underscore the point.

A striking example exists in the Roman fascination for Pythagoreanism. Not that this went deep. Nor will many have immersed themselves in the philosophic teachings of the sect. But a popular tale had it that the second king of Rome, Numa Pompilius, had studied with Pythagoras himself at Croton in southern Italy, whence he came to take up the throne in Rome. Pythagoras had instructed him in the proper manner of worshipping the gods and much else besides, lessons that Numa transferred to Rome, where he laid the foundation of its religious institutions.[196] The king, himself from the Sabine country, thus gained his intellectual training from a Greek sage, and brought the Pythagorean combination of austerity, abstinence, and learning to Rome. The link between these two figures was, of course, a fiction. Chronology alone ruled it out, as many ancient writers themselves observed. Numa, according to conventional calculations, died a century and a half before Pythagoras moved from his native Samos to southern Italy. And the idea that a Sabine had ever heard of him, let alone imbibed philosophy from him, struck some as preposterous. The refutation of this purported contact held importance for certain Roman intellectuals who sought to affirm that the virtues and moral qualities of Numa Pompilius were homegrown, a product of Sabine upbringing rather than alien teachings.[197] All the more surprising and significant then that the story persisted. Discrepancy in the dates did not derail it. Ovid's retelling of the legend, whatever he may have thought of it, shows its continuing popularity.[198] And other writers addressed the incongruity by devising dodges or reaching for parallels that would keep the Pythagoras/Numa bond alive.[199] That itself tells us much.[200]

The story doubtless had its roots in Hellenic speculation. Biographers of Pythagoras, like Aristoxenus of Tarentum in the early third century, made

---

[195] See Moatti (1997), 263–287.
[196] Dion. Hal. 2.59.1; Diod. Sic. 8.14.
[197] Cic. *Rep.* 2.28–29; Livy 1.18.1–3; Dion. Hal. 2.59.
[198] Ov. *Fast.* 3.151–154; *Met.* 15.1–8, 15.60–72; *Pont.* 3.341–344.
[199] Plut. *Num.* 1.3–4, 8.2–8, 11.1–2, 22.3–4.
[200] Garbarino (1973), II, 223–244; Gruen (1990), 158–162.

him teacher or counselor to a host of Italic peoples from Lucanians to Romans.[201] It seemed suitable enough to have him as mentor to Numa, the father of Roman religious law. Pythagoras took central place in this form of the legend. What carries special interest, however, is the Roman adoption of that legend. Willingness to appropriate and convey a story that conceived the revered lawgiver from the Sabine country as pupil of the Hellenic sage has revealing implications for the Roman self-image. Cicero, who disbelieved the tale, nevertheless recognized its force and significance. He saw it as consequence of Roman engagement in Magna Graecia, acquaintance with Pythagoras' repute, and readiness to find in the sound judgment and sagacity of Numa a counterpart to the Greek wise man.[202]

Pythagoras' high esteem in Rome can be viewed from a different angle. The oracle at Delphi, so we are told, advised the Romans, in the course of the Samnite wars, to erect statues to the wisest and bravest of the Greeks. The Senate chose to install an image of Pythagoras in the first category, Alcibiades in the second.[203] That Rome would be taking counsel with the oracular shrine of Apollo as early as the Samnite wars can be questioned. And the Romans may have embraced the philosopher as a means of appeal to the Greeks of southern Italy, who could be useful in a contest against Samnites. But the statue of Pythagoras in the *comitium* stood until the time of Sulla, who needed the space for his expanded Senate house. The story itself attests to the reputation that Pythagoras continued to enjoy among Romans. Cato the Elder, so it was said, found the sect appealing enough to gain instruction from a Pythagorean philosopher in Tarentum.[204] One report even had it that Pythagoras received an award of Roman citizenship.[205] Here again the tale itself carries more value than whatever truth it might contain. One can legitimately question the proposition that Pythagoras became a Roman citizen. The concept perhaps reflects Hellenic and Hellenistic practices of granting honorary citizen privileges to distinguished individuals. But the story, whatever its origins, would have found favor among the Romans. It had the added dimension of reference to Rome's liberality in expansion of the franchise to "aliens."

The sphere of religion provides still more illumination. Roman religious consciousness from an early stage acknowledged ingredients that were ostensibly non-Roman. Legend dated the arrival in Rome of the Sibylline books, a collection of Greek oracles in verse, to the time of Tarquinius Superbus. The books, supervised by a Roman college of priests, were frequently consulted on matters of religion affecting state interest and were

---

[201] Diog. Laert. 8.14; Porph. *Pyth.* 22.
[202] Cic. *Tusc.* 4.2–3.
[203] Plin. *HN* 34.26; Plut. *Num.* 8.10.
[204] Plut. *Cat. Mai.* 2.3; cf. Cic. *Sen.* 41.
[205] Plut. *Num.* 8.9.

treated *Graeco ritu*, in Greek mode of ritual.²⁰⁶ The temple of Ceres, Liber, and Libera received authorization from the Sibylline books in the early fifth century, according to tradition, its rites eventually governed by Greek priestesses from southern Italy, another indication of official welcome to Hellenic elements in Roman practice.²⁰⁷ In comparable fashion, Rome embraced Etruscan diviners. The haruspices claimed (or were conceived as having) access to ancient Etruscan skill in interpreting prodigies. At least from the time of the early third century BCE they were consulted frequently by Rome to disclose the meaning of bizarre prodigies and to examine the entrails of sacrificial animals. Haruspices eventually became an organized body of diviners fitted into the structure of Rome's religious establishment, while retaining their character or image as Etruscans steeped in native lore.²⁰⁸

State action could take more direct form. Romans reached out explicitly to the Greek world in 293, in the wake of an epidemic. On the recommendation of the Sibylline books, an official delegation went to Epidaurus, there to summon the healing god Aesculapius for assistance. As the tale goes, the god, in the form of a snake, slithered voluntarily onto the Roman vessel and then slithered off again at the Tiber Island. That would mark the spot for a new temple to Aesculapius, whose powers had terminated the plague.²⁰⁹ Whatever the truth of the story, the shrine is a fact. And concoction of the tale itself demonstrates the readiness of Roman writers to ascribe religious institutions to Hellenic authority. In 217, during the dark days of the Hannibalic war, Rome turned again to foreign divinities. The goddess Venus Erycina moved from Sicily to a new shrine on the Capitoline Hill in Rome. The deity blended Hellenic and Punic elements, a combination evidently acceptable to Rome.²¹⁰ In the next decade a still more dramatic transfer took place. On the advice of the Sibylline books Roman authorities had the Magna Mater shipped from Asia Minor to Rome in the form of a black stone that emblematized her cult. This Hellenized Anatolian divinity received a new temple on the Palatine Hill, with annual games to be celebrated in her honor. Magna Mater or Cybele had the great advantage not only of reinforcing Rome's links with the Hellenistic kingdom of Pergamum but of symbolizing the nation's roots in Troy.²¹¹ The gyrating

---

²⁰⁶ Dion. Hal. 4.62; Aul. Gell. 1.19.1; Varro *Ling*. 7.8; Gruen (1990), 7–8; Scheid, (1995), 25–26; Orlin (1997), 76–97; Beard, North, and Price (1998), 62–63.
²⁰⁷ Dion. Hal. 6.17.2; Cic. *Balb*. 55; Beard, North, and Price (1998), 64–66.
²⁰⁸ MacBain (1982), 43–59; Beard, North, and Price (1998), 19–20.
²⁰⁹ Livy 10.47.6–7; Val. Max. 1.8.2; Orlin (1997), 106–108.
²¹⁰ Livy 22.9–10, 23.30–31; Schilling (1954), 233–266; Erskine (2001), 198–205. On the mixture of elements, see Schilling (1954), 233–239.
²¹¹ Livy 29.10.4–11.8; Ov. *Fast*. 4.247–348; Gruen (1990), 5–33. Erskine (2001), 205–224, emphasizes the Pergamene initiative here rather than the Roman. But the Romans were

castrated priests who serviced the cult with wild dancing and clashing cymbals, to be sure, needed to be controlled. And regulations banned citizens from the cult's priesthood, for Roman sensitivities found the behavior unbecoming.[212] But the temple occupied a prominent place on the Palatine, and the annual festivals continued to be central events on the Roman calendar.[213]

A notorious episode seems, on the face of it, to contradict Roman openness to alien cults. In 186 BCE the Senate came down with thunderous fury against the rites of Bacchus, dissolving the cult's associations, persecuting its leaders, hunting down its adherents, and firmly suppressing its worship.[214] The reasons for this explosion of state power targeting the Bacchic sect remain obscure. A concern for the highly organized structure of the cells that cut across conventional social groups, representing a powerful religious community outside the control of the state, may have played a role.[215] Or else Roman leaders exaggerated the threat presented by the Bacchants and utilized the opportunity to make public demonstration of their own authority and the collective ascendancy of the Senate.[216] Whatever the explanation, it needs to be stressed that this episode is quite extraordinary, lacked real precursors, and set no precedents. The Bacchic cult had long been familiar to Romans prior to this period. And it did not disappear thereafter. The actions of 186 in no way signaled a crackdown on alien cults generally.

Occasional demonstrations of state authority over alternative forms of religious expression did occur periodically. Jews were expelled from Rome in 139 BCE, together with astrologers. And the Senate took action against the shrines of Isis several times in the 50s and 40s BCE.[217] The actions, however, had no lasting effects, and very likely intended none. Jews were back in Rome (if they ever left) in substantial numbers before the late Republic. And the continued existence of the Isis cult in the city holds greater significance than temporary state hostility.[218] The exhibit of Roman authority had its uses from time to time, when ad hoc circumstances called for it. But there was no enduring repression of foreign rites.

---

hardly innocent bystanders. For a different interpretation, see P. Burton (1996), 36–63, who plays down the Trojan connection. See further Borgeaud (1996), 108–117; L. Roller (1999), 263–285.

[212] Dion. Hal. 2.19.
[213] Goldberg (1998), 1–20.
[214] Livy 39.8–19; *ILS* 18.
[215] North (1979), 92–97.
[216] Gruen (1990), 34–78; Takács (2000), 301–310. The fullest discussion of the affair may be found in the massive volume of Pailler (1988), especially 125–324. See also Cancik-Lindemaier (1996), 77–96.
[217] Val. Max. 1.3.3–4; Tert. *Ad Nat.* 1.10; Dio Cass. 40.47.3, 42.26.
[218] On Isis worshippers, see Takács (1995), 57–63; on Jews, Gruen (2002a), 15–19, followed by Goodman (2007), 369–371. Cf. also Isaac (2004), 456–458.

How then to characterize a Roman outlook on external religions and national identity? "Tolerance" of other sects is a term often applied. But that misconceives the essential disposition. The very notion of tolerance (no Latin word exists for it in this sense) implies a central and uniform religious structure that indulged in lenience toward deviant sects or practices. The concept simply does not apply to the fundamentally pluralist and polytheist society of Rome. Romans were neither tolerant nor intolerant.[219] The embrace of ostensibly alien cults was an ingredient of Roman identity, not a matter of broad-mindedness or liberality. The Romans, as a celebrated tale has it, defeated their bitter foe, the Etruscan city of Veii, in 396 by calling out (*evocatio*) its patron deity Juno and installing her in a temple on the Aventine Hill.[220] The Etruscan divinity thus became a Roman one, not a defeat of the other's god but an appropriation of it. The Sibylline books may have been inscribed in Greek as a repository of Greek oracular wisdom, but they were integrated seamlessly into a Roman system. And when senators summoned the Magna Mater from the Troad, the act signified that this purportedly foreign cult was, in fact, fundamentally Roman. The Great Mother had her home on Mount Ida, where Aeneas had repaired after the fall of Troy and from which he set forth to lay the foundations of Roman identity.

The acquisition of the Magna Mater, not coincidentally, had the sanction of the Delphic oracle. Roman envoys visited that most sacred and venerable of Greek shrines and operated in part under its instructions.[221] Recognition of the power and prestige of Delphi may have had multiple motives in the Mediterranean world of the late third century. But it is vital to note that this was far from the first time that Rome had resort to Pythian Apollo. Various tales record consultations of the oracle that go back to the era of the Roman kings. Tarquin the Proud purportedly sent to Delphi for interpretation of an ominous portent—and got a fuller response than he had bargained for.[222] At the siege of Veii a miraculous rise in the waters of the Alban lake prompted another embassy to Apollo to solicit a rendering of its meaning.[223] And after the fall of Veii, Rome redeemed the vow of its victorious commander to Apollo by purchasing gold for a splendid offering to Delphi.[224] The Samnite war provided a further occasion: Delphi advised Rome to erect statues of the most valorous Greek and the wisest. The Roman Senate duly complied.[225] The historicity of these visits

---

[219] Beard, North, and Price (1998), 212.
[220] Livy, 5.21.1–7.
[221] Livy 29.10.6, 29.11.5–7.
[222] Livy 1.56.4–13; Ov. *Fast.* 2.711–720.
[223] Livy 5.15–17; Val. Max. 1.6.3.
[224] Livy 5.21.1–2, 5.23.8–11, 5.25.4–10, 5.28.1–5.
[225] Plin. *HN* 34.26; Plut. *Num.* 8.10.

is questionable.[226] But no matter. They held a firm place in the tradition. More reliable is the notice that Rome's great victory over the Gauls at Clastidium in 222, a turning point in the contest for northern Italy, prompted the dispatch of a golden bowl to Delphi to commemorate the triumph.[227] That gesture implies an open acknowledgment of the Hellenic shrine's authority and of Roman deference to it.

A still more pointed declaration of this relationship came a few years later. The Hannibalic war threatened to bring Rome to its knees, and frightful omens followed the calamity at Cannae in 216. The Romans forthwith sent an embassy to the Delphic oracle, headed by the formidable statesman and historian Q. Fabius Pictor. Whatever he may have heard at Delphi, Fabius returned with a list of prescriptions detailing the proper means to propitiate the gods and the specific deities to whom entreaties should be made. Promises of success accompanied the advice, and a request that gifts be sent to Apollo from the spoils that were to come. Fabius returned home, conspicuously displaying the laurel crown he had worn to Delphi, and deposited it on Apollo's altar in Rome.[228] The act emblematized an identification of Pythian Apollo with the divinity worshipped in Rome. All fell out as predicted. Rome emerged victorious against Hannibal, and a new embassy returned to Delphi with a handsome gift fashioned out of the spoils of war. A reciprocal gesture from the oracle forecast still greater successes for the future.[229] The interchanges carried notable significance. Rome had proclaimed, through one of its most distinguished representatives, a close and fruitful association with Greece's holiest shrine—from which the western power had been a signal beneficiary.

Rome benefited too, as a famous story recounts, from Greek stimulus in the fashioning of the Twelve Tables, the very foundation of Roman law. According to the narrative, internal strife in the mid–fifth century BCE led to the appointment of a commission to draw up a legal code. The Senate therefore assigned three men as envoys to Athens, there to transcribe the laws of Solon and employ them as models for Rome's legislation. The task was appropriately discharged. The envoys returned with a copy of the Solonian measures in hand and employed it in framing the Roman counterpart.[230] Rome thus owed the origin of its law code to Athenian inspiration. An alternative tradition had it that the Greek philosopher Hermodorus of Ephesus conveniently happened to be in Rome, in exile from his native city, and acted as adviser to the Romans in drafting the

---

[226] Fontenrose (1978), 65, 314, 334, 342–343.
[227] Plut. *Marc.* 8.6.
[228] Livy 22.57.4–5, 23.11.1–6.
[229] Livy 28.45.12, 29.10.6; Gruen (1990), 10.
[230] Livy 3.31.8, 3.32.6, 3.33.3–5; Dion. Hal. 10.51.5, 10.52.4, 10.55.5.

Twelve Tables, for which service he received a statue set up in the *comitium* at public expense.[231]

The tales have no claim on historicity. Indeed they are hardly compatible with one another. The similarity of at least parts of the Twelve Tables to certain Solonian laws was recognized by Cicero, who saw even a near-verbatim translation in one instance—though he knows nothing of a mission to Athens.[232] That legend may have been made up in the late Republic, when writers elaborated the parallels to invent an actual trip resulting in an Athenian pattern for Roman legislators.[233] The similarities more likely came from interaction with the Greeks of southern Italy. But creation of the tales carries the real significance. The idea that Rome's most venerable laws, the basis for its whole legal system, derived inspiration, influence, or intellectual input from Greeks offers important insight. Roman mythmakers constructed or enhanced the narratives without embarrassment, even had their leaders actively seek and take advice from Hellenic sources. The debt was not only acknowledged; it was fantasized.

The assemblage of testimony here, drawing on Greek, Jewish, Phoenician, and Roman lore, provides no neat pattern or linear development. It represents a miscellany of tall tales, symbolic gestures, and even state actions that encompass acknowledged or concocted overlap of cultural influences, reciprocal reading of independent traditions, embellished associations with foreign figures of eminence, incorporation of alien rites and institutions, and the staking of rival claims that imply mutual regard. But all testify to a marked and meaningful tendency in each of these cultures: an association with others that brings not devaluation but elevation.

[231] Plin. *HN* 34.21; cf. Strabo 14.1.25; *Dig.* 1.2.2.4.
[232] Cic. *Leg.* 2.59, 2.64.
[233] Siewert (1978), 331–344; Cornell (1995), 274–275.

CONCLUSION

⊚ ⊚ ⊚ ⊚ ⊚ ⊚ ⊚ ⊚ ⊚ ⊚ ⊚ ⊚ ⊚ ⊚ ⊚ ⊚

The fashioning of a collective consciousness defies articulation. It constitutes no deliberative process or calculated design. To attempt a narrative tracing gradual evolution or developing constructs of a people's sense of itself would be a fruitless venture. Patterns elude recovery or depend on artificial impositions. The jagged course of shaping a national identity depends on the dynamic of circumstances and the complex interrelations with diverse peoples and cultures. It resists a simple formula and requires repeated reconceptualization. This study offers an alternative vision to the widespread idea that framing the self requires postulating the "Other." The expression of collective character in antiquity, so it is here argued, owes less to insisting on distinctiveness from the alien than to postulating links with, adaptation to, and even incorporation of the alien.

The subject is vast. It receives treatment here through soundings rather than survey. But the selected texts and themes draw on writers of sensitivity and insight, and explore topics of central significance for ancient mentalities. A picture emerges quite different from the standard image of "us" and "them."

The paradigm case of cultural clash would seem to come in the confrontation of Greece and Persia in the fifth and fourth centuries BCE. That struggle for survival or supremacy has become, in both scholarly and popular imagination, a defining feature of the contest between east and west. Yet a closer scrutiny of eloquent contemporary voices points in a different direction. Aeschylus' arresting play the *Persae* was composed by a proud participant in the wars and appeared onstage when memory of the fierce fray was still fresh—and its resumption imminent. Yet the playwright eschews jingoism or denigration. While not disguising the differences between the contestants or denying the justice of the cause, Aeschylus' portrayal of the Persian court shows sensitivity to the human condition and to the tragic forces that cut across cultural divides. The central subject of Herodotus' great history itself was the clash of arms between Hellas and Persia. The historian's attitude toward the "enemy," however, was multilayered and subtle. It has little to do with balancing positive and negative features, an issue of minimal concern for Herodotus. He provides a mosaic of personages, principles, and conventions (sometimes honored in the breach) that shed a refracted light on Persians and Greeks alike, advancing a portrait of entanglement rather than an agenda of enmity.

The Athenian military man and intellectual Xenophon served in the ranks of both Greek and Persian armies. But his remarkable and largely fanciful treatise, the *Cyropaedia*, represented the Iranian king as model ruler, an archetype for the finest governance of an empire. Xenophon's treatise, a mixture of the serious and the sardonic, both set up the Persian king as an exemplar of admirable statecraft and heaped scorn on critics who conveyed the clichés of eastern decadence. The literary representations impinged on reality when Alexander marched Greek and Macedonian troops through the length and breadth of the Persian empire. The great conqueror, whatever he may have felt about Persians at the outset of his campaign, swiftly incorporated many of them into his forces, appointed some as officers and administrators, and, most significantly, promoted intermarriage from the top echelons (including himself) to the rank and file of his soldiery. A mixture of motives determined Alexander's actions. Politics and pragmatism may have taken precedence over sentimentality. But ferocious fights on the battlefield did not entail an enduring commitment to hostility and alienation. A persistent strain in Greek thinking on the values and attainments of the foreigner matched or outmatched any sense of an inveterate clash of cultures.

Egypt remained an exotic, mysterious, and intriguing land to most Greek and Roman intellectuals. It was, in many ways, the alien culture par excellence. Differences, however, need not translate into disdain. Random and sporadic comments by individual writers, especially satirists, stressed the peculiar practices of Egyptians and delivered the occasional sneer. But serious investigations produced a far more judicious, if not always accurate, depiction. Here again, the issue is not that of weighing positive and negative aspects in order to reach a balanced appraisal. Judgment is immaterial. Herodotus duly delineates the conspicuous contrasts between Hellenic and Egyptian practices, but more subtly calls attention to crosscurrents and intersections in religious rites, compatible divinities, and even mythology. Diodorus similarly skirts judgments of praise or blame, pointing instead to the overlap of legends and the reciprocal appropriation of traditions. That analysis found further affirmation in Plutarch's study of Egyptian beliefs, which stressed parallels with Hellenic conceptualization and comparable institutions. In the hands of writers who probed the subject rather than indulged in offhand sniping, Egypt shed some of its strangeness and even gained an air of familiarity.

The enemies of Rome too could be treated with circumspection and nuance by Roman intellectuals, no mere objects of abuse and slander. Even the fiercest and most tenacious of foes, the Carthaginians, earned a respect that defied stereotypes. The slur of *Punica fides* turns out to have had far less purchase on the Roman mentality than has customarily been thought—even in the era of the Punic wars themselves. Bloody contests did not eradicate

Roman regard for Carthaginian institutions, accomplishments, and learning. The construct of Punic treachery came late and never predominated. Carthage's image was multifaceted and heterogeneous. Two other Roman adversaries came under scrutiny by careful historians, the Gauls by Caesar and the Germans by Tacitus. Neither fell prey to simplistic stereotype or caricature. Caesar's account conveys some negative conventions about Celts. But he transcends them in a shaded portrait that entangles Roman and Gallic traits, ascribing comparable values and motives, blurring rather than sharpening the boundaries. Tacitus performs an analogous dissection of the Germans. He has less interest in displaying their alien nature than in employing both Romans and Germans to reflect on one another and to draw out the shortcomings of both. The cynical historian soft-pedals the alienness of the Germans, thereby to highlight the failings of his countrymen. Both Caesar and Tacitus offer calculated and complex visions that subvert any facile dichotomies.

Of all alien peoples in the experience of the classical world, perhaps the most noticeable and conspicuous were the Jews and the blacks. The habits of the former and the appearance of the latter made them unmistakable. Classical authors singled them out on numerous occasions for comment, often in unflattering or parodic fashion. Here, if ever, the disparagement of the "Other" ought most readily to be found. Yet ambiguity enters even into this realm of the nonconformist and the dissimilar. Snide remarks about Jews exhibit more mockery than malice. The one extended discussion that we possess, a lengthy excursus by Tacitus, normally taken as the most virulent attack, actually carries a more ambivalent and more ironic message. The historian, while duly derogatory about Jewish traits, beliefs, and practices, has a wider set of targets. He aims his critique as much against misinformed, preposterous, and self-contradictory attitudes *about* Jews as against Jews themselves. As so often, the skewering of his countrymen takes precedence over animosity toward the non-Roman. The sardonic cast of Tacitus' mind turns this digression into something less than an anti-Jewish tract and more like an acerbic reflection on misguided opinions among fellow-Romans. The distinctive looks of the black Africans lent themselves to curiosity, comment, and even occasional caricature. But the ancients were remarkably free of racist bigotry with regard to blacks. Greek literature elevated the Ethiopians. Classical writers in general remarked on the peculiarity of their appearance but rarely descended to derision. That was left largely to the satirists, for whom it was stock-in-trade. What evidence exists on the position of blacks in classical society suggests that they entered a wide variety of occupations without prejudice, had access to Roman citizenship, and did not face exclusion from intermarriage. Visual representations reinforce the impression. Negroid features might provide material for mockery, but the overwhelming proportion of images, including the juxtaposition of blacks and whites, show a remarkable absence of disdain or distancing.

The assessment of particular "alien" peoples from Persians to Africans by classical authors shows a more complex set of attitudes than is commonly supposed. The complexity becomes still more striking when one moves from individual texts and authors to a thematic approach. The second part of the book explores a variety of means whereby ancients, particularly Greeks, Romans, and Jews (whence derives the vast bulk of our evidence), expressed affiliations with other cultures and societies. The phenomenon appears, quite prominently, in imaginative foundation tales. Peoples all over the Mediterranean indulged in the invention of fictive founders, a common feature in establishing group identity. What bears special notice, however, is the frequency with which such legends associated nations with foreign founders. Some of the more celebrated cities and regions of Hellas took pride in heroes who had settled them from abroad: Cadmus in Thebes, Danaus in Argos, Pelops in the Peloponnese. And the reverse too could hold. Greek legendary figures stood at the beginnings of other nations, like Perseus in Persia, Armenus in Armenia, and Scythes in Scythia. Egyptians too could play this game, claiming as their own some celebrated figures who had peopled places in Babylon, Palestine, Colchis, and Macedon. Romans took pride in Trojan ancestry and an Arcadian background. Jews not only embraced the origins of Abraham in Mesopotamia and Moses in Egypt but prompted speculation that linked them with Assyria, Crete, and Asia Minor. And even Athenian autochthony was compromised by the prior presence of Pelasgians. The willingness of peoples to adopt, even to invent, forebears from elsewhere suggests a powerful penchant for interconnection.

This penchant manifests itself also in another arresting form: the fabrication of fictitious kinships. Greeks and Egyptians retailed stories that tied Athens to Saïs. Osiris and Herakles became linked in legend. The fable of Nectanebos, which had the last pharaoh sire Alexander the Great, produced a genealogical connection that served the interests of Greek and native alike in Ptolemaic Egypt. In North Africa a tangled tale associated Numidians and Libyans with immigrants from Persia, Media, and Armenia as their forefathers. And the legendary Perseus, Hellenic hero though he was, became the centerpiece for a host of fictions that gave him ancestral affiliations with Persians, Egyptians, Ethiopians, Assyrians, and Jews. The cross-Mediterranean associations are rich and remarkable. Even the Jews, who had a widespread reputation for separatism and estrangement, manufactured traditions that affiliated themselves with an impressive array of gentiles. Intermarriage between Israelites and non-Israelites began with the patriarchs. It included none other than Abraham, Joseph, other sons of Jacob, Moses, and David—not to mention Solomon and his nest of foreign wives. The biblical story of Judah and Tamar and the moving tale of Ruth brought Canaanites and Moabites into intimate association with Israelites. The stock of Ishmael became identified with Arabs, thus tracing that nation's roots to the house of Abraham. The inventiveness struck out in further directions in the postbiblical era, postulating kinships even between Abraham and Herakles, and between Jews and Spartans. The intermingling of family ties with the foreigner is a notable feature, no aberration, in Jewish tradition.

The final portion of this work adduces a plethora of associations reinforcing the theme of constructed connections that crossed ethnic boundaries. Fascinating reciprocal concoctions imagined Jews as purveyors of Greek philosophy or, conversely, Greek philosophers as the heirs of Mosaic teachings. The trade-off here has less to do with competition for precedence than with a claim on mutual underpinnings. Jewish writers in the Hellenistic period, sometimes with tongue in cheek, represented Greeks, Egyptians, or Arabs as dependent on Israelite learning or skill; mingled Babylonian, biblical, and Hellenic lore; and appropriated the image of the Sibylline oracle to convey Jewish prophecy. Phoenicians showed similar intellectual agility, asserting (if not conceiving) their claim on the origins of Thebes, the ancestry of Thera, and a link to the celebrated tyrannicides in Athens. They took credit not only for the Greek alphabet, a widely acknowledged boast, but also for the Hesiodic cosmogony and the formulation of atomic theory. Chauvinism plays a part here. But the professions of priority fit comfortably within a long tradition of Hellenic bows to Near Eastern wisdom. Romans shared this mentality of outreach as well. Although Latin texts contain numerous slurs that smear aliens of all stripes from Greeks to Sardinians, they decidedly do not exemplify broader Roman perspectives, principles, or policy. The Romans themselves, in fact, proclaimed their mongrel heritage; awarded citizenship to the manumitted from all over the Mediterranean; embraced the tales that connected them to the personage and teachings of Pythagoras; remolded a range of Greek and Etruscan cults, rituals, and rites to bring them under the umbrella of Roman religion; and proclaimed unabashedly their deference to the oracle at Delphi.

To be sure, the story told here does not tell all. Greeks, Romans, and Jews took strong pride in their own cultures, could disparage the different and abuse the alien, and periodically found reason to accentuate distinctions between themselves and the "Other." But an alternative strand exists in the ancient mentality, a significant and telling element too often overlooked and requiring emphasis. The establishment of a collective identity is an evolving process, intricate and meandering. To stress the stigmatization of the "Other" as a strategy of self-assertion and superiority dwells unduly on the negative, a reductive and misleading analysis. The lens here is turned on inclusion rather than exclusion. Many ancients took the affirmative route, set the alien in a softer light, found connections among peoples, appropriated the traditions of others, inserted themselves into the genealogies and legends of foreigners, and enhanced their own self-image by proclaiming their participation in a broader cultural scene.

BIBLIOGRAPHY

◉ ◉ ◉ ◉ ◉ ◉ ◉ ◉ ◉ ◉ ◉ ◉ ◉ ◉ ◉ ◉

Africa, T. W. "Herodotus and Diodorus on Egypt," *JNES*, 22 (1963), 252–259.
Aitken, J. K. "Review Essay on Hengel, *Judaism and Hellenism*," *JBL*, 123 (2004), 331–341.
Alexanderson, B. "Darius in the Persians," *Eranos*, 65 (1967), 1–11.
Alexandre, C. *Oracula Sibyllina*, 2 vols. (Paris, 1841–1856).
Alter, R. *The Art of Biblical Narrative* (New York, 1981).
———. *Genesis* (New York, 1996).
Ambler, W. *Xenophon: The Education of Cyrus* (Ithaca, 2001).
Anderson, A. A. "The Marriage of Ruth," *JSS*, 23 (1978), 171–183.
Anderson, J.G.C. *Cornelii Taciti, De Origine et Situ Germanorum* (Oxford, 1938).
Ando, C. "*Interpretatio Romana*," *CP*, 100 (2005), 41–51.
Andreotti, R. "Per una critica dell' ideologia di Alessandro Magno," *Historia*, 5 (1956), 257–302.
Anti, C. "Il vaso di Dario e i Persiani di Frinico," *ArchClass*, 4 (1952), 23–45.
Applebaum, S. "Economic Life in Palestine," in S. Sarai and M. Stern, *The Jewish People in the First Century*, vol. II (Philadelphia, 1976), 631–700.
Arafat, K. W. "State of the Art—Art of the State: Sexual Violence and Politics in Late Archaic and Early Classical Vase-painting," in S. Deacy and K. Pierce, *Rape in Antiquity* (London, 1997), 97–121.
Astin, A. E. *Scipio Aemilianus* (Oxford, 1967).
Attridge, H. W. "Fragments of Pseudo-Greek Poets," in J. H. Charlesworth, *The Old Testament Pseudepigrapha*, vol. II (Garden City, 1985), 821–830.
Attridge, H. W., and R. A. Oden. *The Phoenician History / Philo of Byblos* (Washington, D.C., 1980).
Avery, H. C. "Dramatic Devices in Aeschylus' *Persians*," *AJP*, 85 (1964), 173–184.
Bacon, H. H. *Barbarians in Greek Tragedy* (New Haven, 1961).
Badian, E. "Alexander the Great and the Unity of Mankind," *Historia*, 7 (1958), 425–444.
———. "Orientals in Alexander's Army," *JHS*, 85 (1965), 160–161.
———. "Alexander in Iran," in I. Gershevitch, *Cambridge History of Iran* (Cambridge, 1985), 420–501.
Bakhos, C. *Ishmael on the Border: Rabbinic Portrayals of the First Arab* (Albany, 2006).
Balsdon, J.P.V.D. *Romans and Aliens* (London, 1979).
Barceló, P. "The Perception of Carthage in Classical Greek Historiography," *Acta Classica*, 37 (1994), 1–14.
Barclay, J.M.G. *Jews in the Mediterranean Diaspora* (Edinburgh, 1996).
———. *Flavius Josephus, Against Apion: Translation and Commentary* (Leiden, 2007).
Bar-Kochva, B. "An Ass in the Jerusalem Temple: The Origins and Development of the Slander," in L. H. Feldman and J. Levison, *Josephus' Contra Apionem: Studies in*

Its Character and Context with a Latin Concordance to the Portion Missing in Greek (Leiden, 1996), 310–326.

———. *The Image of the Jews in Greek Literature: The Hellenistic Period* (Berkeley, 2010).

Barlow, J. "Noble Gauls and Their Other in Caesar's Propaganda," in K. Welch and A. Powell, *Julius Caesar as Artful Reporter* (London, 1998), 139–170.

Barrett, D. S. "Tacitus, *Hist.* 5.13.2 and the Dead Sea Scrolls Again," *RhM*, 119 (1976), 366.

Barringer, J. "Skythian Hunters on Attic Vases," in C. Marconi, *Greek Vases, Images, Contexts, and Controversies* (Leiden, 2004), 13–25.

Baumgarten, A. *The Phoenician History of Philo of Byblos: A Commentary* (Leiden, 1981).

Beard, M., J. North, and S. Price. *Religions of Rome*, 2 vols. (Cambridge, 1998).

Beardsley, G. H. *The Negro in Greek and Roman Civilization: A Study of the Ethiopian Type* (New York, 1929).

Beare, W. "Tacitus on the Germans," *Greece and Rome*, 11 (1964), 64–76.

Beattie, D.R.G. "The Book of Ruth as Evidence for Israelite Legal Practice," *VT*, 21 (1974), 251–267.

Beck, J.-W. "*Nec impune C. Marius . . .*: Zu Tacitus' Sicht der römischen Erfolge gegen die Germanen in 37. Kapitel seiner 'Germania,'" *Philologus*, 139 (1995), 97–132.

Bellen, H. *Metus Gallicus—Metus Punicus. Zum Furchtmotiv in der römischen Republik* (Wiesbaden, 1985).

Benario, H. W. "Tacitus and the Fall of the Roman Empire," *Historia*, 17 (1968), 37–50.

———. "Tacitus, *Germania*. A Third of a Century of Scholarship," *QS*, 9 (1983), 209–230.

Benbessa, E. and J.-C. Attias. *The Jew and the Other* (Ithaca, 2004).

Bérard, C. "The Image of the Other and the Foreign Hero," in B. Cohen, *Not the Classical Ideal* (Leiden, 2000), 390–412.

Berman, D. W. "The Double Foundation of Boiotian Tebes," *TAPA*, 134 (2004), 1–22.

Bernal, M. *Black Athena: The Afroasiatic Roots of Classical Civilization*, vols. I–II (New Brunswick, 1987, 1991).

———. "Response to Edith Hall," *Arethusa*, 25 (1992), 203–214.

Bernays, J. *Theophrastos' Schrift über Frömmigkeit* (Berlin, 1866).

Berndt, T. *Bemerkungen zu Platon's Menexenos* (Herford, 1888).

Berthelot, K. "The Use of Greek and Roman Stereotypes of the Egyptians by Hellenistic Jewish Apologists, with Special Reference to Josephus' *Against Apion*," in J. U. Kalms, *Internationales Josephus-Kolloquium* (Aarhus, 1999), 185–221.

———. *Philanthropia Judaica: Le débat autour de la "misanthropie" des lois juives dans l'antiquité* (Leiden, 2003).

Bertholet, A. *Die Stellung der Israeliten und der Juden zu den Fremden* (Freiburg and Leipzig), 1896.

Bickermann, E. "Origines Gentium," *CP*, 47 (1952), 65–81.

Bieber, M. *The History of the Greek and Roman Theater*, 2nd ed. (Princeton, 1961).

Biers, W. R. "Some Thoughts on the Origins of the Attic Head Vase," in W. G. Moon, *Ancient Greek Art and Iconography* (Madison, 1993), 119–126.

Billault, A. "Remarques sur l'origine des Éthiopiens dans la littérature antique," in V. Fromentin and S. Gotteland, *Origines Gentium* (Bordeaux, 2001), 347–354.
Bleicken, J. "Zur Entstehung der Verfassungstypologie im 5. Jahrhundert v. Chr.," *Historia*, 27 (1979), 148–172.
Blenkinsopp, J. *Ezra-Nehemiah* (Philadelphia, 1988).
Bloch, R. S. "Geography without Territory: Tacitus' Digression on the Jews and Its Ethnographic Context," in J. U. Kalms, *Internationales Josephus-Kolloquium* (Münster, 2000), 38–54.
———. *Antike Vorstellungen vom Judentum: Der Judenexkurs des Tacitus im Rahmen der griechisch-römischen Ethnographie* (Stuttgart, 2002).
Boccacini, G. *Middle Judaism: Jewish Thought, 300 BCE to 200 CE* (Minneapolis, 1991).
Boedeker, D. "Protesilaos and the End of Herodotus' *Histories*," *CA*, 7 (1988), 30–48.
Bohak, G. *Joseph and Aseneth and the Jewish Temple in Heliopolis* (Atlanta, 1996).
———. "The Ibis and the Jewish Question: Ancient Anti-Semitism in Historical Perspective." in M. Mor and A. Oppenheimer, *Jewish-Gentile Relations in the Second Temple Period* (Jerusalem, 2003), 27–43.
———. "Ethnic Portraits in Greco-Roman Literature," in E. S. Gruen, *Cultural Borrowings and Ethnic Appropriations in Antiquity* (Stuttgart, 2005), 207–237.
Bollansée, J. *Hermippos of Smyrna and His Biographical Writings: A Reappraisal* (Leuwen, 1999).
Borchhardt, J., and G. Mader. "Der triumphierende Perseus in Lykien," *Antike Welt*, 3 (1972), 3–16.
Borgeaud, P. *La Mère des dieux de Cybèle à la Vierge Marie* (Paris, 1996).
Bosworth, A. B. "Alexander and the Iranians," *JHS*, 100 (1980), 1–21.
———. *A Historical Commentary on Arrian's History of Alexander*, vols. I–II (Oxford, 1980, 1995).
———. *Conquest and Empire: The Reign of Alexander the Great* (Cambridge, 1988).
———. "Alexander the Great," in D. M. Lewis, J. Boardman, S. Hornblower, and M. Ostwald, *Cambridge Ancient History*, vol. VI (Cambridge, 1994), 791–875.
Bourgeois, A. *La Grèce antique devant la negritude* (Paris, 1971).
Bovon, A. "La représentation des guerriers perses et la notion de barbare dans la première moitié du cinquième siecle," *BCH*, 87 (1963), 579–602.
Bowen, A. *Plutarch, The Malice of Herodotus* (Warminster, 1992).
Bradley, K. R. *Slaves and Masters in the Roman Empire: A Study in Social Control* (Brussels, 1984).
———. *Slavery and Society at Rome* (Cambridge, 1994).
Braund, D. "In Search of the Creator of Athens' Scythian Archer Police: Speusis and the 'Eurymedon Vase,'" *ZPE*, 156 (2006), 109–113.
Brenner, A. "Ruth as a Foreign Worker and the Politics of Exogamy," in A. Brenner, *Ruth and Esther* (Sheffield, 1999), 158–162.
Briant, P. "Institutions perses et histoire comparatiste dans l'historiographie grecque," in H. Sancisi-Weerdeburg and A. Kuhrt, *Achaemenid History*, vol. II: *The Greek Sources* (Leiden, 1987), 1–10.
———. "History and Ideology: The Greeks and 'Persian Decadence,'" in T. Harrison, *Greeks and Barbarians* (Edinburgh, 2001), 193–210.

———. *From Cyrus to Alexander: A History of the Persian Empire* (Winona Lake, Ind., 2002).
Bringmann, K. "Die Verfassungsdebatte bei Herodot, 3.80–82, und Dareios' Aufstieg zur Königsherrschaft," *Hermes*, 104 (1976), 266–279.
———. "Topoi in taciteischen Germania," in H. Jankuhn und D. Timpe, *Beiträge zum Verständnis der Germania des Tacitus*, vol. I (Göttingen, 1989), 59–78.
Broadhead, H. D. *The Persae of Aeschylus* (Cambridge, 1960).
Brosius, M. "Alexander and the Persians," in J. Roisman, *Brill's Companion to Alexander the Great* (Leiden, 2003), 169–193.
Brunner, H. *Die Geburt des Gottkönigs* (Wiesbaden, 1964).
Brunnsaker, S. *The Tyrant Slayers of Kritios and Nesiotes* (Stockholm, 1971).
Buitenwerf, R. *Book III of the Sibylline Oracles and Its Social Setting* (Leiden, 2003).
Bunnens, G. "La distinction entre Phéniciens et Puniques chez les auteurs classiques," in *Atti del I. Congr. Int. di Studi Fenici e Punici* (Rome, 1983), 233–238.
Burchard, C. *Untersuchungen zur Joseph und Aseneth* (Tübingen, 1965).
Burck, E. "Das Bild der Karthager in der römischen Literatur," in J. Vogt, *Rom und Karthago* (Leipzig, 1943), 297–345.
———. "Fides in den 'Punica' des Silius Italicus," in *Munera philologica et historica Mariano Plezia oblata* (1988), 49–60.
Burkert, W. "Herodot als Historiker fremder Religionen," *FondHardt*, 35 (1990), 1–32.
Burns, T. S. *Barbarians, 100 B.C.–A.D. 400* (Baltimore, 2003).
Burstein, S. *Graeco-Africana: Studies in the History of Greek Relations with Egypt and Nubia* (New Rochelle, 1995).
———. "Images of Egypt in Greek Historiography," in A. Lopriano, *Ancient Egyptian Literature* (Leiden, 1996), 591–604.
Burton, A. *Diodorus Siculus, Book I: A Commentary* (Leiden, 1972).
Burton, P. J. "The Summoning of the Magna Mater to Rome (205 B.C.)," *Historia*, 45 (1996), 36–63.
Buruma, I., and A. Margalit. *Occidentalism: The West in the Eyes of Its Enemies* (New York, 2004).
Buxton, R. *Imaginary Greece: The Contexts of Mythology* (Cambridge, 1994).
Caizzi, F. D. *Antisthenis Fragmenta* (Milan, 1966).
Calame, C. "Poétique du 'mythe' dans la littérature grecque: Hélène, Hérodote et la pragmatique de l'historiographie," *Lalies*, 18 (1998), 71–107.
Campbell, E. F. *Ruth* (New York, 1975).
Cancik, H. "Religionsgeschichtsschreibung bei Tacitus," in W. Spickermann, *Religion in den germanischen Provinzen Roms* (Tübingen, 2001), 49–69.
Cancik-Lindemaier, H. "Der Diskurs Religion im Senatsbeschluss über die Bacchanalia von 186 v. Chr. und bei Livius (B. XXXIX)," in H. Cancik et al., *Geschichte-Tradition-Reflexion*, vol. II (Tübingen, 1996), 77–96.
Capomacchia, A.M.G. "L'Avidità dei Fenici," *Atti del II Congr. Int. di Studi Fenici e Punici* (Rome, 1991), 267–269.
Carmichael, C. "A Ceremonial Crux: Removing a Man's Sandal as a Female Gesture of Contempt," *JBL*, 96 (1977), 321–336.
Carney, E. D. *Women and Monarchy in Macedonia* (Norman, Okla., 2000).
Cartledge, P. *The Greeks* (Oxford, 1993).

———. "The Machismo of the Athenian Empire—or the Reign of the Phaulus?" in L. Foxhall and J. Salmon, *When Men Were Men: Masculinity, Power, and Identity in Classical Antiquity* (London, 1998), 54–67.

———. *Alexander the Great* (Woodstock, 2004).

Cassola, F. "Tendenze filopuniche e antipuniche in Roma," in *Atti del I Congr. Int. di Studi Fenici e Punici* (Rome, 1983), 35–59.

Cavalli, M. *De Iside et Osiride* (Milan, 1985).

Chamoux, F. "L'Égypte d'après Diodore de Sicile," *Entre Égypte et Grèce, Cahiers de la villa "Ke'rylos,"* 5 (1995), 37–50.

Chesnutt, R. *From Death to Life: Conversion in Joseph and Asenath* (Sheffield, 1995).

Chilver, G.E.F. *A Historical Commentary on Tacitus' Histories IV and V* (Oxford, 1985).

Clarke, J. R. *Looking at Laughter: Humor, Power, and Transgression in Roman Visual Culture, 100 B.C.–A.D. 250* (Berkeley, 2007).

Clavel-Lévéque, M. "La domination romaine en Narbonnaise et les formes de re-présentation des Gaulois," in *Modes de contacts et processus de transformation dans les sociétés anciennes*, Collection de l'École Francaise de Rome, 67 (Rome, 1983), 607–633.

Clifton, G. "The Mood of the *Persai* of Aeschylus," *Greece and Rome*, 10 (1963), 111–122.

Coats, G. W. "Widow's Rights: A Crux in the Structure of Genesis 38," *CBQ*, 34 (1972), 461–466.

Cogrossi, C. "Preocccupazioni etniche nelle leggi di Augusto sulla manumissio ser-vorum?" in M. Sordi, *Conoscenze etniche e rapporti di convivenza nell' antichità* (Milan, 1979), 158–177.

Cohen, A. "The Self as Other: Performing Humor in Ancient Greek Art" (forthcoming).

Cohen, E. *The Athenian Nation* (Princeton, 2000).

Cohen, S.J.D. *The Beginnings of Jewishness* (Berkeley, 1999).

———. *From the Maccabees to the Mishnah*, 2nd ed. (Louisville, 2006).

Cohn, R. L. "Before Israel: The Canaanites as Other in Biblical Tradition," in L. Silberstein and R. L. Cohn, *The Other in Jewish Thought and History* (New York, 1994), 74–90.

Collins, J. J. *Between Athens and Jerusalem: Jewish Identity in the Hellenistic Diaspora*, 2nd ed. (Grand Rapids, 2000).

———. *Jewish Cult and Hellenistic Culture: Essays on the Jewish Encounter with Hel-lenism and Roman Rule* (Leiden, 2005).

Collins, N. L. *The Library in Alexandria and the Bible in Greek* (Leiden, 2000).

Cornell, T. J. "Aeneas and the Twins: The Development of the Roman Foundation Legend," *PCPS*, 21 (1975), 1–32.

———. *The Beginnings of Rome: Italy and Rome from the Bronze Age to the Punic Wars (c. 1000–264 BC)* (London, 1995).

Courtney, E. *A Commentary on the Satires of Juvenal* (London, 1980).

Cracco Ruggini, L. "Il negro buono e il negro malvagio nel mondo classico," in M. Sordi, *Conoscenze etniche e rapporti di convivenza nell' antichità* (Milan, 1979), 108–133.

Croissant, F. "Collection Paul Canellopoulos IV: Vases plastiques attiques en forme de têtes humaines," *BCH*, 97 (1973), 205–225.

Curty, O. *Les parentés légendaires entre cités grecques* (Geneva, 1995).
Dahlinger, S. C. "Gorgo, Gorgones," *LIMC*, 4.1 (1988), 284–330.
Dauge, Y. A, *Le barbare: recherches sur la conception romaine de la barbarie et de la civilization* (Brussels, 1981).
Davidson, J. N. *Courtesans and Fishcakes: The Consuming Passions of Classical Athens* (New York, 1998).
Davies, E. W. "Inheritance Rights and the Hebrew Levirate Marriage," *VT*, 31 (1981), 138–144, 257–268.
Dee, J. H. "Black Odysseus, White Caesar: When Did 'White People' Become 'White'?" *CJ*, 99 (2003–2004), 157–167.
Delebecque, É. *Essai sur la vie de Xénophon* (Paris, 1957).
Demand, N. *Thebes in the Fifth Century: Heracles Resurgent* (London, 1982).
Dench, E. *From Barbarians to New Men: Greek, Roman, and Modern Perceptions of Peoples of the Central Appenines* (Oxford, 1995).
———. *Romulus' Asylum: Roman Identities from the Age of Alexander to the Age of Hadrian* (Oxford, 2005).
Denis, A.-M. *Fragmenta Pseudepigraphorum Quae Supersunt Graeca* (Leiden, 1970).
Desanges, J. "L'Afrique noire et le monde méditerranéen dans l'Antiquité (Éthiopiens et Gréco-Romains)," *Revue francaise d'histoire d'outre-mer*, 62 (1975), 391–414.
———. "The Iconography of the Black in Ancient North Africa," in J. Vercoutter et al., *The Image of the Black in Western Art*, vol. I (Houston, 1976), 246–268.
———. "Diodore de Sicile et les Éthiopiens d'Occident," in *Comptes rendues des séances* (1993), 525–541.
Devallet, G. "*Perfidia plus quam punica*: L'image des Carthaginois dans la littérature latine, de la fin de la République à l'époque des Flaviens," *Lalies*, 16 (1996), 17–28.
Devillers, O. "L'utilisation des sources comme technique de déformation: le cas de la *Germanie*," *Latomus*, 48 (1989), 845–853.
Dewald, C. "Form and Content: The Question of Tyranny in Herodotus," in K. Morgan, *Popular Tyranny* (Austin, 2003), 25–58.
Dihle, A. "Herodot und die Sophistik," *Philologus*, 106 (1962a), 207–220.
———. "Zur hellenistischen Ethnographie," in H. Schwabl et al., *Fondation Hardt: Entretiens sur l'antiquité classique*, 8 (1962b), 214–215.
Dillery, J. "Review of Nadon, *Xenophon's Prince*," *BMCR* (2002).
Di Lorenzo, E. "Il discorso di Critognato (*B.C.* 7.77): struttura narrativa e ideologia," in D. Poli, *La cultura in Cesare*, vol. II (Rome, 1993), 553–575.
Doran, R. "Cleodemus Malchus," in J. H. Charlesworth, *Old Testament Pseudepigrapha*, vol. II (Garden City, 1985a), 883–887.
———. "Pseudo-Eupolemus," in J. H. Charlesworth, *Old Testament Pseudepigrapha*, vol. II (Garden City, 1985b), 873–882.
Dover, K. J. *Greek Homosexuality* (Cambridge, Mass., 1978).
Drews, R. "Aethiopian Memnon: African or Asiatic?" *RhM*, 112 (1969), 191–192.
———. *The Greek Accounts of Eastern History* (Washington, D.C., 1973).
Drexler, H. "Die *Germania* des Tacitus," *Gymnasium*, 59 (1952), 52–70.
Dubuisson, M. "L'image du Carthaginois dans la littérature latine," in E. Gubel, E. Lipinski, and B. Servais-Soyez, *Studia Phoenicia*, vols. I–II (Leuven, 1983), 159–167.

Due, B. *The Cyropaedia: Xenophon's Aims and Methods* (Aarhus, 1989).
Dueck, D. *Strabo of Amasia* (London, 2000).
Edwards, R. B. *Kadmos the Phoenician: A Study in Greek Legends and the Mycenaean Age* (Amsterdam, 1979).
Eichler, G. *De Cyropaediae capite extremo* (Leipzig, 1880).
Emerton, J. A. "Some Problems in Genesis XXXVIII," *VT*, 25 (1975), 338–361.
———. "An Examination of a Recent Structuralist Interpretation of Genesis XXXVIII," *VT*, 26 (1976), 79–98.
———. "Judah and Tamar," *VT*, 29 (1979), 403–415.
Endres, J. *Biblical Interpretation in the Book of Jubilees* (Washington, D.C., 1987).
Eph'al, I. "Ishmael and 'Arab(s)': A Transformation of Ethnological Terms," *JNES*, 35 (1976), 225–231.
Erickson, B. "Fallen Masts, Rising Masters: The Ethnography of Virtue in Caesar's Account of the Veneti," *AJP*, 123 (2002), 601–622.
Erskine, A. *Troy between Greece and Rome: Local Tradition and Imperial Power* (Oxford, 2001).
———. "Unity and Identity: Shaping the Past in the Greek Mediterranean," in E. S. Gruen, *Cultural Borrowings and Ethnic Appropriations in Antiquity* (Stuttgart, 2005), 121–136.
Evans, J.A.S. *Herodotus, Explorer of the Past* (Princeton, 1991).
Fabre, P. "La date de la rédaction du Périple de Scylax," *LEC* 33 (1965), 353–366.
Fabre-Serris, J. *Rome, l'Arcadie et la mer des Argonautes* (Villeneuve d'Ascq, 2008).
Faller, S. "Punisches im *Poenulus*," in T. Baier, *Studien zu Plautus' Poenulus* (Tübingen, 2004), 165–202.
Farney, G. *Ethnic Identity and Aristocratic Competition in Repubican Rome* (Cambridge, 2007).
Fehling, D. *Die Quellenangaben bei Herodot* (Berlin, 1971).
Fehr, B. *Die Tyrannentöter, oder kann man der Demokratie ein Denkmal setzen?* (Frankfurt, 1984).
Feldman, L.H. "Pro-Jewish Intimations in Tacitus' Account of Jewish Origins," *REJ*, 150 (1991), 331–360.
———. *Jew and Gentile in the Ancient World* (Princeton, 1993).
———. "Reflections on Jews in Graeco-Roman Literature," *JSP*, 16 (1997), 39–52.
———. *Flavius Josephus: Translation and Commentary*, vol. III: *Judaean Antiquities 1–4* (Leiden, 2000).
Ferris, I. M. *Enemies of Romans: Barbarians through Roman Eyes* (Stroud, 2000).
Fishbane, M. *Biblical Interpretation in Ancient Israel* (Oxford, 1985).
Fitzmyer, J. A. *The Acts of the Apostles* (New York, 1998).
———. *Tobit* (Berlin, 2003).
Flach, D. "Die Germania des Tacitus," in H. Jankuhn und D. Timpe, *Beiträge zum Verständnis der Germania des Tacitus*, vol. I (Göttingen, 1989), 27–58.
Flory, S. "Laughter, Tears, and Wisdom in Herodotus," *AJP*, 99 (1978), 145–153.
Flower, M "Herodotus and Persia," in C. Dewald and J. Marincola, *The Cambridge Companion to Herodotus* (Cambridge, 2006), 274–289.
Flower, M. and J. Marincola. *Herodotus, Histories, Book IX* (Cambridge, 2002).
Flusser, D. "Paganism in Palestine," in S. Safrai and M. Stern, *The Jewish People in the First Century* (Philadelphia, 1987), 1065–1100.

Flusser, D., and S. Amorai-Stark. "The Goddess Thermuthis, Moses, and Artapanus," *JSQ*, 1 (1993–1994), 217–233.
Fontenrose J. *The Delphic Oracle* (Berkeley, 1978).
Fornara, C. W. *Herodotus: An Interpretative Essay* (Oxford, 1971).
———. *The Nature of History in Ancient Greece and Rome* (Berkeley, 1983).
Fowler, R. L. *Early Greek Mythography* (Oxford, 2000).
Franko, G. "The Use of *Poenus* and *Carthaginiensis* in Early Latin Literature," *CP*, 89 (1994), 153–158.
———. "Incest and Ridicule in the *Poenulus* of Plautus," *CQ*, 45 (1995), 250–252.
———. "The Characterization of Hanno in Plautus' *Poenulus*, *AJP* 117 (1996), 425–452.
Fraser, P. M. *Ptolemaic Alexandria*, 3 vols. (Oxford, 1972).
———. *Cities of Alexander the Great* (Oxford, 1996).
Freudenthal, J. *Alexander Polyhistor* (Breslau, 1874–1875).
Friis Johansen, H., and E. W. Whittle. *Aeschylus, the Suppliants* (1980).
Froidefond, C. *Le mirage Égyptien dans la littérature grècque d'Homère à Aristote* (Aix-en-Provence, 1971).
———. *Isis et Osiris* (Paris, 1988).
Gabba, E. "The Growth of Anti-Judaism or the Greek Attitude towards the Jews," in W. D. Davies and L. Finkelstein, *The Cambridge History of Judaism*, vol. II: *The Hellenistic Age* (Cambridge, 1989), 614–656.
Gagarin, M. *Aeschylean Drama* (Berkeley, 1976).
Gager, J. G. *Moses in Greco-Roman Paganism* (Nashville, 1972).
———. *The Origins of Anti-Semitism: Attitudes toward Judaism in Pagan and Christian Antiquity* (Oxford, 1985).
Galinsky, K. *Augustan Culture* (Princeton, 1996).
Garbarino, G. *Roma e la filosofia greca dalle origini alla fine del II sec. a.C.* (Turin, 1973).
Garbini, G. "La letteratura dei Fenici," *Atti del II Congr. Int. di Studi Fenici e Punici* (Rome, 1991), 489–494.
Gardner, J. F. "Blameless Ethiopians and Others," *Greece and Rome*, 24 (1977), 185–193.
———. "The 'Gallic Menace' in Caesar's Propaganda," *Greece and Rome*, 30 (1983), 181–189.
———. *Being a Roman Citizen* (London, 1993).
Garland, R. *The Eye of the Beholder* (Ithaca, 1995).
Garvie, A. F. *Aeschylus Persae* (Oxford, 2009).
Gauer, W. "Penelope, Hellas und der Perserkönig," *JDAI*, 105 (1990), 31–65.
Gehrke, H.-J. "Gegenbild und Selbstbild: Das europäische Iran-Bild zwischen Griechen und Mullahs," in T. Hölscher, *Gegenwelten: zu den Kulturen Griechenlands und Roms in der Antike* (Leipzig, 2000), 85–109.
Georges, P. *Barbarian Asia and the Greek Experience* (Baltimore, 1994).
Gera, D. *Xenophon's Cyropaedia* (Oxford, 1993).
Ghiron-Bistagne, P. "A propos du 'vase des Perses' au Musée de Naples. Une nouvelle interpretation," in P. Ghiron-Bistagne et al., *Les Perses d'Eschyle* (Gita, 1992–1993), 145–158.
Gibson, E. L. *The Jewish Manumission Inscriptions of the Bosporan Kingdom* (Tübingen, 1999).

Goldberg, S. "Plautus on the Palatine," *JRS*, 88 (1998), 1–20.
Goldenberg, D. "Racism, Color Symbolism, and Color Prejudice," in M. Eliav-Feldon, B. Isaac, and J. Ziegler, *The Origins of Racism in the West* (Cambridge, 2009), 88–108.
Goldenberg, R. *The Nations That Know Thee Not: Ancient Jewish Attitudes towards Other Religions* (Sheffield, 1997).
Goldhill, S. "Battle Narrative and Politics in Aeschylus' Persae," *JHS*, 108 (1988), 189–193.
Gomme, A. W. "The Legend of Cadmus and the Logographi," *JHS*, 33 (1913), 53–72, 223–245.
Good, E. M. *Irony in the Old Testament* (Sheffield, 1981).
Goodman, M. "Jewish Proselytizing in the First Century," in J. Lieu, J. North, and T. Rajak, *Jews among Pagans and Christians* (London, 1992), 53–78.
———. *Mission and Conversion: Proselytizing in the Religious History of the Roman Empire* (Oxford, 1994).
———. *Rome and Jerusalem: The Clash of Ancient Civilizations* (New York, 2007).
Gorman, P. "Pythagoras Palestinus," *Philologus*, 127 (1983), 30–42.
Gould, J. *Herodotus* (New York, 1989).
Goulder, M. "Ruth, a Homily on Deuteronomy 22–125?" in H. A. McKay and D.J.A. Clines, *Of Prophets, Visions, and the Wisdom of the Sages* (Sheffield, 1993), 307–319.
Grabbe, L. *Ezra and Nehemiah* (London, 1998).
Graft-Hanson, J. O. "Africans in the Rome of Juvenal's Day," in *Afrique noire et monde méditerranéen dans l'antiquité* (1978), 171–181.
Green, C.M.C. "*De Africa et eius incolis*: The Function of Geography and Ethnography in Sallust's History of the Jugurthine War (*BJ* 17–19)," *Ancient World*, 24 (1993), 185–197.
Griffin, J. "Augustus and the Poets: 'Caesar qui cogere posset,'" in F. Millar and E. Segal, *Caesar Augustus: Seven Aspects* (Oxford, 1984), 189–218.
Griffith, M. "The King and Eye: The Rule of the Father in Greek Tragedy," *PCPS*, 44 (1998), 20–84.
Griffiths, J. G. *Plutarch's De Iside et Osiride* (Cambridge, 1970a).
———. "Tacitus, *Hist.* 5.13.2 and the Dead Sea Scrolls," *RhM*, 113 (1970b), 363–368.
———. "Tacitus and the *Hodayot* in the Dead Sea Scrolls," *RhM*, 122 (1979), 99–100.
Gruen, E. S. *Studies in Greek Culture and Roman Policy* (Leiden, 1990).
———. *Culture and National Identity in Republican Rome* (Ithaca, 1992).
———. "The Purported Jewish-Spartan Affiliation," in R. W. Wallace and E. M. Harris, *Transitions to Empire: Essays in Greco-Roman History, 300–146 B.C., in Honor of E. Badian* (Norman, Okla., 1996), 254–269.
———. *Heritage and Hellenism: The Reinvention of Jewish Tradition* (Berkeley, 1998).
———. *Diaspora: Jews amidst Greeks and Romans* (Cambridge, Mass., 2002a).
———. "Roman Perspectives on the Jews in the Age of the Great Revolt," in A. M. Berlin and J. A. Overman, *The First Jewish Revolt: Archaeology, History, and Ideology* (London, 2002b), 27–42.

———. "Greeks and Jews: Mutual Misperceptions in Josephus' *Contra Apionem*," in C. Bakhos, *Ancient Judaism in Its Hellenistic Context* (Leiden, 2005), 31–51.
———. "Greeks and Non-Greeks," in G. R. Bugh, *The Cambridge Companion to the Hellenistic World* (Cambridge, 2006a), 295–314.
———. "Romans and Others," in N. Rosenstein and R. Morstein-Marx, *A Companion to the Roman Republic* (Oxford, 2006b), 459–477.
———. "The Letter of Aristeas and the Cultural Context of the Septuagint," in M. Karrer and W. Kraus, *Die Septuaginta—Texte, Kontexte, Lebenswelten* (Tübingen, 2008), 134–156.
———. "Hellenism and Judaism: Fluid Boundaries" (forthcoming).
Gutman, Y. *The Beginnings of Jewish-Hellenistic Literature*, 2 vols. (Jerusalem, 1958, 1963) (Hebrew).
Gutschmidt, A. von. "Skylax von Karyanda," *RhM*, 9 (1854), 141–146.
Haarhoff, T. J. *The Stranger at the Gate* (Oxford, 1948).
Hahn, I. "Aischylos und Themistokles. Bemerkungen zu den Persern," in E. G. Schmidt, *Aischylos und Pindar* (Berlin, 1981), 73–86.
Hall, E. *Inventing the Barbarian: Greek Self-definition through Tragedy* (Oxford, 1989).
———. "When Is a Myth Not a Myth?" *Arethusa*, 25 (1992), 181–201.
———. "Asia Unmanned: Images of Victory in Classical Athens," in J. Rich and G. Shipley, *War and Society in the Greek World* (London, 1993), 107–133.
———. *Aeschylus Persians* (Warminster, 1996).
———. "When Is a Myth Not a Myth?" in M. R. Lefkowitz and G. M. Rogers, *Black Athena Revisited* (Chapel Hill, 1996), 333–348.
Hall, J. A. "A Black Note in Juvenal: Satire V 52–55," *PACA*, 17 (1983), 108–113.
Hall, J. M. *Ethnic Identity in Greek Antiquity* (Cambridge, 1997).
———. *Hellenicity: Between Ethnicity and Culture* (Chicago, 2002).
———. "*Arcades His Oris*: Greek Projections on the Italian Ethnoscape?" in E. S. Gruen, *Cultural Borrowings and Ethnic Appropriations in Antiquity* (Stuttgart, 2005), 259–284.
Hamilton, J. R. *Plutarch, Alexander: A Commentary* (Oxford, 1969).
———. "Alexander's Iranian Policy," in W. Will and J. Heinrichs, *Zu Alexander der Grosse: Festschrift G. Wirth* (Amsterdam, 1987), 467–486.
Hammond, N.G.L. "The Text and the Meaning of Arrian vii.6.2–5," *JHS*, 103 (1983), 139–144.
Hani, J. *La religion égyptienne dans la pensée de Plutarch* (Paris, 1976).
Hanson, J. A. "Plautus as a Sourcebook for Roman Religion," *TAPA*, 90 (1959), 48–101.
Harrison, E. B. "The South Frieze of the Nike Temple and the Marathon Painting in the Painted Stoa," *AJA*, 76 (1972), 354–378.
———. "The Glories of the Athenians: Observations on the Program of the Frieze of the Temple of Athena Nike," in D. Buitron-Oliver, *The Interpretation of Architectural Sculpture in Greece and Rome* (Washington, D.C., 1997), 109–125.
Harrison, T. *Divinity and History: The Religion of Herodotus* (Oxford, 2000a).
———. *The Emptiness of Asia: Aeschylus' Persians and the History of the Fifth Century* (London, 2000b).
———. *Greeks and Barbarians* (New York, 2002).

———. "Upside Down and Back to Front: Herodotus and the Greek Encounter with Egypt," in R. Matthews and C. Roemer, *Ancient Perspectives on Egypt* (London, 2003), 145–155.
Hartog, F. *The Mirror of Herodotus* (Berkeley, 1988).
———. "The Greeks as Egyptologists," in T. Harrison, *Greeks and Barbarians* (New York, 2002), 211–228.
Harvey, P. "The Death of Mythology: The Case of Joppa," *JECS*, 2 (1994), 1–14.
Haubold, J. "Xerxes' Homer," in E. Bridges, E. Hall, and P. J. Rhodes, *Cultural Responses to the Persian Wars* (Oxford, 2007), 47–63.
Hayman, P. "Monotheism—a Misused Word in Jewish Studies?" *JJS*, 42 (1991), 1–15.
Heidel, W. A. "Hecataeus and the Egyptian Priests in Herodotus, Book II," *Memoirs of the American Academy of Arts and Sciences*, 18 (1935), 53–134.
Heinen, H. "Ägyptische Grundlagen des antiken Antijudaismus: Zum Judenexkurs des Tacitus, Historien, V 2–13," *Trierer Theologische Zeitschrift*, 101 (1992), 124–149.
Hemingway, S. *The Horse and Jockey from Artemision* (Berkeley, 2004).
Hendel, R. S. "Israel among the Nations: Biblical Culture in the Ancient Near East," in D. Biale, *Cultures of the Jews* (New York, 2002), 43–75.
Henderson, J. "Hanno's Punic Heirs: Der *Poenulus*-Neid des Plautus," in J. Henderson, *Writing Down Rome* (Oxford, 1999), 3–37.
Hengel, M. *Judaism and Hellenism*, 2 vols. (London, 1974).
Henrichs, A. "Graecia Capta: Roman Views of Greek Culture, *HSCP*, 97 (1995), 243–261.
Heubner, F. "Das Feindbild in Caesars *Bellum Gallicum*," *Klio*, 56 (1974), 103–182.
Heubner, H. and W. Fauth, *P. Cornelius Tacitus: Die Historien Band V: Fünftes Buch* (Heidelberg, 1982).
Hexter, R. "Sidonian Dido," in R. Hexter and D. Selden, *Innovations of Antiquity* (New York, 1992), 332–384.
Higgins, W. E. *Xenophon the Athenian: The Problem of the Individual and the Society of the Polis* (Albany, 1977).
Hirsch, S. W. *The Friendship of the Barbarians: Xenophon and the Persian Empire* (Hanover, 1985).
Holladay, C. R. *Fragments from Hellenistic Jewish Authors*, vol. I: *The Historians* (Chico, Calif., 1983).
———. "Jewish Responses to Hellenistic Culture in Early Ptolemaic Egypt," in P. Bilde et al., *Ethnicity in Hellenistic Egypt* (Aarhus, 1992), 139–163.
———. *Fragments from Hellenistic Jewish Authors*, vol. III: *Aristobulus* (Atlanta, 1995).
———. *Fragments from Hellenistic Jewish Authors*, vol. IV: *Orphica* (Atlanta, 1996).
———. *Theios Aner in Hellenistic Judaism: A Critique of the Use of This Category in New Testament Christology* (Missoula, 1977).
Hölscher, T. *Griechische Historienbilder des 5. und 4. Jahrhunderts v. Chr.* (Würzburg, 1973).
———. "Feindwelten—Glückswelten: Perser, Kentauren und Amazonen," in T. Hölscher, *Gegenwelten zu den Kulturen Griechenlands und Rom in der Antike* (Leipzig, 2000a), 287–320.

———. *Gegenwelten zu den Kulturen Griechenlands und Rom in der Antike* (Leipzig, 2000b).
Holt, F. H. *Alexander the Great and Bactria: The Formation of a Greek Frontier in Central Asia* (Leiden, 1988).
Honig, B. "Ruth, the Model Emigrée: Mourning and the Symbolic Politics of Immigration," in A. Brenner, *Ruth and Esther* (Sheffield, 1999), 50–74.
Honigman, S. *The Septuagint and Homeric Scholarship in Alexandria* (London, 2003).
Hornblower, S. *The Greek World 479–323 BC* (London, 1991).
Horsfall, N. "Dido in the Light of History," *PVS*, 13 (1973–1974), 1–13.
How, W. W., and J. Wells. *A Commentary on Herodotus*, 2 vols. (Oxford, 1912).
Hoyos, B. D. "Cato's Punic Perfidies," *AHB*, 1 (1987), 112–121.
Hubbard, R. L. *The Book of Ruth* (Grand Rapids, 1988).
Huntington, S. *The Clash of Civilizations and the Remaking of World Order* (New York, 1996).
Huss, W. *Der makedonische König und die Ägyptische Priester* (Wiesbaden, 1994).
Hutzfeldt, B. *Das Bild der Perser in der griechischen Dichtung des 5. Vorchristlichen Jahrhunderts* (Wiesbaden, 1999).
Isaac, B. *The Invention of Racism in Classical Antiquity* (Princeton, 2004).
Ivanchik, A. I. "Who Were the 'Scythian' Archers on Archaic Attic Vases?" in D. Braund, *Scythians and Greeks* (Exeter, 2005), 100–113.
Jacobson, H. "Hermippus, Pythagoras, and the Jews," *REJ*, 135 (1976), 145–149.
———. "Artapanus Judaeus," *JJS*, 57 (2006), 210–221.
Jacoby, F. "Ktesias," *RE*, 11.2 (1922), 2032–2073.
Jaeger, W. "Greeks and Jews: The First Greek Records of Jewish Religion and Civilization," *Journal of Religion*, 18 (1938), 127–143.
Johnson, S. R. *Historical Fictions and Hellenistic Jewish Identity: Third Maccabees in Its Cultural Context* (Berkeley, 2004).
Jones, C. P. *Kinship Diplomacy in the Ancient World* (Cambridge, Mass., 1999).
Jouanna, J. *Hippocrate, Airs, eaux, lieux* (Paris, 1996).
Kahn, C. H. "Plato's Funeral Oration: The Motive of the *Menexenus*," *CP*, 58 (1963), 220–234.
Kaimio, J. *The Romans and the Greek Language* (Helsinki, 1979).
Kannicht, R. *Tragicorum Graecorum Fragmenta*, 5.1 (Göttingen, 2004).
Kantzios, I. "The Politics of Fear in Aeschylus' *Persians*," *CW*, 98 (2004), 3–19.
Kelley, D. R. "*Tacitus Noster*: The *Germania* in the Renaissance and Reformation," in T. J. Luce and A. J. Woodman, *Tacitus and the Tacitean Tradition* (Princeton, 1993), 152–167.
Kennedy, D. F. "'Augustan' and 'Anti-Augustan': Reflections on Terms of Reference," in A. Powell, *Roman Poetry and Propaganda in the Age of Augustus* (London, 1992), 26–58.
Kennell, N. M. *The Gymnasium of Virtue* (Chapel Hill, 1995).
Kenner, H. "Die Trauernde von Persepolis," *WS*, 79 (1966), 572–592.
King, A. "The Emergence of Romano-Celtic Religion," in T. Blagg and M. Millett, *The Early Roman Empire in the West* (Oxford, 1990), 220–241.
Knauf, E. A. *Ismael: Untersuchungen zur Geschichte Palästinas und Nordarabiens im I Jahrtausend v. Chr.* (Wiesbaden, 1985).

Köhnken, A. "Das Problem der Ironie bei Tacitus," *MH*, 30 (1973), 32–50.
Konstan, D. "Persians, Greeks, and Empire," *Arethusa*, 20 (1987), 59–73.
Kontorini, V. N. "Le roi Hiempsal II de Numidie et Rhodes," *AC*, 44 (1975), 87–99.
Koskenniemi, E. "Greeks, Egyptians, and Jews in the Fragments of Artapanus," *JSP*, 13 (2002), 17–31.
Kossatz-Deissmann, "Memnon," *LIMC*, 6.1 (1992), 448–461.
Kraemer, R. S. *When Aseneth Met Joseph* (New York, 1998).
Kranz, W. *Stasimon* (Berlin, 1933).
Krebs, C. *Negotiatio Germaniae* (Göttingen, 2005).
———. "*Suffugium hiemis... rigorem frigorum*: Tacitus (*Germ.* 16.3) and Seneca (*de ira* 1.11.3)," *RhM*, 150 (2007), 429–434.
Kremer, B. *Das Bild der Kelten bis in Augusteische Zeit* (Stuttgart, 1994).
Kugler, R. "Hearing the Story of Moses in Ptolemaic Egypt: Artapanus Accommodates the Tradition," in A. Hilhors and G. H. van Kooten, *The Wisdom of Egypt: Jewish, Early Christian, and Gnostic Essays in Honour of Gerard P. Luttikhuizen* (Leiden, 2005), 67–80.
Kühr, A. *Als Kadmos nach Boiotien kam* (Stuttgart, 2006).
Kurke, L. "The Politics of ἁβροσύνη in Archaic Greece," *CA*, 11 (1992), 91–120.
———. *Coins, Bodies, Games, and Gold: The Politics of Meaning in Archaic Greece* (Princeton, 1999).
Lacocque, A. *The Feminine Unconventional* (Minneapolis, 1990).
———. *Ruth* (Minneapolis, 2004).
Lacroix, L. "La légende de Pélops et son iconographie, *BCH*, 100 (1976), 327–341.
Langlotz, E. "Zur Deutung der 'Penelope,'" *JDAI*, 76 (1961), 72–99.
Larkin, K.J.A. *Ruth and Esther* (Sheffield, 1996).
Lassere, F. "Hérodote et Protagoras: le débat sur les constitutions," *MH*, 33 (1976), 65–84.
Lateiner, D. "Herodotean Historiographical Patterning: The Constitutional Debate," *QS*, 20 (1984), 257–284.
———. "Polarità: il principio della differenza complementare," *QS*, 11 (1985), 79–103.
———. *The Historical Method of Herodotus* (Toronto, 1989).
Lattimore, R. "Aeschylus on the Defeat of Xerxes," in *Classical Studies in Honor of W.A. Oldfather* (Urbana, 1943), 82–93.
Laurens, A.-F. "Bousiris," *LIMC*, 3.1 (1986), 147–152.
Leclant, J. "Egypt, Land of Africa, in the Greco-Roman World," in J. Vercoutter et al., *The Image of the Black in Western Art*, vol. I (Houston, 1976), 269–285.
Leigh, M. *Comedy and the Rise of Rome* (Oxford, 2004).
Lesky, A. *A History of Greek Literature* (London, 1966).
Letta, C. "I *mores* dei romani e l'origine dei sabini in Catone," in B. Riposati, *Preistoria, storia e civiltà dei Sabini* (Rieti, 1985), 15–34.
Levenson, J. D. "The Universal Horizon of Biblical Particularism," in M. G. Brett, *Ethnicity and the Bible* (Leiden, 1996), 143–169.
Levine, L. I. *Judaism and Hellenism in Antiquity: Conflict or Confluence?* (Seattle, 1998).

Levinskaya, I. *The Book of Acts in its Diaspora Setting* (Grand Rapids, 1996).
Levy, E. "Hérodote *Philobarbaros* ou la vision du barbare chez Hérodote," in R. Lonis, *L'étranger dans le monde grec*, vol. II (Nancy, 1992), 193–244.
Lévy, I. "Tacite et l'origine du people juif," *Latomus*, 5 (1946), 331–340.
Lewis, D. M. *Sparta and Persia* (Leiden, 1977).
Lewy, H. "Aristotle and the Jewish Sage according to Clearchus of Soli," *HTR*, 31 (1938), 205–235.
Lewy, Y. "Tacitus on the Jews," in J. Dan, *Binah*, vol. I: *Studies in Jewish History* (New York, 1989), 15–46.
Lieberg, G. *Caesars Politik in Gallien: Interpretation zum Bellum Gallicum* (Bochum, 1998).
Lightfoot, J. L. *The Sibylline Oracles, with Introduction, Translation, and Commentary on the First and Second Books* (Oxford, 2007).
Lissarague, F. "Identity and Otherness: The Case of Attic Head Vases and Plastic Vases," *Source: Notes in the History of Art*, 15 (1995), 4–9.
———. "The Athenian Image of the Foreigner," in T. Harrison, *Greeks and Barbarians* (New York, 2002), 101–124.
Livingstone, N. *A Commentary on Isocrates' Busiris* (Leiden, 2001).
Llewelyn-Jones, L. and J. Robson. *Ctesias' History of Persia: Tales of the Orient* (London, 2010).
Lloyd, A. B. "Perseus and Chemmis (Herodotus, II 91)," *JHS*, 89 (1969), 79–86.
———. "Nationalistic Propaganda in Ptolemaic Egypt," *Historia*, 31 (1982), 33–55.
———. *Herodotus. Book II: Commentary 99–182* (Leiden, 1988).
———. *Herodotus, Book II: Introduction*, 2nd ed. (Leiden, 1994a).
———. *Herodotus, Book II: Commentary, 1–98*, 2nd ed. (Leiden, 1994b).
———. "Book II," in D. Asheri, A. Lloyd, and A. Corcella, *A Commentary on Herodotus Books I–IV* (Oxford, 2007), 219–378.
Lonis, R. "Les trois approches de l'Éthiopien par l'opinion gréco-romaine," *Ktema*, 6 (1981), 69–87.
Loraux, N. *The Invention of Athens: The Funeral Oration in the Classical City* (Cambridge, Mass., 1986).
———. *Born of the Earth: Myth and Politics in Athens* (Ithaca, 2000).
Lund, A. A. "Zur Glaubwürdigkeit der Germania des Tacitus (Tac. Germ. 12 u. 27)," *Eranos*, 82 (1984), 205–210.
———. *P. Cornelius Tacitus, Germania* (Heidelberg, 1988).
———. "Gesamtinterpretation der *Germania* des Tacitus," *ANRW*, II.33.3 (Berlin, 1991a), 1858–1988.
———. "Kritischer Forschungsbericht zur *Germania* des Tacitus," *ANRW*, II.33.3 (Berlin, 1991b), 1989–2222, 2341–2382.
———. "Caesar als Ethnograph," *Der Altsprachliche Unterricht*, 39 (1996), 12–23.
———. "Zum Germanenbegriff bei Tacitus," in H. Beck et al., *Germanenprobleme in heutiger Sicht* (Berlin, 1999), 53–87.
MacBain, B. *Prodigy and Expiation: A Study in Religion and Politics in Republican Rome* (Brussels, 1982).
Machinist, P. "Outsiders or Insiders: The Biblical View of Emergent Israel and Its Contexts," in L. J. Silberstein and R. L. Cohn, *The Other in Jewish Thought and History* (New York, 1994), 35–60.

Maehler, H. "Roman Poets on Egypt," in R. Matthews and C. Roemer, *Ancient Perspectives on Egypt* (London, 2003), 203–215.
Malaise, M. *Les conditions de pénétration et de diffusion des cultes égyptiens découverts en Italie* (Leiden, 1972).
Malitz, J. *Die Historien des Poseidonios* (Munich, 1983).
Marincola, J. "Plutarch's Refutation of Herodotus," *AncWorld*, 20 (1994), 191–203.
Matthews, V. J. "The *Libri Punici* of King Hiempsal," *AJP*, 93 (1972), 330–335.
Mattogno, G. P. *L'antigiudaismo nell' antichità classica* (Padua, 2002).
Maurice, L. "The Punic, the Crafty Slave and the Actor: Deception and Metatheatricality in the *Poenulus*," in T. Baier, *Studien zu Plautus' Poenulus* (Tübingen, 2004), 267–290.
Mavrogiannis, T. "Herodotus and the Phoenicians," in V. Karageorghis and I. Taifacos, *The World of Herodotus* (Nicosia, 2004), 53–71.
Mazza, F. "The Phoenicians as Seen by the Ancient World," in S. Moscati, *The Phoenicians* (New York, 1988), 548–567.
McCall, M. "Aeschylus in the *Persae*: A Bold Stratagem Succeeds," in M. Cropp, E. Fantham, and S. Scully, *Greek Tragedy and Its Legacy: Essays Presented to D. J. Conacher* (Calgary, 1986), 43–49.
McDonnell, M. *Roman Manliness: Virtus and the Roman Republic* (Cambridge, 2006).
McNeal, R. A. "How Did Pelasgians Become Hellenes? Herodotus I.56–58," *Illinois Classical Studies*, 10 (1985), 11–21.
Meier, C. *Die politische Kunst der griechischen Tragödie* (Munich, 1988).
Mélèze-Modrzejewski, J. "L'Image du Juif dans la pensée grecque vers 300 avant notre ère," in A. Kasher et al., *Greece and Rome in Eretz Israel* (Jerusalem, 1990), 105–118.
Mellor, R. *Tacitus* (London, 1993).
Mendels, D. *Memory in Jewish, Pagan and Christian Societies of the Graeco-Roman World* (London, 2004).
Menn, E. M. *Judith and Tamar (Genesis 38) in Ancient Jewish Exegesis: Studies in Literary Form and Hermeneutic* (Leiden, 1997).
Michelini, A. *Tradition and Dramatic Form in the Persians of Aeschylus* (Leiden, 1982).
Millar, F. "Hagar, Ishmael, Josephus, and the Origins of Islam," *JJS*, 44 (1993), 23–45.
Miller, M. C. "Persians: The Oriental Other," *Source: Notes in the History of Art*, 75 (1995), 39–44.
———. *Athens and Persia in the Fifth Century BC: A Study in Cultural Receptivity* (Cambridge, 1997).
———. "The Myth of Bousiris: Ethnicity and Art," in B. Cohen, *Not the Classical Ideal* (Leiden, 2000), 413–442.
———. "Barbarian Lineage in Classical Greek Mythology and Art: Pelops, Danaos, and Kadmos," in E. S. Gruen, *Cultural Borrowings and Ethnic Appropriations in Antiquity* (Stuttgart, 2005), 68–89.
———. "Persians in the Greek Imagination," *MeditArch*, 19 (2006), 109–123.
———. "I Am Eurymedon: Tensions and Ambiguities in Athenian War Imagery" (forthcoming).
Mitchell, L. "Greeks, Barbarians, and Aeschylus' *Suppliants*," *Greece and Rome*, 53 (2006), 205–223.

———. *Panhellenism and the Barbarian in Archaic and Classical Greece* (Swansea, 2007).
Moatti, C. *La Raison de Rome* (Paris, 1997).
Momigliano, A. *Alien Wisdom: The Limits of Hellenization* (Cambridge, 1975).
Montanari, E. *Il mito dell'autoctonia: linee di una dinamica mitico-politico ateniense* (Rome, 1981).
Moore, C. A. *Tobit* (New York, 1996).
Morenz, S. "Die orientalische Herkunft der Perseus-Andromeda-Sage," *Forschungen und Fortschritte*, 36 (1962), 307–309.
Moretti, L. *Iscrizione agonistiche greche* (Rome, 1953).
Morstein-Marx, R. "The Myth of Numidian Origins in Sallust's African Excursus (*Iugurtha* 17.7–18.12)," *AJP*, 122 (2001), 179–200.
Moyer, I. "Herodotus and an Egyptian Mirage," *JHS*, 122 (2002), 70–90.
Much, R. *Die Germania des Tacitus* (Heidelberg, 1937).
Mueller-Goldingen, C. *Untersuchungen zu Xenophons Kyrupädie* (Stuttgart and Leipzig, 1995).
Muhly, J. D. "Homer and the Phoenicians: The Relations between Greece and the Near East in the Late Bronze and Early Iron Ages," *Berytus*, 19 (1970), 19–64.
Müller, C. W. "Fremderfahrung und Eigenerfahrung: Griechische Ägyptenreisende von Menelaos bis Herodot," *Philologus*, 141 (1997), 200–214.
Munson, R. *Telling Wonders: Ethnographic and Political Discourse in the Work of Herodotus* (Ann Arbor, 2001).
———. *Black Doves Speak: Herodotus and the Languages of Barbarians* (Washington, D.C., 2005).
Murray, M. *Playing a Jewish Game: Gentile Christian Judaizing in the First and Second Centuries CE* (Waterloo, 2004).
Murray, O. "Aristeas and Ptolemaic Kingship," *JTS*, 18 (1967), 337–371.
———. "Hecataeus of Abdera and Pharaonic Kingship," *JEA*, 56 (1970), 141–171.
Mussies, G. "The Interpretatio Judaica of Thot-Hermes," in M. Voss et al., *Studies in Egyptian Religion* (Leiden, 1982), 87–120.
Musti, D. *Strabone e la Magna Grecia* (Padua, 1988), 235–257.
Muth, S. "Zwischen Pathetisierung und Dämpfung: Kampfdarstellungen in der attischen Vasenmalerei des 5. Jhs. v. Chr," in G. Fischer and S. Moraw, *Die andere Seite der Klassik: Gewalt im 5. und 4. Jahrhundert v. Chr.* (Stuittgart, 2005). 185–209.
Nadeau, J. Y. "Ethiopians," *CQ*, 20 (1970), 339–349.
———. "Ethiopians Again, and Again," *Mnemosyne*, 30 (1977), 75–78.
Nadon, C. *Xenophon's Prince: Republic and Empire in the Cyropaedia* (Berkeley, 2001).
Nash, D. "Reconstructing Posidonius' Celtic Ethnography: Some Considerations," *Britannia*, 7 (1976), 112–126.
Naumann, H. "Die Glaubwürdigkeit des Tacitus," *Bonner Jahrbücher*, 139 (1934), 21–33.
Nesselhauf, H. "Tacitus und Domitian," *Hermes*, 80 (1952), 222–245.
Neumann, G., and H. Seemann. *Beiträge zum Verständnis der Germania des Tacitus*, vol. II (Göttingen, 1992).
Neville, J. W. "Herodotus on the Trojan War," *Greece and Rome*, 24 (1977), 3–12.

Nickelsburg, G.W.E. *I Enoch* (Minneapolis, 2001).
Nielson, K. *Ruth: A Commentary* (Louisville, 1997).
Nikiprowetsky, V. *La Troisième Sibylle* (Paris, 1970).
Nimis, S. "Egypt in Greco-Roman History and Fiction," *ALIF*, 24 (2004), 34–67.
Nippel, W. *Griechen, Barbaren und "Wilde"* (Frankfurt am Main, 1990).
Norden, E. *Germanische Urgeschichte in Tacitus' Germania* (Leipzig, 1923).
North, J. A. "Religious Toleration in Republican Rome," *PCPS*, 25 (1979), 85–103.
Ober, J. "Tyrant-Killing as Therapeutic Conflict: A Political Debate in Images and Texts," in K. Morgan, *Popular Tyranny* (Austin, 2003), 215–250.
Ogden, D. *Perseus* (London, 2008).
O'Gorman, E. "No Place Like Rome: Identity and Difference in the Germania of Tacitus," *Ramus*, 22 (1993), 135–154.
———. *Irony and Misreading in the Annals of Tacitus* (Cambridge, 2000).
Ohly, D. "Dia Gynaikon," in E. Boehringer and W. Hoffmann. *Robert Boehringer, Eine Freundesgabe* (Tübingen, 1957), 433–460.
Oliver, J. H. *Demokratia, the Gods, and the Free World* (Baltimore, 1960).
Ollier, F. *Le mirage spartiate*, 2 vols. (Paris, 1933–1943).
Olmstead, C. M. "A Greek Lady from Persepolis," *AJA*, 54 (1950), 10–18.
Oniga, R. *Sallustio e l'etnografia* (Pisa, 1995).
Orlin, E. M. *Temples, Religion, and Politics in the Roman Republic* (Leiden, 1997).
Osborne, R. "Images of a Warrior on a Group of Athenian Vases and Their Public," in C. Marconi, *Greek Vases, Images, Contexts, and Controversies* (Leiden, 2004), 41–54.
Ostwald, M. *Oligarchia: The Development of a Constitutional Form in Ancient Greece* (Stuttgart, 2000).
Ozick, C. "Ruth," in J. A. Kates and G. Twersky, *Reading Ruth: Contemporary Women Reclaim a Sacred Story* (New York, 1994), 211–232.
Pagden, A. *Worlds at War: The 2,500-year Struggle between East and West* (New York, 2008).
Pailler, J. M. *Bacchanalia: la répression de 186 avant J.-C. à Rome et en Italie* (Rome, 1988).
Paladino, I. "Marcii e Atilii tra *fides* romana e *fraus punica*," in *Atti del II Congr. Int. di Studi Fenici e Punici* (Rome, 1991), 179–185.
Palagia, O. "The Marble of the Penelope from Persepolis and Its Historical Implications," in S.M.R. Darbandi and A. Zournatzi, *Ancient Greece and Ancient Iran: Cross-cultural Encounters* (Athens, 2008), 223–237.
Palmer, R.E.A. *Rome and Carthage at Peace* (Stuttgart, 1997).
Paratore, E. "I Germani e i loro rapporti con Roma dalla *Germania* agli *Annales* di Tacito," *Romanobarbarica*, 2 (1977), 149–182.
Parente, F. "La lettera di Aristea come fonte per la storia del Giudaismo Alessandrino durante la prima metà del 1 secolo a.C.," *AnnPisa*, 2.1–2 (1972), 177–237, 517–567.
Parke, H.W.E. *Sibyls and Sibylline Prophecy in Classical Antiquity* (London, 1988).
Parker, G. *The Making of Roman India* (Cambridge, 2008).
Paul, G. M. *A Historical Commentary on Sallust, Bellum Jugurthinum* (Trowbridge, 1984).
Pearce, S.J.K. *The Land of the Body* (Tübingen, 2007).

Peek, W. *Griechische Versinschriften* (Berlin, 1955).
Pelling, C. R. "Aeschylus' *Persae* and History," in C. R. Pelling, *Greek Tragedy and the Historian* (Oxford, 1997a), 1–19.

———. "East Is East and West Is West—or Are They? National Stereotypes in Herodotus," *Histos*, 1 (1997b), 1–12 (electronic publication), http://www.dur.ac.uk/Classics/histos.

———. "Speech and Action: Herodotus' Debate on the Constitutions," *PCPS*, 48 (2002), 123–158.

———. "Bringing Autochthony Up-to-Date: Herodotus and Thucydides," *CW*, 102 (2009), 471–483.

Perl, G. "Die 'Germania' des Tacitus: Historisch-politische Aktualität und ethnographische Tradition," *Acta Classica Univ. Scient. Debrecen.*, 19 (1983), 79–89.

———. "Zur Methode des Vergleichs und der Analogie in der antken Ethnographie (Tacitus, *Germania* 25–26; 10,2; 39,1), *Wissenschaftliche Zeitschrift der Wilhelm-Pieck-Universität Rostock*, 37.2 (1988), 25–28.

———. *Tacitus, Germania* (J. Herrmann, *Griechische und lateinische Quellen zur Frühgeschichte Mitteleuropas bis zur Mitte des 1. Jahrtausends U.Z.* 2) (Berlin, 1990).

Perrotta, G. *I tragici greci* (Bari, 1931).
Petrochilos, N. *Roman Attitudes to the Greeks* (Athens, 1974).
Pfeiffer, R. *Callimachus* (Oxford, 1949).

———. *History of Classical Scholarship from the Beginnings to the End of the Hellenistic Age* (Oxford, 1968).

Phillips, K. "Perseus and Andromeda," *AJA*, 72 (1968), 1–23, with plates 1–20.
Philonenko, M. *Joseph et Aséneth* (Leiden, 1968).
Pinney, G. F. "For the Heroes Are at Hand," *JHS*, 104 (1984), 181–173.
Plass, P. *Wit and the Writing of History: The Rhetoric of Historiography in Imperial Rome* (Madison, 1988).
Podlecki, A. *The Political Background of Aeschylean Tragedy* (Ann Arbor, 1966).
Poinsotte, J.-M. "L'Image du Carthaginois à Rome," in *L'Afrique du nord antique et Médiévale* (Rouen, 2002), 77–86.
Potter, D. *Prophets and Emperors* (Cambridge, Mass., 1994).
Poucet, J. "Les origines mythiques des Sabins," in *Études Étrusco-Italiques* (Louvain, 1963), 155–225.
Prag, J. "*Poenus plane est*—but Who were the 'Punickes'?" *PBSR*, 74 (2006), 1–37.
Prandi, L. "La 'fides punica' e il pregiudizio anticartaginese," in M. Sordi, *Conoscenze etniche e rapporti di convivenza nell' antichità* (Milan, 1979), 90–97.
Pressler, C. *Joshua, Judges, and Ruth* (Louisville, 2002).
Pritchett, W. K. *The Liar School of Herodotus* (Amsterdam, 1993).
Propp, W.H.C. *Exodus 1–18* (New York, 1999).
Raeck, W. *Zum Barbarenbild in der Kunst Athens im 6. und 5. Jahrhundert v. Chr.* (Bonn, 1981).
Rajak, T. *The Jewish Dialogue with Greece and Rome: Studies in Cultural and Social Interaction* (Leiden, 2001).

———. "Translating the Septuagint for Ptolemy's Library: Myth and History," in M. Karrer and W. Kraus, *Die Septuaginta—Texte, Kontexte, Lebenswelten* (Tübingen, 2008), 176–193.

———. *Translation and Survival: The Greek Bible of the Ancient Jewish Diaspora* (Oxford, 2009).
Rambaud, M. *L'Art de la déformation historique dans les Commentaires de César* (Paris, 1966).
Rasmussen, D. *Caesars Commentarii: Stil und Stilwandel am Beispiel der direkten Rede* (Göttingen, 1963).
Rawlings, L. "Caesar's Portrayal of Gauls as Warriors," in K. Welch and A. Powell, *Julius Caesar as Artful Reporter* (London, 1998), 171–192.
Rawson, E. *Intellectual Life in the Late Roman Republic* (London, 1985).
Redfield, J. "Herodotus the Tourist," *CP*, 80 (1985), 97–118.
Reed, J. *Virgil's Gaze: Nation and Poetry in the Aeneid* (Princeton, 2007).
Reinhold, M. "Roman Attitudes toward Egyptians," *AncSoc*, 3 (1980), 97–103.
Retsö, J. *The Arabs in Antiquity: Their History from the Assyrians to the Umayadds* (London, 2003).
Rhomiopoulou, K. "Attikos Amphiprosopos kantharos apo tapho tes arxaias akanthou," in *Ametos* (Festschrift for M. Andronikos) (Thessaloniki, 1987), 723–728.
Richter, D. "Plutarch on Isis and Osiris: Text, Cult, and Cultural Appropriation," *TAPA*, 131 (2001), 191–216.
Ridgway, B. S. *The Severe Style in Greek Sculpture* (Princeton, 1970).
———. *Fifth-Century Styles in Greek Sculpture* (Princeton, 1981).
Riggsby, A. *Caesar in Gaul and Rome: War in Words* (Austin, 2006).
Ritter, H.-W. "Iranische Tradition in Numidien," *Chiron*, 8 (1978), 313–317.
Rives, J. *Tacitus, Germania* (Oxford, 1999).
Robin, P. *L'Ironie chez Tacite* (Lille, 1973).
Roccos, L. J. "Perseus," *LIMC*, 7.1 (1994), 332–348.
Rokeah, D. "Tacitus and Ancient Antisemitism," *REJ*, 154 (1995), 281–294.
Roller, D. W. *The World of Juba II and Kleopatra Selene: Royal Scholarship on Rome's African Frontier* (London, 2003).
Roller, L. E. *In Search of God the Mother: The Cult of Anatolian Cybele* (Berkeley, 1999).
Romm, J. *Herodotus* (New Haven, 1998).
Rose, C. B. "Re-evaluating Troy's Links to Rome," *JRA*, 16 (2003), 479–481.
Rosen, K. "Der Historiker als Prophet: Tacitus und die Juden," *Gymnasium*, 103 (1996), 107–126.
Rosenbloom, D. *Aeschylus: Persians* (London, 2006).
Rosenmeyer, T. G. *The Art of Aeschylus* (Berkeley, 1982).
Rosivach, V. J. "Autochthony and the Athenians," *CQ*, 37 (1987), 294–306.
Rzach, A. "Sibyllen," *RE*, IIA.2 (1923), 2073–2183.
Sacks, K. S. *Diodorus Siculus and the First Century* (Princeton, 1990).
Sage, P. W. "Dying in Style: Xenophon's Ideal Leader and the End of the *Cyropaedia*," *CJ*, 90 (1994), 161–174.
Said, E. *Orientalism* (New York, 1978).
Said, S. "Darius et Xerxes dans les *Perses* d'Eschyle," *Ktema*, 6 (1981), 17–38.
Sakellariou, M. B. *Peuples preéhelléniques d'origine indo-européene* (Athens, 1977).
Salmon, A. "L'expérience de Psammétique (Hérodote, II, 2)," *LEC*, 24 (1956), 321–329.

Salmon, P. "L'image du noir dans l'antiquité gréco-romaine," in M. Sordi, *Emigrazione e immigrazione nel mondo antico* (Milan, 1994), 283–302.
Sancisi-Weerdenburg, H. "Decadence in the Empire or Decadence in the Sources," in H. Sancisi-Weerdenburg, *Achaemenid History*, vol. I: *Sources, Structures, and Synthesis* (Leiden,1987), 33–45.
Sandin, P. *Aeschylus' Supplices: Introduction and Commentary on vv. 1–523* (Lund, 2005).
Sänger, D. "Erwägungen zur historischen Einordnung und zur Datierung von 'Joseph und Aseneth,'" *ZNW*, 76 (1985), 86–106.
Sasson, J. M. *Ruth: A New Translation with a Philological Commentary and a Formalist-Folklorist Interpretation* (Sheffield, 1989).
Satlow, M. L. "Theophrastus's Jewish Philosophers," *JJS*, 59 (2008), 1–20.
Savino. E. "Per una reinterpretazione della 'Germania' di Tacito," *Annali dell' Istituto Italiano per gli Studi Storici*, 11 (1989–1990), 83–107.
Sawyer, D. T. *God, Gender, and the Bible* (London, 2002).
Schadee, H. "Caesar's Construction of Northern Europe: Inquiry, Contact and Corruption in *De Bello Gallico*," *CQ*, 58 (2008), 158–180.
Schäfer, P. *Judeophobia: Attitudes toward the Jews in the Ancient World* (Cambridge, Mass., 1997).
Schauenburg, K. *Perseus in der Kunst des Altertums* (Bonn, 1960).
———. "Eurymedon eimi," *AthMitt*, 90 (1975), 97–121.
———. "Siegreiche Barbaren," *AthMitt*, 92 (1977), 91–100.
———. "Andromeda," *LIMC*, 1.1 (1981), 774–790.
Scheid, J. "*Graeco ritu*: A Typically Roman Way of Honoring the Gods," *HSCP*, 97 (1995), 15–31.
Schieffer, R. "Die Rede des Critognatus (B.G. VII 77) und Caesars Urteil uber den Gallischen Krieg," *Gymnasium*, 79 (1972), 477–494.
Schilling, R. *La religion romaine de Vénus* (Paris, 1954).
Schmal, S. *Feindbilder bei den frühen Griechen* (Frankfurt, 1995).
Schmidt, M. "Asia und Apate," in *Aparchai. Nuovi ricerche e studi sulla Magna Grecia e la Sicilia Antica in onore di Paulo Enrico Arias*, vol. II (Pisa, 1982), 505–520.
Schürer, E. *The History of the Jewish People in the Age of Jesus Christ*, vol. II, rev. ed. by G. Vermes, F. Millar, and M. Black (Edinburgh, 1979).
———. *The History of the Jewish People in the Age of Jesus Christ*, vol. III.1, rev. ed. by G. Vermes, F. Millar, and M. Goodman (Edinburgh, 1986).
———. *The History of the Jewish People in the Age of Jesus Christ*, vol. III.2, rev. ed. by G. Vermes, F. Millar, and M. Goodman (Edinburgh, 1987).
Schwartz, E. "Hekataeos von Teos," *RhMus*, 40 (1885), 223–262.
Schwartz, R. M. *The Curse of Cain* (Chicago, 1997).
Scott, K. "The Political Propaganda of 44–30 B.C.," *MAAR*, 2 (1933), 7–49.
Scott, S. and J. Webster. *Roman Imperialism and Provincial Art* (Cambridge, 2003).
Scullion, S. "Tragic Dates," *CQ*, 52 (2002), 81–101.
Seager, R. "Caesar and Gaul: Some Perspectives on the *Bellum Gallicum?*" in F. Cairns and E. Fantham, *Caesar against Liberty? Perspectives on His Autocracy* (Cambridge, 2003), 19–34.
Segal, C. "The Two Worlds of Euripides' *Helen*," *TAPA*, 102 (1971), 553–614.
Seibert, J. *Alexander der Grosse* (Darmstadt, 1972).

Serrati, J. "Neptune's Altars: The Treaties between Rome and Carthage (509–226 B.C.)," *CQ*, 56 (2006), 113–134.
Sevenster, J. N. *The Roots of Anti-Semitism in the Ancient World* (Leiden, 1975).
Shapiro, H. A. "Autochthony and the Visual Arts in Fifth-Century Athens," in D. Boedeker and K. Raaflaub, *Democracy, Empire, and the Arts in Fifth-Century Athens* (Cambridge, Mass., 1998), 127–151.
———. "The Invention of Persia in Classical Athens," in M. Eliav-Feldon, B. Isaac, and J. Ziegler, *The Origins of Racism in the West* (Cambridge, 2009), 57–87.
Sherwin-White, A. N. *Racial Prejudice in Imperial Rome* (Cambridge, 1967).
Sherwin-White, S. and A. Kuhrt. *From Samarkhand to Sardis* (London, 1993).
Shields, M. E. "'More Righteous Than I,' The Comeuppance of the Trickster in Genesis 38," in A. Brenner, *Are We Amused? Humour about Women in the Biblical Worlds* (London, 2003), 31–51.
Siewert, P. "Die angebliche Übernahme solonischer Gesetze in die Zwölftafeln. Ursprung und Ausgestaltung einer Legende," *Chiron*, 8 (1978), 331–344.
Silberstein, L. J. and L. R. Cohn. *The Other in Jewish Thought and History* (New York, 1994).
Silverman, D. "The Nature of Egyptian Kingship," in D. O'Connor and D. Silverman, *Ancient Egyptian Kingship* (Leiden, 1995), 49–94.
Skutsch, O. *The Annals of Quintus Ennius* (Oxford, 1985).
Smelik, K.A.D. and E. A. Hemelrijk. "Egyptian Animal Worship in Antiquity," in H. Temporini and W. Haase, *Aufstieg und Niedergang der römischen Welt*, II.17.4 (1984), 1852–2000.
Smith, A. "Eurymedon and the Evolution of Political Personifications in the Early Classical Period," *JHS*, 119 (1999), 128–141.
Smith, J. Z. "What a Difference a Difference Makes," in J. Neusner and E. Frerich, *To See Ourselves as Others See Us: Christians, Jews, "Others" in Late Antiquity* (Chico, 1985), 3–48.
Smith, M. *Palestinian Parties and Politics That Shaped the Old Testament* (New York, 1971).
Smith-Christopher, D. L. "The Mixed Marriage Crisis in Ezra 9–10 and Nehemiah 13: A Study of the Sociology of the Post-exilic Judaean Community," in T. C. Eskenazi and K. H. Richards, *Second Temple Studies*, vol. 2: *Temple Community in the Persian Period* (Sheffield, 1994), 243–265.
———. *A Biblical Theology of Exile* (Minneapolis, 2002).
Snowden, F. M. "The Negro in Classical Italy," *AJP*, 68 (1947), 266–292.
———. "The Negro in Ancient Greece," *American Anthropologist*, 50 (1948), 31–44.
———. "Some Greek and Roman Observations on the Ethiopian," *Traditio*, 16 (1960), 19–38.
———. *Blacks in Antiquity: Ethiopians in the Greco-Roman Experience* (Cambridge, Mass., 1970).
———. "Iconographical Evidence on the Black Populations in Greco-Roman Antiquity," in J. Vercoutter et al., *The Image of the Black in Western Art*, vol. I (Houston, 1976), 133–245, 298–307.
———. *Before Color Prejudice: The Ancient View of Blacks* (Cambridge, Mass., 1983).
———. "Review of Thompson, *Romans and Blacks*," *AJP*, 111 (1990), 543–557.

———. "Misconceptions about African Blacks in the Ancient Mediterranean World: Specialists and Afrocentrists," *Arion*, 4 (1997), 28–50.
Sonnabend, H. *Fremdenbild und Politik: Vorstellungen der Römer von Ägypten und dem Partherreich in der späten Republik und frühen Kaiserzeit* (Frankfurt, 1986).
Sourvinou-Inwood, C. "Herodotos (and Others) on Pelasgians: Some Perceptions of Ethnicity," in P. Derow and R. Parker, *Herodotus and His World: Essays from a Conference in Memory of George Forrest* (Oxford, 2003), 103–144.
Speiser, E. A. *Genesis* (New York, 1964).
Spencer, F. S. "Those Riotous—Yet Righteous—Foremothers of Jesus: Exploring Matthew's Comic Genealogy," in A. Brenner, *Are We Amused? Humour about Women in the Biblical Worlds* (London, 2003), 7–30.
Spickermann, W. "Interpretatio Romana? Zeugnisse der Religion von Römern, Kelten und Germanen im Rheingebiet bis zum Ende des Bataveraufstandes," in D. Hopp and C. Trumpler, *Die frühe römische Kaiserzeit im Ruhrgebiet* (Essen, 2001), 94–106.
Spina, F. *The Faith of the Outsider: Exclusion and Inclusion in the Biblical Story* (Grand Rapids, 2005).
Städele, A. "Neues von der Germania des Tacitus. Oder: Das Ende einer Legende?" *Anregung*, 36 (1990), 156–168.
Stadter, P. A. "Fictional Narrative in the *Cyropaideia*," *AJP*, 112 (1991), 461–491.
Stähler, K. "Die Freiheit in Persepolis? Zum Statuentypus der sog. Penelope," *Boreas*, 13 (1990), 5–11.
Standhartinger, A. *Das Frauenbild im Judentum der hellenistischen Zeit: Ein Beitrag anhand von "Joseph und Aseneth"* (Leiden, 1995).
Starks, J. H. "*Fides Aeneia*: The Transference of Punic Stereotypes in the Aeneid," *CJ*, 94 (1999), 255–283.
———. "*Nullus me est hodie Poenus Poenior*: Balanced Ethnic Humor in Plautus' *Poenulus*," *Helios*, 27 (2000), 163–186.
Stephens, S. A. *Seeing Double: Intercultural Poetics in Ptolemaic Alexandria* (Berkeley, 2003).
Sterling, G. E. *Historiography and Self-Definition: Josephos, Luke-Acts, and Apologetic Historiography* (Leiden, 1992).
Stern, M. *Greek and Latin Authors on Jews and Judaism*, vols. I–III (Jerusalem, 1974, 1980, 1984).
Stewart, A. F. "History, Myth, and Allegory in the Program of the Temple of Athena Nike, Athens," in H. I. Kessler and M. Shreve Simpson, *Pictorial Narrative in Antiquity and the Middle Ages* (Washington, D.C., 1985), 53–83.
Stoneman, R. *The Greek Alexander Romance* (London, 1991).
———. *Alexander the Great: A Life in Legend* (New Haven, 2008).
Swain, S. *Hellenism and Empire: Language, Classicism, and Power in the Greek World, AD 50–250* (Oxford, 1996).
Syed, Y. "Romans and Others," in S. Harrison, *A Companion to Latin Literature* (Oxford, 2005a), 360–371.
———. *Vergil's Aeneid and the Roman Self: Subject and Nation in Literary Discourse* (Ann Arbor, 2005b).
Syme, R. *The Roman Revolution* (Oxford, 1939).
———. *Tacitus*, 2 vols. (Oxford, 1958).

Takács, S. *Isis and Sarapis in the Roman World* (Leiden, 1995).
———. "Politics and Religion in the Bacchanalian Affair of 186 B.C.E.," *HSCP*, 100 (2000), 301–310.
Taplin, O. *Pots and Plays* (Los Angeles, 2007).
Tarn, W. W. *Alexander the Great*, vols. I–II (Cambridge, 1948).
Tatum, J. *Xenophon's Imperial Fiction* (Princeton, 1989).
Taylor, W. M. *The Tyrant Slayers: The Heroic Age in Fifth Century B.C. Athenian Art and Politics*, 2nd ed. (Salem, N.H., 1991).
Tcherikover, V. "The Ideology of the Letter of Aristeas," *HTR*, 51 (1958), 59–85.
Ternes, C.-M. "Tamdiu Germania Vincitur. La critique tacitéenne de la politique romaine en Germanie," *Colloque Historie et Historiographie: Clio*, 15 (1980), 165–176.
Thalmann, W. "Xerxes' Rags: Some Problems in Aeschylus' *Persians*," *AJP* 101 (1980), 260–282.
Thiel, J. H. "Punica Fides," in H. Wallinga, *J. H. Thiel, Studies in Ancient History* (Amsterdam, 1994), 129–150.
Thielscher, P. "Das Herauswachsen der 'Germania' des Tacitus aus Câsars 'Bellum Gallicum,'" *Das Altertum*, 8 (1962), 12–25.
Thomas, C. "Alexander the Great and the Unity of Mankind," *CJ*, 63 (1968), 258–260.
Thomas, R. *Herodotus in Context: Ethnography, Science, and the Art of Persuasion* (Cambridge, 2000).
———. "Ethnicity, Genealogy and Hellenism in Herodotus," in I. Malkin, *Ancient Perceptions of Greek Ethnicity* (Washington, D.C., 2001), 213–233.
Thompson, L. A. "Observations on the Perception of 'Race' in Imperial Rome," *PACA*, 17 (1983), 1–21.
———. *Romans and Blacks* (Norman, Okla., 1989).
Thompson, T., and D. Thompson. "Some Legal Problems in the Book of Ruth," *VT*, 18 (1968), 79–99.
Tierney, J. J. "The Celtic Ethnography of Posidonius," *Proceedings of the Royal Irish Academy*, 60 (1960), 189–275.
Tigerstedt, E. N. *The Legend of Sparta in Classical Antiquity*, 3 vols. (Stockholm, 1965, 1974, 1978).
Timpe, D. "Zum politischen Charakter der Germanen in der 'Germania' des Tacitus," in P. Kneissl und V. Losemann, *Alte Geschichte und Wissenschaftsgeschichte* (Darmstadt, 1988), 502–525.
———. "Die Absicht der Germania," in H. Jankuhn and D. Timpe, *Beiträge zum Verständnis der Germania des Tacitus*, vol. I (Göttingen, 1989), 106–127.
———. "Tacitus' Germania als religionsgeschichtliche Quelle," in H. Beck et al., *Germanische Religionsgeschichte: Quellen und Quellenprobleme* (Berlin, 1992), 434–485.
Tiverios, M. A. "Kadmos," *LIMC*, 5.1 (1990), 863–882.
Tobin, V. A. "Isis and Demeter: Symbols of Divine Motherhood," *Journal of the American Research Center in Egypt*, 28 (1991), 187–200.
Too, Y. L "Xenophon's *Cyropaedia*: Disfiguring the Pedagogical State," in Y. L. Too and N. Livingstone, *Pedagogy and Power: Rhetorics of Classical Learning* (Cambridge, 1998), 282–302.

Tourraix, A. "L'image de la monarchie achéménide dans les Perses," *REA*, 86 (1984), 123–134.
———. "Le Vase des Perses, le mythe et l'histoire," *REG*, 110 (1997), 295–324.
———. *Le mirage grec, L'Orient du mythe et de l'épopée* (Paris, 2000).
Trebilco, P. R. *Jewish Communities in Asia Minor* (Cambridge, 1991).
Treggiari, S. *Roman Freedmen during the Late Republic* (Oxford, 1969).
Triantis, I. "Pelops," *LIMC*, 7 (1994), 282–287.
Troiani, L. "*I Fenici e la tradizione storica classica*," in *Atti del II Congr. Int. di Studi Fenici e Punici* (Rome, 1991), 213–216.
Tsitsiridis, S. *Platons Menexenos: Einleitung, Text und Kommentar* (Stuttgart, 1998).
Tuplin, C. "Persian Decor in *Cyropaedia*: Some Observations," in H. Sancisi-Weerdenburg and J. W. Drijvers, *Achaemenid History*, vol. V: *The Roots of the European Tradition* (Leiden, 1990), 17–29.
———. "Xenophon, Sparta and the Cyropaedia," in A. Powell, *The Shadow of Sparta* (London, 1994), 127–181.
———. "Xenophon's *Cyropaedia*: Education and Fiction," in A. H. Sommerstein and C. Atherton, *Education in Greek Fiction* (Bari, 1997), 65–162.
———. "Greek Racism? Observations on the Character and Limits of Greek Ethnic Prejudice," in G. R. Tsetskhladze, *Ancient Greeks, West and East* (Leiden, 1999), 47–75.
Urban, R. "Aufbau und Gedankengang der Germania des Tacitus," in H. Jankuhn and D. Timpe, *Beiträge zum Verständnis der Germania des Tacitus*, vol. I (Göttingen, 1989), 80–105.
VanderKam, J. C. *The Book of Jubilees* (Sheffield, 2001).
Van Minnen, P. "Drei Bemerkungen zur Geschichte des Judentums in der griechisch-römischen Welt," *ZPE*, 100 (1994), 253–258.
Van Wolde, E. "Intertextuality: Ruth in Dialogue with Tamar," in A. Brennner and C. Fontaine, *A Feminist Companion to Reading the Bible: Approaches, Methods, and Strategies* (Sheffield, 1997), 426–451.
Vasunia, P. *The Gift of the Nile: Hellenizing Egypt from Aeschylus to Alexander* (Berkeley, 2001).
Vessey, D. "Silius Italicus: The Shield of Hannibal," *AJP*, 96 (1975), 391–405.
Vian, F. *Les origines de Thèbes: Cadmos et les Spartes* (Paris, 1963).
Vicenzi, R. "Cartagine nell' 'Eneide,'" *Aevum*, 59 (1985), 97–106.
Villanueva-Puig, M. C. "Le Vase des Perses," *REA*, 91 (1989), 277–298.
Vittmann, G. *Ägypten und die Fremden im ersten vorchristlichnen Jahrtausend* (Mainz, 2003).
Vogt, J. "Die Hellenisierung der Perser in der Tragödie des Aischylos," in R. Stiehl and G. Lehmann, *Antike und Universalgeschichte* (Münster, 1972), 131–145.
von Rad, G. *Genesis: A Commentary* (Philadelphia, 1972).
von See, K. *Barbar, Germane, Arier* (Heidelberg, 1994).
Voutiras, E. "Individuum und Norm: Bemerkungen zum Menschenbild der frühen Klassik," in D. Papenfuss and V. M. Strocka, *Gab es das griechische Wunder?* (Mainz, 2001), 21–37.
Wacholder, B. Z. "Pseudo-Eupolemus' Two Greek Fragments on the Life of Abraham," *HUCA*, 34 (1963), 83–113.

———. *Eupolemus: A Study of Judeo-Greek Literature* (Cincinnati, 1974).
Waldherr, G. H. "'Punica fides'—das Bild der Karthager in Rom," *Gymnasium*, 107 (2000), 193–222.
Walser, G. *Caesar und die Germanen: Studien zur politischen Tendenz römischer Feldzugsberichte* (Wiesbaden, 1956).
———. *Hellas und Iran* (Darmstadt, 1984).
Walter, N. *Der Thoraausleger Aristobulos* (Berlin, 1964).
———. "Kann man als Jude auch Grieche sein? Erwägung zur jüdisch-hellenistischen Pseudepigraphie," in J. C. Reeves and J. Kampen, *Pursuing the Text: Studies in Honor of Ben Zion Wacholder* (Sheffield, 1994), 148–163.
Wannagat, D. "'Eurymedon eimi': Zeichen ethnischer, sozialer und physischer Differenz in der Vasenmalerei des 5. und 4. Jahrhunderts v. Chr.," in R. von den Hoff and S. Schmidt, *Konstruktion von Wirklichkeit. Bilder im Griechenland des 5. und 4. Jahrhunderts v. Chr.* (Stuttgart, 2001), 51–71.
Ward, A. *Herodotus and the Philosophy of Empire* (Waco, 2008).
Wardman, A. *Rome's Debt to Greece* (London, 1976).
Wardy, B. "Jewish Religion in Pagan Literature during the Late Republic and Early Empire, *ANRW*, II.19.1 (1979), 592–644.
Wasserstein, A., and D. J. Wasserstein. *The Legend of the Septuagint from Classical Antiquity to Today* (Cambridge, 2006).
Waters, K. H. *Herodotus on Tyrants and Despots* (Wiesbaden, 1971).
Watts, W. J. "Race Prejudice in the Satires of Juvenal," *Acta Classica*, 19 (1976), 83–104.
Webster, J. "At the End of the World: Druidic and Other Revitalization Movements in Post-conquest Gaul and Britain," *Britannia*, 30 (1999), 1–20.
Wehrli, F. *Die Schule des Aristoteles. 3: Klearchos* (Basel, 1948).
West, M. L. *Hesiod's Theogony* (Oxford, 1966).
———. *The Hesiodic Catalogue of Women: Its Nature, Structure, and Origins* (Oxford, 1985).
———. *The East Face of Helicon: West Asiatic Elements in Greek Poetry and Myth* (Oxford, 1997).
West, S. "*Joseph and Aseneth*: A Neglected Greek Romance," *CQ*, 68 (1974), 70–81.
———. "Herodotus' Portrait of Hecataeus," *JHS*, 111 (1991), 144–160.
Westermann, C. *Genesis 12–36: A Commentary* (Minneapolis, 1985).
———. *Genesis 37–50: A Commentary* (Minneapolis, 1986).
Whedbee, J. W. *The Bible and the Comic Vision* (Cambridge, 1998).
White, P. *Promised Verse: Poets in the Society of Augustan Rome* (Cambridge, Mass., 1993).
Wiedemann, T. "The Regularity of Manumission at Rome," *CQ*, 35 (1985), 162–175.
Wiesehöfer, J. *Die "dunklen Jahrhunderte" der Persis* (Munich, 1994).
———. *Iraniens, Grecs et Romains* (Paris, 2005).
Wiesen, D. S. "Juvenal and the Blacks," *ClassMed* 31 (1970), 132–150.
Williams, J.H.C. *Beyond the Rubicon: Romans and Gauls in Republican Italy* (Oxford, 2001).
Williamson, H.G.M. *Ezra, Nehemiah* (Waco, 1985).

Wills, L. M. *The Jewish Novel in the Ancient World* (Ithaca, 1995).
———. *Not God's People* (Lanham, Md., 2008).
Winkes, R. "Physiognomonia: Probleme der Charakterinterpretation römischer Porträts," *ANRW*, 1.4 (1973), 899–926.
Winter, I. J. "Homer's Phoenicians: History, Ethnography, or Literary Trope (A Perspective on Early Orientalism)," in J. B. Carter and S. P. Morris, *The Ages of Homer* (Austin, 1995), 247–271.
Wirth, G. "Hellas und Ägypten: Rezeption und Auseinandersetzung im 5. bzw. 4 Jht. v. Chr.," in M. Görg and G. Hölbl, *Ägypten und der östliche Mittelmeerraum im 1. Jahrtausend v. Chr.* (Wiesbaden, 2000), 281–319.
Wiseman, T. P. *Remus: A Roman Myth* (Cambridge, 1995).
Wissowa, G. "*Interpretatio Romana:* Römische Götter im Barbarenlande," *Archiv für Religionswissenschaft*, 19 (1916–1919), 1–49.
Witt, R. E. *Isis in the Greco-Roman World* (London, 1971).
Wolff, E. "Das geschichtliche Verstehen in Tacitus' *Germania*," *Hermes*, 69 (1934), 121–164.
Woolf, G. *Becoming Roman: The Origins of Provincial Civilization in Gaul* (Cambridge, 1998).
Worthington, I. *Alexander the Great: Man and God* (London, 2004).
Yavetz, Z. "Judeophobia in Classical Antiquity: A Different Approach," *JJS*, 44 (1993), 1–22.
———. *Judenfeindschaft in der Antike* (Munich, 1997).
———. "Latin Authors on Jews and Dacians," *Historia*, 47 (1998), 77–107.
Zakovitch, Y. *Das Buch Rut: Ein jüdischer Kommentar* (Stuttgart, 1999).
Zehnacker, H. "Les intentions de Plaute dans le *Poenulus*," in H. Zehnacker, *Dramatische Wäldchen* (Zürich, 2000), 415–430.
Zellentin, H. "The End of Jewish Egypt: Artapanus and the Second Exodus," in G. Gardner and K. L. Osterloh, *Antiquity in Antiquity: Jewish and Christian Pasts in the Greco-Roman World* (Tübingen, 2008), 27–73.
Ziegler, R. "Der Perseus-Mythos im Prestigedenken kaiserzeitlicher städtischer Eliten Kilikiens," in R. von Haehling, *Griechische Mythologie und frühes Christentum* (Darmstadt, 2005), 85–105.

INDEX OF CITATIONS

⊙ ⊙ ⊙ ⊙ ⊙ ⊙ ⊙ ⊙ ⊙ ⊙ ⊙ ⊙ ⊙ ⊙ ⊙ ⊙

Hebrew Bible

Genesis
9.18–19, 339n158
9.18–27, 279n17
11.27–12.1, 250n155
12.1–3, 279n14
16.1–3, 287n60
16.1–16, 299n130
16.12, 302n144
19.30–38, 280n21
21.8–13, 300n131
21.13, 302n147
21.14–21, 300n132
21.18, 302n147
23.6, 320n61
24.3–4, 280n18
24.37, 280n18
25.1, 287n61
25.1–4, 303n151
25.12–17, 300n133
25.12–18, 302n148
25.18, 302n144
26.34–35, 282n34
27.40, 319n60
27.46–28.2, 282n34
34, 283n36
36.2, 282n34
37.25, 302n145
37.28, 326n101
38.1–6, 291n87
38.1–11, 290n82
38.11–14, 291n88
38.12–19, 290n83
38.20–23, 290n84
38.24–30, 291n85
41.45, 285n49, 287n62
41.50–52, 285n49
43.32, 286n54
43:32, 77n5
46.20, 285n49
49.5–7, 283n36

Exodus
2.16–22, 287n64
6.7, 279n14
12.37–38, 288n69
12.43–49, 288n72
22.21, 288n75
23.9, 288n75
23.23–28, 280n19
33.16, 279n14
34.11–16, 280n19
Leviticus
17.8–16, 289n77
18.15, 292n97
18.16, 292n96
19.9–10, 293n102
19.33–34, 288n75
20.21, 292n96
20.26, 279n14
22.17–25, 289n77
23.22, 293n102
25.23–25, 296n110
Numbers
9.14, 288n72
11.4, 288n70
12.1–8, 287n64
15.13–16, 289n77
15.15–16, 288n72
23.7–10, 279n14
36, 284n40
Deuteronomy
5.14–15, 288n75
7.1–3, 282n30
7.1–6, 280n19
7.6, 279n14
10.15, 279n14
10.19, 288n75
14.2, 279n14
16.11–12, 288n75
23.1, 289n77
23.4, 281n27

386   INDEX OF CITATIONS

Deuteronomy (*cont.*)
   23.4–9, 280n20, 282n30
   23.8–9, 289n76
   24.18–22, 288n75
   24.19–22, 293n102
   25.5–10, 284n44, 292n96, 296n110
   27.19, 288n75
   29.10, 288n70
Joshua
   8.35, 288n70
Judges
   8.24, 302n146
   8.30–31, 287n65
   14.3, 287n66
   14–16, 287n65
Ruth, 293–99 *passim*
   4.12–22, 291n86
1 Samuel
   22.3–4, 297n115
2 Samuel
   3.3, 287n67
   11.2–3, 287n67
   11.27, 287n67
1 Kings
   5–7, 117n13
   8.41–43, 289n77
   9.10–13, 117n13
   11.1–11, 287n68
   22.4, 305n159
2 Kings
   3.7, 305n159

1 Chronicles
   2.3–5, 296n113
   2.4–15, 291n86
   2.9–15, 296n113
Ezra
   9.1–3, 281n25
   10.1–12, 281n26
Nehemiah
   10.29–31, 281n26
   13.1–3, 281n27
   13.23–30, 281n28
Esther
   3.8, 278n11
   Add. B.3–5, 279n13
Psalms
   83.4–8, 302n146
Isaiah
   42.1–6, 306n163
   49.1–6, 306n163
   51.4, 306n163
   56.4–7, 289n77
   60.7, 289n77
   66.18–22, 289n77
Jeremiah
   32.6–12, 296n110
Ezekiel
   44.5–9, 289n77
   47.22–23, 289n80
Amos
   9.7, 289n79
Malachi
   1.11, 289n78

Other Jewish Writings

Assumption of Moses
   1.12–13, 279n14
2 Baruch
   48.20–23, 279n13
2 Esdras
   6.53–59, 279n14
Joseph and Asenath
   1.5, 286n57
   7.1, 286n54
   7.5, 286n56
   8.4–7, 286n55
   9–13, 285n51
   14–17, 285n52
   19–20, 285n53
   20.6–21.8, 286n59

Josephus
   Ant.
      1.121, 223n1
      1.158, 329n112
      1.159–160, 250n158
      1.189–190, 302n149
      1.191–193, 301n143
      1.214, 301n143
      1.220–221, 301n140
      1.239, 301n141
      1.239–241, 303n153
      2.32, 301n142
      2.213, 301n141
      7.67, 192n86, 251n162
      8.55, 138n123

INDEX OF CITATIONS 387

8.76, 117n13
8.144–149, 138n122
9.283, 138n122
12.225–227, 304n155–304n156
13.164–170, 304n156
13.167–168, 305n160
13.245, 278n5
15.371, 324n89
BJ
  3.420, 263n46
  6.300, 195n105
  6.333–336, 186n45
CAp.
  1.12–120, 138n122
  1.71, 250n157
  1.106–107, 138n123
  1.162, 320n66, 323n85
  1.164, 321n70
  1.165, 322n71, 323n86
  1.168–171, 86n57
  1.172–174, 192n86
  1.172–175, 251n162
  1.175, 321n67
  1.176–183, 311n14
  1.179, 311n16, 313n21
  1.180, 312n17
  1.181, 312n18
  1.234, 288n70
  1.248, 251n162
  1.290, 288n70
  2.28–31, 226n12
  2.165, 322n72
  2.168–169, 320n66
  2.225–235, 306n162
  2.257, 321n68
  2.281, 321n67
Jubilees
  15.20, 302n147
  20.1, 300n136
  20.4, 282n32
  20.11–13, 300n136
  22.16–20, 282n33
  25.1–10, 282n35
  27.8–10, 282n35
  30.1–17, 283n37
  34.20, 287n63
  41, 291n89
  41.1–2, 292n94
Letter of Aristeas, 314–17 passim,
  333–37 passim
  131–139, 279n12

1 Maccabees
  12.6–18, 304n156
  12.9–15, 305n160
  12.20–23, 304n155
  12.23, 305n159
  14.16–23, 304n156
2 Maccabees
  5.6–10, 304n156
  14.3, 279n13
  14.38, 279n13
3 Maccabees
  3.4, 278n11
Philo Judaeus
  Aet.
    13–19, 319n58
  Leg.
    4, 250n156
  Leg. All.
    1.105–108, 319n57
    2.15, 320n62
  Mos.
    1.23, 320n64
    2, 319n59
    2.31, 250n156
    2.40, 250n156
  Mut.
    152, 320n61
  Prob.
    53–57, 319n60
    72–75, 324n90
  Q. Gen.
    2.6, 320n63
  Somn.
    2.244, 320n61
  Spec. Leg.
    1.1–2, 184n39
    1.51–53, 306n164
    1.308–309, 306n164
    4.177–178, 306n164
  Virt.
    21, 292n91
    102–103, 306n164
Qumran
  1 QM 1.1–2, 280n24
Sibylline Oracle, 3, 338–41 passim
Testament of Job
  45.1–3, 283n39
Testament of Judah
  10.1, 291n90
  10–11, 292n95

388 INDEX OF CITATIONS

Testament of Levi
  9.10, 283n38
  14.6, 283n38
Tobit
  1.9, 284n41
  3.15, 284n42

4.12–13, 284n43
5.11–13, 284n47
6.11–13, 284n44
6.16–18, 284n45
7.10–12, 284n45

Greek and Latin Authors

Acusilaus
  FGH 2 F25a, 241n116
Ad Herennium
  4.20, 130n75, 132n81
  4.66, 132n81
Aelian
  Varia Historia
    8.7, 71n101
Aeschylus
  Persae, 9–21 passim
    79–80, 256n13
    765, 225n6
    768–772, 54n6
  Hyp. to Aeschylus' *Persae*, 10n3
  Prom. Bound
    561–886, 257n19
    787–856, 230n38
    787–869, 232n57
    808–809, 201n37
    851, 201n37
    853–869, 258n22
    858, 232n53
    869, 232n58
  Suppliants, 258n22
    70–71, 230n41
    119, 230n41
    130, 230n41
    154–155, 201n37, 230n41
    176–203, 232n53
    234–237, 231n42
    236–237, 241n115
    250–259, 241n115
    274–275, 232n55
    279–289, 231n43
    291–326, 232n55
    325–326, 232n56
    365–369, 232n54
    370–375, 232n54
    393–395, 232n53
    397–401, 232n54
    496–498, 231n44

    517–519, 232n53
    719–720, 201n37
    741, 231n50
    741–742, 231n46
    798–799, 232n53
    817–818, 231n50
    817–821, 231n46
    836–965, 231n51
    911–914, 231n47, 241n115
    952–953, 231n48
    954–965, 232n54
    972–974, 231n45
    994–995, 231n45
    1031–1032, 232n53
    1052–1053, 232n53
    1062–1064, 232n53
Agatharchides
  Mar. Erythr.
    16, 205n78
Airs, Waters, Places, 39n168
Alexander Romance (Ps. Callisthenes),
  267–72 passim
  3.18.6, 206n86
  3.21–23, 199n20
Ammianus Marcellinus
  22.15.8, 272n85, 274n91
  22.15.24, 262n45
Anthologia Latina
  No. 182, 206n85
  No. 183, 206n85
Apion
  apud Jos. CAp. 2.21, 191n79
  apud Jos. CAp. 2.121, 278n7
Apollodorus
  Bibliotheca
    1.9.11–12, 85n52
    2.1.1, 241n116
    2.1.3, 257n19, 258n21
    2.1.3–4, 230n38
    2.1.4, 230n35–230n36
    2.1.4–5, 258n22

INDEX OF CITATIONS 389

2.1.5, 201n37
2.2.1–2, 258n23
2.4.1–4, 255n3
2.4.1–5, 37n159
2.4.3, 200n35, 258n25
2.5.11, 303n152
3.4.1–2, 233n60
31.1, 233n60
Apollonius Molon
  apud. Jos. CAp. 2.148, 182n23, 278n4
  apud. Jos. CAp. 2.258, 278n4
Apollonius Rhodius
  2.357–359, 228n25
  2.790, 228n25
Schol. Apollonius Rhodius
  1248, 96n111
Appian
  Pun.
    53, 136n117
    62–64, 136n117
    69, 130n73
    250, 132n79
  Syr.
    10, 126n55
Aristophanes
  Birds
    504–507, 102n142
  Frogs
    1026–1027, 12n12
    1406, 102n142
  Peace
    1253, 102n142
  Thesm.
    855–857, 102n142
    921–922, 102n142
  Vesp.
    1075–1080, 236n84
Aristotle
  De Gen. Anim.
    1.722a, 203n56
    5.3.782b, 203n53, 204n61
  Met.
    10.105ba–b, 206n81
    981B, 107n169
  Pol.
    1269b, 144n27
    1272b, 120n26–120n27
    1273a, 120n25
    1273b, 120n27
    1286A, 107n169
    1329B, 107n169

[Aristotle]
  De. Mir. Ausc.
    135, 121n34
  Physiognomica
    6.812a–b, 205n77
Arrian
  Anab.
    1.24.1, 70n99
    2.14.7, 66n72
    3.3.2, 264n55
    3.16.7–8, 51n204
    4.1.3–5, 69n91
    4.4.1, 67n77
    4.7.4, 67n79
    4.8.4, 67n82
    4.9.9, 67n79
    4.10.5–12, 69n92
    4.12.1, 69n92
    4.12.2, 68n88
    4.14.2, 67n82, 69n92
    4.17.3, 66n73
    4.19.5–6, 70n93
    4.20.4, 70n93
    4.22.5, 67n77
    4.24.7, 67n77
    5.2.2–4, 66n74
    5.3.6, 66n74
    5.4.4, 202n50
    5.11.3, 66n74
    5.12.2, 66n74
    5.29.3, 67n77
    6.25.5, 70n98
    6.29.4–11, 68n87
    7.2–3, 313n22
    7.4.4–8, 71n101
    7.4.8, 70n98, 72n112
    7.5.1–3, 73n114
    7.6.1, 66n75, 73n115
    7.6.2, 72n108
    7.6.2–5, 74n117
    7.6.3, 67n82
    7.8.2, 67n82, 73n115, 74n117
    7.8.2–7.12.4, 73n116
    7.11.6–7, 74n121
    7.11.9, 74n122
    7.12.2, 74n120
    7.23.1, 74n119
    7.29.4, 68n84, 68n86
Athenaeus
  7.299e, 103n143
  7.299f–300a, 103n144

390 INDEX OF CITATIONS

Athenaeus (cont.)
  7.300b, 103n145
  12.537d–540a, 71n101
Bacchylides
  8.31, 227n20
  18.39–48, 235n69, 235n72
Caesar
  B Gall., 147–58 passim
    1.1, 167n46
    2.4, 145n30
    6.17.1, 175n101
    6.21–24, 159n1
    6.22, 164n29
    6.23.9, 164n31
[Caesar]
  B Alex.
    24, 108n176
Callimachus
  fr. 655, 264n56
Cato
  Orig.
    F1.4–15, 245n132
    F1.19, 245n134, 247n144
    F2.3, 146n34
    F2.12, 146n35
    F2.15, 249n153
    F2.22, 248n148, 248n151
    F2.24, 249n153
    F2.26, 245n134, 249n153
    F3.2, 249n153
Catullus
  37.20, 344n192
  39.17–21, 344n192
Chares
  FGH 125 F 4, 71n101
Cicero
  Balb.
    55, 347n207
  Cat.
    4.5, 147n43
    4.10, 147n43
  De Div.
    1.90, 146n37
  De Inv.
    1.71, 132n81
  De Off.
    1.38, 132n82
    1.108, 133n85
  De Rep.
    2.28–29, 345n197
    3.14, 109n187

  Flac.
    65, 344n185
    67, 181n17, 344n189
  Font.
    12, 147n41
    13, 147n39
    23, 147n41
    26, 147n41
    29–30, 147n41
    30, 147n39
    31, 147n42
    32–33, 147n39
    35, 147n39
    41, 147n39
    43, 147n39
    44, 147n40
    46, 147n40
    49, 147n40
  Har. Resp.
    19, 133n86
  Leg.
    2.59, 351n232
    2.64, 351n232
  Leg. agr.
    2.87, 131n78
    2.95, 132n84
  Nat. Deor.
    1.43, 109n184
    1.81–82, 109n190
    1.83–84, 175n97
    1.101, 110n191, 113n215
    3.47, 109n189
  Prov. Cons.
    10, 344n187
  Q Fr.
    1.1.23, 54n4
    1.1.27, 344n191
  Rab. Post.
    34–36, 108n175
  Red. Sen.
    14, 344n186
  Scaur.
    42, 132n83, 344n190
  Sen.
    41, 346n204
  Sest.
    141, 344n184
  Tusc.
    4.2–3, 346n202
    5.78, 109n188

Columella
 De Re Rust.
  1.1.13, 129n72
Ctesias
 FGH 688, 55n8
 FGH 688 F16, 38n164
Curtius Rufus
 4.1.30, 109n185
 4.8.3, 200n32
 6.2.11, 68n86
 6.6.1–8, 67n79
 6.6.7, 67n83
 6.6.9, 67n81
 7.3.23, 67n77
 8.4.22–30, 70n93
 8.4.25–26, 70n95
 8.5.1, 66n75–66n76
 8.5.5–24, 69n92
 8.5.20–21, 69n92
 8.5.22–24, 69n89
 8.7.12, 67n82
 9.2.24, 66n74
 10.2.9–11, 73n114
 10.2.12, 73n115
 10.2.13–10.4.3, 73n116
 10.3.7–14, 75n123
 10.3.12, 71n101, 71n104
Deinias
 FGH 306 fr. 7, 256n16, 259n26
Demosthenes
 Epitaph.
  4, 236n84
 Digesta
  1.2.2.4, 351n231
Dio Cassius
 40.47.3, 348n217
 42.26, 348n217
 50.24.6–25.3, 109n183
 50.27.1, 109n183
 67.4.1, 164n28
Dio Chrysostomus
 11.14, 200n27
Diodorus Siculus, 90–99 *passim*
 1.17.1–3, 267n64
 1.18.1, 225n8
 1.20.1–3, 225n8
 1.23.8, 223n2
 1.24.1–7, 267n65
 1.28.1, 226n9
 1.28.2, 226n10, 230n39
 1.28.2–3, 226n11–226n12

1.28.4, 235n71, 265n59
1.29.5, 266n61
1.38.6–29.1, 266n60
1.60.2–5, 202n44
1.65.2–8, 202n44
1.67.11, 104n152
1.86.3–5, 113n213
1.87, 113n215
1.88.4–5, 104n153
1.96–98, 270n80
2.22, 38n164
2.22.1–5, 200n29
2.43.3, 225n7
3.2.1, 200n23
3.2.2–4, 198n10
3.3.1, 198n11
3.3.2, 200n24
3.5.2–3, 202n44
3.6.3–4, 202n44
3.8.1–2, 204n62
3.8.2–6, 205n71
3.9.1–2, 199n12
3.9.1–4, 205n72
3.10–33, 205n75
3.14.6, 204n68
3.32–33, 204n68
3.67.1, 240n105
4.17.4–5, 303n152
4.18.1, 104n153
4.27.2–3, 104n153
4.56.1, 225n6
4.73.6–4.74.1, 228n26
5.26.3, 143n14
5.27.4, 143n15
5.28.1–3, 143n16
5.28.4, 143n17
5.28.5, 143n18
5.28.5–6, 144n19
5.29.4–5, 144n20
5.29.5, 144n21
5.31.1, 144n22, 146n36
5.31.1–3, 144n23
5.31.3–4, 144n24
5.31.5, 144n25
5.32.3–6, 144n26
5.32.7, 144n27
5.33.2–5, 156n94
5.35.4, 121n34
5.38.3, 122n38
5.57.4–5, 266n61
5.57.5, 265n58

392   INDEX OF CITATIONS

Diodorus Siculus (cont.)
   5.80.1, 241n112
   7.5.4–5, 244n129
   8.14, 345n196
   10.27, 225n6
   11.41.1, 51n206
   17, 70n97
   17.77.4, 68n86
   17.77.4–7, 67n79
   17.77.5, 67n80, 67n83
   17.78.1, 67n81
   17.83.2, 67n77
   17.94.4, 70n98
   17.107.6, 71n101, 72n107
   17.108.1–2, 66n75
   17.108.3, 73n115
   17.109.2, 73n114
   17.109.2–3, 73n116
   17.110.1–2, 74n119
   17.110.3, 70n98, 74n120
   30.7.1, 133n91
   34/5.1.1–4, 278n5
   34/5.35, 274n92
   40.3.2, 226n10, 230n39
   40.3.3, 226n11
Diogenes Laertius
   1.1, 156n93, 313n24
   1.3, 277n1
   1.9, 313n23
   2. 125–144, 316n38
   4.67, 137n120
   5.1, 322n77
   8.3, 323n82
   8.7, 322n77
   8.14, 346n201
   8.32, 322n78
   8.36, 322n77
   8.41, 322n76
   9.1, 322n77
Dionysius Halicarnassensis
   1.10–13, 246n137
   1.11.1, 245n133, 247n143
   1.13.2, 245n133, 247n143
   1.28.4, 240n107
   1.31, 246n139
   1.34.1, 246n140
   1.41–44, 246n140
   1.49.1–2, 247n146
   1.60–62, 247n145
   1.72.2, 244n126
   1.74.1, 244n129

   1.89.1–2, 246n137
   1.89.2, 246n139
   2.19, 348n212
   2.49.2, 248n148
   2.49.4–5, 248n149
   2.59, 345n197
   2.59.1, 345n196
   4.62, 347n206
   6.17.2, 347n207
   10.51.5, 350n230
   10.52.4, 350n230
   10.55.5, 350n230
Ennius
   Ann.
      221V, 122n40
      274–275V, 123n43
      286V, 123n42
      325V, 122n41
Ephorus
   apud Strabo 5.2.4, 240n104
Euripides
   apud Apollod. 2.1–4, 19n68
   Bacch.
      170–172, 119n22, 236n80,
         341n173
   Erechth.
      apud Lyc. Leok. 100, 236n84
   fr. 145, 258n25
   fr. 147, 258n25
   Helen
      1–67, 89n73
      224, 102n141
      295, 102n141
      666, 102n141
      769, 259n29
      863–864, 102n141
      1100, 102n141
      1507, 102n141
Ion
   589–592, 236n84
Phoen.
   4–6, 236n79
   5–6, 119n22, 341n173
   216–219, 236n79
   244–248, 236n79
   280–282, 236n79
   291, 236n79
   638–639, 119n22, 341n173
   638–648, 236n79
Phrixus
   fr. 819, 236n80

INDEX OF CITATIONS 393

Schol. Eur.
  Or.
    4, 227n17
Fabius Pictor
  F1–2, 125n54, 244n130
  F2, 246n142
Florus
  1.22.2, 138n128
Gellius
  1.19.1, 347n206
  10.1.10, 123n44
Hecataeus of Abdera
  1 fr. 286, 225n6
  apud Diod. Sic., *40.3.2*, 235n71
  apud Diod. Sic., *40.3.4*, 182n23, 277n2
  apud Strabo 7.7.1, 228n21, 229n34, 240n102
  FGH 1 F119, 242n122
  FGH 1 F307–309, 89n71
Heliodorus
  Aeth.
    4.8, 199n17
    4.12, 199n14
    8.1, 199n16
    8.16, 199n17
    8.16–17, 199n16
    9.1, 199n18
    9.5–6, 199n16
    9–10, 202n45
    9.13, 199n16
    9.20–23, 199n16
    9.24–26, 199n18
    9.26, 199n16
    10.4, 199n15
    10.6, 199n15
    10.7, 199n18–199n19
    10.9, 199n19
    10.16–17, 199n19
Hellanicus
  apud Dion. Hal. 1.28.3, 241n108
  FGH 4 F51, 235n70
  FGH 4 F59–60, 224n3, 256n15, 260n32
  FGH 4 F153, 89n72
  FGH 4 FF53–55, 159n2
  FGH 4 FF173–176, 159n2
Herodotus, 21–39 *passim*, 76–90 *passim*
  1.1, 117n14–117n15
  1.1.1–3, 235n74
  1.1–2, 258n20
  1.2, 118n16
  1.2.1, 235n74

  1.4–5, 118n16
  1.5, 258n20
  1.56.2, 240n100
  1.56–58, 239n94
  1.57.1, 241n109
  1.57.2, 239n95
  1.57–58, 242n122
  1.58, 239n96, 240n101
  1.86.6, 54n7
  1.90, 54n7
  1.127.1–2, 54n7
  1.141.1–3, 54n7
  1.146.1, 241n111, 242n118
  1.153.1–2, 56n17
  1.153.1–3, 54n7
  2.1.37, 201n41
  2.22, 203n53–203n54
  2.41, 258n21
  2.43, 267n66
  2.45, 104n149–104n150
  2.49, 119n22, 341n173
  2.49.3, 235n76
  2.51, 242n118
  2.51.2, 242n122
  2.52.1, 241n113
  2.54–57, 118n17
  2.56.1, 239n98, 240n103
  2.91, 258n24, 259n27, 259n29
  2.91.5, 230n39, 232n57
  2.139, 201n42
  2.171.3, 232n57
  2.182.2, 232n57
  3.1–2, 270n78
  3.19, 118n19
  3.19–24, 202n46
  3.20, 201n40
  3.25, 202n47
  3.89.3, 54n7
  3.107, 117n14
  4.5, 225n7
  4.8–10, 225n7
  4.42, 117n14
  4.44, 117n14
  4.45.4–5, 235n75
  4.95, 323n83
  4.145.2, 241n109, 242n118
  4.147.1–148.1, 342n175
  4.147.4, 235n76
  4.183, 204n68
  4.196, 117n14, 119n20
  4.197, 200n22

394 INDEX OF CITATIONS

Herodotus (cont.)
  5.17, 175n101
  5.53–54, 200n29
  5.57, 341n173, 342n176
  5.57–59, 119n21
  5.57–61, 235n77
  5.58, 342n177
  6.47, 117n14
  6.53, 264n53
  6.54, 260n31
  6.137, 241n109
  6.137–140, 240n99, 242n118
  7.8.g.1, 228n23, 229n29
  7.11.4, 228n23, 229n29
  7.23, 119n23
  7.42, 242n118
  7.43, 50n201
  7.61, 19n68, 224n3, 256n14
  7.62.1, 225n6
  7.70, 204n60
  7.89, 118n18
  7.90, 117n14
  7.94, 232n57
  7.94–95, 242n119
  7.150, 257n17
  7.150–152, 19n68
  7.151, 200n29
  7.161.3, 236n84
  8.44.2, 239n98
  8.74–76, 14n27
  9.122, 54n7
Hesiod
  fr. 296, 230n37
  fr. 358, 88n68
  Theog.
    274–281, 255n6
    985–986, 200n26
    1000–1001, 225n6
    1011–1016, 243n123
[Hesiod]
  Cat.
    fr. 129, 255n9
    fr. 135, 255n9
  Shield of Herakles
    216–237, 255n6
Homer
  Il.
    1.423–425, 198n5
    2.100–108, 227n15
    2.681, 241n112
    2.701–702, 38n164

    2.840–841, 241n112
    4.376–409, 234n65
    6.184, 251n162
    6.288–295, 116n6
    6.289–292, 87n62
    10.285–289, 234n65
    14.319–320, 255n5
    14.321–322, 234n66
    16.233–234, 241n113
    23.205–207, 198n6
    23.677–680, 234n65
    23.740—743, 116n6
  Od.
    1.22–25, 198n7
    4.81–85, 88n67, 198n8
    4.125–132, 88n66–88n67
    4.227–230, 87n62, 88n67
    4.351–352, 87n62, 88n67
    4.614–619, 116n6–116n7
    5.282–287, 198n7
    5.283, 251n162
    5.333, 234n64
    11.271–276, 234n65
    11.281–297, 85n52
    13.200–220, 117n12
    13.250–286, 117n12
    13.271, 116n9, 121n35
    13.271–284, 116n8
    13.272, 116n5
    14.285–297, 116n8
    14.287–297, 117n10
    15.225–242, 85n52
    15.415, 116n8–116n9, 121n35
    15.415–484, 117n11
    19.177, 241n112
Horace
  Carm.
    1.37.6–10, 108n181
    3.5.33, 133n93
    4.4.49, 133n93
  Epodes
    9.11–16, 108n181
  Odes
    3.16.1–11, 264n54
  Sat.
    1.4.139–143, 183n29
    1.5.97–101, 181n17
    1.9.70, 184n36
Hypereides
  Against Athenogenes
    3, 107n171

INDEX OF CITATIONS 395

Iamblichus
  Vita Pyth.
    14–15, 323n83
    146, 323n84
Ion of Chios
  FGH 392 F7, 12n12
Isocrates
  Busiris
    9, 104n154
    10, 104n155
    15–25, 105n156
    26–27, 105n157
    28–29, 105n158
    30–33, 105n159
    36–37, 105n160
  Helen
    68, 229n34, 237n86, 238n91
  Nic.
    24, 119n24
  Panath.
    80, 229n34, 237n86, 238n92
    124, 236n84
  Paneg.
    24, 236n84
    110–128, 53n2
    150–152, 53n1
    157–158, 53n1
  Peace
    49, 236n84
Justin
  12.3.8–11, 67n79
  12.4.1, 67n81
  12.4.1–6, 70n98
  12.4.2, 72n112
  12.4.2–6, 71n100
  12.4.5–6, 74n120
  12.7.3, 69n92
  12.10.10, 71n101, 71n104
  12.11.1–3, 73n114
  12.11.4–5, 73n115
  12.11.6–12.12.10, 73n116
  12.12.4, 74n119
  20.1.14–15, 248n150
  36.2.1, 250n158
  36.2.14, 191n79
  42.2.7–10, 225n5
  42.3.6, 225n6
  42.3.8, 225n5
[Justin]
  De Monarch.
    2, 332n127, 333n129
    2–3, 333n128
    2–5, 333n130
Juvenal
  1.26–29, 111n199
  1.26–30, 208n94
  2.20–28, 207n92
  2.23, 202n51
  3.10–16, 183n30
  3.296, 183n30
  4.1–33, 208n94
  4.108–109, 208n94
  5.49–64, 208n94
  6.159–160, 184n34
  6.522–541, 111n199
  6.542–547, 183n30
  6.592–601, 208n95
  8.30–39, 209n99
  13.162–173, 209n101
  13.163, 204n65
  14.96–106, 179n6
  14.98–99, 184n34
  14.100–102, 182n22
  14.103–104, 278n9
  14.104, 182n24
  15.1–8, 110n192
  15.4–6, 111n198
  15.10–11, 110n193
  15.13, 110n194
  15.77–92, 110n195
  15.119–131, 110n196
  15.131–174, 110n197
Livy
  1.18.1–3, 345n197
  1.56.4–13, 349n222
  3.31.8, 350n230
  3.32.6, 350n230
  3.33.3–5, 350n230
  5.15–17, 349n223
  5.21.1–2, 349n224
  5.21.1–7, 349n220
  5.23.8–11, 349n224
  5.25.4–10, 349n224
  5.28.1–5, 349n224
  10.47.6–7, 347n209
  21.4.9, 133n88
  22.6.12, 133n89
  22.9–10, 347n210
  22.22.15, 133n86
  22.57, 158n107
  22.57.4–5, 350n228
  23.11.1–6, 350n228

396 INDEX OF CITATIONS

Livy (*cont.*)
  23.30–31, 347n210
  28.44.4, 133n89
  28.45.12, 350n229
  29.10.4–11.8, 347n211
  29.10.6, 349n221, 350n229
  29.11.5–7, 349n221
  30.22.6, 133n89
  30.30.27, 133n92
  30.42.17, 132n79
  34.31.2–4, 133n90
  34.61.13, 133n89
  35.14.5–12, 126n55
  35.49.8, 344n188
  36.17.4–5, 344n188
  38.17.5–11, 344n193
  38.47.12, 147n46
  39.8–19, 348n214
  42.47.7, 133n91
  Per.
    48, 274n95
Lucan
  8.542–549, 108n182
  10.63, 108n182
Lucian
  Astr.
    3–5, 199n13
  Sacr.
    2, 198n9
  Zeus Trag.
    37, 198n9
    42, 111n201
Lycophron
  Alex.
    1413–1414, 256n16
Lysias
  Epitaph.
    17, 236n84
Manilius
  4.723–724, 202n50
Martial
  3.34, 207n92
  6.8.8, 184n37
  6.39.1–9, 207n90
  7.30, 111n199
  7.30.5, 184n38
  11.94, 184n38
  12.57.13, 183n30
  102.14, 184n37
  De Spect.
    3.10, 204n60

Megasthenes
  FGH 715, 159n2
Menander
  fr. 612, 203n53, 206n79
  Sam.
    589–591, 256n11
Nepos
  Hann.
    9.2, 133n85
Nicolaus Damascenus
  FGH 90 F6, 224n4
  FGH 90 F10, 227n19
Nonius
  s.v. duodevicesimo, 123n44
Ovid
  Ars Amat.
    1.53, 201n36
    3.191, 201n36
  Fast.
    1.260, 248n150
    2.711–720, 349n222
    3.151–154, 345n198
    3.545–550, 136n114
    4.247–348, 347n211
  Her.
    7.7–8, 136n114
    7.18, 136n114
    7.30, 136n114
    7.57, 136n114
    7.81–82, 136n114
    7.195–196, 136n114
  Met.
    1.747, 258n21
    3.1–137, 233n60
    4.668–681, 201n36
    4.669, 200n35, 258n25
    4.764, 200n35
    5.1, 200n35
    15.1–8, 345n198
    15.60–72, 345n198
    185.826, 108n179
    583–750, 257n19
  Pont.
    3.341–344, 345n198
Pausanias
  1.8.5, 51n205
  1.28.3, 240n107, 241n111
  1.33.4, 205n74
  2.6.5, 227n17
  2.15.1, 227n17
  2.16.1, 230n35

2.19.3–4, 230n35
2.22.2–3, 227n19
2.26.2, 227n17
2.30.8, 227n17
3.17.3, 258n24
3.20.5, 241n111
4.35.9, 262n42
4.36.1, 241n111
5.8.2, 227n17–227n18
8.1.4–6, 241n111
8.4.1, 241n111
8.46.3, 51n202
10.10.4, 230n35
10.31.7, 200n27, 200n30
Petronius
  fr. 37, 184n33
  Sat.
    102, 203n52, 207n88
Pherecydes
  FGH 3 F17, 103n146
  FGH 3 F21, 232n57, 235n70
  FGH 3 F26, 255n4
  FGH 3 F38, 228n22
  FGH 3 F114, 85n52
Philostratus
  Her.
    207–214, 319n56
  Imagines
    1.29, 201n36, 258n25, 262n42
  Vita Apoll.
    3.1, 211n107
    6.4.1–3, 200n31
  Vita soph.
    2.588, 211n107
Phrynichus
  Phoenissae, 10
Pindar
  Ol.
    1.24, 227n18
    1.35–94, 228n28
    1.36–38, 227n19
    1.93, 227n18
    9.9, 227n18
  Pyth.
    10.44–48, 255n10
    12.6–16, 255n10
Schol. Pindar
  Ol.
    1.35, 228n27

Plato
  Critias
    110A–b, 106n165
    133A–b, 106n165
  Crito
    52E, 119n24
  Laws
    656D–E, 107n168
    747B–C, 107n168
    953E, 107n168
  Menex.
    234C–235C, 237n87
    235C–236D, 237n88
    245C–D, 229n34, 237n85
    249D–E, 237n89
  Phaedrus
    274C–D, 107n168
  Rep.
    3.414B–C, 121n35
    5.473D, 319n59
    586c, 88n69
  Timaeus
    21E, 106n163, 265n57–265n58, 266n63
    22B, 106n164
    22C–23B, 106n165
    23D–25D, 106n166
Plautus
  Poen., 126–29 passim
    1289–1291, 202n50, 203n52
    1309–1310, 126n57
Pliny the Elder
  HN
    2.169, 137n119
    2.189, 203n55, 204n60
    5.13.67, 138n125
    5.43–46, 205n75
    5.46, 275n97
    5.67, 138n127
    5.69, 262n41, 262n43
    5.128, 262n43
    6.70, 203n55
    6.182, 200n35, 258n25, 263n49
    6.187–195, 205n75
    6.189, 204n68
    6.190, 205n76
    7.6, 201n39
    7.51, 203n56
    9.11, 262n45
    15.46, 264n55
    18.5.22, 129n72

398 INDEX OF CITATIONS

Pliny the Elder (*cont.*)
   18.22, 274n90
   29.52, 156n98
   30.4, 156n98
   31.24, 183n32
   34.16–17, 51n203
   34.21, 351n231
   34.26, 346n203, 349n225
   34.69–70, 51n204
Pliny the Younger
  Pan.
   16, 164n28
   31.2–5, 109n185
Plutarch
  Alex.
   42.4, 70n98
   43.3, 68n86
   45.1, 68n84
   45.2, 67n80
   45.3, 67n81
   47.3, 66n75–66n76
   47.4, 70n93–70n94
   47.5, 67n80
   51.3, 67n82
   54.2, 69n92
   54.3–55, 69n91
   65, 313n22
   69, 313n22
   70.2, 70n98, 71n101, 72n112, 73n114
   71.1, 66n75
   71.1–3, 73n115
   71.3–5, 73n116
   71.5, 74n120
   74.1–2, 69n90
  Cam.
   22.2, 243n124, 246n138
  Cat. Mai.
   2.3, 346n204
   12.5, 343n183
   26–27, 130n73
  De Is. et Osir., 111–14 *passim*
   31, 191n79, 192n83
   354e, 100n129
  De Malignitate Herodoti
   857A, 30n115, 81n32
  De Stoic. Rep
   38, 181n17
  De Superst.
   69C, 181n17
  Marc.
   3.4, 158n107

   8.6, 350n227
  Mor.
   328 E, 67n78
   329 B–D, 65n71
   329 C, 71n103
   329 E, 71n101–71n102
   330 A, 67n80, 68n84
   332 E, 70n93
   338 D, 70n94
   678 C, 112n205
   799 D, 136n118
  Num.
   1.3, 248n150
   1.3–4, 345n199
   8.2–8, 345n199
   8.9, 346n205
   8.10, 346n203, 349n225
   11.1–2, 345n199
   22.3–4, 345n199
  Quaest. Conv.
   4.4–5, 184n35
   5.5.5, 112n205
  Rom.
   3.1–3, 244n129
   16.1, 248n150
  Sert.
   9.3–5, 303n152
   9.4–5, 274n93
  Thes.
   3.1, 227n17
Polybius
   1.14, 123n47
   1.14–15, 123n46
   1.15.12, 123n47
   2.7.5–6, 142n3
   2.15.7, 142n9
   2.17.9–12, 142n6
   2.18.1–2, 142n8–142n9
   2.19.3–4, 142n3
   2.19.4, 142n4
   2.21.9, 143n11
   2.29.5, 142n10
   2.31.7, 142n8
   2.32.7–8, 142n4
   2.33.2–3, 142n5
   2.35.2, 142n9
   2.35.6, 142n5
   3.2.6, 123n46
   3.6.1–7, 123n48
   3.8.1–3.9.5, 124n49
   3.10.3–5, 125n52

INDEX OF CITATIONS 399

3.15.5, 124n50
3.15.7, 124n50
3.15.10, 125n52
3.21.1–8, 124n51
3.30.4, 125n52
3.34.2, 142n7, 142n9
3.70.4, 142n4
3.78.1, 121n36
3.78.2, 142n4
3.78.5, 142n7
6.43.1, 120n29
6.47.9, 120n30
6.51.1–2, 120n30
6.51–52, 120n31
6.52.1, 117n14
6.56.1–5, 120n31
9.11.2, 122n38
9.22.8–10, 125n53
9.26.1–11, 125n53
15.24–33, 107n174
15.33.10, 107n172
27.13.1, 107n172
36.9, 131n76
36.9.16, 131n77
38.21.22, 139n130
39.7.7, 107n172
apud Dion. Hal. 1.32.1, 246n141
Pomponius Mela
  1.62–64, 262n40, 262n44
  1.65, 138n126
  3.46, 274n94
  3.103, 275n97
Porphyry
  De Abstinentia
    2.5.1, 107n170
    2.26, 309n3, 310n5
  Vita Pyth.
    6, 323n82
    11–12, 323n82, 323n87
    22, 346n201
Posidonius
  apud Diod. Sic. 34/5.1–3, 182n23
  apud Strabo 16.2.24, 343n181
Proclus
  FGH 72 F20b, 266n63
  FGH 124 F 51, 265n58
Propertius
  2.27.1–4, 138n125
  2.33a.20, 108n180
  3.11.33–42, 108n180
  4.6.78, 200n35

Ptolemy
  Tetrabib.
    2.2, 203n53
Quintilian
  3.7.2, 182n20
  3.7.21, 181n17
  9.3.31, 130n75
Quintus Smyrnaeus
  2.30–32, 200n27, 200n33
  2.100–161, 200n27
  2. 211–647, 200n27
Sallust
  Cat.
    50.1, 147n43
    52.36, 147n43
  Fragmenta dubia vel falsa
    3, 275n97
  Iug.
    17.7, 138n124, 272n84
    18.1–8, 273n86
    18.9–10, 273n87
    18.11–12, 273n88
    108.3, 132n80
[Scylax]
  104, 260n34, 261n35
Seneca
  Ad Helviam
    19.6, 109n185
  apud Augustine CD 6.11, 181n17,
    181n19, 183n26, 183n28, 183n31
  De Ira
    1.11.34, 159n1
    3.20.2–4, 202n48
    3.26.3, 209n102
Servius
  Ad Aen.
    1.273, 245n135
    3.167, 247n147
    7.207, 247n147
    8.638, 248n148, 249n152
Sextus Empiricus
  Adv. Math.
    9.359–364, 343n181
    9.363, 121n33
    11.43, 203n59
Silius Italicus
  3.231–234, 136n116
  8.414–415, 249n152
  156–157, 129n69
Solinus
  31.6, 275n97

400 INDEX OF CITATIONS

Solinus (*cont.*)
   32.2, 272n85, 274n91
Sophocles
  Ajax
    1228, 229n31
    1262–1263, 229n31
    1288–1289, 229n32
    1291–1292, 229n30
    1292, 227n20
  Ant.
    82–825, 227n20
  fr. 270, 241n110
Statius
  Silvae
    3.2.113, 111n201
  Theb.
    5.426–428, 198n9
Stesichorus
  fr. 15, 88n69
Stobaeus
  86, 206n79
  493, 206n79
Strabo, 100–101 *passim*
  1.1.13, 203n53
  1.2.27, 201n37, 203n55
  1.2.35, 258n25, 261n37, 263n48
  1.4.9, 65n70, 120n28
  3.5.5, 121n37
  4.1.5, 146n36
  4.4.2, 145n31, 146n36
  4.4.2–5, 145n28
  4.4.4, 156n95
  4.4.5, 145n29, 145n32
  5.2.4, 230n36, 240n106, 241n112–241n113
  5.3.3, 246n139
  7.3.5, 323n83
  7.7.1, 240n106, 242n122
  7.7.10, 241n114
  8.4.4, 228n27
  8.5.5, 228n27
  8.6.9, 230n36, 240n106
  8.6.14, 227n17
  9.2.3, 240n107
  11.11.4, 68n87
  11.14.12, 225n5
  13.1.53, 247n146
  14.1.25, 351n231
  15.1.24, 204n63
  15.1.40, 203n55
  15.1.59, 314n26

  15.1.61–68, 313n22
  15.3.2, 200n29
  16.1.39, 324n91
  16.1.68, 311n12
  16.1.70, 311n12
  16.2.24, 120n32, 121n33, 138n125
  16.2.28, 261n35, 261n38
  16.2.39, 311n12
  16.4.17, 204n68
  17.1.12, 107n172
  17.1.18, 259n29
  17.1.19, 104n151
  17.1.42, 200n29
  17.1.46, 200n29
  17.2.1–3, 205n73
  17.2.3, 199n12
  17.3.7, 275n98
  17.3.13, 274n92
Suetonius
  Aug.
    40.3, 210n105
  Claud.
    25, 156n98
Tacitus
  Agr.
    16, 166n43
    21, 165n37
    39.1, 164n28
    42, 152n78
  Annals
    1.9–10, 190n75
    1.10, 193n90
    1.51.1, 176n104, 177n113
    1.69, 159n1
    2.12.1, 174n95
    2.85, 181n17
    3.27, 163n20
    4.73.4, 176n104
    11.11, 194n99
    14.12, 195n102
    15.74, 193n91
    16.33, 195n103
  Germania, 159–78 *passim*
  Hist., 179–96 *passim*
    1.11.1, 109n185
    5.2, 200n35
    5.2.1, 250n160
    5.2.1–5.3.1, 251n164
    5.2.2, 263n50
    5.2.3, 251n162
    5.5.1–2, 278n8

INDEX OF CITATIONS

Theophrastus
  apud Porphyry *On Abstinence* 2.5.1,
    107n170
Thucydides
  1.2.4, 162n16
  1.2.5, 236n84
  1.3.2, 240n103
  1.9.2, 228n24, 229n33
  1.94–95, 28n106
  1.128–135, 28n106
  2.36.1, 236n84
  4.109.4, 241n109, 242n122
Timagenes
  apud Amm. Marc.15.9.8, 156n96
Trogus
  apud Justin 36.2.15, 278n6
Tyrtaeus
  fr. 2, 227n16
Valerius Maximus
  1.3.3–4, 348n217
  1.6.3, 349n223
  1.8.2, 347n209
  2.10.ext.1, 51n205
  7.4.4, 136n115
Varro
  apud Aug. CD 4.31, 177n117, 181n16
  apud Aug. De Consensu Evangelistarum
    1.30, 181n15
  apud Aug. De Consensu Evangelistarum
    1.31, 181n15

  apud Aug. De Consensu Evangelistarum
    1.42, 181n15
De Re Rust.
  1.1.10, 129n72
Ling.
  7.8, 347n206
  8.38, 202n51
  8.41, 202n51
  9.42, 202n51
Vergil
  Aen., 134–36 passim
  1.489, 200n33
  1.661, 129n68
  2.351–352, 195n105
  6.853, 132n79
  7.372, 264n54
  8.688, 108n179
  Book I, 129
Vitruvius
  6.1.4, 204n63
Xanthus
  FGH 765, 159n2
Xenophanes
  fr. 16, 203n58
Xenophon
  Anabasis
    1.9, 55n11
    1.9.1, 55n10
  Cyropaedia, 53–65

Christian Writings

Augustine
  Ep.
    17.2, 138n129
Clement of Alexandria
  Protr.
    6.68.3, 333n129
  Strom.
    1.15.70.2, 311n14
    1.15.71.4, 313n24
    1.15.72.4, 317n45
    1.15.72.5, 313n25, 314n27
    1.22.150.1, 318n49
    1.22.150.1–3, 331n118
    1.22.150.2, 318n54
    1.22.150.3, 317n48
    5.11.75.1, 333n129
    5.14.97.7, 317n47
    5.14.99.3, 318n50

    5.14.101.4b, 318n51, 332n125
    5.14.107.1–3, 332n123
    5.14.111.4–6, 333n128
    5.14.113.2, 333n128
    5.14.119.2, 333n130
    5.14.121.1–3, 333n130
    5.14.123, 332n121
    5.14.131.2–3, 332n127
    5.14.133.3, 333n130
    5.114.121.4–122.1, 333n128
    6.3.33.2, 156n93
Cyril of Alexandria
  Contra Jul.
    4, 156n93
Eusebius
  Chron.
    I, 23, 338n152
    Ol.151, 317n47

Eusebius (*cont.*)
  PE
    7.13.7, 317n47
    7.32.16, 317n47
    9.6.6, 317n45
    9.6.8, 317n48
    9.6.9, 325n93
    9.7.1, 324n92
    9.17.1–9, 329n109
    9.17.2–3, 329n111
    9.17.3, 329n112
    9.17.4, 330n113
    9.17.8, 330n113
    9.17.8–9, 330n114
    9.18.1, 326n99
    9.18.2, 330n116
    9.19.1–2, 301n138
    9.20.2–4, 303n153
    9.23.1, 300n137
    9.23.1–4, 326n100
    9.27.3–4, 327n102
    9.27.4–5, 328n105
    9.27.6, 327n103
    9.27.7–8, 328n107
    9.27.9–10, 328n106
    9.27.12, 328n106
    9.27.16, 328n106
    9.27.18, 328n107
    9.27.19, 328n108
    9.27.23–25, 328n107
    9.27.28, 328n106
    9.27.32, 328n106
    13.11.3, 317n45
    13.12.1, 317n48, 318n49, 318n54, 324n88, 331n118
    13.12.4, 318n50
    13.12.5, 331n120
    13.12.6–7, 318n51, 332n125
    13.12.8, 318n52–318n53, 331n119
    13.12.12, 332n122
    13.12.13–15, 332n123
    13.12.16, 332n124
    13.13.38, 333n128
    13.13.40, 333n128
    13.13.45–47, 333n130
    13.13.60, 332n127
    13.13.62, 333n130
    13.30.48, 333n128
Isidorus
  Etym.
    17.7.7, 264n56
Jerome
  Comm. In Ionam.
    1.3, 263n47
  Ep.
    108.8, 263n47
  In Rufinum
    3.22, 263n47
Matthew
  1.1–6, 297n116
  1.3–16, 291n86
Origen
  CCelsum
    1.15.334, 323n87, 324n88
Photius
  FGH I 26 fr. 1, 262n39
Tertullian
  Ad Nat.
    1.10, 348n217

Other Sources

Manetho
  apud Jos. CAp. 1.239, 182n23, 278n3
Metz Epitome
  31, 70n97

Philo of Byblos
  in Euseb. PE 1.10.40, 342n179
  in Euseb. PE 1.10.50, 343n180

SUBJECT INDEX

Abraham, 280, 282, 287, 299–301, 303–4, 326, 329–30, 332
abstention from pork, Jews and, 184
Achaeans, use of term, 230
Achaemenes, 224
Achaemenids, 10, 51–52, 55, 224; and Alexander the Great, 65–75. *See also names of rulers*
Achilles, 70, 200
Acilius, C., 125
Acrisius, 254–55, 260
Actisanes, 202n44
Actium, battle of, 108–9
Acusilaus, 241
Adherbal, 273
Aduatuci, 151
Aedui, 154–55
Aegyptus, 201, 258
Aeneas, 134–36, 243–45, 247
Aeolic dialect, 245, 247
Aeschylus, 255, 257; experience at Salamis, 12n12; Jewish authors on, 332–33; *Persae*, 9–21, 49n195, 54, 256, 352; *Suppliants*, 101, 201, 230, 241, 258
Aesculapius, 347
aesthetic, Persian, 11
Aestii, 161, 167
African nations. *See names of nations*
Agatharchides of Cnidus, 205
Agrippina the Younger, 195
Agroitas, 96n111
Airs, Waters, Places, 39n168
Aithiops, use of term, 197
Akianthos, necropolis of, 219
Alba Longa, 245
Alci, 176
Alesia, 152, 154–55
Alexander Polyhistor, 300, 303n153, 325, 329, 330n116, 338n152
Alexander Romance, 199, 206, 267–72
Alexander the Great, 49–50, 125, 200, 353; letter to Darius, 66; and mass wedding at Susa, 71–74; and Perseus, 264–65; and the Persians, 65–75

Alexandria, 107–8
Allobroges, 147
alphabet, introduction of, 119, 125, 244, 246, 342
Amasis, 78, 84
"Amazon" rhyton, 46 (fig. 3)
Ambiorix, 154, 154n84
Ammon, 95, 269
Ammonites, 280–81, 282n30, 288–89
Amon-Re, 270
Amos, 289
Amphion and Zethios, 234n62
Anaxagoras, 320
Anaxandrides, 103
Anaxarchus, 69n92
Anaximenes of Lampsacus, 266n63
ancestral values, Gauls and, 151, 155
Andromeda, 19, 200–201, 224, 254–55, 260–64; depiction of, 213–16
aniconism: German, 176–77, 177n112; Jewish, 181, 188–89, 193, 310; Persian, 32
animal sacrifice, Jews and, 192–93, 309
animal worship, Egyptians and, 77–78, 82, 92–93, 92n92, 102, 105, 109–10, 112–13, 188, 328, 328n105
Antaeus, 267, 303
Antenor, statue group of Athenian "Tyrannicides," 51–52
Anthologia Latina, 206
Antigonus Gonatas, 316n38
Antinoe, inscription, 206
Antiphanes, 102
antiquity: of Athens, 106; contested, 79–81; of Egypt, 79–81, 83–84, 91–92; of Phrygians, 80
anti-Semitism: Jews and, 278; Tacitus and, 179–80, 184–88
Antisthenes, 55
Antonius Felix, 193–94
Anubis, 98
Apate, 48
Apher and Aphran, 303
Aphra, 303
Aphrodite, 50n197

404 SUBJECT INDEX

Apion, 189, 191, 278
Apollo, 32–33, 47, 158; "Musegetes," 95
Apollodorus, 257–58; *Bibliotheca*, 254
Apollonius Molon, 278, 301
Apollonius of Rhodes, 228
Appendix Vergiliana, 204
Appian, 136
appropriation, and collective identity, 3–5. See also cultural appropriation
Arabs, 299–302, 327–28, 356
Aratus of Soli, 332; *Phaenomena*, 318
Arcadia, 241, 245–46
Arcobarzanes, 274
Areus, 304–6
Argives, use of term, 230
Argos, 98, 201, 240–41, 254–55, 257–58; foundation legend, 226, 229–33, 249
Ariovistus, 152, 152n73
Aristagoras of Miletus, 99
Aristobulus, 317–19, 321, 331–33
Aristogeiton, 51, 342
Aristophanes, 12, 102
Aristotle, 65, 107, 119–20, 155, 204, 206, 311–13
Aristoxenus of Tarentum, 345–46
Armenia and Armenians, 273, 275–76; foundation legend, 224–25
Armenus, 224–25
army of Alexander the Great, 66; and intermarriage, 70–73; and mutiny, 73–75. See also military; *names of Companions*
Arrian, 51, 66, 66n72, 67, 69n92, 72–74
Artabanus, 35–36
Artapanus, 300, 325–29
Artapanus, as Persian name, 325–26
Artaxerxes, 60n37
Artaxerxes II, 55
Artaxerxes Ochus, daughter of, 71
Artayctes, 33
Artemidorus of Ephesus, 205
Artemis, 32, 47
Arverni, 152, 154
Asia: as origin of Pelops, 227–29; portrayal of, 48. See also Europe-Asia dichotomy; *place names*
ass, cult of, ascribed to Jews, 188–89
assimilation, Ethiopians and, 209–11
ass-libel, 188–89
Assouri, 303
Assyria, 303
Assyrians, 192, 251, 260, 264

astrology/astrologers, 310, 330, 348
astronomy, 138
Astyages, 33
Ate, in Aeschylus' *Persae*, 16–17
Athena, 47, 106–7, 254; in Aeschylus' *Persae*, 17n45
Athenaeus, *Deipnosophists*, 102
Athenians: in Aeschylus' *Persae*, 13; and battle of Salamis, 22–23; foundation legend, 236–43
Athens: antiquity of, 106; and Egypt, 98, 265–67; and Saïs, 106–7, 265–66
athletes, blacks portrayed as, 212
Atlantis legend, 106n166
Atlas, 247, 330
atomic theory, 121–22, 138, 343
Augustine, 138, 183; *City of God*, 182
Augustus, Emperor, 108, 156, 193
autochthony: of Athenians, 236, 239–40, 355; of Ethiopians, 199–200; of Germans, 162; Jews and, 250; Romans and, 249
avarice, as Celtic characteristic, 143

Babylon, 329; foundation legend, 226
Bacchic cult, Roman repression of, 348
Bacchylides, 227, 235
Bactrians, 66, 69–70
Baduhenna, 176
Balsdon, J.P.V.D., 2
barbarians: in *Alexander Romance*, 272n83; concept of, as Roman borrowing, 345; Egyptians and, 76–77; Germans as, 161; Greeks and, 65–67, 76–77, 236–38; Pelasgians as, 242–43; Tacitus' use of term, 161. See also Greek-barbarian dichotomy
Batavi, 163–64, 172–73
Bathsheba, 287
battle scenes, of Greeks and Persians, 40–45
Belgae, 149, 151
Bellovaci, 151
Bellum Alexandrinum, 108
Belos/Belus (Baal), 226, 330
Ben-Ammi, 280
Berossus, 329
Bible, Hebrew: as foundation for Greek philosophy, 317; Greek translation of, 314–15, 318–19, 331, 333–37; Phoenicians in, 117
bilingualism: Greek-Latin, 129–30; Latin-Punic, 128–29

blackness, Ethiopians and, 202–3
blacks. *See* Ethiopia and Ethiopians
black/white dichotomy, 203, 206
Boaz, 294–95
Bocchus, 132
Boeotia, 85
Boges, 31
Boudicca, 166n43
Brahmans, Indian, 313–14, 324
Britons, Tacitus on, 196n107
bronzes, depicting blacks, 211–13, 214 (fig. 5), 215 (fig. 5)
burial customs: Egyptian, 94; German, 163
Busiris, 81, 100, 103–5, 103n148, 267; depiction of, 216n134

Cadmeians, Thebans as, 234
Cadmus/Kadmos, 85, 97, 119, 226, 229, 341; depiction of, 235n78; as founder, 233–36
Calanoi, 312–13
Calanus, 313
Caligula, Emperor, 186, 193
Calliphon of Croton, 321
Callisthenes, 69, 69n92, 265
Cambyses, 34, 118, 202, 270
Canaan, 279, 330
Canaanites, 282; as Jewish "Other," 279–80; Tamar as, 291–92
Cannae, 350
cannibalism: Celts and, 144; Egyptians and, 93, 110
caricature: in depictions of blacks, 213; of Jews by Romans, 182–83
Carthage: destruction of, 130–31, 139; Roman colonization of, 135; as Roman "Other," 115
Carthaginian, use of term, 116n2
Carthaginians: Roman depictions of, 132–37; as treaty violators, 123–25, 130, 132–33, 136
Cartledge, Paul, 2
Cassander, 69
Cassiopeia, 254
Castor and Pollux, 174–76
Catalogue of Women, 234
Cato the Elder, 129–30, 146, 244–49, 343, 346
Catullus, 344
Celts. *See* Gauls

Cepheus, 200, 251, 254, 256, 258, 260–61, 263
Chaldeans, 98, 226, 250, 256, 313
Chandragupta, 313
charioteers, blacks portrayed as, 212
chariot races, 62
chariots, scythed, introduction of, 61, 64
Chatti, 164–65, 173
Chauci, 165–66, 173
Chemmis, 85–86, 259
Cherusci, 166
Cicero, 108–10, 132–33, 146–47, 175, 343–44, 346, 351
Cimbri, 169–70
Circe, depicted with negroid features, 213
circumcision: Arabs and, 301; Colchians and, 86, 226; Egyptians and, 83–84, 86; Ethiopians and, 86, 328; Jews and, 184, 226, 288, 301; Phoenicians and, 86; Syrians and, 86
Clastidium, 350
Claudius, Emperor, 156, 193–94, 249
Clearchus, 311, 324; *On Sleep*, 311–13
Clement of Alexandria, 317, 331; *Stromateis*, 313–14
Cleodemus Malchus, 303–4
Cleopatra and Antony, 108–9
Coele-Syria, 311
coinage, depicting blacks, 212
Colchians, 86, 98, 226
collective identity: and appropriation, 3–5; and the Other, 1–5
colonies: Egyptian, 98–99, 226; established by Alexander the Great, 66–67; Greek, 99
comedy, Greek, 205–6, 256; Egypt in, 102–3
comic imagery, 44, 44n182
communis libertas, Gauls and, 154
Companions of Alexander the Great, 67–68, 71–72
Conon, 261–62
constitution, Carthaginian, 120
"constitutional debate," in Herodotus, 23–25, 34–35;
conversion: call for; 340, to Judaism, 182–83, 185, 189–90, 280, 286
conversion narrative, book of Ruth as, 297–98
Craterus, 71
Crete, 120, 191–92, 241, 250
Critognatus, 152–53, 152n73, 154–55, 155n92

406 SUBJECT INDEX

Croesus, 27, 33–34
Ctesias of Cnidus, 64; *Persica*, 54–55
cultural appropriation: Egyptians and, 85–86, 225–26, 270; Greeks and, 96, 223–25; Jews and, 304; Romans and, 139–40, 343–51. *See also* identity theft
cultural competition, Greek-Phoenician, 342–43
cultural convergence, in *Letter of Aristeas*, 333–37
cultural interconnection: Greek-Egyptian, 84–90, 106–7; in Plutarch, 113–14
cultural relativism: in depictions of gods, 203; Herodotus and, 30–35
Curtius Rufus, 66n75, 70–71, 75
customs: Celtic, 144–45, 158n110; Egyptian, 77–79, 83–84, 94, 109–11 (*see also* animal worship); German, 164; Jewish, 183–84 (*see also* abstention from pork; circumcision); Persian, 14, 29–30, 60–63 (see also *proskynesis*)
Cybebe, 32
Cybele, Roman cult of, 347–49
Cyrus the Great, 68, 270; in Herodotus, 26–28, 33–34; in Xenophon's *Cyropaedia*, 53–65
Cyrus the Younger, 55

Daedalus, 95
Damascus, and origins of Jews, 250
Danae, 254–55, 258, 264, 264n54
Danaids, 83n42, 201, 229–33, 258
Danaoi, use of term, 230
Danaus, 201, 201n37, 226, 240n106, 258–59; as founder, 229–33
Dardanus, 247
Darius, 13n20, 14, 48, 76, 92n89; in Aeschylus' *Persae*, 12–13, 17–18; daughters of, 71; in Herodotus, 24–25, 34–35
"Darius painter" vase, 45–50, 47 (fig. 4)
Datis, 32
Dauge, Y. A., 2
David, house of, 293, 296–97
Dead Sea Scrolls, 185n44
defeat, Persian, in Aeschylus' *Persae*, 15–17
Deinias, 258
Deioces, 25n94
Delphi, plundered by Gauls, 144, 146
Delphic oracle, 346, 349–50
Demaratus, 21–22, 37

Demeter, 95, 98
Demetrius of Phalerum, 314–17, 334, 336
democracy, Athenian, 51–52
democracy, in Herodotus' "constitutional debate," 23–25
Democritus, 95
despotism, Persian, 12–13
Deuteronomy, 280
Dictys, 254–55
Dinah, rape of, 283
Dio Cassius, 109
Diodorus of Sicily, 72, 109, 240; on Athens and Egypt, 265–66; on Celts, 143–45, 157; on the Egyptians, 90–99, 112–13, 159, 225, 353; on the Ethiopians, 198, 200–202, 204–5; on the Gauls, 141, 143, 156; on the Jews, 189, 278; on legend of Busiris, 104; sources, 91, 99
Dionysiac rites: Diodorus on, 96–98; Greek and Egyptian, 84–85
Dionysius of Halicarnassus, 245–46
Dionysius Skytobrachion, 240
Dionysus/Dionysos, 95–98, 198
Diphilus, 333
Dius, 138
divine intervention, in Aeschylus' *Persae*, 16–19
diviners, Etruscan, 347
divinities, Egyptian and Greek, 82–84
divinity of rulers. *See* kingship, divine
Divitiacus, 146
Dodona, as oracular center, 83, 118
Domitian, Emperor, 164
Dorotheus of Sidon, 138
dress: "barbarian," 67; Persian, 11
drink, excessive: as characteristic of Celts, 142–43; as characteristic of Germans, 165
druids, 144, 146, 155–58
Dumnorix, 155, 155n91

East-West dichotomy, 39n168
Eburones, 154
Edomites, 280, 288–89
education: among Gauls, 157; Egyptian, 95; Persian, 56–57
Egypt and Egyptians, 101, 280, 324; in Aeschylus' *Suppliants*, 230–32; antiquity of, 79–81, 83–84, 91–92; Athens and, 265–67; and "barbarians," 76–77; and cultural appropriation, 85–86; Greek borrowings from, 95; in

Greek drama, 101–3; Greek fascination with, 99–100; Greek visitors to, 95; Herodotus and, 76–90; Jews and, 190–91, 251, 285–86, 288–89; in Moses story, 327–28; and origin of Cadmus, 235; and origin of Danaus, 229–33; and Perseus myth, 257–59, 264; under Ptolemies, 267–72; settled by Ethiopians, 200; as source of wisdom, 95; wonders of, 81. *See also* Diodorus of Sicily; Plutarch; Strabo
elders, chorus of, in Aeschylus' *Persae*, 13–14, 16–17, 20–21
Eleazer, 279, 335
Eleusinian mysteries, 98
eleutheria, personification of, 50n197
emperor worship, Tacitus and, 193
endogamy, Jews and, 284–85
Ennius, 122–23, 245
Enoch, 330
environmental determinism, in *Airs, Waters, Places*, 39n168
Ephorus, 240
Epicureans, 110n191
Epigoni, 73
equites, 156
Eratosthenes, 65, 65n71, 100, 104, 120, 289–90
Erechtheus, 98, 266
Esau, 282
Essenes, 324
Ethiopia and Ethiopians, 197–211, 354–55; and blackness, 202–3; in Greek myth, 198–202, 220; Jews as, 251; and origin of Jews, 192; and Perseus myth, 254–55, 258–59, 263; personification of, 215n132; and practice of circumcision, 86, 328; role in Greco-Roman society, 209–11; as slaves, 210; visual images of, 210–20, 214 (fig. 5), 215 (fig. 5)
ethnic differences, between Greeks and Persians, 25–30
ethnography, 141; Caesar and, 141–42, 147–50, 155, 157; Diodorus and, 91, 143–45; and Ethiopians, 204–6, 220; Herodotus and, 25, 29; Sallust and, 273; Tacitus and, 159–61, 160n9, 161–62, 169, 196, 196n107
Eudoxus of Cnidus, 99–100
Eumaeus, 117
Eumenes, 71

Euripides: *Andromeda*, 215n132, 256, 258; *Danae*, 256; *Helen*, 89, 102; Jewish authors on, 333; *Phoenissae*, 236; *Phrixus*, 236
Europa, 234–35
Europe-Asia dichotomy, 39n168
Eurymedon, 43n176
Eurymedon River, battle of, 42
Eurymedon vase, 42–44, 43 (fig. 2)
Eusebius, 300, 317, 325, 331
Evander, 125, 244, 246
Exodus, 190–91, 288
exogamy, and Jewish separatism, 280–87
Ezekiel, 289
Ezra, 281, 297
Ezra-Nehemiah composition, 281

Fabius Pictor, 123–25, 244, 246, 350
factionalism, among Gauls, 153–54
family feud, Germans and, 168–69
fatherhood, divine, in *Alexander Romance*, 268–70
ferocity, as Celtic characteristic, 144
fictive founders, 224–27; of Israel, 250–51. *See also* foundation legends; *names of founders*
fictive kinship, 253, 355; of Greeks and Jews, 302–6; of Greeks and Persians, 19–20, 38
flood stories, 106
Florus, 138, 186
Fonteius, M., 146–47
foreigners: dwelling among Jews, 288–89; as fictive founder, 227–36
foreign troops, in army of Alexander, 66
foundation legends, 224–27, 303, 355; Argos, 226, 229–33, 249; Armenia, 224–25; Athenians and, 236–43; Babylon, 226; Egyptians and, 98–99; Jerusalem, 226; Jewish, 250–51; Macedonia, 225; Media, 225; Peloponnesus, 227–29; Persians and, 224; Pisa, 249; Politorium, 249; Rome, 243–49; Thebes, 85, 226, 233–36; Tibur, 249
freedmen: as Roman citizens, 210; Roman vs. German, 163, 171; Tacitus on, 171, 193–94

Gades, 274
Gaetulians, 272–73
Galba, Emperor, 187

408 SUBJECT INDEX

Gallo-Grecians, 344
Gauls: as adversaries of Rome, 142–43, 146–47, 153; as contrast to Romans, 149–53; and German origins, 165, 165n38; and *libertas*, 153–55; stereotypes of, 141–47. *See also names of tribes*
Gellius, Aulus, 122
Gellius, Cn., 248
Gelon, 23n83
genealogical connections: Argive-Persian, 257; Greek-Persian, 19–20, 37–38; in tales of founding of Rome, 243–49
genealogies. *See* fictive founders; foundation legends
Genesis, 280, 282–83, 289–92, 299, 303, 319–20, 329
gentiles, Jewish presentations of, 325–41
genus hominum invisum deis, Jews as, 191
Gephyraioi clan, 342
Germans, 149, 152, 161–62, 196n107; and Romans, 159–71. *See also names of tribes*
Gideon, 287
Gigantomachia, 329
gods: Gallic, 158; German, 174–78; Greek and Egyptian, 82–84, 95. *See also names of deities;* religion
Gorgon, 254–55
Gotones, 171–72
governance: Carthaginian system of, 119–20; Spartan system of, 120
Greek-barbarian dichotomy, 76–77; Alexander's rejection of, 65–67
Greek literature, Aristobulus on, 331–32
Greek mythology, 94–95; Egypt and, 96–98; Ethiopians in, 198–202, 220; Persians and, 38–39, 50–51. *See also names of mythical figures*
Greek persona, used by Jewish author, 334, 339
Greeks: attitudes to non-Greeks, 237–38; and barbarian contamination, 236–38; and Celts, 141–46; and cultural appropriation, 223–24; and Egypt, 92, 95; and Jews, 302–6, 308–25; opposition to *proskynesis*, 69; and Phoenicians, 116–22, 137–38, 341–43; and purity of blood, 236–38; reactions to Third Punic War, 131; roles in Persian empire, 11; and Roman foundation legends, 243–44; visual representations, 40–52
gymnosophists, Indian, 313, 324

Hadrumetum inscription, 206
Hagar, 287, 299–300
Hall, Edith, 2
Hall, Jonathan, 2
Hannibal, 121, 123–26, 132–33
Hanno the Carthaginian: *Periplus*, 137; in Plautus' *Poenulus*, 126–29
Harmodius, 51, 342
Harmonia, 233
Hartog, François, 2
haruspices, 347
Hasdrubal, 124, 137
head vases, depicting blacks, 211–12
Hecataeus of Abdera, 91, 100, 226, 265–66, 277, 335
Hecataeus of Miletus, 79–80, 89, 89n75, 99, 228, 240
Helen of Troy, Egyptian story of, 86–90, 102
Heliodorus, *Aethiopica*, 199, 202
Hellanicus, 89, 99, 159, 229n33, 241, 256, 260
Hellas: mourning, 50n197; portrayal of, 47
Hellenes. *See* Greeks
Hellespont, 17, 20, 36
Helvetii, 150–51
Hephaestion, 71
Heracleides Ponticus, 243, 246
Heraclides Lembus, 322
Heraclitus, 319
Herakles/Hercules, 83, 244, 303–4; and Arcadian connection, 246; and Busiris, 103, 105; contested origins of, 83–84; death of, 273; depiction of, 216; dual figure of, 96; as Egyptian, 267; Egyptian story of, 96; Ethiopians and, 198; Germans and, 174–75, 177; as kinsman of Osiris, 98; as mythical forefather of Numidian royal line, 274–75; and Osiris, 266–67; and Scythians, 225
herm, 214 (fig. 5), 215 (fig. 5)
Hermes: and Moses, 326–27; and Perseus, 254; Thracians and, 175n101
Hermippus of Smyrna, 321–24
Hermodorus of Ephesus, 350–51
Hermopolis, 328
Herodes Atticus, 211
Herodotus, 21–39, 49n195, 54, 56, 228, 232, 257, 341–42; anecdote of Hecataeus' visit to Thebes, 79–80; on Busiris, 104;

"constitutional debate," 23–25, 34–35; and cultural relativism, 30–35; dialogue between Xerxes and Demaratus, 21–22; and Diodorus, 91, 92n84; on Egypt, 76–90, 112–13, 159, 267, 353; on Ethiopians, 199–201, 203–4; on ethnic differences between Greeks and Persians, 25–30; on Herakles, 96; and myth of Perseus, 259; on Pelasgians, 239–42; on Persians, 21–39, 224, 256–57, 352; as *philobarbaros*, 30, 81, 90; on Phoenicians, 117–19, 235; on Scythians, 225; story of Psammetichus, 80
Hesiod, 88, 90, 200, 234, 241, 255, 319, 332; *Theogony*, 339, 342
Hiempsal II, 272–74, 274n90; *Punici libri*, 138
Hipparchos, 51
Hippias, 48n188, 51–52
Hippodameia, 228
Hiram, 117
Histiaeus, 48n188
Homer, 88, 95, 116–17, 121, 143, 198, 227, 230, 255, 332; *Iliad*, 50, 241; *Odyssey*, 50, 84–85, 241
homosexuality, Celts and, 144
Horace, 133, 184; "Cleopatra Ode," 108
horsemanship, Persian, 61, 64
hospitality: of Celts, 143; Ethiopian, 198, 205; German, 164; Greek, 88
human sacrifice, 105; Celts and, 144, 147; Egyptians and, 103; Ethiopians and, 199; Gauls and, 157–58; Germans and, 161; Jews and, 309; Romans and, 158
hunters, blacks portrayed as, 212
hunting, Persians and, 63, 63n64
Huntington, Samuel, 1–2
Hydarnes, 23
Hyginus, 248–49
Hypereides, 107

ideal ruler, Cyrus as, 53–54
identity theft: Egyptians and, 225–26, 266; Greeks and, 223–25
imperial cult, Tacitus on, 193
Inachus, 241
inclusiveness, Jews and, 287–99, 306
India and Indians, 66, 311–13
intermarriage: Alexander the Great and, 69–74; Jews and, 280–87, 355–56; race and, 208–9, 211

interpretatio graeca, 82, 251, 259, 312, 314, 320
interpretatio judaica, 304, 320
interpretatio romana, 158, 169–78, 174n96, 195, 195n105; as Tacitean coinage, 175
inversion: Herodotus and, 27–28; Plautus and, 128; Tacitean, 159–69
Io, 117–18, 230, 236n83, 257
Ionians, and burning of Sardis, 32
Ion of Chios, 12n12
Iranians, 66
Iris, 198
irony, Tacitean, 161–62, 165–67, 178, 187–96
Isaac, Benjamin, 3
Ishmael, 299–302
Ishmaelites, 299–302
Isis, 95; Ethiopians and, 211; Germans and, 174, 176; Roman cult of, 111, 348
Isocrates, 64, 104–5, 237; *Panathenaicus*, 238; *Panegyricus*, 53
Israel, fictive founders of, 250–51. *See also* Jews
Italy, and Perseus myth, 264n54

Jacob, 282
Jaffa/Joppa, as locus of Perseus myth, 260–64
Janus vases, 216–19, 217 (fig. 6), 218 (fig. 7), 219 (fig. 8), 220
Jason and Argonauts, 224–25
Jerusalem/Hierosolyma, 192–93, 250–51; foundation legend, 226
Jewish identity, and kinship relations, 299–307
Jewish rebellion, against Rome, 194–95
Jews, 98; as chosen people, 279; expelled from Rome, 348; and Greek kinship, 302–6; and Hellenistic diaspora, 302–6; origins of, 190–92, 250–51, 287–88; and Perseus myth, 260–64; as philosophers, 308–25; and Spartans, 304–6; as threat to Rome, 185. *See also* proselytism; separatism
jockeys, blacks portrayed as, 212
Jonah, 261n36
Jonathan (Hasmonean High Priest), 304
Joseph, 287, 300; Artapanus on, 326–27; and Aseneth, 285–86, 327
Joseph and Aseneth, 285–86

410 SUBJECT INDEX

Josephus, 86n57, 138, 189, 195n105, 223, 262–63, 305–6, 311–13, 312n19; *Antiquities*, 301; *contra Apionem*, 320–21
Juba II, 274
Jubilees, Book of, 282–83, 291–92, 300
Judah, 287; and Tamar, 289–93
Judea, as Roman province, 193–94
Jugurtha, 273
Julius Caesar: *De Bello Gallico*, 147–58 *passim*, 162n14; on Gauls, 147–59, 354; on Germans, 159
Juno, Roman cult of, 349
Jupiter/Zeus, 47, 95, 97, 158, 198, 254–55
Justin, 71
Juvenal: on the Ethiopians, 202, 207–9; on the Jews, 182–83, 278; *Satire 2*, 207; *Satire 15*, 110–11

kantharos: in form of conjoined heads, 217 (fig. 6); with Janiform heads, 219, 219 (fig. 8)
Keturah, 287, 303
kingship, Persian, 13–15, 35–37, 48–49, 53–65
kingship treatises, 315
kinship relations, and Jewish identity, 299–307. *See also* fictive kinship
Kronos, 330, 342
Kush, 197, 330

Laetus/Laitos, 137, 343
language: Pelasgian, 239; Phrygian, 80; in Plautus' *Poenulus*, 127–29; Punic, 274. *See also* bilingualism
Larissa, 255
laws, Persian, 56–57
laziness, as German characteristic, 164–65, 169
Lemovii, 172
Leonidas, 28, 31
Leonnatus, 68
lethargy, Jewish, 183, 189
Letter of Aristeas, 278–79, 314–17, 333–37
Levi, 283
levirate marriage, 289–93, 295–96
libertas: Gauls and, 153–55; Germans and, 169–72
libri Punici, 272, 272n85, 273–74, 274n90
Libya and Libyans, 118, 250, 272–73, 275–76
Linus, 332

Litaviccus, 154
Livy, 125–26, 133, 344
Lot, 280
Lucan, 108
Lucian, 198–99
Lutatius, treaty of, 124
luxury/softness motif: applied to Alexander the Great, 67–69; applied to Celts, 149–50; applied to Gauls, 152; in Herodotus, 26–28; Persians and, 63–64; in Xenophon's *Cyropaedia*, 58–60
Lycurgus, 95
Lydians, 27, 30
Lynceus, 259

Macedon/Macedonia, 225, 268–69
Macedon (son of Osiris), 98, 225
Macedonians, 65–75
magi, Persian, 313, 324
Magna Mater, Roman cult of, 347–49
Mago, 129–30
Malachi, 289
Manetho, 91, 191, 277–78
manumission, 210–11
Marcomani, 167, 172
Mardonius, 25–26, 25n95, 26, 28
Maroneia, 225
marriage practices, German, 168–69
Mars: Gauls and, 158; Germans and, 174–75
Martial, 183–84
Massagetae, 27
Medes, 273, 275–76
Media, foundation legend, 225
Medizers, 10
Medus, 225
Medusa, 254–55
Megabyzus, 24–25
Megasthenes, 159, 311, 324; *Indica*, 313–14
Melampus of Pylos, 84–85, 97
Melqart, 274
Memnon, 200, 211; depiction of, 213–16
Memnonion, 200
Menander, 138, 333; *Samia*, 256
Menedemus of Eretria, 316, 316n38
Menelaus, 87–90, 116, 198
Menestheus, 98
Mercury: Gauls and, 158; Germans and, 174–75, 175n101
Meroe, 211, 328
metus gallicus, 147

military: Greek, in Aeschylus' *Persae*, 18–19; Persian, 64
Minerva, 158
miscegenation, 208–9
Mizraim, 330
Moab and Moabites, 280–81, 282n30, 288–89; in book of Ruth, 293–99
Mochus of Sidon, 120–21
Momigliano, Arnaldo, 3
monarchy: Egyptian, 78, 82; in Herodotus' "constitutional debate," 23–25; Persian, 13–15, 35–37, 48–49, 53–65
money, Germans and, 166–67
monotheism: Jewish, 181, 195, 310; Orphic, 331–32
morality, Tacitus on, 162–63
Moretum, 204, 207
Mosaic law, Aristobulus on, 331
Moses, 191, 279–80, 284, 287, 319–21, 327–28; as Chaldean, 250; as Egyptian, 226
Mount Ida, Crete, 191–92, 250
Mount Sipylus, 227
multiculturalism, 253; Jews and, 287–99, 306; of Perseus myth, 264–65
Muses, 95
Myrtilos, 228

Nabatene, 301
Nabis, 133
Naevius, 122, 245
Nahanarvali, 175–76
Naomi and Ruth, 293–99
Naphtali, 287
Nearchus, 71
Near East, Numidians and, 272–76
Nechos, 76
Nectanebos II, legend of, 267–72
Nehemiah, 281–82, 297
Neith, 107
Nepos, Cornelius, 133n92
Nero, Emperor, 193
Nerthus, 175–76
Nervii, 149, 151, 165
Nicaeus of Byzantium, 203
nicknames, humorous, 209
Nike, 47
Nile, 235
Noah, 339
Nubia, 197
Numa Pompilius, 345–46

number seven, 332
Numenius of Apamea, 324–25
Numidians, and the Near East, 272–76

Occidentalism, 1
Odysseus/Ulysses, 116–17, 174, 177; depicted with negroid features, 213; and founding of Rome, 243–44
officials, Persian, portrayal of, 48
oinochoe: of "Eurymedon," 43 (fig. 2); showing Greek warrior and Persian archer, 41 (fig. 1)
oligarchy, in Herodotus' "constitutional debate," 23–25
Olympias, Queen, 268–69, 271
Onan, 290
Onescritus, 204
Onias, 304–6
oratory, Egyptian, 94
Orientalism, 1
Orientalizing: as behavior of Alexander the Great, 67, 73–75; of figure of Pelops, 228; of Persians, 9, 11
oriental wisdom, Jews and, 311
Origen, 323
origins: of Athens, 98; of Gauls, 165, 165n38; of Germans, 162; of Herakles, 83–84; of Jews, 190–92, 250–51, 287–88; of Sibylline oracle, 339–40; of Thebes, 119; of Veneti, 146n35. *See also* fictive founders; foundation legends
Orpheus, 95, 327, 331–32
Orphism, 323
Osiris, 95–98, 104, 200, 225; and Herakles, 266–67
Otanes (speaker in Herodotus' "constitutional debate"), 24
Other, the: Canaanites as, 279–80; Carthage as, 115; and collective identity, 1–5; Egyptians as, 78–79, 81–82
Otho, Emperor, 187, 194
Ovid, 200–201, 257, 345

Pagden, Anthony, 2
Painted Stoa, Marathon painting, 40
Pallantion, 246
paradox: in career of Alexander the Great, 65; Herodotus and, 77, 89; Tacitean, 161, 165–66, 168, 187–88, 190, 195–96
Paris and Helen, 86–90
Passover, 288

SUBJECT INDEX

patriarchs, Jewish, marriages of, 285–87. *See also names of figures*
Pausanias, 205, 241
Pausanias (king of Sparta), 26, 28–29
Pelasgian, use of term, 242
Pelasgians, 230, 239–43
Pelasgus, 241
Pella, 268
Peloponnesus, 227; foundation legend, 227–29
Pelops, as founder, 227–29
Penelope, 50
Penes, 98
Perdiccas, 71
performers, blacks portrayed as, 212
Peripatetics, 317
Persepolis, Alexander's sacking of, 50
Perses, as progenitor of Persians, 19, 37, 224, 256
Perseus, 19–20, 37, 97n119; and Andromeda, 200–201, 224, 254–55; associated with Persia, 256–57; as Assyrian, 260, 264; and Egypt, 257–58; and Ethiopia, 258–59; as Greek hero, 254–56, 264; legends of, 85–86, 253–65
Persians: in Africa, 273; Alexander the Great and, 65–75; foundation legend, 224; and Greek culture, 50–52; and Greek legends, 38–39, 50–51; and Numidians, 274–76; Orientalizing of, 9, 11; and Perseus myth, 260, 264; visual representations, 40–52. *See also* Herodotus; Xenophon
personifications: in early classical visual representations, 43n177; of Ethiopia, 215n132
"Pesach rule," 288
Petronius, 184, 202–3, 207
Phanodemus, 265
Pharusii, 274
Pherecydes, 103n146, 228, 232, 235, 255, 343
Philinus, 123, 333
Philip II of Macedon, 268–69
Philo, 184, 250, 291–92, 306, 319, 324
philobarbaros, Herodotus as, 30
Philo of Byblos, 342–43
Phoenicia and Phoenicians, 85, 107n168, 116n2, 117–18, 353–54; and Greeks, 341–43; and Herakles, 274; intellectual activities, 119–21, 125, 137–38; and "noble lie," 121; as origin of Cadmus, 233–36; and Perseus myth, 260–64; and practice of circumcision, 86; as sailors, 117–18; as traders, 118–19; and Trojan War, 117–18, 257–58. *See also* Carthaginians
"Phoenician lie," 121–22
Photius, 261
Phrygians, 80
Phrynichus, *Phoenissae*, 10, 49n195
physical appearance: of Celts, 142–43; of Ethiopians, 203–6. *See also* skin color
Pindar, 227–28, 235n69, 255
Pisa, foundation legend, 249
Plataea, battle of, 18, 31–32, 37
Plato, 64, 95, 100, 107n168, 318–21, 331; *Menexenus*, 236–38; *Republic*, 121; *Symposium*, 315; *Timaeus*, 106–7, 265
Plautus, *Poenulus*, 126–29
Pliny, 138, 263, 274–75; on Ethiopians, 201, 203, 205; on Germans, 159; on Jews, 183
Plutarch, 30, 65, 65n71, 66n75, 67, 70; on Egypt, 353; on Herodotus, 81, 90; *On Isis and Osiris*, 111–14; on the Jews, 184; *Life of Alexander*, 71; *Symposium of the Seven Wise Men*, 315
politics: in Herodotus, 23–25; in Tacitus' *Germania*, 163–64
Politorium, foundation legend, 249
Polybius, 107, 120–21, 123, 131, 139; on Arcadians, 246; on Carthaginians, 123–25; on Celts, 142–43; on Gauls, 141
Polydectes, 254
Polyperchon, 69
Pompeius Trogus, 278
Pompey, 108n182, 188
Pomponius Mela, 138, 274
Pontus, 226
Poseidon, 198, 254
Posidonius, 120–22, 138, 141, 143, 145, 157, 157n104, 343
Priam, 200
priests: Jewish, 310; of Memphis, 86–90; Theban, 79–80, 118
priority: Egyptian, 83–84; of Jewish learning, 318–19, 333–37; of Phoenician learning, 342
Proclus, commentary on Plato, *Timaeus*, 266
prodigies: Jews and, 194–95; Tacitus on, 194–95
Prometheus, Egyptian story of, 96
Propertius, 108

prophecy. *See* Sibylline oracles
proselytism, Jewish, 182–83, 183n29, 185, 189–90
proskynesis: at court of Alexander the Great, 68–69; as Egyptian practice, 93; as Persian practice, 14–15, 57
Proteus, 86–90
Pseudo-Aristotle, *Physiognomica*, 205
Pseudo-Callisthenes, 199
Pseudo-Eupolemus, 329–30
Pseudo-Hesiod, *Catalogue of Women*, 255
Pseudo-Phocylides, 306
Ptolemies, the, 264–65, 267–72; Ptolemy I, 71; Ptolemy II (Philadelphus), 314–17, 334; Ptolemy VI (Philometor), 317, 338n152
Punic, use of term, 116n2
Punica astu, 126
Punica fides, 132, 139–40, 353–54; and manipulation of Carthaginian image, 132–37; as stereotype, 115–16, 125
Punic Wars, 115, 122–32, 353–54; First Punic War, 123–24; Second Punic War, 123–25; Third Punic War, 130–31, 139
punishment, Persian practice of, 29–30, 30n118
Pyrrhus, 126
Pythagoras, 95, 105, 317–24, 331, 346
Pythagoreanism, Romans and, 345–46
Pythagoreans, 113, 144

Quadi, 167, 172
Queen Mother, Persian, in Aeschylus' *Persae*, 17

"race," as category, 197–98. *See also* skin color
Rahab, 297
Rebecca, 282
recklessness, as Celtic characteristic, 148
religion: Ethiopian, 198–99; of Gauls, 155–58; German, 174–78; Persian, 32; Roman, and non-Roman elements, 346–50
rhyton, "Amazon," 46 (fig. 3)
Rigii, 172
Roman influence, Germans and, 166–67, 171–72
Roman law, Tacitus on, 163
Rome and Romans: and Arcadia, 245–46; and Carthaginians, 122–32; cultural adaptation and appropriation, 343–51; and

Egypt, 107–11; foundation legends, 243–49; and Gauls, 142, 144, 146, 149–53; and Germans, 159–71, 178; and Jewish customs, 183–84; and Trojan origins, 243–45, 247–48
Romulus and Remus, 244
Roxane, 69–70
Ruth and Naomi, 293–99

Sabakos (Shabaka), 201–2
Sabbath, sanctification of, 332
Sabbath observance, Jews and, 183, 189
Sabines, Spartan origins of, 248–49
Sabus, 248–49
Said, Edward, 1
Saïs, 106–7; as Athenian colony, 265–66
Salamis, naval battle of, 10, 14n27, 17–19
Sallust, 138, 159, 272–73, 272n85
Samnite wars, 346, 349
Samson, 287
Sanchuniathon, 342
Sarah, 284, 299–300
Sardinia, Roman seizure of, 124
satire, in Xenophon's *Cyropaedia*, 62–65
satirists, Roman, and portrayal of Ethiopians, 207–9
Scaurus, M. Aemilius, 262
Scipio Aemilianus, 139
Scipio Africanus, 125–26
Scipio Nasica, 130
Scylax, 260
scythed chariots, introduction of, 61, 64
Scythes, 225
Scythians, 43–44, 225n7; foundation legend, 225
Second-Isaiah, 306
Seleucus I, 71–72, 313
self-representation, Jewish, 250–51
Semele, 97
Semnones, 161
Seneca, 181–83, 189, 202
Senones, 151
separatism: Egyptian, 77, 82, 85; Jewish, 182, 277–99
Seriphos, 255
seven (number), 332
Seven Sages of Greece, 324
Sextus Empiricus, 203
sexual imagery, 42–44
shared values, of Romans and Gauls, 149–55
Shechem, 283

414 SUBJECT INDEX

Shem, Ham, and Japheth, 279
Sibylline books, in Rome, 346–47, 349
Sibylline oracles, Jewish writers and, 337–41
Sidon: inscription from, 341; king of, 116
Silanus, D., 129–30
Silius Italicus, 129, 136
Simeon, 283, 287
sisters, Greece and Persia as, 20
Sitones, 166, 172
Siwah, as oracular center, 83
skin color, 214 (fig. 5), 215 (fig. 5); symbolized by Scythians and Ethiopians, 203; textual images, 197–211; visual images, 211–20
slave, term used for officials serving a monarch, 23
slavery, dissociated from blackness, 210–11
social hierarchy, German, 174
Socrates, 121, 318, 320
Socratic approach, 315
Sogdians, 66, 69–70
Solomon, 117, 287
Solon, 84, 95, 106
Solymoi, Jews as, 186, 192, 250–51
Sophocles, 255–56; *Acrisius*, 256; *Ajax*, 229; *Danae*, 256; Jewish authors on, 332–33; *Larissaeans*, 256
Sparta and Spartans, 21–23, 26, 28, 31; and founding of Rome, 248–49; governance, 120; and Jews, 304–6
spies, Persian (King's Eyes and Ears), 57n24
state policy, Persian, in Xenophon's *Cyropaedia*, 61–62
statue group, of Athenian "Tyrannicides," 51–52
statues, Greek, 50–52
Stephanus of Byzantium, 263n52
stereotypes: of Gauls, 141–47; *Punica fides* as, 115–16; Roman use of, 343–45
Stesichorus, 88, 90
Stoicism and Stoics, 315, 318–20
Strabo, 104, 114, 120–21, 261, 263, 314; on Celts, 145; on Ethiopians, 203–5; on Gauls, 141, 143, 156–57; *Geography*, 100–101; on Pelasgians, 240–41
Suebi, 176
Suiones, 172
Susa, 10, 200; mass wedding at, 71–74
symposium, in *Letter of Aristeas*, 315–16, 334–37
Syrians, 86, 310

Tacitus, 109, 354; *Annals*, 187, 190; *Germania*, 159–78; *Histories*, 179–96; on the Jews, 179–96, 250–51, 263, 278, 354
Tamar and Judah, 289–93
Tanfana, 176
Targitaus, 225n7
Tarquinius Priscus, 249
Temple in Jerusalem, 117; destruction of, 184–86; images in, 188–89
Temple of Athena Nike, south frieze, 40–42
Temple of Hephaistos (Ptah) at Memphis, 80
terra-cotta masks, depicting blacks, 211–12
terra-cotta vase, with Janiform heads, 218 (fig. 7)
Tertullian, 308
Testament of Job, 283
Testament of Judah, 291–92
Testament of Levi, 283
Thebes and Thebans, 92, 97, 119, 341; foundation legend, 85, 226, 233–36
Themistocles, 14n27, 19
Theodectes/Theodectus, 204, 336
Theophrastus, 107; *Peri Eusebeias*, 309–11
Theopompus, 266, 266n63, 336
Theras, 341–42
Thesmophoria of Demeter (Isis), 83n42
Theuth/Thoth, 107n168, 327
Third-Isaiah, 289
Third Sybilline Oracle, 338–41
Thonos, 89
Thracians, 321–24
Thucydides, 228–29
Tiberius, 156
Tibur, foundation legend, 249
Timagenes, 145n30, 156–57
Timocles, *The Egyptians*, 103
Tiryns, 255
Titus, Emperor, 185–86, 193–94
Tobias, 284
Tobit, Book of, 284
tolerance, Roman, 349
Tomyris, 27
tourism, 262–64
Tower of Babel, 223, 329
tragedy, Greek: Aeschylus' *Persae* as, 20–21; and story of Perseus, 255
transmigration of souls, as Celtic belief, 144
treachery, Carthaginians and, 122–25, 131–37

treaty violations, Carthaginians and, 123–25, 130, 132–33, 136
Treveri, 165
triumph, Roman, 164
Trogodutai, 204
Trojan Cycle, 200
Trojan War, 134, 241, 257–58; Egyptian story of, 86–90; Ethiopians and, 200; Persian legend of, 38–39, 117–18; Phoenicians and, 117–18. *See also* Aeneas; Helen
Troy, and Roman origins, 243–45, 247–48
truth-telling: Persians and, 29–30; Phoenicians and, 121–22
Turnus, 264n54
Twelve Tables, 350–51
tyranny, Persian, opposed to Greek freedom, 21–25
Tyre, 233–36
Tyrrhenoi, 241
Tyrtaeus, 227

Ubii (Agippinenses), 165n38
universalism, Jewish, 336–37
untrustworthiness, Celtic, 142, 147–48
utopian fantasy, Ethiopian setting for, 199

Valerius Maximus, 136
valor: Celtic, 142–43, 145–46, 149; German, 164; Persian respect for, 31
Varro, 177, 181, 202, 247
vase, with Janiform heads, 218 (fig. 7)
vase paintings, 40–50, 41 (fig. 1), 103, 228n28; Amazon rhyton, 46 (fig. 3); depicting blacks, 212–13; "Eurymedon" vase, 43 (fig. 2); story of Perseus, 256
Veii, 349
Veneti, Trojan origins of, 146n35
Venus Erycina, Roman cult of, 347
Vercingetorix, 150n66, 154, 154n85

Vergil, 108, 200; *Aeneid*, 129, 134–36
Vespasian, Emperor, 194
virtus: Caesar's use of, 149–53; Gallic, 149–53; German, 149, 172; as Roman virtue, 150; Tacitus' use of term, 172–74; and *virtutes*, 151–52
visitors, Greek, to Egypt, 95
visual images: of Greeks and Persians, 40–52; skin color, 211–20
Vitellius, Emperor, 187, 194
volute krater, of "Darius painter," 45–50, 47 (fig. 4)

wall paintings, depicting blacks, 213
warriors: black, 212; German, 167–68; Persian, 40n169, 66
Watchtower of Perseus, 259
weapons, in Aeschylus' *Persae*, 18n61
Wepwawet, 98
wit: as Celtic characteristic, 146; Tacitean, 187
women: German, 163; Roman, deification of, 163

Xanthippus (Athenian commander), 33
Xanthus, 159
Xenophanes, 203
Xenophon: *Anabasis*, 55; *Cyropaedia*, 53–65, 353; *Res Publica Lacedaemoniorum*, 57n19, 59
Xerxes, 12, 14, 50–51, 228–29, 257; in Aeschylus' *Persae*, 15n39, 18; and Greek culture, 50–52; in Herodotus, 21–22, 25–26, 29–31, 35–38

Yahweh, as god of all nations, 289

Zeno, 120, 319